The Palgrave Handbook of Managing Family Business Groups

Marita Rautiainen · Maria José Parada ·
Timo Pihkala · Naveed Akhter ·
Allan Discua Cruz · Kajari Mukherjee
Editors

The Palgrave Handbook of Managing Family Business Groups

palgrave
macmillan

Editors
Marita Rautiainen (iD)
School of Engineering Science
LUT University
Lahti, Finland

Timo Pihkala (iD)
School of Engineering Science
LUT University
Lahti, Finland

Allan Discua Cruz (iD)
Department of Entrepreneurship
and Strategy
Lancaster University Management School
Lancaster, UK

Maria José Parada (iD)
Department of Strategy and General
Management
ESADE Business School
Sant Cugat del Vallès, Spain

Naveed Akhter (iD)
Jönköping International Business School
(JIBS)
Jönköping, Sweden

Kajari Mukherjee (iD)
Department of Organisation Behavior
and Human Resources Management
Indian Institue of Management Indore (IIM)
Indore, India

ISBN 978-3-031-13205-6   ISBN 978-3-031-13206-3   (eBook)
https://doi.org/10.1007/978-3-031-13206-3

© The Editor(s) (if applicable) and The Author(s), under exclusive license to Springer Nature
Switzerland AG 2023
This work is subject to copyright. All rights are solely and exclusively licensed by the Publisher, whether
the whole or part of the material is concerned, specifically the rights of translation, reprinting, reuse
of illustrations, recitation, broadcasting, reproduction on microfilms or in any other physical way, and
transmission or information storage and retrieval, electronic adaptation, computer software, or by similar
or dissimilar methodology now known or hereafter developed.
The use of general descriptive names, registered names, trademarks, service marks, etc. in this publication
does not imply, even in the absence of a specific statement, that such names are exempt from the relevant
protective laws and regulations and therefore free for general use.
The publisher, the authors, and the editors are safe to assume that the advice and information in this book
are believed to be true and accurate at the date of publication. Neither the publisher nor the authors or
the editors give a warranty, expressed or implied, with respect to the material contained herein or for any
errors or omissions that may have been made. The publisher remains neutral with regard to jurisdictional
claims in published maps and institutional affiliations.

Cover credit: KTSDESIGN/SCIENCE PHOTO LIBRARY

This Palgrave Macmillan imprint is published by the registered company Springer Nature Switzerland AG
The registered company address is: Gewerbestrasse 11, 6330 Cham, Switzerland

Acknowledgments

This book about family business groups would not have been possible without the families who invited us into their business life. We have met family businesses of all sizes from all over the world. We are grateful to all those family business owners with whom we have had the pleasure to work during this and other related projects that helped us to compile this book.

Writing a book requires the work of large numbers of people. It is important to us as editors in this developing professional field to acknowledge the influence and contributions of our colleagues. We want to thank all the authors for their effort in writing and finishing the chapters in this book.

Specifically, we want to express our gratitude for financial and other forms of support for the following institutions. In Finland, Foundation for Entrepreneurship Research and Foundation for Economic Education have supported the research of this topic in several projects. In Spain, thanks to l'Agencia Estatal de Investigación PID2020-112648GA-I00/AEI/10.13039/501100011033, for their support via a grant to pursue this research. To the ESADE Entrepreneurship Institute team, and the Strategy and General Management Department director and the secretary for giving all kinds of support to pursue this project.

The Palgrave Macmillan press has our sincere thanks for helping us turn our research into a publication.

Contents

**1   Growing, Developing, and Performing Family Business
Groups: Introduction to the Handbook**   1
*Naveed Akhter, Allan Discua Cruz, Kajari Mukherjee,
Maria José Parada, Timo Pihkala, and Marita Rautiainen*
The Origins: (Family) Business Groups?   3
   Innovation   4
   Entrepreneurship   5
   Management and Resource Allocation   5
   Family Ownership Arrangements   6
The Vision and Organization of the Book   7
Studies on Strategy, Entrepreneurship, & Business
Transformation in FBGs   7
Studies on Ownership, Governance, and Management
in FBGs   8
Studies on Innovation Strategies in Family Business Groups   9
Studies on Identity, Values, and Sustainability in FBGs   10
References   11

Part I   Strategy, Entrepreneurship & Business Transformation

2   Ambidexterity in Family Business Groups   15
Salvador Cerón de la Torre, Cristina Cruz, and Maria José Parada
Introduction   15
Theoretical Background   20
   Organizational Ambidexterity in Family Firm Research   21

vii

viii   Contents

The Family Business Group Ambidexterity Framework	23
Tensions and Paradoxes Involved in Managing an FBG	24
Business-Owning Families' Transgenerational Intentions and Individual Drivers of OA	25
Organizational-Level Drivers and FBG Ambidexterity	27
Toward an Integrated Framework of OA and IA in Developing Ambidextrous FBGs	28
The FBG Ambidexterity Framework in Practice: An Illustration from a Mexican Ambidextrous FBG	30
Case Description	30
Case Observations in Connection to the FBG Ambidexterity Framework	32
Discussion and Concluding Remarks	42
References	43

3   The Role of Internal Capital Market in Business Groups   49
Valentina Giannini and Donato Iacobucci

Introduction	49
Literature Background	52
The Survival to External Shocks	52
The Allocation of Resources in Innovative Investments	55
Discussion and Conclusions	57
References	61

4   Exit and Resource Management in a Family Business Portfolio   65
Naveed Akhter and Xavier Lesage

Introduction	65
Theoretical Background	67
Portfolio Entrepreneurship	67
Business Exit	68
Research Methods	69
Data Collection and Analytical Strategy	69
Findings	71
Resource Management as a Lever for Restructuring	72
Resource Management as a Lever for Creating Opportunities	72
Resource Management as a Lever for Recycling	73
Discussion and Contributions	74
Limitations and Future Research	75
Conclusion Remarks	76

Contents ix

References 76

5 Corporate Strategy in Family Business Groups in Developed Economies 81

Xavier Mendoza, Paula M. Infantes, Maria José Parada, Marita Rautiainen, and Jan Hohberger

Introduction	81
Literature Review	84
Family Business Groups (FBGs)	84
Corporate Strategies of Family Business Groups	85
Structure of FBG	85
Diversification in FBG	86
Methods	89
Research Setting	89
Sample	89
Profile of FBGs	91
Parent Characteristics	91
FBGs Characteristics	93
Mapping Corporate Strategies of Family Business Groups	95
FBGs and Ownership. How Do FBGs Control Their Investee Companies?	95
Product Diversification	98
Geographic Diversification	106
Mixing Strategies: Product and Geographic Diversification	114
Discussion and Conclusion	117
References	118

6 Entrepreneurship in Family Business Groups in Latin America Under Organizational Ambidexterity Lens 125

Claudio G. Muller

Introduction	125
Literature Analysis	127
Entrepreneurship and Family Business	127
Institutional Quality in Latin America	128
Family Business Groups in Latin America	130
Organizational Ambidexterity	133
Methodological Approach	134
Case Studies	135
Grupo Carso—Mexico	136
Grupo Poma—El Salvador	138
Motta Group—Panama	139

x   Contents

Carvajal Group—Colombia	140
Romero Group—Peru	140
Gerdau—Brazil	141
Jacto Group—Brazil	143
Techint—Argentina	144
Cencosud—Chile	145
Falabella—Chile	146
Fortaleza Group—Bolivia	147
Analysis	148
Conclusion and Future Research	151
References	153

7   Family Business Groups in India: Perspectives on Their Roles, Strategies, and Innovations   159
Santanu Bhadra, Sougata Ray, Sankaran Manikutty, and Kavil Ramachandran

Introduction	159
Formation of Family Business Groups: The Indian Story	162
Roles of Family Business Groups	171
Family Business Group Strategy	173
Innovations at Family Business Groups	177
Conclusion	181
References	183

Part II   Ownership, Governance and Management

8   The Moderating Role of Governance in Promoting Transgenerational Entrepreneurship and Value Creation in Latin Family Business Groups   189
Neus Feliu and Fernanda Jaramillo

Introduction	189
Transgenerational Entrepreneurship in Latin American Family Business Groups	192
Transgenerational Entrepreneurship	192
Governance in FBG	194
Method and Case Studies	194
Three Models for Entrepreneurship in Family Business Groups	202
Model 1. Entrepreneurship at the Subsidiary Level	202
Model 2. Entrepreneurship at the Business Group Level	203

Model 3. Entrepreneurship Through Separate Investment
Vehicle ... 204
Framework for the Moderating Role of Governance
in Promoting Transgenerational Entrepreneurship and Value
Creation ... 205
   Antecedents for Entrepreneurship ... 206
   The Moderating Role of Governance ... 210
   Entrepreneurship Outcomes ... 212
Conclusions ... 213
   Insights for Owning Families and Practitioners ... 213
   Limitations of the Study and Future Research Questions ... 217
References ... 218

**9   Ownership Strategies in Family Businesses: A Conceptual
Framework** ... 223
*Jari Sorvisto, Marita Rautiainen, Timo Pihkala,
and Maria José Parada*
Introduction ... 223
Ownership Strategies: Typology and Examples ... 226
   The Target of Control ... 227
   The Unit of Analysis ... 228
   The Typology ... 228
Discussion ... 233
   The Drivers of Ownership Strategy ... 233
   Dysfunctions of Ownership Strategy ... 234
Conclusions ... 235
References ... 236

**10 Family Business Groups in Advanced Asian Economies
and the Politics of Institutional Trust** ... 241
Michael Carney and Zhixiang Liang
Introduction ... 241
Institutional Trust & Mistrust ... 243
The Emergence of FBGs: Entrepreneurial Dynamism
and Technology Assimilation ... 245
Corporate Governance by Personal Rule in FBGs ... 247
The Politics of Institutional Trust: Divisions Between Groups
Based on Economic, Political, and Ethnic Stratification ... 250
Political Inequality: Sources of Institutional Mistrust
in China ... 252
Korea Economic Inequality ... 253

xii   Contents

Malaysian Ethnic Inequality		255
The Complicated Politics of Institutional Trust		256
Conclusion		259
References		260

11 Conceptualising the Governing Ownership System in a Family Business Group   267

Tuuli Ikäheimonen, Marita Rautiainen, and Sanjay Goel

Introduction	267
Literature Review	271
Governing Ownership System in a Complex Family Business Group	271
Elements of Governance in the Family Business Group	273
Towards Conceptualising Governing Ownership	276
Methodology	280
The Case Study Approach	280
Context	280
Data Collection	281
Case Description	281
Discussion—Governing Ownership in a Family Business Group	287
Conclusions and Suggestions for Future Research	292
References	294

12 Informal Governance Practices in Family Business Groups: A Framework and Suggestions for Research   299

Tom Liljeström, Tuuli Ikäheimonen, and Timo Pihkala

Introduction	299
Literature Review	300
Features of Informal Governance	300
The Origin of Informal Practices	302
The Temporality of Informal Practices	303
The Accountability of Informal Practices	304
Informal Governance in FBGs	305
Hidden or Open Informal Governance	305
Temporary or Continuous Informal Governance	307
Delegated Versus Emerged Informal Governance Practices	308
Conclusions and Implications	309
Avenues for Future Research	310
References	312

Contents   xiii

13 Territoriality in Family Business Groups: The Impact of Ownership in Sharing Territories   317
Noora Heino, Marita Rautiainen, and Tuuli Ikäheimonen
Introduction   317
Literature   320
   Ownership in Business Organisations   320
   Ownership in Family Businesses and Family Business Groups   321
   Territories and Territoriality   322
   Territorial Behaviours of Marking and Defending   325
   Territories and Territoriality in Family Businesses and Family Business Groups   327
Methodology   329
   Case Selection   329
   Data Collection   330
Data Analysis   330
   Brief Description of the Cases   333
Analysis   336
   The Effect of Different Dimensions of Ownership on Territorial Behaviour and Territory Division   340
   Territory Division and Territoriality in Critical Incidents   342
Discussion and Conclusions   346
References   351

Part III   Innovation Strategies in Family Business Groups

14 The Temporal Evolution of Innovation Management in a Family Business Group   361
Timo Pihkala, Marita Rautiainen, and Naveed Akhter
Introduction   361
Innovation Management in Family Business Groups   364
Methodology   366
   The Case Study Approach   366
   Case Selection   367
   Data Collection   367
   Data Analysis   378
   Case Description   379
Analysis   380
Discussion and Conclusions   383
References   385

xiv Contents

15 Open Innovation and Family Business Groups: Anomalies Arising from the Context? 389
Suvi Konsti-Laakso, Tuomo Uotila, and Martti Mäkimattila

Introduction 389
Literature 391
Open Innovation 391
The Family Effect on Innovation 393
Family Business Groups as a Context for Innovation 394
Discussion and Conclusion 398
Limitations and Further Research 399
References 400

16 Innovation in Family Business Groups 403
Sabyasachi Sinha and Vinod Thakur

Introduction 403
Family Business Groups and Innovation 405
Innovation Process in Family Business Groups 407
Methodology 408
Cases of Innovation in Family Business Groups 409
Tata Group 409
Reliance Group 411
Aditya Birla Group 413
Mahindra Group 415
Discussion 416
Direction for Future Research 418
Conclusion 419
References 420

Part IV Sustainability, Identity, Values and Beyond

17 Business Groups Owned by Family and Sustainability Embeddedness: Understanding the Family Sustainability Spectrum 429
Marcela Ramírez-Pasillas, Ulla A. Saari, and Hans Lundberg

Introduction 429
An Introduction to Corporate Sustainability 432
Corporate Sustainability Embeddedness 436
Corporate Sustainability in Business Groups Owned by Family 438
Sustainability Embeddedness of Business Groups Owned by Family 441

Contents xv

Theoretical Implications 448
Future Research 449
References 450

18 Socioemotional Wealth and the Development of Family Business Group 459
Dony Abdul Chalid and Mira Kartika Dewi Djunaedi
Introduction 459
FBG and Socioemotional Wealth 461
Case Studies 463
    Case 1: Mr. Pan FBG 463
    Case 2: Mr. Fan FBG 466
Findings 468
    Socioemotional Wealth Heterogeneity 468
    Socioemotional Wealth and FBG Development 481
Conclusions and Implications 487
    Conclusions 487
    Limitations and Future Research 488
References 493

19 Explaining FBGs' Influence and Actions via a Sensemaking Lens 497
Sanjay Goel, Marita Rautiainen, Tuuli Ikäheimonen, and Hikari Akizawa
Introduction 497
Sensemaking and Sensegiving as a Process of Reality Construction 499
Illustrative Cases 505
    Toyoda Family Business House of Japan 505
    The Tata Family Business House of India 507
    The John Nurminen Family Business from Finland 508
Discussion 509
Conclusion 513
References 514

20 Intergenerational Flourishing: Sharing Knowledge from Generation to Generation in Mexican Family Business Groups 517
Fernando Sandoval-Arzaga, María F. Fonseca, and Maria José Parada
Introduction 517
Literature Review 520

xvi   **Contents**

Knowledge-Sharing Mechanisms in FBGs	520
Methodology	524
Findings—Case Description	527
Knowing that Mechanisms	527
Knowing How Mechanisms	530
Collective Knowing	531
Intergenerational Flourishing	535
Conclusions and Discussion	536
Knowledge Flow in an FBG	536
Flourishing of Enterprising Families—A Framework of 4C's to Attain a Sense of Purpose	538
Limitations and Further Research	542
References	542

21 Transition from Family Business to Business Family: Managing Paradoxical Tensions in Organizational Identities and Portfolio Entrepreneurship   549

Jeremy Cheng and Roger King

Introduction	549
Theoretical Background	552
Business Family as a Unit of Entrepreneurial Analysis	552
Transition as Managing Paradoxical Tensions	556
Identifying the Paradoxical Tensions	558
The Transition Trigger: Raising the Paradoxical Cognition	561
Methods	562
Findings and Propositions	564
The Business Family Cases	564
Shifting Organizational Identities	566
Embracing Portfolio Entrepreneurship	571
Transition Catalysts	574
Discussion	577
Shifting Identity or Building a Portfolio First?	578
Not All Will Become Business Families?	579
Theoretical Contributions	579
Practical Implications	580
Limitations and Future Research	581
Conclusion	582
References	582

22	**From Founder Identity to Family Business Group (FBG) Meta-Identity: Identity Development in the Journey from a Founder's Firm to an Entrepreneurial Family with a Portfolio of Businesses**	587
	Marta Widz and Maria José Parada	
	Introduction	587
	Identity Development in Family Business Groups	591
	Identity and Family Business	591
	Founder's Firm and Founder's Identity	592
	Identity Conflicts: Collective Family-Owners Identity Versus Organizational Identity	595
	FBG Identity Development	604
	Discussion and Conclusions	607
	Recommendations for Further Research	611
	References	612

Part V Conclusions

23	**Understanding the Dynamics of FBGs: Avenues for Further Research**	619
	Naveed Akhter, Allan Discua Cruz, Kajari Mukherjee, Maria José Parada, Timo Pihkala, and Marita Rautiainen	
	Innovation	620
	Entrepreneurship	621
	Strategy and Resources	624
	Identity	625
	Sustainability	626
	Ownership and Governance	627
	References	628

Index	631

Notes on Contributors

Akhter Naveed is an assistant professor at CeFEO and JIBS with research focusing on family business groups and exit strategies. He is also an affiliate researcher at EU Asia Institute ESSCA France. He has experience working for his own family business in his early career and later joined academia working on the topics of family business, entrepreneurship, and strategy. He is serving on the editorial review boards of the *Journal of Family Business Strategy* and *Journal of Small Business and Management*.

Akizawa Hikari is the president of Oikos Research. She was a professor at Chuo University, visiting scholar at HEC Montreal, and the president of the Japan Academy of Family Business. She received her Ph.D. from Department of Value and Decision Science at Tokyo Institute of Technology. She has written many publications; her articles are grounded on Japanese cases and mostly written in Japanese. She studies traditional practices in family firms and their relationship with a market economy. Moreover, she regularly holds executive seminars and dialogues with family business managers and owners.

Dr. Bhadra Santanu is currently appointed as an assistant professor in the area of Strategic Management at Indian Institute of Management Raipur, India. He completed his Ph.D. in Strategic Management from Indian Institute of Management Calcutta and has also worked as a Research Associate at the Thomas Schmidheiny Centre for Family Enterprise, Indian School of Business. Previously, he had received his Bachelor of Engineering degree

xx **Notes on Contributors**

from Jadavpur University, Kolkata, India, and worked as an IT consultant in India and USA. His research and teaching interests are in the area of strategic management, corporate sustainability, and family business. He has presented his papers in top international conferences including Academy of Management and Strategic Management Society. ORCID: 0000-0001-7640-101X.

Chalid Dony Abdul is a lecturer at Universitas Indonesia's Faculty of Economics and Business. He earned his Ph.D. in 2013 from the University of Bologna. His research focuses on finance, corporate governance, and family business. His recent publications include the *Review of Accounting and Finance*, *Journal of Economic Studies*, and the *Review of Behavioral Finance*.

Carney Michael is a professor of Management at the John Molson School of Business, Concordia University. He has published extensively on the corporate and organizational strategies of Asia's family-owned business groups. His research focuses on entrepreneurship and the comparative analysis of business, financial, and governance systems and their influence upon the development of firm capabilities and national competitiveness. He is the former Editor-in-Chief of *Asia Pacific Journal of Management*. He has published in journals such as the *Academy of Management Journal*, *Academy of Management Review*, *Asia Pacific Journal of Management*, *Entrepreneurship: Theory and Practice*, *Family Business Review*, *Journal of Management Studies*, *Journal of World Business*, *Management and Organization Review*, *Organization Studies*, and *Strategic Management Journal*.

Cerón de la Torre Salvador is partner and head of the business transformation practice at Ceron&Co, the leading family governance consulting firm in Mexico. He is member of a second-generation enterprising family. He holds a master's degree in international management and advanced certificates in Family Wealth and Business Advising by the Family Firm Institute. Currently, he is a doctoral candidate in Business Administration at IE Business School. His research interests concern family business strategy, entrepreneurship, and business model innovation. ORCID: 0000-0003-3536-3883.

Cheng Jeremy is a researcher at the Center of Family Business at the Chinese University of Hong Kong. He is a faculty member of the Global Education Network of Family Firm Institute (FFI). An FFI Fellow, he is the Founding Chair of the FFI Asian Circle, member of the Research Applied Board of Family Business Review, and the recipient of the FFI Barbara Hollander Award 2021. He is also a member of Research Committee of the Successful

Transgenerational Entrepreneurship Practices (STEP) Project Global Consortium. To inform his research, he founded GEN+ Family Business Advisory & Research and advises ethnic Chinese families-in-business, family offices, and other professional firms in Asia. His research focuses on governance, family office, and family advisory practices. His co-edited book *Family Business Case Studies Across the World: Succession and Governance in a Disruptive Era* is published by Edward Edgar in May 2022. ORCID: 0000-0003-4320-4233.

Cruz Cristina, Ph.D. in Economics from Carlos III University (Madrid) is Full Professor of Entrepreneurship and Family business at IE University. She is the Academic Director of the IE Center for Families in Business, an excellence research center at IE University. She leveraged her expertise in family business to conduct research on business families in different areas, including strategy, entrepreneurship, finance, and human resources. Her academic work, published in leading academic journals such as *Academy of Management*, *Administrative Science Quarterly* and *Entrepreneurship Theory and Practice*, has contributed to enhance the legitimacy of the family business as a research field. She is associate editor of Family Business Review since 2017. ORCID: 0000-0002-3011-2607.

Discua Cruz Allan (Ph.D.) is a Senior Researcher and the Director of the Centre for Family Business at Lancaster University Management School (UK). His research focus relates to stewardship, paradox, and relational lenses. His work has appeared in *Entrepreneurship Theory and Practice*, *Journal of Business Ethics*, *Journal of Business Research*, *Business History*, *Journal of Family Business Strategy*, *International Journal of Entrepreneurship and Behaviour Research*, *Entrepreneurship and Regional Development* and the *International Small Business Journal*.

Djunaedi Mira Kartika Dewi is a lecturer at Universitas Esa Unggul, Faculty of Economics and Business in Indonesia. She earned her doctoral degree from the University of Indonesia in 2020. She is the second generation of her father's family business, having witnessed its growth and decline. She has a strong interest for research in the broad areas of family business, finance, and corporate governance.

Dr. Feliu Neus is a consultant, researcher, and educator in the area of family enterprises. She is a partner at Lansberg Gersick Advisors. Building on her background in economics and organizational psychology, she has developed an expertise in the governance, long-term sustainability planning, and ownership strategies of family enterprise, specializing in large Latin American and European Family Businesses. She holds an M.A. in Family Mediation and a

xxii   Notes on Contributors

Postgraduate in Family Systems (Georgetown Family Center, Washington, DC). She obtained her Ph.D. from ESADE Business School (Barcelona, Spain) with a specialization in philanthropy in family enterprises from a governance perspective. ORCID: 0000-0003-0308-3211.

Fonseca María F. is Executive Director of the Institute of Enterprising Families for Mexico and Latin America at Tecnologico de Monterrey. She holds a Ph.D. in Industrial Relations by the University of Toronto. She was a founding researcher in the global applied research initiative on entrepreneurship and family businesses: The STEP Project. She has published some chapters in books related to leadership, family business, and entrepreneurship. She has been a consultant and counsellor in more than 20 medium-sized companies in Mexico and Latin America. Her current research focuses on leadership and multigenerational perspectives in enterprising families. ORCID: 0000-0002-9065-8230.

Giannini Valentina is a post-doc researcher at the Centre for Innovation and Entrepreneurship, Polytechnic University of Marche (Ancona, Italy). She holds a Ph.D. in Applied Economics at Faculty of Engineering (Department of Information Engineering, Polytechnic University of Marche) with the Ph.D. thesis on resource allocation mechanisms and the innovative performance in business groups. She graduated in Economy and Management at Polytechnic University of Marche, after a period of study abroad as an exchange student at University of Applied Sciences Upper Austria (Austria). In 2017, she was a visiting research scholar at Fuqua School of Business (Duke University, North Carolina, USA), where she focused her studies on firms' innovative performance. Her main research interests are business groups, entrepreneurship, and innovation. ORCID: 0000-0002-7027-247X.

Goel Sanjay is Professor and Burwell Endowed Chair in Entrepreneurship at the University of North Dakota. His research interests are in the broad of governance, family business, corporate strategy, and entrepreneurship. He was born in Dehradun, India.

Heino Noora works as a post-doctoral researcher at LUT University, School of Engineering Science, Finland. She holds a Doctoral Degree in Economics and Business Administration from LUT University and a Professional Educator Degree from JAMK University of Applied Sciences. Her main research themes include different aspects of entrepreneurship and ownership, organizational behavior, firm performance, and strategic management, especially among family businesses and co-operatives. Her research has been published in journals such as *Journal of Family Business Strategy*,

International Journal of Entrepreneurial Venturing and *International Journal of Co-operative Management*. She has a wide teaching experience in topics related to management, organizations, and business research methods as she has taught bachelor's and master's level courses at LUT University since 2009. She is closely involved with business practice through research projects and professional education programs. ORCID: 0000-0003-2585-1971.

Dr. Hohberger Jan is an associate professor of Strategic Management at ESADE business school. His research lies in the intersection of strategy and innovation and has been published in journals such as *Journal of Management*, *Journal of Management Studies*, *Research Policy*, *Industrial & Corporate Change*, *Journal of International Business Studies*, and *Strategic Organization* as well as in scholarly books. As a trainer and consultant, he has worked with companies in the USA, Europe, Asia, and Africa including, FIA, SK Group, RioTinto, Bayer, Bertelsmann, Almirall, DeBaak, and Grifols. ORCID: 0000-0002-1177-8147.

Iacobucci Donato is a full professor of Applied Economics at the Faculty of Engineering of the Polytechnic University of Marche and Rector's Delegate for Entrepreneurship. He is promoter and present director of the Center for Entrepreneurship and Innovation at Univpm (CII). He is the coordinator of Fondazione Aristide Merloni and member of the EUA Expert group on Innovation Ecosystems. He holds an M.B.A. from the Istao and a Ph.D. from the University of Stirling (UK). His main research interests are in the following fields: entrepreneurship, business groups, technology clusters, and innovation. ORCID: 0000-0001-8463-1106.

Infantes Paula M. is Postdoctoral Researcher at the Esade Center for Corporate Governance. She earned her Ph.D. from Universitat de les Illes Balears. Before joining Esade, she was teaching human resources management and family business for undergraduates. She has been co-teaching business and international strategy course in the EMBA at Esade Business School. She was visiting Northeastern University. Her research primarily focuses on business groups and their corporate governance: namely, the composition of boards of directors, ownership structures, and gender issues. Her research has been published in top-tier academic journals and book chapters. She also has numerous practitioner reports on ESG and corporate governance. ORCID: 0000-0002-4446-3555.

Ikäheimonen Tuuli, D.Sc. (Econ. & Bus.Adm.) is a post-doctoral researcher in LUT University. She is the director of LUT University's Entrepreneurship Master program, where she also teaches course business

xxiv Notes on Contributors

governance and strategic renewal. She has a strong background in family businesses and family business research, especially in the fields of family business ownership, governance, and board of directors. Her current research interests focus on informal governance practices, board of directors, growth business governance, and family business group governance. ORCID: 0000-0001-5835-3114.

Jaramillo Fernanda is a partner at Lansberg Gersick Advisors working primarily in Latin America, supporting multigenerational family enterprises in their continuity efforts throughout generations, including the development and implementation of complex corporate and family governance structures. She has developed a particular interest and expertise on the development of shared vision for the family enterprise and the promotion and governance of the entrepreneurial activity in business families. She is featured in several episodes of LGA Lighthouse, a podcast series about the challenges and dilemmas of family enterprises. She is also a frequent speaker in for institutions that support the education of business families and serves on several boards of family business as independent director. She holds a B.S. degree in Industrial Engineering, an M.B.A. degree from the Haas School of Business, University of California at Berkeley, and a Masters' degree in Family Advisory from the Javeriana University in Cali, Colombia. ORCID: 0000-0002-8851-4086.

King Roger, Ph.D. is Adjunct Professor of Finance and Founding Director and Senior Advisor of the Tanoto Center for Asian Family Business and Entrepreneurship Studies and the Thompson Center for Business Case Studies at the Hong Kong University of Science and Technology (HKUST). He leads a unique journey from an engineer of the Bell Labs to a serial entrepreneur and a family business scholar. He served as a family executive of the global shipowner Orient Overseas (International) Limited, as an outsider CEO of a family-owned cosmetics retailer and wholesaler listed in Hong Kong Stock Exchange, as a supervisory board member of TNT Express, to name but a few. He is currently an editorial board member of *Journal of Family Business Strategy*; Honorary Court member of HKUST; member of the Board of Governors of Tel Aviv University; and member of SKOLKOVO Academic Council. His research interests include family business, family office, entrepreneurship, and governance.

Konsti-Laakso Suvi, D.Sc. (Econ. & Bus. Adm.) works as a post-doctoral researcher in LUT University, Lahti Campus, Finland. Her primary research interest concerns innovation, which she studies in different contexts such as public sector, family business groups, entrepreneurial ecosystems, and sustainability. In addition, she teaches multiple master level courses and has strong experience in applying research funding and managing research projects as PI and project manager.

Lesage Xavier, Ph.D. is an Associate Professor in Strategy and Entrepreneurship at Essca School of Management, Paris Campus, France. He is the head of the M.Sc. Entrepreneurship & Design Thinking, a dual degree program in collaboration with the Design School of Québec (Canada). In charge of the school incubator (2015-2018), he has been acting as a mentor and coach for 10 years and is recognized as an expert in entrepreneurial support, innovation and business models, internationalization strategies of traditional SMES, creation, and innovation ecosystems. He recently specialized in new approaches to sustainable entrepreneurship and innovation through design by joining ENSCi Les ateliers, and the CRD, Centre de Recherche en Design of ENS Paris Saclay. He is member of the editorial board of Entreprendre & Innover. ORCID: 0000-0003-0916-1671.

Liang Zhixiang is Assistant Professor of Management and teaches strategic management and international business at York University. His research interests focus on how institutional environments interact with corporate governance and strategies in different business contexts. His recent works address such issues as comparative corporate governance, business groups, market-entry, and foreign direct investment. He has publications in a wide range of academic journals, including *Journal of World Business, Industrial and Corporate Change*. Before joining academic, he served multiple positions in finance industry, non-profit organizations, and consulting firms in China. ORCID: 0000-0002-9776-0588.

Liljeström Tom is a doctoral student at Lappeenranta-Lahti University of Technology in Finland. He holds a Master of Science in engineering from Helsinki University of Technology and a Master of Science in economics from Hanken School of Economics in Helsinki. He conducts research within corporate governance with a focus on informal governance practices, defined as activities outside board meetings. The aims of his research are to create a framework of dimensions for informal practices, to understand why boards use informal practices and how boards learn through these. His interest for this theme came from three decades of board work in many different companies, most presenting various forms of informal corporate governance practices. ORCID: 0000-0001-9878-9254.

Dr. Lundberg Hans is Senior Lecturer in Entrepreneurship and Innovation at the School of Business and Economics of Linnaeus University, Kalmar and Växjö, Sweden. His research focus on early stage venturing in entrepreneurial practices constituted of hybrid logics. His work is published in about 30 books and book chapters with leading publishers (i.e., Routledge, Edward Elgar, Springer, Palgrave Macmillan) and in various journals (i.e., Journal of Management Studies, International Journal of Entrepreneurship and Innovation Management). He has extensive practical experience from early stage venturing from various sectors, many countries and on different levels. ORCID: 0000-0002-4951-4171.

Manikutty Sankaran graduated in strategic management in 1987 from Indian Institute of Management, Ahmedabad, India, was a faculty member at the same institute for 22 years teaching strategy and leadership, and after retirement in 2012, continues to teach at the Institutes of Management Ahmedabad and Bangalore. His interests include strategic management, leadership through study of literature and family businesses. He has published in *Entrepreneurial Theory and Practice and Family Business Review*.

Mendoza Xavier is General Director of ESADE Business School and Professor in the Strategy and General Management department and the former director of the Observatory of Spanish Multinational Companies (OEME), a research unit jointly promoted by ESADE and ICEX. He served as dean of ESADE Business School (2000-2008) and as deputy director general of ESADE (2008-2011). His research studies internationalization processes of firms, strategic management of multinational companies, and management education. His work has been published in journals such as *Corporate Governance, Long Range Planning*, or *Journal of Business Research* and in books such as the *Handbook of Research on Family Business* or the OEME Annual Reports. He currently teaches Executive, M.B.A., and M.Sc. students at ESADE in the areas of corporate strategy and international business. He has lectured and presented conference papers at several academic institutions and professional associations in Europe, North and South America, and Asia.

Muller Claudio G. is Professor of Management at the School of Business and Economics at the University of Chile. He received his Ph.D. in Business Economics from Universidad Autónoma de Madrid, Spain. His research focuses on the field of family business, entrepreneurship, and corporate governance. Several of his researches have been published in international academic journals such as *Cross Cultural & Strategic Management, Academia Revista Latinoamericana de Administración, British Food Journal*, and *Global Journal* *of Flexible Systems Management*. He is Co-Author and Co-Editor of the book *Family Firms in Latin America* (Routledge, 2018), one of the first books of its kind to highlight family firms in a Latin American context and Co-Author of the book *Family Business Heterogeneity in Latin America* (Springer, 2021). He has given presentations throughout the USA, Spain, France, Italy, UK, Mexico, Colombia, Peru, Ecuador, Argentina, and Brazil and leads the FERC Spanish Discussion Group, a study group with members from America, Europe, and Asia. ORCID 0000-0003-3412-1946.

Mukherjee Kajari is Professor in OB&HRM Area of Indian Institute of Management Indore, India. Her area of research is organization design using paradigm of complexity theory; professionalization, HRM practices and growth of Family Businesses; and corporate social responsibility. Her various books, articles, and case studies reflect her wide-ranging research interest. Before joining academics, she has worked in a wide gamut of industries for over two decades holding various senior positions. She was Principal Consultant in one of the largest consultancy firms in the world. She consults in areas of change management, with specific focus on family-run businesses, end-to-end HR process design, and corporate social responsibility. She has master's degree in mathematics and master's and Ph.D. in management. She was one of the twelve senior managers of India selected for Chevening Scholarships (UK) in 2004. She has won "Best Teacher" award and numerous research grants.

Mäkimattila Martti, D. Sc. (Tech.) works as a start-up accelerator manager in LAB University of Applied Sciences in Lahti, Finland. His research interests include technology and innovation management, systemic innovation, and intellectual property rights. He has strong professional background from technology industry, as he has worked in several positions international technology companies in Finland and abroad.

Parada Maria José is Associate Professor at the Strategy and General Management Department at ESADE and Academic co-Director of the ESADE Global Business Family Initiative. She holds a Ph.D. from Jönköping International Business School and a Ph.D. from ESADE Business School. She teaches family business courses and strategy in different programs. She has been a visiting researcher of the INSEAD Global Leadership Centre in France and a visiting scholar in HEC Paris. Her research interests cover strategizing, governance, professionalization, values, next gen development, and entrepreneurship in family businesses, emergence, and development of family business groups which appears in various academic journals, co-edited books, and book chapters. Prior to her academic career, she worked several years for a

xxviii Notes on Contributors

multinational corporation in the telecom industry and in her family business in the tourism industry.

Pihkala Timo is a professor of Management and Organizations, specializing in entrepreneurship and small business management. He is currently heading an entrepreneurship research group at LUT University, Finland. His research interests include entrepreneurship, entrepreneurship education, ownership, and family businesses.

Ramachandran Kavil is Professor and Senior Advisor of the Thomas Schmidheiny Centre for Family Enterprise at the Indian School of Business. He received his Ph.D. in Business Management from Cranfield University, UK. For the next 15 years, he served as Professor at the Indian Institute of Management, Ahmedabad. His areas of specialization are family business, entrepreneurship, and strategic management. He has done extensive research on various aspects of family business and has published in *Journal of Business Venturing*, *Global Strategy Journal*, and *Journal of Business Ethics*. His special areas of interest are strategy, governance, and professionalization; he has been a consultant to family businesses in India and outside. He is a frequent speaker on family business and regularly contributes to the media. ORCID: 0000-0002-5044-3673.

Ramirez-Pasillas Marcela is doctor and assistant professor in entrepreneurship and sustainability. She is affiliated to the Centre for Family Enterprise and Ownership (CeFEO) at JIBS. She has been Director of the Bachelor Programme in Sustainable Enterprise Development. She was the UN PRME Manager at JIBS for which she obtained two international awards. She has served as a chair of the STEP European Leadership Council of the Global STEP Project for Family Enterprising from 2013 to 2016. She also served as a co-chair of the doctoral colloquium at the European Academy of Management (EURAM) from 2013 to 2016. She has published in the *Journal of Management Studies*, *Entrepreneurship and Regional Development: An International Journal*, *International Journal of Entrepreneurial Behavior & Research*, the *European Planning Studies Journal*, the *Corporate Communications: An International Journal* and the *International Journal of Entrepreneurship* and *Small Business*. Her research interests within entrepreneurship and sustainability include venturing and innovation practices across family generations, migration, and developing countries. ORCID: 0000-0001-9248-3705.

Rautiainen Marita is Associate Professor at LUT University, Finland. She is a co-director of the Entrepreneurship Master's program in School of Energy

Science in which she teaches growth management and strategic ownership. Her research focuses on the dynamics of the family business groups with a particular attention to five main areas: ownership, entrepreneurship, strategy, innovations, and group development. She has more than twenty years of experience in entrepreneurship both in a family business and as a self-employed entrepreneur. She is CeFEO Affiliated Researcher at Jönköping Business School and a member of the expert advisory group in a number of ownership and entrepreneurship working groups hosted by various entrepreneurship organizations.

Ray Sougata is Thomas Schmidheiny Chair, Professor of Strategy and Entrepreneurship Practice, and Executive Director of the Thomas Schmidheiny Centre for Family Enterprise. He has researched extensively on strategy, internationalization, entrepreneurship, innovation, corporate sustainability, governance, and digital transformation of firms in high growth economies. Since the past few years, he has been spearheading a mega program involving multiple research projects toward developing a solid research-based understanding of family firms, business groups, and business families in India and South Asia. He has also been leading a research program involving multiple research projects for nearly a decade focusing on the areas of social entrepreneurship, corporate sustainability strategy, base of the pyramid initiatives, and involvement of corporations in sustainable development. His research has appeared in journals such as *Global Strategy Journal, Journal of International Business Studies, Journal of Business Ethics, Journal of Business Research, Management International Review*, and *Organization Science*. ORCID: 0000-0003-4829-0193.

Saari Ulla A. is Senior Research Fellow at the Unit of Industrial Engineering and Management, Tampere University, Finland. She has received a D.Sc. (Tech) degree in Industrial Engineering & Management and a M.Sc. in Environmental Engineering from the Tampere University of Technology. She also has a M.A. degree in Languages and Social Sciences from the University of Helsinki, Finland. She is a research affiliate at Jönköping University, Sweden. Her research topics include technology and innovation management, sustainability-oriented innovation, sustainable production and consumption, and sustainable business models. She has 20 years of experience in the high-tech industry in senior management level roles. ORCID: 0000-0003-4007-5341.

Sandoval-Arzaga Fernando is Academic Director of the Institute of Enterprising Families for Mexico and Latin America at Tecnologico de Monterrey. He holds a Ph.D. in Administrative Sciences by ESADE Business School and studied a Postdoctoral Fellowship at London Business School. He is professor and consultant on family businesses and strategy for more than 15 years. He is pioneer on teaching and designed massive online courses (MOOCS) both in Coursera as in edX on Family Businesses with more than 15 thousand students from 20 countries. His current research focuses on intergenerational dynamics, next gen education and development, sharing knowledge in family groups, and governance mechanisms in Latin American countries. ORCID: 0000-0001-7889-11163.

Sinha Sabyasachi is Associate Professor of Strategic Management, Innovation and Entrepreneurship at the Indian Institute of Management (IIM), Lucknow (India). He obtained his Ph.D. from IIM, Ahmedabad (India), and his M.B.A. from the Indian Institute of Technology (ISM), Dhanbad (India). Before joining academics, he had worked with Nestlé S.A. and 3M. His areas of interest include strategic management, corporate entrepreneurship and innovation, organizational ambidexterity, family businesses, start-ups, and qualitative research methods. He has published several research papers in international journals and has received awards for his research from the Industrial Finance Corporation of India, the European Group of Organization Studies, and Society for the Advancement of Management Studies (UK). He is also involved in training programs for senior executives and provides consulting services to a variety of organizations, including the government, public enterprises, multinational corporations, and family businesses. He also provides consultancy services to several organizations. ORCID: 0000-0003-2016-032X.

Sorvisto Jari, M.Sc. works on business development position in global business environment and has held a number of various international technology management positions. He is a doctoral candidate at the LUT University, Finland, and his research focuses on ownership strategy, owners' strategic capabilities, and family businesses.

Thakur Vinod is Assistant Professor in Strategy area at FORE School of Management, New Delhi, India. He is Ph.D. from Indian Institute of Management Lucknow, India. His doctoral dissertation focuses on the family constitution as a family governance tool for business families. He has also worked with KPMG, EY, and other consulting firms in different cultural contexts such as India, the Middle East, and Africa. His research interests lie in the field of governance, internationalization, and innovation with a focus on family firms.

Uotila Tuomo, D.Sc. (Tech.) works as a professor of Industrial Engineering and Management, especially Innovation Management at Lappeenranta-Lahti University of Technology (LUT University). His current research interests are related to futures research and organizational foresight activities, networked innovation processes, networked knowledge generation processes, and knowledge transfer in networks and absorptive capacity. He is also an adjunct professor (Economic Geography, especially Regional innovation Systems) at University of Turku. His publications include altogether some 40 scientific and other publications in international and national publication series. ORCID: 0000-0001-7859-8450.

Widz Marta is Director in Family Office Research at the Wealth Management Institute (WMI) and a key member of WMI's Global-Asia Family Office (GFO Circle) leadership team, responsible for research and development. She is also Affiliated Faculty at the Family Business Institute at the Grossman Business School of the University of Vermont, Executive in Residence at the INSEAD Wendel International Centre for Family Enterprise, Affiliated Expert of the Institute of Family Business, Poland, and Regional Governance Partner at International Board Foundation. She obtained her Ph.D. at the Centre for Family Business at the University of St. Gallen, Switzerland, and was the Research Fellow at IMD Business School, Switzerland, where she worked closely with the winners and jury members of the IMD Global Family Business Award as well as the IMD-Pictet Sustainability in Family Business Award. She is member of International Family Enterprise Research Academy (IFERA), Academy of Management (AOM), and the Family Firm Institute (FFI), where she served as the Co-Chair of the 2020 FFI Global Conference's Program Committee.

List of Figures

Fig. 2.1	The FBG Ambidexterity Framework	29
Fig. 2.2	SONI FBG ambidextrous evolution over time	31
Fig. 5.1	Classification of FBGs by their geographic diversification	106
Fig. 6.1	Levels of ambidexterity in Latin American family businesses (*Source* Canale et al., [2021])	135
Fig. 6.2	Ambidexterity levels found in our sample	150
Fig. 7.1	Logics behind emergence of family business groups	161
Fig. 7.2	Foreign direct investment trend as indicator of India's economic reform (*Source* World Bank)	166
Fig. 7.3	Total market cap trend as indicator of business growth (*Source* Bang et al., 2020) (*Note* FBGF: family business group; SFF: stand-alone family firm)	167
Fig. 7.4	The bajaj family tree	176
Fig. 8.1	Antecedents and outcomes of transgenerational entrepreneurship pursuits in family business groups and the moderating role of governance	206
Fig. 9.1	Four types of ownership strategies	229
Fig. 11.1	Fan model of the family business governance conceptualisation	278
Fig. 15.1	FBG as an underlying variable for innovation perspectives	396
Fig. 16.1	A model of FBGs innovation activities	417
Fig. 17.1	Sustainability embeddedness of business groups owned by family	442

xxxiv   **List of Figures**

Fig. 18.1	Pan family genogram (*Note* The Genogram of the Pan Family illustrates the Pans' primary family tree and the emotional bonds between Pan's siblings during their formative years. The red dashes represent sibling rivalry. Conflicts between Pan's siblings began when Brother B decided to leave the family businesses founded by Pan's brothers. There were no conflicts with Pan's sister because they were not affiliated with the family businesses. Mr. Pan exercised indirect control over his son as CEO for the duration of his life to ensure that his son's decisions regarding the family business did not significantly increase the firm's survival risk. Mrs. Pan inherited the majority of the company after Mr. Pan's death, but she had no influence in how her son ran the family businesses	465
Fig. 18.2	The Pan family business group structure (*Note* *Warehouses are part of the real estate industry. The majority of the shares are owned by the father [Mr. Pan]. The founder held a 3% stake in the logistics company prior to his passing. It is now in the son's possession. Two friends own the remaining 65% of Heavy Equipment Company, with each owning 35% and 30%. Following Mr. Pan's demise, the majority of the shares pass to his widow. It is not permitted for in-laws to own stock)	466
Fig. 18.3	Fan family genogram (*Note* The Fan family did not experience any intrafamily conflict. Throughout our interviews, the family attempted to align the vision of the family business with stewardship values)	467
Fig. 18.4	Mr. Fan family business group structure (*Notes* The ownership of Cottage public company is as per 2012. There is a dilution of Fan family ownership after 2012, but the Fan family is still the ultimate shareholder. We suspect there is more than one company under Mr. Fan Business Group. Due to a lack of information, the picture of the family business group is based on interviews done before the founder died and documents.)	468
Fig. 18.5	The Pan family firm socioemotional wealth	483
Fig. 18.6	The Fan family firm socioemotional wealth	486
Fig. 19.1	Layers of sensemaking in FBGs relative to the external environment	504
Fig. 20.1	FBGs Knowledge-sharing strategies (*Source* Own elaboration)	538

Fig. 20.2	Impact of the FBGs knowledge-sharing strategies in the intergenerational flourishing competencies (*Source* Own elaboration)	541
Fig. 21.1	Data structure	568
Fig. 21.2	Paradoxical tensions embedded in the transition	577
Fig. 22.1	Family and founder's firm identities anchored in founder's entrepreneurial identity	595
Fig. 22.2	Family-owners collective identity anchored in legacy business	603
Fig. 22.3	Family Business Group (FBG) meta-identity	607
Fig. 22.4	Identity development. From founder's identity to FBG meta-identity	610
Graph 5.1	Distribution of FBGs by number of sectors	102
Graph 5.2	Distribution of FBGs (by size of the FBG) by number of sectors. **a** Distribution of small FBGs by number of sectors. **b** Distribution of medium FBGs by number of sectors. **c** Distribution of large/v.large FBGs by number of sectors	104
Graph 5.3	Distribution of internationalized FBGs (by size of the FBG) by OEME classification. **a** Distribution of small FBGs by OEME classification. **b** Distribution of medium FBGs by OEME classification. **c** Distribution of large/v.large FBGs by OEME classification	109
Graph 5.4	Distribution of internationalized FBGs (by size of the FBG) by regional focus. **a** Distribution of small FBGs by regional focus. **b** Distribution of medium FBGs by regional focus. **c** Distribution of large/v.large FBGs by regional focus	113
Graph 5.5	Distribution of foreign investees by regional focus and size of the FBG. **a** Distribution of foreign investees (small FBGs) by regional focus. **b** Distribution of foreign investees (medium FBGs) by regional focus. **c** Distribution of foreign investees (large/v.large FBGs) by regional focus	115

List of Tables

Table 2.1	Selected Family-Firm Ambidexterity Studies	17
Table 2.2	Managing tensions in a FBG context	24
Table 2.3	GRUPO QD Stages of Development and Consolidation	33
Table 4.1	Snapshot of the cases	70
Table 4.2	Data collection	70
Table 5.1	Distribution of Spanish FBGs by administrative and political division (regions)	91
Table 5.2	Classification of parent companies according to their typology	92
Table 5.3	Average number of investee companies by typology of parent company	92
Table 5.4	Average age of parent companies by typology of parent company	93
Table 5.5	Breakdown of FBGs by size (number of investees)	93
Table 5.6	Average number of investees and total employees by FBGs size	94
Table 5.7	Breakdown of FBGs by size and age	94
Table 5.8	Breakdown of FBGs by corporate structure (organizational levels)	95
Table 5.9	Breakdown of FBGs by size and corporate structure	95
Table 5.10	Classification of investees in FBGs (ownership-level criteria)	96
Table 5.11	Breakdown of investees by FBG size and investee type (ownership level criteria)	97
Table 5.12	Distribution of FBGs (GUO industry) by sector	98
Table 5.13	Breakdown of FBGs by sector and size	99

xxxviii List of Tables

Table 5.14	Breakdown of FBGs by subsector and size	99
Table 5.15	Breakdown of FBGs by sector and GUO typology (holding or with sectorial activity)	99
Table 5.16	Breakdown of FBGs by subsector and GUO typology (holding or with sectorial activity)	100
Table 5.17	Distribution of investees by sector	100
Table 5.18	Distribution of investees by subsector	101
Table 5.19	Breakdown of investees by type of investee (commercial or productive)	102
Table 5.20	Average number of sectors by FBGs' size	103
Table 5.21	Average industrial distance in a FBG by sector	105
Table 5.22	Average industrial distance in a FBG by subsector	105
Table 5.23	Average industrial distance in a FBG by GUO age	105
Table 5.24	Breakdown of FBGs by geographic diversification and size	107
Table 5.25	Breakdown of FBGs by corporate structure and geographic diversification	107
Table 5.26	OEME classification of internationalized FBGs	108
Table 5.27	Breakdown of internationalized FBGs by OEME classification and size	108
Table 5.28	Classification of investee companies by their geographic diversification	110
Table 5.29	Classification of FBGs according to the number of foreign investees	110
Table 5.30	Breakdown of foreign investees by country (Top 10 countries)	111
Table 5.31	Classification of internationalized FBGs by multinationalization	111
Table 5.32	Breakdown of internationalized FBGs by regional focus	112
Table 5.33	Breakdown of internationalized FBGs by regional focus and size	112
Table 5.34	Breakdown of foreign investees by region	114
Table 5.35	Breakdown of FBGs by product and geographic diversification	116
Table 6.1	Ranking of net entrepreneurial in Latin America	129
Table 6.2	Data set	137
Table 6.3	Cases of exploratory and exploitative companies	148
Table 7.1	Typical formation of family business groups in India	168
Table 7.2	Advantage of business group structure for business family needs	174
Table 8.1	Description of the latin American FBGs analyzed	197
Table 8.2	Fundamental governance themes the framework addresses	214
Table 8.3	Application of framework to models of entrepreneurship	215
Table 10.1	Summary of three institutional mistrust in Asian economies	257
Table 11.1	Description of data	282

Table 11.2	Principles guiding the composition of the board at different levels of the FBG	286
Table 11.3	Ownership governance system in the case company	290
Table 13.1	Data sources and case characteristics	331
Table 13.2	Family owners' actions and behaviour during and after critical events	337
Table 14.1	Data collection and analysis	368
Table 14.2	Innovation activities in the Case FBG	370
Table 18.1	SEW and FBG	489
Table 19.1	Key elements in constructing an entrepreneurial narrative and action via sense making in illustrative cases	511
Table 20.1	Sharing knowledge mechanisms in FBGs	525
Table 20.2	FBGs Characteristics	526
Table 20.3	Formal and informal contact in the last five years	528
Table 20.4	Quotations examples	529
Table 21.1	Definitions of a cluster of terms related to "business families" in the literature	553
Table 21.2	Differences between family business and business family	557
Table 21.3	Participants and key facts of their business families and business groups	567

List of Boxes

Box 7.1.	Advantage of the family legacy	169
Box 7.2.	Group split to manage family conflicts	170
Box 7.3.	Formalizing roles to manage succession	176
Box 7.4.	Innovation as group culture	179
Box 7.5.	Innovation guided by family's aspirations	180

1

Growing, Developing, and Performing Family Business Groups: Introduction to the Handbook

Naveed Akhter, Allan Discua Cruz, Kajari Mukherjee, Maria José Parada, Timo Pihkala, and Marita Rautiainen

Family business groups (FBGs) are a fascinating phenomenon. They exist everywhere under different names and guises (Parada et al., 2016; Tu et al., 2002). Their emergence and development showcase the dynamics of families in business and the decisions they proactively, or reactively, take to business opportunities or institutional and contextual challenges. More recent accounts underscore that we are just beginning to understand how they grow, develop, and perform over time (Rosa et al., 2019). FBGs are relevant contexts of study as they challenge the myth that family businesses cease to exist within a few generations, particularly in developed economies, where they are seldom studied.

N. Akhter
Jönköping International Business School (JIBS), Jönköping, Sweden
e-mail: naveed.akhter@ju.se

A. D. Cruz
Department of Entrepreneurship and Strategy, Lancaster University Management School, Lancaster, UK
e-mail: a.discuacruz@lancaster.ac.uk

K. Mukherjee
Department of Organisation Behavior and Human Resources Management, Indian Institue of Management Indore (IIM), Indore, India
e-mail: kajari@iimidr.ac.in

© The Author(s), under exclusive license to Springer Nature Switzerland AG 2023
M. Rautianen et al. (eds.), *The Palgrave Handbook of Managing Family Business Groups*,
https://doi.org/10.1007/978-3-031-13206-3_1

What we have observed is that FBGs bring to the surface the often-overlooked approach of family members to the complex decisions that lead to allocating efficiently existing resources within a business. The strategies of families in business related to shape a constellation of businesses over time may run counter to expected market approaches (Rosa et al., 2014). Such strategies demand a high level of complexity that becomes more intricate as family members have to decide about aspects of ownership, management, and governance. Further decisions become complex over time as a constellation of firms may be created, acquired, merged, and some even divested. Such decisions, often crossing national borders, are influenced not only by business objectives but also by the objectives of family owners who look for ways to balance efficiently emotional and rational impulses in business. It is because of such an intricate and yet fascinating journey that this book emerged.

FBGs have a unique feature. They embody the marriage between a known phenomenon in the business literature, a business group, and the characteristics that underscore the control of such business by members of a family (Rautiainen et al., 2019). Such control allows family members to draw a blueprint for those entrusted to lead and manage the diverse companies within a business group in ways that balance both business and family aspirations. Such features will demand not only business acumen but also ways in which to keep family members committed to building on existing assets and developing family skills.

This book stresses that turning one family business into a business portfolio that may span across diverse business sectors is not an easy task. It requires factors such as a unique approach to ownership, governance, innovation, entrepreneurship, emotions, and the appropriate resources deployment strategies. In addition to the mere understanding of the FBG phenomenon, we offer a portrayal of the FBG as an ideal context to theorize different dimensions that may explain their emergence and survival. We unpack diverse dynamics in a way that shows how the family business group is an evolving

---

M. J. Parada
Department of Strategy and General Management, ESADE Business School, Sant Cugat del Vallès, Spain
e-mail: mariajose.parada@esade.edu

T. Pihkala (✉) · M. Rautiainen
School of Engineering Science, LUT University, Lahti, Finland
e-mail: timo.pihkala@lut.fi

M. Rautiainen
e-mail: marita.rautiainen@lut.fi

phenomenon, where different factors influence its development, growth, and performance.

The reader will find that exemplary FBGs are not behemoths that remain set in their ways over time. Rather they evolve in ways that denote an intricate intertwinement between family members dreams, concerns, and skills and the opportunities to develop a constellation of businesses. The insights provided by scholars in this volume show how our current understanding is fragmented and, in some cases, disconnected from an in-depth comprehension of FBGs. Throughout the book, the reader will find that the FBG becomes an ideal context to extend our theoretical understanding of how, why, what, and by whom FBGs grow, develop, and perform in ways that challenge prior academic conversations. Hence, this provides us an opportunity to bring them together into a compilation that extends such conversations and increases our understanding.

The Origins: (Family) Business Groups?

FBGs are often considered as an exception within the phenomenon of business groups. Business groups, defined as "*a collection of firms bound together in some formal and informal ways*" (Granovetter, 1994, p. 454), are largely a phenomenon that is found in developing economies, a vehicle to manage with the uncertainties of the economy and the society (Carney & Gedajlovic, 2002; Khanna & Yafeh, 2007). The externalities related to business groups build on three main logics:

a. In the absence of businesses operating in the supply chain, internalizing the supply in the business group is a way of securing the resources. That is, in the case of resource scarcity, internalizing the sourcing activities within the same ownership structure may be an effective way to lower transaction costs. Reacting to the problems of resource supply, business groups are likely to benefit from vertical integration and growing the value chain (Chang & Hong, 2000). The downside of this mode of operation is the increasing internal complexity of the business group, and subsequently, the rising costs of ownership.

b. In the absence of a developed financial market, creating an internal capital structure to provide financial opportunities for new businesses may prove an efficient approach (e.g., Keister, 1998). This problem with the undeveloped financial infrastructure has led to identifying of major efficiencies of the business groups. That is, the business group would concern a financing structure—with some of the businesses operating as financiers and some businesses in need of financing. Lending money within the same ownership structure would lower the agency costs related to the external financing institutions' control and fasten the decision-making process in the financing processes. Furthermore, the terms of financing may be built on collaterals provided by the group.

c. In the absence of the developed economy, the national or regional governments may offer FBGs subsidies, privileges, priorities, etc., to secure the emergence of the economy. In these cases, the business groups' viability would depend on the governmental incentives rather than their internal efficiencies (e.g., Guillén, 2000). Should the privileges be owner-specific, these business groups are likely to benefit from diversifying horizontally into a wide range of industries, making the best use of the subsidies. Along with the growth of the economy and the societal development, the subsidies are likely to be reduced, leading to the dissolvement of the business groups.

Due to the contextual reasoning for the existence and growth of business groups in developing economies, business groups are expected to disappear with the development of an economy. However, a number of FBG studies conducted in developed economies have shown that FBGs continue to grow and prevail (e.g., Parada et al., 2019) as they are embedded and aligned with contextual factors (Manikutty, 2000).

Therefore, this book presents FBGs as a unique case—one that extends contextual explanations of the phenomenon and argues for the inherent capabilities, mechanisms, and logics that may explain their importance. That is, we suggest that since there are no external conditions for the FBGs to prevail in developed economies, their existence, growth, and success must be explained through the analysis of their internal characteristics. The theoretical point is largely centered around the ways in which FBGs create competitiveness and effectiveness indigenously, through innovation, entrepreneurship, management and resource allocation, and concentrated ownership arrangements.

Innovation

Innovation is needed in any organization. In the family business field, innovation has been linked to aspects such as ownership, management, willingness, and ability of current and next-generation family members (Calabro et al., 2019; De Massis et al, 2014). Innovation is a multidimensional phenomenon,

1 Growing, Developing, and Performing Family Business Groups ... 5

and it helps businesses to survive and adapt to the changing business landscape. In family businesses innovation is affected by the unique ownership and management structures. In this book, topics such as open innovation, innovation sourcing, financing of innovations, ownership innovations, and innovation patterns are especially targeted. As we study not only one firm but an entity that embodies several firms over time, some of these studies also challenge current assumptions about innovation in family firms, particularly the lower level of innovation or the fact that the presence of the family can hinder innovation.

Entrepreneurship

Family is considered as the oxygen that feeds the fire of entrepreneurship (Roggoff & Heck, 2003). In the family business field, scholars have suggested how entrepreneurship develops in diverse ways within a single-family firm (Howorth et al., 2014). Entrepreneurship becomes crucial to develop FBGs. In prior studies, scholars have pinpointed that the DNA behind the development of a portfolio of businesses lies in the way teams of family members act (Discua Cruz et al., 2013, 2017) and the way family dynamics may influence the pace and breadth of development of a portfolio of businesses (Rosa et al., 2014). In this book, aspects such as transgenerational entrepreneurship, new venture creation and development, diversification, risk, exits, portfolio entrepreneurship, and ambidexterity are analyzed in the FBG context. The picture of entrepreneurship in FBGs is rich due to simultaneous entrepreneurial initiative, parallel exit, and entry dynamics and multiple endeavors, launched by multiple owners.

Management and Resource Allocation

In single-family businesses, the management of resources is key for survival (Chirico et al., 2011). The appropriate decisions about how to allocate resources and manage them efficiently may allow an FBG to leverage a unique take on both tangible and intangible assets over time. The task of managing and allocating resources in a multi-business family firm does not only come with several complex processes but also provided opportunities. Indeed, sometimes efficient resource management allows family owners leverage existing resources to explore or invest in new opportunities (Akhter et al., 2016). In this book, FBG forms such as pyramid-shape, portfolios, conglomerates, dynasties, and synergetic group structures suggest that resource management requires further exploration of aspects linked to re-directing, reallocating, and recycling resources.

Family Ownership Arrangements

Ownership provides control. Such control, by family members, is a key characteristic of any family business (Howorth et al., 2010). Family businesses differentiate from other types of organizations for the particular arrangements with regard to ownership that tends to be concentrated, retaining voting power (Aguilera & Crespi-Cladera, 2012), and the multiple family owners that combine economic and non-economic goals (Zellweger et al., 2013). Owners have decision-making power over the FBG resources and their use over time. In the family business group context, we can imagine that such approach may become complicated as diverse firms may demand unique combination and orchestration of resources. There are different ownership permutations that can emerge as results of creating a new firm or deciding in an expansion strategy that will create new ventures over time led by family members.

In this book, we find that ownership strategies that allow to balance ownership within the family, management of the business, and professionalization of management which play an important role in terms of FBG development. As the business develops confirming a portfolio of businesses, FBGs need to organize themselves to manage this growing complexity by defining their structure as a business. Simultaneously, as the family grows in complexity and more owners appear, the FBGs need to organize their ownership governing system, allowing them to be more efficient in all realms.

In the case of FBGs, the question of governance becomes essential. Here, the issue is not predominantly on the agency relationship between the owner and the agent. In FBGs with concentrated ownership, the owning family participates closely in the management of the FBG. Instead, governance issues are related to the ownership, territoriality, and maintaining balance in the complex company structures. The theoretical perspective does not lean on transaction cost theory, agency theory, or the institutional theory but instead on the ownership theory, entrepreneurship theory, resource-based theory, innovation theory, and systems theory.

The Vision and Organization of the Book

Our earlier book "The Family Business Group Phenomenon" (Rautiainen et al., 2019) introduced the phenomenon, the concept and the variety and richness of FBG. In this book, the main message of the book is progressive—the chapters concern growth, innovation, management of complexity, strategic renewal, and mechanisms for effective governance of the complex FBG.

In the following paragraphs, we introduce the various sections and chapters therein. The chapters flow from *why* FBGs develop and *what* are the paradigms, alternate logics and strategies adopted to *how* these complex interlocked entities achieve a coherent whole within the holy trinity of family, business and management, while traversing the range of governance challenges. Thereafter, the chapters concentrate on various innovative interventions that allow the FBGs to *grow and sustain, create value* and *future-proof* against the changing societal, ecological and regulatory expectations. The family in FBGs make a strong comeback by the last few chapters by taking up issues related to identity, socio-emotional wealth, and values. The thematic grouping of chapters and their diversity and flow is likely to make an absorbing reading, while providing a holistic overview of FBGs.

Studies on Strategy, Entrepreneurship, & Business Transformation in FBGs

The growth and development of FBGs are not haphazard. Instead, they are the outcome of owners' growth strategies and continuous entrepreneurship. While the size and accumulated wealth of FBGs could suggest that the owning families would be inclined toward wealth securing activities, the studies on FBG strategies, entrepreneurship, and business transformation are suggesting otherwise. In terms of growth strategies, research related to FBGs has been surprisingly sparse. In their quantitative study on corporate strategies of Spanish FBGs, *Parada, Mendoza, Infantes, Rautiainen, and Hohberger* map the diversification and internationalization of FBGs. Their exploratory study creates a basis for further quantitative studies on the strategic management in FBGs.

The papers by *Ceron, Cruz and Parada,* and by *Müller* suggest FBGs are ambidextrous in the pursuit of exploiting the existing resources and exploring new opportunities for wealth. As a dynamic capability, ambidexterity is path-dependent and benefits from the continuity of explorative activities.

8   N. Akhter et al.

The explorative activities often require reconfiguration of the FBG resources and processes. In their paper on business exits and resource management, *Akhter and Lesage* show how owners manage resources through exits and redirect the resources back to the business. In this sense, the business renewal requires the owners' active participation in the recycling of resources within the FBG. From this perspective, the study by *Giannini and Iacobucci* highlights the interconnectedness of the companies within same groups. They suggest that FBGs form internal capital markets that provide the FBGs superior capacity for overcoming external shocks and to finance innovative projects. The paper by *Bhadra, Ray, Manikutty, and Ramachandran* shows how the Indian FBGs respond and persist despite significant changes in their institutional environment.

Studies on Ownership, Governance, and Management in FBGs

As large multi-business organizations, the question of governance and control of FBGs is growing. To maintain their competitiveness, efficiency, and benefits related to size, scale, internal synergies, and internal capital market, FBGs need to have well-functioning governance systems. These governance systems are affected by the institutional environment of the FBGs. In their study of FBGs in Advanced Asian Economies, *Liang and Carney* suggest that FBGs retain personalized governance structures as a defense mechanism against the political uncertainty in the economy. Parallel to the governance needs communicating the trustworthiness of the FBGs to the external stakeholders, the internal circumstances may lead to development of governance practices. *Ikäheimonen, Rautiainen, and Goel* conceptualize a governing ownership system in an FBG and show that along with the growth of complexity of ownership in the FBG, new needs for governing the ownership may arise. Should the governance of ownership be successful, it benefits the business as well as the owners equally. If the governance of ownership is not considered satisfactory, the co-ownership in the FBG may incur unwanted behavior from the FBG owners. In their paper on territorial behavior in FBGs, *Heino, Rautiainen, and Ikäheimonen* argue that family business owners are strongly motivated to participate the development of ownership and governance structures of the FBG, marking and defending their possessions.

A large majority of governance studies focus on governance actors such as board of directors or the management team. Yet limited insight is often found around ownership strategies in FBGs. The paper by *Sorvisto, Rautiainen, Pihkala, and Parada* presents a conceptual framework on ownership strategies in FBGs, highlighting the perspective on owners. Their framework suggests a new approach to understanding the owners' ability to guide the managerial and governance systems in the business.

The study by *Feliu and Jaramillo* shows how governance practices may moderate the transgenerational entrepreneurship and value creation in FBGs. They point out that there are no predetermined solutions for FBG governance but that the governance choices need to respond to the existing governance needs in the FBG. Supporting this perspective, *Liljeström, Ikäheimonen, and Pihkala* raise the issue of informal governance practices in FBGs. They suggest that FBGs may respond to the emerging governance needs through informal rather than formal approaches, adding thus to the speed, agility, and effectiveness of the FBG governance. Their analysis shows that the informal governance practices may in fact be crucial for the success and survival of FBGs.

Studies on Innovation Strategies in Family Business Groups

Innovation is one of the most effective routes for business renewal and competitiveness. From this perspective, the innovation strategies and innovation activities need careful analysis. FBGs have been suggested to embark on more riskier and diversifying innovation projects due to their ability to finance the project internally and build internal synergies between group companies. Yet, little is known about the management of innovation in FBGs. *Sabyasachi and Thakur* raise the issue of innovation initiatives as questions of centralization or decentralization. Should the innovation activities take place in group companies, they may lack institutional support from the group level. On the other hand, those innovation activities taking place at the group level may stay too abstract or unconcerned with the actual needs and opportunities in the group companies. Widening the perspective on innovation to include also external world, *Konsti-Laakso, Mäkimattila, and Uotila* discuss open innovation in FBGs. They argue that FBG innovation research would benefit from the lessons of open innovation—that is, in the present literature of FBG innovation, the reasons, mechanisms, and timing of innovation seem too simplistic. Supporting this view, *Pihkala, Akhter, and Rautiainen* analyze the temporal development of innovation management in an FBG. They show how the FBG owners are guiding the innovation management in the FBG and introducing new approaches to renew the businesses in the group. Furthermore, their study highlights the owners' central role in spotting innovative opportunities both in- and outside the FBG.

Studies on Identity, Values, and Sustainability in FBGs

The major difference between business groups and family business groups is the presence of the family as owners in the FBG. Along with the inclusion of the family in the analysis, the family-dependent aspects such as personal and collective knowledge, values, identity, transition, or legacy grow in importance for understanding of the FBG. These issues emphasize the intra-family processes, especially in cases of business succession, or growth of the FBG in wealth. In their papers, *Cheng and King* and *Widz and Parada* discuss the family identity development in the process where the family business is transforming the family into a business family. Cheng and King suggest that the process is characterized by paradoxical tensions that need to be solved to make the transition successful. On the other hand, Witz and Parada emphasize the social nature of the transition process and analyze it as a consecutive evolution of self- and external narratives. In this sense, it is also important how the narratives of the external stakeholders evolve during the process. *Chalid and Djunaedi* analyze the dynamics of socio-emotional wealth and suggest that in the process of the family business transforming into a medium-sized FBG, the family experiences shape their socio-emotional wealth and thereby the family members' attachment to their business. The changing nature of the family may also take new routes. Discussing the perspective of sustainability embeddedness, *Ramirez-Pasillas, Saari, and Lundberg* raise the important issue of sustainability as a response to the ecological, social and ethical challenges. They argue that their proposed model of sustainability embeddedness is useful for analyzing the degree and form of involvement of the owning family in their pursuit of sustainability.

Finally, two papers focus on the knowledge creation and sharing processes in FBGs. *Goel, Rautiainen, and Ikäheimonen* suggest that the evolution of an FBG is characterized by the sense-making and sense-giving processes by the controlling coalition. From this perspective, understanding the growing complexity and institutional environment require subjective knowledge creation, and interpersonal knowledge sharing. In line with this, *Sandoval-Argaza, Fonseca and Parada* analyze intergenerational flourishing through the perspective of knowledge sharing. With their case analysis of three

FBGs, they show that the knowledge sharing mechanisms help explain the intergenerational flourishing of the FBGs and their long-term survivability.

Taken together, the chapter of this book underscores the need to understand more about FBGs around the world. We acknowledge that our work may just be the tip of the iceberg, yet it opens the door for academics interested in exploring more about this fascinating phenomenon.

References

Aguilera, R. V., & Crespi-Cladera, R. (2012). Firm family firms: Current debates of corporate governance in family firms. *Journal of Family Business Strategy, 3*(2), 66–69.

Akhter, N., Sieger, P., & Chirico, F. (2016). If we can't have it, then no one should: Shutting down versus selling in family business portfolios. *Strategic Entrepreneurship Journal, 10*(4), 371–394.

Calabrò, A., Vecchiarini, M., Gast, J., Campopiano, G., De Massis, A., & Kraus, S. (2019). Innovation in family firms: A systematic literature review and guidance for future research. *International Journal of Management Reviews, 21*(3), 317–355.

Carney, M., & Gedajlovic, E. (2002). The co-evolution of institutional environments and organizational strategies: The rise of family business groups in the ASEAN region. *Organization Studies, 23*(1), 1–29.

Chang, S. J., & Hong, J. (2000). Economic performance of group-affiliated companies in Korea: Intragroup resource sharing and internal business transactions. *Academy of Management Journal, 43*, 429–448.

Chirico, F., Sirmon, D. G., Sciascia, S., & Mazzola, P. (2011). Resource orchestration in family firms: Investigating how entrepreneurial orientation, generational involvement, and participative strategy affect performance. *Strategic Entrepreneurship Journal, 5*(4), 307–326.

De Massis, A., Kotlar, J., Chua, J. H., & Chrisman, J. J. (2014). Ability and willingness as sufficiency conditions for family-oriented particularistic behavior: Implications for theory and empirical studies. *Journal of Small Business Management, 52*(2), 344–364.

Discua Cruz, A., Howorth, C., & Hamilton, E. (2013). Intrafamily entrepreneurship: The formation and membership of family entrepreneurial teams. *Entrepreneurship Theory and Practice, 37*(1), 17–46.

Discua Cruz, A., Hadjielias, E., & Howorth, C. (2017). Family entrepreneurial teams. In *Research Handbook on Entrepreneurial Teams* (pp. 187–207). Edward Elgar Publishing.

Granovetter, M. (1994). Business groups. *The Handbook of Economic Sociology, 1*, 453–475.

Guillén, M. F. (2000). Business groups in emerging economies: A resource-based view. *Academy of Management Journal, 43*, 362–380.

Howorth, C., Rose, M., Hamilton, E., & Westhead, P. (2010). Family firm diversity and development: An introduction. *International Small Business Journal, 28*(5), 437–451.

Howorth, C., Jackson, J., & Cruz, A. D. (2014). Entrepreneurship in family businesses. In *Handbook of Research on Small Business and Entrepreneurship* (pp. 333–357). Edward Elgar Publishing.

Keister, L. A. (1998). Engineering growth: Business group structure and firm performance in China's transition economy. *American Journal of Sociology, 104*(2), 404–440.

Khanna, T., & Yafeh, Y. (2007). Business groups in emerging markets: Paragons or parasites? *Journal of Economic Literature, 45*(2), 331–372.

Manikutty, S. (2000). Family business groups in India: A resource-based view of the emerging trends. *Family Business Review, 13*(4), 279–292.

Parada, M. J., Akhter, N., Basco, R., Discua Cruz, A., & Fitz-Koch, S. (2019). Understanding the dynamics of business group development: A transgenerational perspective. In *The family business group phenomenon* (pp. 201–222). Palgrave Macmillan.

Parada, M. J., Müller, C., & Gimeno, A. (2016). Family firms in Ibero-America: An introduction. *Academia Revista Latinoamericana De Administración, 20*(3), 19–30.

Rautiainen, M., Rosa, P., Pihkala, T., Parada, M. J., & Discua Cruz, A. (2019). *The family business group phenomenon*. Palgrave Macmillan.

Rogoff, E. G., & Heck, R. K. Z. (2003). Evolving research in entrepreneurship and family business: Recognizing family as the oxygen that feeds the fire of entrepreneurship. *Journal of Business Venturing, 18*(5), 559–566.

Rosa, P., Howorth, C., & Discua Cruz, A. (2014). Habitual and portfolio entrepreneurship and the family in business. *The Sage handbook of family business*, 364–382.

Rosa, P., Rautiainen, M., Pihkala, T., Parada, M. J., & Discua Cruz, A. (2019). Conclusions: Researching family business groups: Lessons learned and avenues for further research. In *The family business group phenomenon* (pp. 387–395). Palgrave Macmillan.

Tu, H. S., Kim, S. Y., & Sullivan, S. E. (2002). Global strategy lessons from Japanese and Korean business groups. *Business Horizons, 45*(2), 39–46.

Zellweger, T. M., Nason, R. S., Nordqvist, M., & Brush, C. G. (2013). Why do family firms strive for nonfinancial goals? An organizational identity perspective. *Entrepreneurship Theory and Practice, 37*(2), 229–248.

Part I

Strategy, Entrepreneurship & Business Transformation

2

Ambidexterity in Family Business Groups

Salvador Cerón de la Torre, Cristina Cruz, and Maria José Parada

Introduction

Family business groups (FBGs) represent one of the most prevalent formal ways to structure multiple ownership among family owners (Cuervo-Cazurra, 2006; Rosa et al., 2019) as part of a survivability and sustainability strategy. Research shows that on average, 19% of listed firms belong to family-controlled business groups, with this figure rising above 40% in some emerging markets (Masulis et al., (2011). Indeed, in Latin America, FBGs are considered an "essential component in explaining the structure of its economic organization" (Del Angel, 2016).

Early research adopted a corporate governance perspective to explain the prevalence of FBGs as a way to overcome external capital constraints and

---

S. Cerón de la Torre (✉) · C. Cruz
IE University, Madrid, Spain
e-mail: sceron@ceronandco.com

C. Cruz
e-mail: cristina.cruz@ie.edu

M. J. Parada
Department of Strategy and General Management, ESADE Business School, Sant Cugat del Vallès, Spain
e-mail: mariajose.parada@esade.edu

© The Author(s), under exclusive license to Springer Nature Switzerland AG 2023
M. Rautianen et al. (eds.), *The Palgrave Handbook of Managing Family Business Groups*, https://doi.org/10.1007/978-3-031-13206-3_2

the associated risk of financial distress in underdeveloped capital markets (Almeida & Wolfenzon, 2006a, 2006b). However, these studies fall short in assessing the role of the business family in the decision to create FBGs (Carter & Ram, 2003). This is why recent attempts have relied on portfolio entrepreneurship (PE) as a theoretical approach to understand the phenomena of business groups in family business contexts (Akhter & Ning, 2019; Rosa et al., 2019). This literature mainly emphasizes how the formation and growth of an FBG are largely determined by the central role that the individual entrepreneur plays in the pursuit of multiple ventures (Iacobucci & Rosa, 2019). While insightful, in the study of FBGs, "there is great scope for adopting a range of currently unexplored theoretical perspectives" (Rosa et al., 2019, p. 395) that accentuate not only the role of family owners behind the founding of new businesses (as emphasized in PE), but also the conditions that are needed to succeed in managing an FBG (which PE fails to fully accentuate).

In this chapter, we argue that to successfully manage an FBG, family owners need to understand how to effectively balance the exploration of new businesses with the exploitation of existing ones within the FBG. Therefore, we build on organizational ambidexterity (OA) literature to further explore the drivers of success in FBGs. OA is defined as the capacity to exploit and explore simultaneously (March, 1991), where optimizing and executing (exploitation) and experimentation and innovation (exploration) (Birkinshaw et al., 2015) go hand in hand. According to family business studies, family firms can put themselves in a better position to survive in the long-term when achieving high levels of ambidexterity by balancing 'sufficient exploitative and explorative activities' (Hiebl, 2015; p. 1062).

Extending this work to the case of FBGs, the aim of this book chapter is to develop a theoretical framework to explain what drives the formation and consolidation of an ambidextrous family business group. Combining insights from macro and micro perspectives of OA and family business studies, we develop the "FBG Ambidexterity Framework." The framework identifies the family conditions that shape the individual and organizational drivers needed to ensure the formation and consolidation of an ambidextrous FBG.

To illustrate our framework, we turn to the analysis of a case study that shows how the FBG Ambidexterity Framework works in practice. Our case study of an FBG exemplifies the development of OA originating at the individual level, through the family leaders' capacity to learn and manage exploration–exploitation tensions, in combination with an effective FBG governance mechanism at the organizational level.

Table 2.1 Selected Family-Firm Ambidexterity Studies

Article	Research Focus	Study Type	Main arguments or findings	Family factors shaping OA
Miller and Le Breton-Miller (2006)	Exploitation and exploration advantages in successful family businesses	Conceptual	Good governance and organizational design enable family firms to obtain potential advantages to exploit and explore	Agency costs
Veider and Matzler (2016)	Ability and willingness to arrive at OA in family firms	Conceptual	Achievement of OA is related to family agency advantages (eg. efficient exploitation,) and facing agency disadvantages (eg. path dependency). Factors such as different systems of governance, resources and goals explain variance in the OA profiles of FFs	Agency costs
Stubner et al. (2012)	OA and Family Firm Performance	Empirical (Quantitative, 104 family firms, Germany)	Family power as well as coordination of firm and family interests can lead to higher OA and also to better financial performance	SEW

(continued)

Table 2.1 (continued)

Article	Research Focus	Study Type	Main arguments or findings	Family factors shaping OA
Arredondo and Cruz (2019)	Value creation across generations	Empirical (Quantitative, 183 family firms, Latin America)	Competitive advantage and value generation in family businesses requires accomplishing a "dual balance" among exploration and exploitation as well as among economic and non-economic objectives	SEW
Kammerlander et al. (2020)	Family involvement and effects on exploration, exploitation and OA	Empirical (Quantitative, 118 family firms, Germany)	Ambidextrous behavior in family firms is influenced by a) the composition and diversity of the top management team and b) the family CEOs' family-centered noneconomic (FCNE) goals	SEW Influence of family leadership
Moss et al. (2014)	Continuity of Exploration and Exploitation strategies in Family Firms	Empirical (Quantitative, 205 firms, 94 family businesses, 4 high-tech industries, 12-year period, USA)	Managers' intentions with regards to the continuation of exploitation or exploration strategies delivers superior performance results. This effect is stronger for family businesses	Influence of family leadership

Article	Research Focus	Study Type	Main arguments or findings	Family factors shaping OA
Kammerlander et al. (2015)	Effect of CEOs' regulatory focus on exploration and exploitation in established SMEs	Empirical (Quantitative, 153 SMEs, Switzerland)	Positive relationship among the promotion focus of the CEO and the firm's engagement in exploitation and exploration. The CEOs' focus of prevention is negatively associated with exploration. Moreover, exploration can be associated with family ownership in SMEs	Influence of family leadership
Mazzelli et al. (2019)	The micro-foundations of ambidextrous search in family and non-family Firms	Simulation Model	Different individuals present different ambidextrous search performance profiles, contingent on social contexts and individual cognitive frameworks. Family businesses still managed by its founder may capitalize from an ambidextrous approach while family businesess managed by outsiders or next-generation CEOs benefit more from an specialization either on exploitation or exploration approach	Influence of family leadership

20 S. Cerón de la Torre et al.

The chapter is organized as follows: First, by integrating concepts from the business group literature, family firm research, and the organizational ambidexterity literature, we define an ambidextrous FBG. Following this, we establish the case for ambidexterity in FBGs. To do so, we drill down on applicable literature connecting family firm research and ambidexterity, both at the organizational and individual level, to explore the drivers behind the formation of ambidextrous FBGs. Based on this exploration, we build propositions and develop our 'FBG Ambidexterity Framework.' Following this, we exemplify our framework through an illustrative FBG case, and finally, we offer some concluding remarks and suggest further research opportunities.

Theoretical Background

Business groups consist of individual firms bound together by economic, family, or social ties that are subject to coordinated action in order to attain common objectives and enhance collective performance (Granovetter, 1995; Khanna & Rivkin, 2001). They typically rely on a central actor or core entity, which provides common administration and managerial coordination between affiliate firms, as well as control over capital, resources, and information (Khanna & Rivkin, 2001; Leff, 1978). For our purposes, we focus on the business-owning family as the central actor that coordinates a group of autonomous ventures. As such, we define an FBG as a group of related businesses with family involvement in ownership and management (Carney & Gedajlovic, 2002; Cuervo-Cazurra, 2006), shaping the strategic direction of the group (Anderson & Reeb, 2003).

FBGs offer family owners multiple financial and socioemotional benefits (Cruz & Justo, 2017). Among other things, they facilitate the transfer of resources between the different business units, leveraging the potential synergies among them (Alsos et al., 2014). They also allow for the replication of known organizational structures (Robson et al., 1993), favoring growth while reducing managerial complexity (Cruz & Justo, 2017). In addition, the creation of a portfolio of interconnected businesses under the control and ownership of the family (Carney et al., 2011) favors transgenerational succession (Goel et al., 2019; Rautiainen & Pihkala, 2019).

By means of an FBG organizational model, business families simultaneously explore new businesses while retaining the businesses that were formed in the past (Rosa et al., 2014). The problem is that it is exceptionally hard to simultaneously allow exploration and exploitation to coexist within a single organization (March, 1991), i.e., to become an ambidextrous organization, as there is a crucial difference between identifying an opportunity and effectively acting to exploit that opportunity (McMullen & Shepherd, 2006). The quest for ambidexterity is even more challenging in the context of FBGs, as in addition to business-related tensions, FBG leaders need to address the potential tensions that emanate from the interaction of the family, the business entities, and the individuals (Habbershon et al., 2003). As Rosa and Pihkala (2019, p. 28) argue, "FBGs grow out of balancing between the strive to keep ownership and control within the family, while at the same time encountering forces of diversification and independent venturing by individual family members." Moreover, as in any family business system, FBGs are also subject to conflicting goals or agendas between the family and the business (Rautiainen et al., 2019; Rosa et al., 2019), or between family members, generations, or branches, when some might be more inclined toward growth while others are more inclined toward wealth accumulation (Goel et al., 2019). This is why while FBGs are prevalent, it is difficult to become—and operate as—an ambidextrous FBG.

While studies of OA in FBGs are absent, family business literature has largely addressed the conditions that favor ambidexterity in family firms. We review these studies in the next section, with the aim of extending these conditions to the particular case of FBGs.

Organizational Ambidexterity in Family Firm Research

OA has been identified as an important driver of family firms' performance and long-term survival (Stubner et al., 2012; Hiebl, 2015; Dolz et al., 2019), so that extant research has focused on the link between ambidexterity and family ownership (Gedajlovic et al., 2012; Kammerlander et al., 2020; Lubatkin et al., 2006). Overall, empirical evidence suggests a positive relationship between family involvement and OA (Allison et al., 2014; Moss et al., 2014; Stubner et al., 2012), although some studies argue that there can be a negative influence between family involvement and ambidexterity, as well as high levels of heterogeneity among family firms with regard to their OA (Hiebl, 2015). This is why Le Breton-Miller and Miller (2006) conclude that specific family conditions may allow family businesses to take advantage of continuity and focus ('exploitation'), while being able to reorient themselves when needed ('exploration').

To account for the heterogeneity in family firms' ambidextrous behavior, several studies have investigated the specific family conditions that may help family firms to achieve OA. Table 2.1 summarizes the findings of studies pointing out specific family factors that may shape OA: (a) distinctive agency costs; (b) socioemotional wealth (SEW); and (c) the influence of family leadership in decision making.

A first set of studies conceptually analyze the organizational conditions that lead to OA in family firms. Both Miller & Le-Breton Miller (2006) and Veider and Matzler (2016) highlight the importance of *good governance systems* as mechanisms that drive and align values and goals as antecedents of OA in family firms, given the unique agency issues derived from family ownership. Ample evidence suggests that family owners have strong monitoring capabilities and a deep knowledge about their firm's operations (Anderson & Reeb, 2003; Villalonga & Amit, 2006). Taken together, these family ownership features reduce agency costs and allow a "long-term view of the business that facilities both exploitation and exploration" to be taken (Miller & Le-Breton Miller, 2006, p. 220). Similarly, Veider and Matzler (2016) argue that reduced owner-manager agency costs in family-controlled firms increase the organizations' ability to achieve OA, considering that they benefit from reduced monitoring costs that favor exploration efforts. They also benefit from a higher motivation to exploit efficiently, given that they have most of their wealth concentrated in one single asset, the family firm. Having a strong governance system would allow family owners to enhance these agency advantages, facilitating the development of OA.

Another aspect that characterizes family firms is that their decision-making processes contemplate achieving a combination of financial and socioemotional wealth (SEW) objectives simultaneously (Gómez-Mejía et al., 2007). Some authors identify the ability to simultaneously pursue economic and non-economic objectives while ensuring exploration–exploitation efforts as a key driver of OA in family firms (Stubner et al., 2012). As such, they may allow for the exploitation of short-term gains (financial and socioemotional), as well as the exploration of new projects with potentially good future (financial and socioemotional) benefits. This is what Arredondo and Cruz (2019) named as achieving the 'double balance' and what Kammerlander et al. (2020) later approached when studying the effect of family-centered non-economic (FCNE) goals on OA, to find that in general, higher levels of FCNE goals generate lower levels of OA. In sum, highlighting the importance of *balancing SEW concerns* as a fundamental family condition can help to manage the tensions that are present in a family business system.

Lastly, family firms are also distinct because of the central role that family leaders have in setting the strategic direction of the firm (Anderson & Reeb, 2003). Some studies identify leadership conditions conducive to OA in family firms. Indeed, while absent in family firm contexts, ambidexterity at the level of the individual has started to emerge as a new research field (Pertusa-Ortega et al., 2020). This emergent stream of research, named individual ambidexterity (IA), analyzes the central position that individuals perform with regard to exploitation or exploration strategies (Gibson & Birkinshaw, 2004; Mom et al., 2009) and highlights some leadership attributes as central in driving ambidexterity, such as (a) the ability to manage contradictions and paradoxical practices such as working in activities pursuing multiple objectives; and (b) a learning orientation and disposition to actively renovate their knowledge (Mom et al., 2007; Kauppila & Tempelaar, 2016; Papachroni & Heracleous, 2020). This literature concludes that as the individual "lies at the heart of managing the organizational tensions between exploration and exploitation" (Papachroni & Heracleous, 2020, pp. 2–3), specific leadership attributes may affect the emergence of ambidextrous strategies such as the leader's search profile (Mazzelli et al., 2019), focus of attention (Kammerlander et al., 2015), and managerial intentionality (Moss et al., 2014).

The Family Business Group Ambidexterity Framework

Building on the previous review, we conclude that an ambidextrous FBG provides a space in which exploration and exploitation of opportunities can coexist, and where integration mechanisms are put in place by the owning family in order to ensure overall group coherence (O'Reilly & Tushman, 2004). Through this organizational design and strategic management process, an ambidextrous FBG would be able to dynamically explore new business ventures while continuing to capitalize on existing businesses, and, as a result, achieve the overall continuity and survival objective of the FBG. Hence, we propose the following definition:

> An ambidextrous FBG consists of a group of distinct ventures managed and controlled by a business family, aiming to ensure long-term family and firm survivability through a dynamic management of the tensions that arise from the simultaneous exploitation of the businesses formed in the past and the exploration of new business opportunities.

Having defined what an ambidextrous FBG is, we now turn to explore what drives the formation and consolidation of these types of organizations.

Tensions and Paradoxes Involved in Managing an FBG

The previous discussion suggested that achieving OA requires being able to resolve the tensions involved in simultaneously dealing with exploration and exploitation (Nosella et al., 2012). Such tensions arise since "in the short-term, ambidexterity is intrinsically inefficient in that it requires the duplication of efforts and the expenditure of resources on innovation, not all of which will be successful" (O'Reilly & Tushman, 2013, p. 333). In addition to these business-related tensions, to achieve OA, family firms need to account for the potential tensions that emanate from the interaction between the family, the business entity, and the individual (Habbershon et al., 2003), which result from the simultaneous pursuit of economic and non-economic goals (Gómez-Mejía et al., 2011). Not surprisingly, family business studies have depicted family-owned firms as a plethora of paradoxes (Ingram et al., 2016), stressing the tensions embedded in managing family firms. In Table 2.2, we highlight the tensions that are most relevant in the study of ambidexterity in FBGs.

Ambidexterity tensions that appear in FBGs can be related to the *family dimension* present when economic and non-economic objectives counteract each other (Arredondo & Cruz, 2019), when the family is not able to strike a balance between the short- and the long-term (Lumpkin & Brigham, 2011), or when power in the family is not necessarily concentrated but dispersed (Gedajlovic et al., 2012). Furthermore, ambidexterity tensions may appear in relation to the *business group dimension*—when different types of skills are demanded for professional management or entrepreneurial endeavors within the group's ventures (Goel et al., 2019), when strategic growth choices have to be made with regard to the integration of value adding processes to

Table 2.2 Managing tensions in a FBG context

Context	AMBIDEXTERITY IN FBGs (Tensions & Paradoxes)		Reference
Family Dimension	← Economic/Non-Economic Profile →		Arredondo & Cruz, 2019
	← Short/Long-term Focus →		Lumpkin & Brigham, 2011
	← Concentrated/Dispersed Ownership →		Gedajlovic, et al., 2012
Business Group Dimension	← Management/Entrepreneurial Competence →		Goel et al., 2019
	← Integration/Diversification Election →		Chrisman et al., 2012
	← Resource Scarcity/Availability →		Iacobucci & Rosa, 2005
	EXPLOIT (Profitability)	**EXPLORE** (Growth)	

existing ventures or the deployment of diversification strategies (Chrisman et al., 2012), and also when the different business units or ventures within the group compete internally for the group's limited capital and resources (Iacobucci & Rosa, 2005) that need to be allocated by the controlling-family.

To balance the aforementioned competing pressures and contradictions, leaders in FBGs should rely on paradoxical thinking in order to transform apparently contradictory demands into synergistic opportunities (Smith & Lewis, 2011). According to paradox thinking, unlike dilemmas, paradoxes must not be resolved with an 'either/or' approach (Ingram et al., 2016) but from a 'both/and' mentality (Miron-Spektor et al., 2018). By embracing a paradoxical mindset, an ambidextrous leader is not confronted with the choice of either exploring or exploiting. Instead, they profit from approaching exploitation as a way to eventually be in a better position to explore and vice versa.

Hence, to become an ambidextrous FBG, family owners need to successfully manage existing paradoxes at both the individual (family) and organizational (business group) level. Our framework proposes that these two levels are highly interconnected, and as such, they need to work together in order to develop an ambidextrous FBG. This leads us to establish our first proposition:

Proposition 1: The development and consolidation of an ambidextrous FBG requires managing paradoxes at the individual and organizational level simultaneously, in order to effectively balance the exploitation-exploration tensions presented in an ambidextrous FBG.

In what follows, we identify specific family conditions that help business families to manage these paradoxes effectively, facilitating individual and organizational drivers of ambidexterity in FBGs.

Business-Owning Families' Transgenerational Intentions and Individual Drivers of OA

We first identify family '*transgenerational intentions*' as a family driver that facilitates the managing of paradoxes at the individual level in FBGs. In an FBG setting, transgenerational intentions are represented by the family's commitment toward transgenerational control of the group of firms (Zellweger et al., 2012). Such long-term orientation and desire to keep the family businesses for the future generations predisposes family business leaders to balance the short-term exploitation requirements with the long-term exploration endeavors required to build ambidextrous leadership capabilities (Veider & Matzler, 2016; Webb et al., 2010).

To provide a fertile ground for developing ambidextrous skills in next-gen leaders, transgenerational families combine a virtuous internal nurturing process with knowledge acquisition outside the family arena (Cruz & Justo, 2017). Family leaders are nurtured internally, by socializing them early into the business dynamics, as well as into the family's shared values and collective identity (Parada & Viladas, 2010; Parada & Dawson, 2017). Exploitative tacit complex knowledge about the business is transferred to incoming generations by means of mentoring processes, shadowing, or early internships (Chirico, 2008; Kandade et al., 2021; Trevinyo-Rodriguez & Bontis, 2010), while explorative profiles are enhanced via formal education, by bringing external knowledge from their experience in other businesses (Cabrera-Suárez et al., 2001; Kellermanns & Eddleston, 2004), as well as fostering entrepreneurial projects of members of subsequent generations (Cruz & Justo, 2017; Nordqvist & Melin, 2010).

Moreover, the desire to keep the family business for future generations predisposes family business leaders to adopt a search profile, forcing them to explore new opportunities that aim to ensure the survivability of family firms (Chrisman & Patel, 2012). It also fosters a long-term orientation that facilitates the development of patient capital (Sirmon & Hitt, 2003), which in turn allows leaders of FBGs to build the capabilities needed to integrate the required knowledge associated with both exploration and exploitation (Veider & Matzler, 2016; Webb et al., 2010).

Hence, business families' transgenerational intentions promote family leaders with a capacity to search and to integrate knowledge, as well as drive their intentionality toward short-term exploration and long-term exploitation. These two leadership capacities are key to developing ambidextrous leaders, and they, therefore, facilitate the development of ambidextrous FBGs. Leadership search profiles, which relate to leaders' capacity to find solutions to problems by identifying and assessing information and knowledge, are closely linked to the acquisition of the relevant management knowledge that eventually leads to the growth and continuity of the group over time (Westhead, Ucbasaran, & Wright, 2003). Moreover, leaders' capacity to learn from past efforts (Papachroni & Heracleous, 2020) and actively seek to renovate their knowledge (Mom et al., 2007) are key for the success of an FBG, since its likelihood of survival is heavily linked to having prior experience in managing business successes and business failures (McGrath, 1999; Ucbasaran et al., 2003).

Lastly, the leader's capacity to simultaneously incorporate '*long- as well as short-term*' perspectives in their decision-making schemes with regard to exploration or exploitation strategies has a significant influence on the development of ambidextrous FBGs. Leaders of families with high transgenerational intentions do not face a dilemma between socioemotional wealth and financial wealth, because they understand that in order to thrive in the long run, financial and non-financial goals should be aligned to ensure the family legacy. Hence, they are better able to manage the paradox between ensuring the long-term continuity of the family business while delivering short-term results (Lumpkin & Brigham, 2011).

Considering the above, we propose that:

Proposition 2a: Business-owning families with high transgenerational intentions are more likely to develop a family leadership profile where focus and intention is directed to maximize and balance short-term profitability with long-term growth, which represents an important individual driver of an ambidextrous FBG.

Proposition 2b: Business-owning families with high transgenerational intentions are more likely to develop a family leadership profile that is continuously searching for solutions and integrating knowledge, which represent important individual drivers of an ambidextrous FBG.

Organizational-Level Drivers and FBG Ambidexterity

According to Tushman and Euchner, (2015): "ambidexterity is marked ...by an overarching set of core values, and by an identity that makes sense of it all" (p. 18). Moreover, according to Sanchez-Famoso et al. (2015): "the family group may contribute to firm performance through family members' strong and enduring ties, shared visions, and goals, and a sense of shared responsibility and collective action" (Sanchez-Famoso et al., 2015, pp. 32–3). Building on these studies, we identify 'family owners' shared identity' as another family condition facilitating the development of ambidextrous FBGs, as it helps them to manage the organizational paradoxes involved in managing an FBG. Families that share a 'common identity and values' would foster strong identification among members and a long-term view of business (Corbetta & Salvato, 2004; De Vries, 1993; Tagiuri & Davis, 1996). Hence, for these families, governance structures are not designed to separate the business and the family dimensions, but to handle the existing tensions between the two (Sundaramurthy, & Kreiner, 2008). As mentioned earlier, managing these tensions is a necessary condition for the development of an ambidextrous FBG. Moreover, a shared family identity would foster the development of governance structures that often look for collective decision making and for preserving family harmony (Canella et al., 2015), enhancing the quality of decision making in family firms (Mustakallio et al., 2002).

The development of strong governance based on a shared identity is essential for the development of FBGs, as they comprise separate ventures in industries that are also potentially different. Hence, "governance needs to develop the requisite expertise to guide the companies' operating managers in order to achieve both each business's and the FBG's overall goals" (Goel et al., 2019, p. 262). Moreover, as Rosa et al. (2019) put it: "the expansion of family members over time, operating at multiple levels within the group, and with multiple roles, differing goals, and ownership stakes, makes it imperative for families to develop systems to control conflicting family interests and agendas" (Rosa et al., 2019, p. 392).

The OA literature on family business contexts highlights the key role of governance in achieving ambidexterity, since "governance provides the ability to shape OA achievement" (Veider & Matzler, 2016, p. 4) through family power and resource control (Chrisman et al., 2012). On the grounds that an ambidextrous family organization requires a balanced management of family and business goals or interests (Stubner et al., 2012; Veider & Matzler, 2016), family owners should develop effective group governance processes and structures if they have the purpose to survive and thrive in the long run. Having the right management tools and governance structures should allow families to conquer a 'double balance'—one that fosters the balance between exploitation and exploration and the balance in the importance of different non-economic goals (Arredondo & Cruz, 2019).

Considering the above, we propose that:

Proposition 3: Business-owning families with a shared identity are more likely to develop an FBG governance structure that serves as a mechanism to coordinate family and firm interests, which represents an important organizational driver of an ambidextrous FBG.

Toward an Integrated Framework of OA and IA in Developing Ambidextrous FBGs

Building on previous OA and IA studies, our propositions suggest that organizational mechanisms are required to support individual ambidexterity. They also imply that ambidextrous individuals enhance the usefulness of organizational mechanisms (Raisch et al., 2009). Our framework proposes that these two levels are highly interconnected, and as such, they need to work together in order to develop an ambidextrous FBG.

When family leadership values knowledge integration and advancement, i.e., when they possess a *search and learning profile,* business families would not only be better positioned to undertake potential improvements in existing ventures, but also to capture new business opportunities. This advantageous but paradoxical situation provided by the profile of family leaders puts the family in a position in which leaders would *focus on the short and the long term* simultaneously, while permanently properly balancing economic and non-economic goals manifested throughout the FBG. Nevertheless, without a proper *FBG governance structure* that is able to conduct and coordinate the group's distinct players and ventures, it would be unviable to attempt to manage the different demands and constraints that are present in this type of organizational structure. Hence, FBG governance must also incorporate and reinforce a previously agreed overall *identity and a set of core shared values* that provide the necessary glue and congruence among the FBG's separated ventures and facilitate the handling of tensions by minimizing differences and maximizing overall goal alignment, which is ultimately represented by long-term family and firm survivability. Taking together these propositions, we now delineate our 'FBG Ambidexterity Framework' (Fig. 2.1). We advocate that the effective management of both paradoxes presented in an FBG—at the individual and organizational levels—is a necessary condition for the development of an ambidextrous FBG.

Our framework identifies high family transgenerational intentions and the existence of family alignment and shared identity as the two main family conditions facilitating the successful management of paradoxes at the individual and organizational levels. This effective management of tensions enhances business families' ability to simultaneously develop exploitation and exploration strategies that allow the FBG to achieve ambidexterity and, as a result, be in a better position to survive in the long term.

In the next section, through the illustrative case of an ambidextrous FBG—the Soni Family Business Group—we show how our FBG Ambidexterity Framework works in practice.

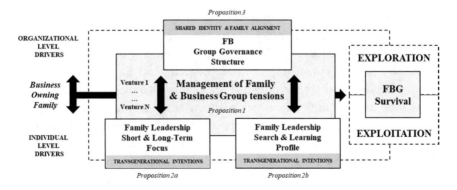

Fig. 2.1 The FBG Ambidexterity Framework

The FBG Ambidexterity Framework in Practice: An Illustration from a Mexican Ambidextrous FBG

Case Description

The Soni Family Business Group is a Mexican FBG comprised of a number of firms that have reached preponderant and relevant positions in their respective markets. This position is the result of a number of organizational configurations attributed to a transgenerational succession strategy aimed at promoting family successors to manage their own business divisions, the family's ability to survive and recover from different crises, as well as a manifested growth ambition supported by a family philosophy of reinvestment. Through this illustrative case, we show how ambidextrous strategies have emerged over time and we highlight the role of individual- and organizational-related factors working together, enhanced by distinctive family features.

Our main data sources were interviews conducted in 2020 and 2021 with Alonso Soni, the CEO of Grupo QD. Moreover, we collected information from company observations of family and business governance bodies, informal discussions with independent board members and non-family managers, as well as analysis of company reports, and websites and records.

The group's origins go back to a painting company called 'PINTURAS SONI,' founded in 1956 by Juan Soni and his brother. In its beginning, the company produced and commercialized different types of painting products. As the company developed, Juan learned that a key success factor was the ability to acquire chemical supplies at lower costs, so he decided to create 'INDUSTRIAS LATINO AMERICANA' and 'INDUSTRIAS QD' in 1973 and 1974 to commercialize chemical products and sell them to the growing Mexican manufacturing industries. The eventual success of Industrias QD served as a family platform for the FBG group to emerge and become an organizational structure consisting of three different and independent business divisions led by the three sons of Juan Soni, as shown in Fig. 2.2 below.

Santiago, who graduated as an architect, was the first and youngest of the brothers to explore uncharted spaces beyond the traditional business, and started his own project with the support of the family; he founded 'SO ARQUITECTOS' in 1992. He developed a successful construction and real estate business, specializing initially in the residential housing market, later

2 Ambidexterity in Family Business Groups   31

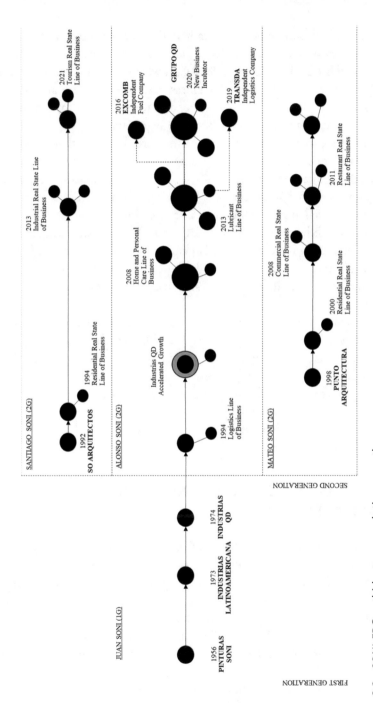

Fig. 2.2 SONI FBG ambidextrous evolution over time

diversifying into industrial real estate and more recently into tourism and hotels.

Moisés, the older son, who also graduated as an architect but initially started working in Industrias QD, also decided to pursue his career to launch 'PUNTO ARQUITECTURA' in 1998. Again with the support of his family, he diversified away from the legacy business and developed an architecture studio into another leading construction and real estate company in the housing, commercial, and restaurant business segments.

Alonso, for his part, was the only one of the three brothers that decided to stay working for Industrias QD, which represents not only the group's origin and core wealth generator for the family, but has now evolved to become a '*business group within the family business group,*' and for this reason, we believe that it deserves special attention. As can be seen in Table 2.3 below, the development and consolidation process of 'GRUPO QD' follows a trajectory in which there have been different periods characterized by instances of exploration and exploitation, illustrating the dynamic ambidextrous process in the group's history, in which different types of tensions have played a role in the configuration of the group.

In 2021, Grupo QD was organized around three independent business divisions—Industrias QD, Excomb, and TransDA—reinforced by an audit and control unit that ensures quality and risk management across the group. Grupo QD has also established a new business incubator office directly managed by Alonso, in which all of the new business ideas are tested and incubated in their initial stages, with three projects close to completion and ready to become independent companies as part of this continuous exploration–exploitation process.

Case Observations in Connection to the FBG Ambidexterity Framework

Given our definition of an ambidextrous FBG provided earlier, we confirm that in the case of the Soni family such a configuration is present because: (a) the Soni family manages and controls a group of distinct ventures; (b) the Soni family has been able to dynamically manage the different types of exploitation-exploration tensions that have been present throughout the group's history; and (c) the Soni family has been able to ensure survivability for almost half a century, and continues to look into the future toward the next generations.

The Soni FBG case exemplifies the development of OA originating at the individual level, through the individual capacity to search, learn, and

Table 2.3 GRUPO QD Stages of Development and Consolidation

Stage	Description	OA as a Dynamic E-E Process	Tensions
Initial stage 1974–1989	After the initial exploration phase, the company grew rather slowly, power was centralized in Juan which had a traditional management style and a team that was too operational. However, even though the company was not large, it was profitable and allowed the family to accumulate an important initial amount of wealth. The company distributed 8,000 tons of chemical products in 1989	Exploration–Exploitation	Management/Entrepreneurial Competence
Separation stage 1989–1994	Family tensions started to emerge between Juan and his brother, who had introduced his sons to the company that lacked the education and competencies to contribute to the business. In 1992, the brothers decided to split, with Juan keeping Industrias QD and his brother the paint factory	Exploitation	Dispersed/Concentrated Ownership

(continued)

Table 2.3 (continued)

Stage	Description	OA as a Dynamic E-E Process	Tensions
Expansion and 1st crisis stage 1994–1997	Juan Soni decided to expand the operations by opening a plant facility in 1994 for which they incurred in a large portion of debt in US dollars. By 1997, there was a substantial currency devaluation which weakened the firms' financial position to the point of near bankruptcy, hadn´t it been for some key suppliers and customers that trusted the family and kept on doing business with them	Exploration	Resource Scarcity/Availability
Reorientation stage 1997–2000	Having survived through the first crisis, Alonso Soni (2G) starts to analyze and understand the risks and weaknesses of the company, which relied only in a few large customers. Having the background of an industrial engineering career, he decides to restructure the business and processes adopting a low-cost operating structure designed to be able to serve an increased customer base. The company distributed 24,000 tons of chemical products in 1999	Exploitation-Exploration	Resource Scarcity/Availability
Accelerated growth stage 2000–2008	In the 2000s, Industrias QD had only a small market share, however it was through their low-cost distribution scheme that allowed them to gain market positions versus their larger competitors that had a high-cost scheme that was twice as costly as Industrias QDs	Exploitation	Resource Scarcity/Availability

Stage	Description	OA as a Dynamic E-E Process	Tensions
Governance and Institutionalization stage 2008–2012	Generational tensions and internal conflicts started to become more prominent between Juan (1G) and Alonso (2G) given their differences in management approaches, with Juan leaning more towards control and cost efficiency while Alonso leaning more towards building a vision and exploring new horizons. In order to dilute the confrontation level, the family decides to hire an external CEO who starts to increase the organizational structure without an encompassing growth in sales, as a result the company started to lose substantial profitability. The external CEO was removed and Alonso took the position of CEO but having decided to stablish an advisory board to mediate between the family members as well as to contribute to the strategy and institutionalization of the business The company distributed roughly 100,000 tons of chemical products in 2009	Exploitation	Short/Long term focus

(continued)

Table 2.3 (continued)

Stage	Description	OA as a Dynamic E-E Process	Tensions
Market upheaval and 2nd crisis stage 2012–2013	By 2013, Industrias QD was already situated among the four largest companies in the chemical distribution market in the country. Two of the largest competitors are merged, and the other is bought by a transnational company that wanted to gain rapid market share. A price war starts and Industrias QD´s revenues were reduced in half. The family, Alonso and the advisory board decided that it was time for rapid expansion and diversification into other profitable lines of business	Exploration	Integration/Diversification Election
Diversification stage 2013 – 2016	Alonso embarks on a thorough market analysis and identifies an opportunity in the lubricant business. In order to rapidly capture the opportunity, Alonso pitches a business plan to one of the largest multinational players in the industry which did not have a local distributor but wanted to enter the market. This company starts a thorough due-diligence of Industrias QD and the honorability of the family and the alliance is consolidated. The lubricant line of business is born	Exploration	Management/Entrepreneurial Competence

Stage	Description	OA as a Dynamic E-E Process	Tensions
Group QD consolidation stage 2016–2020	In 2016, derived from the continued power struggles between father and son, the group decides to embark on a second attempt to bring another external CEO, in order to accelerate the institutionalization process, to establish the internal controls that Juan demanded and in order to allow Alonso to have more time to engage new business opportunities. In 2016, a new business division "EXCOMB" is born aimed at the commercialization of fuels through a joint venture with a global energy trading company. It was also at this stage that the company "TRANSDA" was spun-off in order to professionalize their own transportation and logistics but also to gain economies of scale by serving third party customers, leveraging their strong capability The group distributed over 320,000 tons of chemical products in 2020	Exploration- Exploitation	Economic/Non-economic profile Short/Long term focus

manage exploration–exploitation tensions with a short- and long-term focus, in combination with an effective FBG governance structure at the organizational level. In what follows, we provide fragments from interviews with Alonso Soni (2G), from which we find evidence regarding important individual-level as well as group-level aspects playing a role in the achievement of ambidexterity in the FBG that illustrates the drivers behind our propositions.

First, the case illustrates how the Soni family has a clear shared vision and alignment of goals, resulting in a very clear philosophy toward continuous investment as a path toward growth:

> "Investment is a medullar point about our family philosophy in business. We all agree that the only way to increase our patrimony is through reinvestments. Another topic on which we agree is that we must be relevant players in the sectors in which we participate, so we work very hard and put all our efforts into enhancing our market positions. We step fully on the accelerator, and to do this, we have clarity that we must invest and reinvest."

Building on this shared vision toward growth, they have developed clear family business group governance mechanisms (Proposition 3) regarding the criteria guiding new investments. Implementing strong governance facilitates the decision making by adding objectivity to the investment process.

> "We have a mandatory frame of governance decisions regarding new projects, in which investments can only be considered if they offer a specific return. When a project doesn't cover these requirements, we don't even bring it to the family table" … "I might be in love with my own projects, but perhaps my brothers or my brother-in-law, who sit on the board, might say that my project has neither feet nor head … and even when I might be emotional about it I don't see that as a necessarily bad thing, I see it as a positive thing … I tell them, let me understand and let me reframe the project" … "As a family we have that capacity …for instance, my brother might bring an investment project but we might not like it because of a specific risk, so he throws a tantrum but we don't go in until he brings something that we like as a family … that's it, you throw a tantrum it brings tensions, but we have the capacity to solve it."

In addition to this, the Soni family also fosters an important set of values that not only comprise a shared family identity, but also contribute to the business group governance by fostering family union and family alignment (Proposition 3):

2 Ambidexterity in Family Business Groups   39

"If they inject you in the blood that you will be successful while you grow, surely when you go out to the world you will do better because that's in you" ... "I was not afraid of anything. Back in time when we were 20 or 30 times smaller than our competitors, I felt like David vs Goliath fighting in the market."

"I think another determinant of our family philosophy consists of always having our feet on the ground; we have received from my father the value of prudence and responsible management of money, to be careful with family spending and to educate our kids in order to make clear that nothing is free, and they have to work to earn money" ..."My father made us understand that nothing is free, everything that we have done is the product of our effort, and I am making the same philosophy for my kids."

"My father taught us that family is the most relevant value and that family union is crucial. For this, we think it is relevant to separate business tensions of family affective issues because when you are unable to do so, the family union could be affected. I think this has to do a lot with our way of organizing ourselves in independent companies in our group."

As stated in this last quote, we can identify that the three brothers' business group division separations appear to have been a key organizational driver, allowing a transgenerational FBG succession strategy to work without increasing family business tensions. As Alonso puts it:

"I think one of the successful factors about our group is that the three of us (the brothers) work independently in our own divisions. Even Santiago and Mateo, who work in construction and real estate, they each manage a different and separate division" ... "Being in different businesses allows us to make decisions easier and to exclude emotions and separate family and business issues" ... "Tensions are reduced when emotions are eliminated."

We can also identify from the case observations that at the individual level, there is a clear long-term vision emanating from the family leadership that has played an important part in the formation of the FBG, yet it is complemented by individual-level skills regarding disciplined execution, which appear to have been key drivers toward generating a *balance between the short and the long term (Proposition 2a)*. The case also illustrates the importance of transgenerational intention in driving this long-term vision, as Soni FBG growth intentionality has a clear origin in the founder's ambition and work philosophy, which has permeated subsequent generations:

"My father wanted to get out of where he was, he did not want to be one of the pack, he wanted to be an important businessman and he was clear about where he wanted to be, that is why you have to have a clear vision of where you want to go."

"Mateo, Santiago, and myself all share some traits. On the one hand we are dreamers, but on the other hand we are also disciplined and work hard for short-term execution. In addition, I believe we are very resilient, we get up when we fall, when our plans and our goals don't come through."

Moreover, this case shows how such transgenerational intention also encourages intergenerational collaboration. Having individuals from the two generations working together helps to manage exploitation-exploration tensions, as the FBG is better able to combine short- and long-term goals:

"In recent years, my dad has acted as the controller whilst I acted as the visionary... When I try to launch something, my father brings me back to the operation because he thinks that if I do not operate, we will lose control, while what I want to do is diversify to make the business larger; what I have learned is that you have to be able to sell the story of the long term to lower this tension."

"My dad, at age 86, is much more focused on the short term, while we (the next-gen) are more focused on the long term ... and all I have to say is that you have to achieve a right balance, you can't go too long nor too short."

Finally, the family leadership's individual experience of *searching for outside knowledge and continuous learning* (Proposition 2b) appears to enhance a growth intentionality and also constitute an important driver in the quest for ambidexterity, as it allows for the exploitation and exploration of business opportunities in current and future ventures. For instance, Alonso exemplifies how he continuously searches, learns, and puts this knowledge to the service of the FBG:

"I have always been an uneasy person, really wanting to learn. Regardless that I have never worked in institutional companies, I decided to study abroad to understand topics that I saw in the market – how companies like Dupont or PPG were handling their structures and processes ... I really wanted to be in those leagues ... The desire was enormous."

"One of our board members told me that I had to do strategic planning, and I was like, what is that? Then I hired someone, we started the strategic planning department, I started to understand what it is and then we started planning mid-term, long-term, growth drivers and competitive advantages. I learned a lot. Then I went to Harvard to understand more about strategy, where I met people that went from nothing to become huge enterprises and that made an impact on the vision of what I wanted to achieve."

"I have never stopped learning, each year I dive into a topic head on and that has become a way of being."

Interestingly, this attitude toward learning is specially directed and practiced in new ventures; it constitutes one of the fundamental drivers in the Soni family strategy toward the group's transgenerational continuity.

"You learn much faster when you launch a new business than in an established company."

"We want the next generation to learn and we encourage them to become entrepreneurs, to feel passion about creating businesses."

In sum, the Soni FBG provides an interesting case in which OA has been able to develop over time, as the family has been able to find the proper behavioral and structural mechanisms to manage paradoxes, and over time at the individual and organizational levels in order to effectively balance the exploitation-exploration tensions (Proposition 1), and by doing so situating the group in a better position to compete and survive over time. As Alonso himself put it when in the last interview we explained to him the concept of OA:

"Our family philosophy about business forces what you call ambidexterity. We have a pressure for delivering returns and at the same time reinvesting and being entrepreneurial for the future."

As manifested in this case, the role of the individual family leaders has been key in the group's exploitation-exploration orientations over time. Complementarily, the organizational design and governance structure have also helped to generate an effective balance between exploitation-orientation instances, so that the group can dynamically capitalize on existing businesses while permanently exploring new business ventures. Alonso interestingly frames the permanent development path behind an ambidextrous FBG:

"Just like my father, I believe that when you encounter an opportunity, you should not let it go. Analyze if it's a good one and even if you already have 18 good businesses, it might be the case that number 19 is more successful than the rest."

Discussion and Concluding Remarks

Family business groups are prevalent all around the world, and their development is receiving increased attention from scholars. A key question that calls for attention is how FBGs are able to develop and thrive over time. Our chapter advances in this direction by theoretically exploring how FBGs develop ambidexterity, which is a sine qua non condition for FBG organizational survival. Combining insights from macro and micro perspectives of OA and family business studies, we develop the 'FBG Ambidexterity Framework,' which identifies the family conditions that shape the individual and organizational drivers needed to ensure the formation and consolidation of an ambidextrous FBG. The framework aspires to signal core family attributes such as transgenerational intentions, as well as family identity and values as pivotal drivers that augment the ambidextrous capabilities of FBGs. All things considered, we intend to push toward a more comprehensive use of a relevant framework (ambidexterity) in a relevant organizational form (FBGs), and to provide a working model for both researchers and practitioners to impel the long-term survivability of family business groups, which can be understood as a strategy for families in business to thrive across generations.

Previous ambidexterity research has used macro-organizational theories or micro-individual approaches to understand ambidexterity, yet few pieces have tried to present these perspectives in combination, which turns "essential to overcome the micro–macro divide between individual ambidexterity and organizational ambidexterity research" (Pertusa-Ortega et al., 2020). We believe that this book chapter provides a starting point for such an endeavor by combining organizational and individual drivers (Raisch et al., 2009) that are highly interconnected in FBG settings. To date, what has been missing in the literature has been a clear understanding of the individual-level factors that can inform the heterogeneity in the levels of engagement in ambidexterity in family firms. In order to extend the contextual and organizational factors that have been signaled in the literature, this work proposes that certain IA characteristics of key family leaders and decision-makers, namely their search and learning profile, as well as their short- and long-term focus, are manifested through an exploration and/or exploitation orientation that affects the firm's level and type of ambidexterity. As such, these capabilities and motivations are important drivers that represent individual aspects of ambidexterity required for OA to arise, which are respectively influenced by important family features related to their transgenerational intentions. However, in an FBG setting, these individual-level factors need to be able to impact and coexist with organizational-level factors related to the FBG governance mechanisms put in place by the family, which are on their part shaped by the identity and values of the family. It is within this interaction that the needed management of family and business tensions resides, these tensions being common in the context of FBGs, manifesting themselves as exploitation or exploration standings.

This work supports the notion that families in business may possess certain abilities to handle tensions (Habbershon & Williams, 1999), and that FBGs are well suited for the nurturing of dualities, and as a result of this aptness to deal with such individual and organizational-level paradoxes, families gain an advantage in terms of adaptability in order to develop ambidexterity over time as a mechanism for enhancing long-term survival (Ingram et al., 2016; Schuman et al., 2010). Yet, how family firm leaders may accommodate ambidexterity in the family firm setting remains poorly understood. That being said, the present work aims to start to fill the gap that exists with regard to how families manage these tensions at different levels and what are the success drivers behind the achievement of ambidexterity in FBGs. We recognize that further investigation will be necessary to better understand the nature of these influences—at the individual and organizational levels of analysis—and to test the propositions indicated in this work.

References

Akhter, N., & Ning, E. (2019). Resourcefulness and informal economy: From pluriactivity to portfolio entrepreneurship. In *The Family Business Group Phenomenon* (pp. 145–174). Palgrave Macmillan.

Almeida, H., & Wolfenzon, D. (2006a). Should business groups be dismantled? The equilibrium costs of efficient internal capital markets. *Journal of Financial Economics, 79*(1), 99–144.

Almeida, H. V., & Wolfenzon, D. (2006b). A theory of pyramidal ownership and family business groups. *The Journal of Finance, 61*(6), 2637–2680.

Allison, T. H., McKenny, A. F., & Short, J. C. (2014). Integrating time into family business research: Using random coefficient modeling to examine temporal influences on family firm ambidexterity. *Family Business Review, 27*(1), 20–34.

Alsos, G. A., Carter, S., & Ljunggren, E. (2014). *Entrepreneurial families and households* (pp. 165–178). The Routledge Companion for Entrepreneurship. Routledge.

Anderson, R. C., & Reeb, D. M. (2003). Founding-family ownership and firm performance: Evidence from the S&P 500. *The Journal of Finance, 58*(3), 1301–1328.

Arredondo, H., & Cruz, C. (2019). How do owning families ensure the creation of value across generations? A "dual balance" approach. In *The Palgrave Handbook of Heterogeneity among Family Firms* (pp. 791–819). Palgrave Macmillan.

Birkinshaw, J., Zimmerman, A., & Raisch, S. (2015). How is ambidexterity initiated? Emergent versus designed processes. *Organization Science, 26*(4), 1119–1139.

Cabrera-Suárez, K., De Saá-Pérez, P., & García-Almeida, D. (2001). The succession process from a resource-and knowledge-based view of the family firm. *Family Business Review, 14*(1), 37–48.

Cannella, A. A., Jr., Jones, C. D., & Withers, M. C. (2015). Family-versus lone-founder-controlled public corporations: Social identity theory and boards of directors. *Academy of Management Journal, 58*(2), 436–459.

Carney, M., & Gedajlovic, E. (2002). The co-evolution of institutional environments and organizational strategies: The rise of family business groups in the ASEAN region. *Organization Studies, 23*(1), 1–29.

Carney, M., Gedajlovic, E. R., Heugens, P. P., Van Essen, M., & Van Oosterhout, J. (2011). Business group affiliation, performance, context, and strategy: A meta-analysis. *Academy of Management Journal, 54*(3), 437–460.

Carter, S., & Ram, M. (2003). Reassessing portfolio entrepreneurship. *Small Business Economics, 21*(4), 371–380.

Chirico, F. (2008). Knowledge accumulation in family firms: Evidence from four case studies. *International Small Business Journal, 26*(4), 433–462.

Chrisman, J. J., & Patel, P. C. (2012). Variations in R&D investments of family and nonfamily firms: Behavioral agency and myopic loss aversion perspectives. *Academy of Management Journal, 55*(4), 976–997.

Chrisman, J. J., Chua, J. H., Pearson, A. W., & Barnett, T. (2012). Family involvement, family influence, and family–centered non–economic goals in small firms. *Entrepreneurship Theory and Practice, 36*(2), 267–293.

Corbetta, G., & Salvato, C. (2004). Self–serving or self–actualizing? Models of man and agency costs in different types of family firms: A commentary on "comparing the agency costs of family and non–family firms: Conceptual issues and exploratory evidence." *Entrepreneurship Theory and Practice, 28*(4), 355–362.

Cruz, C., & Justo, R. (2017). Portfolio entrepreneurship as a mixed gamble: A winning bet for family entrepreneurs in SMEs. *Journal of Small Business Management, 55*(4), 571–593.

Cuervo-Cazurra, A. (2006). Business groups and their types. *Asia Pacific Journal of Management, 23*(4), 419–437.

De Vries, M. F. K. (1993). The dynamics of family-controlled firms: The good and the bad news. *Organizational Dynamics, 21*(3), 59–71.

Del Angel, G. A. (2016). The nexus between business groups and banks: Mexico, 1932–1982. *Business History, 58*(1), 111–128.

Dolz, C., Iborra, M., & Safón, V. (2019). Improving the likelihood of SME survival during financial and economic crises: The importance of TMTs and family ownership for ambidexterity. *BRQ Business Research Quarterly, 22*(2), 119–136.

Gedajlovic, E., Cao, Q., & Zhang, H. (2012). Corporate shareholdings and organizational ambidexterity in high-tech SMEs: Evidence from a transitional economy. *Journal of Business Venturing, 27*(6), 652–665.

Gibson, C. B., & Birkinshaw, J. (2004). The antecedents, consequences, and mediating role of organizational ambidexterity. *Academy of Management Journal, 47*(2), 209–226.

Goel, S., Ikäheimonen, T., & Rautiainen, M. (2019). Governance in family business groups: Resolving multiple contingencies to sustain entrepreneurial capability. In *The Family Business Group Phenomenon* (pp. 253–283). Palgrave Macmillan.

Gómez-Mejía, L. R., Cruz, C., Berrone, P., & De Castro, J. (2011). The bind that ties: Socioemotional wealth preservation in family firms. *Academy of Management Annals, 5*(1), 653–707.

Gómez-Mejía, L. R., Haynes, K. T., Núñez-Nickel, M., Jacobson, K. J., & Moyano-Fuentes, J. (2007). Socioemotional wealth and business risks in family-controlled firms: Evidence from Spanish olive oil mills. *Administrative Science Quarterly, 52*(1), 106–137.

Granovetter, M. (1995). Coase revisited: Business groups in the modern economy. *Industrial and Corporate Change, 4*(1), 93–130.

Habbershon, T. G., & Williams, M. L. (1999). A resource-based framework for assessing the strategic advantages of family firms. *Family Business Review, 12*(1), 1–25.

Habbershon, T. G., Williams, M., & MacMillan, I. C. (2003). A unified systems perspective of family firm performance. *Journal of Business Venturing, 18*(4), 451–465.

Hiebl, M. R. (2015). Family involvement and organizational ambidexterity in later-generation family businesses. *Management Decision.*

Iacobucci, D., & Rosa, P. (2005). Growth, diversification, and business group formation in entrepreneurial firms. *Small Business Economics, 25*(1), 65–82.

Iacobucci, D., & Rosa, P. (2019). Managing portfolio entrepreneurship: A case study. In *The Family Business Group Phenomenon* (pp. 89–110). Palgrave Macmillan.

Ingram, A. E., Lewis, M. W., Barton, S., & Gartner, W. B. (2016). Paradoxes and innovation in family firms: The role of paradoxical thinking. *Entrepreneurship Theory and Practice, 40*(1), 161–176.

Kammerlander, N., Burger, D., Fust, A., & Fueglistaller, U. (2015). Exploration and exploitation in established small and medium-sized enterprises: The effect of CEOs' regulatory focus. *Journal of Business Venturing, 30*(4), 582–602.

Kammerlander, N., Patzelt, H., Behrens, J., & Röhm, C. (2020). Organizational ambidexterity in family-managed firms: The role of family involvement in top management. *Family Business Review, 33*(4), 393–423.

Kandade, K., Samara, G., Parada, M. J., & Dawson, A. (2021). From family successors to successful business leaders: A qualitative study of how high-quality relationships develop in family businesses. *Journal of Family Business Strategy, 12*(2), 100334.

Kauppila, O. P., & Tempelaar, M. P. (2016). The social-cognitive underpinnings of employees' ambidextrous behaviour and the supportive role of group managers' leadership. *Journal of Management Studies, 53*(6), 1019–1044.

Kellermanns, F. W., & Eddleston, K. A. (2004). Feuding families: When conflict does a family firm good. *Entrepreneurship Theory and Practice, 28*(3), 209–228.

Khanna, T., & Rivkin, J. W. (2001). Estimating the performance effects of business groups in emerging markets. *Strategic Management Journal, 22*(1), 45–74.

Leff, N. H. (1978). Industrial organization and entrepreneurship in the developing countries: The economic groups. *Economic Development and Cultural Change, 26*(4), 661–675.

Lubatkin, M. H., Simsek, Z., Ling, Y., & Veiga, J. F. (2006). Ambidexterity and performance in small-to medium-sized firms: The pivotal role of top management team behavioral integration. *Journal of Management, 32*(5), 646–672.

Lumpkin, G. T., & Brigham, K. H. (2011). Long–term orientation and intertemporal choice in family firms. *Entrepreneurship Theory and Practice, 35*(6), 1149–1169.

March, J. G. (1991). Exploration and exploitation in organizational learning. *Organization Science, 2*(1), 71–87.

Masulis, R. W., Pham, P. K., & Zein, J. (2011). Family business groups around the world: Financing advantages, control motivations, and organizational choices. *The Review of Financial Studies, 24*(11), 3556–3600.

Mazzelli, A., De Massis, A., Petruzzelli, A. M., Del Giudice, M., & Khan, Z. (2019). Behind ambidextrous search: The microfoundations of search in family and non-family firms. *Long Range Planning*, 101882.

McGrath, R. G. (1999). Falling forward: Real options reasoning and entrepreneurial failure. *Academy of Management Review, 24*(1), 13–30.

McMullen, J. S., & Shepherd, D. A. (2006). Entrepreneurial action and the role of uncertainty in the theory of the entrepreneur. *Academy of Management Review, 31*(1), 132–152.

Miller, D., & Le Breton-Miller, I. (2006). The best of both worlds: Exploitation and exploration in successful family businesses. *Advances in Strategic Management, 23*(3), 215–240.

Miron-Spektor, E., Ingram, A., Keller, J., Smith, W. K., & Lewis, M. W. (2018). Microfoundations of organizational paradox: The problem is how we think about the problem. *Academy of Management Journal, 61*(1), 26–45.

Mom, T. J., Van Den Bosch, F. A., & Volberda, H. W. (2007). Investigating managers' exploration and exploitation activities: The influence of top-down, bottom-up, and horizontal knowledge inflows. *Journal of Management Studies, 44*(6), 910–931.

Mom, T. J., Van Den Bosch, F. A., & Volberda, H. W. (2009b). Understanding variation in managers' ambidexterity: Investigating direct and interaction effects of formal structural and personal coordination mechanisms. *Organization Science, 20*(4), 812–828.

Moss, T. W., Payne, G. T., & Moore, C. B. (2014). Strategic consistency of exploration and exploitation in family businesses. *Family Business Review, 27*(1), 51–71.

Mustakallio, M., Autio, E., & Zahra, S. A. (2002). Relational and contractual governance in family firms: Effects on strategic decision making. *Family Business Review, 15*(3), 205–222.

Nordqvist, M., & Melin, L. (2010). Entrepreneurial families and family firms. *Entrepreneurship & Regional Development, 22*(3–4), 211–239.

Nosella, A., Cantarello, S., & Filippini, R. (2012). The intellectual structure of organizational ambidexterity: A bibliometric investigation into the state of the art. *Strategic Organization, 10*, 450–465.

O'Reilly, C. A., III., & Tushman, M. L. (2004). The ambidextrous organization. *Harvard Business Review, 82*(4), 74.

O'Reilly, C. A., III., & Tushman, M. L. (2013). Organizational ambidexterity: Past, present, and future. *Academy of Management Perspectives, 27*(4), 324–338.

Papachroni, A., & Heracleous, L. (2020). Ambidexterity as practice: Individual ambidexterity through paradoxical practices. *The Journal of Applied Behavioral Science, 56*(2), 143–165.

Parada, M. J., & Dawson, A. (2017). Building family business identity through transgenerational narratives. *Journal of Organizational Change Management, 30*(3), 344–356.

Parada, M. J., & Viladàs, H. (2010). Narratives: A powerful device for values transmission in family businesses. *Journal of Organizational Change Management, 23*(2), 166–172.

Pertusa-Ortega, E. M., Molina-Azorín, J. F., Tarí, J. J., Pereira-Moliner, J., & López-Gamero, M. D. (2020). The microfoundations of organizational ambidexterity: A systematic review of individual ambidexterity through a multilevel framework. *BRQ Business Research Quarterly*, 2340944420929711.

Raisch, S., Birkinshaw, J., Probst, G., & Tushman, M. L. (2009). Organizational ambidexterity: Balancing exploitation and exploration for sustained performance. *Organization Science, 20*(4), 685–695.

Rautiainen, M., & Pihkala, T. (2019). The emergence of a family business group: The role of portfolio entrepreneurship. In *The Family Business Group Phenomenon* (pp. 65–87). Palgrave Macmillan.

Rautiainen, M., Rosa, P., Pihkala, T., Parada, M. J., & Cruz, A. D. (2019). *The family business group phenomenon.* Springer.

Robson, G., Gallagher, C., & Daly, M. (1993). Diversification strategy and practice in small firms. *International Small Business Journal, 11*(2).

Rosa, P., & Pihkala, T. (2019). Theoretical insights into the nature, diversity and persistence of business groups. In *The Family Business Group Phenomenon* (pp. 17–35). Palgrave Macmillan.

Rosa, P., Howorth, C., & Cruz, A. D. (2014). Habitual and portfolio entrepreneurship and the family in business. *The Sage Handbook of Family Business*, 364–382.

Rosa, P., Rautiainen, M., Pihkala, T., Parada, M. J., & Cruz, A. D. (2019). Conclusions: Researching Family Business Groups: Lessons learned and avenues for further research. In *The Family Business Group Phenomenon* (pp. 387–395). Palgrave Macmillan.

Sanchez-Famoso, V., Akhter, N., Iturralde, T., Chirico, F., & Maseda, A. (2015). Is non-family social capital also (or especially) important for family firm performance? *Human Relations, 68*(11), 1713–1743.

Schuman, A., Stutz, S., & Ward, J. (2010). *Family business as paradox.* Springer.

Sirmon, D. G., & Hitt, M. A. (2003). Managing resources: Linking unique resources, management, and wealth creation in family firms. *Entrepreneurship Theory and Practice, 27*(4), 339–358.

Smith, W. K., & Lewis, M. W. (2011). Toward a theory of paradox: A dynamic equilibrium model of organizing. *Academy of Management Review, 36*(2), 381–403.

Stubner, S., Blarr, W. H., Brands, C., & Wulf, T. (2012). Organizational ambidexterity and family firm performance. *Journal of Small Business and Entrepreneurship, 25*(2), 217–229.

Sundaramurthy, C., & Kreiner, G. E. (2008). Governing by managing identity boundaries: The case of family businesses. *Entrepreneurship Theory and Practice, 32*(3), 415–436.

Tagiuri, R., & Davis, J. (1996). Bivalent attributes of the family firm. *Family Business Review, 9*(2), 199–208.

Trevinyo-Rodríguez, R. N. & Bontis, N. (2010). Family ties and emotions: a missing piece in the knowledge transfer puzzle. *Journal of Small Business and Enterprise Development.*

Tushman, M., & Euchner, J. (2015). The challenges of ambidextrous leadership. *Research-Technology Management, 58*(3), 16–20.

Ucbasaran, D., Wright, M., & Westhead, P. (2003). A longitudinal study of habitual entrepreneurs: Starters and acquirers. *Entrepreneurship & Regional Development, 15*(3), 207–228.

Veider, V., & Matzler, K. (2016). The ability and willingness of family-controlled firms to arrive at organizational ambidexterity. *Journal of Family Business Strategy, 7*(2), 105–116.

Villalonga, B., & Amit, R. (2006). How do family ownership, control and management affect firm value? *Journal of financial Economics, 80*(2), 385–417.

Webb, J. W., Ketchen, D. J., Jr., & Ireland, R. D. (2010). Strategic entrepreneurship within family-controlled firms: Opportunities and challenges. *Journal of Family Business Strategy, 1*(2), 67–77.

Westhead, P., Ucbasaran, D., & Wright, M. 2003. Differences between private firms owned by novice, serial and portfolio entrepreneurs: Implications for policy makers and practitioners. *Regional Studies, 37.*

Zellweger, T. M., Kellermanns, F. W., Chrisman, J. J., & Chua, J. H. (2012). Family control and family firm valuation by family CEOs: The importance of intentions for transgenerational control. *Organization Science, 23*(3), 851–868.

3

The Role of Internal Capital Market in Business Groups

Valentina Giannini and Donato Iacobucci

Introduction

The aim of this chapter is to discuss the role played by the internal capital market in business groups and open new lines of research on how these internal flows influence the relations between companies belonging to the same group and in particular the relation between the head and its subsidiaries (or affiliated companies). The internal capital market is a peculiarity of business groups; it refers to several mechanisms that allow the transfer of funds between companies belonging to the same group.

The internal capital market may play a dual role. The first is that the presence of internal capital flows within a group can make it easier for companies to survive an external shock, such as an economic or a financial crisis. The second is that the internal capital market facilitates the allocation of resources to investment projects, in particular innovative projects, for which it could be difficult to raise external funds.

V. Giannini (✉) · D. Iacobucci
Centre for Innovation and Entrepreneurship, Polytechnic University of Marche, Ancona, Italy
e-mail: v.giannini@staff.univpm.it

D. Iacobucci
e-mail: d.iacobucci@univpm.it

© The Author(s), under exclusive license to Springer Nature
Switzerland AG 2023
M. Rautianen et al. (eds.), *The Palgrave Handbook of Managing Family Business Groups*,
https://doi.org/10.1007/978-3-031-13206-3_3

As regards the first aspect, an underperforming or economically distressed company belonging to a group could have easier access to capital (e.g., financial loans from the head or from another subsidiary) or could obtain an external loan (e.g., bank loan) more easily given the guarantee of belonging to a group. In the latter case, the head could act as guarantor for the bank loan.

Regarding the second point, literature shows that companies belonging to groups are less dependent on internal cash flows to finance their investments. This is particularly relevant for investments in innovation activities where information asymmetries between managers and investors are higher. The internal capital market may be an instrument for the group to mitigate information problems (Mota & Coutinho dos Santos, 2020). As a result, the presence of an internal capital market is considered one of the main reasons for the superior innovativeness of firms belonging to a group compared to standalone firms (Belenzon & Berkovitz, 2010). Indeed, belonging to a group may have a significant effect on the direction and results of R&D activity (Belenzon & Berkovitz, 2010 ; Cefis et al., 2009; Hsieh et al., 2010). This result is particularly relevant given the increasing importance attributed by policymakers to R&D and patent activities of firms.

More generally, literature has shown that business groups are widespread not only in emerging markets where they are supposed to substitute the deficiency of market institutions (Gorodnichenko et al., 2009; Khanna & Yafeh, 2005; Samphantharak, 2003), but also in developed countries given their ability to improve the efficiency and innovative performance of affiliated companies compared to standalone ones (Cainelli & Iacobucci, 2011; Hamelin, 2011; Sharon Belenzon et al., 2013). In all countries, business groups are responsible for the allocation of significant amounts of resources in the private sector. Managers and entrepreneurs tend to adopt the group form to develop business activities. In fact, this form can increase the effective management of diversified portfolio of products and markets. In the small firm sector, the business group is also a mechanism for facilitating the start-up of new businesses (Rosa & Iacobucci, 2010). Business groups are seen as a way to experiment new entrepreneurial activities, thanks to their superior investment capacity than standalone companies. Bena and Molina (2013) suggest that business groups facilitate the financing of entrepreneurial activities. This aspect is highlighted also by Almeida and Wolfenzon (2006): For controlling shareholders, it is easier to create new firms when the original companies start to decline.

This capacity of business groups to expand and develop in new business activities is also a consequence of the possibility to benefit from the internal capital market. For example, business groups may have a greater capacity to invest in one sector using the cash flow generated in other sectors (Boutin et al., 2013).

However, the internal capital market and its function are part of a wider discussion on how business groups are viewed. In this regard, there are two streams of literature that consider the "nature" of the business group in a different way: (a) business group as a substitute of inefficient institutions; (b) business group as a financial device.

According to the former, the development of business groups may be favored by underdeveloped financial markets or institutional and political instability or the lack of entrepreneurial power in private companies. There are several papers about that. Khanna and Palepu (1997, p. 41) argue that "highly diversified business groups can be particularly well suited to the institutional context in most developing countries...."

According to this view, business groups should develop most frequently in countries with market inefficiencies, usually emerging countries with significant market information asymmetries (Kock & Guillén, 2001; Yiu et al., 2005).

Similarly, Chang (2006) referring to East Asian countries states that: "business groups are creatures of market imperfections, government intervention, and socio-cultural environments. I expect that as long as markets, especially capital markets, are imperfect and the East Asian governments influence resource allocation, business groups will continue to exist and even prosper in this region. As markets become more efficient and government intervention subsides, business groups may lose their reason for existence and see their influence decline" (p. 413).

However, this interpretation on the presence of business groups in inefficient market contexts is contradicted by the large number of business groups in advanced economies, a growing rather a declining trend in recent years.

In fact, Khanna and Yafeh (2005), using a sample of large groups in several emerging countries, argue that "...other reasons are more likely to explain the ubiquity of business groups around the world" (p. 301).

Researches in developed countries stress the interpretation of the group as a financial device in order to separate ownership and control (Cainelli & Iacobucci, 2011).

The control of companies derives from negotiated relationships between the main stakeholders, such as entrepreneurs, banks, or managers, which may guarantee more stable control and may exploit the activities controlled through the equity capital invested by the controlling owners.

Controlling firms allocate resources in a more efficient way compared to the capital market and this aspect may justify the presence of groups.

Hence, the interest in the internal capital market in business groups. It represents an evident advantage of the affiliation to a group, i.e., the easiest possibility to renegotiate in case of financial problems. Moreover, the possibility to manage an internal capital market allows business groups to maintain a good reputation in the external market (Gopalan et al., 2007).

Most of this literature on business groups is focused mainly on large groups, undervaluing the relevance and the implications of small and medium-sized business groups.

Given these premises, this work aims to investigate the results so far achieved by the literature on the internal capital market, focusing on the dual role that it may play:

1) The superior capacity of firms belonging to a business group to survive and overcome external shocks;
2) The superior capacity to finance investment projects, in particular innovative projects.

The chapter is organized as follows. Section 2 reviews the existing literature. Section 3 discusses its results and then draws the main conclusions and highlights future extensions of research in this area.

Literature Background

The Survival to External Shocks

The first aspect we investigate is whether the internal capital market can be a way for companies to survive and overcome external shocks, such as an economic and financial crisis.

Given the presence of these internal funds between affiliated companies, belonging to a group may allow low-performance firms to survive compared to standalone ones. This is particularly true in case of crisis or market shocks (Cainelli et al., 2019). Easier access to financial resources is expected to facilitate investment and growth by affiliated companies but may not result in superior financial performance. Several studies show lower performance of affiliated firms compared to independent firms (Bae et al., 2002; Claessens et al., 2000; George & Kabir, 2008; Lins, 2003) and this is more evident in the case of larger groups. The lower performance of affiliated firms compared

3 The Role of Internal Capital Market in Business Groups   53

to independent ones is caused by the redistribution of profits from high to low performing firms. Some authors (Almeida & Wolfenzon, 2006) argue that one of the reasons for a lower performance of affiliated firms might be that standalone firms, which have fewer available resources, invest them in more profitable projects, while affiliated firms that benefit from greater amounts of internal resources, invest also in less profitable projects. However, Hamelin (2011), conducting a study on French SMEs, finds that affiliated firms reach higher performance than non-affiliated ones. Khanna and Yafeh (2007) argue that in diversified groups, the performance of affiliated firms may be country-specific: In emerging markets, it is easier to find diversified groups where the performance of affiliated firms is sacrificed in favor of maintaining the stability of the overall group.

In general, belonging to a business group favors innovation and continuity, rather than profitability (Cainelli et al., 2019). This is especially true in a situation of a real or financial crisis, when group firms, even with a poor performance, survive, thanks to the support provided by their controlling companies (heads), while poorly performing standalone firms in the same context may be forced to leave the market.

In the short-term, the financial support provided by the group may result in the survival of inefficient firms thus producing a negative welfare effect (Almeida & Wolfenzon, 2006). However, the overall effect is not clear since, in the longer run, it may avoid the dispersion of productive resources that follow the dissolution of firms. This role of business groups is especially relevant in periods of economic crisis. Affiliated firms may be able to withstand the effect of a real or financial shock for a longer period, thanks to the support provided by the other companies of the group. For example, a study on emerging markets during the 2008 financial crisis has shown that affiliated firms were supported by a sharp increase of intra-group loans (David Buchuk et al., 2019).

When considering the performance rather than the survival of firms during a recession, the effect of belonging to a business group may not be straightforward because of opposing effects at work. The first one can be the advantages of belonging to a group compared to standalone firms thanks to the sharing of resources and easier access to finance. The other effect is that the group can also guarantee the survival of firms with poor performance in terms of both growth and profitability (Cainelli et al., 2019).

Literature agrees that the presence of an internal capital market is specifically relevant when there are difficulties in raising external finance, consequently firms belonging to business groups are less financially constrained than the corresponding standalones (Fan et al., 2005; Iacobucci, 2012; Lee et al., 2009; Lensink et al., 2003). For example, Buckuk et al. (2014) underline that it is more convenient for a group to use internal debt than internal equity in the case of financial problems, because the first can be used immediately by the firm that borrows, while for internal equity the controlling shareholders have to contribute with their shares of dividends.

However, the group has the possibility to increase external finance sources, since capital (debt and equity) can be collected by both the controlling firms and controlled firms (Cainelli & Iacobucci, 2011). According to Buzzacchi and Pagnini (1994), this mechanism of resource allocation may generate inefficiencies due to the so-called tunneling.

This phenomenon is not possible in the case of multidivisional companies since shareholders have the same shares in all divisions of the firm.

The conflict of interests between controlling and minority shareholders was a topic of specific interest for a stream of literature that considers the group as a mechanism for separating ownership and control (Bae et al., 2002; Bertrand & Mullainathan, 2003; Claessens et al., 2000; Friedman et al., 2003; Johnson et al., 2000; Morck & Yeung, 2003). Controlling shareholders have interests in all the companies of the group while minority shareholders have shares in individual companies. This interpretation is more appropriate for groups including listed firms and with a relevant divergence between control and cash flow rights (Cainelli & Iacobucci, 2011).

However, empirical evidence shows that most of the groups are composed of unlisted companies and do not show a significant divergence between control and cash flow rights (Faccio & Lang, 2002; Franks & Mayer, 2001). Moreover, Buchuk et al., (2014) find that financial flows do not typically go from the bottom of the control pyramid straight to the top of the pyramid, as tunneling suggests. On the contrary, controlled companies within groups often get loans from the top of the pyramid. This evidence is in contrast with the idea of a widespread presence of tunneling in business groups, in which resources are supposed to move from the bottom to the top of the pyramid (Bae et al., 2002; Gopalan et al., 2007; Jian & Wong, 2010). Moreover, Almeida et al. (2015) show that belonging to a business group allows firms to transfer cash from low-growth to high-growth companies, but they don't mention the phenomenon of tunneling, as this transfer of resources is not influenced by the position of the firm (i.e., top, intermediate, or bottom of the pyramid).

Hamelin (2011) analyzes the "expropriation" hypothesis of minority shareholders in small groups. She finds that controlling shareholders develop groups mainly to preserve their value and wealth rather than to expropriate minority shareholders. Moreover, the author underlines that tunneling

3 The Role of Internal Capital Market in Business Groups   55

is positively related to group size: While in smaller groups the controlling shareholders are involved in firm management, in larger groups they are not directly connected in management activities; this is particularly true when the cash flow is low. The idea is that the risk of tunneling is correlated negatively by group size, due to the presence of "patrimony securitization" strategies in small groups. The controlling shareholders may tunnel funds away from the minority shareholders, when the market is not favorable or when there are negative shocks (Hamelin, 2011).

Moreover, as mentioned above, the presence of business groups is also justified when entrepreneurs intend to attract capital for new companies from outside investors (Almeida & Wolfenzon, 2006).

Given the role played by the internal capital market on the survival and resilience of firms belonging to groups, we propose some hypotheses and policy implications for future research that we believe are worthwhile to investigate.

The first line of empirical research would be to study the role of the internal capital market in small and medium-sized groups during external shocks (such as the recent pandemic crisis) and whether there are differences in behavior between smaller and larger groups.

Another interesting line of research would be to understand the flows of financial transfers between firms, which in a group may take several directions: bottom-up, from controlled firms to the head; top-down, from the head or controlling firms to controlled ones; horizontal, i.e., exchanges at the same hierarchy level of groups.

Up to now some of the literature on business groups has cast doubts on the desirability of this organizational form. We believe that the role of business groups in increasing the resilience and the likelihood of survival of firms to external shocks should induce policymakers to reverse this view and even favor this organizational form.

The Allocation of Resources in Innovative Investments

Affiliated companies may invest in projects, such as innovative projects, that would be difficult to finance for standalone companies due to financial constraints in raising external funds (Belenzon & Berkovitz, 2010; Boutin et al., 2013; Masulis et al., 2020). Several papers demonstrate that companies belonging to business groups show a superior innovative performance compared to their standalone companies. In fact, affiliated companies show a higher propensity to be involved in R&D (Belenzon & Berkovitz, 2010; Blanchard et al., 2005; Cefis et al., 2009; Guzzini & Iacobucci, 2014). This result is explained by considering the advantages of groups in providing resources to affiliated companies. Guzzini and Iacobucci (2014) also show that the R&D propensity of affiliated companies depends on their position within the group. Heads and intermediate companies show a higher R&D propensity than the corresponding standalone companies, while there are no differences in R&D propensity between standalone companies and those at the bottom of a group. For these authors, the higher propensity to invest in R&D activities by the heads of groups depends on the possibility to internalize the knowledge spillovers that flow to controlled companies.

Companies belonging to a business group can share financial, technological, and marketing resources (Carney et al., 2011; Hamelin, 2011). There is an extended stream of literature underlining how belonging to a group favors the propensity of companies to invest in R&D and boosts their innovation capabilities and economic performance (Blanchard et al., 2005; Cefis et al., 2009; Chang et al., 2006; Filatotchev et al., 2003; Karim & Mitchell, 2004; Sharon Belenzon & Berkovitz, 2010). Belenzon et al. (2010) find that belonging to a business group is important for innovation in industries that rely on external funding and in more diversified groups; these findings are in line with the view that the presence of an internal capital market may facilitate the financing of R&D projects. In particular, the internal capital market is expected to mitigate the asymmetry of information, which is considered one of the main problems when financing R&D projects. The head of a group is supposed to have a better knowledge about innovative projects of its affiliated companies than external investors (such as banks, private investors, or the market). Masulis et al. (2020) find that business groups use internal capital to manage projects that are hard to finance, making them easily scalable. Moreover, the head of a group may be facilitated in collecting financial resources by centralizing the flow of funds within the group and using the "portfolio effect" for the acquisition of external resources (Maksimovic & Phillips, 2007). Group heads may provide financial resources to affiliated companies in several ways. The most important for the financing of innovative projects is equity capital. Equity capital may be provided in two ways: directly, through the issue of new shares; indirectly, by restraining the distribution of dividends and allowing controlled companies to retain profits. The easier access to equity capital by an affiliated company is expected to play a relevant role for the innovative performance because R&D investments are preferably financed with equity capital, given the risk attached to such investments. This is explained by the advantages of groups in providing resources to affiliated companies.

Unlike standalone companies that cannot benefit from an internal capital market, companies in groups may have a greater capacity to invest in one sector using cash generated in other sectors. The easier access to financial resources by affiliated companies may affect their propensity and intensity on R&D activities (Boutin et al., 2013). Moreover, empirical studies show that affiliated companies have a lower amount of cash compared to their corresponding standalone companies, since the former can have the access to the internal capital market of the group (Locorotondo et al., 2014). Almeida et al. (2015) show how Korean business groups (*chaebol*) transferred cash among affiliated companies using equity investments during the 1997 Asian financial crisis and this mechanism allowed them to alleviate the negative effects of the crisis compared to the corresponding standalone companies.

Even in this case, we may outline some research hypotheses for future developments about the role played by the internal capital market on innovative projects, which have relevant management implications.

Empirical evidence demonstrates that companies belonging to groups show a greater capacity for innovation, thanks also to the possibility of using the internal capital market. On this issue, there are several aspects which are worthwhile to be further investigated.

A first issue to investigate would be the most efficient way of raising and allocating financial resources between companies in terms of directions and centralization of financial flows.

Connected to the above issue, another important research question would be to understand whether it is more efficient to centralize or decentralize R&D activities and how R&D results are shared between the affiliated companies.

For both the above issues it will be interesting to analyze the similarities and differences between large groups and small and medium-sized groups.

Discussion and Conclusions

The previous section has examined the dual role of the presence of an internal capital market in business groups. The first one is the capacity of business groups to help affiliated firms when facing external shocks such as economic and financial crisis and allowing them to survive. The second role is the superior ability of business groups to provide financial resources to sustain the investment of affiliated companies, specifically to sustain R&D investment and the innovative performance of the firms belonging to the group.

In so doing, it highlights the shift that occurred in the literature during the last decade about the role of business groups.

Most of the literature considers business groups as a suitable organizational form in the presence of inefficient and unstable markets. On the contrary, this chapter starts with the idea that groups may represent an efficient mechanism of resource allocation, which allows affiliated companies to foster their economic and innovative performance. Unlike standalone companies, firms belonging to business groups may benefit from the internal capital market, i.e., the transfer of resources between affiliated firms. This may help them to overcome financial constraints in sustaining their investment and cope with external shocks.

In particular, during the economic and financial crisis, the strength of external relations is expected to have a positive impact on survival even if this results in an ambiguous effect on firm performance. This is because the softening of the selection effect provided by belonging to a group may allow poor performing firms to survive. On the contrary, in the case of standalone firms, only the best performing ones remain in the market (Cainelli et al., 2019).

The presence of groups may reduce the selection effects produced by the market mechanism and allow the survival of firms with lower performance. This is particularly relevant during periods of economic and financial crises. Although this implies the survival of inefficient firms in the short run, in the longer run the overall welfare effect can be positive as the survival of firms may prevent the dispersion of productive resources. Moreover, in "normal" times, the internal capital market of business groups may sustain the investments in R&D and in innovative activities.

Indeed, the increasing relevance of the latter generates a competitive advantage for firms. Consequently, there is an increasing need to allocate financial resources to invest in such activities, which are difficult to finance because of the high risk attached to them and the information asymmetry between firms and the provider of financial resources. For these reasons, belonging to a business group may facilitate this type of investments.

On the one hand, the internal capital market is an easier way to transfer resources between affiliated firms, without referring to external investors, thus benefiting in terms of cost and time in obtaining financial resources. On the other hand, belonging to a business group may represent an implicit guarantee for external investors in case of financing.

Innovation represents a key factor for achieving long-run economic growth. In developed countries, the innovative performance of firms is increasingly dependent on R&D investments and patent activities. Business

3 The Role of Internal Capital Market in Business Groups 59

groups represent a way to foster the innovative performance of affiliated firms, given the benefits from belonging to a group, such as the use of internal capital markets. Recent contributions consider that the role of this organizational form is to support the innovative performance of affiliated firms compared to standalone firms, for example by guaranteeing a superior capacity in R&D investments and in patent activities. It is not a coincidence that in the last decade, we have witnessed an increasing relevance of business groups in developed countries.

The main advantages of belonging to a business group may be summarized as follows:

- the possibility to internally share resources through the internal capital market;
- the possibility to transfer R&D results between controlled firms;
- the possibility to benefit from the portfolio diversification in order to reduce the risk of activities;
- the possibility to obtain external financing more easily, given the implicit guarantee of the group.

For these reasons, the group should not be considered as an anomalous organization resulting from inefficient market institutions but as an efficient mechanism of resource allocation. Belonging to a business group brings several benefits to affiliated firms, especially when operating in turbulent times and when innovation and change are the main drivers of the company's performance.

In conclusion, we may suggest some policy and management implications resulting from this analysis.

Regarding "policy" implications, the main debate is whether taxation and corporate law should favor or discourage the development of business groups.

Contrary to the US legislation, in the majority of countries, law does not discourage the presence of business groups, and in some cases, it may favor them. For example, in 1986, Italy introduced the fiscal consolidation, that is the possibility for a group to compensate profits and loss between affiliated companies, thus reducing the overall taxation of the group. Although this introduction was aimed at making the Italian tax system homogeneous with the most efficient ones in the EU Member States, it also contributed to the tax recognition of firms belonging to business groups. There are two ways of tax consolidation: (a) national consolidation between firms localized in Italy; and (b) world consolidation in case of affiliated firms localized abroad.

The main advantages of fiscal consolidation are:

- the opportunity to offset tax profits and losses between affiliated firms of the same group;
- the possibility to offset tax credits and debts between firms involved in fiscal consolidation;
- there are no tax liabilities for controlled firms because the only firm responsible for the payment of taxes is the head of the group.

In general, the Italian legislation seems to recognize the positive role played by business groups. Indeed, the increasing relevance of business groups in the Italian economy during the last decade may represent an indirect demonstration of a favorable Italian legislation.

Regarding the "management" implications, it is important to raise the awareness of managers and management researchers toward the group as an efficient organization structure. Indeed, it is important for managers to have a better understanding of specific characteristics of business groups and the role played by firms belonging to them. One of the key elements is that in a business group firms remain legally independent. For this reason, the degree of autonomy of each affiliated firm is a crucial aspect, which influences the efficiency of the firm and of the group as a whole. On the one hand, to give total autonomy to affiliated firms may mean losing the meaning of the group and the possibility to share resources internally. On the other hand, the total loss of their autonomy may mean considering the group as a multidivisional firm. Consequently, the management should find the most efficient balance between autonomy and centralization, considering the specific characteristics of the group.

We think that there is additional scope for a better understanding of the group's potentials on how to manage the internal capital market and share resources between affiliated firms.

A better awareness on the part of managers controlling the group about the different mechanisms of resource allocation and sharing within the group may have great relevance in the efficient managing of the portfolio of activities and in decisions about R&D investment and other innovative activities.

This means also understanding how and to what extent innovative results, developed in an affiliated firm, may be shared with other companies of the group.

Regarding long-term effects in resource allocation, a further development may be to examine whether the advantages arising from the possibility to sustain the survival of underperforming firms in the short run are offset by an increase in the growth capabilities in the long-term. This means investigating to what extent the decisions taken in the short-term to sustain underperforming firms may affect the performance of the whole group in the long-term.

These future research developments and policy implications appear to be even more relevant for SMEs, given their relevance in all European countries. The group form can represent a tool for the growth of SMEs by supporting their competitiveness and strengthening their innovation capacity. Moreover, in case of external shocks (such as the pandemic crisis), belonging to a group can raise the likelihood of survival for smaller firms, which have fewer resources and may be less resilient compared to larger companies. In a long-term perspective, the bailout of distressed affiliated companies may allow the group to be more resilient while the overall entrepreneurial system avoids the dispersion of resources and maintains its stability.

References

Almeida, H., Chang, S., & K, H. B. (2015). Internal capital markets in business groups: Evidence from the Asian Financial Crisis. *The Journal of Fin, LXX* (6).

Almeida, H., & Wolfenzon, D. (2006). A theory of pyramidal ownership and Family Business Groups. *Journal of Finance, LXI* (6), 2637–2680.

Bae, K. H., Kang, J. K., & Kim, J. M. (2002). Tunneling or value added? Evidence from mergers by Korean Business Groups. *Journal of Finance, 57* (6), 2695–2740.

Belenzon, S., & Berkovitz, T. (2010). Innovation in business groups. *Management Science, 56* (3), 519–535. https://doi.org/10.1287/mnsc.1090.1107

Belenzon, S., Berkovitz, T., & Rios, L. a. (2013). Capital markets and firm organization: How financial development shapes European corporate groups. *Management Science, 59* (6), 1326–1343.https://doi.org/10.1287/mnsc.1120.1655.

Bena, J., & Ortiz-Molina, H. (2013). Pyramidal ownership and the creation of new firms. *Journal of Financial Economics, 108* (3), 798–821. https://doi.org/10.1016/j.jfineco.2013.01.009

Bertrand, M., & Mullainathan, S. (2003). Pyramids. *Journal- European Economic Association, 1* (2/3), 478–483.

Blanchard, P., Huiban, J. P., & Sevestre, P. (2005). R&D and productivity in corporate groups: An empirical investigation using a panel of French firms. *Annales d'économie et de Statistique,* (79/80), 461–485. https://doi.org/10.2307/20777585.

Boutin, X., Cestone, G., Fumagalli, C., Pica, G., & Serrano-Velarde, N. (2013). The deep-pocket effect of internal capital markets. *Journal of Financial Economics, 109* (1), 122–145. https://doi.org/10.1016/j.jfineco.2013.02.003

Buchuk, D., Larrain, B., Muñoz, F., & Urzúa I., F. (2014). The internal capital markets of business groups: Evidence from intra-group loans. *Journal of Financial Economics, 112*(2), 190–212.https://doi.org/10.1016/j.jfineco.2014.01.003.

Buchuk, D., Larrain, B., Prem, M., & Urz, F. (2019). *How do internal capital markets work ? Evidence from the Great Recession.*

Buzzacchi, L., & Pagnini, M. (1994). *I meccanismi di funzionamento dei circuiti interni dei capitali: un'indagine empirica del caso italiano. Banca d'Italia Temi Di Discussione No. 240.*

Cainelli, G., Giannini, V., & Iacobucci, D. (2019). Agglomeration, networking and the Great Recession. *Regional Studies.* https://doi.org/10.1080/00343404.2018.1511892

Cainelli, G., & Iacobucci, D. (2011). Business groups and the boundaries of the firm. *Management Decision, 49*(9), 1549–1573. https://doi.org/10.1108/002517 41111173989

Carney, M., Gedajlovic, E. R., Heugens, P. P. M. A. R., Van Essen, M., & Van Oosterhout, J. (2011). Business group affiliation, performance, context, and strategy: A meta-analysis. *Academy of Management Journal, 54*(3), 437–460.

Cefis, E., Rosenkranz, S., & Weitzel, U. (2009). Effects of coordinated strategies on product and process R&D. *Journal of Economics/ Zeitschrift Fur Nationalokonomie, 96*(3), 193–222. https://doi.org/10.1007/s00712-008-0041-z

Chang, S.-J. (2006). Business groups in East Asia: Post-crisis restructuring and new growth. *Asia Pacific Journal of Management, 23*(4), 407–417.

Chang, S.-J., Chung, C.-N., & Mahmood, I. P. (2006). When and how does business group affiliation promote firm innovation? A tale of two emerging economies. *Organization Science, 17*(5), 637–656. https://doi.org/10.1287/orsc.1060.0202

Claessens, S., Djankov, S., & Lang, L. H. (2000). The separation of ownership and control in East Asian Corporations. *Journal of Financial Economics, 58*(1–2), 81–112.

Faccio, M., & Lang, L. H. (2002). The ultimate ownership of Western European corporations. *Journal of Financial Economics, 65*(3), 365–395.

Fan, J. P. H., Wong, T. J., & Zhang, T. (2005). The emergence of corporate pyramids in China.

Filatotchev, I., Piga, C., & Dyomina, N. (2003). Network positioning and R&D activity: A study of Italian groups. *R & D Management, 33*, 37–48. https://doi.org/10.1111/1467-9310.00280

Franks, J., & Mayer, C. (2001). Ownership and control of German Corporations. *The Review of Financial Studies, 14*(4), 943–977.

Friedman, E., Johnson, S., & Mitton, T. (2003). Propping and tunneling. *Journal of Comparative Economics, 31*(4), 732–750.

George, R., & Kabir, R. (2008). Business groups and profit redistribution: A boon or bane for firms? *Journal of Business Research, 61*, 1004–1014. https://doi.org/10.1016/j.jbusres.2007.12.002

Gopalan, R., Nanda, V., & Seru, A. (2007). Affiliated firms and financial support: Evidence from Indian business groups. *Journal of Financial Economics, 86*(3), 759–795. https://doi.org/10.1016/j.jfineco.2006.09.008

Gorodnichenko, Y., Schaefer, D., & Talavera, O. (2009). Financial constraints and continental business groups: Evidence from German Konzerns. *Research in International Business and Finance, 23*(3), 233–242.

Guzzini, E., & Iacobucci, D. (2014). Ownership as R&D incentive in business groups. *Small Business Economics, 43*(1), 119–135. https://doi.org/10.1007/s11187-013-9529-1

Hamelin, A. (2011). Small business groups enhance performance and promote stability, not expropriation. Evidence from French SMEs. *Journal of Banking & Finance, 35*(3), 613–626.

Hsieh, T.-J., Yeh, R.-S., & Chen, Y.-J. (2010). Business group characteristics and affiliated firm innovation: The case of Taiwan. *Industrial Marketing Management, 39*(4), 560–570.

Iacobucci, D. (2012). Internal capital market and investment decisions in small and medium-sized groups. In G. Calcagnini and I. Favaretto I. (Eds.), *Small businesses in the aftermath of the crisis. Contributions to Economics* (Physica, H, pp. 211–227). https://doi.org/10.1007/978-3-7908-2852-8.

Jian, M., & Wong, T. J. (2010). Propping through related party transactions. *Review of Accounting Studies, 15*(1), 70–105. https://doi.org/10.1007/s11142-008-9081-4

Johnson, S., La Porta, R., Lopez-de-Silanes, F., & Shleifer, A. (2000). Tunneling. *The American Economic Review, 90*(2), 22–27. http://www.jstor.org/stable/117185.

Karim, S., & Mitchell, W. (2004). Innovating through acquisition and internal development: A quarter-century of boudary evolution at Johnson & Johnson. *Long Range Planning, 37*(6), 525–547.

Khanna, T., & Palepu, K. (1997, July–August). Why focused strategies may be wrong for emerging markets. *Harvard Business Review.*

Khanna, T., & Yafeh, Y. (2005). Business groups and risk sharing around the world. *Journal of Business, 78*(1), 301–340.

Khanna, T., & Yafeh, Y. (2007). Business groups in emerging markets: Paragons or parasites? *Journal of Economic Literature, 45*(2), 331–372.

Kock, C. J., & Guillén, M. F. (2001). Strategy and structure in developing countries: Business groups as an evolutionary response to opportunities for unrelated diversification. *Industrial and Corporate Change, 10*(1), 77–113.

Lee, S., Park, K., & Shin, H. H. (2009). Disappearing internal capital markets: Evidence from diversified business groups in Korea. *Journal of Banking and Finance, 33*(2), 326–334. https://doi.org/10.1016/j.jbankfin.2008.08.004

Lensink, R., van der Molen, R., & Gangopadhyay, S. (2003). Business groups, financing constraints and investment: The case of India. *Journal of Development Studies, 40*(2), 93–119. https://doi.org/10.1080/00220380412331293787

Lins, K. V. (2003). Equity ownership and firm value in emerging markets. *Journal of Financial and Quantitative Analysis, 38*(1), 159–184.

Locorotondo, R., Dewaelheyns, N., & Van Hulle, C. (2014). Cash holdings and business group membership. *Journal of Business Research, 67*(3), 316–323. https://doi.org/10.1016/j.jbusres.2013.01.019

Maksimovic, V., & Phillips, G. (2007). Conglomerate firms and internal capital markets. In B. E. Eckbo (Ed.), *Handbook of empirical corporate finance* (pp. 423–479). Elsevier. https://doi.org/10.1016/B978-0-444-53265-7.50022-6.

Masulis, R. W., Pham, P. K., & Zein, J. (2020). Family Business Group expansion through IPOs: The role of internal capital markets in financing growth while preserving control. *Management Science.* https://doi.org/10.1287/mnsc.2019.3418.

Morck, R., & Yeung, B. (2003). Agency problems in large family business groups. *Entrepreneurship Theory & Practice, 27*(4), 367–382.

Mota, J. H., & Coutinho dos Santos, M. (2020). *Does internal capital market membership matter for financing behavior? Evidence from the euro area.*

Rosa, P., & Iacobucci, D. (2010). The growth of business groups by habitual entrepreneurs: The role of entrepreneurial team. *Entrepreneurship Theory & Practice, 34*(2), 351–377.

Samphantharak, K. (2003). *Internal capital markets in business groups.*

Yiu, D., Bruton, G. D., & Lu, Y. (2005). Understanding business group performance in an emerging economy: Acquiring resources and capabilities in order to prosper. *Journal of Management Studies, 42*(1), 183–206.

4

Exit and Resource Management in a Family Business Portfolio

Naveed Akhter◉ and Xavier Lesage◉

Introduction

The entrepreneurial exit has been studied by a growing number of scholars in the past three decades, crossing the field of strategy (Burgelman, 1994, 1996; Elfenbein & Knott, 2014; Elfenbein et al., 2016), entrepreneurship (Akhter et al., 2016; DeTienne, 2010; DeTienne & Cardon, 2012; DeTienne et al., 2016), organization (Albert & DeTienne, 2016; Chen et al., 2019; Kolarska & Aldrich, 1980; Withers et al., 2012), and family business (Bird & Wennberg, 2016; DeTienne & Chirico, 2013; Hsu et al., 2016; Salvato et al., 2010). Exit refers to a situation where owners leave the firm they have created or the firm leaves the market (DeTienne & Chirico, 2013; Wennberg et al., 2010). Some studies have shown that owners embark on exit due to retirement, absence of a successor, financial distress, or perusing another opportunity (Dehlen et al., 2014; Ronstadt, 1986; Shepherd, 2003; Wennberg & DeTienne, 2014). Indeed, research suggests that

---

N. Akhter (✉)
Jönköping International Business School (JIBS), Jönköping, Sweden
e-mail: naveed.akhter@ju.se

X. Lesage
ESSCA School of Management, Angers, France
e-mail: xavier.lesage@ju.se

© The Author(s), under exclusive license to Springer Nature
Switzerland AG 2023
M. Rautianen et al. (eds.), *The Palgrave Handbook of Managing Family Business Groups*,
https://doi.org/10.1007/978-3-031-13206-3_4

exit is a common phenomenon, especially in times of adversity, business decline, and even in times of prosperity (Akhter, 2016a; Porter, 1976).

Despite the importance of business exits, a notable feature of the existing literature is that it does not focus on how resources are managed through exited businesses (Baert et al., 2016; Sieger et al., 2011). Similarly, the substantial strategy literature examines business entry (see Elfenbein & Knott, 2014; Lee & Lieberman, 2010), yet significantly less attention has been devoted to business exit. Although evidence shows that exits are highly consequential, the relative lack of attention in the literature is surprising (Elfenbein & Knott, 2014; Elfenbein et al., 2016). Some scholars, on the other hand, have recently emphasized the need to study business exit in family firms (Nordqvist & Melin, 2010; Sharma & Manikutty, 2005)—organizations in which trans-generational entrepreneurship and succession are very important; and where shedding (*often* unproductive) assets is challenging due to social, emotional, and psychological factors (DeTienne & Chirico, 2013). Furthermore, with few exceptions, current research has focused primarily on entrepreneurial exit of a firm from a single firm perspective, while overlooking the process of exit occurring within a portfolio of firms (Akhter et al., 2016; Cruz & Justo, 2017). Portfolios are very common in many of the world's developed and emerging economies (Carter & Ram, 2003; Carter et al., 2004; Cruz & Justo, 2017; Huovinen & Tihula, 2008). Thus, the ownership of multiple businesses is common in family firms, which provides an interesting setting to look at multiple exits and resource management in family firms (Sieger et al., 2011). We address this gap and ask: how family owners manage resources while exiting the business in the multi business firms? We address the calls for the need to examine not only the creation of businesses but also their ultimate exit.

Given limited extant theory on business exits and family business portfolios, we use a theory-building approach. The setting is the exit from the subsequent activities of two cases of family business portfolios in Pakistan. Our study offers three key insights concerning the resource management processes in family businesses exits. First, family owners re-direct the resources back to the business portfolio while exiting subsequent businesses to restructure their overall portfolio. Second, they manage resources to provide the next generation with the opportunity to start businesses that follow their passion and renew the business portfolio with a new set of ideas. Third, they manage resources by recycling in the family business portfolios in times of crisis, enabling the business to withstand critical times. With these findings, this study offers some important contributions. First, this study adds new insights to exit in terms of family owners opting of exiting from subsequent businesses for different reasons in response to adversity. Second, we add to family business portfolios and multiple exit strategies that is how family owners embark on exiting from multiple firms. Third, our work underlines the importance of the resource management process that is shedding light on productive and unproductive resources.

The article is organized as follows. The next section presents the theoretical background by reviewing the literature on portfolio entrepreneurship and business exits. Further on, we give details about our research method, design, setting, data collection, and analytical strategy. We then present the emerging findings and themes with interview quotes and create the overall story of the paper. Finally, we engage in the discussion and put forward the study's contributions together with future research avenues and limitations.

Theoretical Background

Portfolio Entrepreneurship

Portfolio entrepreneurship means the concurrent ownership and management of many businesses (Alsos, 2007; Carter, 1998; Carter & Ram, 2003). The socio-economic benefit and impact of portfolio entrepreneurship is agreed upon by scholars and there has been a surge of interest in this phenomenon in the past two decades (Akhter, 2016b; Sieger et al., 2011; Wiklund & Shepherd, 2008). One reason why portfolio entrepreneurship has captured the interest of scholars of entrepreneurship is that it is widespread in many developed and developing countries while offering specific contexts of study (Akhter et al., 2016; Akhter, 2016b; Carter & Ram, 2003; Wiklund & Shepherd, 2008). One such context is family firms where portfolio entrepreneurship is a common form of owning and managing the business. Indeed as noted by Zellweger et al. (2012), there is a misconception that family firms only consist of a single business and this assumption is not in line with the actual consideration that family firms are often comprised of multiple businesses. Therefore, while reviewing the previous literature, it becomes evident that family firms as a context carry important insights when it comes to multiple ownership of businesses (Akhter, 2016b; Baert et al., 2016; Sieger et al., 2011). For instance, family firms leverage on portfolio entrepreneurship to create employment opportunities for next generations, diversify risk through multiple businesses, ensure sustainability for business across generations (Carter, 2001; Cruz & Justo, 2017; Cruz et al., 2013). Indeed, portfolio entrepreneurship is specifically appropriate for family firms where family related dynamics support multiple business ownership and management and lead to long-term success of family firms (Manikutty, 2000; Ward, 2000). Despite the growing interest in family business portfolios and its characteristics, ownership modes and how it is managed and grow, there are still gaps to be filled (Akhter, 2016b; Carter & Ram, 2003). For example, since the growth process is not linear and surely business portfolios can realistically be assumed to follow "natural" economic cycles with phases of growth and decline (Michael-Tsabari et al., 2014), family firms often start on exit strategies to renew and restructure the portfolio for sustainable growth (Akhter et al., 2016; DeTienne & Chirico, 2013). In for that reason engage in resource redeployment process or re-directing resources to other businesses when exiting and prior research has not explored resource management when exiting in family business portfolios.

Business Exit

Business exit is a critical component of the organizational process (Rouse, 2016) and has a lasting impact on economies, firms, families, and individuals (DeTienne, 2010). It is also a process that nearly all firms and all founders will eventually undertake. However, the scholarly exit research has emerged, somewhat independently, from varying disciplines (e.g. entrepreneurship, strategy, economics, psychology), and has drawn upon numerous theoretical perspectives resulting in a myriad of conceptualizations and a proliferation of terms for similar constructs. The seminal work of Porter (1976) on business exit raised interest among scholars; however, the bulk of the research has been published since the late 1990s when research on business exit, especially in the field of strategy and entrepreneurship, escalated. Several terms (e.g. business exit, firm exit, firm closure) have been used over the last two decades to examine this phenomenon, but, it is important that we first distinguish exit from failure. Entrepreneurial exit is a volitional, cognitive decision-making process that is not purely financial in nature (e.g., Jenkins et al., 2014). Failure (involuntary exit) however occurs when a venture has not met a minimum threshold for economic viability (Ucbasaran et al., 2013). Scholars argue that they have focused their attention on business failure due to its wide prevalence (Rouse, 2015; Shepherd, 2009; Shepherd & Cardon, 2009). Another observation from the literature is the fact that researchers often appear to describe the exit occurring in different modes (does exit refer to the owner exiting the business or business exiting the markets or both?). In fact, firms and entrepreneurs often exit simultaneously, for example, in the case of liquidation of a firm (Akhter et al., 2016; Wennberg, 2008). The context of our study, family business portfolios, offers a unique perspective on this issue, as subsequent businesses are often created, acquired, liquidated or sold, as part of a broader family entrepreneurial exit strategy.

In sum, the literature on exit/divestments, family firms, and resource management offer us the opportunity to understand how family owners manage resources while exiting the business. However, despite the strategic importance of resource management in the exit process we still know very little about how exit and resource management unfolds in family business portfolios. We address this gap and ask: how do family owners manage resources while exiting the business in multi-business firms? The analysis of two-family business portfolios from Pakistan (18 businesses that experienced 10 exits) aims to unravel this dynamic and address these open issues.

Research Methods

To generate new insights on entrepreneurial exit and resource management processes in family business portfolio, we investigate how family owners manage resources while exiting the business. The research design we followed is multiple case study method (Yin, 2009, 2010, 2011). Multiple case study allows the "replication" logic where the cases are treated as a series of experiments and compared or linked together to get a greater picture (Eisenhardt, 1989, 1991; Yin, 2009, 2010, 2011). The context for this research is family business portfolios, where we had a chance to examine multiple exits. As in the case of this research, the chosen setting offered some distinctive evidence of observing a total number of 10 exits in the sample of 18 businesses in 2 family business portfolios (see Table 4.1). The two cases selected namely Beta and Zeta are third-generation firms with the active involvement of the third generation. The firm's Beta and Zeta started with a single legacy business of constructions and wholesales respectively and later gradually reached ten and eight firms at their peak times.

Data Collection and Analytical Strategy

When collecting data, we opted for multi-sources of data collection with interviews, observations, and archival documents. However, we mainly rely on interviews as the primary source of data collection method (see Table 4.2). We interviewed family owners and always started with the current family CEO for the information we were looking for. We adopted open and closed-ended interview strategies. We followed an open-ended interview strategy for

70   **N. Akhter and X. Lesage**

Table 4.1 Snapshot of the cases

Case	Legacy business	Maximum number of subsequent businesses owned	Number of exits	Founding year	Generation in the business
Beta	Construction	10	6	1970s	3rd generation
Zeta	Wholesale	8	4	1960s	3rd generation

the initial rounds, where respondents were first asked to describe the family firm's history and background information chronologically, but we opted for a close-ended interview strategy in the following rounds. We collected data in two rounds dated November 2013 and January 2014 respectively. In the first round, we carried out ten in-depth interviews followed by five additional interviews in a total of fifteen interviews. We also collected data through company websites mainly linked to the number of businesses and information. We also spend time at company offices to collect information in the form of brochures and carry out observations linked to how family owners manage everyday activities and issues related to resource management by informally engaging in talks with employees at the company.

Consistent with multiple-case analysis (Eisenhardt, 1989), we began with transcribing the interviews. The interview texts were then integrated for each

Table 4.2 Data collection

Case	Total number of interviews	Respondents	Interviews per person	Interview duration	Other data types
Beta	7	Family CEO 1 (2 gen)	3	80 min	Company website, brochures, news articles and onsite observations
		Family owner 1 (2 gen)	2	75 min	
		Family owner 2 (3 gen)	2	67 min	
Zeta	8	Family CEO 1 (2 gen)	4	55 min	Company website, brochures, and onsite observations
		Family owner 1 (2 gen)	1	64 min	
		Family owner 2 (3 gen)	1	60 min	
		Family owner 3 (3 gen)	2	75 min	

firm leading to individual case stories being developed. Writing the detailed case history for each firm helped us follow the exit process in each portfolio (Eisenhardt, 1989; Miles & Huberman, 1994). The case studies were 60 to 80 pages in length, comprising of respondent's quotes and events, chronologically. Case histories helped us engage in a data-reduction process (Miles & Huberman, 1994; Miles et al., 2013) to distill higher-order constructs, which we later linked to the extant literature. We followed the exit and resource management process by tracking the events, the motivations, and the strategies adopted when exiting. The description of the cases through the analysis of the transcripts of the interviews led us identify the core themes and coherent narratives from the raw data. For instance, we identified three important resource management activities (i.e., restructuring, opportunity for next generation and recycling resources under crises and prosperity) that explain why they showed different exit strategy in different circumstances. Further, through the first (within-case) level of analysis, we categorized the patterns and themes, and once we were sure that we had a substantial understanding of each case, we moved on to the next (cross-case) level of analysis. The cross-case analysis helped to foster the emergence of similar themes and patterns. Through the process of iterating between theory and data, we also investigated related research and we were able to unfold the link between exit and resource management in family business portfolios.

Findings

The key insights of our study are that family owners, when embarking on business exit in family business portfolios, engage in three types of resource management processes, each leading to a unique outcome. First, family owners re-direct the resources back to the business portfolio while exiting subsequent businesses to restructure their overall portfolio. Second, they manage resources to provide the next generation with the opportunity to start businesses that follow their passion and renew the business portfolio with a new set of ideas. Third, they manage resources by recycling of the family business portfolios in times of crisis, enabling the business to withstand critical times.

Resource Management as a Lever for Restructuring

We had learned that family owners had entered several subsequent businesses when the legacy business was growing in both of our cases. It mainly happened in the flow as the opportunity arose, and the family owners accepted this prospect without giving too much thought to the process. Our family owners reflected that the business was flourishing, and when you have a growing business and the profit is pouring in, one would like to seize any business opportunity that comes up. The business portfolios in our study both grew and diversified in many different unrelated businesses. At some point, they realized that holding on too many businesses was perhaps not a wise idea and that they probably had to focus on businesses that were in line with what they wanted to do and that could be managed by the family owners. Noted by the CEO of Beta: "*I think we were all over the place at one point and running five businesses entirely different in nature….we did not have a problem with the types of businesses we owned but it was more about owning what makes sense and we wanted to re-evaluate ourselves and perhaps re-brand in the area we had mostly made our reputation…we exited two of the businesses we thought didn't really make sense to any of us.*" By exiting the business, family owners restructured their business portfolio, which happened through resource management by re-directing resources back to the legacy business or other subsequent businesses. In one case, the owner exited the businesses to enter other businesses. Similarly, stated by Owner 1 of Zeta: "*I discussed things with my brother about streamlining things at one point due to unavailability of who will run the business from the family as some of the businesses were started by our father, and we had no interest in them anymore, and most of the family was engaged in our core/legacy business, and others were either managed by the non-family managers or partners. We decided to come out of the business managed by partners and focused entirely on our fully managed and owned businesses.*" The process of restructuring is commonly found in business portfolios, especially when owned by family owners who have long-term orientation with the business.

Resource Management as a Lever for Creating Opportunities

Our data also led us to the insight that family owners also engage in the resource management process to create opportunities for their current and next-generation family members. In a family business portfolio, family owners take advantage of multiple businesses and introduce new businesses by exiting non-productive businesses. When introducing the new business, family owners create opportunities for their current members or next-generation members in the area they are interested in working. This allows the family members to re-direct the resources in activities that are meaningful to family owners. Reflected by the current CEO of Zeta: *"After graduation, I was asked by my father to continue with the family business. Still, with the active involvement in the business, I also wanted to continue with the idea I started during my university days to start the coding institute and software development. I suggested to my father that when I took over as CEO to close the businesses, in my opinion, they had reached their full potential or not as profitable as they should have been to invest in the software house. Similarly, we also started a trading company for e-commerce, where my younger brother contributed since his interest and education were aligned with the businesses."* The exit works two ways, one to manage unproductive resources and the other to lead to the new projects in the form of entering new businesses. Similarly, the CEO of Beta reflected: *"We plan to exit one of our businesses in the auto sector to start farming for my younger brother. His passion for hunting and farming always kept him away from the city, so our family decided to invest in something new close to what he wanted to do. My brother started the business and now added a couple of additional types of crops to the business, with the growing interest expanded further with the help of a partnership".* In another instance, Owner 2 of Zeta replied: *"Entering into the art shop was my passion, and with the help of family, I set up a small gallery and craft shop together with a designer friend."* This is in line with the existing literature that portfolio entrepreneurship allows next-generation enragement in the business. However, in our cases, it also portrays that it will enable us to also grab on the opportunities by exiting existing businesses and replacing them with new businesses meaningful to the next generation owners.

Resource Management as a Lever for Recycling

Another interesting insight emerged in the form of resource recycling which happens both at the time of prosperity and crises. Recycling in times of prosperity happens by exiting from the unproductive assets, but during crises, family owners tend to exit from both unproductive and productive businesses by recycling the resources. Recycling occurs when family owners "temporarily shift the firm's resources (e.g., tangible assets and human and financial capital) to other businesses" (Akhter et al., 2016, p. 385). The CEO of Zeta commented on one occasion about recycling resources: *"When we were under pressure due to our constant low profits for a prolonged period, we decided to let go of two of our businesses to shift the resources to our other businesses [mainly core business]. The transfer of assets from the closed businesses helped revive the overall losses."* In a similar way, Beta also exited businesses both at the time of prosperity and crises mainly to manage the unproductive resources through the transfer of resources to the legacy or other subsequent businesses.

The CEO of Beta reflected: "*We cut costs by closing businesses and moved the leftover resources to our main business. The closing also allowed us to focus on what is interesting and how to manage crises, which we also continued during the times when we didn't really have to exit, but we also knew the advantages of closing the business.*" The strategy of re-directing resources to the core/legacy business in times of crises is what entrepreneurs often do but is more prominent in the case of family firms where the emotional and identity-related issues derive from such actions (Akhter et al., 2016). Noted by Owner 1 of Beta: "*For us during the times when we were going downhill, the most important things were to find a solution to save our family business (core/legacy)...and we had not come across another idea then to close down the other businesses and focus on the family's main business (core/legacy).*" In sum, our data show that family owners due to attachment with the core/legacy business stick with it (even when it is suffering) and manage resources by redirecting to their main business.

Discussion and Contributions

We wanted to understand how family owners manage resources while exiting the business. Interestingly, our data led us to reveal that family owners engage in three types of resource management processes in family business portfolios. These processes are triggered by different reasons and lead to unique outcomes. Our study with these insights has threefold contributions.

First, our key contribution lies in the entrepreneurial exit literature and, more specifically, addresses the exit issue in family business portfolios. There has been a surge in researching the topic on entrepreneurial exit in entrepreneurship and strategy literature (Burgelman, 1996; Wennberg et al., 2010), but there are very few studies that offer insights on exit in the context of family firms and specifically on family firms' portfolios (Rosa et al., 2014; Seaman, 2015; Sieger et al., 2011). We have addressed that gap in the literature by shedding light on how exit leads to unique resource management processes in family business portfolios. In this respect, we have shown how the exit in firm business portfolios can be seen as an intentional, strategic decision to free up resources and re-direct them or even recycle them in order to turn around the declining business or create opportunities for family members and next generations in a more conducive and friendly-business environment or recycle resources back to the core/legacy or other subsequent businesses in times of crises or prosperity.

Second, the study also contributes to the *portfolio entrepreneurship* literature by investigating it in the context of family firms. Research focusing on the process of portfolio entrepreneurship, along with all the factors influencing this phenomenon, lacks development in the literature. Therefore, the research will provide a holistic picture of portfolio entrepreneurship, with the addition of the family firm context, overall providing a contribution to literature (Sieger et al, 2011). We contribute to the literature on family business portfolios, an important area in which very little is known about firm exit and portfolio entrepreneurship (Nordqvist & Melin, 2010). In particular, our study is in line with the works of Salvato et al. (2010) and DeTienne and Chirico (2013). We have observed from our family business portfolios that it is crucial to provide opportunities for the next generations to explore their own desired endeavors, not only to keep them attached to the business but also to sustain the development of the portfolio in the long term through portraying how exiting business leads to an opportunity for next generation.

Third, we contribute to the *resource management* literature (Santamaria, 2022; Sirmon & Hitt, 2003; Sirmon et al., 2007) in the context of family business portfolios. In doing so, we have integrated three kinds of literature that is exit, portfolio entrepreneurship, and family firms, to shed light on the unique resource management processes and show how resource shedding in family business portfolios contributes to business continuations. We highlight that it's that resource shedding in times of crisis and prosperity could be an important strategy for firms to move forward.

Limitations and Future Research

Our study has not come without the constraints of the qualitative research carried out with a limited sample. There are limitations to the extent of the generalization of the study results as the study is conducted in a specific context. However, owing to the nature of the portfolio firms, we suggest that key findings from this study could be applied to a broader setting of portfolio entrepreneurship. Nevertheless, our findings and the resulting propositions are analytical rather than statistical generalizations. Thus, it would be interesting to compare our findings with the studies from Europe or the United States in a similar setting of portfolio firms. We hope that the insights from this study will help to inform both research and practice in this important setting of portfolio entrepreneurship.

Conclusion Remarks

How do family owners manage resources while exiting the business in multi-business firms? Our study of two cases of family business portfolios from Pakistan with eighteen businesses and ten exits shows and identifies three distinct resource management processes as levers of action for family owners to better manage their business portfolio in times of crisis or renewal, as we currently experience. We hope to inspire further studies on this topic.

References

Akhter, N. (2016a). *Family business portfolios: Enduring entrepreneurship and exit strategies* (Publication Number 108) [Doctoral Dissertation, Jönköping University]. Jönköping.

Akhter, N. (2016b). Portfolio entrepreneruship in family firms: Taking stock and moving forward. In F. Kellermanns & F. Hoy (Eds.), *The Routledge companion to family business.* Taylor & Francis Ltd.

Akhter, N., Sieger, P., & Chirico, F. (2016). If we can't have it, then no one should: Shutting down versus selling in family business portfolios. *Strategic Entrepreneurship Journal, 10*(4), 371–394.

Albert, L. S., & DeTienne, D. R. (2016). Founding resources and intentional exit sales strategies: An imprinting perspective. *Group & Organization Management, 41*(6), 823–846.

Alsos, G. A. (2007). *Portfolio entrepreneurship: General and farm contexts* [Universitetet i Nordland]. Bodo, Norway.

Baert, C., Meuleman, M., Debruyne, M., & Wright, M. (2016). Portfolio entrepreneurship and resource orchestration. *Strategic Entrepreneurship Journal, 10*(4), 346–370.

Bird, M., & Wennberg, K. (2016). Why family matters: The impact of family resources on immigrant entrepreneurs' exit from entrepreneurship. *Journal of Business Venturing, 31*(6), 687–704.

Burgelman, R. A. (1994). Fading memories: A process theory of strategic business exit in dynamic environments. *Administrative Science Quarterly*, 24–56.

Burgelman, R. A. (1996). A process model of strategic business exit: Implications for an evolutionary perspective on strategy. *Strategic Management Journal, 17*(S1), 193–214.

Carter, S. (1998). Portfolio entrepreneurship in the farm sector: Indigenous growth in rural areas? *Entrepreneurship & Regional Development, 10*(1), 17–32.

Carter, S. (2001). Multiple business ownership in the farm sector—Differentiating monoactive, diversified and portfolio enterprises. *International Journal of Entrepreneurial Behavior & Research, 7*(2), 43–59.

Carter, S., & Ram, M. (2003). Reassessing portfolio entrepreneurship. *Small Business Economics, 21*(4), 371–380.

Carter, S., Tagg, S., & Dimitratos, P. (2004). Beyond portfolio entrepreneurship: Multiple income sources in small firms. *Entrepreneurship & Regional Development, 16*(6), 481–499.

Chen, J. S., Croson, D. C., Elfenbein, D. W., & Posen, H. E. (2019). The impact of learning and overconfidence on entrepreneurial entry and exit. *Organization Science, 29*(6), 989–1009.

Cruz, A., Howorth, C., & Hamilton, E. (2013). Intrafamily entrepreneurship: The formation and membership of family entrepreneurial teams. *Entrepreneurship Theory and Practice, 37*(1), 17–46.

Cruz, C., & Justo, R. (2017). Portfolio entrepreneurship as a mixed gamble: A winning bet for family entrepreneurs in SMEs. *Journal of Small Business Management, 55*(4), 571–593.

Dehlen, T., Zellweger, T., Kammerlander, N., & Halter, F. (2014). The role of information asymmetry in the choice of entrepreneurial exit routes. *Journal of Business Venturing, 29*(2), 193–209.

DeTienne, D. R. (2010). Entrepreneurial exit as a critical component of the entrepreneurial process: Theoretical development. *Journal of Business Venturing, 25*(2), 203–215.

DeTienne, D. R., Alicia, R., McKelvie, A., & Miller, J. (2016, June 8–11). *Exits and the effect on entrepreneurial recycling*. Babson College Entrepreneurship Research Conference, University of Nordland, Business School, Bodo, Norway.

DeTienne, D. R., & Cardon, M. S. (2012). Impact of founder experience on exit intentions. *Small Business Economics, 38*(4), 351–374.

DeTienne, D. R., & Chirico, F. (2013). Exit strategies in family firms: How socioemotional wealth drives the threshold of performance. *Entrepreneurship Theory and Practice, 37*(6), 1297–1318.

Eisenhardt, K. M. (1989). Building theories from case study research. *Academy of Management Review, 14*(4), 532–550. http://search.ebscohost.com/login.aspx?direct=true&db=buh&AN=4308385&loginpage=Login.asp&site=ehost-live

Eisenhardt, K. M. (1991). Better stories and better constructs: The case for rigor and comparative logic. *Academy of Management Review, 16*(3), 620–627.

Elfenbein, D. W., & Knott, A. M. (2014). Time to exit: Rational, behavioral, and organizational delays. *Strategic Management Journal, 36*(7), 957–975.

Elfenbein, D. W., Knott, A. M., & Croson, R. (2016). Equity stakes and exit: An experimental approach to decomposing exit delay. *Strategic Management Journal, 36*(7), 957–975.

Hsu, D. K., Wiklund, J., Anderson, S. E., & Coffey, B. S. (2016). Entrepreneurial exit intentions and the business-family interface. *Journal of Business Venturing, 31*(6), 613–627.

Huovinen, J., & Tihula, S. (2008). Entrepreneurial learning in the context of portfolio entrepreneurship. *International Journal of Entrepreneurial Behavior & Research, 14*(3), 152–171.

Jenkins, A. S., Wiklund, J., & Brundin, E. (2014). Individual responses to firm failure: Appraisals, grief, and the influence of prior failure experience. *Journal of Business Venturing, 29*(1), 17–33.

Kolarska, L., & Aldrich, H. (1980). Exit, voice, and silence: Consumers' and managers' responses to organizational decline. *Organization Studies, 1*(1), 41–58.

Lee, G. K., & Lieberman, M. B. (2010). Acquisition vs. internal development as modes of market entry. *Strategic Management Journal, 31*(2), 140–158. https://doi.org/10.1002/smj.804

Manikutty, S. (2000). Family business groups in India: A resource-based view of the emerging trends. *Family Business Review, 13*(4), 279–292.

Michael-Tsabari, N., Labaki, R., & Zachary, R. K. (2014). Toward the cluster model the family firm's entrepreneurial behavior over generations. *Family Business Review, 27*(2), 161–185.

Miles, M. B., & Huberman, A. M. (1994). *Qualitative data analysis: An expanded sourcebook*. Sage.

Miles, M. B., Huberman, A. M., & Saldaña, J. (2013). *Qualitative data analysis: A methods sourcebook*. Sage.

Nordqvist, M., & Melin, L. (2010). Entrepreneurial families and family firms. *Entrepreneurship and Regional Development, 22*(3–4), 211–239.

Porter, M. B. (1976). Please note location of nearest exit: Exit barriers and planning. *California Management Review, 19*(2), 21–33.

Ronstadt, R. (1986). Exit, stage left why entrepreneurs end their entrepreneurial careers before retirement. *Journal of Business Venturing, 1*(3), 323–338.

Rosa, P., Howorth, C., & Discua Cruz, A. (2014). Habitual and portfolio entrepreneurship and the family in business. In L. Melin, M. Nordqvist, & P. Sharma (Eds.), *The Sage handbook of family business* (pp. 364–382). Sage.

Rouse, E. D. (2015). Beginning's end: How founders psychologically disengage from their organizations. *Academy of Management Journal, 59*(5), 1605–1629.

Rouse, E. D. (2016). Beginning's end: How founders psychologically disengage from their organizations. *Academy of Management Journal, 59*(5), 1605–1629.

Salvato, C., Chirico, F., & Sharma, P. (2010). A farewell to the business: Championing exit and continuity in entrepreneurial family firms. *Entrepreneurship and Regional Development, 22*(3–4), 321–348.

Santamaria, S. (2022). Portfolio entrepreneurs' behavior and performance: A resource redeployment perspective. *Management Science, 68*(1), 333–354.

Seaman, C. (2015). *In search of the business family: Exploring rural portfolio entrepreneurship*. Rural Entrepreneurship Conference: Acquiring Community Assets, Islay.

Sharma, P., & Manikutty, S. (2005). Strategic divestments in family firms: Role of family structure and community culture. *Entrepreneurship Theory and Practice, 29*(3), 293–311.

Shepherd, D. A. (2003). Learning from business failure: Propositions of grief recovery for the self-employed. *Academy of Management Review, 28*(2), 318–328.

Shepherd, D. A. (2009). Grief recovery from the loss of a family business: A multi- and meso-level theory. *Journal of Business Venturing, 24*(1), 81–97.

Shepherd, D. A., & Cardon, M. S. (2009). Negative emotional reactions to project failure and the self-compassion to learn from the experience. *Journal of Management Studies, 46*(6), 923–949.

Sieger, P., Zellweger, T., Nason, R. S., & Clinton, E. (2011). Portfolio entrepreneurship in family firms: A resource-based perspective. *Strategic Entrepreneurship Journal, 5*(4), 327–351.

Sirmon, D. G., & Hitt, M. A. (2003). Managing resources: Linking unique resources, management, and wealth creation in family firms. *Entrepreneurship Theory and Practice, 27*(4), 339–358.

Sirmon, D. G., Hitt, M. A., & Ireland, R. D. (2007). Managing firm resources in dynamic environments to create value: Looking inside the black box. *Academy of Management Review, 32*(1), 273–292.

Ucbasaran, D., Shepherd, D. A., Lockett, A., & Lyon, S. J. (2013). Life after business failure the process and consequences of business failure for entrepreneurs. *Journal of Management, 39*(1), 163–202.

Ward, J. L. (2000). Reflections on Indian family groups. *Family Business Review, 13*(4), 271–278.

Wennberg, K. (2008). Entrepreneurial exit. In J. P. Dana (Ed.), *Encyclopedia of entrepreneurship*. Edward Elgar.

Wennberg, K., & DeTienne, D. R. (2014). What do we really mean when we talk about 'exit'? A critical review of research on entrepreneurial exit. *International Small Business Journal, 32*(1), 4–16.

Wennberg, K., Wiklund, J., DeTienne, D. R., & Cardon, M. S. (2010). Reconceptualizing entrepreneurial exit: Divergent exit routes and their drivers. *Journal of Business Venturing, 25*(4), 361–375.

Wiklund, J., & Shepherd, D. A. (2008). Portfolio entrepreneurship: Habitual and novice founders, new entry, and mode of organizing. *Entrepreneurship Theory and Practice, 32*(4), 701–725.

Withers, M. C., Corley, K. G., & Hillman, A. J. (2012). Stay or leave: Director identities and voluntary exit from the board during organizational crisis. *Organization Science, 23*(3), 835–850.

Yin, R. K. (2009). *Case study research: Design and methods*. Sage.

Yin, R. K. (2010). *Qualitative research from start to finish*. Guilford Press.

Yin, R. K. (2011). *Applications of case study research*. Sage.

Zellweger, T., Nason, R. S., & Nordqvist, M. (2012). From longevity of firms to transgenerational entrepreneurship of families introducing family entrepreneurial orientation. *Family Business Review, 25*(2), 136–155.

5

Corporate Strategy in Family Business Groups in Developed Economies

Xavier Mendoza⬭, Paula M. Infantes⬭, Maria José Parada⬭, Marita Rautiainen⬭, and Jan Hohberger⬭

Introduction

Family Business Groups (FBGs), defined as a collection of businesses bound together by shared family ownership and management control (Rautiainen et al., 2019), are characterized by family involvement in management and ownership, intertwined with economic and non-economic objectives (Anderson & Reeb, 2003; Arregle et al., 2007; Gómez-Mejía et al., 2007).

X. Mendoza · M. J. Parada (✉) · J. Hohberger
Department of Strategy and General Management, ESADE Business School, Sant Cugat del Vallès, Spain
e-mail: mariajose.parada@esade.edu

X. Mendoza
e-mail: xavier.mendoza@esade.edu

J. Hohberger
e-mail: jan.hohberger@esade.edu

P. M. Infantes
Center for Corporate Governance, ESADE Business School, Madrid, Spain
e-mail: paulamaria.infantes@esade.edu

M. Rautiainen
School of Engineering Science, LUT University, Lahti, Finland
e-mail: marita.rautiainen@lut.fi

© The Author(s), under exclusive license to Springer Nature Switzerland AG 2023
M. Rautiainen et al. (eds.), *The Palgrave Handbook of Managing Family Business Groups*,
https://doi.org/10.1007/978-3-031-13206-3_5

FBGs are ubiquitous and a global phenomenon mostly studied in emerging economies focusing on their existence, competitive strategies, and organizational structures (Colpan & Jones, 2016; Rautiainen et al., 2019). Research states (e.g., Khanna & Yafeh, 2007) that business group structures are supporting the development of economic activities to compensate imperfect markets and poor institutional quality and fill institutional vacuums.

The existence of FBGs is frequently explained as a reaction to market failure in emerging economies (Khanna & Yafeh, 2007). However, anecdotal evidence shows the importance of FBGs in developed economies, and they are also highlighted for the capacity to create new businesses, exit others, and recompose their portfolio of businesses for the long run (c.f. Parada et al., 2019) These examples highlight family entrepreneurship, entrepreneurial ability, and the competence to mobilize resources (Granovetter, 2005) for the existence of FBG.

FBGs are not single homogeneous units, instead they are a large variety of groups with diverse strategic roles often with complex ownership structures. Yet, the family business literature has seldom studied their presence and dynamics as most research has focused on the family firm as a single business.

Family business research commonly argue that family firms tend to diversify less than non-family firms (Gómez-Mejía et al., 2007), are slower to enter new markets, concentrate on fewer countries when they internationalize, and grow more slowly when entering new markets (e.g., Gomez-Mejia et al. 2010; Graves & Thomas, 2004; Schulze et al., 2003). While family businesses leverage the family reputation (Deephouse & Jaskiewicz, 2013), they often are burdened by old traditions, resistant to change (Dyer, 1994; Gersick et al., 1997), and preserve the social-emotional endowment invested in the firm by maintaining the control over generations (e.g., Gomez-Mejia et al., 2010). Studies also show that if entrepreneurial capacity is low it will hamper further developments (Hall et al., 2001). According to various studies, it seems that later generations are less entrepreneurial than founding generations (Block et al., 2013; Cruz & Nordqvist, 2012; Miller et al., 2007; Miller & Le Breton–Miller, 2011).

Although there appears to be a conversation around the planned, strategic evolution of family businesses (Rautiainen et al., 2019) and what managerial principles might enable them to endure and perform well, there has been limited systematic research on the corporate strategy attributes of FBGs, particularly combining diversification strategies (Hafner, 2021) and structure (Almeida & Wolfenzon, 2006; Masulis et al., 2011). This chapter aims to address these research gaps by answering the following questions: Which structures do FBGs present? Which corporate strategies do they follow? More

5 Corporate Strategy in Family Business Groups in Developed Economies

specifically this study provides a profile of FBGs in Catalonia and maps their corporate strategies in terms of (i) their structure—how are they structured and the degree of control on their investee companies and (ii) their diversification strategies—product diversification strategy (related or unrelated), industries in which they are more prevalent, and their geographical footprint.

We focus on Catalonia for two reasons, first, given their economic relevance. By 2021, the estimated growth of the Catalan GDP exceeds the one in the Eurozone (5.8% vs 5.3%) and its economy (€212.93bn in 2020) is larger than that of most countries in the euro area. Second, Catalonia has a solid predominance of family-owned businesses, with a long-lasting tradition of developing business tissues and opening to other regions and countries given its size. Catalan family firms represent 88% of all companies in the region and account for 76% of private employment.

We follow a two-step procedure starting with the SABI database to identify FBGs in Spain and obtain most of the information on their corporate strategies. Then we use the Amadeus database to complement the information on their international investee companies. We follow the definition of family business by the European Commission(2009), which defines a family business based on the following criteria: (i) there is a presence of the family in ownership bodies, (ii) there is a presence of at least one person from the family in the management or governance bodies, such as the board of directors, and (iii) there is permanence and continuity of the company (according to the concept of Socioemotional Wealth), approximately the business has been around 20–25 years in the hands of the same family. Then we analyze whether there are significant differences among FBGs according to their age, size, and ownership (public and privately held). This exploratory study describes *what* are the contents of the corporate strategies of FBGs in Spain leaving the door open for further studies focusing on *how* investee companies benefit from group affiliation.

Thereby, our study contributes in three distinct ways to the current discussion on family business and family business groups in particular. First, our chapter raises awareness of the prevalence of family business groups by getting out from the narrow view of a single business, thus broadening the perspective of the phenomenon. Second, it expands knowledge about the type of growth strategies used by these groups owned and controlled by families. Thus, our study may shed light on specific corporate strategies that may be different from mainstream listed companies. Third, we pursue our study in a developed economy showing the prevalence of this type of organization, contradicting the assumption that these groups prevail only in emerging economics to cover institutional voids. Our results allow us to present a future research agenda that will contribute to our understanding of the issue.

Literature Review

Family Business Groups (FBGs)

FBGs are ubiquitous and relatively common organizational forms that are present globally in emerging and developing economies. FBGs can be defined as collections of legally independent firms bounded with formal and informal ties (Granovetter, 1995) where ownership is shared across several family members and/or their companies (Pihkala et al., 2019). FBGs are an interesting and important research context because of the endogenous sources of complexity that characterize their structure and management (Mäkimattila et al., 2016). However, the characteristics of FBG are frequently tightly connected with the local environment. In Japan, family-controlled business networks, called *Zaibatsu*, were pre-war establishments that resembled a closed intra-family corporation, where family businesses could be undivided for more than 300 years as the family was not able to take back their own investments (Todeva, 2005). *Keiretsus* took place in the post-war period, and represent a web of overlapping financial, commercial, and governance networks where two varieties of these networks are relevant: industrial or vertical Keiretsus, and financial, or horizontal Keiretsus (Gedajlovic & Shapiro, 2002). The Korean economy has relied heavily on *Chaebols*, i.e., the descendants of the individuals who founded Korean BGs, which are family conglomerates of Korea, that have exerted enormous influence on the country's fast-growing economy (Chang, 1988). *Chaebols* are family controlled, family managed, paternalistic leadership, and financially controlled by the founders or their family members (Chang, 2003; Cho & Yoon, 2001). In Latin America, the dominant corporate form among large private domestic firms has been the family owned and controlled, diversified BGs, named as a *grupo económico* that involves multiple generations of managers and overlays generational hierarchy on managerial relations (Schneider, 2009). There are also many other, i.e., Asian, and European countries, where BGs represent a phenomenon of great practical importance.

Although we have a vast knowledge about family businesses in developed countries, we have surprisingly little knowledge about FBGs in such contexts and even less insights in the corporate strategies they follow. In that regard, Spain, and particularly Catalonia, offers a fertile research ground to study the corporate strategies of FBGs. Most SMEs and many large companies in Spain are family owned and those which are more successful and dynamic tend to engage in product and international diversification (IEF, 2015), evolving toward a FBG structure.

Corporate Strategies of Family Business Groups

There have been initial studies characterizing FBGs (Rautiainen et al., 2019) but rarely focusing on FBGs' corporate strategies in the context of developed economies. The fact that they are long lasting in developed economies, not necessarily linked to market failure or institutional voids, calls for more studies on what makes them prevail. Corporate strategy is focused on the whole group and is a pattern of different decisions defining the businesses in which the company will be in and the way how resources are transferred between business. Corporate strategy in organizations, that are using varied forms and structures, is important in enabling competitive advantage and enhancing corporate performance. In strategy literature, different perspectives determine how we understand and measure corporate strategies. This chapter brings forward the knowledge of FBGs corporate strategies in a developed economy context by concentrating on identifying FBGs structures and diversification strategies.

Structure of FBG

FBGs are structurally different compared to conglomerate organizations. In conglomerates, the coordination takes place through the unified internal control of a portfolio of firms (Davis et al., 1994), whereas in FBGs, the coordination is frequently a more complex web of mechanisms (Granovetter, 2005; Rosa & Pihkala, 2019). In FBGs, the corporate structure is frequently a hybrid between fully integrated conglomerates and stand-alone companies e.g., Keiretsu groups (Chang et al., 2010). According to Morck et al. (2005), the use of family ownership structures is one central character in FBG. A characteristic feature is also the pyramidal ownership structure to control the multiple affiliate firms (Claessens et al., 2000a; La Porta et al., 2002; Morck et al., 2005; Young et al., 2008). The larger the FBG is, the more likely it will rely on a pyramidal ownership structure to achieve control (Morck et al., 2005). For example, Chung (2013) showed how ownership structures affect diversification decisions in Taiwanese large family business groups concluding that the pyramidal ownership structure enhanced diversification in these family business groups. The uniqueness and higher complexity of FBG emerge from the overlapping systems of family, ownership, and business where multiple roles are held, and business and family goals collide (Lansberg, 1983; Mukherjee et al., 2019). Through different dynamic processes, the family business system grows both in size and in complexity. Rosa and Pihkala (2019) suggest that FBGs are the cumulative outcomes of short-term reactions to both internal and external opportunities and threats. As a result, in agency theory, FBGs are seen as fraught with agency costs (Morck et al., 2005) which wealthy families use to appropriate private benefits through a variety of tactics (Carney et al., 2011). It is not clear which structures FBGs follow, therefore we aim to map the type of structures they form.

Diversification in FBG

FBGs are by definition diversified companies, as they are composed of several businesses that are usually legally independent. Diversification is related to changing the characteristics of the products the firm has or the markets in which the firm is (Ansoff, 1957). The motives for diversification vary from other types of business groups. For instance, state-owned business groups may be interested in diversifying to cover market imperfections, whereas FBGs are driven by the entrepreneurial behavior of their owners in different generations who may detect opportunities in other countries (c.f. Parada et al., 2019), family dynamics may push for diversification (Anderson & Reeb, 2003), and their diversification process might be even faster as they might be owner-managers shortening the decision-making structure (Cuervo-Cazurra, 2006).

The strategy literature emphasizes two modes of diversification: geographic diversification (e.g., internationalization, globalization) (e.g., Mendoza et al., 2019), or product diversification (e.g., Ansoff, 1957), which we use for our analysis.

Product Diversification

FBGs tend to be highly diversified due to a high level of product diversification that emanates primarily from transaction costs and institutional theory considerations (Kumar et al., 2012). Product diversification has brought several benefits for business groups e.g., strong and flexible internal markets (Kim et al., 2004; Manikandan & Ramachandran, 2015; Morck, 2010), competitive advantages while going into new markets (Lamin, 2013; Wan

5 Corporate Strategy in Family Business Groups in Developed Economies

et al., 2011), and reduced risks by spreading their investments across a portfolio of businesses (Mahmood & Mitchell, 2004). Diversification is one of the characteristics of FBGs and an important rationale behind many activities undertaken by large family corporations (Akhter et al., 2021).

In general, strategy theories often consider unrelated diversification as an unstable and inefficient arrangement (Kock & Guillén, 2001). However, diversification has been associated with managers' behavior and their preference for growth (Iacobucci & Rosa, 2005). Research on corporate diversification and firm performance has concentrated on two factors that are playing an important part in selecting a diversification strategy: diversification into a related business where the emphasis is on strategic control (Markides & Williamson, 1994; Miller, 2006; Palepu, 1985) and diversification into unrelated business (Hoskisson & Johnson, 1992; Kogut & Zander, 1992; Rumelt, 1982) where the emphasis is more on financial control (Baysinger & Hoskisson, 1989). Diversification can be a survival strategy (Robson et al., 1993) or a result of entrepreneurial behavior (Iacobucci & Rosa, 2005).

Focusing on family businesses, research has stated that family firms are strategically conservative and risk-averse (Carney et al., 2015; Zahra, 2005) and are concerned about losing control (González et al., 2013), reluctant to invest in new ventures (Schulze et al., 2001; Zahra, 2005), introverted, and resistant to change (Hall et al., 2001). Diversification exposes to greater uncertainty and risks, and from a family business perspective, the ownership structure influences FBG diversification for several reasons. Differences in identity and resource endowments among owners determine their power and ability to monitor ownership. There may be several family owners with divergent goals, and this has different influences on group structures. Relationships between companies within a group can be determined in many ways. However, diversification requires that FBGs have entrepreneurial or managerial coordination, and common ownership ties that are usually the result of the aging of the group. In mature family firms, diversification can also be the result of family capital accumulation (Scott & Rosa, 1996) and most large FBGs have emerged over a long period of time (Rautiainen, 2012).

Geographic Diversification

Geographic diversification is the second important diversification dimension in FBG's. Despite the recent discussion of deglobalization (e.g., Witt, 2019), international business activities have been an important aspect of modern companies. International business research has a long-standing tradition to explain the underlying drivers, benefits, and challenges of international business activities from a theoretical and practical perspective (Buckley & Casson, 1976; Kogut & Zander, 1993). Similarly, the diversification literature has investigated geographic diversification and frequently focuses on the impact on firm performance (Lu & Beamish, 2004; Qian et al., 2010) and recent innovation research highlighted the importance of international activities to access geographically dispersed knowledge despite modern information technology (Ferraris et al., 2020; Hohberger & Wilden, 2022).

It is also notable that internationalization has been an important aspect of investigations in the family business literature (e.g., Banalieva & Eddleston, 2011; Cirillo et al., 2021; Gallo & Pont, 1996; Fernández & Nieto, 2005; Pukall & Calabrò, 2014). However, even though diversification is central to the definition of FBG, and certain geographic issues translate between product and geographic diversification (e.g., transaction cost arguments, agency costs) geographic diversification has been explored to a much more limited extent than product diversification. A notable exception is a study by Chung (2013) who showcase that family business groups may decide to enter new geographic spaces when there is a higher degree of ownership based on a pyramidal structure form along with greater family management in the subsidiary. Moreover, their results show that the presence of family in management and the specific pyramidal ownership structure in the subsidiary leads to entering into regions that present higher differences from the region of origin. Despite the various studies about diversification in the family business field, our understanding about the breadth of geographic diversification in FBGs, and the type of structure they employ to pursue this strategic goal, is still limited.

To address some of these gaps, our study examines which structures and which diversification strategies FBGs in Catalonia follow and where we might contradict prior assumptions about the inability of family businesses to internationalize (Crespí-Cladera & Bru, 2006). Additionally, we expand current studies about Spanish family businesses and their capacity to grow in international markets (Guillen, 2005).

Methods

Research Setting

The study is set in the context of the region of Catalonia. We focus on Catalonia for two reasons. First, its economic relevance. By 2021, the estimated growth of the Catalan GDP exceeds the one in the Eurozone (5.8% vs 5.3%) and its economy (€212.93bn in 2020) is larger than that of most countries in the euro area. Second, Catalonia has one of the highest ratios of family businesses in Spain and Europe. Catalan family firms represent 88% of all companies in the region, contribute 69% of the Catalan GDP, and account for 76% of private employment. Nearly 5% of family businesses in Catalonia are centenarians and exports account for 20% of sales, whose main foreign market is Europe.

Sample

The data comes primarily from the publicly available SABI and AMADEUS Bureau van Dijk databases. For the identification of the FBGs in Catalonia, we follow two different approaches: a purely quantitative and a more qualitative one. First, we use machine learning techniques based on algorithms to identify FBGs. Algorithms allow through iterations to massively identify ownership and governance connections between firms. In the case of the FBGs, the use of algorithms helps to tie firms based on ownership links and overlapping between board members, creating the structure of the business group. We also use an iterative classification for family firms, mainly based on the ownership percentage owned by the family and the presence of family members on the board of directors, but also identifying keywords in the name of the company (for example, if the company name includes the Spanish word "hermanos", which means "siblings", it may be the case of a family firm). Second, we valid the initial sample using a manual expert-based approach. To be rigorous and do a good identification of FBGs, it is critical to know the business ecosystem and who is behind each family business to trace the companies down to create a good composition of the FBG. We have the privilege to be highly involved with the family business ecosystem and be embedded in Catalonia, which allowed us to know in-depth the families that owned, govern, and manage the companies. This double-check gives us the possibility to refine our sample and ensure accuracy.

For the inclusion of companies in the sample, these had to meet the following requirements:

1. The Global Ultimate Owners (GUOs) of the FBGs are not physical entities, that is, they are not individuals, but companies. Global Ultimate Owners refer to the parent companies of the FBG. We define an investee company as a company directly/indirectly owned by the GUO (parent company).[1]
2. The GUOs are located in Spain, although they may have corporate investees abroad.[2]
3. The GUOs have been identified as family firms and non-listed companies.
4. We start identifying the GUOS from a sample of Catalan firms included in ORBIS; so, the initial sample of GUOs are the GUOs of Catalan firms. We also filter the universe of Catalan firms in ORBIS as follows:

   - Location: Firms located in Catalonia, whose GUOs are located in Spain. For example, a firm located in Catalonia but whose GUO was a multinational entity was excluded from the sample
   - Ownership chain: Firms with at least one corporate investee
   - Size: Firms with a minimum turnover of 2 million € and with more than 10 employees
   - Industry: Firms not operating in the following NACE Code 4-digits: 6420, 6499, 7010, or 8299, since these industry codes denote
   - Status: Active firms
   - Type: Non-listed companies

5. When we retrieve this sample of Catalan firms meeting the previous requirements, we identify which of them were family and non-family firms.
6. From a bounded sample of Catalan family firms, we move one step up in the ownership chain and identify their GUOs. We follow an iterative process to check the classification of these GUOs between FFs and NFFs (see points 1, 2, and 3).

Consequently, the final sample is composed of 238 FBGs investing in 9161 companies, located either nationally or internationally. Of the 238 Catalan FBGs, there are only 86 FBGs operating only in Spain, while 153 FBGs operate in both Spain and abroad (defined as internationalized FBGs).

---

[1] In the literature, the concepts of "headquarters", "apex firm," and "parent company" have been used indistinctively to refer to the company at the top of the organizational structure in a business group. The same for the concepts of "subsidiaries", "affiliates," and "investees" for the member firms in a business group, although we stress some of the main differences between them in the sections below.

[2] Technical note. Ownership and other information about the 238 GUOs were retrieved from SABI database, but these 238 GUOs must appear in Amadeus database in order to track international (mostly European) investees.

5 Corporate Strategy in Family Business Groups in Developed Economies

Table 5.1 Distribution of Spanish FBGs by administrative and political division (regions)

Spanish region	Number of GUOs	Percentage (%)
Catalonia	201	84.45
Madrid	21	8.82
Aragon	6	2.52
Andalusia	3	1.26
Valencian community	2	0.84
Galicia	2	0.84
Estremadura	1	0.42
Murcia	1	0.42
Navarre	1	0.42
Total	238	100

As we start the identification of FBGs and their respective GUOs from a sample of Catalan firms, it is not surprising to find that most of these GUOs are located in the region of Catalonia. However, it is important to note that the GUOs may be based outside Catalonia and be located in other Spanish regions. In the following table, we show the distribution of the GUOs by the Spanish regions (Table 5.1). We observe that 84% of the GUOs are located in Catalonia, followed by Madrid (9%), which includes the capital city of Spain, and Aragon (3%), given the geographic proximity to Catalonia.[3]

Profile of FBGs

Parent Characteristics

As we mentioned before, in our definition of FBGs, the GUO is the parent company of the group. According to the industry NACE codes, we can differentiate between holding companies (whose NACE codes can be 6420, 6499, 7010, or 8299 and are the family holding companies), pseudo-holding companies (whose NACE codes can be 6810, 6820, 6920, or 7022 and are real estate services and business services), and parent companies with sectorial activity (belonging to the remaining NACE codes).[4] Table 5.2 exhibits the distribution of the 238 parent companies according to the previous typology.

---

[3] Disclaimer. For the sample of FBGs, we have considered firms in Catalonia after October 2017, date when the Catalonia Independence Referendum was proclaimed.

[4] Pseudo-holding companies refer to real estate holding companies, which are a popular mechanism that some business groups use to avoid risks from owning investment properties, providing also asset protection, privacy, and, sometimes, even tax benefits.

Table 5.2 Classification of parent companies according to their typology

Typology	Number of GUOs	Percentage (%)
Holding	112	47
Pseudo-holding	56	24
Sectorial activity	70	29
Total	238	100

We find that over 71% of parent companies can be identified as holding or pseudo-holding companies and 29% are parent companies with sectorial activity.

When we cross this classification regarding the typology of the parent with the number of investee companies that each FBG has, we observe that, on average, holding parents have fewer investees than parents with sectorial activity, but the difference in means is not statistically significant (Panel A, Table 5.3). However, the median for the two types of parents is around 10. That is, 50% of groups whose parent company is a holding has 12 investees and for the case of parents with sectorial activity is 10. For both cases, the minimum number of investees is 2 and the maximum is around 600 investees.

When we repeat the previous analysis without considering large FBGs (we remove FBGs with more than 150 investees), we observe that the average number of investees is larger for the case of holding parents (Panel B, Table 5.3). However, the difference in means is not statistically significant.

Regarding the mean age of parent companies, we find that, on average, the 238 parent companies in our sample are 24 years old. If we separate the parent companies by typology, we observe in Table 5.4 that, on average, holding parents are younger than parents with sectorial activity, 20 years versus 32.

Table 5.3 Average number of investee companies by typology of parent company

Typology	Mean	Median	Std. Dev	Min	Max
Panel A: All FBGs					
Holding	31.51	12	77.15	5	597
Sectorial activity	41.71	10.5	108.16	5	654
Total	34.51	11.5	87.30	5	654
Panel B: Without large FBGs (those with more than 150 investees)					
Holding	19.12	11	23.04	2	138
Sectorial activity	15.78	9	16.50	2	76
Total	18.17	11	21.40	2	138

5 Corporate Strategy in Family Business Groups in Developed Economies

Table 5.4 Average age of parent companies by typology of parent company

Typology	Mean	Median	Std. Dev	Min	Max
Holding	20.98	19.46	14.78	1.67	77.51
Sectorial activity	32.21	28.01	24.36	1.62	122.30
Total	24.28	21.77	18.78	1.62	122.30

FBGs Characteristics

Size of FBGs

In terms of size, measured as the number of corporate investees that integrate the FBG, we find that, on average, FBGs invest in 35 companies. 50% of the FBGs analyzed invest in 12 companies and 75% invest in 23 companies. The minimum number of investees is 2 (to avoid economically insignificant business groups with less than 2 firms) and the maximum number of investees is 654.

We establish three categories of types of FBGs in terms of size. The first group includes FBGs of "Small size" and low internal complexity, with a maximum of 10 investees. We find 110 FBGs to be categorized as "Small size". The second group includes FBGs of "Medium size" and medium internal complexity, with a minimum of 11 investees and a maximum of 50 investees. We find 99 FBGs to be considered as "Medium size". The third group includes "Large/very large" and high/very high internal complexity, with more than 50 investees. The remaining 29 FBGs fit this category. The breakdown of FBGs by size is included in Table 5.5.

Investees in FBGs have, on average, 72 employees for the case of small FBGs, 87 employees for the case of medium FBGs and 132 employees for the case of large/very large FBGs. It is not a measure of the average number of total employees per FBGs, but the average number of employees per investee (Table 5.6).

In Table 5.7, we observe that the average number of investees of those FBGs whose parent's age is less than 10 years is 12. On the contrary, and

Table 5.5 Breakdown of FBGs by size (number of investees)

Size	Number of FBGs	Percent (%)
Small	110	46
Medium	99	42
Large/very large	29	12
Total	238	100

X. Mendoza et al.

Table 5.6 Average number of investees and total employees by FBGs size

Size	Average number of investees	Average number of total employees (per investee)
Small	5.74	72.91
Medium	21.06	87.86
Large/very large	189.55	132.58
Total	34.51	86.40

Table 5.7 Breakdown of FBGs by size and age

Parent age	Average number of investees
Up to 10 years	12.09
10–19 years	37.6
20–34 years	28.89
More than 34 years	69.46
Total	34.51

as expected, the average number of investees is higher for those FBGs whose GUOs are older (from 37.6 investees to 69.46 investees).

Corporate Structure of FBGs

According to the structure of business groups, in terms of where the investees are located within the group hierarchy, we establish three typologies. First, simple groups are composed of the parent company (level 0 in the hierarchy) and investees directly owned by the parent (all the investees are at level 1 in the hierarchy). The graphical depiction of this typology would seem like a "hair comb". Second, semi-pyramidal groups have investees up to levels 2 or 3 of the hierarchical structure. Investees at level 2 are directly owned by investees at level 1 and indirectly owned by the parent through investees at level 1. Finally, pyramidal groups have corporate investees up to level 4 or higher, representing then a pure pyramid.

Table 5.8 shows the breakdown of FBGs by their corporate structure. We find that more than 70% of groups can be categorized as semi-pyramidal and 27% of business groups whose structure is strictly pyramidal. Simple business groups are those with all the corporate investees at level 1.

When we cross this information on corporate structure with the size of the FBG, we observe in Table 5.9 that almost 96% (98 + 64) of 169 semi-pyramidal groups are composed of between 2 and 50 investees. Unlike, 34% of pyramidal FBGs are composed of more than 50 investees. We find a positive and significant correlation between the corporate structure of the FBG

5 Corporate Strategy in Family Business Groups in Developed Economies

Table 5.8 Breakdown of FBGs by corporate structure (organizational levels)

Corporate structure	Number of FBGs	Percent (%)
Simple	5	2
Semi-pyramidal	169	71
Pyramidal	64	27
Total	238	100

Table 5.9 Breakdown of FBGs by size and corporate structure

Size/Structure	Simple	%	Semi-pyramidal	%	Pyramidal	%	Total
Small	4	4	98	89	8	7	110
Medium	1	1	64	65	34	34	99
Large/very large	0	0	7	24	22	76	29
Total	5	2	169	71	64	27	238

and the size (0.4892*). The larger the size of the FBG (from the first category "Small size" to the third category "Large/very large size"), the more hierarchical/vertical the structure (from the most horizontal "Simple" to the most vertical "Pyramidal").

Mapping Corporate Strategies of Family Business Groups

FBGs and Ownership. How Do FBGs Control Their Investee Companies?

The World Investment Report (by UNCTAD) define the following classification of investments, regarding the percentage of ownership that the parent company has in its investees[5]:

- Affiliates: when the parent company owns 10%–49.99% of shares
- Joint venture: when the parent company exactly owns 50% of shares
- Subsidiary: when the parent company owns 50.01%–95% of shares
- Wholly owned: when the parent company owns more than 95% of shares

In Panel A of Table 5.10, we observe that of the total number of investee companies in the FBGs, one out of four investees are jointly controlled (as

---

[5] Note that any investment below 10% is a financial investment, thus, we do not consider financial investments as affiliates or subsidiaries.

affiliates or joint ventures). About three out of four are majority or fully controlled (as subsidiaries or wholly owned investees).

The first question we want to answer is how many domestic investee companies belong to each of the types of investments described above. In Panel B of Table 5.10, we show that most of the investees are wholly owned by the parent company (54%), but there is still 46% of investees that may fall in one of the other three categories. Affiliates represent more than 20% of the sample, followed by subsidiaries (16%) and joint ventures (10%).

When we replicate the same analysis but restricted to only those foreign investee companies, the results are pretty similar with some small differences (Panel C of Table 5.10). Now the number of wholly owned investees and subsidiaries is slightly larger, to the detriment of the percentage of affiliates and joint ventures. It seems that parent companies in our sample may prefer to wholly own companies when they invest abroad to ensure control of these foreign investees.

In Table 5.11, we observe that in large/very large FBGs there is a larger presence of affiliates (22%) and fewer wholly owned investees (55%). In small FBGs, there is a larger propensity to control group investees (subsidiary plus wholly owned investees) compared to large FBGs (subsidiary plus wholly owned investees).

Table 5.10 Classification of investees in FBGs (ownership-level criteria)

Type of investee	Number of FBGs	Percentage (%)
Panel A. All investee companies		
Affiliate	1831	20
Joint venture	698	8
Subsidiary	1478	16
Wholly owned	5154	56
Total	9161	100
Panel B. Domestic companies		
Affiliate	990	20
Joint venture	506	10
Subsidiary	753	16
Wholly owned	2615	54
Total	4864	100
Panel C. Foreign companies		
Affiliate	839	20
Joint venture	192	4
Subsidiary	721	17
Wholly owned	2532	59
Total	4284	100

Table 5.11 Breakdown of investees by FBG size and investee type (ownership level criteria)

Size/Type of investees	Affiliate	%	Joint venture	%	Subsidiary	%	Wholly owned	%	Total
Small	80	12.35	37	5.71	120	18.52	411	63.43	648
Medium	374	16.82	163	7.33	398	17.90	1288	57.94	2223
Large/very large	1377	21.89	498	7.92	960	15.26	3455	54.93	6290
Total	1831	19.99	698	7.62	1478	16.13	5154	56.26	9161

Product Diversification

Industrial Location of GUOs (Parent Companies) of FBGs

First, we analyze in which sectors the parent companies of the FBGs are located. Table 5.12 exhibits the distribution of FBGs by sector of activity (Panel A). We observe a high prevalence of FBGs in Services. When we divide the sectors into subsectors in Panel B, we find the largest presence of FBGs in the wholesale industry.

Table 5.13 shows the breakdown of FBGs by sector and size. We observe that in the industry sector, almost 50% of the FBGs are small. However, in the construction around 30% of the FBGs are large. Table 5.14 shows a closer look at the distribution of FBGs by subsector and size.

In Table 5.15, we can find the breakdown of FBGs by sector and typology of the GUO. We observe how FBGs whose GUO is a holding company are prevalent in all the sectors, except for the construction industry. Table 5.16 shows a zoom in the breakdown of FBGs by subsector and GUO typology.

Table 5.12 Distribution of FBGs (GUO industry) by sector

Sector	Number of FBGs	Percentage (%)
Panel A: Sector level		
Construction	14	6
Energy	4	2
Industry	86	36
Services	134	56
Total	238	100

Subsector	Number of FBGs	Percentage (%)
Panel B: Subsector level		
Food, beverages, and tobacco	29	12
Wholesale and retail trade	60	25
Construction	14	6
Manufacture of machinery and equipment	12	5
Hospitality	11	5
Real estate	4	2
Financial intermediation and insurance	5	2
Other manufactures	45	19
Other services	14	6
Business services	26	11
Electricity and gas supplies	4	2
Telecommunications	4	2
Transportation	10	4
Total	238	100

5 Corporate Strategy in Family Business Groups in Developed Economies 99

Table 5.13 Breakdown of FBGs by sector and size

Sector/Size	Small	%	Medium	%	Large/very large	%	Total
Construction	6	44	4	29	4	29	14
Energy	2	50	2	50	0	0	4
Industry	42	49	33	38	11	13	86
Services	60	45	60	45	14	10	134
Total	110	46	99	42	29	12	238

Table 5.14 Breakdown of FBGs by subsector and size

Subsector/Size	Small	%	Medium	%	Large/very large	%	Total
Food, beverages and tobacco	12	41.38	11	37.93	6	20.69	29
Wholesale and retail trade	32	53.33	24	40.00	4	6.67	60
Construction	6	42.86	4	28.57	4	28.57	14
Manufacture of machinery and equipment	5	41.67	6	50.00	1	8.33	12
Hospitality	4	36.36	5	45.45	2	18.18	11
Real estate	2	50.00	2	50.00	0	0.00	4
Financial intermediation and insurance	2	40.00	3	60.00	0	0.00	5
Other manufactures	25	55.56	16	35.56	4	8.89	45
Other services	8	57.14	6	42.86	0	0.00	14
Business services	9	34.62	14	53.85	3	11.54	26
Electricity and gas supplies	2	50.00	2	50.00	0	0.00	4
Telecommunications	1	25.00	1	25.00	2	50.00	4
Transportation	2	20.00	5	50.00	3	30.00	10
Total	110	46.22	99	41.60	29	12.18	238

Table 5.15 Breakdown of FBGs by sector and GUO typology (holding or with sectorial activity)

Sector/GUO typology	W. sectorial activity	%	Holding	%	Total
Construction	8	57	6	43	14
Energy	1	25	3	75	4
Industry	13	15	73	85	86
Services	48	36	86	64	134
Total	70	29	168	71	238

100   X. Mendoza et al.

Table 5.16 Breakdown of FBGs by subsector and GUO typology (holding or with sectorial activity)

Subsector/GUO typology	W. sectorial activity	%	Holding	%	Total
Food, beverages and tobacco	5	17	24	83	29
Wholesale and retail trade	10	17	50	83	60
Construction	8	57	6	43	14
Manufacture of machinery and equipment	1	8	11	92	12
Hospitality	3	27	8	73	11
Real estate	3	75	1	25	4
Financial intermediation and insurance	4	80	1	20	5
Other manufactures	7	16	38	84	45
Other services	6	43	8	57	14
Business services	19	73	7	27	26
Electricity and gas supplies	1	25	3	75	4
Telecommunications	2	50	2	50	4
Transportation	1	10	9	90	10
Total	70	29	168	71	238

Industrial Location of Investee Companies of FBGs

Table 5.17 shows the distribution of investee companies by the industrial sector. We observe that there is a larger proportion of investee companies among domestic investees versus foreign investees. On the contrary, there is a larger proportion of investees in industry and construction in the case of foreign investees. Table 5.18 zooms in on the distribution of investees by subsector.

According to their NACE code of sectorial activity, we classify investee companies between commercial (wholesale or retail trade; they are retail point

Table 5.17 Distribution of investees by sector

Sector	All investees		Only foreign investees		Only domestic investees	
	Number of investees	Percent (%)	Number of investees	Percent (%)	Number of investees	Percent (%)
Services	5560	71	1966	62	3594	76
Industry	1358	17	694	22	664	14
Construction	674	8	401	13	273	6
Energy	282	4	97	3	185	4
Total	7874	100	3158	100	4716	100

5 Corporate Strategy in Family Business Groups in Developed Economies 101

Table 5.18 Distribution of investees by subsector

Subsector	All investees		Only foreign investees		Only domestic investees	
	Number of investees	Percent (%)	Number of investees	Percent (%)	Number of investees	Percent (%)
Wholesale and retail trade	1302	17	520	16	782	17
Other services	924	12	77	2	847	18
Business services	897	11	442	14	455	10
Construction	674	9	401	13	273	6
Other manufactures	660	8	353	11	307	7
Hospitality	601	8	174	6	427	9
Financial intermediation and insurance	565	7	292	9	273	6
Food, beverages and tobacco	472	6	200	6	272	6
Transportation	453	6	93	3	360	8
Real estate	417	5	157	5	260	6
Telecommunications	325	4	167	5	158	3
Electricity and gas supplies	282	4	97	3	185	4
Manufacture of machinery and equipment	226	3	141	4	85	2
Water supply, sanitation and management	76	1	44	1	32	1
Total	7874	100	3158	100	4716	100

of sales or services and do not produce) and productive (rest of sectors; they produce). Table 5.19 exhibits the classification of investees into commercial or productive investees. 17% of investee companies are commercial and 83% are productive. We observe that when we differentiate between foreign and domestic investees, the proportion of commercial and productive investees is pretty similar.

Product Diversification of FBGs

One way to measure product diversification is to calculate how many sectors/subsectors FBGs have their investees. On average, the 238 FBGs

Table 5.19 Breakdown of investees by type of investee (commercial or productive)

Typology	All investees		Only foreign investees		Only domestic investees	
	Number of investees	Percent (%)	Number of investees	Percent (%)	Number of investees	Percent (%)
Commercial	1302	17	520	16	782	17
Productive	6572	83	2638	84	3934	83
Total	7874	100	3158	100	4716	100

have investees in more than 4 subsectors. The largest number of different subsectors equals 14.

In Graph 5.1, we observe the distribution of FBGs depending on the number of sectors where they have located their investees. For example, we see that there are 55 FBGs with investees in 3 subsectors.

Table 5.20 shows the average number of sectors by FBG size. We observe that small FBGs are present, on average, in fewer sectors than medium or large/very large FBGs. As small FBGs are composed of fewer firms, it is not surprising that the average number of sectors is smaller than for medium and large FBGs.

Graph 5.2 represents the distribution of small, medium, and large/very large FBGs by the number of sectors, respectively.

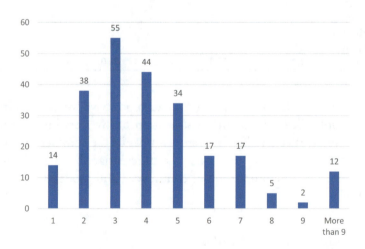

Graph 5.1 Distribution of FBGs by number of sectors

5 Corporate Strategy in Family Business Groups in Developed Economies   103

Table 5.20 Average number of sectors by FBGs' size

FBGs size	Average number of sectors
Small	2.8
Medium	4.7
Large/very large	8.6
Total	4.3

Industrial Distance

Besides industrial diversification, we also consider industrial distance for each dyad of the parent company and the investee. This helps us to understand how far or close is the parent company of the FBG with their investees in terms of the sector where they operate. To do so, we use the following criteria, which establishes five levels of industrial distance according to the differences between the NACE 4-digits' codes:

- Value of 4: the first digit of the parent NACE code and the investee NACE code is different (maximum level of industrial distance; the parent company and the investee operate in unrelated industries)
- Value of 3: the first digit is equal but the second digit is different
- Value of 2: the first two digits are equal but the third digit is different (medium level of industrial distance; the parent company and the investee operate in related industries)
- Value of 1: the first three digits are equal but the fourth digit is different
- Value of 0: all four digits are equal (minimum level of industrial distance; the parent company and the investee operate in the same industries)

We calculate the average industrial distance by FBG, considering all the dyads parent-investee. Results show that, on average, the average industrial distance by FBG is 2.7 (close to 3). This means that the average value of the industrial distance between the GUOs and all of the investees in a FBG is close to 3, that is, the NACE codes are only equal for the first digit.

Regarding the sectorial distribution, in Table 5.21 we observe that the sector with the largest average industrial distance is construction, and the sector with the smallest average industrial distance is energy.

The sub-sectorial distribution of the industrial distance by FBG shows that those subsectors with a larger industrial distance by FBGs are real estate, financial, and business services (Table 5.22). On the contrary, subsectors with a smaller industrial distance are other services, energy supplies, and hospitality.

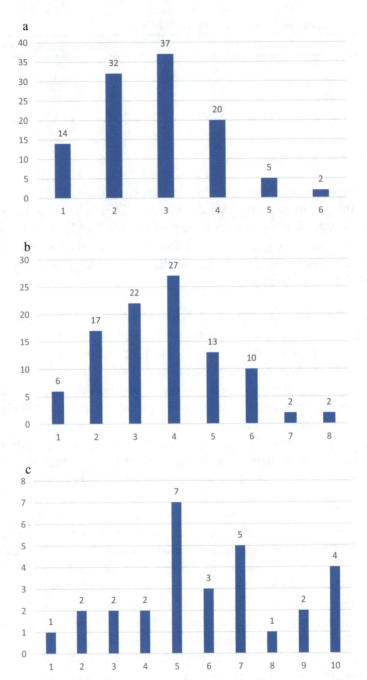

Graph 5.2 Distribution of FBGs (by size of the FBG) by number of sectors. **a** Distribution of small FBGs by number of sectors. **b** Distribution of medium FBGs by number of sectors. **c** Distribution of large/v.large FBGs by number of sectors

5 Corporate Strategy in Family Business Groups in Developed Economies

Table 5.21 Average industrial distance in a FBG by sector

Sector	Average industrial distance
Construction	3.3
Energy	2.2
Industry	2.8
Services	2.6
Total	2.7

Table 5.22 Average industrial distance in a FBG by subsector

Subsector	Average industrial distance
Food, beverages, and tobacco	2.7
Wholesale and retail trade	2.4
Construction	3.3
Manufacture of machinery and equipment	2.9
Hospitality	2.2
Real estate	3.8
Financial intermediation and insurance	3.8
Other manufactures	2.8
Other services	2.0
Business services	3.4
Electricity and gas supplies	2.2
Telecommunications	3.0
Transportation	2.4
Total	2.7

When we combine the average industrial distance with the age of the GUO, in Table 5.23 we find that older FBGs exhibit a larger average industrial distance than younger FBGs (there is a positive and significant correlation: 0.1972, $p < 0.01$).

Table 5.23 Average industrial distance in a FBG by GUO age

GUO age	Average industrial distance
Up to 10 years	2.5
10–19 years	2.7
20–34 years	2.8
More than 34 years	3.0
Total	2.7

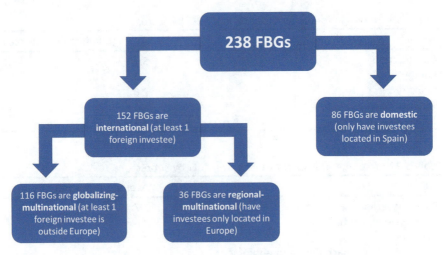

Fig. 5.1 Classification of FBGs by their geographic diversification

Geographic Diversification

Geographic diversification can be analyzed from two different angles: (i) the breadth of the geographic diversification as the number of different countries where the FBG invests and (ii) the breadth of geographic diversification as the number of different geographic regions where the FBG invests.[6]

Figure 5.1 summarizes the classification of the FBGs in the sample. Internationalized FBGs represent 64% of the sample (152 FBGs). Among these 152 internationalized FBGs, we divide them into globalizing-multinational FBGs (116), in which there is at least one foreign investee outside the region of the parent company, Europe, and regional-multinational FBGs (36), whose foreign investees are all located in Europe. The remaining 36% belong to FBGs whose all their investees are domestic.

When we cross the information related to the geographic diversification of FBGs with their size, we observe in Table 5.24 that, among internationalized FBGs, the percentage of large/very large business groups (17%) is larger than for the case of domestic FBGs (4%).

We also analyze the intersection between corporate structure (simple, semi-pyramidal, pyramidal) and geographic diversification. We observe that 52 out of 64 pyramids are internationalized (81%) and the remaining 12 pyramids only have investees in Spain (19%) (Table 5.25).

---

[6] As we deal with non-listed companies, we do not have information about company assets, sales, and employees abroad. Therefore, due to data limitations, it is not possible for us to estimate the depth of internationalization.

5 Corporate Strategy in Family Business Groups in Developed Economies 107

Table 5.24 Breakdown of FBGs by geographic diversification and size

Internationalization/Size	Small	%	Medium	%	Large/very large	%	Total
Domestic	57	66	26	30	3	4	86
Internationalized	53	35	73	48	26	17	152
Total	110	46	99	42	29	12	238

Table 5.25 Breakdown of FBGs by corporate structure and geographic diversification

Structure/Internationalization	Domestic	%	Internationalized	%	Total
Simple	4	80.00	1	20.00	5
Semi-pyramidal	70	41.42	99	58.58	169
Pyramidal	12	18.75	52	81.25	64
Total	86	36.13	152	63.87	238

Breadth of Geographic Diversification (Number of Different Countries)

The breadth of internationalization depends on the number of different countries where a FBG has foreign investees. On average, the foreign investees of the 152 internationalized FBGs are located in 7 different countries. These 152 FBGs are located in up to 54 different countries, although the majority (50%) have foreign investees in up to four countries. Regarding the remaining 86 domestic FBGs, there are 10 of them that carry out export and/or import activities.

The Observatory of Spanish Multinational Companies (OEME) establishes a classification of four levels of internationalization in terms of the number of foreign countries where companies locate. The OEME classification follows this aggrupation:

– From 1–4 foreign countries (level 1)
– From 5–9 foreign countries (level 2)
– From 10–19 foreign countries (level 3)
– More than 20 foreign countries (level 4).

When we classify our FBGs according to the OEME aggrupation, we find in Table 5.24 that 60% of them are located in the first level (from 1–4 foreign countries), which suggests that Catalan FBGs are not widely geographic diversified. Only 9% of analyzed FBGs are based in more than 20 foreign countries. Table 5.26 also includes the average number of foreign

Table 5.26 OEME classification of internationalized FBGs

OEME classification	Number of FBGs	Percentage (%)	Average number of foreign countries
From 1–4 foreign countries	91	60	2.1
From 5–9 foreign countries	30	20	6.6
From 10–19 foreign countries	17	11	13.8
More than 20 foreign countries	14	9	32.2
Total	152	100	7.1

Table 5.27 Breakdown of internationalized FBGs by OEME classification and size

OEME classification/Size	Small	%	Medium	%	Large/very large	%	Total
From 1 to 4 countries	53	58.24	34	37.36	4	4.40	91
From 5 to 9 countries	0	0.00	28	93.33	2	6.67	30
From 10 to 19 countries	0	0.00	11	64.71	6	35.29	17
More than 20 countries	0	0.00	0	0.00	14	100.00	14
Total	53	34.87	73	48.03	26	17.11	152

countries in each of the OEME categories. Obviously, the average number of foreign countries increases when we move along the categories.

When we cross the OEME classification with the size of the internationalized FBG (Table 5.27), we observe that more than half of internationalized FBGs in the range of 1–4 countries are small. Moreover, there is a hegemony of large/very large internationalized FBGs in the category of more than 20 countries, suggesting that those FBGs that are more internationalized are the largest ones. We can visualize the previous pattern in the set of Graph 5.3.

At the investee level, we can classify how many are domestic or foreign. In Table 5.28, we find a balanced number of domestic and foreign investee companies, although the percentage of domestic is slightly higher (53% versus 47%).[7]

---

[7] There is a small difference between the total number of investee companies ($N = 9161$) and the total number reported in Table 5.28. The difference equals 0.14% of the sample without information about the geographic location.

5 Corporate Strategy in Family Business Groups in Developed Economies

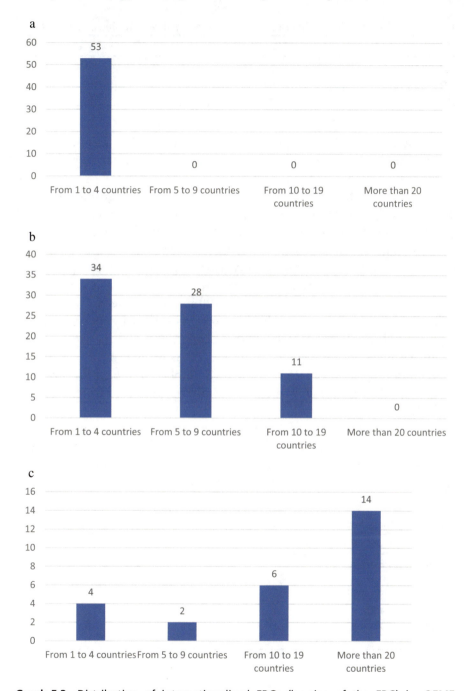

Graph 5.3 Distribution of internationalized FBGs (by size of the FBG) by OEME classification. **a** Distribution of small FBGs by OEME classification. **b** Distribution of medium FBGs by OEME classification. **c** Distribution of large/v.large FBGs by OEME classification

110   X. Mendoza et al.

Table 5.28 Classification of investee companies by their geographic diversification

Type of investees	Number of investees	Percentage (%)
Domestic	4864	53
Foreign	4284	47
Total	9148	100

We have measured the geographic diversification of FBGs in terms of how many countries they are located. Moreover, we can also measure geographic diversification according to the number of foreign investees. We establish five categories: (i) no foreign investees; (ii) between 1–10 foreign investees; (iii) between 11–50 foreign investees; (iv) between 51–100 foreign investees; and (v) more than 100 foreign investees. In Table 5.29, we observe that over 64% of business groups have at least one corporate investee abroad, whereas 36% of groups invest in the home country, that is, Spain. Forty-five percent of business groups have between one and 10 foreign investees. It is worthy to mention that 10 groups have more than 100 foreign investees.

Table 5.30 exhibits the breakdown of foreign investees by country. For the sake of brevity, only the 10 most relevant countries in terms of the number of foreign investees are included. Our 238 FBGs mainly invest in Portugal, this country represents 25.75% of the total number of foreign investees (see column 3). Portugal is followed by Italy (8.52%), the United States (5.35%), and Mexico (4.95%).

From these results, we can extract that our 239 FBGs, headquartered in Spain, invest in close countries in terms of geographic proximity (Portugal and Italy), but also in terms of cultural proximity (Mexico and Peru). Also, the size of the market matters, as in the case of the United States.

Table 5.29 Classification of FBGs according to the number of foreign investees

Number of foreign investees	Number of FBGs	Percentage (%)
No foreign investees	86	36
Between 1–10	108	45
Between 11–50	30	13
Between 51–100	4	2
More than 100	10	4
Total	238	100

5 Corporate Strategy in Family Business Groups in Developed Economies 111

Table 5.30 Breakdown of foreign investees by country (Top 10 countries)

Foreign investee country	Number of foreign investees	Percent out of total # of foreign investees (%)
Portugal	1103	25.75
Italy	365	8.52
United States	229	5.35
Mexico	212	4.95
Great Britain	172	4.01
Peru	151	3.52
Germany	141	3.29
France	138	3.22
Poland	127	2.96
Chile	97	2.26

Breadth of Geographic Diversification (Number of Different Regions)

The depth of internationalization depends on the number of different regions where a FBG has foreign investees. Out of the 152 FBGs that are internationalized, we observe that 116 have at least one investee outside the parent's region, that is, Europe (Table 5.31). On average, these 116 business groups have investees in two different regions, with a maximum of 7 different regions. The remaining 36 internationalized FBGs only have investees within Europe (regional-multinational FBGs).

A firm's geographical focus is determined based on the number of regions where it has foreign affiliates as follows: Regional focus, all foreign affiliates located in the same region; Bi-regional focus, when affiliates are located in 2 regions; Semi-global focus, when they are located in 3 or 4 regions; and Global focus, when foreign affiliates are in 5 or more regions. This classification is similar to the one proposed by Collinson and Rugman (2008) and Oh and Rugman (2012), although we have added the semi-global category proposed by some authors (Banalieva & Eddleston, 2011; Flores & Aguilera, 2007). Of the 152 multinational FBGs that have both investees in Europe and outside Europe (for example, they have an investee in Europe and another in Latin America), there are 77% FBGs that are in more than

Table 5.31 Classification of internationalized FBGs by multinationalization

Type of FBG	Number of FBGs	Percentage (%)
Regional-multinational	36	24
Globalizing-multinational	116	76
Total	152	100

Table 5.32 Breakdown of internationalized FBGs by regional focus

Regional focus	Number of internationalized FBGs	Percentage (%)
Regional	36	24
Bi-regional	54	35
Semi-global	35	23
Global	27	18
Total	152	100

one region, that is, globalized (a BG has an investee in Europe and another one in Latin America, it is a globalized group and specifically Bi-regional). We can observe the breakdown of internationalized FBGs by the number of regions in Table 5.32.

When we cross the regional focus of the internationalized FBGs with the size, we observe in Table 5.33 that the predominant size among FBGs with a regional focus is small. More than 3 out of 4 semi-global FBGs are of medium size. FBGs with a global focus are predominantly large or very large FBGs. We can visualize the previous pattern in the set of Graph 5.4.

At the investee level, we can observe in which countries foreign investee companies of the FBGs are located. These countries are classified into eight regions: (1) Europe; (2) Latin America and the Caribbean; (3) the USA and Canada; (4) sub-Saharan Africa; (5) South, East, and Southeast Asia; (6) Northern Africa and the Middle East [includes Turkey]; (7) Oceania; and (8) Community of Independent States and Southeast Europe (former communist countries) [includes Russia]. This classification of regions closely mirrors the one used by the Spanish Registry of Foreign Investments (which is very similar to the classification of UNCTAD, 2018).

In Table 5.34, we find that 59% of foreign investees of FBGs are located in Europe. The remaining 41% of investees are regionally distributed as follows: around 18% are located in Latin America and the Caribbean, and 6% are located in USA and Canada.

Table 5.33 Breakdown of internationalized FBGs by regional focus and size

Regional focus/Size	Small	%	Medium	%	Large/very large	%	Total
Regional	21	58.33	15	41.67	0	0.00	36
Bi-regional	26	48.15	23	42.59	5	9.26	54
Semi-global	6	17.14	27	77.14	2	5.71	35
Global	0	0.00	8	29.63	19	70.37	27
Total	53	34.87	73	48.03	26	17.11	152

5 Corporate Strategy in Family Business Groups in Developed Economies

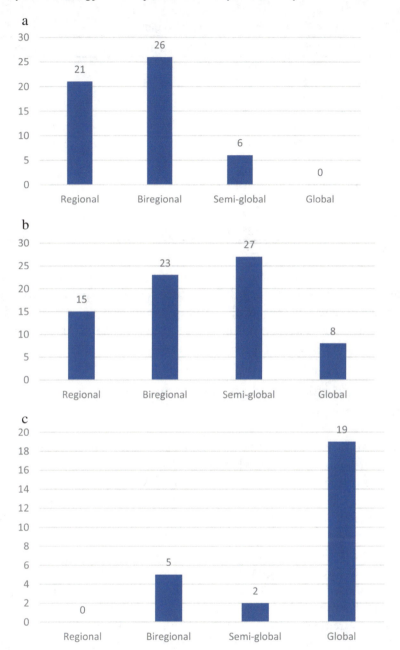

Graph 5.4 Distribution of internationalized FBGs (by size of the FBG) by regional focus. **a** Distribution of small FBGs by regional focus. **b** Distribution of medium FBGs by regional focus. **c** Distribution of large/v.large FBGs by regional focus

114   X. Mendoza et al.

Table 5.34 Breakdown of foreign investees by region

Foreign investee region	Number of foreign investees	Percentage (%)
Europe	2521	59
Latin America and the Caribbean	776	18
USA and Canada	253	6
CIS and Southeast Europe	193	4
South, East and Southeast Asia	167	4
sub-Saharan Africa	166	4
Northern Africa and Middle East	161	4
Oceania	47	1
Total	4284	100

In the set of Graph 5.5, we observe the number of foreign investees by region and by size of the FBG. We find a similar regional distribution of foreign investees by size, with a strong presence of investees from both small, medium, and large/very large FBGs in Europe, Latin America and the Caribbean, and the United States and Canada.

Mixing Strategies: Product and Geographic Diversification

In our sample, we observe a positive and significant correlation between the number of foreign countries where FBGs have investees and the number of different subsectors where these investees operate (0.4922, $p < 0.01$).

In Table 5.35, we observe that a large proportion of FBGs operating in a few different sectors (from one to four different subsectors) do not have foreign investees. For example, 71% of FBGs operating in only one subsector do not have investees located abroad. On the contrary, the largest concentration of more internationalized FBGs (with more than 100 foreign investees) is among those FBGs that are also more diversified (operating in more than 9 industrial subsectors).

When we remove the largest FBGs (with more than 100 investees), the correlation between the number of foreign investees and the number of different subsectors where the FBGs operate is still positive and significant (0.5241, $p < 0.01$).

5 Corporate Strategy in Family Business Groups in Developed Economies

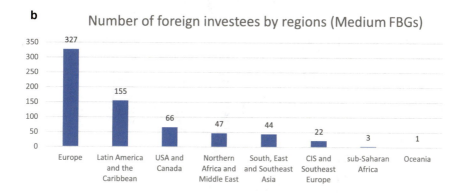

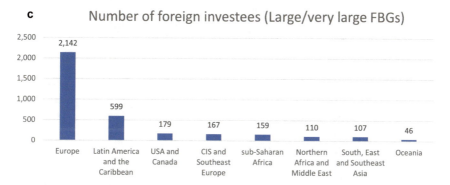

Graph 5.5 Distribution of foreign investees by regional focus and size of the FBG. **a** Distribution of foreign investees (small FBGs) by regional focus. **b** Distribution of foreign investees (medium FBGs) by regional focus. **c** Distribution of foreign investees (large/v.large FBGs) by regional focus

Table 5.35 Breakdown of FBGs by product and geographic diversification

Product diversification	No foreign investees	%	1–10 foreign investees	%	11–50 foreign investees	%	51–100 foreign investees	%	More than 100 foreign investees	%	Total
1	10	71.43	4	28.57	0	0.00	0	0.00	0	0.00	14
2	17	44.74	21	55.26	0	0.00	0	0.00	0	0.00	38
3	24	43.64	28	50.91	3	5.45	0	0.00	0	0.00	55
4	19	43.18	19	43.18	6	13.64	0	0.00	0	0.00	44
5	11	32.35	17	50.00	6	17.65	0	0.00	0	0.00	34
6	3	17.65	9	52.94	4	23.53	1	5.88	0	0.00	17
7	0	0.00	7	41.18	6	35.29	1	5.88	3	17.65	17
8	1	20.00	2	40.00	2	40.00	0	0.00	0	0.00	5
9	0	0.00	1	50.00	1	50.00	0	0.00	0	0.00	2
More than 9	1	9.09	0	0.00	2	18.18	2	18.18	6	54.55	11
Total	86	36.13	108	45.38	30	12.61	4	1.68	10	4.20	238

Discussion and Conclusion

The data collected in this chapter provides insights, concerning what structures do FBGs present and which corporate strategies they follow. While there has been an increasing interest in understanding diversification strategies in the context of family firms (Hafner, 2021), there is still limited research on FBGs, particularly in what concerns both combined, product, and geographic diversification. Many family firms use diversification and the establishment of wholly owned subsidiaries to organically grow (Hafner, 2021). We argue that understanding how FBGs are structured and how they diversify is key for the current state of the art of family firms. While literature on business group has described them as old business dinosaurs who only play locally and are highly specialized (Dyer, 1988; McCann et. al., 2001), it seems that Catalonian FBGs are indeed robust organizational forms using corporate strategies to cope with strong, dynamic changing forces.

Our exploratory analysis exhibits some interesting insights into the Catalonia FBGs' corporate strategies and provides preliminary findings on FBGs' corporate strategies. For example, from an ownership perspective, the literature argues that a system of minority shareholders squatting, i.e., owners of a critical mass, can use a share for their own exploitation. If the power hypothesis holds (Claessens et al., 2000b), all or most of the FBGs should be pyramids. Based on our analysis, it seems that this is not the case as the predominant structure of Catalonian FBGs is very variegated. This may be linked to the fact that family business groups are heterogeneous among them, as they have a family behind making strategic choices, and their goals and preferences will affect the way they decide (Arregle et al., 2012) to structure their ownership as well as their decisions with regards to where to enter and how much to diversify in terms of product. Catalan FBGs are mainly small in terms of the number of investee companies—and semi-pyramidal—with up to three hierarchical levels.

Regarding their product diversification, Catalan FBGs operate in more than four subsectors on average, and their parent-investee dyads exhibit a high level of industrial distance. Concerning their geographic diversification, two-thirds of these FBGs are internationalized and almost half of them can be considered as globalizing-multinationals. These results are in line with previous studies that suggest that family businesses look for opportunities in terms of product and international diversification given the highly global competitive environment (Pukall & Calabrò, 2014).

Overall, our study contributes to the growing interest in understanding the strategies that follow FBGs (Rosa et al., 2019). We present one of the few studies in diversification in family business groups that compares and connects product and geographic diversification (Hafner, 2021).

We expand knowledge with regards to diversification in FBGs by also depicting the structure that FBGs deploy to build their FBG. This chapter connects with mainstream literature in corporate strategy by bringing a context that entails not only diversification strategies but also different modes of structuring ownership to pursue such strategies. Moreover, we pursue our study in a developed economy showing the prevalence of this type of organization, contradicting the assumption that these groups prevail only in emerging economics to cover institutional voids.

Finally, our chapter maps out the Catalonian FBG universe identifying them and their corporate strategies, which allows for reaching out to policy makers and practitioners alike for the awareness of the contribution they have in the economic landscape as well as the practices they utilize to grow. Contrary to previous studies who focus on publicly traded business groups (c.f. Hernández-Trasobares & Galve-Górriz, 2017), this chapter analyzes privately held companies along with publicly traded companies, which is seldom the case.

There are also many possibilities for further analysis and research well beyond those provided in this chapter, which gives a unique opportunity to collect quantitatively grounded data about FBGs based upon a homogeneous methodology of data collection and analysis. For example, future studies could follow a similar analysis in other countries to compare results to find cross-cultural differences in the way FBGs structure themselves and their product and geographic diversification. We hypothesize that in countries like Finlandia, where the market is rather small, the internationalization strategy might be more intense. We also see opportunities to dig deeper into the motives for choosing related or unrelated diversification, the countries in which they are in and with which mode of entry and why they develop a specific ownership structure to build their FBG. This would bring to the table the combination of economic and non-economic goals (Gómez-Mejía et al., 2007) that are present in FBGs, particularly when there are many owners running different business units that are expanding either independently or interdependently.

References

Akhter, N., Rautiainen, M., Pihkala, T., & Ikäheimonen, T. (2021). The risk that became true: Case study of a Pakistani family business portfolio diversification. In *The Routledge companion to Asian family business* (pp. 478–493). Routledge.

5 Corporate Strategy in Family Business Groups in Developed Economies   119

Almeida, H. V., & Wolfenzon, D. (2006). A theory of pyramidal ownership and family business groups. *The Journal of Finance, 61*(6), 2637–2680.

Anderson, R. C., & Reeb, D. M. (2003). Founding-family ownership and firm performance: Evidence from the S&P 500. *The Journal of Finance, 58*(3), 1301–1328.

Ansoff, H. I. (1957). Strategies for diversification. *Harvard Business Review, 35*(5), 113–124.

Arregle, J. L., Hitt, M. A., Sirmon, D. G., & Very, P. (2007). The development of organizational social capital: Attributes of family firms. *Journal of Management Studies, 44*(1), 73–95.

Arregle, J. L., Naldi, L., Nordqvist, M., & Hitt, M. A. (2012). Internationalization of family-controlled firms: A study of the effects of external involvement in governance. *Entrepreneurship Theory and Practice, 36*(6), 1115–1143.

Banalieva, E. R., & Eddleston, K. A. (2011). Home-region focus and performance of family firms: The role of family vs non-family leaders. *Journal of International Business Studies, 42*(8), 1060–1072.

Baysinger, B., & Hoskisson, R. E. (1989). Diversification strategy and R&D intensity in multiproduct firms. *Academy of Management Journal, 32*(2), 310–332.

Block, J., Miller, D., Jaskiewicz, P., & Spiegel, F. (2013). Economic and technological importance of innovations in large family and founder firms: An analysis of patent data. *Family Business Review, 26*(2), 180–199.

Buckley, P. J., & Casson, M. (1976). A long-run theory of the multinational enterprise. In *The future of the multinational enterprise* (pp. 32–65). Palgrave Macmillan.

Carney, M., Gedajlovic, E. R., Heugens, P. P., Van Essen, M., & Van Oosterhout, J. H. (2011). Business group affiliation, performance, context, and strategy: A meta-analysis. *Academy of Management Journal, 54*(3), 437–460.

Carney, M., Van Essen, M., Gedajlovic, E. R., & Heugens, P. P. (2015). What do we know about private family firms? A meta-analytical review. *Entrepreneurship Theory and Practice, 39*(3), 513–544.

Chang, C. S. (1988). Chaebol: The South Korean conglomerates. *Business Horizon, 31*(2), 51–57.

Chang, S. J. (2003). Ownership structure, expropriation, and performance of group-affiliated companies in Korea. *Academy of Management Journal, 46*, 238–254.

Chang, X., Hilary, G., Shih, C. M., & Tam, L. H. K. (2010). Conglomerate structure and capital market timing. *Financial Management, 39*, 1307–1338.

Cho, Y.-H., & Yoon, J. (2001). The origin and function of dynamic collectivism: An analysis of Korean corporate culture. *Asia Pacific Business Review, 7*(4), 70–88.

Chung, H. M. (2013). The role of family management and family ownership in diversification: The case of family business groups. *Asia Pacific Journal of Management, 30*(3), 871–891.

Cirillo, A., Maggi, B., Sciascia, S., Lazzarotti, V., & Visconti, F. (2021). Exploring family millennials' involvement in family business internationalization: Who should be their leader? *Journal of Family Business Strategy*, 100455.

Claessens, S., Djankov, S., & Lang, L. H. P. (2000a). The separation of ownership and control in East Asian corporations. *Journal of Financial Economics, 58*, 81–112.

Claessens, S., Djankov, S., Fan, J., & Lang, L. (2000b). *Expropriation of minority shareholders in East Asia* (Vol. 4). Institute of Economic Research, Hitotsubashi University.

Collinson, S., & Rugman, A. M. (2008). The regional nature of Japanese multinational business. *Journal of International Business Studies, 39*(2), 215–230.

Colpan, A. M., & Jones, G. (2016). Business groups, entrepreneurship and the growth of the Koç group in Turkey. *Business History, 58*(1), 69–88.

Crespí-Cladera, R., & Bru, L. (2006). *Diversification of family business groups and board control*. Available at SSRN 924845.

Cruz, C., & Nordqvist, M. (2012). Entrepreneurial orientation in family firms: A generational perspective. *Small Business Economics, 38*(1), 33–49.

Cuervo-Cazurra, A. (2006). Business groups and their types. *Asia Pacific Journal of Management, 23*(4), 419–437.

Davis, G. F., Diekman, K., & Tinsley, C. H. (1994). The decline and fall of the conglomerate firm in the 1980s: The deinstitutionalization of an organizational form. *American Sociological Review, 59*, 547–570.

Deephouse, D. L., & Jaskiewicz, P. (2013). Do family firms have better reputations than non-family firms? An integration of socioemotional wealth and social identity theories. *Journal of Management Studies, 50*(3), 337–360.

Dyer, W. G. (1988). Culture and continuity in family firms. *Family Business Review, 1*(1), 37–50.

Dyer, W. G. (1994). Potential contributions of organizational behaviour to the study of family-owned businesses. *Family Business Review, 7*(2), 109–131.

Fernández, Z., & Nieto, M. J. (2005). Internationalization strategy of small and medium-sized family businesses: Some influential factors. *Family Business Review, 18*(1), 77–89.

Ferraris, A., Bogers, M. L., & Bresciani, S. (2020). Subsidiary innovation performance: Balancing external knowledge sources and internal embeddedness. *Journal of International Management, 26*(4), 100794.

Flores, R. G., & Aguilera, R. V. (2007). Globalization and location choice: An analysis of US multinational firms in 1980 and 2000. *Journal of International Business Studies, 38*(7), 1187–1210.

Gallo, M. A., & Pont, C. G. (1996). Important factors in family business internationalization. *Family Business Review, 9*(1), 45–59.

Gedajlovic, E., & Shapiro, D. M. (2002). Ownership structure and firm profitability in Japan. *Academy of Management Journal, 45*(3), 565–575.

Gersick, K. E., Davis, J. A., Hampton, M., & Lansberg, I. (1997). *Generation to generation—Lifecycles of the family business*. Harvard Business School Press.

Gómez-Mejía, L. R., Haynes, K. T., Núñez-Nickel, M., Jacobson, K. J., & Moyano-Fuentes, J. (2007). Socioemotional wealth and business risks in family-controlled firms: Evidence from Spanish olive oil mills. *Administrative Science Quarterly, 52*(1), 106–137.

Gomez-Mejia, L. R., Makri, M., & Kintana, M. L. (2010). Diversification decisions in family-controlled firms. *Journal of Management Studies, 47*(2), 223–252.

González, M., Guzmán, A., Pombo, C., & Trujillo, M.-A. (2013). Family firms and debt: Risk aversion versus risk of losing control. *Journal of Business Research, 66*(11), 2308–2320.

Granovetter, M. (1995). Coase revisited: Business groups in a modern economy. *Industrial and Corporate Change, 4*, 93–140.

Granovetter, M. (2005). Business groups and social organization. In N. J. Smelser & R. Swedberg (Eds.), *The handbook of economic sociology* (2nd ed., pp. 429–450). Princeton University Press.

Graves, C., & Thomas, J. (2004). Internationalisation of the family business: A longitudinal perspective. *International Journal of Globalisation and Small Business, 1*(1), 7–27.

Guillen, M. F. (2005). *The rise of Spanish multinationals.* Cambridge University Press.

Hafner, C. (2021). Diversification in family firms: A systematic review of product and international diversification strategies. *Review of Managerial Science, 15*(3), 529–572.

Hall, A., Melin, L., & Nordqvist, M. (2001). Entrepreneurship as radical change in the family business: Exploring the role of cultural patterns. *Family Business Review, 14*(3), 193–208.

Hernández-Trasobares, A., & Galve-Górriz, C. (2017). Diversification and family control as determinants of performance: A study of listed business groups. *European Research on Management and Business Economics, 23*(1), 46–54.

Hohberger, J., & Wilden, R. (2022). Geographic diversity of knowledge inputs: The importance of aligning locations of knowledge inputs and inventors. *Journal of Business Research, 145*, 705–719.

Hoskisson, R. O., & Johnson, R. A. (1992). Corporate restructuring and strategic change: The effect on diversification strategy and R & D intensity. *Strategic Management Journal, 13*, 625–634.

IEF. (2015). https://www.iefamiliar.com/wp-content/uploads/2019/07/La-Empresa-Familiar-en-Espan%CC%83a-2015.pdf

Iacobucci, D., & Rosa, P. (2005). Growth, diversification and business group formation in entrepreneurial firms. *Small Business Economics, 25*(1), 65–82.

Khanna, T., & Yafeh, Y. (2007). Business groups in emerging markets: Paragons or parasites? *Journal of Economic Literature, 45*(2), 331–372.

Kim, H., Hoskisson, R. E., Tihanyi, L., & Hong, J. (2004). The evolution and restructuring of diversified business groups in emerging markets: The lessons from chaebols in Korea. *Asia Pacific Journal of Management, 21*, 25–48.

Kock, C. J., & Guillén, M. F. (2001). Strategy and structure in developing countries: Business groups as an evolutionary response to opportunities for unrelated diversification. *Industrial and Corporate Change, 10*, 77–113.

Kogut, B., & Zander, U. (1992). Knowledge of the firm, combinative capabilities, and the replication of technology. *Organization Science, 3*(3), 383–397.

Kogut, B., & Zander, U. (1993). Knowledge of the firm and the evolutionary theory of the multinational corporation. *Journal of International Business Studies, 24*(4), 625–645.

Kumar, V., Gaur, A. S., & Pattnaik, C. (2012). Product diversification and international expansion of business groups: Evidence from India. *Management International Review, 52*(2), 175–192.

Lamin, A. (2013). Business groups as information resource: An investigation of business group affiliation in the Indian software services industry. *Academy of Management Journal, 56*(5), 1487–1509.

Lansberg, I. (1983). Managing human resources in family firms: The problem of institutional overlap. *Organizational Dynamics, 12*, 39–46.

La Porta, R., Lopez-de-Silanes, F., Shleifer, A., & Vishny, R. W. (2002). Investor protection and corporate valuation. *Journal of Finance, 57*, 1147–1170.

Lu, J. W., & Beamish, P. W. (2004). International diversification and firm performance: The S-curve hypothesis. *Academy of Management Journal, 47*(4), 598–609.

Mahmood, I. P., & Mitchell, W. (2004). Two faces: Effects of business groups on innovation in emerging economies. *Management Science, 50*(10), 1348–1365.

Mäkimattila, M., Rautiainen, M., & Pihkala, T. (2016). Systemic innovation in complex business portfolios—A case study. *International Journal of Business Innovation and Research, 10*(2–3), 363–379.

Manikandan, K. S., & Ramachandran, J. (2015). Beyond institutional voids: Business groups, incomplete markets, and organizational form. *Strategic Management Journal, 36*(4), 598–617.

Markides, C. C., & Williamson, P. J. (1994). Related diversification, core competences and corporate performance. *Strategic Management Journal, 15*, 149–165.

Masulis, R. W., Pham, P. K., & Zein, J. (2011). Family business groups around the world: Financing advantages, control motivations, and organizational choices. *The Review of Financial Studies, 24*(11), 3556–3600.

Mccann, J. E., III., Leon-Guerrero, A. Y., & Haley, J. D., Jr. (2001). Strategic goals and practices of innovative family businesses. *Journal of Small Business Management, 39*(1), 50–59.

Mendoza, X., Espinosa-Méndez, C., & Araya-Castillo, L. (2019). When geography matters: International diversification and firm performance of Spanish multinationals. *BRQ Business Research Quarterly*.

Miller, D. (2006). Technological diversity, related diversification, and firm performance. *Strategic Management Journal, 27*, 601–619.

Miller, D., & Le Breton–Miller, I. (2011). Governance, social identity, and entrepreneurial orientation in closely held public companies. *Entrepreneurship Theory and practice, 35*(5), 1051–1076.

5 Corporate Strategy in Family Business Groups in Developed Economies   123

Miller, D., Le Breton-Miller, I., Lester, R. H., & Cannella Jr, A. A. (2007). Are family firms really superior performers? *Journal of Corporate Finance, 13*(5), 829–858.

Morck, R. (2010). The riddle of the great pyramids. In A. M. Colpan, T. Hikino, & J. R. Lincoln (Eds.), *The Oxford handbook of business groups* (pp. 602–628). Oxford University Press.

Morck, R., Wolfenzon, D., & Yeung, B. (2005). Corporate governance, economic entrenchment, and growth. *Journal of Economic Literature, 43*, 655–720.

Mukherjee, K., Rautiainen, M., Pihkala, T., & Rosa, P. (2019). The dynamics and complexity of family business groups. In M. Rautiainen, P. Rosa, T. Pihkala, M.-J. Parada, & A. Discua Cruz (Eds.), *The family business group phenomenon—Emergence and complexities* (pp. 177–200). Palgrave Macmillan.

Oh, C. H., & Rugman, A. M. (2012). Regional integration and the international strategies of large European firms. *International Business Review, 21*(3), 493–507.

Palepu, K. (1985). Diversification strategy, profit performance and the entropy measure. *Strategic Management Journal, 6*(3), 239–255.

Parada, M. J., Akhter, N., Basco, R., Discua Cruz, A., & Fitz-Koch, S. (2019). Understanding the dynamics of business group development: A transgenerational perspective. In *The family business group phenomenon* (pp. 201–222). Palgrave Macmillan.

Pihkala, T., Goel, S., Rautiainen, M., Mukherjee, K., & Ikävalko, M. (2019). Deciphering ownership of family business groups. In M. Rautiainen, P. Rosa, T. Pihkala, M.-J. Parada, & A. Discua Cruz (Eds.), *The family business group phenomenon—Emergence and complexities* (pp. 223–252). Palgrave Macmillan.

Pukall, T. J., & Calabro, A. (2014). The internationalization of family firms: A critical review and integrative model. *Family Business Review, 27*(2), 103–125.

Qian, G., Khoury, T. A., Peng, M. W., & Qian, Z. (2010). The performance implications of intra-and inter-regional geographic diversification. *Strategic Management Journal, 31*(9), 1018–1030.

Rautiainen, M. (2012). Dynamic ownership in family business system—A portfolio business approach.

Rautiainen, M., Rosa, P., Pihkala, T., Parada, M. J., & Discua Cruz, A. F. (2019). *The family business group phenomenon—Emergence and complexities.* Palgrave Macmillan.

Robson, G., Gallagher, C., & Daly, M. (1993). Diversification strategy and practice in small firms. *International Small Business Journal, 11*(2), 37–53.

Rosa, P., & Pihkala, T. (2019). Theoretical insights into the nature, diversity and persistence of business groups. In M. Rautiainen, P. Rosa, T. Pihkala, M.-J. Parada, & A. Discua Cruz (Eds.), *The family business group phenomenon—Emergence and complexities* (pp. 17–35). Palgrave Macmillan.

Rosa, P., Rautiainen, M., Pihkala, T., Parada, M. J., & Discua Cruz, A. (2019). Conclusions: Researching family business groups: Lessons learned and avenues for further research. In *The family business group phenomenon*(pp. 387–395). Palgrave Macmillan, Cham.

Rumelt, R. P. (1982). Diversification strategy and profitability. *Strategic Management Journal, 3*(4), 359–369.

Schneider, B. R. (2009). Hierarchical market economies and varieties of capitalism in Latin America. *Journal of Latin American Studies, 41*(03), 553–575.

Schulze, W. S., Lubatkin, M. H., & Dino, R. N. (2003). Toward a theory of agency and altruism in family firms. *Journal of Business Venturing, 18*(4), 473–490.

Schulze, W. S., Lubatkin, M. H., Dino, R. N., & Buchholtz, A. K. (2001). Agency relationships in family firms: Theory and evidence. *Organization science, 12*(2), 99–116.

Scott, M., & Rosa, P. (1996). Opinion: Has firm level analysis reached its limits? Time for a rethink? *International Small Business Journal, 14*(4), 81–89.

Todeva, E. (2005). Governance, control and co-ordination in network context: The cases of Japanese Keiretsu and Sogo Shosha. *Journal of International Management, 11*, 87–109.

Wan, W. P., Hoskisson, R. E., Short, J. C., & Yiu, D. W. (2011). Resource-based theory and corporate diversification: Accomplishments and opportunities. *Journal of Management, 37*(5), 1335–1368.

Witt, M. A. (2019). De-globalization: Theories, predictions, and opportunities for international business research. *Journal of International Business Studies, 50*(7), 1053–1077.

Young, M. N., Peng, M. W., Ahlstrom, D., Bruton, G. D., & Jiang, Y. (2008). Corporate governance in emerging economies: A review for the principal-principal perspective. *Journal of Management Studies, 45*(1), 196–220.

Zahra, S. A. (2005). Entrepreneurial risk taking in family firms. *Family Business Review, 18*(1), 23–40.

6

Entrepreneurship in Family Business Groups in Latin America Under Organizational Ambidexterity Lens

Claudio G. Muller

Introduction

In this chapter, we present the dynamics of entrepreneurship in family business groups from the framework of organizational ambidexterity. The concept of emerging countries has become generalized and widespread in recent years, especially in studying a notably dynamic region such as Latin America (Parada et al., 2016). The region has seen a growing flow of foreign direct investment (Trevino et al., 2002), highlighting the increasing prominence of companies and business groups in the rankings of the world's largest businesses (Family Business Index, 2021). Understanding the various reasons for the rise and relative success of Latin America's leading business actors and their context is a relatively recent topic in the literature (Botero et al., 2018). However, for many experts, the peak of acceleration of this process has taken place since the end of the 1980s, with the latest financial globalization and the rise of deregulation, privatization, and global capital flows (Ramírez-Solís et al., 2021). Other authors attribute the development and birth of economic groups to the historical milestone of independence in most Latin American countries, around the 1800s (Müller & Sandoval-Arzaga, 2021), as this was

---

C. G. Muller (✉)
School of Business and Economics, University of Chile, Santiago, Chile
e-mail: cmuller@fen.uchile.cl

© The Author(s), under exclusive license to Springer Nature
Switzerland AG 2023
M. Rautianen et al. (eds.), *The Palgrave Handbook of Managing Family Business Groups*,
https://doi.org/10.1007/978-3-031-13206-3_6

when budding family businesses managed to flourish with the support of the new governments. It is, therefore, a growing field of study.

Other lines of research consider the increase in the number of large family businesses and business groups in the Latin American economy as an opportunity for investment funds and sometimes as a threat to European, Asian, and US groups and multinationals. This is the case of Carrefour and its exit from the Chilean market, selling all its assets to a local family group, Familia Ibáñez, in 2001 (Bianchi & Reyes, 2005).

Further research has focused on resilience and family business groups in uncertain environments, such as Cruz et al. (2019). They seek to explain that family businesses apply various strategies to mitigate risks in unstable environments and remain resilient. Other works have conducted a macro review of the phenomenon. In Reynolds et al. (1999), a model is presented which argues that nationally established entrepreneurial activity varies with the number of variables, referred to as general national framework conditions, while entrepreneurial activity varies with entrepreneurial framework conditions. These conditions are related to the social, cultural, and political context of a country. Entrepreneurial framework conditions, on the other hand, include the specific policies and plans of the government that enhance the entrepreneurial dynamics (Amorós, 2009). Nevertheless, it is noted by Coyne and Boettke (2006) that only recently has research begun to pay attention to the role of institutions and how they influence entrepreneurial behavior.

This chapter focuses on a crucial determinant of entrepreneurship in developing countries, that is, how entrepreneurship is affected in a context of low institutional quality in family-controlled business groups in a region such as Latin America. In a sense, this chapter goes a step back from the study of family business entrepreneurship by explicitly considering a more general perspective on the influence of institutional quality in developing countries. The "rules of the game" (North, 1990) have an impact on economic outcomes, including entrepreneurship, essentially through the general role of government in providing or failing to provide institutions that underpin the effective rule of law (Alvarez & Urbano, 2011; Friedman, 2014). We focus on Latin American countries because there is a consensus that low- and middle-income countries have a relatively low degree of institutional quality compared to more developed nations (Gwartney et al., 2004).

Our research question addresses the issue of how family groups in Latin America adapt to an unstable environment in contexts of low institutional quality through balancing exploitation and exploration.

The remaining part of the paper proceeds as follows: The next section presents a general framework on the concept of entrepreneurship and family business. The following section is concerned with the methodology used for this study. Then, analysis, conclusion, and future research are presented.

Literature Analysis

Entrepreneurship and Family Business

Those scholars who have addressed entrepreneurship have tended to underestimate the contribution of family systems to entrepreneurial success (Lumpkin et al., 2011). Many existing family business scholars have focused on wealth preservation rather than wealth-creating activities such as opportunity recognition, innovation, strategy, and growth. On the other hand, Aldrich and Cliff (2003) suggest that family has a pervasive effect on entrepreneurship. This means that family ties can have a positive or negative effect on entrepreneurial performance. Family kinship ties within a family often extend to the management teams followed by family members. Hence, it can be argued that family members can have a long-term effect on entrepreneurship. Jaskiewicz et al. (2015) have found that family firms foster transgenerational entrepreneurship by actively involving younger family members. As a result, it is vital to assess how younger family members influence the entrepreneurship of the firm at a micro-level.

Another facet of entrepreneurship and family business is related to the ability to take risks. There has been some debate in the family business literature about whether families are too conservative about taking risks (Berrone et al., 2012). The reason, the authors argue, is that families want to protect their wealth and reputation in the market. Short et al. (2009) found that risk-taking in family businesses can be negatively associated with performance, given that in most family businesses, financial and non-financial objectives affect performance, influencing the type and level of entrepreneurial activity.

Because some family members are more entrepreneurial than others, it is crucial to evaluate both individual and team forms of entrepreneurship. Family entrepreneurial teams are groups of people from the same family who engage in entrepreneurial activities (Discua-Cruz et al., 2012), given that families tend to have shared values and a level of trust among members. Such elements can help in entrepreneurial endeavors. This entrepreneurial behavior can be fostered through the involvement in family-based social interactions;

an example of this is a family where members learn from observation and interaction based on social factors.

Family businesses are entrepreneurial through their collective and individual actions. Following social learning theory, beliefs and attitudes are passed on to others through interaction. That is, information and resources are transmitted when people interact in the environment, whether it is business or family interaction. By emulating others, individuals are motivated to behave in a certain way. Consequently, by being exposed to other behaviors, one can influence another to engage in an entrepreneurial action (Dou et al., 2020).

Other studies such as Arzubiaga et al. (2019) have approached the subject from the entrepreneurial orientation and concluded that, in family businesses, drivers are linked to resources, attitudes, and values. In this chapter, we addressed the concept of Entrepreneurship and Family Business.

Institutional Quality in Latin America

The study of the institutional environment has taken on great relevance, especially since the 1990s, particularly with North (1990) and Weingast (1993). Although it has been a relevant variable for the exercise of economic transactions in recent centuries, as reflected in Greif's (1994) work on the merchants of Genoa, Italy in the twelfth century. His work indicated that "it is misleading to expect that a beneficial organization in one society will yield the same results in another." He argued that as early as medieval times, there was a strong belief that trading in one or another would have different effects using the same resources invested, depending on the political and legal system prevailing in that society. The study of institutions as determinants of individual behaviors that influence the performance of the economy focuses on the understanding of societies and their economic systems through what North (1990) called the "rules of the game," which define and constrain the set of choices that individuals have to make decisions.

In this context, it is worth noting that there is little applied research (Camargo, 2021; Stosberg, 2018). Among the few studies is the work of Müller and Sandoval-Arzaga (2021), in which they replicate a Sobel (2008) study in Latin America, calculating a *net entrepreneurial rate*, which by definition is equal to the sum of net productive entrepreneurship rate minus the unproductive entrepreneurship rate (Sobel, 2008). An inherent problem with this type of calculation is the lack of variables for the analyzed phenomena, institutional quality, and productive and unproductive entrepreneurship. Müller and Sandoval-Arzaga (2021) use the economic freedom indicator as a proxy of institutional quality, estimated by The Heritage Foundation each year for 186 countries. At the Latin American level, they conclude that Chile is the best ranked concerning the net entrepreneurship rate with 21.92 points in 28th position worldwide, followed by Uruguay ranked 38th, with 2.92 points. Our concept of net entrepreneurial rate is used to show that, in a low-quality institutional environment, the conditions for entrepreneurship are of low probability and firms are more likely to make profit than to make the economy grow. Table 6.1 shows the Latin American Net Entrepreneurship Ranking.

These findings confirm the assumptions that the Latin American institutional environment is low in comparison with other regions, similar even to countries in the sub-Saharan African zone. Most of the countries in this sample are in the lowest percentile of the study, eight out of fourteen economies in the region; this indicates not only low institutional quality but also an incentive to the informal economy, contributing to the emergence of a culture and codes of conduct, in many cases outside the legal framework.

This is in line with studies such as Gedajlovic et al. (2012), which indicate that institutional conditions moderate performance differences among family firms. More specifically, they suggest adverse effects of institutional conditions experienced by family firms when operating in an emerging economy.

Table 6.1 Ranking of net entrepreneurial in Latin America

World Rank	Latin American Rank	Country
28	1	Chile
38	2	Uruguay
39	3	Costa Rica
46	4	Brasil
58	5	Panamá
60	6	Colombia
61	7	Trinidad y Tobago
62	8	México
63	9	Perú
72	10	Guatemala
75	11	Argentina
79	12	Honduras
85	13	Ecuador
86	14	Paraguay

Source Müller and Sandoval-Arzaga (2021)

Family Business Groups in Latin America

Business groups are defined in the literature as an organization with a plurality of companies, which may be autonomous, with a leading company that exercises control over all the companies that make up the aggregation itself (Morck & Yeung, 2003). Similarly, Khanna and Rivkin (2001) indicate that business groups are associations of firms consisting of several legally independent firms united by formal and informal ties and subject to coordinated action.

Research on business groups in emerging markets has proliferated as developing countries have grown economically (Khanna & Palepu, 2000). Moreover, although business groups are most often legally independent entities, they often "take coordinated action" (Khanna & Rivkin, 2001), leading to negative externalities in the markets in which they operate. Other studies indicate that the share of group-affiliated firms is substantial in certain regions, such as an Asia Pacific sample, with prevalence ranging from 25% of listed firms in the Philippines to 65% in Indonesia (Carney & Gedajlovic, 2002).

Rautiainen et al.'s (2019) recent publication indicates that family-owned economic groups are even more complex than the traditional multi-divisional form of corporate organization. Also, it points out that this type of conglomerate is more prevalent in developing countries as regulatory and legal institutions are weak, encouraging risk dilution through legally independent smaller companies. A similar conclusion was reached by Carney et al. (2018) by indicating that the two most common perspectives on the encouragement and proliferation of economic groups are generated by institutional gaps and entrenchment/exploitation in their industry sector. In fact, these authors suggest that the inability of governments and the state to create institutions and the ability of business groups to adapt to institutions foster these types of organizations.

In emerging markets, governments are heavily involved in business decisions (Granovetter, 1995) and play an essential role for family-owned conglomerates. Kim et al. (2004) provide the example of the Siam Cement Group in Thailand and the Salim and Astra companies in Indonesia, especially in the business growth phase. This government-family business proximity is also reflected in the case of Mexico. The commercial banking sector in the late 1800s underwent a process of "Mexicanization" when, with the help of state forces, foreign control was eliminated, and powerful family conglomerates or holding groups were established around national private banks.

By and large, Latin American countries share many characteristics such as specialization in natural or agricultural resources, heterogeneous productive structures of low productivity, and the persistence of a substantial informal sector against the background of weak state capacities. This has resulted in opposing capitalist socioeconomic regimes. In some countries, there is a reliance on markets to organize value creation and income distribution. In contrast, in others, there is a mediating role for socio-political commitments embedded in a series of institutional forms. Such criteria have led to the definition of four types of capitalism in Latin America: international outsourcing—as in the case of Mexico—socio developmentalist—as in Brazil—rentier/liberal—in the example of Chile— and rentier/redistributive—as in Ecuador (Bizberg, 2019). Many weak states have been entrenched in rent-seeking behavior, with control exercised by elites who exploit their political and economic power for their own benefit. Acemoglu and Robinson (2012) have termed it "extractive institutions," i.e., institutions designed to benefit elites.

One of the aspects related to the growth and consolidation of family business groups in Latin America has been the predominant role of the state in the region, which was strongly reflected in the implementation of intervention and import substitution industrialization policies. This period began at the end of the 1930s and continued until after World War II, in different Latin American countries and at varying intensity levels. These initiatives contributed to diversifying industrial capacity and meeting their needs for consumer goods and part of the intermediate and capital goods with domestic production. All this came hand in hand with a process of investment and a productive and technological transformation. Agriculture, especially in Argentina, Brazil, and Chile, benefited from applying technologies and forms of production in land cultivation. Many of the landowning families that were engaged in basic agricultural production benefited from these innovations. While the Central American countries, Ecuador, and Peru, lagged as they did not modernize their agriculture and remained with the primary export model.

The next step was the establishment of concentration processes in family-owned companies that went on to form the first diversified business groups in Mexico, Argentina, Colombia, Chile, and Brazil. Most of these family-owned companies came from the early stages of development during the incorporation into the world market for agricultural and livestock products. Many of these families had been rooted since the end of the colonial period. Many moved toward integration processes, alliances with other families, and permanent adaptation to changing and irregular cycles.

Family businesses in Argentina were concentrated in the manufacturing industry, especially in the automotive parts manufacturing industry and more innovative industrial sectors such as pharmaceuticals and chemicals. In Mexico, family groups of family businesses benefitted from the post-1920 reforms, which fostered institutional conditions for entrepreneurial action, particularly in the industrial sector. These incentives were oriented toward protectionist economic nationalism. Business families linked to the oligarchy that had supported the political system before the 1910 revolution suffered expropriation (Cerutti et. al., 2000).

In the case of Colombia, early in the twentieth century, the rise of family businesses rapidly shaped the first economic groups. In the process, the activity of regional business families that came to control specific economic groups was of great relevance. In this period, the most important companies correspond to six of the economic groups founded as family businesses (Rodríguez-Satizábal, 2014).

Later, and at different times depending on the country, privatizations, a process contrary to import substitution, were implemented. Some countries with important state-owned sectors, such as Costa Rica, Ecuador, and Uruguay, barely privatized some companies, while others, such as Chile, Argentina, Bolivia, Panama, and Peru, carried out sales of state-owned companies for more than 15% of their GDP (Bruton et al., 2015). In Latin America, 75% of the revenues obtained from privatizations came from public utilities and infrastructure companies' sales; 11% corresponded to the financial sector and the rest to oil, gas, and manufacturing. Most Latin American countries have privatized their telecommunications, electricity, gas, and water and sanitation services to a lesser extent. On the other hand, the sale of state-owned railways, airlines, airports, and highways has not been as important. As for the financial and industrial sectors, privatizations were not as notable because private participation was already widespread. Besides, most countries kept at least one official bank and retained control of companies linked to natural resources such as oil, gas, and copper. Even in Chile, it was decided not to privatize companies in critical sectors, such as copper, oil, banking, mail, railroads, and ports. A peculiar case is Argentina, which did not keep any significant company in the state's hands, except some national and provincial banks and some local health companies. In contrast, Uruguay, which is comparable to Argentina in other respects, was the least advanced in the privatization process in the entire region.

The profitability and efficiency of state-owned enterprises now in private hands increased considerably, by more than 15%. Company production also increased as a result of privatization. The largest increases were recorded in

6 Entrepreneurship in Family Business Groups ...

Mexico and Colombia, where average production increased by 68% and 59%, respectively.

During this process, many state-owned companies were transferred to the control of family businesses or family economic groups, in the search for diversification and growth and due to their historical closeness and favoritism to different governments (Müller & Sandoval-Arzaga, 2021). It can be seen that, since the mid-1850s, family businesses went from being mere producers of semi-finished agricultural products (and in very exceptional cases, exporters of other raw materials) to being located in intermediate production sectors because of import substitution policies. This gave birth to the first diversified economic groups until the new impulse to purchase state-owned companies—privatization processes—which, depending on the country, took on relevance at the end of the 1960s.

Organizational Ambidexterity

Organizational ambidexterity is the capability that enables organizations to achieve high levels of exploitation, focused on the current product/market mix to gain efficiency, and exploration or search for new opportunities to generate innovation (Raisch & Birkinshaw, 2008).

Exploration is related to search and prospecting activities (March, 1991). Its purpose is to respond to and drive latent trends by focusing on new opportunities, skills, markets, and/or relationships (Lavie & Rosenkopf, 2006). To develop exploration, knowledge is gathered from outside the company with the intention of building new competencies (Webb et al., 2010). In contrast, exploitation is related to learning activities (March, 1991); its purpose is to be responsive to current circumstances and meet the needs of existing customers (Lubatkin et al., 2006), strengthening core competencies (Shane & Venkataraman, 2000).

Organizational ambidexterity is vital for the long-term success of family businesses (Kammerlander et al., 2020) and has been used in different contexts, including the role of family engagement in this context. A reason for this is the transgenerational intention of family firms and their focus on long-term survival (McAdam et al., 2010).

The literature suggests that family influences organizational ambidexterity in different dimensions. From family values, shared principles guiding the behavior of family members, shared vision for the family and the business, and a set of family-owners committed to the strategy that defines both exploration and exploitation activities (Jansen et al., 2006).

Methodological Approach

We used the lens of Organizational Ambidexterity (O.A.) to explain entrepreneurship in family business groups. It is an appropriate concept to study this dynamic (Hughes et al., 2018; Stubner et al., 2012). The paradox of this framework addresses that organizations must be flexible, stable, and simultaneously adaptive, achieve short-term profits without forgetting long-term growth (Tushman & O'Reilly, 1996). Many gaps still exist in family business research regarding this topic (Kammerlander et al., 2020). The existing knowledge stems mainly from regions with solid institutions such as Western Europe and the United States. This leaves behind emerging economies with lower institutional quality, whose environments generate significant variations influencing the strategies and behavior of family businesses (Vázquez et al., 2020).

We followed a recent study by Canale et al. (2021), which used a sample of eleven countries and 21 cases of family businesses in Latin America. They assessed how exploration and exploitation are informed by specific decisions and manifested through strategic actions at the family and firm levels. The study found two family dimensions that act as drivers of ambidexterity in contexts of low institutional quality: family social responsibility and a sense of belonging to a region. It also provides evidence supporting the existing literature on the positive impact of family cohesion, shared values, commitment to exploration and exploitation strategies, shared vision, and long-term orientation toward ambidexterity.

Figure 6.1 shows the findings of the Canale et al. (2021) sample in a matrix based on their levels of exploration and exploitation. In line with the combined perspective of ambidexterity, understood as the firm's simultaneous focus on exploratory and exploitative orientations (Jansen et al., 2006), Canale et al.'s study presents twelve cases of ambidextrous family firms within our sample. Seven more cases are ranked as medium or low in their exploration levels, while the two remaining cases showed medium or low levels of both exploration and exploitation, so we classify them as non-ambidextrous firms.

In Canale et al. (2021) findings, there are no exclusively exploratory companies. A possible explanation for this is based precisely on the influence of the institutional context. According to Goel and Jones (2016), in different institutional contexts, one can find different benefits related to exploration versus exploitation, as is in this business environment.

Although from a small sample, these findings are counterintuitive to what is indicated by Müller & Sandoval-Arzaga (2021) on the ranking of net

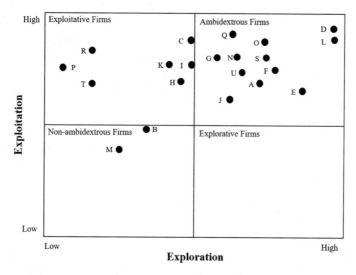

Fig. 6.1 Levels of ambidexterity in Latin American family businesses (*Source* Canale et al., [2021])

entrepreneurial in Latin America. According to the literature, in environments of low institutional quality, we should find a relatively low capacity for ambidextrousness, i.e., low exploitation and low exploration, much like in countries of sub-Saharan Africa (Olagboye et al., 2022).

Case Studies

Family businesses in Latin America offer a suitable context to study entrepreneurship and institutional quality, given the heterogeneity of uncertain settings. To better understand the phenomenon in the context of family business groups, we focused on the intensity of their orientation toward exploration and exploitation activities, considering both primary and secondary data. For this process, the primary sources were web pages and archival data from the companies; these played an essential role in triangulating and confirming what was stated by interviewed experts.

To classify the orientation and exploratory activities of the companies, we considered the intensity with which they engage in searching activities and gather knowledge from outside the company in pursuit of new horizons. In line with the existing literature, we assigned high levels of exploration to firms heavily involved in activities such as experimenting, risk-taking, seeking new knowledge from outside, creating technology, focusing on new products, services, and markets, and building new competencies (Lavie & Rosenkopf,

2006; Webb et al., 2010). Likewise, we attributed lower levels of exploration to the firms that were less involved in such activities and those that allocated considerably fewer resources (e.g., investment, structure, time, focus).

To define the exploitation orientation of firms, we analyzed the degree to which they were involved in strengthening core competencies. According to the existing literature, we assigned high levels of exploitation to firms strongly committed to activities such as efficiency, refinement, incremental improvements, fulfillment of existing customer needs, and complementing or enhancing existing competencies (Lubatkin et al.,2006; March, 1991; Webb et al., 2010). We also attributed lower levels of exploration to companies that are not engaged in exploitation initiatives and allocated considerably fewer resources to them.

Case studies of companies were purposively selected and provided a systematic way to view processes and events, observe phenomena within real-life contexts, collect and analyze data, and report results (Leppäaho et al., 2016). Case studies from several countries were selected to provide cross-sectional information on the Entrepreneurship and Institutional Quality phenomenon. These cases were selected on the basis of where the processes under study are most likely to occur (Hollifield & Coffey, 2006). We studied eleven Family Economic Groups from nine Latin American countries (see Table 6.2). Such diversity addressed the concept of external validity (Riege, 2003) and helped better to examine the complex dynamics of family business groups. As access to family firms is difficult, especially in those countries with high levels of personal security, we approached the firms by drawing on primarily public information, personal contacts, and interviews with experts, using a qualitative narrative approach.

Grupo Carso—Mexico

Grupo Carso, owned by the Slim Family, includes hotels, mines, railroads, shopping centers, among others. The various sectors of this conglomerate have served it well in times of crisis to offset the losses of one sector against the rest. The company was founded in Mexico in 1980 when it was initially constituted as Grupo Galas. Between 1980 and 1989, the company acquired most of the shares of Cigatam, Artes Gráficas Unidas, Fábricas de Papel Loreto y Peña Pobre, Galas de México, Sanborns, Empresas Frisco, Industrias Nacobre, and Porcelanite Holding. In 1990, the company changed its name to Grupo Carso, and in June, the company's shares were listed on the Mexican Stock Exchange. In the same year, Carso, together with Southwestern Bell

6 Entrepreneurship in Family Business Groups ... 137

Table 6.2 Data set

Case	Country	Brand	Founding year	Gen	Family	Main industry	Employees
A	Mexico	Grupo Carso	1980	2nd	Slim	Telecomunications	72.000
B	El Salvador	Grupo Poma	1919	3th	Poma	Real Estate	10.000
C	Panama	Grupo Motta	1939	3th	Motta Cardoze	Retail	2.500
D	Colombia	Grupo Carvajal	1905	3th	Carvajal	Pulp & Paper	35.000
E	Peru	Grupo Romero	1888	4th	Romero	Food & Finance	N/A
F	Brazil	Gerdau Aza	1901	3th	Gerdau Johan-npeter	Iron and steel	30.000
G	Brazil	Jacto Group	1948	3th	Nishimura	Agro-industrial	3.400
G	Argentina	Techint	1945	3th	Rocca	Engineering & Construction	19.500
H	Chile	Cencosud	1960	2nd	Paulmann	Retail	140.000
I	Chile	Falabella	1889	4th	Solari	Retail	96.000
J	Bolivia	Fortaleza	1975	2nd	Hinojosa - Vargas	Finance	2.500

International Holding Corp., France Cables Et Radio, and a group of investors, gained control of Telmex through a public bidding process. Indeed, this acquisition was the first step toward becoming a multinational company.

From 1991 to 1995, Carso acquired shares in companies from various industrial sectors: Compañía Euzkadi, Grupo Condumex, Grupo Aluminio and General Tire de México, and 80% of the capital of Sears Mexico. It also has a 49.9% interest in Philip Morris Mexico. In 1999, Grupo Sanborns redefines its corporate structure as the commercial unit of Grupo Carso and acquires Pastelería El Globo, which was sold to Grupo Bimbo sometime later. Carso also purchases the share capital of Ferrosur, the holding company of the operating rights of the Mexico-Veracruz railroad. During 2003, Grupo Sanborns buys 6 JC Penney stores and 13 Pastelerías Monterrey stores. Grupo Condumex ventured into the oil platform construction business. In 2004, Sanborns acquired all of the shares of Dorian's Tijuana and opened three stores in El Salvador. In 2005, Carso Infraestructura y Construcción carried out a public offering through the Mexican Stock Exchange. In 2007, the automotive piston rings and liners manufacturing business in Condumex was sold, the shareholding in the tobacco business is reduced, and Porcelanite is sold. The first Saks Fifth Avenue store is opened. In 2010, Grupo Carso sold the mining and real estate business of Minera Frisco e Inmuebles Carso. In 2013, Grupo Sanborns placed a public offering of shares in Mexico and abroad. Carso then sold the remainder of its shares in Philip

138 C. G. Muller

Morris Mexico. In this brief account, it is possible to see Carlos Slim's profile as a serial entrepreneur through Grupo Carso, one of the largest and most important conglomerates of Latin America.

Grupo Poma—El Salvador

Grupo Poma's business activities include car dealers, real estate development and construction, industrial manufacturing, and hotels. The automotive division operates under Excel Automotriz with branches in El Salvador, Guatemala, Honduras, Nicaragua, Costa Rica, and Panama. It represents some leading companies such as Toyota, BMW, Mitsubishi, Chevrolet, Ford, and KIA. It is considered the largest automotive distribution company in Central America. The real estate development division is Grupo Roble, a construction subsidiary that builds and manages shopping centers, residential, and office housing. Some of the accomplishments of this division include the construction of more than 19 shopping centers in Central America. The hotel division covers 19 InterContinental, Marriott International, and Choice Hotels franchises. Another business unit is the industrial division, Solaire, which manufactures windows and aluminum products in four factories in El Salvador.

Grupo Poma was founded in 1919 by Bartolomé Poma, who originally began the business of vehicle distribution agencies. The group's vision has been one of innovation, which is why they began distributing Hudson and Essex automobiles and providing services for the automotive industry. Today, they are engaged in the global competition in several productive sectors. In the early 1930s, Luis and Didine, sons of Don Bartolomé, assumed the leadership of the business, renaming it Poma y Cía. and focused on the distribution of General Motors automobiles. In 1950, Ricardo Poma's management introduced Toyota to its automotive distribution business, and in 1970, the company ventured into the shopping mall business with the construction of Metrocentro in San Salvador and also started the hotel project. Currently, the group has operations in Central America, Panama, the Dominican Republic, Miami (USA), Mexico, and Colombia. They operate a total of 20 five-star hotels and international franchises. Its current president is José Ricardo Poma Delgado.

Among the most emblematic projects of the Poma Family is the Escuela Superior de Economía y Negocios (ESEN), a private educational institution in El Salvador that offers undergraduate studies (Bachelor's Degree). ESEN was created in 1993, aiming to become the best business school in the country. In 2003, it expanded its educational services to include a bachelor's degree in Legal Sciences. Since its foundation, Ricardo Poma, who is also president of Grupo Roble, has held the position of rector.

Motta Group—Panama

The Motta Group is a conglomerate that includes ASSA insurance company, Banco Continental de Panamá, Telecarrier telecommunications firm, GBM Corporation, Motta International S.A., BG Financial Group, S.A., Televisora Nacional S.A., as well as investments in shopping centers and real estate. Motta is chairman of Copa Holding since 1986 and of Inversiones Bahía Ltda. Since 1990, Motta has strengthened its position as an importer and distributor of international consumer goods. The company owns duty-free stores in airports in over 20 Latin American countries. COPA, the most emblematic company, was founded in 1947 under the name Compañía Panameña de Aviación. Initially, it flew domestic flights to 3 cities in Panama using Douglas DC-47 airplanes. In 1970, the company's directors decided to withdraw from the domestic market and focus on operating international destinations. Its growth did not stagnate, and in the 1990s, the group decided to expand its international coverage with flights from Mexico to Santiago de Chile. In 1998, Continental Airlines bought 49% of Copa Airlines' shares. Following this purchase, Copa Airlines and Continental Airlines formed an alliance that allowed Copa to leverage Continental's relationship with Boeing to acquire new aircrafts. Its chairman is Stanley Motta, who is also chairman of Grupo Financiero Continental.

Alberto Motta Cardoze is its founder. In 1936 with the opening of the Motta store in Colon, Panama, he moved to and resided in that city. In 1940, he began selling duty-free liquors and perfumes to tourist ships transiting through the Panama Canal. In 1947, after World War II ended, the area of Colon began to struggle economically with the closing down of the military bases and its effect on business, that is when the idea of creating a duty-free zone arose. Alberto Motta was one of the visionaries who promoted the Colon Free Zone. In 1949, Motta International began operations by opening the first Duty Free in the western hemisphere in the Tocúmen airport. In 1972 Banco Continental began operations. In 2005, Copa Holdings (NYSE: CPA) was listed on the New York Stock Exchange, becoming the third Latin American airline listed on this significant market.

Carvajal Group—Colombia

Grupo Carvajal is one of the best-known economic groups in Colombia and is currently still in the founding family's hands. The company has operations in more than 15 countries in Latin America, Spain, and the United States, including publishing, printing, paper, school products, office products, packaging, and other sectors. Since its foundation in the furniture sector, the company has diversified into process outsourcing, information management, ambient music, and business services.

The origins of Grupo Carvajal date back to 1869 when Manuel Carvajal, together with some friends, bought an old printing press that was used to publish a weekly newspaper called La Opinión. With this newspaper, they disseminated political ideas of the Colombian Conservative Party, which was engaged in a conflict with the liberals. Nevertheless, these initial motivations would never have been projected to what it is today, with operating profits of over 100 million dollars as of 2018.

One of Carvajal's most internationalized companies is Grupo Editorial Norma, which is engaged in the creation, design, production, and marketing of books for education and entertainment across all genres and formats, and for all sorts of audiences. In 1961 Manuel Carvajal Sinisterra transferred 40% of the shares to the Hernando Carvajal Borrero Foundation, renamed Fundación Carvajal in 1977. Since then, it has been the largest shareholder of the company. The foundation dedicates much of its work to improving living conditions in impoverished areas of Cali.

Romero Group—Peru

This family-owned company defines itself as a "Peruvian investment group that seeks to generate value in the participating sectors" (Memorias Grupo Romero, 2013).

It all began in 1874 when the immigrant Calixto Romero Hernández left Spain to dedicate himself to trade in Central America and the Caribbean. In 1888 he settled in Peru, dazzled by the commercial activity of Catacaos, in the north of Peru and very near the city of Piura, starting a straw-hat business. By 1893, he was starting a new business: the export of cattle and goat hides, and by 1896, his first exports began. As early as 1897, he started the cotton business. However, it was not until 1902 that Calixto Romero acquired shares of Banco Italiano, currently the Banco de Crédito del Perú and the second-largest bank in terms of clients and transactions.

Soon after, in 1917, the business was taken over by the nephew and son of the founder, Feliciano del Campo Romero and Dionisio Romero Iturrospe. Between 1927 and 1949, operations were focused and expanded into the agricultural sector. In 1950 Almacenes Romero began operations, later renamed Interamérica de Comercio, and currently Plaza del Sol, one of Peru's most important shopping centers.

The third generation, Dionisio Romero Seminario, José Antonio Onrubia Romero, Calixto Romero Seminario and Manuel Romero Seminario, took over in 1965. Under this generation's leadership, substantial expansion and diversification were carried out through purchases, mergers, and acquisitions in various industrial sectors. One of the most relevant companies is Anderson Clayton & Co., currently Alicorp S.A., a consumer goods company with operations in several countries in the Americas, employing 35,000 workers as of 2018. In 1983 José Antonio Onrubia was kidnapped by terrorists and held captive for more than six months.

With the fourth generation at the helm, the group diversified into other sectors such as the Terminal Internacional del Sur in 1999, and it was granted the franchise for the port of Matarani, the second busiest port in Peru after Callao. The company's management is left in the hands of Dionisio Romero Paoletti, Luis Romero Belismelis, and José Antonio Onrubia Holder. From this moment on, its international presence is consolidated with the expansion of the purchase of the Repsol chain in Ecuador and 188 service stations, among others. In 2009, an ethanol plant made from sugarcane was started up, and the first shipment was made abroad. It also ventured into Argentina with the purchase of Alicorp Italo Manera and Pastas Especiales in 2011.

Gerdau—Brazil

Joo Gerdau was a German immigrant who arrived in southern Brazil in 1869 and set up a nail factory in Porto Alegre. In succession, he passed on the business to his son Hugo Gerdau, who passed it on to his son-in-law Curt Johannpeter in 1946.

By the time World War II ended, the family was still manufacturing nails. But commodity imports were severely restricted in the early postwar years, and the nail factory had trouble finding raw materials. To secure steel supplies, Johannpeter acquired a controlling share in a local steel mill in 1948. It turned out that steelmaking suited Johannpeter well. By the late 1960s, the steel mill had saturated local demand. Johannpeter decided to expand.

In 1967 it acquired a steel mill in São Paulo and added more foundries throughout Brazil over the next decade. To raise expansion capital, Johannpeter in 1970 listed one of the mills on the Rio de Janeiro and São Paulo stock exchanges. Later his other companies followed suit. In the 1980s, Gerdau actively participated in the privatization of state-owned Brazilian steel companies. By the end of the decade, Gerdau's market share in steel was about 40%, and Brazilian antitrust regulators were making it difficult for Gerdau to acquire more.

Curt Johannpeter passed away in 1983; his sons had studied business careers and were ready to take over. Fortunately for the family and the company, each son had pursued a major career that they were happy to follow, sparing Gerdau from the internal strife between brothers that has destroyed many a family business.

Jorge is CEO of the company, overseeing human resources and planning; Germano handles the commercial division (Gerdau also has the largest steel trading operation in Brazil); Klaus is responsible for technology, the industrial area, and investments in mills; and Frederico oversees finance and administration.

Eventually, the brothers were not willing to rest and expanded outside Brazil. They had learned a valuable lesson in 1981 when Gerdau acquired a small steel mill in Uruguay. In 1989, Gerdau acquired Courtice Steel, a steelmaker in Canada. The brothers bought it cheaply, so they could invest heavily in new equipment that improved productivity. Today, Courtice Steel profits handsomely and produces 250,000 metric tons of products a year.

Acquisitions in Argentina and another in Canada followed. However, Gerdau's most prominent merger and acquisition were AmeriSteel, based in Tampa, Florida, paying $262 million and assuming $200 million in debt. With more production in North America (AmeriSteel's production capacity is 1.8 million metric tons of crude steel annually), Gerdau now has more stable, dollar-based revenues and earnings. Another advantage is that Gerdau's Canadian and US operations can shift production to respond to market demands.

The current succession is in the 16 fifth-generation children, five of whom are now working at Gerdau, some for 15 years. Jorge and his brothers are in a succession process, but only after they have cleaned things up and expanded a bit more.

Jacto Group—Brazil

According to Cintra (1971), Japanese migration to Brazil was initially aimed at relocating Japan's population increase in the mid-1850s. To this end, the Japanese government promoted migration by funding part of their relocation, particularly to the state of Sao Paulo, where the government signed corporation agreements to work in coffee plantations. However, a second objective was to incorporate the Japanese private sector as a stakeholder in promoting and subsidizing groups of citizens seeking to migrate to Brazil. Japan developed a strategy to enable the supply of raw materials. Japanese interests visualized Brazil as more than a mere territory that could solve population problems. Following the example of England, which controlled the foreign coffee trade through The São Paulo Railway Company, Japanese industrialists initiated a broad investment policy, mainly in the agricultural sector. Organized as institutions in which capital and labor were purely Japanese, these companies were bound to play the role of authentic enclaves of the Japanese economy in Brazilian territory.

One hundred years later, there are around 1.5 million Japanese descendants in Sao Paulo alone, whose influence on society has extended from farming land to martial arts, architecture, and business.

The young Japanese Shunji Nishimura case represents this wave of migration and how they turned into unique family businesses while maintaining their tradition. Nishimura decided to leave Japan in 1932 to work in Brazil. Like other migrants, his goal was to earn money quickly and return to Kyoto, his hometown. Thousands of other Japanese migrants had made the same journey before him to Brazilian coffee plantations where they had the prospect of a better life. For 22-year-old Nishimura, at that time, it was all different. "One of the things they used to tell people that attracted them here is that in Brazil, you could find money hanging on trees," says Jorge Nishimura, who is second generation in the company. The family lives in a remote village in the state of Sao Paulo, now running a company with 4,500 employees built on Shunji Nishimura's invention of a machine to spray pesticides on crops, an example of the strong Japanese influence on farming techniques.

Within weeks of his arrival in Brazil, young Shunji began harvesting coffee on the Santa Maria farm in the town of Botucatu. The work was hard, and the pay was small. Eventually, Shunji decided to go to Rio de Janeiro, where he worked as a butler for a couple in Petrópolis. He saved some money with the intention of resuming his studies, improving his Portuguese, getting to know Brazil, and exploring its opportunities.

In 1934, he returned to São Paulo and enrolled in elementary school. He studied eight hours a day and worked at the school. A year later, he ran out of money. He left school and found work as a lathe operator and welder in a factory. The salary was so low that sometimes he only had bread and banana for breakfast. At the Brazilian Episcopal Church, he met his wife, Chieko Suzukayama. In 1939 Shunji decided to try his luck in the countryside. He took a train from São Paulo to the Alta Paulista region and then got off 472 km at the last stop: Pompéia, at that time, was a small village of wooden houses. Shunji Nishimura rented a house and hung a sign that read, "We fix everything." He fixed bowls, transformed lubricant oil cans into buckets and jugs, invented an alembic for distilling menthol, fixed farm machinery, and trucks, adapted gasoline engines to gas, among other things. In this workshop, farmers also asked Nishimura to fix their imported agrochemical sprinklers, which had no technical assistance in the region. By fixing so many of them, he designed a new model that was better and easier to use. It was the first sprinkler created in Brazil and the first product of the Jacto brand in 1948. Shunji Nishimura ran Jacto Agricultural Machines until 1972, when the company formed its first board of directors, and his son, Jiro Nishimura, was elected president. The founder then turned his attention to designing new products, such as the first coffee harvester. He continued to guide the company's strategies and decisions. Nishimura died in April 2010 at the age of 99.

Techint—Argentina

Founded in 1945, Techint Group has grown to become the world's largest steel pipes manufacturer, mainly for the oil industry and other engineering and construction services. The Buenos Aires-based company is one of the largest steel companies in Latin America. Italian immigrant Agostino Rocca founded the precursor company Compagnia Tecnica Internazionale in 1945. Techint won a contract to build a 1,000-mile gas pipeline from Comodoro Rivadavia to Buenos Aires and became a government contractor a few years later. Rocca retired in 1975 and transferred control of the company to his eldest son, Roberto. By that time, it had become an international conglomerate. The patriarch's original philosophy for the Techint Group was a long-term presence. As a result, Techint describes its companies as deeply rooted in the communities in which it operates. The firm says it can recognize and leverage local strengths to manage highly complex projects through that knowledge of local cultures.

The family's vision has been the concept of reinvesting in communities. Working in a very competitive market with low margins, Techint intends to remain competitive through continuous training of its employees. With more than 58,000 employees, its unique approach seems to be withstanding Argentine's poor economic performance.

The third-generation brothers are Paolo and Gianfelice Mario Rocca, who lead the company today. Paolo became CEO of the company in 2002 after the tragic 2001 plane crash that killed Agostino. He remains CEO of the Techint Group and chairman of the company's holdings, Tenaris and Ternium. Paolo's brother Gianfelice runs Techint's healthcare company Humanitas.

Cencosud—Chile

Little is known about this second-generation company. Founder Horst Paulmann managed to transform a small neighborhood store into a retail empire, with an internationalization process that reaches five Latin American countries. Born in the German city of Kassel in 1935, Horst Paulmann is the son of Hilde Kemna and Karl Werner Paulmann. When World War II ended, the family emigrated to Latin America, landing first in Argentina. They lived for two years in Buenos Aires until 1950, when they settled permanently in Chile. The Paulmann family took up residence in Temuco, in southern Chile. They started Las Brisas restaurant, which was gradually transformed into a delicatessen, managed by Horst and his brother Jurgen Paulmann, who turned the small business into a well-known company. The Paulmann brothers were partners until the 1970s when they went their separate ways. Horst Paulmann continued with the self-service business, but his vision went further. The businessman focused his efforts on creating Jumbo, the country's first hypermarket, which opened its doors in the Las Condes neighborhood of Santiago in 1976. Little by little, the company grew in Chile, which led the entrepreneur to explore business opportunities in other sectors such as construction, founding the company Centros Comerciales Sudamericanos Cencosud in 1978. Currently, the group owns complexes such as Costanera Center and Alto Las Condes in Santiago, Unicenter in Buenos Aires, Santa Ana in Bogotá, and Plaza Lima, in the Peruvian capital.

In 2005, the business conglomerate added the Paris department stores (owned by another third-generation family business). These stores distribute international fashion lines of companies such as Topshop, Miss Selfridge, Women'Secret, and All Saints and a range of its own brands.

146   C. G. Muller

The group's presidency is currently in the hands of Heike, the only daughter of his marriage to Helga Koepfer: Manfred, Heike, and Peter. Manfred Paulmann was vice-president from 2008 to 2010, upon his resignation from his post and his position on the board of directors of Cencosud, due to disagreements with his father. Currently, the executive is away from the company's activities. The other two siblings, Peter and Heike, have held their positions on the group's board since 1996 and 1999, respectively. Currently, Peter Paulmann is the general manager of the Genial gift stores. Before becoming chairman of the board, his sister Heike was in charge of various corporate social responsibility projects.

Falabella—Chile

The Solari family is the name behind one of the most important companies in the retail world. Since its founding, four generations have led the business founded by an Italian immigrant in the late nineteenth century. Since then, the family has maintained control of the company and consolidated one of Chile's most enormous fortunes. The Solari family have been the architects of turning a tailor's shop into a conglomerate of companies that has a presence in Argentina, Brazil, Colombia, and Peru. The Falabella Group also includes another Chilean family, the Del Rio-Goudie family, a shareholder since 2003, when the group bought Sodimac, the home improvement store.

The Solari family dates its beginnings as a family business to 1899, when Salvatore Falabella opened a tailor's shop in Santiago (Chile's capital). Over time, the business grew with the help of his son Arnaldo Falabella. Then in 1937, Alberto Solari Magnasco, who was married to Eliana Falabella, granddaughter of the group's founder, joined the company and made the first significant contribution by diversifying production from the tailoring business to the sale of women's clothing and home accessories.

Falabella's first official store opened in Santiago in 1958. The Solari Falabella couple had three daughters: María Luisa, Liliana, and Teresa, the principal heirs. The business grew in Chile, and in 1962, the company opened its first store outside the Chilean capital in the city of Concepción. It began its local expansion from then on, which led the group to have points of sale in almost the entire country. Before his death, Alberto Solari appointed his brother Reinaldo Solari Magnasco as the protector of his daughters María Luisa, Liliana, and Teresa, the group's majority shareholders. In 1980, Reinaldo Solari Magnasco took over the group's management with his nephew, Juan Cúneo Solari. The two built up the group's other lines of business, such as CMR, Falabella's credit card, and promoted international expansion in Peru, Argentina, Brazil, and Colombia. Uncle and nephew built the economic group that includes a travel agency, an insurance company, and Banco Falabella. Although the family men were at the helm of the business, the three Solari-Falabella sisters always kept abreast of the group's operations. They served on its board of directors until their children stood in for them.

Liliana Solari expanded her wealth by investing in new businesses in 1987. The businesswoman is the founder of Bethia, an investment fund from which she controls her shares in Falabella and other businesses such as the Latam airline and the Chilean Equestrian Club, among other companies. Her son, Carlos Heller, currently holds one of Falabella's board positions, while her daughter, Andrea Heller, works alongside her at Bethia.

In 2014, another phase began in the generational replacement of the group, which until then had been led by Reinaldo Solari Magnasco and Juan Cúneo Solari. That year, Carlo Solari Donaggio, son of Reinaldo, assumed the group's presidency, while Juan Carlos Cortés, son of Teresa Solari, was appointed vice-president.

Today, the chain is one of the 100 largest retail companies globally in terms of turnover and is present in several countries in the region. As of 2020, it had ten branches of Falabella stores in Argentina and nine branches of Sodimac, the construction and household goods business. It also has a presence in Buenos Aires, Mendoza, San Juan, Córdoba, and Santa Fe. The group has been expanding into Peru, Colombia, Brazil, and Mexico.

Fortaleza Group—Bolivia

Aseguradora Fortaleza and later, Grupo Fortaleza, was created in 1975 as Cruceña Cooperativa de Seguros, as a result of the initiative of the Cooperativa de Ahorro y Crédito La Merced, to provide regionally an additional financial service to its members. This financial group is led by the Hinojosa Family, the patriarch being Guido Hinojosa Cardoso. Patricio Hinojosa Jimenez, one of the sons, is the General Manager.

In 1999, after enacting the new insurance law, the Cooperativa became part of the Fortaleza Financial Group due to a strategic decision. Thus, the legal structure was changed with the transformation from a cooperative to a corporation and adapting the name of Fortaleza Seguros y Reaseguros S.A. to focus on the SME and individual insurance market segment. These strategic changes helped to achieve a broad national presence in seven of the nine departments of Bolivia.

148   C. G. Muller

In 2005, the company expanded operations to the United States by purchasing Anchor Bank based in Florida. Nelson Hinojosa, one of the four sons of the founder, is the CEO of this company. In 2015, Aseguradora de Vida Fortaleza was incorporated to complete the portfolio of products offering life insurance.

Fortaleza, one of the largest groups in the financial sector in Bolivia, is now in its second generation at the helm.

Analysis

Following Canele et al.'s (2021) methodology, the evidence in Table 6.3 suggests classifying the cases in exploration and exploitation companies according to the very low, low, medium, high, and very high categories.

We ranked each case based on the intensity of its orientation toward exploration and exploitation activities, taking into account available information and interviews with experts. In this process, public sources, i.e., websites, interviews, company reports, played an essential role in triangulation. To classify the orientation and exploratory activities of the companies, we considered the intensity with which they engage in search activities and gather knowledge from outside the company in pursuit of new horizons. Following the existing literature, we assigned high levels of exploration to companies heavily involved in activities such as experimentation, diversification, external relationships, searching new external knowledge, technology creation, focus on new products, services, and markets, and building new competencies (March, 1991; Shane & Venkataraman, 2000).

Table 6.3 Cases of exploratory and exploitative companies

Case	Country	Brand	Exploration	Exploitation	Ambidextrous
A	Mexico	Grupo Carso	Very High	Medium	Yes
B	El Salvador	Grupo Poma	High	Medium	Yes
C	Panama	Grupo Motta	Very High	Medium	Yes
D	Colombia	Grupo Carvajal	High	High	Yes
E	Peru	Grupo Romero	Very High	High	Yes
F	Brazil	Gerdau	Low	High	No
G	Brazil	Jacto Group	Medium	High	Yes
H	Argentina	Techint	High	High	Yes
I	Chile	Cencosud	Low	High	No
J	Chile	Falabella	Low	High	No
K	Bolivia	Fortaleza	Low	Medium	No

To define the orientation of firms toward exploitation, we analyzed the degree to which they were involved in strengthening core competencies and the degrees of vertical integration in their own industry cluster. In accordance with the existing literature, we assigned high levels of exploitation to firms highly committed to activities such as efficiency, improvements in meeting current customer needs, and complementing or enhancing existing competencies (Lubatkin et al., 2006; March, 1991). Equally, we attribute lower levels of exploration to companies that are not as committed to exploitation initiatives and have allocated considerably fewer resources to them.

Figure 6.2 shows all cases in a matrix according to their exploration and exploitation levels. It is worth noting that we employed a combined perspective of ambidexterity, that is, the concurrent focus of the firm on exploratory and exploitative orientations (Jansen et al., 2006). Seven cases of ambidextrous family firms were found in the sample, from which two were distinguished by very high levels of exploration. We ranked four more cases as medium or low in their exploration levels, but they were highly exploitative and thus placed in the exploitative quadrant.

A business strategy may, as a result, be more focused on seeking new business opportunities, referred to as exploration, or on refining current competitive advantages, also known as exploitation, or a combination of the two. Long-term financial wealth creation is possible through a business strategy that can balance exploitation and exploration. This balance is complicated, as implementing each action requires different business structures and calls for leaders with vastly different skill sets. Companies that can address this dilemma and find a strategy that balances, on the one hand, the continuous improvement of current strengths (exploitation) and, on the other hand, the search for new business opportunities (exploration) are known as ambidextrous companies.

Ambidextrous business groups have demonstrated the ability to explore and exploit in a balanced way and have been able to combine the entrepreneurial mindset with the implementation of the strategy. What drives ambidexterity? On the one hand, to develop new opportunities for long-term success, which we know as exploration, and on the other hand, to strengthen existing capabilities, referred to as exploitation. From this perspective, Latin America provides a suitable environment to do so, as family-owned companies in the cases mentioned above face significant institutional challenges to engage in exploratory and exploitation activities. Latin America's legal and political systems present many inefficiencies and obstacles to operating and expanding companies, particularly when companies face arbitrary barriers and have to deal with high levels of uncertainty. By the same token,

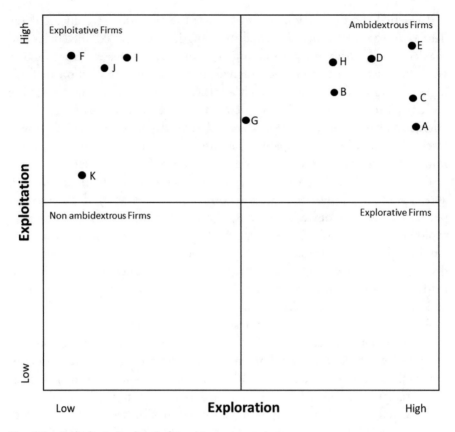

Fig. 6.2 Ambidexterity levels found in our sample

widespread corruption and security threats lead families and businesses to commit to additional costs and pursue more cautious strategies for ambidextrousness. Despite these challenges in a context of low institutional quality, family businesses in the cases above are unwilling to engage in corrupt practices or illegal political lobbying and instead focus on strengthening their core competencies and exploring new growth opportunities.

Another observed feature in the sample is the balance in the exploitation of existing competitive advantages with the exploration of new lines of business, as in the cases of Grupo Carso, Grupo Motta, and Grupo Romero. A further characteristic of these business groups is the family's strong desire to exert control and influence over the company's decision-making through solid leadership, agile decision-making, and a shared vision. Another variable is the desire for family continuity and the passing on of the company to future generations as a legacy. Except for the Romero Group, which is in the

4th generation, the other two groups could be considered as recent, since the second generation is working together with the first generation.

On the other hand, the groups oriented to exploitation are shown with strategies based on the continuous improvement of current strengths, the creation of an organizational culture based on efficiency, low risk, and quality, which is the case of Falabella and Cencosud groups in Chile. In the cases of the four groups in this quadrant, it is noteworthy that the pursuit of new business opportunities, but without departing from their industrial sector and a medium degree of organizational flexibility.

Conclusion and Future Research

Throughout this chapter, we have examined entrepreneurship in family business groups in Latin America under the organizational ambidexterity lens. Our findings suggest that medium and high degrees of exploratory capacity are present in all the companies studied, but not all of them become ambidextrous.

Creating long-term economic value is a great challenge facing every company. This challenge is affected by constant fluctuations in the business environment. Markets, consumers, and institutional environments undergo changes that force companies to redefine their business models in the process of continuous adaptation. This is why concepts such as innovation and the entrepreneurial mindset have become a mainstay of business discussions in recent years. However, intense competition also puts pressure on delivering a unique value proposal backed by operational excellence defined by ever-lower cost structures.

In this competitive landscape, leaders of Latin American companies must be able to guide their companies through what, at first glance, might appear to be a contradiction: perfecting their current competitive advantage and at the same time challenging it in pursuit of new sources of value creation.

The above is about an appropriate balance between implementing the necessary mechanisms to manage existing assets more professionally and fostering an entrepreneurial mindset within the group or conglomerate. This balance between exploiting existing resources and exploring new opportunities for wealth allows these types of companies to be ambidextrous, successful in stable periods, but able to adapt to changes in the environment such as that experienced during the year 2020. Hence, entrepreneurial families and groups must make their companies ambidextrous: They must pursue operational excellence while driving innovation to create value across generations.

The Latin American context is ideal for analyzing the challenges faced by entrepreneurial families for several reasons. First, it is a business environment with enormous uncertainty. This uncertainty is partly due to the frequency and impact of economic cycles and partly due to political changes, complicating medium- and long-term decision-making. On top of this, the lack of institutional aspects such as the fragilities and inflexibility of legal systems, access to funding, and corruption complicate doing business in Latin America. And yet, it is precisely this uncertain environment that creates unique opportunities for entrepreneurship and exploration. These opportunities have not gone unnoticed by many international firms, which have invested in the region in search of higher returns on investment. This also impacts the region's groups, which must compete not only with their Latin American peers but also with transnational companies with greater financial resources. In this context, the need to fine-tune their current competitive operating advantages also becomes a relevant strategic imperative. This is why Latin American companies need to be flexible but at the same time efficient and effective. It also means that Latin American groups need to strike a balance.

This chapter contributes to the understanding of entrepreneurship in family business groups in Latin America under the organizational ambidexterity lens (Canale et al., 2021; Hiebl, 2015). In this regard, the family business groups in Latin America have managed to implement business models that combine innovation with tradition, on the one hand, and generational entrepreneurship processes that foster growth and family ties among the new generations, on the other. In doing so, they have also become more efficient among their competitors and stood out in industry sectors such as food, finance, pulp, and paper. The best practices identified among these business groups suggest that the key to successfully managing these paradoxes rests in creating a multigenerational vision among family members, an ambidextrous strategic direction in their companies, and an investment mindset in their capital.

Future exploratory research may be necessary. A comprehensive and balanced approach to family, business, and equity constituents, both in terms of mindset and overall toolkit, is necessary to become a family with solid transgenerational potential (Arredondo & Cruz, 2019).

One final contribution of this chapter is showing that ambidexterity is all about a delicate balance, since overlooking or overemphasizing either of these aspects (exploration vs. exploitation) may jeopardize the future of the business group. An example of this is that business groups with low entrepreneurship potential exhibit particularly low levels of sectoral diversification.

References

Acemoglu, D., & Robinson, J. A. (2012). *Why nations fail: The origins of power, prosperity, and poverty.* Currency.

Aldrich, H. E., & Cliff, J. E. (2003). The pervasive effects of family on entrepreneurship: Toward a family embeddedness perspective. *Journal of Business Venturing, 18*(5), 573–596.

Alvarez, C., & Urbano, D. (2011). Environmental factors and entrepreneurial activity in Latin America. *Academia Revista Latinoamericana De Administración, 48*, 126–139.

Amorós, J. E. (2009). *Entrepreneurship and quality of institutions: A developing-country approach* (No. 2009/07). WIDER Research Paper.

Arredondo, H., & Cruz, C. (2019). How do owning families ensure the creation of value across generations? A "dual balance" approach. In *The Palgrave handbook of heterogeneity among family firms* (pp. 791–819). Palgrave Macmillan, Cham.

Arzubiaga, U., Maseda, A., & Iturralde, T. (2019). Entrepreneurial orientation in family firms: New drivers and the moderating role of the strategic involvement of the board. *Australian Journal of Management, 44*(1), 128–152.

Berrone, P., Cruz, C., & Gomez-Mejia, L. R. (2012). Socioemotional wealth in family firms: Theoretical dimensions, assessment approaches, and agenda for future research. *Family Business Review, 25*(3), 258–279.

Bianchi, C. C., & Reyes, C. (2005). Defensive strategies of local companies against foreign multinationals: Evidence from Chilean retailers. *Latin American Business Review, 6*(2), 67–85.

Bizberg, I. (2019). Four types of capitalism in Latin America. In *Diversity of capitalisms in Latin America* (pp. 27–51). Palgrave Macmillan, Cham.

Botero, I. C., Cruz, A. D., & Müller, C. G. (2018). Family firms in Latin America: Why are they important and why should we care? In *Family firms in Latin America* (pp. 1–7). Routledge.

Bruton, G. D., Peng, M. W., Ahlstrom, D., Stan, C., & Xu, K. (2015). State-owned enterprises around the world as hybrid organizations. *Academy of Management Perspectives, 29*(1), 92–114.

Camargo, M. I. B. (2021). Institutions, institutional quality, and international competitiveness: Review and examination of future research directions. *Journal of Business Research, 128*, 423–435.

Canale, F., Muller, C., Lavere, E., & Cambre, B. (2021), Ambidextrous Family Firms in Low Institutional Quality Contexts. *IFERA Annual Conference*, ISBN 9791220089487.

Carney, M., & Gedajlovic, E. (2002). The co-evolution of institutional environments and organizational strategies: The rise of family business groups in the ASEAN region. *Organization Studies, 23*(1), 1–29.

Carney, M., Van Essen, M., Estrin, S., & Shapiro, D. (2018). Business groups reconsidered: Beyond paragons and parasites. *Academy of Management Perspectives, 32*(4), 493–516.

Cerutti, M., Ortega, I., & Palacios, L. (2000). Entrepreneurs and enterprise in Northern Mexico. Monterrey: From oligarchical state to globalization. *European Review of Latin American and Caribbean Studies, 69*, 3–29.

Cintra, J. T. (1971). *La migración japonesa en Brasil (1908-1958)*. El Colegio de México. pp. 116.

Coyne, C. J., & Boettke, P. J. (2006). The role of the economist in economic development. *The Quarterly Journal of Austrian Economics, 19*(1).

Cruz, A. D., Basco, R., Parada, M. J., Fierro, A. M., & Alvarado-Alvarez, C. (2019). Resilience and family business groups in unstable economies. In *The Family business group phenomenon* (pp. 315–352). Palgrave Macmillan, Cham.

Cruz, A. D., Hamilton, E., & Jack, S. L. (2012). Understanding entrepreneurial cultures in family businesses: A study of family entrepreneurial teams in Honduras. *Journal of Family Business Strategy, 3*(3), 147–161.

Dou, J., Wang, N., Su, E., Fang, H., & Memili, E. (2020). Goal complexity in family firm diversification: Evidence from China. *Journal of Family Business Strategy, 11*(1), 100310.

Friedman, B. A. (2014). The relationship between effective governance and the informal economy. *International Journal of Business and Social Science, 5*(9).

Gedajlovic, E., Carney, M., Chrisman, J. J., & Kellermanns, F. W. (2012). The adolescence of family firm research: Taking stock and planning for the future. *Journal of Management, 38*(4), 1010–1037.

Goel, S., & Jones, R. J., III. (2016). Entrepreneurial exploration and exploitation in family business: A systematic review and future directions. *Family Business Review, 29*(1), 94–120.

Granovetter, M. (1995). Coase revisited: Business groups in the modern economy. *Industrial and Corporate Change, 4*(1), 93–130.

Greif, A. (1994). On the political foundations of the late medieval commercial revolution: Genoa during the twelfth and thirteenth centuries. *The Journal of Economic History, 54*(2), 271–287.

Grupo Romero. (2013). accessed November 30. 2021 http://www.gruporomero. com.pe/es-PE/el_grupo_romero/memorias_gestion_empresarial/

Gwartney, J. D., Holcombe, R. G., & Lawson, R. A. (2004). Economic freedom, institutional quality, and cross-country differences in income and growth. *Cato Journal, 24*, 205.

Hiebl, M. R. (2015). Family involvement and organizational ambidexterity in later-generation family businesses: A framework for further investigation. *Management Decision.*

Hollifield, C. A., & Coffey, A. J. (2006). Qualitative research in media management and economics. In *Handbook of media management and economics* (pp. 572–599). Routledge.

Hsueh, J. (2021). *Family Business Index*. Compiled by the Center for Family Business at the University of St.Gallen, Switzerland in cooperation with EY. Accessed 1 October 2021. https://familybusinessindex.com/

Hughes, M., Filser, M., Harms, R., Kraus, S., Chang, M. L., & Cheng, C. F. (2018). Family firm configurations for high performance: The role of entrepreneurship and ambidexterity. *British Journal of Management, 29*(4), 595–612.

Jansen, J. J., Van Den Bosch, F. A., & Volberda, H. W. (2006). Exploratory innovation, exploitative innovation, and performance: Effects of organizational antecedents and environmental moderators. *Management Science, 52*(11), 1661–1674.

Jaskiewicz, P., Combs, J. G., & Rau, S. B. (2015). Entrepreneurial legacy: Toward a theory of how some family firms nurture transgenerational entrepreneurship. *Journal of Business Venturing, 30*(1), 29–49.

Kammerlander, N., Patzelt, H., Behrens, J., & Röhm, C. (2020). Organizational ambidexterity in family-managed firms: The role of family involvement in top management. *Family Business Review, 33*(4), 393–423.

Khanna, T., & Palepu, K. (2000). The Future of Business Groups in Emerging Markets: Long-Run Evidence from Chile. *Academy of Management Journal, 43*(3), 268–285.

Khanna, T., & Rivkin, J. W. (2001). Estimating the performance effects of business groups in emerging markets. *Strategic Management Journal, 22*(1), 45–74.

Kim, D., Kandemir, D., & Cavusgil, S. T. (2004). The role of family conglomerates in emerging markets: What western companies should know. *Thunderbird International Business Review, 46*(1), 13–38.

Lavie, D., & Rosenkopf, L. (2006). Balancing exploration and exploitation in alliance formation. *Academy of Management Journal, 49*(4), 797–818.

Leppäaho, T., Plakoyiannaki, E., & Dimitratos, P. (2016). The case study in family business: An analysis of current research practices and recommendations. *Family Business Review, 29*(2), 159–173.

Lubatkin, M. H., Simsek, Z., Ling, Y., & Veiga, J. F. (2006). Ambidexterity and performance in small-to medium-sized firms: The pivotal role of top management team behavioral integration. *Journal of Management, 32*(5), 646–672.

Lumpkin, G. T., Steier, L., & Wright, M. (2011). Strategic entrepreneurship in family business. *Strategic Entrepreneurship Journal, 5*(4), 285–306.

March, J. G. (1991). Exploration and exploitation in organizational learning. *Organization Science, 2*(1), 71–87.

McAdam, R., Reid, R., & Mitchell, N. (2010). Longitudinal development of innovation implementation in family-based SMEs: The effects of critical incidents. *International Journal of Entrepreneurial Behavior & Research, 16*(5), 437–456.

Morck, R., & Yeung, B. (2003). Agency problems in large family business groups. *Entrepreneurship Theory and Practice, 27*(4), 367–382.

Müller, C. G., & Sandoval-Arzaga, F. (2021). *Family business heterogeneity in latin America: A historical perspective* (pp. 71–98). Palgrave Macmillan.

North, D. C. (1990). *Institutions, institutional change and economic performance.* Cambridge University Press.

Olagboye, D., Obembe, D., & Okafor, G. (2022). Enterprise survival and growth: A conceptual exposition of entrepreneurial activities in Sub-Saharan Africa. In *The Palgrave handbook of African entrepreneurship* (pp. 93–114). Palgrave Macmillan, Cham.

Parada, M. J., Müller, C., & Gimeno, A. (2016). Family firms in Ibero-America: An introduction. *Academia Revista Latinoamericana de Administración.*

Raisch, S., & Birkinshaw, J. (2008). Organizational ambidexterity: Antecedents, outcomes, and moderators. *Journal of Management, 34*(3), 375–409.

Ramírez-Solís, E. R., Fonseca, M., Sandoval-Arzaga, F., & Amoros, E. (2021). Survival mode: How Latin American family firms are coping with the pandemic. *Management Research: Journal of the Iberoamerican Academy of Management.*

Rautiainen, M., Rosa, P., Pihkala, T., Parada, M. J., & Cruz, A. D. (2019). *The family business group phenomenon.* Springer International Publishing.

Reynolds, P. D., Hay, M., & Camp, S. M. (1999). *Global entrepreneurship monitor.* Kauffman Center for Entrepreneurial Leadership.

Riege, A. M. (2003). Validity and reliability tests in case study research: a literature review with "hands-on" applications for each research phase. *Qualitative Market Research: An International Journal.*

Rodríguez-Satizábal, B. E. (2014). Grupos económicos en Colombia (1974–1998): entre pequeña empresa familiar y gran familia de empresas. *Grupos económicos y mediana empresa familiar en America Latina.*

Shane, S., & Venkataraman, S. (2000). The promise of entrepreneurship as a field of research. *Academy of Management Review, 25*(1), 217–226.

Short, J. C., Moss, T. W., & Lumpkin, G. T. (2009). Research in social entrepreneurship: Past contributions and future opportunities. *Strategic Entrepreneurship Journal, 3*(2), 161–194.

Sobel, R. S. (2008). Testing Baumol: Institutional quality and the productivity of entrepreneurship. *Journal of Business Venturing, 23*(6), 641–655.

Stosberg, J. (2018). *Political risk and the institutional environment for foreign direct investment in Latin America: An empirical analysis with a case study on Mexico* (p. 342). Peter Lang International Academic Publishers.

Stubner, S., Blarr, W. H., Brands, C., & Wulf, T. (2012). Organizational ambidexterity and family firm performance. *Journal of Small Business & Entrepreneurship, 25*(2), 217–229.

Trevino, L. J., Daniels, J. D., & Arbelaez, H. (2002). Market reform and FDI in Latin America: An empirical investigation. *Transnational Corporations, 11*(1), 29–49.

Tushman, M. L., & O'Reilly, C. A., III. (1996). Ambidextrous organizations: Managing evolutionary and revolutionary change. *California Management Review, 38*(4), 8–29.

Vázquez, P., Carrera, A., & Cornejo, M. (2020). Corporate governance in the largest family firms in Latin America. *Cross Cultural & Strategic Management.*

Webb, J. W., Kistruck, G. M., Ireland, R. D., & Ketchen, D. J., Jr. (2010). The entrepreneurship process in base of the pyramid markets: The case of multinational enterprise/nongovernment organization alliances. *Entrepreneurship Theory and Practice, 34*(3), 555–581.

Weingast, B. R. (1993). Constitutions as governance structures: The political foundations of secure markets. *Journal of Institutional and Theoretical Economics (JITE)/Zeitschrift für die gesamte Staatswissenschaft*, 286–311.

7

Family Business Groups in India: Perspectives on Their Roles, Strategies, and Innovations

Santanu Bhadra⬨, Sougata Ray⬨, Sankaran Manikutty, and Kavil Ramachandran⬨

Introduction

The dominance of business groups in certain parts of the world is an intriguing phenomenon to business scholars. Business groups in India and other emerging economies, in particular, have attracted considerable attention from researchers in the past three decades. The main thesis explaining the emergence and dominance of business groups in certain emerging economies is that these economies had underdeveloped market structures and weak legal enforcement, and the business groups filled those institutional voids and thereby gained competitive advantage (Khanna & Palepu, 2000a, 2000b). This stream of research has overlooked one very interesting feature of the Indian economy, namely, that Indian business groups are primarily family business groups. Indian businessmen lived in interlinked social structures, and the primary entity was the extended joint family (Dutta, 1997; Tripathi,

---

S. Bhadra
Indian Institute of Management, Raipur, India

S. Ray · K. Ramachandran (✉)
Indian School of Business, Hyderabad, India
e-mail: K_RAMACHANDRAN@ISB.EDU

S. Manikutty
Indian Institute of Management, Ahmedabad, India

© The Author(s), under exclusive license to Springer Nature
Switzerland AG 2023
M. Rautianen et al. (eds.), *The Palgrave Handbook of Managing Family Business Groups*,
https://doi.org/10.1007/978-3-031-13206-3_7

2004). In fact, family business groups have been an integral part of the Indian economy since formal industrial activity took root in the country around the latter half of the nineteenth century. Khanna and Palepu (2000a) stated that "Indian business groups are collections of publicly traded firms in a wide variety of industries, with a significant amount of common ownership and control, usually by a family." Our definition of a family business group is adapted from this view in the sense that effective control has to be in the hands of a family through either direct family ownership or indirect corporate ownership (i.e., a pyramidal structure with a holding company), and public listing is not a necessary condition to identify the collections of firms. It is important to note that a business group may or may not be owned by a family. Family business groups are those that are controlled by families through generations and are characterized by the strong bonding of the family name with the business, such as the Tata Group and the Birla Group in India. On the other hand, there are Indian business groups such as L&T and ITC, which are not family-owned and can be characterized as non-family business groups.

Indian business groups have not only originated and expanded under strikingly different institutional environments, first during the colonial period under British rule, then in the post-independence years when private sector economic activity was regulated with an inbuilt bias against business groups, and finally during the increasingly liberalized and globalized policy environment since the 1990s, but they also have remarkably diverse sociological roots in terms of communities, family structures, languages, regions, etc. The unique composition, structure, values, and governance of the family, its collective motivations, and the individual motivations of its members to own as well as expand their businesses have significant bearing on the emergence, evolution, continuation, and resilience of a family business group, unlike a non-family business group. Therefore, the "institutional voids" logic stemming from institutional economics may at best be a partial explanation for the existence and dominance of business groups in India. Against the prevailing view that family businesses are the result of a negative condition, namely, the absence of strong institutional structures, and hence, that the need for them would disappear once these voids were addressed, we argue that business groups in India also arose and exist because these family business connections in themselves form a strong source of strength and hence will be still relevant even after the institutional issues are addressed and strengthened. We call this "family and business logic." We argue that this logic could greatly enrich our understanding of family business groups in India (Fig. 7.1).

7 Family Business Groups in India: Perspectives on Their ...

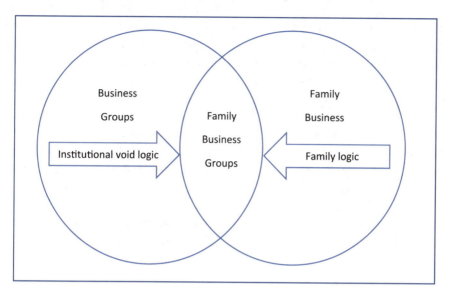

Fig. 7.1 Logics behind emergence of family business groups

The present chapter presents an analysis of the strategic evolution of family business groups in India with special emphasis on the period since the early 1990s when India started to embrace the path of economic liberalization, which significantly impacted the country's social structure and strengthened its institutions. It highlights important elements of family business groups such as their *raison d'être*, factors motivating the adoption of a business group structure, ownership, governance and management, strategies, innovations, relevance, and impact.

The chapter is organized as follows. First, we provide the background story of how family business groups came into existence in India. We highlight their dominance in both the pre-economic reform and post-economic reform phases, and thus make a strong case for understanding the "family logic" (Bertrand & Schoar, 2006; Reay et al., 2015) behind this dominance. This historical context is important, because an organization's present and future are influenced by its evolution in the past (Boeker, 1989; Stinchcomb, 1965), and this is more likely to occur in family businesses due to the preservation of values through the family system (Koiranen, 2002). We go on to discuss the role of family business groups in supporting both business needs and family needs and present a framework to understand how business group structure can benefit business families in supporting their family needs, and vice versa. This groundwork is important for understanding the different organizational goals of business families before delving into some of the strategies used to achieve those goals. Here, we analyze family business group strategies in terms of legacy resources and succession planning. Even if we concede that Indian family firms might have derived their *raison d'être* from the existence of institutional voids at one point of time, their subsequent progress in an intensely competitive environment as exists in India suggests that there were many other factors working in their favor, such as the ability to employ coherent strategies across the groups, make clear choices for succession, and innovate. Innovation being one of the essential components of business strategy (Davenport et al., 2007; Li et al., 2013), we look into the innovation strategies adopted by Indian family firms and illustrate our discussion with brief cases from different Indian family business groups. Although we focus on India, a key purpose of this chapter is to extend the theoretical conversation around family business groups, using the Indian context merely as empirical guidance to build our argument. We conclude this chapter by summarizing the new approach to understanding the evolution and behavior of family business groups at a conceptual level.

Formation of Family Business Groups: The Indian Story

Family business groups exist in many countries, though they are most prevalent, but by no means restricted to, emerging economies. For example, China has its *qiyejituan*, Japan its *kieretsus*, and South Korea its *chaebols*. South American, Middle Eastern, and African countries also have their respective family business groups. However, they all evolved differently, and the path of their development has influenced their structure, strategies, and growth vectors. In this chapter, we shall confine ourselves to Indian family business groups.

The economic and industrial scenario in India in 2021 is drastically different from what it was in 1990 when India was on the threshold of liberalization, which, in turn, was vastly different from the forties and fifties when India became independent and commenced its own journey of growth. Since the economic reforms in 1991 mark a major milestone in the path of India's institutional development, we use the event as an analytical reference.

Pre-reform phase: In pre-independence India, most of the families that became the drivers of Indian industry had a background in trade (Tripathi, 2004). They sensed and capitalized on opportunities in the environment, the earliest of which were in textile and jute, and set up manufacturing and trading companies. In the face of a hostile imperial government, they took great risks and piloted their firms' growth. Nationalism also played a part in their entrepreneurial motivations, beyond a mere desire to make profit. Faced with abundant opportunities, these entrepreneurs started multiple businesses, giving rise to the formation of the earliest business groups. The main driver for such expansion in scope was the attractiveness of the individual ventures, rather than any relationships among the businesses. They were controlled by the "promoters" (a term peculiar to India) who ran them all personally, appointing trusted managers. They were not yet family businesses, since there was usually no family involvement until the promoters' sons (as dictated by the patriarchal social system) were of an age to assist them. There was coordination among the group companies when such coordination was called for, and this was mainly in the area of financing their requirements.

So long as the businesses remained private, there were no other issues. The promoters invested their capital, raised money through debt and even equity, reaped rewards for good performance, and suffered punishment when performance was bad, whether due to improper running of the businesses or bad luck. But soon the companies grew, requiring the mobilization of public equity, and some of the firms became public and independent companies legally, each with its own set of boards, managers, and shareholders. By the time of India's independence, many of the business families had a varied portfolio of businesses, primarily through acquisitions of British interests in coal, tea, and other industries at the time of Britain's departure from India.

Newly independent India embraced a Soviet-style planned economy, with a high level of government control and regulation. Concerns about the monopolistic control of many industries by the private sector intensified. In pursuit of a socialist dream, crippling restrictions were placed on the expansion of private businesses, and state enterprises occupied the "commanding heights of the economy." This put a limit on the scope for expansion of the existing businesses, and all activities were subject to a licensing regime known as the "License Raj," which specified what items a business could produce and how much. Unable to expand in their own existing fields, Indian business groups sought to expand their activities by exploring new areas.

With elaborate licensing requirements for starting and running companies, many business families grew by cornering licenses in multiple industries. They adopted a business group structure and dominated by virtue of entering a business before others. Consequently, they ended up with increasingly diverse portfolios. Licensing also seems to have had the effect of increasing the concentration of existing business groups since they had better access to the corridors of power, and they could use it not only to get licenses for themselves, but also to deny them to others. Understanding of the regulatory framework and relationships with bureaucrats and politicians became the critical success factors for businesses.

Competition was limited, and hence, profitability was assured. The lack of competitiveness was largely due to the inherent lack of incentives to become more efficient, and while the groups prospered financially, they were highly inefficient and uncompetitive internationally. This did not matter due to the high degree of protection the government gave to the domestic industry.

The Tatas and Birlas were the two major groups in India at that time. Both were in a large variety of businesses with very little in common, and they were not looking for any commonalities either. Other relatively smaller groups also had diverse businesses, such as the DCM group and the Sundaram group.

In these groups, control remained with the families. There were succession issues and splits among families, but it was well-understood that they were all controlled by the family members and that management would pass on control to members of the family. The Indian business groups were characterized by another feature: unlike the United States, many families did not have majority or even substantial shareholdings in their group firms, but controlled them effectively through crossholdings, the formation of holding companies, creation of trusts, and so on. A substantial proportion of their shares (and debt) lay with financial institutions such as LIC, IDBI, and banks, who generally played a passive role in the affairs of the company and typically supported the management. Consequently, the family had a free rein while shareholders had little say in company matters due to their dispersed holdings.

This pattern of control had its strengths as well. Khanna and Palepu (Khanna & Palepu, 2000a) have argued in their landmark paper that the groups substituted for the weaknesses in the institutional infrastructure. For example, they could reallocate funds across their companies, develop common training programs, and through brand names, access finance and build relationships, which were important with a weak legal system in place. The groups thus had enormous economic power. Even the groups that developed later, in the seventies and eighties, such as the Reliance Group, developed on the same lines. There is a lot of truth in Khanna and Palepu's argument. But even in this phase, the family business groups were not merely filling up institutional voids; they were actively pursuing entrepreneurial opportunities in the particular environment prevailing then. They can be more accurately described not as filling up institutional voids and making up for deficiencies, but as the products of the prevalent institutional and regulatory structure of the time.

These were not just business groups, but family business groups. Apart from the control exerted through the mechanisms outlined above, the boards had members who were trusted by the family; all the top positions were filled not only through tests of competence, but also loyalty to the family, and succession was almost entirely in the family. At the bottom of these priorities was the fear of loss of control.

Post-reform phase: India has been on a continuous path of institutional development since independence, arriving at an inflection point in 1991, with the liberalization of the economy and opening of the domestic market to global competition. Since then, both the market structure and the legal environment have improved in parallel with the surge in foreign investor participation (see Fig. 7.2). Financial and legal institutions, among many others, saw major improvements, although they are by no means perfect. Many new companies, such as Infosys, HCL, and Wipro, which cannot be labeled as family businesses, emerged in new areas including information technology (IT), retail, and logistics, but family groups also entered these fields in a big way (for example, the Tatas established Tata Consultancy Services, or TCS). A natural corollary of the institutional void logic (Khanna & Palepu, 2000a, 2000b) is that Indian business groups would lose their advantage in a post-reform environment and gradually give way to stand-alone companies. Yet, this has not happened even after three decades of economic liberalization (see Fig. 7.3). Despite the emergence of new companies that themselves became groups (but not necessarily family business groups), family businesses also thrived. We observe many Indian business groups evolving and emerging stronger in the post-liberalization era, suggesting the need for a relook at the argument for their certain demise. Apart from the Tatas and the Birlas, many other families from different parts of the country established multiple businesses, such as the Mahindras from the North, the Goenkas from the East, the Godrej and the Bajaj Groups from the West, and the Murugappas from the South. The Reliance Group started as a textile company in the mid-seventies, got into the petroleum business, and later ventured into retail and telecom in a big way. The post 2000 years also saw the emergence of big family business groups focusing on infrastructure; the Adanis, for example, are in a variety of businesses ranging from power and roads to ports and mining.

The end of the License Raj paved the way for the entry of foreign investment and multinational companies and the emergence of a new breed of Indian entrepreneurs. However, defying the popular logic, not only did some of the old family business groups such as the Tatas, Birlas, and Ambanis (Reliance) continue their dominance, but a large and growing number of

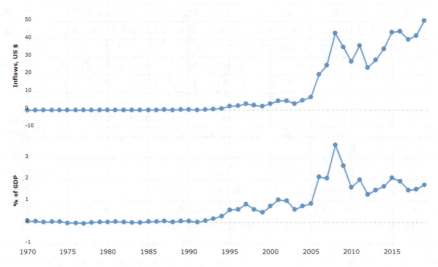

Fig. 7.2 Foreign direct investment trend as indicator of India's economic reform (*Source* World Bank)

new family business groups gained prominence in the 1990s, including the Nambiars (BPL), the Guptas (Lloyds Steel), the Jindals (Jindal Steel, Power and Cement), the Oswals (OWM and Vardhman), the Mittals (Bharti Telecom), the Munjals (Hero Motor), the Shahras (Ruchi Soya), the Mehtas (Torrent), the Lohias (Indo Rama), the Dhoots (Videocon), and the Premjis (Wipro). Most of these new groups had grown steadily in the eighties but rose in importance in the nineties and thereafter the economy rapidly developed and new institutions were put in place.

Other than the emergence of new business families, the splits in the established business families led to the formation of new family business groups. The split of the Goenka family in the eighties led to the formation of the RPG group of R.P. Goenka and the Duncans group led by J.P. Goenka. Similarly, divisions in the Bajaj, Ambani, Jindal, and R.P. Goenka families in recent years led to the creation of additional family business groups. Sometimes, these splits sparked greater competitive entrepreneurialism among the splintered groups, leading to higher growth and value creation of each of the new entities. They became separate businesses, but with the same familial roots. In Table 7.1, the evolution of the Goenka Group provides a typical example of how Indian family business groups have come into existence.

Taken in combination, the rise of new family business groups, revitalization of some older and established ones, and continued growth and dominance of several business groups, despite family splits and undoubted

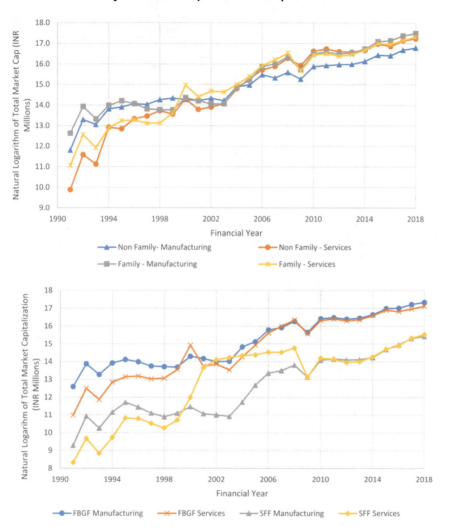

Fig. 7.3 Total market cap trend as indicator of business growth (*Source* Bang et al., 2020) (*Note* FBGF: family business group; SFF: stand-alone family firm)

improvements in the institutional structure, cast serious doubts on the institutional void argument as the sole, or even the major, reason for the existence and dominance of family business groups. Evidently, the institutional void logic does not explain the dominance of business groups in an emerging economy like India. We argue that the missing link lies in the fact that most Indian business groups are family-owned and that there are distinctive family motivations for their sustenance and prosperity. These business families, of course, found the advantage in a developing institutional environment in terms of access to resources, but the real motivations to use that

168   S. Bhadra et al.

Table 7.1 Typical formation of family business groups in India

Evolution of the Goenka Group	
1800s	Ramdutt Goenka started as a banker in Kolkata and then became a successful agent for British business houses. He was later assisted by his son Ramkissendas to form a company trading in jute and tea
1900s	The fourth-generation owners, Sir Badridas Goenka and Sir Hariram Goenka, were knighted by the Emperor of India for their contribution to business and society
1947	Soon after India's independence, the Goenkas crossed into manufacturing by acquiring Octavius Steel from a company moving out of India
1950s	In 1951, the Goenkas picked up a stake in Duncan Brothers, a trading company that owned substantial holdings in jute and tea. 1n 1957, Keshav Prasad Goenka became the Chairman of Duncan Brothers
1960s	Keshav Prasad transitioned the group's business from trading to manufacturing through acquisitions of companies in textiles, power, cables, and engineering, and started a carbon black company. In 1963, he retained Duncan Brothers as his inheritance, while another branch of the family inherited Octavius Steel
1979	Keshav Prasad Goenka split his business empire among his three sons, Rama Prasad, Jagadish Prasad, and Gouri Prasad. Rama Prasad Goenka established RPG Enterprises in 1979 with Philips Carbon Black, Asian Cables, Agarpara Jute, and Murphy India as the constituents
1980s	The Group acquired CEAT Tires in 1981, KEC International (transmission tower maker) in 1982, and Searle India (drug company) in 1983. The tire giant Dunlop India was acquired in 1984 from Dunlop Holdings, UK. The group acquired a stake in the drug firm Bayer in 1985 and the iconic music company Gramophone Company of India in 1986. In 1988, Harrison Malayalam (tea and rubber plantations) and ICIM (computer services) were acquired. In 1989, the group's acquisitions included CESC (power), Raychem Technologies (advanced materials), and Spencer's (retail)
1990s	Remington Rand (typewriter maker) was acquired in 1990. In 1993, NPCL was formed as a joint venture between the group and Greater Noida Industrial Development Authority. The group ventured into music retailing with Music World in 1997
2000s	The group entered the media business with the launch of *Open Magazine* in 2009. Au Bon Pain Café was set up the same year. The Mundra unit, a greenfield project of PCBL, was commissioned in October 2009
2010	The group's businesses were divided between Rama Prasad Goenka's sons, Harsh and Sanjiv

(continued)

Table 7.1 (continued)

Evolution of the Goenka Group

2011	Harsh Goenka took over RPG Enterprises (also known as RPG Group) and Sanjiv Goenka formed the RP-Sanjiv Goenka Group. Their children are now involved in the respective groups and are being groomed to be future leaders supported by professionals

advantage came from the families' economic, social, and emotional aspirations. These family aspirations, in effect, are reflected in the family business group structure that we see today.

In other words, beyond the outside-in approach suggested by the institutional void logic, we posit an inside-out approach from a family logic to describe the family business groups (Fig. 7.1). This approach can also partially explain why, given a similar institutional environment, some family business groups flourish and others face challenges. A case in point could be the standout features of the Aditya Birla Group compared with the M.P. Birla Group and the C.K. Birla Group (refer to Box 7.2); another is the recent divergence between the Reliance Group (led by Mukesh Ambani) and the ADA Group (led by Anil Ambani) (refer to Box 7.5).

Box 7.1. Advantage of the family legacy
Branding the family name: The case of the Tata Group

The name Tata is associated with trust and values in Indian society. This was achieved through generations of ethical business leadership by the Tata family for over a century. Their commitment to social value creation while doing business has earned them recognition and respect in the community. This legacy is one of the key advantages for Tata Group affiliates over their stand-alone competitors.

There are three connected mechanisms by which the Tata leaders were able to transform the family name into a famous brand. First, by naming their companies "Tata." This started with the setup of Tata Iron and Steel Company (now Tata Steel) in 1907 by Sir Dorabji Tata, son of Jamsetji Nusserwanji Tata who made the initial move from trading to manufacturing. Thereafter, other companies were formed, such as Tata Hydroelectric Power Supply Company (now Tata Power) in 1910, Tata Oil Mills Co. in 1917 (sold to HUL in 1984), Tata Chemicals in 1939, Tata Engineering and Locomotive Company (now Tata Motors) in 1945, Tata Finlay (later Tata Tea; now Tata Global Beverages) in 1962, and Tata Computer Systems (now Tata Consultancy Services) in 1968, and so on. All of these entities were independently run but controlled by the Group through the holding company, Tata Sons.

Second, by associating the name with social endeavors. In 1892, Jamsetji Tata established the JN Tata Endowment Fund to help Indian students pursue higher studies abroad. The Tata Institute of Social Sciences was established in 1936, the Tata Memorial Hospital in 1941, and the Tata Institute of Fundamental Research in 1945. These institutions are still regarded as among the best in their respective areas.

Third, by articulating the Tata identity. Under the leadership of Ratan Tata, a common ethical guideline for the group companies was formalized as the Tata Code of Conduct. He also restructured the group to give more control to Tata Sons, the holding company, and made the affiliates accountable for using the Tata name. Tata, as a superbrand, both safeguards values in decision-making and multiplies goodwill for its affiliates (Ramachandran et al., 2013).

Today, while individual Tata companies are run by independent boards and professional managers, group-level control is in the hands of the Tata Trusts, which have invested in Tata Sons. The Tata Trusts are philanthropic organizations committed to social value creation in the country. The current chairman of the Tata Trusts is Ratan Tata, and a few other family members are also on the Board of Trustees. Thus, it is not difficult to imagine that the strategic direction of the Tata Group will be influenced to a great extent by how the Tata family wants to identify with the name in times to come.

Box 7.2. Group split to manage family conflicts
Formation of subgroups within the Birla Group

The pioneering industrialist of the Birla Group was Ghanshyam Das Birla, who not only invested in industries ranging from jute and textile to cement and chemicals, but also made a name for himself through his patriotic and philanthropic endeavors, much as the Tatas did. His sons and nephews led various group companies and helped expand the Birla Group. After Ghanshyam Das's demise in 1983, ownership of the companies was rearranged within the family to allow for more independent leadership by the brothers. This is one of the strategies adopted by family business groups to distribute entrepreneurial opportunities along with family wealth. However, such exercises are not without their share of tension and conflict over questions of right and fairness.

For example, a conflict within the group arose when Priyamvada Devi Birla, the widow of Madhav Prasad Birla (nephew of Ghanshyam Das), having no children of her own, bequeathed her estate to her loyal associate Rajendra Singh Lodha through a controversial will disclosed after her death. The Birla family was taken aback by this arrangement and a long legal battle ensued. Despite this, Rajendra Singh Lodha became the next chairman of Birla Corporation, the flagship company of the M.P. Birla Group (named after Madhav Prasad), and his son Harsh Vardhan Lodha succeeded him as chairman of the company. This episode reveals the sensitive nature of family expectations in the distribution of ownership of the business empire.

Meanwhile, the other Birla brothers forged ahead independently with their own set of companies, and their sons took over from there. Aditya Vikram Birla, the grandson of Ghanshyam Das, made his mark as an industry leader, having demonstrated his entrepreneurial abilities from a young age. His dream of international expansion is being carried forward by his son, Kumar Mangalam Birla, the current chairman of the Aditya Birla Group. Similarly, Chandra Kant Birla, son of Ganga Prasad Birla, a nephew of Ghanshyam Das, formed the C.K. Birla Group with his share of the empire.

Roles of Family Business Groups

In this section, we move from the historical context to the conceptual domain of family business groups so that family logic can be discussed within a framework. We contend that family business groups fulfill not only business needs determined by economic concerns, but also family needs determined by socio-emotional motives (Berrone et al., 2012; Gómez-Mejía et al., 2007). Understanding the multiple goals of family business groups can help us appreciate the strategic choices they make, which we discuss in the following sections.

Supporting business needs: Family business groups, like any other business group, lend some structural advantages to their affiliate companies (Granovetter, 1995; Masulis et al., 2011). First, the "group headquarters"— usually a holding company governed by owning family members and their close associates—holds responsibility for identifying new opportunities and financing across the group companies (Chang & Hong, 2000). The group companies, while adept at identifying areas for related diversification, typically are not equally skilled at identifying unrelated areas, and the group-level executives (and owners) are able to do this job better. For example, it is doubtful if Titan, a watch retailer turned watch and jewelry retailer, could have been identified by Tata Steel or Tata Motors; it was an idea entirely originating from Tata Sons, the group holding company of Tata. The entry of groups into completely new areas was invariably driven by the vision of their founders or group-level executives rather than executives at the company level, unless the new opportunities were closely related to the existing businesses. The financing of these new companies was almost entirely the responsibility of the group. Groups used multiple means to finance the ventures, such as raising debt and issuing shares through initial public offerings (IPOs), but where the role of the group was crucial was through cross investments across the group companies in the new company. Various resources from the existing companies were reallocated to the new companies, for instance, managers from the group companies were appointed to the new company. This redistribution of resources, along with the backing of the group headquarters, made the start-up process of the new companies smoother and their existence more secure. At first glance, it may appear that the group companies were following Khanna and Palepu's model. However, on closer inspection, we see that this was not due to any failure of the capital market or institutions as such; rather, it was much easier to fund the new companies from the group companies and retain control over their strategy, especially in their early years.

The group's role as financier and even as a sort of venture capitalist (without the selling out of stakes) continues today. Group heads at the top still prospect and approve the group's entry into new areas and finance the new ventures. These investments reduce both the cost of capital and the risks involved, thus placing the companies under a group at a competitive advantage compared to stand-alone new ventures (Chittoor et al., 2015).

Its second role is the establishment of the values and codes of conduct for the group companies, making it clear what their brand names stand for (Ramachandran et al., 2013). None has done this better than the Tata Group, which capitalizes on its brand name (and even charges its group companies for using it). The established reputation of any group becomes a competitive advantage, as seen from the willingness of giants such as Facebook to invest in the Reliance Group.[1] Apart from its formal code of values, the group's brand and reputation is built on the perception of how it treats its employees, vendors, and the larger community; the kinds of litigation in which it is involved; and the alliances it is able to command.

Its third role is setting standards for corporate governance, both at the group level and at the constituent companies' level. Though it could be argued that much still needs to be done in this area, especially in terms of resolving the contradictions of the interests of minority and other shareholders, their willingness to invest in Indian family companies indicates their confidence in the corporate standards laid down by these businesses.

Supporting family needs: Family business groups benefit as much from the group structure as their non-family counterparts in the absence of a strong institutional environment. At the same time, this structure also serves the owning family's needs, which is not the case with non-family business groups. In other words, the business group structure may be advantageous to the family business owners beyond supplementing institutional weaknesses, and the families' aspirations can become the primary driving force for the success of the family business groups. In Table 7.2, we show how the business group structure fulfills the owning family's economic, social, and emotional needs. This forms the basis of the family logic for the sustenance of family business groups.

Family Business Group Strategy

Family business groups have unique advantages and disadvantages over non-family domestic firms and foreign companies with respect to their ability to formulate their long-term strategy (Bertrand et al., 2008; Manikutty, 2000). We will first consider the advantages enjoyed by family business groups. First, the continuity of tradition over generations of a family can create a strong legacy for the family name that can be transformed into shared brand equity among the affiliate companies. The intrinsic motivation of the family members to uphold their identity can produce business leaders committed to their businesses. This helps in maintaining continuity as well as commonality of strategy across units and generations.

Second, business families forge relationships through marriages and friendships. This allows them to create formal and informal alliances in their businesses, giving them a strategic advantage over their competitors. Among business families in Indian society, marriages are often arranged keeping in mind the business alliances between the two families. Having multiple businesses increases the possibilities for such alliances. Many strategy conflicts that might take place otherwise can be resolved more smoothly.

Third, families work based on trust. A trusted network of family members and loyal non-family associates can help each other in times of personal crisis. The family as a support system makes the leadership team, consisting of multiple family members, more resilient. This replaces market-based, arm's length transactions with trust-based ones, making it possible for the family leaders to take greater strategic risks.

Family businesses have a distinctive advantage over foreign companies in that families are rooted in the local culture, which gives them a deeper understanding of consumer preferences as well as the broader social behavior in the country. Further, unlike foreign companies, family business groups can validate and complement their understanding of the country's social dynamics

174   S. Bhadra et al.

Table 7.2 Advantage of business group structure for business family needs

Family needs		Business implications	Advantage of BG
Economic	• Present living standard • Wealth for future	• Sources of income • Investment planning	• Diversified businesses to maintain family income level through business cycles • Enter new business areas to secure family's future
Social	• Power • Respect • Relationship	• Authority/control • Responsible business • Alliances	• Hierarchical holdings to expand family control • Create socially responsible ventures to uphold family name • Multiple possibilities with the new partners
Emotional	• Tradition/legacy • Entrepreneurial spirit • Children's well-being • Values	• Protect older firms • New venture • Succession planning • Business ethics and brand building	• Supporting older companies by pooling resources • Support from existing companies while creating new ones • Multiple avenues to launch children into their careers and fair distribution of wealth • Propagation of values through common charter and spillover of brand value

with knowledge gathered from their own business experiences, including past experience.

The above advantages can become disadvantages for family business groups in different settings or when handled improperly. For instance, one wrong step by one family member can tarnish the entire group's image and reputation, carefully built over decades. Similarly, family business groups might face serious challenges in foreign countries if they fail to appreciate social and cultural differences. In terms of relational strategy, a bad marriage or an

7 Family Business Groups in India: Perspectives on Their ...   175

incompetent relative trusted to run a business can backfire, with a lasting impact. Finally, the very support system on which the group relies—the family—can break down in times of conflict among the members, taking attention away from business growth to resolving the tension.

It must be noted that the advantages enjoyed by family business groups arise not from external institutional deficiencies, but from the nature of the family group itself. They reinforce these advantages through two mechanisms: (i) gaining from the past, and (ii) managing and securing the future.

Gaining from the past: The path of "the family name becoming a brand in itself" is followed by many family businesses around the world. Personal identification with the business not only keeps the family members motivated to succeed, but also provides a natural platform for the next generation to join the business. The business group structure is then maintained by the extended family members as the family name becomes a strategic asset for the affiliate companies. Though such strong group identity can exist for non-family business groups also, we think family-level cohesion and pride in the name make it more achievable (Ramachandran et al., 2013; Sundaramurthy & Kreiner, 2008). Box 7.1 showcases one of the leading examples of identity creation among Indian family business groups, namely, the branding of the Tata name.

Securing the future: The future course of family business groups depends heavily upon their succession strategy (Chittoor & Das, 2007). The existence of multiple companies and multiple potential successors allows for many different possible combinations, making succession a complex issue, especially given the varied expectations and abilities of the successors (Friedman, 1991). Well-known devices such as regular family meetings, setting up of family councils, and drafting constitutions for the family businesses are used in many cases to ensure smooth transitions (Dutta, 1997). The key to a good succession strategy for the family business is to find a balance between what is good for the company and what is good for the family, but this is not always easy to achieve. In fact, family interests need to be managed carefully to protect the future of the business (Reay, 2009). One of the main family motives for succession planning in family businesses, which does not exist in other businesses, is the universal parental desire to secure an uninterrupted livelihood for their offspring. On paper, this can be done by giving equitable shares, but not control, to all family members. However, in India, parental obligation usually extends beyond the equitable distribution of wealth to the running of the businesses themselves. Indian family business groups have handled the dilemmas of succession in different ways and learned from their experiences in the process. In the past, within the joint family structure, extended family members worked closely together to make a fortune for themselves and their children. Sons were expected to join the business, and daughters were married into other business families (today, daughters from progressive families are given an equal opportunity to participate in the business). As the generations passed and families grew bigger, sibling rivalry became more common, and family members sought greater independence. In some cases, the groups were split into subgroups (though carrying the same legacy), and in others, holding companies were created to distribute ownership.[2] In Boxes 7.2 and 7.3, we show two ways of managing family conflicts generally seen among family business groups.

> **Box 7.3. Formalizing roles to manage succession**
> **Maintaining cohesion in the Bajaj Group**
>
> In 1931, inspired by the nationalist movement at the time and responding to a national need, Jamnalal Bajaj set up his first company—a sugar plant called Hindustan Sugar Mills Limited. He was also known to be a philanthropist, and his sons continued his legacy of both industrial and social development. The Bajaj Foundation was set up in 1963 to participate in development activities. The group was known for its pioneering efforts and leadership in the two-wheeler market, which made the name "Bajaj" synonymous with scooters and autorickshaws across India. In 1988, Hindustan Sugar Mills Limited was renamed Bajaj Hindustan Limited, another step toward upholding the family name.
>
> The Bajaj Group remained together for almost three generations until 2008 when Shishir Bajaj parted ways from his four brothers (highlighted in Fig. 7.4 below) to lead his separate sugar and consumer goods group. It is believed that he took this decision to accommodate the entrepreneurial aspirations of his

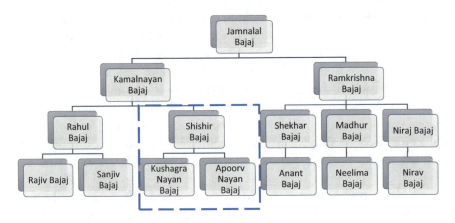

Fig. 7.4 The bajaj family tree

son Kushagra.[3] This incident encouraged the rest of the extended family to formalize their roles in the group so that succession would be transparent.[4] A holding company called Bajaj Holdings and Investment Limited was formed in 2009 to build more alignment in the group.

Succession planning and securing the future can be both an advantage and a disadvantage for family firms as compared to non-family firms. With a strong and decisive patriarch (or matriarch) at the head who clearly articulates the succession plan during their lifetime, a family firm could avoid the struggles commonly seen in non-family firms, which often results in many competent people leaving the firms. This need not happen in family firms. However, if the patriarch does not make the choices well in time or makes the wrong choices, it can be a disadvantage.

As may be seen in Boxes 7.2 and 7.3, whatever may be the outcomes, they do not seem to have anything to do with the institutional environment, but only with the nature of family businesses themselves. Many firms have learned to leverage their strengths as family businesses (though many have not), but even with the further strengthening of institutions, the ability to plan succession will be a major strength of family businesses.

Innovations at Family Business Groups

Innovation has become an integral part of firm strategy. There is a fair degree of agreement among scholars as well as practitioners that in today's intensely competitive world, innovation is a key strength for any company (Davenport et al., 2007). However, there is less clear agreement on whether family ownership facilitates or impedes innovation (De Massis et al., 2013). The major arguments in favor of the former view are the long-term orientation of family firms and the unique social capital they possess (De Massis et al., 2013). The opposing view argues that captive knowledge and resistance to change in order to retain control are factors that could hinder innovation. However, new avenues for innovation open up when family owners adopt the business group structure. Exploration and innovation efforts by business group affiliates can be triggered by marginal performance concerns (Vissa et al., 2010), but these can also be driven by the family owners' motivations when such business groups are family-controlled (Ray & Bhadra, 2021).

Business group structure offers certain advantages for innovation. Group-level pooling provides the extra resources necessary for "slack" search leading to innovation (Greve, 2003). Further, research finds that inter-organizational alliances can help in innovation through sharing of complementary knowledge and resources (Ahuja, 2000; Cowan & Jonard, 2009; Goes & Park, 1997), and business groups facilitate such collaborations among their affiliates. Business group affiliates operating in different parts of the value chain are better suited for innovation through collaborations (Hess & Rothaermel, 2011). Studies show that such inter-organizational collaborations are more important for innovation in a rapidly changing technological environment (Powell et al., 1996).

Family business groups can facilitate innovation in two additional ways. First, by encouraging family members to lead new ventures to support experimentation, and second, through the participation of next-generation family members in setting the future direction.

Experimental ventures are more effectively handled by family members because of their higher risk tolerance; there is little fear of losing their jobs in case of failure. The risk profile of the family owners plays an important role in this regard. Many family business group owners focus their energies on new investment opportunities to grow the family wealth or to satisfy their entrepreneurial spirit, thereby opening themselves to innovative ideas. In such cases, they seem to be happy to delegate operational activities to professional managers. Managerial attention to distant or novel areas as a cause for innovation is also supported by research (Li et al., 2013). This attitude to experimentation is another major reason why family business groups may continue to morph and exist.

Next-generation family members are important agents for innovation as they bring in modern ideas and push for change. Among Indian family business groups, younger-generation members are well educated (many from Ivy League universities in the US) and likely to possess a global identity, and therefore, more capable of fostering innovation in a multicultural setup (Lisak et al., 2016). As members of the family, these young leaders can be more persuasive and exercise greater influence in decision-making than young outsiders.

In Boxes 7.4 and 7.5, we depict the innovation strategies followed by two family business groups, realized in two different ways. In both cases, family needs, whether in the form of sustaining family values or upholding family aspirations, played an important role in their innovation journey.

Box 7.4. Innovation as group culture
Pursuit of innovation in the Godrej Group

Godrej, with a long string of successful products, is a household name in India. The group presents itself as innovation-driven, declaring, "we are only as good as what we do next."[5] The Godrej journey started in 1897, with the founding of a lock company by Ardeshir Godrej. His brother Pirojsha joined him, and since Ardeshir had no children, Pirojsha's sons became the second-generation successors. In the third generation, Adi Godrej took over as chairman and manages the group alongside his brother Nadir Godrej and cousin Jamshyd Godrej. The fourth-generation members are now involved in the management of the group companies, showcasing a rare example of solidarity in an extended family business.

Much credit for their growth and success goes to their continuous endeavors to pick up on the needs of the masses and innovate with their products. Godrej locks and Godrej *almirahs* (steel cupboards), among their earliest products, are still considered among the best in the market a century later. In 1918, Godrej launched the world's first vegetable oil soap (today Godrej is the second largest soap manufacturer in India); they introduced refrigerators in 1958 and hair color products in 1974, both of which were successful. In 1990, the group established Godrej Properties, which brought the "group's philosophy of innovation and excellence"[6] to the real estate industry in India. Godrej Agrovet, a R&D backed agri-business company, was incorporated in 1991.

Continuing on their innovation journey, in 2007, they built India's first key with a chip and the first lock with two separate keys. In 2018, they partnered with the World Green Building Council to accelerate the concept of net-zero carbon buildings. The diversity of the group's business ventures shows their relentless attention to scanning consumer needs, and the longevity of their product lines owes much to continuous improvements made to remain relevant. When these practices are followed (and believed to be the key to success) through generations, innovation becomes the group culture

Innovation also becomes a tool to provide space for growth for future generations. The Godrej Group has implemented this strategy very well so far.[7] Over the years, as they created companies in diverse industries, the younger members were able to take active leadership roles in various group companies.[8] Their recent ventures into housing finance, gourmet retail, and lifestyle solutions signal their interest in further expansion in the services sector. The establishment of Godrej India Culture Lab in 2011 as a fluid, experimental space to cross-pollinate ideas and people seems a fitting next step in their innovation journey.

Box 7.5. Innovation guided by family's aspirations
A family business group in the making: Reliance Industries

Reliance Industries, led by Mukesh Ambani, is on a transformational journey from being a conglomerate to becoming a family business group—a testament to the importance of family business groups in modern India. What makes the story more interesting is that his brother Anil Ambani, having inherited a similar fortune from their father, the self-made billionaire Dhirubhai Ambani, is witnessing the downfall of his part of the empire. This divergence can be partly attributed to the difference in aspirations between the two brothers and shows how family-level factors can be as important as institutional factors in the prosperity of family business groups.

Reliance started as a textile business in the 1960s, moved into oil refining in the 1980s, and then entered the communications sector in the early 2000s. After Dhirubhai Ambani's death in 2002, his two sons decided to divide the wealth and operate independently. In 2005, Reliance made the decision to reorganize its businesses through a demerger; power generation and distribution, financial services, and telecommunication services were demerged into separate entities. Mukesh stayed at Reliance Industries with the textile and petroleum refining divisions, while Anil Ambani took over the group of companies dealing with power, communication, and finance.

The petroleum refining and petrochemicals business led by Mukesh has been generating massive revenues for years, making him one of the richest businessmen in the world. However, the oil sector is now being considered a sunset industry, given the rapid transition to renewable energy globally. His textile business was also suffering from a lack of desired growth.[9] To remain at the top of the Indian business landscape, he had to reinvent his company to make it future proof. Driven by this aspiration, he is not only in the process of creating new age businesses, but also considering separate companies, perhaps to facilitate the "one-to-many succession" of his three children, Akash, Isha, and Anant. Indeed, Akash and Isha have already started participating in decision-making, and the youngest, Anant, is likely to join them soon.

This journey of reinventing the company began with Mukesh's realization that "data is the new oil." Though it was Anil who had inherited the communications business initially, it was Mukesh who envisioned a data revolution in India. He launched Reliance Jio in 2007 and invested heavily in the country's digital communication infrastructure, especially in voice over internet technology. The pan-India launch of 4G services by Reliance Jio in 2016 disrupted the telecommunications industry and challenged the dominance of incumbent heavyweights such as Airtel and Vodafone.

The 2006 launch of his other venture, Reliance Retail, was also part of Mukesh's aspiration to transform Reliance into a large consumer-oriented

> group. With companies such as Facebook and Google as strategic investors in Reliance Jio, more disruptive business models are in sight for Reliance Retail as well, such as hyperlocal delivery powered by the digital infrastructure.
>
> It is believed that Reliance Industries will soon list the two subsidiaries—Reliance Jio and Reliance Retail—to become a family business group of publicly listed companies. The way Mukesh has utilized his entrepreneurial mindset to disrupt and progress seems absent in his brother Anil's case. Even Mukesh's wife Nita Ambani is more visible in the public domain through the work of Reliance Foundation than Anil's wife Tina Ambani. Mukesh and Nita's intention to remain at the top of their empire is clearly visible in the billion-dollar house they built in Mumbai in 2010. The aspirations of Mukesh and his family seem to drive a large part of the exploration and innovation efforts by Reliance Industries in multiple directions.

Again, while there is no doubt that the institutional environment is crucial in supporting innovation, this applies to all business in a country. What Boxes 7.4 and 7.5 show are the ways that "familiness" has been exploited to enhance the firm's innovation capabilities.

Conclusion

This chapter provides a family logic for the emergence of family business groups, which is different from the dominant institutional void logic. Our contention is that family business groups should be analyzed in a more nuanced way than business groups in general. We argue that an inside-out approach is also necessary to understand the variations among business groups in a similar institutional environment. We took examples from different family business groups in India to initiate the conversation around their roles, strategies, and innovations.

Indian family business groups followed a pattern of making money through trade in the British era and then investing in industrial opportunities as India started to become self-reliant after independence. India's joint family culture helped in creating a common pool of financial and human capital for the families to venture into different domains. This approach also ensured career opportunities for future generations of the extended family. Thus, the formation of family business groups was a natural phenomenon arising out of the growth of the family.

The weak institutional environment certainly gave an added advantage to these family business groups but was in no way the only advantage they had.

Business families also derived benefits from the business group structure for economic, social, and emotional reasons and will continue to do so even when the institutional environment improves.

Their identity and reputation, built on the family's goodwill in the past and its concern for its future well-being, contributed to the prosperity of family business groups. For these groups, the major challenges related to differences among the members on matters of succession planning or strategic direction. In such cases, some groups restructured themselves to allow for independent entrepreneurial pursuits and others consolidated further to distribute ownership via holding companies.

We also find family legacy and motivations at the root of innovations in family business groups. While we see a continuous push for innovation as the key to success for the Godrej Group, we also see how Reliance Industries is on its way to business model innovation by creating new age companies.

There are many more cases from India and abroad where family reasons have directly or indirectly reflected on the structure or conduct of the family business groups. Be it the decision to enter into new business verticals, or the decision to internationalize, or the decision to restructure ownership and management, most have some link to the family dynamics and aspirations of the group. There are historical narratives on many such events, but what is missing is a theoretical consolidation of these cases. We contend that the "family logic" behind the behavior of family business groups, not only in India, but around the world, is deserving of greater scholarly attention and conversation.

Notes

1. https://techcrunch.com/2020/04/21/facebook-reliance-jio/.
2. https://www.forbesindia.com/article/india-rich-list-10/family-businesses-and-splitting-heirs/18242/1.
3. https://www.livemint.com/Companies/Q1yt1hDIr9FrJM3lDkwMvM/How-the-Bajajs-split-and-made-up-after-7-yrs.html.
4. https://www.livemint.com/Companies/W1KcASuM6q2liXL3ALmJRJ/Bajaj-Group-plans-for-Gen-Next-with-a-family-settlement.html.
5. https://www.godrej.com/our-story#1997.
6. https://www.godrej.com/our-story#1990.
7. https://economictimes.indiatimes.com/news/company/corporate-trends/godrej-group-locks-its-future-crafts-succession-plan/articleshow/51336198.cms.
8. https://economictimes.indiatimes.com/news/company/corporate-trends/genext-taking-on-active-role-at-godrej-group/articleshow/5692308.cms.
9. https://www.firstpost.com/business/corporate-business/goodbye-vimal-why-mukesh-ambani-is-selling-his-fathers-first-major-business-1999363.html.

References

Ahuja, G. (2000). Collaboration networks, structural holes, and innovation: A longitudinal study. *Administrative Science Quarterly, 45*, 425–455. https://doi.org/10.2307/2667105

Bang, N. P., Bhatia, N., Ray, S., & Ramachandran, K. (2020). *Family businesses and India's transition to a services led economy (1991–2018)*. Indian School of Business.

Berrone, P., Cruz, C., & Gomez-Mejia, L. R. (2012). Socioemotional wealth in family firms: Theoretical dimensions, assessment approaches, and agenda for future research. *Family Business Review, 25*(3), 258–279. https://doi.org/10.1177/0894486511435355

Bertrand, M., & Schoar, A. (2006). The role of family in family firms. *Journal of Economic Perspectives, 20*(2), 73–96. https://doi.org/10.1257/jep.20.2.73

Bertrand, M., Johnson, S., Samphantharak, K., & Schoar, A. (2008). Mixing family with business: A study of Thai business groups and the families behind them. *Journal of Financial Economics, 88*(3), 466–498. https://doi.org/10.1016/j.jfineco.2008.04.002

Boeker, W. (1989). Strategic change: The effects of founding and history. *Academy of Management Journal, 32*(3), 489–515.

Chang, S. J., & Hong, J. (2000). Economic performance of group-affiliated companies in Korea: Intragroup resource sharing and internal business transactions. *Academy of Management Journal, 43*(3), 429–448.

Chittoor, R., & Das, R. (2007). Professionalization of management and succession performance—A vital linkage. *Family Business Review, 20*(1), 65–79.

Chittoor, R., Kale, P., & Puranam, P. (2015). Business groups in developing capital markets: Towards a complentarity perspective. *Strategic Management Journal, 36*, 1277–1296. https://doi.org/10.1002/smj

Cowan, R., & Jonard, N. (2009). Knowledge portfolios and the organization of innovation networks. *Academy of Management Review, 34*(2), 320–342. https://doi.org/10.5465/AMR.2009.36982634

Davenport, T. H., Leibold, M., & Voelpel, S. C. (2007). *Strategic management in the innovation economy: Strategic approaches and tools for dynamic innovation capabilities*. John Wiley & Sons.

De Massis, A., Frattini, F., & Lichtenthaler, U. (2013). Research on technological innovation in family firms: Present debates and future directions. *Family Business Review, 26*, 10–31. https://doi.org/10.1177/0894486512466258

Dutta, S. (1997). *Family business in India*. Sage Publications.

Friedman, S. D. (1991). Sibling relationships and intergenerational succession in family firms. *Family Business Review, 4*(1), 3–20. https://doi.org/10.1111/j.1741-6248.1991.00003

Goes, J. B., & Park, S. H. (1997). Interorganisational links and innovation: The case of hospital services. *Academy of Management Journal, 40*(3), 673–696.

Gómez-Mejía, L. R., Haynes, K. T., Núñez-Nickel, M., Jacobson, K. J. L., & Moyano-Fuentes, J. (2007). Socioemotional wealth and business risks in family-controlled firms: Evidence from Spanish olive oil mills. *Administrative Science Quarterly, 52*, 106–137.

Granovetter, M. (1995). Coase revisited: Business groups in the modern economy. *Industrial and Corporate Change, 4*(1), 93–130. https://doi.org/10.1093/icc/4.1.93

Greve, H. R. (2003). A behavioral theory of R&D expenditures and innovations: Evidence from shipbuilding. *Academy of Management Journal, 46*(6), 685–702.

Hess, A. M., & Rothaermel, F. T. (2011). When are assets complementary? Star scientists, strategic alliances, and innovation in the pharmaceutical industry. *Strategic Management Journal, 32*, 895–909. https://doi.org/10.1002/smj

Khanna, T., & Palepu, K. (2000a). Is group affiliation profitable in emerging markets? An analysis of diversified Indian business groups. *Journal of Finance, 55*(2), 867–891.

Khanna, T., & Palepu, K. (2000b). The future of business groups in emerging markets: Long-run evidence from Chile. *Academy of Management Journal, 43*(3), 268–285.

Koiranen, M. (2002). Over 100 years of age but still entrepreneurially active in business: Exploring the values and family characteristics of old Finnish family firms. *Family Business Review, 15*(3), 175–187. https://doi.org/10.1111/j.1741-6248.2002.00175.x

Li, Q., Magiitti, P. G., Smith, K. G., Tesluk, P. E., & Katila, R. (2013). Top management team attention to innovation: The role of search selection and intentsity in new product introductions. *Academy of Management Journal, 56*(3), 893–916. https://doi.org/10.5465/amj.2010.0844

Lisak, A., Erez, M., Sui, Y., & Lee, C. (2016). The positive role of global leaders in enhancing multicultural team innovation. *Journal of International Business Studies, 47*(6), 655–673. https://doi.org/10.1057/s41267-016-0002-7

Manikutty, S. (2000). Family business groups in India: A resource-based view of the emerging trends. *Family Business Review, 13*(4), 279–292. https://doi.org/10.1111/j.1741-6248.2000.00279

Masulis, R. W., Pham, P. K., & Zein, J. (2011). Family business groups around the world: Costs and benefits of pyramids. *Review of Financial Studies, 24*, 3556–3600. http://ssrn.com/abstract=1363878

Powell, W. W., Koput, K. W., & Smith-Doerr, L. (1996). Interorganizational collaboration and the locus of innovation: Networks of learning in biotechnology. *Administrative Science Quarterly, 41*(1), 116–145. https://doi.org/10.2307/2393988

Ramachandran, J., Manikandan, K. S., & Pant, A. (2013). Why conglomerates thrive. *Harvard Business Review*, 1–11.

Ray, S., & Bhadra, S. (2021). Indian family firms in an emerging digital economy: An analysis of digital technology adoption. In H.-D. Yan & F.-L. T. Yu

(Eds.), *The Routledge companion to Asian family business* (1st ed., pp. 445–460). Routledge.

Reay, T. (2009). Family-business meta-identity, institutional pressures, and ability to respond to entrepreneurial opportunities. *Entrepreneurship Theory and Practice, 33*(6), 1265–1270.

Reay, T., Jaskiewicz, P., & Hinings, C. R. (2015). How family, business, and community logics shape family firm behavior and "rules of the game" in an organizational field. *Family Business Review, 28*(4), 292–311. https://doi.org/10. 1177/0894486515577513

Stinchcomb, A. L. (1965). Social structure and organizations. In J. G. March (Ed.), *Handbook of organizations* (pp. 142–194). Rand-McNally & Co.

Sundaramurthy, C., & Kreiner, G. E. (2008). Governing by managing identity boundaries: The case of family businesses. *Entrepreneurship: Theory and Practice, 32*(3), 415–436. https://doi.org/10.1111/j.1540-6520.2008.00234.x

Tripathi, D. (2004). *The Oxford history of Indian business.* Oxford University Press.

Vissa, B., Greve, H. R., & Chen, W.-R. (2010). Business group affiliation and firm search behavior in India: Responsiveness and focus of attention. *Organization Science, 21*(3), 696–712. https://doi.org/10.1287/orsc

Part II

Ownership, Governance and Management

8

The Moderating Role of Governance in Promoting Transgenerational Entrepreneurship and Value Creation in Latin Family Business Groups

Neus Feliu and Fernanda Jaramillo

Introduction

FBGs represent a small proportion of all family firms; however, in some regions, such as Latin America, they account for a large portion of jobs and annual GDP. Their economic relevance, especially in developing countries, is notable. Moreover, many such groups have already spanned several generations, moving from founder-owned businesses to sibling partnerships, and now transitioning to cousin consortiums (Gersick et al., 1997). The transition to cousin consortium stages represents a momentum shift for many FBGs, as (1) distribution of ownership/wealth across family branches and households is likely to be unequal due to differences in size; (2) job opportunities become more scarce as the number of family shareholders/owners increases; (3) owners with no active role in the business have liquidity needs/expectations. If not well managed, this transition may risk the continuity of the FBG. Together, these factors underscore the case for further research on features that enable enterprising families, such as Latin American ones, to create value over

---

N. Feliu (✉) · F. Jaramillo
Lansberg Gersick Advisors, New Haven, CT, USA
e-mail: feliu@lga.global

F. Jaramillo
e-mail: jaramillo@lga.global

© The Author(s), under exclusive license to Springer Nature
Switzerland AG 2023
M. Rautianen et al. (eds.), *The Palgrave Handbook of Managing Family Business Groups*,
https://doi.org/10.1007/978-3-031-13206-3_8

generations, including through ongoing entrepreneurial dynamics. This study aims to shed light on the governance of entrepreneurial activity of FBGs.

FBGs are heterogeneous, with large diversity of business forms. A business group is a collection of firms bound together in some formal and/or informal ways, in which there are generally personal and operational ties between all the firms, with a long-term strategic component. They are known in many countries under various names: the old "zaibatsu" and its modern successors, the "keiretsu," in Japan; the "chaebol" in Korea; the "grupos económicos" in Latin America; the "twenty-two families" in Pakistan. FBGs are those business groups that are the outcome of investments by a single family or a small number of allied families, who keep the businesses together as a coherent group and between which personnel and resources may be shifted as needed. That being said, the individual companies still retain a separate identity (Granovetter, 1995). This definition extends to conglomerates (network of (legally) independent companies held by a core owner, with high engagement between ownership and management (Ramachandran et al., 2013); multi-divisional holdings (parent companies that own or control subsidiary companies that function as single economic entities); or portfolios of enterprises (stable owner groups that run multiple firms, each of which can control internal allocation of financial resources). For the purposes of our study, the groups are family-owned and controlled.

Importantly, FBGs feature specific psychological, interpersonal elements that non-family firms don't. Among such elements, there is an atmosphere of loyalty and trust normally associated with families or kinship groups (Strachan, 1976). We have observed sense of belonging, which entails the ability to benefit from the group's assets/resources; cohesion among FBG owners based on psychological factors such as solidary, long-term vision, and sense of entrepreneurial tradition, but also challenges to this cohesion based on rivalry, divergent expectations among family employees and those uninvolved, and others; confusion of family and business roles; and succession-related challenges. Such factors affect FBG behaviors including entrepreneurship.

Most business groups originate through business expansion, or establishment of an effective economic-financial structure to diversify risk, mainly risk capital, resource dependence, and market barriers through ownership of multiple businesses. These groups are thus often established when it stands to reason that they'll lead to improved outcomes. Enterprising families adapt business groups to the needs of the people within the owning family, enabling effective fiscal planning while generating opportunities for involvement of rising generations in innovation, creativity, risk-taking, and professional development. The entrepreneurial activity, defined as proactive pursuit of potentially risky business opportunities within and outside the legacy firm's sector or geography, is a hallmark of FBGs and common to long-lived enterprising families (Le Breton-Miller & Miller, 2018).

FBGs owning families have the resources that allow them to engage in entrepreneurial initiatives across multiple businesses simultaneously, creating value within and over generations. Such families may evolve from operational controlling leaders to governing owners, stewarding the value of entrepreneurship and leveraging available resources (e.g., Gersick et al., 1997; Rosa & Pihkala, 2017; Zellweger et al., 2012). Multiple family-influenced resources affect entrepreneurship, including financial capital (i.e., inexpensive and patient), human capital (diverse, loyal, proactive), relational capital (reputational, community, political) (Le Breton-Miller & Miller, 2018), and formal governance (Habbershon et al., 2010). Most of these resources have flexibility and broad application, which extends their scope and durability, and broadens the range of possible entrepreneurial options. Recent reviews of governance research concur that one size does not fit all family-enterprise configurations and pathways to transgenerational value creation (Gersick & Feliu, 2014). We build on the definition of governance as "the means of stewarding the multigenerational family organization ... [It] establishes the processes whereby: strategic goals are set, key relationships are maintained, the health of the family is safeguarded, accountability is maintained, and achievement and performance are recognized" (Goldbart & DiFuria, 2009: 7), to explore its role in stewarding, promoting, and governing multigenerational FBG entrepreneurial pursuits.

While the literature has broadly covered the mindsets and capabilities that potentiate entrepreneurship within family business (role models, culture, familiness, others), it has largely neglected the role of governance in promoting it (Habbershon et al., 2010). Previous studies have analyzed the influence of multiple factors on family business entrepreneurship: the business family (Sciascia et al, 2013) and its attitudes (Casillas et al, 2011); family involvement (De Massis et al, 2014) and number of family generations in business operations (Kraiczy et al., 2014); and education levels of board members (Talke et al, 2010). In addition, the management literature has focused on publicly traded FBGs due partly to easier access to reliable data (Chen & Smith, 1987). Therefore, we still know little about the impact of governance on FBG entrepreneurship. Clarity in this area, including how multigenerational FBGs maintain entrepreneurial drive, can promote the development of recommendations for enterprising families to deploy their family-oriented resources to their businesses through effective governance practices.

We base our study on case research into three Latin American FBGs. Specifically, we explore the role of FBG governance mechanisms, structures, processes, and policies in fostering and institutionalizing an entrepreneurial mindset and activities across generations. We are especially interested in the transfer of this mindset from one development stage to the next and identify potential applications of governance practices within three models for governing transgenerational FBG pursuits. We focus on established, family-controlled FBGs with a vision of family influence beyond the founders (Chua et al., 1999), arguing that entrepreneurship is key to performance, value-generation, and success over generations.

We proceed as follows. First, we position our analysis in the business groups, transgenerational entrepreneurship, and governance literatures. Second, we describe our method and three cases of successful entrepreneurial family business groups and their governance systems. Third, we present a framework for governing FBG transgenerational entrepreneurship initiative. We conclude with practical implications, study limitations, and future research avenues.

Transgenerational Entrepreneurship in Latin American Family Business Groups

Transgenerational Entrepreneurship

The *Oxford Dictionary* defines "entrepreneurship" as making money by starting or running businesses, typically while taking financial risks—a commonly agreed-upon core definition. In the business family context, entrepreneurship has been defined as the proactive pursuit of potentially risky business opportunities within, and often outside, the legacy firm's sectoral/geographic boundaries, with actions aimed at product-market and technology innovation to maintain a competitive edge across generations (Miller, 1983). Enterprising families are incubators of new ventures by nature, conceiving, developing, and funding these (Lansberg & Jaramillo, 2021). Indeed, studies show that enterprising families are the primary financing source for very early-stage businesses. Further, creation of new streams of economic/social value is critical for both new and established firms, for longevity.

Therefore, entrepreneurship is an ongoing process through which enterprising families use and develop entrepreneurial mindsets and family-influenced capabilities to create new streams of entrepreneurial, financial, and social value (Habbershon et al., 2010). Enterprising capabilities are the resources a family possesses or accesses that may facilitate or constrain entrepreneurial activities (Habbershon & Pisturi, 2002; Sirmon & Hitt, 2003). We see that enterprising families that successfully maintain cross-generational entrepreneurial pursuits (whether the result of economic need, market pressure, shifting family demographics, or entrepreneurial spirit) grow their businesses by adding new ventures as new opportunities are accessed—a process termed "portfolio entrepreneurship" (Rosa & Pihkala, 2017).

Moreover, from a demographic perspective, many families grow at a faster pace than businesses they own, requiring seeking new ventures to provide economic well-being for rising generations. If families are not able to match business growth with demographic growth, the equity value for each owner will be diluted in subsequent generations, risking the loss of the business's economic significance for family members. Without economic relevance or a sense of emotional ownership, owners' commitment to the legacy business may attenuate, often resulting in the company's sale, against previous generations' continuity aspirations.

From a business perspective, most companies follow a predictable growth cycle as they move from early ventures to growth to more mature businesses, and eventually to decline, unless they consistently tap new value-creation sources. Authors of the book *The Alchemy of Growth: Practical Insights for Building the Enduring Enterprise* articulate this process: "A company must maintain a continuous pipeline of business-building initiatives. Only if it keeps the pipeline full will it have new growth engines ready when existing ones begin to falter." As such, sustainable value creation requires simultaneous management of three strategic governance-related horizons: Horizon 1 focused on extending and defining the core business; Horizon 2 on targeting and developing emerging opportunities; Horizon 3 on creating viable long-term options (Baghai et al., 1999). The search for new growth opportunities requires competitive resource allocation processes aimed at value creation over generations, to convert new ideas into viable businesses, with inherent financial risk (Sirmon & Hitt, 2003). As such, business development deployed as mergers and acquisitions, diversification, internationalization, and expansion into new markets counts as entrepreneurship, even if it doesn't always involve founding new businesses or obvious forms of product-market innovation (Le Breton-Miller & Miller, 2018). While this is also true for non-family businesses, one advantage of family businesses is their ability to make long-term decisions, thus giving them a leg-up when it comes to managing the three parallel strategic horizons. Entrepreneurial FBGs, moreover, possess valuable, rare, inimitable, and non-substitutable resources and manage them appropriately to produce value (Sirmon & Hitt, 2003: 341). In this context, we pose that FBG decisions regarding entrepreneurship and the management of related resources are made at the governance level, and the planning process and governance required to manage each planning horizon may differ.

Governance in FBG

Since Morck and Yeung study of "agency problems in large family business groups" (2003), research on governance has proliferated in the family business field (Gersick & Feliu, 2014; Suess-Reyes, 2017).

The classical three circle model suggests that family businesses are composed of three interacting systems—the business, the family, and the ownership (Tagiuri & Davis, 1996). The lack of separation between management and ownership in many family businesses has traditionally led them to be considered organizations with low or zero agency cost (Ang et al., 2000). However, as they evolve, so does the agency equation. Major research efforts have overlooked the governance specificities of family business groups, despite a few exceptions (e.g., Carney & Gedajlovic, 2002; Discua Cruz et al., 2013; Piana et al., 2018). Because of the multiplicity of owners in a FBG, the ways in which they are connected to each other and the differing goals they may strive for, a FBG is a context in which good governance can be critical. Setting risk and return parameters, generating capital from whatever sources are more advantageous, determining distribution amounts and formats, and driving and managing entrepreneurial initiatives while maintaining value creation, are specific governance tasks that further the owners' confidence in and commitment to the FBG as an investment. Therefore, the study of critical aspects of governance, such as the entrepreneurial activity, is an important contribution to the development of knowledge about the effectiveness of FBGs in various dimensions.

Method and Case Studies

We engaged in qualitative exploratory research using a multiple-case-study methodology (Yin, 2009). We conducted semi-structured interviews of CEOs and chairs of three Latin American FBGs, and multiple other primary and secondary sources to understand the firms' entrepreneurial histories (Miles & Huberman, 1994). We complemented this research with our findings from 20 + years of advising Latin American FBGs.

FBGs are especially common in developing regions such as Latin America. Many Latin American FBGs originated in the post-World War II era, due to the need to produce domestically rather than relying on developed-country imports. Moreover, Latin America has been a market economy with dynamic private sectors. From Mexico's Monterrey group to large Brazilian conglomerates, founders saw part of their mission as advancing the country through state-of-the-art technology and other offerings. Some Latin American FBGs, like Pantaleón (Guatemala), FEMSA (Mexico), Carvajal (Colombia), Simán (El Salvador), among others, have survived 100 + years despite multiple economic crises.

Their development, in general, centered on three pillars: expansion based on development of natural resources (mining, oil, agriculture, others); diversification of an industrial base; acquisition of financial, construction, and service firms. In the 1980s, the "Lost Decade," many Latin American governments stopped paying their debt, accompanied by contraction of GDP due to zero/negative growth. Privatization reforms of the 1980s/1990s gave rise to a second wave of large domestic FBGs. Moreover, just before the 1990s, domestic economies closed and FBGs' excess cash had to be reinvested locally, reinforcing diversification. Concurrently, foreign multinationals entered. This entry catalyzed international expansion of domestic FBGs. Some followed the path of free trade agreements: Argentina, Brazil, Paraguay, and Uruguay, for example, agreed to the Southern Common Market (Mercosur); Mexico forged a 1994 agreement with the US and Canada. The years between 2002 and 2008 saw Latin American FBGs go global—the age of "emerging markets."

Most large Latin American business groups are owned by multigenerational families and vary in form: extremely diversified versus concentrated with regard to their businesses, vertically controlled (pyramidal groups) versus horizontally controlled through cross-participation. Families' involvement also varies. Well-known examples of highly involved enterprising families include Luksic, Matte, and Solari (Chile), Romero and Brescia (Peru), Cisneros and Mendoza (Venezuela), Poma and Simán (El Salvador), Gutiérrez and Castillo (Guatemala), Camargo and Moraes (Brazil), and Slim and Bailleres (México).

Family-owned groups represent the most common organizational form in countries with volatile economies, market failures, poor regulatory/legal institutions, and corruption; these features incentivize internalization of transactions and risk-mitigation through smaller legally independent companies rather than in one large unaffiliated institution. FBGs' cost of capital is low, which was especially critical previously, when Latin American capital markets were small. Moreover, in volatile economies, family ownership with a long-term focus yields better results than traditional public firms at the mercy of short-term-oriented investors. FBG features including decisiveness, shared values, employee loyalty, understanding of local markets and consumer preferences, and connections with government agencies translate into strong competitive advantages. These groups are also seen as family organizations with objectives connected to the social/family milieu and related to succession, family harmony, pride, and national ideology (Del Giudice, 2017). For example, faced with the difficulty of managing sibling rivalry related to family employment/succession, many FBGs pursue development of business units or companies in different industries, providing each sibling a visible leadership role.

We placed particular emphasis on understanding the family legacies, values, and mindset influencing entrepreneurship. The three FBGs profiled are successful family business groups from Latin America, founded at least 100 years ago, and currently in the stage of development of advanced cousin consortium, with ownership control in the 4th generation of the founding family. Their family businesses span all areas of Latin America and operate in over a dozen different industries. They have their operating companies organized under a single Holding Company and have sophisticated governance structures and processes in place for their businesses and families. They have successfully—and sometimes unsuccessfully—pursued entrepreneurial activities at different levels of their business structure, and yet their reasons to become a group vary. They have been mostly influenced by the business context, the family risk appetite, and the availability of excess liquidity to reinvest in new endeavors. Table 8.1 provides descriptions of the three FBGs analyzed.

The profiled FBGs have consistently been characterized by an entrepreneurial orientation and desire for continuity of family ownership. Our research reveals how the FBGs' governance mechanisms have enabled them to transfer an entrepreneurial mindset across generations.

The data collected through the interviews was analyzed by creating categories for the different themes that emerged from the interviews and then segmenting these categories according to the models of entrepreneurship of each FBG case for further analysis. The analysis was complemented by our own observations on numerous Latin American FBGs over the years. The segmentation of findings by entrepreneurial model allowed for a better understanding of the role of governance in promoting intergenerational entrepreneurship given the unique role played by the antecedents to entrepreneurship in each case.

Table 8.1 Description of the latin American FBGs analyzed

Feature	Case I	Case II	Case III
Geographic presence	Central and South America, Mexico	Central and South America, US, Caribbean	Central America
Year founded	1904	1921	1906
Generation/Branches	6th; 4 branches	5th; 5 branches	6th; 4 branches
Development stage	Advanced Cousin Consortium, ownership mostly in G4	Advanced Cousin Consortium, ownership transitioning from G3 to G4	Advanced Cousin Consortium, ownership mostly in G4
Family values and mindset	Family Union; Respect; Integrity; Professional development; Spirituality; Trust; Social responsibility; Creativity; Modesty Global view of doing business. Reliance on innovation and cutting-edge technology. Reinvestment in business is optimal investment. Share ownership with good partners. Ownership-focused culture. Willing to accept failure as part of entrepreneurship	Family union; Preservation of family legacy; Prudence; Humility; Responsibility; Respect for differences of opinion; Excellence; Commitment to work/family Longtime diversification in market and industry. Strong leadership and autonomy of each subsidiary. Use of cutting-edge technology and expert knowledge/advice. Professional management hired and compensated for entrepreneurship. Increasing number of G4s with investor's mindset	Effort and tenacity; Social responsability; Ethics; Entrepreneurial spirit lost in transition from G3 to G4 "Entrepreneurial spirit with perseverance and social impact" inherited from ancestors (as per G3 member). G5 drives entrepreneurial agenda. G5 members have investor's rather than entrepreneur's mindset. "Family of entrepreneurs rather than entrepreneurial family" (G5 member)

(continued)

Table 8.1 (continued)

Feature	Case I	Case II	Case III
Business values	Innovation for value-creation; Winning attitude; Professional development; Impeccable execution; Collaborative spirit; Visionary and strategic; Sustainable relationships	Integrity; Sustainability; Quality; Responsibility; Honesty; Respect; Solidarity	Innovation for value-creation; Integrity; Excellence; Social responsibility
Industries	Longtime diversification; current focus on Packaging, Real Estate, Technology Services)	Diversified (mainly Retail, Real Estate, Manufacturing)	Hospitality, Shopping Malls, Real Estate, Vehicle Sales/Leasing
Role of family in business	Mostly engaged and governing owners, with some family executives including CEO. All operating business heads are non-family Employment of family formerly wide open, now selective by merit	Engaged owners, governors, and executives, including all subsidiary CEOs	Engaged and governing owners. Non-family CEO. Limited G5 engagement in corporate and ownership governance G5 members not expected to work in business. G5 manages venture fund

Feature	Case I	Case II	Case III
Legal structure	Portfolio of enterprises owned fully or partially by Holding Company. Separate investment vehicle for Family Office	Portfolio of enterprises legally bound by Holding Company (patrimonial)	Portfolio of enterprises owned by Holding Company. Separate investment vehicle for venture fund
Ownership governance structure	Holding Board that controls and directs all operating businesses. Majority independent (non-family) members	Institutionalized governance at ownership level with role of strategic architect for FBG. Holding Board with family and independent board members	Holding Board makes most ownership-related decisions
Business governance	Dedicated governance committee for each operating business, with regular meetings between committees and Holding Board. Separate board for Family Office with family members and majority independent directors; non-family Chairman	Board of Directors for each subsidiary, with family and independent directors, makes all business decisions	Single Board of Directors, all family members, controls/directs all business units. Venture Fund has its own board (de facto investment committee) with G5 members and independent directors
Family governance	Family Council, Family Assembly	Institutionalized Family Council, Family Assembly	Family Council (with Entrepreneur-ship Committee), Family Assembly

(continued)

Table 8.1 (continued)

Feature	Case I	Case II	Case III
FBG policies	Family Constitution that includes ownership-related agreements	Shareholders Agreement, Family Constitution	Shareholders Agreement
Definition of entrepreneurship	While innovation requires creating something new, entrepreneurship involves seizing opportunity and risking financial/human resources	Beyond innovation in existing businesses, entrepreneurship involves creating new endeavors within existing businesses or new companies in new industries/regions	Innovation applies to products/processes and requires creativity; entrepreneurship involves creating a new business venture idea from scratch, with risk-taking
Path & motivation to become FBG	Opportunities to use spare capacity and restriction on US imports motivated new export business alliances. When economies opened to international markets (new competition), shifted from diversification to innovation aimed at strengthening existing business. M&A is part of entrepreneurial activity	Aim to diversify by geography and industry, to mitigate risks, increase value creation for growing ownership, and harness knowledge/capabilities of family owners	Sale of original core business generated significant liquidity to support new ventures and invest in other industries

Feature	Case I	Case II	Case III
FBG entrepreneurship policy	Incentives for managers to act like owners. Some independent members chosen for entrepreneurial mindset. Entrepreneurial Fund supports family members' ventures, with goal of generating opportunities for family members (versus business growth)	Incentives for family/non-family executives when entrepreneurship is part of their role No specific policy on entrepreneurship, but Holding Board reviews/approves investments that involve new ventures	Long-term strategic planning process led by the two boards Operating business fairly conservative regarding new ventures, but G3 shareholders granted funds for G5 to create venture capital fund now owned by G5. Fund's investment policy includes rules for investing in family members' ventures

Three Models for Entrepreneurship in Family Business Groups

Our analysis of Latin American FBG evolution suggests three models of entrepreneurship based on underlying business structures. A specific FBG can demonstrate one, two, or all three models at different development points; they are not mutually exclusive. The three models do not cover all configurations used by any business to pursue entrepreneurial efforts, but are the most common ones we observed in Latin American FBGs. All participating FBGs used at least one of the three models. The models are:

1. Entrepreneurship at the subsidiary level.
2. Entrepreneurship at the business group level.
3. Entrepreneurship through separate investment vehicle such as a Family Office.

Model 1. Entrepreneurship at the Subsidiary Level

Here, companies seek expansion/growth aligned with any core business, mainly through innovation in their processes, products, or services, or through investments in the whole business value chain. The resulting, organic growth is more conservative and carries lower risk than that associated with new ventures. The entrepreneurial activity is typically embedded in the business's strategic planning process, through conversations between top executives and the board. In companies with several business lines, exploration of innovative ideas may be a responsibility of a corporate office or specialized committee. This is particularly helpful in multi-business companies with a single board of directors, given the time and expertise required to explore innovation across multiple disparate businesses. However, in companies where each business has its own corporate governance structure, each board is typically expected to discuss entrepreneurial innovation with the management team it oversees. Thus, it is important that those involved be highly familiar with the industry, market opportunities, and the company's resources and capabilities. As an example, our FBG Case #2 has diversified into multiple businesses in the real-estate space, each with its own industry-specific board.

Model 2. Entrepreneurship at the Business Group Level

The second model involves integrating all new ventures within the family business group, creating synergies among FBG resources and capabilities and institutionalizing their development within the group. This is the case, for example, for the creation of new subsidiaries or business units under the same holding company or conglomerate structure, with ownership distributed the same as any other business on the platform. The aim is usually to diversify by industry and region, and to deploy different talents (family and non-family) within distinct opportunities. In this model, entrepreneurship is pursued outside the traditional/legacy business.

The platform, in the case of our FBG Case #2, is a Holding Board with the role of "strategic architect." It offers resources (financial, technical, administrative), knowledge, and expertise for new ventures and supports entrepreneurs (family and non-family) while monitoring their performance. Once a new venture is created and has its own team and governance body, the platform's role shrinks, providing the new company more autonomy.

Also important in this model is to have a clear FBG mission or vision and an investment policy, or in its absence, a clear process through which entrepreneurial opportunities are presented, discussed, and approved, to ensure alignment of entrepreneurial efforts with shareholders' long-term vision.

For example, our FBG Case #1 initially diversified to decrease exposure to their country-of-origin risk, the preferred strategy of the owning family rather than the business. As motives can change over time, this second model is appropriate for families with medium risk-tolerance and a vision of more aggressive, diversification-fueled value creation. The process of entrepreneurship, moreover, requires clarity on who is responsible for seeking new opportunities; in our FBG Case #1, the drive to create and contribute to the FBG's value creation has become a true organizational feature. Family and non-family executives share the entrepreneurial mindset, and it is a criterion for ascending to relevant positions.

Also, the holding board is responsible for finding, analyzing, and recommending new ventures or investments, and decides allocation of resources and liquidity among the new ventures, current businesses, and dividends. The owners may or may not be involved in approving these pursuits, depending on the financial risk and level of authority delegated to the holding company board. When the FBG does not have a Holding Board, because it is formed by legally independent companies, but has shared family ownership, a committee or de facto board can be appointed to make all decisions related to and monitor new ventures.

In general, this model first requires investment in an adequate governance structure (Holding Board, Entrepreneurship Committee, others) at the business-group level, with sufficient collective knowledge, experience, and skills to guide the FBG through their vision and allocate group resources. Second is investing in developing family members to become good governors, to learn about family legacy and entrepreneurship (particularly its governance: to assess risks, evaluate key metrics, and manage talent); third is frequent reassessment of the FBG's vision and, within it, new opportunities for next-generation members. This model carries risk when the common platform fails to function well, such as bureaucracy or poor preparation among board/committee members, which may consequently fail to attract next-generation members to pursue/lead new ventures.

Two examples of this model are FBG Cases #1 and #2, which pursued multiple expansion opportunities with deep family involvement as operators/governors and oversight of a single board of directors.

Model 3. Entrepreneurship Through Separate Investment Vehicle

Under this form of entrepreneurship, the business family creates an investment vehicle independent from the operating businesses but capitalized with shareholders' funds, frequently called a Family Office. To create liquidity or diversify the investment portfolio, the vehicle typically pursues investments in equities or other instruments as guided by an investment policy stipulating asset allocation strategy. Since the investment vehicle serves a different purpose than the operating business, it is best to have a separate director group (or committee) with investment knowledge providing direction/control and defining investment parameters including risk (industry, currency, geography, stage of development, etc.), liquidity, and financial return, among others.

In some cases, families also use separate investment funds to finance new ventures launched by family members. Many businesses reach a point where they can't absorb more participants, and not all family members may be interested in working for the family firm, due in part to increasing geographic dispersion. But rising extended-family members often have an ancestral entrepreneurial spirit and will likely need capital, know-how, and other resources a family can provide for new ventures. For example, the fifth generation of FBG Case #3 provided a cash gift for fifth-generation members to create an independent investment vehicle for entrepreneurial pursuits.

Such investment strengthens emotional links within and between generations, along with collective motivation to further the family legacy, improving chances of continuity. Our research suggests it is paramount to define the fund's purpose clearly from the outset and to align all related rules, policies, and practices with interests of the family, owners, and business. For example, if the fund's goal is to grow the family's wealth, it may be advisable for the fund to own a larger stake of new ventures, such that success may benefit all shareholders, not just the entrepreneur. Or if the fund's main purpose is to support family entrepreneurs, then it should be associated with clear ownership exit mechanisms, to free up financial resources for future investments. Establishing a clear fund purpose will also provide guidelines for deciding fund sources, financing policies, participation of business/family in governance, and others; these should be transparent to all stakeholders and applied consistently. Finally, we recommend that families institute a dedicated governance body for an entrepreneurship fund, like an Investment Committee, preferably with external independent members experienced with early-stage investments.

Two examples of this model are FBG Cases #1 and #3, which established independent vehicles of investment.

Framework for the Moderating Role of Governance in Promoting Transgenerational Entrepreneurship and Value Creation

Using our case studies and observations of multiple Latin American FBGs, we have developed a framework for understanding the moderating role of governance in providing direction, control, and accountability for family-enterprise entrepreneurial activity. The framework illuminates the relationship between antecedents both internal and external to the family and outcomes for the business and family, including the moderating role of governance (see Fig. 8.1).

Our analysis shows that the motivations behind transgenerational entrepreneurship can be divided into three different categories: one related to the owning family (values and mindset), another to the business (family's vision for the business) and the last to the context in which the FBG operates at different points in time (economic, political, social, and family demographics). Overall, our analysis reflects how these input variables shape

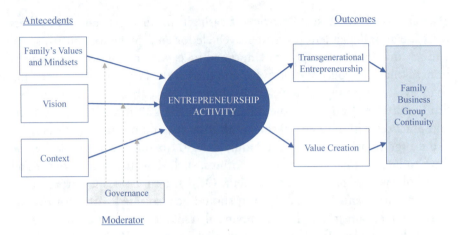

Fig. 8.1 Antecedents and outcomes of transgenerational entrepreneurship pursuits in family business groups and the moderating role of governance

the decisions around which model(s) of entrepreneurship to pursue and what structures/processes of governance to establish in order to govern the entrepreneurial activity.

Antecedents for Entrepreneurship

The antecedents/motivations behind transgenerational entrepreneurship include the family's values, mindsets, and vision regarding the FBG—which may differ by development stage—and the economic, political, and social context in which the FBG operates.

Enterprising Family Values and Entrepreneurial Mindset

We see the entrepreneurial mindset as the attitudes, values, and beliefs that orient a person or group toward pursuit of entrepreneurial activities (Lumpkin & Dess, 1996; Miller, 1983). Core values, mindset, and personality traits shape strategic options enterprising families consider for the future of their businesses, as influenced by narratives of the family business's history and longtime values and principles, typically those of the founder(s). Many families consider entrepreneurship a core value, an admired feature that often becomes part of their identity and DNA.

Research on family firms suggests family values and mindset can promote or constrain entrepreneurial activities. The decision to invest in entrepreneurship is unique in family firms because family interest and values are an integral part of the goals/strategies of a family business (Sharma et al., 1997). While some enterprising families demonstrate a culture that supports innovation and change, others may seek to maintain the status quo (Gersick et al., 1997) or may not perceive opportunities in their environments, suggesting the range of entrepreneurship-influencing mindsets in this domain.

More specifically, some families have an Entrepreneurial Orientation (EO) they are able to embed in their enterprise and make part of organizational culture—Alvesson defines organizational culture "as a shared and learned world of experiences, meanings, values and understandings which inform people and which are expressed, reproduced and communicated in a partly symbolic form" (1993, p. 2, 3). EO refers to the attitudes and practices within an organization that make it innovative, proactive, and risk-taking (Miller, 1983), and able to identify and exploit opportunities (Sirmon & Hitt, 2003). Some family enterprises tend to develop cultures that support inflexibility and adherence to path-dependent traditions, diminishing reliance on proactive entrepreneurial strategies (Hall et al., 2001). That might mean barring inputs from non-family executives or refusing to work with suppliers from outside the country of origin. EO, in contrast, enables an FBG to promote entrepreneurial activities, including through strategic governance decisions aimed at driving vision-consistent change and innovation.

We have also identified willingness to change as a core part of entrepreneurial families' mindsets. The literature has highlighted this as an important attribute of family enterprises to adapt to global competition and survive environmental shifts by capitalizing on new opportunities through rapid, effective change (Miller, 1983; Zahra et al., 2004). Some enterprising families avoid change because they believe it will cause conflict or be costly, or because they are unwilling to modernize. Such fear is associated with stagnation and loss of market share (Miller et al., 2003). In contrast, willingness to change is associated with innovation, organizational adaptation, and long-term viability, and distinguishes entrepreneurial families from less entrepreneurial counterparts (Hedberg, 1981).

In general, every family business was once a new venture, created by an entrepreneur with vision, will, and capability. Founders' passion, commitment, ability to take wise risks, and willingness to surround themselves with people who complement their weaknesses lead them to undertake new ventures, some of which may become viable businesses and thrive. In early stages, the venture's primary focus is to grow through a dynamic process of value-creating innovation. In this phase, it is straightforward to pass an entrepreneurial mindset from parents to children, including through modeling (example-setting) behavior, family narratives emphasizing entrepreneurship, and mentorship of children to develop aspirational ideas. Family business leaders can easily incorporate such antecedents to entrepreneurship into the family experience (Lansberg & Jaramillo, 2021).

As the family business system evolves (ownership atomizes as family grows over generations, business expands and becomes more complex), leaders' priorities shift. In the ownership circle, the business transitions from controlling owner to sibling partnership and then to cousin consortium and advanced cousin consortium. In this developmental process, business families often lose their original entrepreneurial spirit. On the one hand, as the business grows, day-to-day activities and long-term planning require a more robust structure, with more human capital, resources, and coordination. Moreover, generational transition typically requires alignment of the rising generation with a shared vision for the enterprise that incorporates their aspirations for the business, family, and governance of both. This increased complexity makes maintenance of entrepreneurial spirit challenging because (i) energy must be directed from entrepreneurship/innovation to address growing needs of the business, family, and ownership; and (ii) as family-members location and interests diverge, it is difficult to transmit the founder's entrepreneurial spirit across members.

Vision for FBG

Vision reflects the family's aspirations of what the FBG will become. Multigenerational FBGs are third- or later-generation groups involved in ownership, management, and governance, typically with collaboration among multiple generations. Such groups must rejuvenate and reinvent themselves to sustain previous generations' value creation and wealth levels (Jaffe & Lane, 2004). As such, entrepreneurship is particularly important. We and fellow researchers have observed that later-generation family members are often the driving force for entrepreneurship (Salvato, 2004; Ward, 1987). While family-firm founders are by definition entrepreneurial, their focus may shift to continuity over time, to steward the business for future generations (Aldrich & Cliff, 2003). Thus, ongoing entrepreneurship will likely depend on the group's ability to enter new markets and revitalize existing operations; family or non-family executives have to lead and manage new efforts and ventures. Moreover, as enterprising families grow, new generations/owners must focus on maintaining and enhancing value creation, to address the needs of the expanding shareholder pool.

In this context, the vision reflects what the family envisions for the future of the FBG: where they are going as a business family, and why. More specifically, the vision refers to what growth the owning family desires for the group, trade-offs between risk and return, desired liquidity, and the role of family in management/governance, among others. Some families seek to grow the family business legacy, for example, while others wish to diversify risk or strengthen bonds among generations. Whatever form it takes, vision can serve as a motivator (or inhibitor) of entrepreneurship.

Economic, Political, and Social Context

The third antecedent we identified is the context: the cultural, geopolitical, and macroeconomic circumstances in which the business operates, and the family's specific stage of development in terms of ownership. Hostile macroeconomic contexts force the business to seek new horizons/options to survive, boosting entrepreneurial spirit and capabilities. As our FBG Case #1 put it, *"necessity forced us to be creative."* In friendlier environments, business families may become more conservative, with no need to diversify risk to survive—that can promote an "if it ain't broke, don't fix it" mentality.

Similarly, the family's developmental stage matters. Earlier-stage, founder-run firms tend to be more flexible and take more risks, so conditions are optimal to innovate and venture, with decisions based on instinct versus complex financial analysis. In the second generation, some members may join the business, but it may be challenging to include all siblings, inducing to family conflict. As we've observed countless times, families in such situations often venture into new business lines to provide each sibling a meaningful professional career path. Since the decision is more family-driven than business-driven, family commitment to this path supersedes potential financial risk; thus, associated investment decisions are made with agility, often with consensus of siblings who work in the business. Later, when families transition into cousin consortiums, it's more common to have governance structures and formalized processes, with decisions based on alignment of opinions. Depending on family vision and entrepreneurial spirit, entrepreneurial activities may be carried through a separate investment vehicle such as a Family Office or Entrepreneurial Fund in advanced cousin consortiums.

Finally, the type of legal organization in place can help define the appropriate governance structure to support entrepreneurial activity. In companies operating as a holding company, without separate boards for subsidiaries, it is common to have specialized committees supporting each general manager in strategic planning and innovation, as the central board will likely lack in-depth knowledge of all businesses. However, in companies where each business has its own board of directors, those boards will work closely with business heads to identify and pursue entrepreneurial activities.

The Moderating Role of Governance

Governance affects whether and how FBGs pursue entrepreneurial activities, influencing the impacts of the antecedents discussed earlier (See Fig. 8.1). Building on Gersick and Feliu's (2014) study of family-enterprise governance, we use Goldbert and Di Furia's definition of governance: "the means of stewarding the multigenerational family organization ... [It] establishes the processes whereby: strategic goals are set, key relationships are maintained, the health of the family is safeguarded, accountability is maintained, and achievement and performance are recognized" (2009, p. 7). Entrepreneurship is likely to be prompted by deliberate governance mechanisms that reflect entrepreneurial family values and mindsets. Indeed, research suggests that governance promotes intergenerational transfer of knowledge and helps later generations offer new, diverse perspectives to modernize organizational objectives/procedures to keep pace with change and plan strategically for success in increasingly competitive landscapes (Handler, 1992; Sirmon & Hitt, 2003).

In general, family-firm governance mechanisms may be more complex than those of non-family firms, due to the interwoven systems of ownership, management, and family (Westhead et al., 2001), especially as the enterprise comprises multiple generations. As a moderator of FBG entrepreneurship, governance mechanisms can heighten the positive impact of the enterprising family's mindset and vision, including through multigenerational involvement. Governance is thus seen as an integrative component enabling individuals and families to better understand where the group is heading, reducing individual biases and facilitating learning, decisiveness, and knowledge transfer, to deploy FBG resources consistent with their entrepreneurial vision.

Overall, our cases reflect that the complexity of FBGs requires a more complex governance system in order for them to create value over time. They also indicate how the family's mindset and vision for the business, along with the business/family context, represent input variables that shape decisions around which model of entrepreneurship to pursue and the governance structures/processes needed to govern the entrepreneurial activity. Good governance is the most effective tool to provide direction/control for decision-making related to new business ideas, but it also requires educating all generations about family history and values as related to entrepreneurship. The cases studied illustrate how effective governance can enhance the transfer of the entrepreneurial spirit across generations, which has an impact on entrepreneurial activity and group growth.

Our analysis shows that governance plays a moderating role in different ways. To begin with, the governance architecture is to be designed taking into consideration the different levels of discussion and decision-making required to suit the chosen model of entrepreneurship. Allocating decision-making responsibilities at the right level is paramount to promoting entrepreneurial activity. It ensures that investment decisions have the adequate level of support and accommodates the family's risk appetite. As was described by our FBG Case #1, "*Our current strategy is for each subsidiary to have a strong and empowered board of directors, and for the holding company to act as an investor in the companies, providing room to each subsidiary board to look for new business opportunities.*" In this case, given that the family has a different risk appetite for the operating businesses and the Family Office, the place where investment decisions are made, and so the principles used in decision-making, are completely different for each.

Secondly, all governance bodies responsible for decision-making need to ensure the appropriate analytical support to make decisions, whether through internal sources or dedicated expert committees. The quality of these decisions, not only in terms of risk/return but also in the discipline with which these conversations and decisions are being addressed, plays a key role in institutionalizing the entrepreneurial activity and passing down the entrepreneurial mindset.

Thirdly, the composition of the governance bodies needs to be considered when addressing the aforementioned variables. The family members elected to the governance bodies have to be carefully selected. In all cases, FBGs also look at incorporating independent members with skills that complement those of the appointed family members. As a whole, these governance bodies are comprised of a group of people capable of supporting the FBG's entrepreneurial model, be it through engaging in conversations with management about innovation, seeking new business opportunities, or making sophisticated investment decisions. We have also observed that these members share the owning family's vision, values, and mindset. They demonstrate the right skillset to interpret the business and family contexts, as highlighted through Case #2, "*we make sure to include trusted former executives who have retired from the operation, as directors on the holding board, where strategic and entrepreneurship-related decisions are made. They have known us and the business group for years, and we respect their voice. And alongside them, we ensure that members of the next generation are involved. The combination of perspectives and learning between shareholders of different generations, and between shareholders and non-family members, has enabled us to get many decisions right.*"

In addition to the above, governance moderates the entrepreneurial activity through policies that support, promote, and incentivize the generation of ideas and search of new opportunities. That can be through incentive plans for management (as in Model #1), through policies that allocate financial resources or encourage the pursuit of new lines of business (as in Model #2), or through financial investment policies that align with the owner's vision / values or that finance family members' ventures (as in Model #3). The latter is exemplified through our FBG Case #1 which expressed, "*Our entrepreneurship fund supports ventures and ideas of family members; the goal is not to grow the FBG but simply to support family members to develop their own businesses, and through this, increase their sense of belonging with the company and reduce their dependence on dividends.*"

Lastly, some governance entities play a key role in educating family members in all aspects related to entrepreneurship in order to create more engagement. This is particularly applicable to Model #3. For instance, our FBG Case #3 explained that "*all family members are welcomed to the board meetings to listen and to learn... we also host meetings of cousins to inform about the investment outlook and the fund's activities so that they all are aware of what's going on.*" They also mentioned that "*the Family Council works actively on educating the large group of cousins about what it means to be an owner of an investment fund... the kind of engagement it has created in the sixth generation had not been possible before we established the investment fund.*"

Entrepreneurship Outcomes

As suggested by our model (Fig. 8.1), the key outcomes of entrepreneurship activity in FBGs are transgenerational entrepreneurship and value creation, which work together to help promote enterprising family continuity.

Transgenerational entrepreneurship is the maintenance of entrepreneurial spirit and business-building activities over generations. Successful FBGs reinvent themselves on small and large scales, within existing business lines and through new ones, as fueled by the entrepreneurial vision and mindset of each new generation. Their governance structures/processes help bring entrepreneurial visions and values to the fore, along with effective decision-making around which risks to take, and how.

Value creation, which goes hand-in-hand with transgenerational entrepreneurship, encompasses both financial and non-financial aspects, as related to the resources and capabilities firms use to gain advantage and earn above-average returns (Kammerlander et al., 2015). FBGs' unique value-creating potential may reside in their capacity to develop and leverage intangible assets such as social capital, trust, reputation, and tacit knowledge (e.g., Sirmon & Hitt, 2003). At the same time, economic and financial performance may be compromised in preference for creating/preserving socioemotional wealth such as perpetuating family name, values, control, and employment (Gómez-Mejia et al., 2007).

Together, transgenerational entrepreneurship and value creation contribute strongly to *continuity*, with the effects of antecedents on entrepreneurial activity moderated by governance.

The Table 8.2 below presents key governance themes our framework addresses.

The following table applies the components of our framework to the three models of entrepreneurship we identified (Table 8.3).

Conclusions

Insights for Owning Families and Practitioners

This paper extends knowledge of family business and entrepreneurship by providing a three-model framework for transgenerational entrepreneurship and value creation as moderated by governance practices. We advance previous research on how governance practices facilitate or hinder entrepreneurship, for instance by institutionalizing strategy work related to new opportunities and the transmission of entrepreneurial spirit and capabilities, as well as values between generations. Moreover, we posit that family businesses move from one entrepreneurship model to another depending on input variables, and can operate in more than one model simultaneously.

When designing governance approaches, the fundamental question is "What must be governed?" For FBG entrepreneurial activity, the answer lies within the input variables: family values and previous entrepreneurship experience, vision regarding growth and risk, and family/ business context—all will shape governance choices. Thus, for owning families and practitioners, our framework (Fig. 8.1) and identified governance-related themes (Table 8.2) provide a useful framework to explore options to foster intergenerational entrepreneurship and value creation. Enterprising families

Table 8.2 Fundamental governance themes the framework addresses

ANTECEDENTS

1. Family Values and Mindset:
- Family's attitude about risk-taking and entrepreneurship
- Family's values regarding entrepreneurship
- Role of entrepreneurship in the family's values, identity and legacy
- Link between the FBG's culture and the family's values regarding entrepreneurship?

2. Vision:
- Family's vision regarding business value-creation and diversification
- Family's role in the enterprise as a whole
- Role of the family in developing the entrepreneurial activity

3. Context:
- Effect of geopolitical, macroeconomic, social, and cultural conditions on existing business growth and on the need to pursue strategic diversification
- Maturity of the company and its industries of operation
- Developmental stage of the ownership (controlling owner, sibling partnership, cousin consortium)

GOVERNANCE
- Governance structures needed to govern the enterprise's entrepreneurial activity
- Role of family and independent members in governance structures
- Skills are needed to participate in governing the enterprise's entrepreneurial activity
- Decision-making responsibility around entrepreneurship
- Incentives in place to promote entrepreneurship (compensation, rewards, incentives, recognition)
- Policies needed to manage owners' involvement with entrepreneurial activity
- Policies to facilitate incorporation of entrepreneurship in FBG culture
- Support of governance to the stewardship of the family's entrepreneurial legacy
- Support of governance to the transfer of entrepreneurship-related knowledge/capabilities to rising generations

OUTPUTS

1. Value Creation:
- Contribution of entrepreneurial activity to creation of FBG value
- Measure of success for entrepreneurship activity
- Measure of value-creation
- Contribution of value creation to family enterprise continuity

2. Transgenerational Entrepreneurship:
- Transfer of entrepreneurial mindset, values, and skills to the next generation
- Incorporation of entrepreneurial mindset, values, and skills in the FBG as core competencies
- Contribution of transgenerational entrepreneurship in reinforcing the family's legacy and identity, thus contributing to continuity

Table 8.3 Application of framework to models of entrepreneurship

Entrepreneurship	At the subsidiary level	At the business group level	Through Separate Investment Vehicle
Family values and mindset	Willingness to take risks in familiar industries. Entrepreneurship or innovation as an embedded family/business value. Family committed to the legacy business. Enterpriser's attitude toward new ventures. Family identifies with founders' entrepreneurial identity	Willingness to take risks with opportunities in less-familiar industries Entrepreneurship as an ownership value (not necessarily transferred to business). Explorer's attitude toward new ventures. Family identifies with founders' entrepreneurial identity	Willingness to make higher-risk investments. Entrepreneurship as a family value. Investor's attitude toward new ventures. Entrepreneurship as tool for developing and empowering family members on managerial, governing, and ownership capabilities, and fostering cohesion/teamwork in next generation. Family identifies with founders' entrepreneurial identity
Vision	Focus value-creation on core business through innovation of products/services; new ventures within value chain of core business, or through geographic diversification Entrepreneurship as core cultural value and skill required in relevant executive positions. Family members promote entrepreneurship through management or governance roles. Strategic and business-driven	Seek incremental value-creation through industry diversification. Family members promote entrepreneurship as pioneers in new ventures or governance. Opportunistic and owner-driven	Use of spare funds to create reserve outside operating businesses. Allocation of funds for private-equity or VC-type investments as diversification strategy or to support individual family-member aspirations Family members promote entrepreneurship as entrepreneurs or through governance. Both strategic and family-driven
Context	Favorable macroeconomic, geopolitical, and cultural factors. Positive industry outlook. Starts with the founder and remains in latter development stages as entrepreneurship becomes organizational value/capability	Stagnation of core business due to increased competition or market saturation. Negative macroeconomic/geopolitical factors. Diverse business interests, skills, and capabilities within siblings/cousins family owners Usually starts in sibling partnership stage or cousin consortium	Investment-friendly environment Typically starts in cousin consortium stage although existence of spare cash and other liquidity aspirations may preempt decision to pursue this model. Likely aimed at keeping next-generation owners not working in core business engaged

(continued)

Table 8.3 (continued)

Entrepreneurship	At the subsidiary level	At the business group level	Through Separate Investment Vehicle
Governance	Decisions made at board level of operating business or subsidiary. Board members with in-depth industry knowledge CEO with high entrepreneurial spirit. Investment-analysis support from internal resources Within business, clear processes for development/approval of new products/services Executive incentive plans for idea generation and implementation Value-creation plans embedded in strategic planning processes, with high management-team involvement	Decisions made at Holding Board level. Holding Board with portfolio-view of business and broad, multi-industry knowledge Board members with high entrepreneurial spirit or clear entrepreneurship mandate Investment-analysis support from dedicated committee High alignment and collaboration between holding board and subsidiaries implementing entrepreneurship. Incentive plans for leaders identifying/pursuing business opportunities aligned with owners' values/vision Holding-level allocation of key financial/human resources to subsidiaries	Decisions made by board of independent vehicle Board members with expertise in PE or VC investments. Support from dedicated investment committee, usually with independent members Operating business as main source of funds for investment vehicle Incentive plans for investment managers recommending investment opportunities Investment policy aligned with owners' values/vision High involvement of next generation Policies for family participation as recipients of investments Communication with family through family-governance forums
Value creation over generations	Contribution to keeping core business growing, avoiding stagnation associated with mature industries/markets Success measured as sustainable short-term business growth and family-enterprise continuity	Contribution to incremental growth from new businesses Success measured as value-creation under medium-term horizon, and equity diversification	Contribution to growing family's wealth through investments in non-operating business Success measured as overall portfolio return under medium/long-term horizon
Transgenerational entrepreneurship	Entrepreneurial spirit and values passed to next generations as part of business culture and through owners' identity	Entrepreneurial spirit and values passed to next generations through their involvement in governance of direct participation in identifying/managing new ventures	Entrepreneurial spirit and values passed on to next generations through their development as entrepreneurs and/or governors of entrepreneurial pursuits

can adopt the model presented herein to diagnose their readiness to undertake entrepreneurial projects that will have a positive impact on the transmission of the family's entrepreneurial spirit and capabilities, as well as on the value creation capacity of their FBG. The model will also enable them to design their governance structures and policies according to which of the three models best suits their current motives and aspirations.

In conclusion, Latin American FBGs are undergoing generational transitions that may require adjustments to their governance models to address the evolving complexities of the family and the FBG. Some FBGs do not manage these governance transitions in a strategic and purposeful manner, as they do when it comes to business. The analysis of the cases herein presented illustrates that the entrepreneurial family's willingness and ultimate commitment to the effective governance of the FBG's entrepreneurial activity drive their ability to remain responsive to the interests of the next generations of owners and continue to create value. On the one hand, FBGs have the capital (financial resources, talent, expertise, access to networks, etc.) to be entrepreneurial; in many cases, their younger generations have been trained in entrepreneurship (which is now a common subject in many business universities), and some aspire to be entrepreneurs. On the other hand, due to political instability in the region, next generations, sometimes by their own initiative, and other times by a collective and strategic family choice, decide not to return to their home countries, instead embarking on entrepreneurial projects in the countries where they reside, study, and/or work, in order to contribute in the future to the shared family project. The framework we present here provides a strategic and systemic approach for owning families aiming to integrate entrepreneurial activity into their FBGs.

Limitations of the Study and Future Research Questions

As far as limitations, though our findings are based on work with many Latin American FBGs, we interviewed three in-depth for this study (one interviewee for each), suggesting the need to extend the research questions here to a broader sample and set of interviewees. Second, we recognize that this research is purely qualitative; future quantitative work could be aimed at areas including understanding the specific links among antecedents, entrepreneurial activity, and outcomes, along with capturing the hypothesized moderating role of governance. Third, in analyzing the role of governance, we included variables such as structure and incentives, leaving examination of others such as number of independent board directors, assessment of entrepreneurial pursuits and/or governance forums themselves, or interaction between formal governance structures in different parts of FBGs, for future study.

The study presents a detailed list of key governance themes related to entrepreneurship and value creation in FBGs that we have found to be relevant in the cases studied. Future research could explore the conditions under which the influence of one of the three antecedents—family values and mindset, vision and context—is dominant over the other two. Another interesting research direction would be to delve into case studies that retroactively trace the evolution of governance as FBGs and their entrepreneurial ventures evolve.

Finally, our framework suggests that the transgenerational entrepreneurship is an outcome of entrepreneurial activity, moderated by governance. However, future studies may address whether transgenerational entrepreneurship could simultaneously act as an input variable by affecting the family mindset regarding entrepreneurship, thus creating a circular framework flow instead of a linear one.

References

Aldrich, H. E., & Cliff, J. E. (2003). The pervasive effects of family on entrepreneurship: Toward a family embeddedness perspective. *Journal of Business Venturing, 18*(5), 573–596.

Alvesson, M. (1993). Organizations as rhetoric: Knowledge-intensive firms and the struggle with ambiguity. *Journal of Management Studies, 30*, 997–1015.

Ang, J. S., Cole, R. A., & Lin, J. W. (2000). Agency costs and ownership structure. *The Journal of Finance, 55*(1), 81–106.

Baghai, M., Coley, S., & White, D. (1999). *The alchemy of growth: Practical insights for building the enduring enterprise.* Ingram Publisher.

Carney, M., & Gedajlovic, E. (2002). The co-evolution of institutional environments and organizational strategies: The rise of family business groups in the ASEAN region. *Organization Studies, 23*(1), 1–29.

Casillas, J., Moreno, A., & Barbero, J. (2011). Entrepreneurial orientation of family firms: Family and environmental dimensions. *Journal of Family Business Strategy, 2*(2), 90–100.

Chen, M., & Smith, K. (1987). Samples used in strategic management research. *Best paper proceedings presented at the 47th Annual Meeting of the Academy of Management*, Athens, Georgia.

Chua, J. H., Chrisman, J., & Sharma, P. (1999). Defining the family business by behavior. *Entrepreneurship Theory and Practice, 23*, 19–40.

De Massis, A., Kotlar, J., Chua, J., & Chrisman, J. J. (2014). Ability and willingness as sufficiency conditions for family-oriented particularistic behavior: Implications for theory and empirical studies. *Journal of Small Business Management, 52*(2), 344–364.

Del Giudice, M. (2017). *Understanding Family-Owned Business Groups*. Palgrave MacMillan.

Discua Cruz, A., Howorth, C., & Hamilton, E. (2013). Intrafamily entrepreneurship: The formation and membership of family entrepreneurial teams. *Entrepreneurship Theory and Practice, 37*(1), 17–46.

Gersick, K. E., Davis, J., Hampton, M., & Lansberg, I. (1997). *Generation to generation: Life cycles of the family business*. Harvard Business School Press.

Gersick, K. E., & Feliu, N. (2014). Governing the family enterprise: Practices, performance, and research. In L. Melin, M. Nordqvist & P. Sharma (Eds.), *Sage handbook of family business*. Sage.

Goldbart, S., & DiFuria, J. (2009). Money and meaning: Implementation of effective family governance structures. *Journal of Practical Estate Planning, 11*(6), 7–9.

Gómez-Mejía, L. R., Takács, K., Núñez-Nickel, M., Jacobson, K. J. L., & Moyano-Fuentes, J. (2007). Socioemotional wealth and business risks in family-controlled firms: Evidence from spanish olive oil mills. *Administrative Science Quarterly, 52*(1), 106–137.

Granovetter, M. (1995). Coase revisited: Business groups in the modern economy. *Industrial and Corporate Change, 4*(1), 93–130.

Habbershon, T. G., & Pistrui, P. (2002). Enterprising families domain: Family-influenced ownership groups in pursuit of transgenerational wealth. *Family Business Review, 15*(3), 223–237.

Habbershon, T. G., Nordqvist, M., & Zellweger, T. M. (2010). Transgenerational entrepreneurship. In M. Nordqvist & T. Zellweger (Eds.), *Transgenerational entrepreneurship: Exploring growth and performance in family firms across generations* (pp. 1–38). Edward Elgar Publishing.

Hall, A., Melin, L., & Nordqvist, M. (2001). Entrepreneurship as a radical change in family business: Exploring the role of cultural patterns. *Family Business Review, 14*(3), 193–208.

Handler, W. C. (1992). Methodological issues and considerations in studying family businesses. *Family Business Review, 2*(3), 257–276.

Hedberg, B. (1981). How organizations learn and unlearn. In P. Nystrom & W. H. Starbuck (Eds.), *Handbook of organizational design* (Vol. 1), Cambridge University Press.

Jaffe, D. T., & Lane, S. H. (2004). Sustaining a family dynasty: Key issues facing complex multigenerational business- and investment-owning families. *Family Business Review, 17*(1), 81–98.

Kammerlander, N., Dessì, C., Bird, M., Floris, M., & Murru, A. (2015). The impact of shared stories on family firm innovation: A multicase study. *Family Business Review, 28*(4), 332–354.

Kraiczy, N., Hack, A., & Kellermanns, F. (2014). New product portfolio performance in family firms. *Journal of Business Research, 67*, 1065–1073.

Lansberg, I., & Jaramillo, F. (2021). *Family Entrepreneurship*. Chapter 10: Antecedents to entrepreneurship: How successful business families nurture agency and kindle the dreams of the next generation. Editors: Matt R. Allen and William B. Gartner, Palgrave Macmillan.

Le Breton-Miller, I., & Miller, D. (2018). Beyond the firm: Business families as entrepreneurs. *Entrepreneurship Theory and Practice, 42*(2), 527–536.

Lumpkin, G. T., & Dess, G. (1996). Clarifying the entrepreneurial orientation construct and linking it to performance. *Academy of Management Review, 21*(1), 135–172.

Miller, D. (1983). The correlates of entrepreneurship in three types of firms. *Management Science, 29*, 770–791.

Miller, D., Le Breton-Miller, I., & Steier, L. L. (2003). Lost in time: Intergenerational succession, change, and failure in family business. *Journal of Business Venturing, 18*(4), 513–531.

Miles, M. B., & Huberman, A. M. (1994). *Qualitative data analysis* (2nd ed.). Sage.

Morck, R., & Yeung, B. (2003). Agency problems in large family business groups. *Entrepreneurship Theory and Practice, 27*(4), 367–382.

Piana, B. D., Vecchi, A., & Jimenez, A. (2018). Embracing a new perspective on the governance of family business groups: A cross-cultural perspective. *European Journal of International Management, 12*(3), 223–254.

Ramachandran, K. S., Manikandan, K. S., & Pant, A. (2013, December). Why conglomerates thrive. *Harvard Business Review*.

Rosa, P., & Pihkala, T. (2017). Theoretical insights into the nature, diversity and persistence of business groups. Chapter 12. In M. Rautiainen, P. Rosa, T. Pihkala, M. J. Parada, & A. Discua Cruz. (Eds.), *The family business group phenomenon emergence and complexities*. Palgrave MacMillan.

Salvato, C. (2004). Predictors of entrepreneurship in family firms. *Journal of Private Equity, 27*(3), 68–76.

Sciascia, S., Mazzola, P., & Chirico, F. (2013). Generational involvement in the top management team of family firms: Exploring nonlinear effects on entrepreneurial orientation. *Entrepreneurship Theory and Practice, 37*(1), 69–85.

Sharma, P., Chrisman, J., & Chua, J. (1997). Strategic management of the family business: Past research and future challenges. *Family Business Review, 10*(1), 1–35.

Sirmon, D. G., & Hitt, M. A. (2003). Managing resources: Linking unique resources, management, and wealth creation in family firms. *Entrepreneurship, Theory and Practice, 27*, 339–358.

Suess-Reyes, J. (2017). Understanding the transgenerational orientation of family businesses: The role of family governance and business family identity. *Journal of Business Economics, 87*(6), 749–777.

Strachan, H. (1976). *Family and Other Business Groups in Economic Development. The Case of Nicaragua*. New York.

Tagiuri, R., & Davis, J. (1996). Bivalent attributes of the family firm. *Family Business Review, 9*(2), 199–208.

Talke, K., Sören, S., & Rost, K. (2010). How top management team diversity affects innovativeness and performance via the strategic choice to focus on innovation fields. *Research Policy, 39*, 907–918.

Ward, J. L. (1987). *Keeping the family business healthy.* Jossey-Bass.

Westhead, P., Wright, M., & Ucbasaran, D. (2001). The internationalization of new and small firms: A resource-based view. *Journal of Business Venturing, 16*(4), 333–358.

Yin, R. K. (2009). *Case study research—Design and methods* (4th ed.). Sage.

Zahra, S. A., Hayton, J. C., & Salvato, C. (2004). Entrepreneurship in family vs. non-family firms: A resource-based analysis of the effect of organizational culture. *Entrepreneurship, Theory and Practice, 28*(4), 363–381.

Zellweger, T., Nason, R. N., & Nordqvist, M. (2012). From longevity of firms to transgenerational entrepreneurship of families introducing family entrepreneurial orientation. *Family Business Review, 25*(2), 136–155.

9

Ownership Strategies in Family Businesses: A Conceptual Framework

Jari Sorvisto, Marita Rautiainen, Timo Pihkala, and Maria José Parada

Introduction

Ownership is an intriguing concept for research—while each business as a legal institution of property has an owner that has the right to protect the value of the business (Bell & Parchomovsky, 2004) and control the resources (Grossman & Hart, 1986), the widespread application of agency theory, and incomplete contracting theories and their strong orientation of incentives (Foss et al., 2021), has led owners to take the position of necessary silent viewers and delegating the direct control of the business to someone else.

J. Sorvisto (✉) · M. Rautiainen · T. Pihkala
School of Engineering Science, LUT University, Lahti, Finland
e-mail: jari.sorvisto@andritz.com

M. Rautiainen
e-mail: marita.rautiainen@lut.fi

T. Pihkala
e-mail: timo.pihkala@lut.fi

M. J. Parada
Department of Strategy and General Management, ESADE Business School, Sant Cugat del Vallès, Spain
e-mail: mariajose.parada@esade.edu

© The Author(s), under exclusive license to Springer Nature Switzerland AG 2023
M. Rautiainen et al. (eds.), *The Palgrave Handbook of Managing Family Business Groups*,
https://doi.org/10.1007/978-3-031-13206-3_9

This paradox of ownership has been dealt with different theoretical perspectives, each seeking to understand the owners' ability and willingness to affect their businesses, and each based on the assumption of cognitively homogenous individuals (Foss et al., 2021). The theoretical perspectives of ownership values, psychological ownership, socio-emotional wealth, and stewardship theory, among others, present approaches through which owners would be guiding the business despite the managerial and governance chain built for the effective management of the business. Foss et al. (2021) present that many alternative theories simply explain how to create and capture value and offer a solution to the ownership paradox as they introduce the concept of ownership competence. They suggest that the concept of "*how to own*" matters as it will define the way decision-making will be delegated to manage the distribution of rents. Competence helps to select the solutions required by the situation. However, when creating a strategy for ownership, the owner needs to look beyond this and create a plan on what the objectives of ownership are for the longer term and how they will be communicated to the organization.

As a relatively new concept, ownership strategy is a promising approach to solving the ownership paradox as it offers the owner a tool that would be directed and applicable to guiding the managerial and governance systems of businesses (Baron & Lachenauer, 2021; Chrisman et al., 2016). Ownership strategies are created for a specific need: the situation in the family, a certain question in the business, the need to control the group of businesses, or the proactive management of the family members' positions in the family business. Shortly, it has been explained as follows.

> The owning family together defines the values, purpose, objectives, and measures guiding the ownership. These, among others, are the basis for ownership strategy that creates the framework for the board of directors' decision making. (Finnish Family Firm Association, Recommendations for Family Firm Ownership, 2020)

Family businesses, ranging from single entrepreneur owned companies to business groups, are different from other types of organizations as well as from each other (Chua et al., 2012). Owners in a widely held public company are often investors while in family businesses relatively small groups of family members are focused on company development (Baron & Lachenauer, 2021). For family business groups, ownership is a major defining issue as groups' ownership arrangements seem highly complex. Jaffe and Lane (2004) suggested that as the company develops from a generation to the next and grows, the family in one way or another tries to maintain control over the company's assets through various agreements, councils, and structures.

9 Ownership Strategies in Family Businesses: A Conceptual Framework 225

Ownership goals and structures also complicate the management of the company. There may be different forms of organizations and levels of ownership which require management to have ability to balance their operations between family owners and public owners (Morck & Yeung, 2003). The complexity arises from several other sources as well. For example, ownership may not involve all family members equally. Furthermore, some or all the businesses within the group may be owned through another company and may involve non-family owners. An important aspect of complexity has to do with the capacity of owners to influence the direction of the company and to keep control in the hands of few members, thus concentrating ownership that allows making strategic decisions. This gives the possibility to succeed in influencing the strategy of the business, but also highlights the challenges of family businesses in dealing with ownership as the business grows and the family expands (Jaffe & Lane, 2004).

At present, a growing number of family businesses are building ownership strategies to meet their practical needs. For researchers, the development of ownership strategies' concepts and tools is still a challenge because the topic has been narrowly researched and there is no comprehensive structuring around it. Astrachan (2010) proposes that because many family-based factors affect the strategy development and implementation in family companies, there is a need for further research on how the family dynamics are influencing risk-taking, setting goals and investment decisions. When defining ownership strategy, we suggest that family businesses purposefully plan and define a path for how to manage their ownership. Therefore, the concept of ownership strategy implies a series of new questions. What is ownership strategy managing? To whom is the strategy aimed for? How is ownership strategy linked to the managerial and governance chain of the business? These questions are fundamental and still unanswered showing a fertile ground for studying ownership strategy issues.

To shed some light on this important yet underexplored concept, we develop a conceptual framework, where we identify four different types of ownership strategies in family businesses: ***ownership strategy targeting a single (simple) business; ownership strategy targeting the family; ownership strategy targeting a multiple (complex) business; ownership strategy targeting a complex family.***

We also suggest that "ownership strategy" may refer to four fundamentally different uses: to communicate the owners' expectations to the operative management of the business; to support family cohesion; to enable a systemic view over an unorganized set of jointly owned businesses; and to enable the systematic management of the family members' personal activities, wealth, and position as owners.

This chapter contributes to the research on family business ownership strategies in two ways. First, we argue that ownership strategies classification may be based on two main dimensions—the unit of analysis (single vs. multiple business) and the target of control (business or family) of the ownership strategy. Second, we introduce a framework of ownership strategies. The analysis of the four different types of ownership strategies leads to two main implications: first, to research ownership strategies, it is necessary to define the type of ownership strategy that is subject to analysis. In doing so, we also highlight the boundaries and main characteristics of each strategy type. Second, and linked to the previous, we point to the fact that each strategy needs a specific context and reason for being. Here, owners as central decision-makers are subject to making mistakes in choosing the type of ownership strategy they want to follow.

The chapter proceeds as follows: first, we introduce the framework to analyze ownership strategies. Next, we raise the issues of ownership strategy origin and ownership strategy dysfunctions into discussion. Finally, we conclude the chapter with practical implications and further research.

Ownership Strategies: Typology and Examples

Tagiuri and Davis (1992) presented a well-known model, where a family business is a business which interconnects three main elements: family, business, and ownership. A key feature of ownership that has been consistently highlighted in different studies is the level of ownership concentration and its consequences for managing and governing the business (e.g., Almeida & Wolfenzon, 2006; Hamadi, 2010; Nordqvist et al., 2014). While non-family businesses are usually characterized by highly dispersed ownership, where the interests of managers and owners diverge (agency theory), family businesses have been acknowledged for their ownership concentration, where the family gives direction to the business (Chua et al., 1999) and imprints values (Bee & Neubaum, 2014) to it. This in turn has important consequences for ownership strategy definition. For a family business, the creation of an ownership strategy is an intervention that seeks to make an effect. The ownership strategy is made by the owners, and it is a voluntaristic, intentional act (Smircich & Stubbart, 1985). Drafting the strategy, the owners act on free will and choose to be involved in the process. As an intervention, the joint

9 Ownership Strategies in Family Businesses: A Conceptual Framework

task of creating the strategy may affect the members' experience of shared understanding and mission.

Family businesses have unique characteristics that stem from the overlap of two distinct yet important social institutions, the family and the business, which portray a logic that can be conflicting but also harmonious (Carlock & Ward, 2001; Miller et al., 2010; Sharma, 2004). This overlap brings along simultaneous roles for family members who end up in governance and management positions. Family and business systems both have their own functions, and the outcome represents the goals, traditions, and values of the stakeholders in the system. In this regard, these features highlight the need to develop ownership strategies that incorporate the business and the family either in isolation or together, and the need to think about the complex nature of the family business as a social system. Based on these assumptions, we build our framework on two analytical dimensions: the target of control (the business or the family) and the unit of analysis (single vs multiple).

The Target of Control

As Barnes and Hershon (1976) already noted, transitions in the business and family can be separate events and there might be different motivations in either side, but they can be linked together as well. Therefore, ownership strategies may be controlling either the business or the family. In the business context, the natural choice would be to design an ownership strategy that tackles the business needs. In this case, ownership strategy would somehow position above competitive and corporate strategies, informing the board of directors or the operational management about the owners' expectations about business performance and lines of action. Following this line of thinking, making a difference between ownership strategy and corporate strategy would create a further challenge. Astrachan (2010) pointed out that the family owners' involvement in the business must be considered throughout the strategic management process. Therefore, the involvement of the family in management positions often overlaps with their roles as owners, making it difficult to separate both strategies.

The target of ownership strategy may also be the family itself. In family business research, the collectiveness and cohesion of the owning family are considered a success factor for the family business (Astrachan, 2003; Mustakallio et al., 2002). In this context, many of the ownership strategies have not been created to have control over the business but to bring unity and alignment to the owning family. In these cases, it is possible that the existence or the contents of the ownership strategy are not communicated to the operational management at all.

The Unit of Analysis

The unit of analysis in ownership strategies relies on a systems approach to the managed target. The system in the family business context can be the business in its different compositions and family in its different generational setups. Researching family business groups may also benefit from taking a systematic view; that is, changes in one element of the organization may affect changes in other elements. The main purpose of the systems theory is *"to describe a system in such a manner that automated control mechanisms can maintain the system's behavior at some desired goal"* (Dooley, 1997). That is, family businesses can be considered ranging from simple to complex organizations (Rautiainen et al., 2012). When the ownership strategy is directed toward the family, ownership strategy would concern, e.g., the collective ownership experience, joint experience of decision-making, or joint understanding of the ownership transitions (e.g., family business succession). Through these efforts, ownership could be *"a tool that, when deployed correctly, aligns incentives among parties and leads to high economic value creation"* (Foss et al., 2021). Communicated for the business, ownership strategy would be directed for the board of directors, the operational management, and the family members participating in the family business management.

On the other hand, ownership strategy may concern complexity in business or in the family. According to Kast and Rosenzweig (1972), systems include synergism. The whole is not just the sum of its parts; instead, there are hierarchical relationships within the system with multiple goals and purposes but at the same time organizations as organisms can be troublesome (Kast & Rosenzweig, 1972). Following the systems theory, to understand the whole system, the intricacies and dependencies of the various subsystems need to be controlled (Rautiainen et al., 2012). That is, ownership strategies building on the notion of complexity seek to take the multiplicity and variety of the managed target into account.

The Typology

Figure 9.1. describes four types of ownership strategies. Tagiuri and Davis (1992) suggested that when ownership and management are separated, the goals of the family and the company are not necessarily the same. The

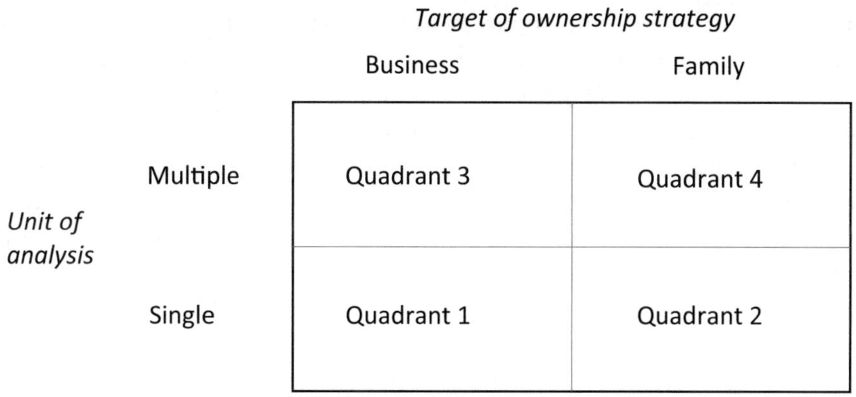

9 Ownership Strategies in Family Businesses: A Conceptual Framework   229

Target of ownership strategy

		Business	Family
Multiple		Quadrant 3	Quadrant 4
Single		Quadrant 1	Quadrant 2

Unit of analysis

Fig. 9.1 Four types of ownership strategies

typology of ownership strategies builds on this notion and suggests that each ownership strategy has been created for a certain purpose and that limits their usefulness for other uses.

Quadrant 1: Ownership Strategy Targeting Single (Simple) Business

At the early stage of the company life, the entrepreneurial process from opportunity recognition and discovery to exploitation and execution focuses on solving the practical challenges of a new business (Shane, 2003; Shane et al., 2003). The founder, usually in charge at this stage, is the main asset of the company and the entrepreneur who gives direction and identity to the company (Miller et al., 2010). Family, company, and individuals form a system that is meant to create wealth by targeting above-average returns (Habbershon et al., 2003) and the main goal for the owner is to get the company to survive and success. At that time, ownership strategy is tightly connected to the business. In many cases, the business is an extension of the owner. This might lead to a latent ownership strategy that can be still recognized, and the objectives of ownership are indirectly connected with the family welfare and how to improve it (Ikävalko et al., 2008).

The owners' strategy and intentions are important guidance for the owned business. Strategy researchers (Holmström, 1979; Katz & Niehoff, 1998; Kite et al., 1996) state that ownership is an important factor in aligning managerial decision-making with the best interests of owners. Yet in this quadrant, usually the owner and the manager are the same person, making this alignment easier. Seth and Thomas (1994) and Katz and Niehoff (1998) underlined particularly the importance of owners in strategy-setting. Strategic decision-making stems from the role of owners and risk-taking incentives of managers (Goold, 1996; Jensen & Meckling, 1976). Ownership strategy is where corporate governance meets strategic management (Wahl, 2015).

The importance of the family for a start-up or small business is considerable and complex. Families can be seen as primary assets in the business (Aldrich & Cliff, 2003) as families bring direction and sense of destiny to their companies (Chua et al., 1999). Through critical processes as decision-making and strategic behavior (Chrisman et al., 2005; Sharma et al., 2014), they inspire and move their companies to share family history, values, and emotions (Bee & Neubaum, 2014). Through ownership, the family as a shareholder has also the right to influence management decisions if necessary (Bethel & Liebeskind, 1993). Family members may participate on the management of the company (Harris et al., 1994; Litz, 1995), which is one critical factor for the company, because internal ownership has been evaluated to have clear positive effect on long-term performance of the business (Oswald & Jahera, 1991). In other words, when there is a clear overlap between ownership and management, the family or founder may appreciate strategy focused on the business rather than on the family.

Quadrant 2: Ownership Strategy Targeting Family

The ownership strategy focuses on the family ownership questions. In this quadrant, the ownership strategy may be kept as an internal document that is not communicated to the business. The collective identity of the family can be strongly built around the founder, and it develops by combining the perspectives of future generations with it (Hall et al., 2001; Parada & Dawson, 2017). The family ownership questions may include, for instance, family business succession, inheritance, joint understanding of the family values, and family or founder legacy. To deal with these, the family may start a strategy process to anticipate the forthcoming ownership challenges. A shared vision of the company's future will improve the owners' strategic decision quality and commitment (Mustakallio et al., 2002). Parada et al. (2019) have recently stated that successful family companies have adopted strong family virtues, like fairness, courage, and moderation which guide their decision-making.

According to Davis and Herrera (1998), the behavior of individual family members as well as the whole owning family is affected also by many psychological factors, such as group cohesiveness, conformance, diffusion of responsibility, deindividualization, and social power. This must be handled

9 Ownership Strategies in Family Businesses: A Conceptual Framework 231

properly, and as Astrachan and Kolenko (1994) noted, strategic planning, professional governance practices, and regular family meetings improve the business survival and success rate.

Quadrant 3: Ownership Strategy Targeting a Complex Business

For many family businesses, ownership strategy is playing an increasingly important role in managing the complex business structure. At the corporate level, the owners are those who need to decide which businesses should be included in the business portfolio and how to direct the units (Porter, 1989). Almeida and Wolfenzon (2006) presented that in this decision process, in the diversified family-owned business groups, the group tends to take pyramidal ownership structures because of economic reasons such as for better return of investment and financing advantages. Especially, if the group of companies is large, enlarged resources generate wealth for the family, and for that reason, owners themselves must evaluate, collect, compose, and use available resources also as a competitive advantage (Sirmon & Hitt, 2003).

Romano et al. (2000) stated that need of funding is necessary while the company grows, and therefore, financial decisions between multiple sources are also one of the most complex but important areas to cover by company owners. In this, for example, retaining the control rights directs decision-making in negotiations with private equity investors (Tappeiner et al., 2012). Usually, those investment decisions are based on controlled risk-taking and reliable outcomes (Patel & Chrisman, 2014), but as Phillips and Kirchhoff (1989) found out, a desire to grow is still one of the most important factors in the company's success and thus influencing the decision-making of the owner as well.

Family businesses that achieve a certain degree of complexity in terms of size, diversification, internationalization, and growth usually lead to wealth accumulation, separation of family and business assets and questions revolve around how to manage the business and the family wealth. In this case, the ownership strategy focuses on managing operational assets in an effective way and developing tools of wealth preservation, and sometimes even wealth distribution (e.g., philanthropy, impact investment, etc.).

Quadrant 4: Ownership Strategy Targeting Family Members and Complex Family

Families grow over time, and so does their complexity in terms of the number of members, interests, or life cycles, often generating misalignment of values and a divergent vision of the company's future. There is less and less room for individualism, but strong personalities or subgroups within the family can still guide ownership quite heavily and against the objectives of the majority (Pihkala et al., 2019).

The way how children view business ownership often, but not always, follows the thinking of their parents; that is, the parents' desire to keep the business ownership within the family will be transmitted to their children (Birley, 2002). Families that find themselves in this situation may become aware of the need to develop a sound ownership strategy that facilitates family cohesion, alignment of values, and the realignment around a common project. In this participative strategy process, altruism can have a positive effect within the family (Eddleston & Kellermanns, 2007).

The complexity of family ownership forces the family to build a more formal and structured way to handle extensive ownership and accumulated wealth (Jaffe & Lane, 2004). The ownership strategy when focusing on families with multiple family owners entails the capacity to dive into individual interests, cohesion building, and joint wealth management. Families may integrate family governance bodies such as family councils and family assemblies, to build cohesion around the common project (Jaffe & Lane, 2004), to develop psychological ownership, and to create bonds among family members. This strategy is also thought to develop responsible owners that aim to take care of their operational business as well as their wealth.

In large, diversified family businesses, all decision-making and ownership solutions related to both the family business and the wealth it generates for the family, require the management of large entities and the strategic planning of long-term ownership. Amit, Liechtenstein, Prats, Millay, and Pendleton (2008) found out that those very wealthy family companies usually have single-family offices (SFO) that act like private investment offices. A family office is one of the instruments, which wealthy families use to handle their social and economic position (Dunn, 1980) and it can be owned by the family or an independently owned tailor-made service provider (Newton, 2002). Zellweger and Kammerlander (2015) present four levels of development of family wealth management: uncoordinated family, embedded family office, single-family office, and family trust, which differ in the way how they govern family assets.

Discussion

The framework of four different ownership strategy types clarifies the concept of ownership strategy in family business. The challenge of any framework seeking to reflect understanding about the strategic nature of ownership in family business is for it to accommodate the diversity of families and business of different settings while retaining conceptual coherence. The framework in this study emphasizes the importance of the unit of analysis (single or multiple) and the target of control (business or family) of the ownership strategy.

The typology of ownership strategies raises a set of issues for further discussion. Due to the diversity of the subject, studying ownership strategy is a challenge. As Kepner (1983) already pointed out, the family business is a complicated dualistic system where the family system is tightly connected with the business system but without clear boundaries. Dyer and Dyer (2009) on their part stated that ownership of family businesses is difficult to research, because inside the owning family different family processes as well as ideologies are largely invisible. It makes ownership strategy research even more complicated that comparing with non-family companies, family businesses are different in the way how the family influences the company and how family members also might participate, in addition to owning, in the management of the company (Harris et al., 1994; Litz, 1995). Moreover, family businesses are heterogeneous (Chua et al., 2012), and therefore, a single ownership strategy might not equally fit all. Because of the challenging research area, we will next discuss the drivers of ownership strategy and some ownership strategy dysfunctions.

The Drivers of Ownership Strategy

The first and most interesting question is, why is ownership strategy created. In this chapter, we argue that ownership strategies are intentionally crafted to manage something. This would mean that ownership strategies are likely to be situation-specific. In another words, they are created for a specific need: a situation in the family, a certain question in the business, a need to control the group of businesses, or proactive management of family members' positions in the family business. For further research, these critical incidents leading to the formation of ownership strategy are of utmost importance as they are likely to affect the form, nature, and function of the ownership strategy. In the theoretical point of view, Flanagan (1954) describes critical incidents as human activities that can be observed and whose meaning and result are clear.

Edvardsson and Roos (2001) later added that those critical incidents need to be researched in the actual context. Pettigrew (1987) saw that changes in the industry are one guiding factor and might lead to critical situations and thus force the company to re-evaluate its strategy. When a family business ends up in a situation where change is needed, it is natural for the family to come together to consider solutions to the need. Whether the change addresses the current need, or whether it also includes long-term strategic planning, is another matter altogether. We encourage explorative empirical studies on the ownership strategies and especially on the motivations and needs leading to the creation of ownership strategy.

As Handler (1994) noted, in the family business context succession is one of the most important critical events. This occurrence has been seen quite complicated because within the family, setting of goals differs depending on unique systemic multidimensional interactions, and it is a dynamic and cyclical process (Kotlar & Massis, 2013). At some level, the family business succession usually means cultural change. Handler and Kram (1988) found out that there are resistances that can be individual, group, organizational, and environmental and they create problems in family succession planning. This process varies according to the generations' common understanding about company future, how experienced the successors are, what the company condition is, and how the older generation will participate in company operations (Harvey & Evans, 1995). Neubauer (2003) also analyzed the succession process and found out that there are also psychological and sociological aspects in the family, leadership, organization, and ownership side in addition to business-related factors that are guiding the business side more heavily. Chua et al. (1999) suggest that the involvement cannot be used as the only differentiable factor but should be supported by factors like vision, intentions, and behavior. All these findings highlight a variety of factors related to the succession situation in the family business that influences the development of the ownership strategy, but at the same time they highlight the differences between distinct ownership strategies.

Dysfunctions of Ownership Strategy

It is evident that the mere existence of ownership strategy is not enough. The strategy needs to deal with the right topics, concern the right targets, be timely, and be communicated to the right audience. From this perspective, ownership strategies are likely to suffer from different dysfunctions.

Chrisman et al. (2016) stated that currently we do not know much about how family firm decisions are made. They open questions related to

9 Ownership Strategies in Family Businesses: A Conceptual Framework

management as well as strategies of family firms, for example how the family formulates strategic goals, how the goals and competitive advantages can be matched, and how the family influences the strategic decisions of the company's resources. Foss et al. (2021) suggest that *what, how, and when to own* are fundamental questions in ownership decisions and they ensure the right kind of skills from the owner. The concept of ownership strategy is building on the assumption that the family or its members would be able to make these decisions and deal with them effectively. However, Akhter et al. (2021) showed that the strategic decisions originating from the family may also include high risks that the family cannot manage due to the different generations, experience, and goals of the family members. Furthermore, the interrelationships between the companies owned by the same family may lead to chain reactions (Akhter et al., 2021). To understand the ownership strategy process more comprehensively, we will need more research of the motives, styles, and driving forces which will affect the strategy decision process.

However, it is likely that many families will face challenges in the process of running the strategic decision-making. In these cases, the decision-makers are affected by their cognitive limits, bounded rationality, and satisficing effects (Cyert & March, 1963). The strategic decisions about ownership are thus important targets for further research. For example, Winter et al. (2004) called for more research on how owners choose to invest their resources in business and whether they stay in or exit from the business. Furthermore, creating or acquiring new ventures may challenge the ownership dynamics that support the survival of a firm in the hands of a family (Johannisson & Huse, 2000). Also managing the dynamics within a growing and multi-generational family is a challenging entity itself, but in the family business context it is further complicated. Therefore, successful transitions of business require good relationships within the family, based on trust and affability between family members (Morris et al., 1997). This is by no means self-evident. According to Davis and Harveston (1999), especially in later generation family businesses, the founders' decision to stay in the company may create conflicts in the extended family. Different entry angles of ownership strategy could be the answers to the way management is able to solve these problems.

Conclusions

To conclude, our study raises a set of ideas to consider in further research. First, in this study, we argue that family and company goals are often of different types (Tagiuri & Davis, 1992), which is why family and company ownership strategies differ. It is difficult, if not impossible, to create a comprehensive ownership strategy that describes the needs and wishes of different companies, families, and individuals.

Furthermore, by dividing ownership strategies into different types, they can be identified and better researched. Ownership strategies are created when the situation so requires and are different from each other due to the heterogeneity of companies and families. In the development and implementation of the ownership strategy, it is advantageous if the family has skills related to the context (Foss et al., 2021), but often this is not the case as the family is mainly an expert in its own business. The growth of both the family (Jaffe & Lane, 2004) and the company (Almeida & Wolfenzon, 2006), on the other hand, forces the creation of more formal structures for defining and managing ownership strategy. An ownership strategy essentially involves detaching oneself from the business strategy and considering the longer-term goals of ownership and how they are communicated to the company or family.

The ownership strategy in the context of a family business, in its complexity and diversity is an interesting but at the same time a challenging field of research. The suggested four ownership strategy types indicating significant changes from each other provide a good basis for further research, where empirical research can identify the distinguishing features of each type and the factors that affect each other.

References

Akhter, N., Rautiainen, M., Pihkala, T., & Ikäheimonen, T. (2021). The risk that became true—Case study of a Pakistani family business portfolio diversification. In F.-L. T. Yu & H.-D. Yan (Eds.), *The Routledge companion to Asian family business—Governance, succession, and challenges in the age of digital disruption.* Routledge.

Aldrich, H. E., & Cliff, J. E. (2003). The pervasive effects of family on entrepreneurship: Toward a family embeddedness perspective. *Journal of Business Venturing, 18*(5), 573–596.

Almeida, H. V., & Wolfenzon, D. (2006). A theory of pyramidal ownership and family business groups. *The Journal of Finance, 61*(6), 2637–2680.

Amit, R., Liechtenstein, H., Prats, M. J., Millay, T., & Pendleton, L. P. (2008). Single family offices: Private wealth management in the family context. In J. Tàpies & J. L. Ward (Eds.), *Family values and value creation. The fostering of enduring values within family-owned business.* Palgrave Macmillan.

Astrachan, J. H. (2003). Commentary on the special issue: The emergence of a field. *Journal of Business Venturing, 18*(5), 567–573.

Astrachan, J. H. (2010). Strategy in family business: Toward a multidimensional research agenda. *Journal of Family Business Strategy, 1*(1), 6–14.

Astrachan, J. H., & Kolenko, T. A. (1994). A neglected factor explaining family business success: Human resource practices. *Family Business Review, 7*(3), 251–262.

Barnes, L. B., & Hershon, S. A. (1976). Transferring power in the family business. *Harvard Business Review, 54*(4), 105–114.

Baron, J., & Lachenauer, R. (2021). *Harvard business review family business handbook: How to build and sustain a successful, enduring enterprise.* Harvard Business Press.

Bell, A., & Parchomovsky, G. (2004). A theory of property. *Cornell Law Review, 90,* 531.

Bee, C., & Neubaum, D. O. (2014). The role of cognitive appraisal and emotions of family members in the family business system. *Journal of Family Business Strategy, 5*(3), 323–333.

Bethel, J. E., & Liebeskind, J. (1993). The effects of ownership structure on corporate restructuring. *Strategic Management Journal, 14*(S1), 15–31.

Birley, S. (2002). Attitudes of owner-managers' children towards family and business issues. *Entrepreneurship Theory and Practice, 26*(3), 5–19.

Carlock, R. S., & Ward, J. L. (2001). *Strategic planning for the family business: Parallel planning to unify the family and business.* Palgrave.

Chrisman, J. J., Chua, J. H., & Sharma, P. (2005). Trends and directions in the development of a strategic management theory of the theory of the family firm. *Entrepreneurship Theory and Practice, 29*(5), 555–575.

Chrisman, J. J., Chua, J. H., De Massis, A., Minola, T., & Vismara, S. (2016). Management processes and strategy execution in family firms: From "what" to "how." *Small Business Economics, 47*(3), 719–734.

Chua, J. H., Chrisman, J. J., & Sharma, P. (1999). Defining the family business by behavior. *Entrepreneurship Theory and Practice, 23*(4), 19–39.

Chua, J. H., Chrisman, J. J., Steier, L. P., & Rau, S. B. (2012). Sources of heterogeneity in family firms: An introduction. *Entrepreneurship Theory and Practice, 36*(6), 1103–1113.

Cyert, R., & March, J. (1963). *A behavioral theory of the firm.* Prentice-Hall.

Davis, J. A., & Herrera, R. M. (1998). The social psychology of family shareholder dynamics. *Family Business Review, 11*(3), 253–260.

Davis, P. S., & Harveston, P. D. (1999). In the founder's shadow: Conflict in the family firm. *Family Business Review, 12*(4), 311–323.

Dooley, K. J. (1997). Complex adaptive systems model of organization change. *Nonlinear Dynamics, Psychology, and Life Sciences, 1*(1), 69–97.

Dunn, M. G. (1980). The family office as a coordinating mechanism within the ruling class. *Insurgent Sociologist, 9*(2–3), 8–23.

Dyer, W. G., Jr., & Dyer, W. J. (2009). Putting the family into family business research. *Family Business Review, 22*(3), 216–219.

Eddleston, K. A., & Kellermanns, F. W. (2007). Destructive and productive family relationships: A stewardship theory perspective. *Journal of Business Venturing, 22*(4), 545–565.

Edvardsson, B., & Roos, I. (2001). Critical incident techniques. *International Journal of Service Industry Management.*

Flanagan, J. C. (1954). The critical incident technique. *Psychological Bulletin, 51*(4), 327.

Foss, N. J., Klein, P. G., Lien, L. B., Zellweger, T., & Zenger, T. (2021). Ownership competence. *Strategic Management Journal, 42*(2), 302–328.

Goold, M. (1996). The (limited) role of the board. *Long Range Planning, 29*(4), 572–575.

Grossman, S. J., & Hart, O. D. (1986). The costs and benefits of ownership: A theory of vertical and lateral integration. *Journal of Political Economy, 94*(4), 691–719.

Habbershon, T. G., Williams, M., & MacMillan, I. C. (2003). A unified systems perspective of family firm performance. *Journal of Business Venturing, 18*(4), 451–465.

Hall, A., Melin, L., & Nordqvist, M. (2001). Entrepreneurship as radical change in the family business: Exploring the role of cultural patterns. *Family Business Review, 14*(3), 193–208.

Hamadi, M. (2010). Ownership concentration, family control and performance of firms. *European Management Review, 7*(2), 116–131.

Handler, W. C. (1994). Succession in family business: A review of the research. *Family Business Review, 7*(2), 133–157.

Handler, W. C., & Kram, K. E. (1988). Succession in family firms: The problem of resistance. *Family Business Review, 1*(4), 361–381.

Harris, D., Martinez, J. I., & Ward, J. L. (1994). Is strategy different for the family-owned business? *Family Business Review, 7*(2), 159–174.

Harvey, M., & Evans, R. (1995). Life after succession in the family business: Is it really the end of problems? *Family Business Review, 8*(1), 3–16.

Holmström, B. (1979). Moral hazard and observability. *Bell Journal of Economics, 10*(1), 74–91.

Ikävalko, M., Pihkala, T., & Jussila, I. (2008). A family dimension in SME owner-managers ownership profiles—A psychological ownership perspective. *Electronic Journal of Family Business Studies.*

Jaffe D., & Lane S. (2004). Sustaining a family dynasty. Key issues facing complex multigenerational business- and investment-owning families. *Family Business Review, 17*(1), 81–98.

Jensen, M. C., & Meckling, W. H. (1976). Theory of the firm: Managerial behavior, agency costs and ownership structure. *Journal of Financial Economics, 3*(4), 305–360.

9 Ownership Strategies in Family Businesses: A Conceptual Framework 239

Johannisson, B., & Huse, M. (2000). Recruiting outside board members in the small family business: An ideological challenge. *Entrepreneurship & Regional Development, 12*(4), 353–378.

Kast, F. E., & Rosenzweig, J. E. (1972). General systems theory: Applications for organization and management. *Academy of Management Journal, 15*, 447–465.

Katz, J. P., & Niehoff, B. P. (1998). How owners influence strategy—A comparison of owner-controlled and manager-controlled firms. *Long Range Planning, 31*(5), 755–761.

Kepner, E. (1983). The family and the firm: A coevolutionary perspective. *Organizational Dynamics, 12*(1), 57–70.

Kite, D., Katz, J., & Zarzeski, M. (1996). Can managers appraise performance too often? *Journal of Applied Business Research, 13*(1), 41–51.

Kotlar, J., & De Massis, A. (2013). Goal setting in family firms: Goal diversity, social interactions, and collective commitment to family-centered goals. *Entrepreneurship Theory and Practice, 37*(6).

Litz, R. A. (1995). The family business: Toward definitional clarity. *Family Business Review, 8*(2), 71–81.

Miller, D. L., Breton-Miller, I., & Lester, R. (2010). Family ownership and acquisition behavior in publicly traded companies. *Strategic Management Journal, 31*, 201–223.

Morris, M. H., Williams, R. O., Allen, J. A., & Avila, R. A. (1997). Correlates of success in family business transitions. *Journal of Business Venturing, 12*(5), 385–401.

Morck, R., & Yeung, B. (2003). Agency problems in large family business groups. *Entrepreneurship Theory and Practice, 27*(4), 367–382.

Mustakallio, M., Autio, E., & Zahra, S. A. (2002). Relational and contractual governance in family firms: Effects on strategic decision making. *Family Business Review, 15*(3), 205–222.

Neubauer, H. (2003). The dynamics of succession in family businesses in western European countries. *Family Business Review, 16*(4), 269–281.

Newton, C. (2002). Adopting the Family Office. *Journal of Financial Planning, 15*(6), 66–74.

Nordqvist, M., Sharma, P., & Chirico, F. (2014). Family firm heterogeneity and governance: A configuration approach. *Journal of Small Business Management, 52*(2), 192–209.

Oswald, S. L., & Jahera, J. S., Jr. (1991). The influence of ownership on performance: An empirical study. *Strategic Management Journal, 12*(4), 321–326.

Patel, P. C., & Chrisman, J. J. (2014). Risk abatement as a strategy for R&D investments in family firms. *Strategic Management Journal, 35*(4), 617–627.

Parada, M. J., & Dawson, A. (2017). Building family business identity through transgenerational narratives. *Journal of Organizational Change Management*.

Parada, M. J., Samara, G., Dawson, A., & Bonet, E. (2019). Prosperity over time and across generations: The role of values and virtues in family businesses. *Journal of Organizational Change Management*.

Pettigrew, A. M. (1987). Context and action in the transformation of the firm. *Journal of Management Studies, 24*(6), 649–670.

Phillips, B. D. & Kirchhoff, B. A. (1989). Formation, growth and survival; Small firm dynamics in the U.S. economy. *Small Business Economics, 1*(1), 65–74.

Pihkala, T. Goel, S. Rautiainen, M. Mukherjee, K., & Ikävalko, M. (2019). Deciphering ownership of family business groups. In M. Rautiainen, P. Rosa, T. Pihkala, M.-J. Parada, & A. Discua Cruz (Eds.), *The family business group phenomenon—Emergence and Complexities* (pp. 223–252). Palgrave Macmillan.

Porter, M. E. (1989). From competitive advantage to corporate strategy. In *Readings in strategic management* (pp. 234–255). Palgrave.

Rautiainen, M., Pihkala, T., & Ikävalko, M. (2012). Family business system models—A Case study and some implications of open systems perspective. *Journal of Small Business & Entrepreneurship, 25*(2), 155–168.

Romano, C. A., Tanewski, G. A., & Smyrnios, K. X. (2000). Capital structure decision making: A model for family business. *Journal of Business Venturing, 16*(3), 285–310.

Seth, A., & Thomas, H. (1994). Theories of the firm: Implications for strategy research. *Journal of Management Studies, 31*(2), 165–191.

Shane, S. (2003). *A general theory of entrepreneurship: The individual-opportunity nexus*. Edward Elgar.

Shane, S., Locke, E. A., & Collins, C. J. (2003). Entrepreneurial motivation. *Human Resource Management Review, 13*(2), 257–279.

Sharma, P. (2004). An overview of the field of family business studies: Current status and directions for the future. *Family Business Review, 17*(1), 1–36.

Sharma, R., Mithas, S., & Kankanhalli, A. (2014). Transforming decision-making processes: A research agenda for understanding the impact of business analytics on organisations. *European Journal of Information Systems, 23*(4), 433–441.

Sirmon, D. G., & Hitt, M. A. (2003). Managing resources: Linking unique resources, management, and wealth creation in family firms. *Entrepreneurship Theory and Practice, 27*(4), 339–358.

Smircich, L., & Stubbart, C. (1985). Strategic management in an enacted world. *Academy of Management Review, 10*(4), 724–736.

Tagiuri, R., & Davis, J. A. (1992). On the goals of successful family companies. *Family Business Review, 5*(1), 43–62.

Tappeiner, F., Howorth, C., Achleitner, A. K., & Schraml, S. (2012). Demand for private equity minority investments: A study of large family firms. *Journal of Family Business Strategy, 3*(1), 38–51.

Wahl, M. F. (2015). Strategic audit and ownership strategy. *International Journal of Business and Social Research, 5*(9), 93–100.

Winter, M., Danes, S. M., Koh, S.-K., Fredricks, K., & Paul, J. J. (2004). Tracking family businesses and their owners over time: Panel attrition, manager departure and business demise. *Journal of Business Venturing, 19*, 535–559.

Zellweger, T., & Kammerlander, N. (2015). Family, wealth, and governance: An agency account. *Entrepreneurship Theory and Practice, 39*(6), 1281–1303.

10

Family Business Groups in Advanced Asian Economies and the Politics of Institutional Trust

Michael Carney and Zhixiang Liang

Introduction

The emblematic corporate structure in Asia's emerging markets is the family-controlled business group (FBG) (Carney et al., 2009). An emblematic form is an organizational structure best adapted to grasp opportunities available in local institutional environments (Boyer, 2005). However, institutions change, and if FBGs are to remain relevant, they should evolve to respond to shifting institutional imperatives. A prominent perspective on BG evolution is the institutional voids (IV) view (Khanna & Rivkin, 2001). The IV view suggests BGs emerge to solve the problem of missing market-supporting institutions' and predicts BGs' competitive advantage will wither when those market institutions develop. Hence, the expectation is that BGs will fade, restructure, and eventually disappear (Carney et al., 2018; Hoskisson et al., 2005).

M. Carney
John Molson School of Management, Concordia University, Montreal, QC, Canada
e-mail: michael.carney@concordia.ca

Z. Liang (✉)
School of Administrative Studies, York University, Toronto, ON, Canada
e-mail: Zliang@yorku.ca

© The Author(s), under exclusive license to Springer Nature Switzerland AG 2023
M. Rautianen et al. (eds.), *The Palgrave Handbook of Managing Family Business Groups*,
https://doi.org/10.1007/978-3-031-13206-3_10

241

However, BGs have displayed unpredicted resilience in the face of institutional development. In a review of the literature Granovetter (2005, p. 445) concludes that 'there is, in fact, considerable evidence that since the mid-twentieth century BGs have typically defied predictions of their imminent demise surviving the conscious attempts by politicians to break them up and the impact of financial crises'. Indeed, a growing body of the literature suggests BGs do certainly adapt to institutional development by internationalizing their scope, learning new capabilities (Mahmood et al., 2011) and adopting modern management practices (Liang & Carney, 2020).

An alternative institutional explanation is offered by advocates of an entrenchment and elite capture (EE) perspective (Fogel, 2006; Morck et al., 2005). In the EE view, developmental states create FBGs to orchestrate a 'big push' toward economic and industrial modernization. If they successfully realize their industrial goal, FBGs become dominant actors in the economy and seek to entrench their market power by forming political ties with political and regulatory elites. Political ties are predicated on the reciprocal giving and granting of favours over long periods. Well-placed state actors can support business groups by introducing policies that protect their interests, such as favourable credit terms, subsidies, and international trade barriers, suggesting business interests co-opt political elites (Fogel, 2006). Subsequently, FBGs retain prominence by diversifying into a wide range of activities that minimize macroeconomic risk (Morck, 2010). In this view, BG's initially emerge under weak institutional conditions, but they rarely restructure and disappear. Instead, through entrenchment and elite capture processes, multigenerational FBGs may gain eternal life, where 'old money' families lose their entrepreneurial vitality but defend and perpetuate their wealth. In Morck's terms, FBGs become 'the undead' (2010) and drag on economic growth (Morck et al., 1998).

This chapter considers the strategic and structural evolution of FBGs in three Asian states, China, Korea, and Malaysia, which have exhibited significant economic growth and institutional advancement in recent decades. In particular, we document how FBGs in these economies have successfully adopted administrative and technical innovations, which have raised their efficiency to levels found in advanced economies. However, we argue that multigenerational FBGs have retained their original personalized governance practices. Established by their founders, FBGs governance structures are now considered anachronistic since they continue to rely upon personal control (Üsdiken, 2012) and traditional authority (Zucker, 1986) rather than adopt rational-legal forms of organizational governance. We explain this typical pattern of FBG governance persistence in three economies with reference to the concept of institutional trust (Bachmann & Inkpen, 2011; Shapiro, 1987; Zucker, 1986). Institutional trust is the extent to which market participants have confidence in robust principal-agent relationships and the impersonal authority that support their functioning (Rousseau et al., 1998). In the context of our study, institutional trust underpins the efficacy of rational-legal forms of authority and the institutions that rest upon this foundation (Portes & Vickstrom, 2011).

Both the IV and EE perspectives of institutional development focus on the state's role in creating solid market-supporting institutions. Despite their social and economic achievements, we argue that the three economies considered here have not yet fully realized the creation of such institutions. Theoretically, we suggest that both IV and EE perspectives on institutional development overlook the political conditions needed to produce institutional trust required for the continuing evolution of FBGs governance structures. We identify persistent economic (Korea), political (China), and ethnic (Malaysia) inequalities that perpetuate low levels of institutional trust in their host country's market-supporting institutions and FBGs' retention of personalized governance structures.

Institutional Trust & Mistrust

We highlight the role of institutional trust because both the IV and EE perspectives depict market-supporting institutions in terms of North's (1990) conception of institutions as the 'rules of the game'. Consequently, research in both the institutional voids (Khanna & Rivkin, 2001) and law and finance traditions (La Porta et al., 1998) use *de jure* institutions. Scholars measure such institutions by the quality of 'rules on the book' in the form of indices that reflect written codes and regulations (Hallward-Driemeier et al., 2015). However, one difficulty with rules on the book standards is that they do not indicate institutional effectiveness, the extent to which market participants have confidence in them. For example, research reports evidence of *de jure* worldwide convergence upon 'best practice' codes of good governance, but much less evidence that the relevant authorities enforce such regulations (Khanna et al., 2006). Further, many states have enacted strong minority investor protection rules (Guillén & Capron, 2016). However, many stock markets exhibit little liquidity, as minority investors refrain from participating because they do not expect their stakes to be protected if the rules are breached (Yenkey, 2018).

Sociologists distinguish between interpersonal and impersonal forms of trust (Shapiro, 1987). Interpersonal trust supports relational forms of contracting and develops from experience, personal familiarity, and frequent interaction (Jeffries & Reed, 2000). In contrast, anonymous arms-length contracting rests upon abstract, impersonal trust. There is an expectation that a third-party agent can intervene when a contract is breached. The third party will act according to predetermined rules. More generally, we may define institutional trust as 'an individual's expectation that some organized system will act with predictability and goodwill' (Maguire & Phillips, 2008, p. 372), described as institution-based trust (Zucker, 1986) or system trust (Bachmann & Inkpen, 2011). The impersonal trust of abstract systems is consistent with the Weberian depiction of rational-legal authority (Zucker, 1986). Compared with traditional forms of authority, such as kinship or charisma, Weber believed that rational-legal authority was innately superior due to the bureaucratic organizational structures it enabled.

Therefore, institutional trust comes from a sociological tradition of authority relations, where trust derives from the diffusion of rational bureaucratic structures. Such structures are ultimately underpinned by state authority, a third-party guarantee, which reduces uncertainty. For example, stock exchanges can produce institutional trust by propagating routines, rules and procedures regarding IPO listings and the professional and ethical certification of stockbrokers, accountants and chartered financial analysts. The custodians of rule-based systems are anonymous and 'trusted' agents exercising delegated power from principals who cannot readily monitor or evaluate their actions. Nevertheless, these individuals may violate the trust charged to them, and the system must respond to these violations to restore confidence in them. Accordingly, social control of impersonal authority requires repair mechanisms (Bachmann et al., 2012), including procedural elaboration to repair lost institutional trust. For example, the Dodds-Frank Act restored confidence in US capital markets in the wake of the 2008 financial crisis.

The level of institutional trust is variable across countries and particular forms of institutions. In particular, the custodians of impersonal authority can be exercised by social groups with different economic, political, or social power (Yenkey, 2015). For example, in the United States, civilian police authority is frequently concentrated in the hands of white citizens. Some black citizens do not expect the police to act impartially in exercising their authority but may discriminate against people of colour. Across countries, social stratification will occur along multiple dimensions, including differences in religion, race, ethnicity, language, economic inequality and political party affiliation. Perceived differences in how dominant social groups exercise impersonal authority relative to other groups can create a sense of exclusion or injustice, resulting in active mistrust in the institutions they represent.

Perceived inequalities in our three countries derive from different forms of social stratification. In Malaysia, the dominant capitalist class with greater economic power and corporate ownership is concentrated in the hands of ethnic Chinese entrepreneurs whose families migrated to Malaysia in the precolonial era (Carney & Gedajlovic, 2002). The majority population is Malay, whose constitutional identity is defined as someone who professes the Islamic religion and habitually speaks Malay. As a democracy, the majority Malay population holds perpetual political power, creating tensions and mistrust with the economically powerful Chinese minority (Gomez, 2012). Indeed, the Chinese FBGs corporate form originates in institutional distrust of the Malaysian state (Carney & Gedajlovic, 2002; McVey, 1992). Compared with Malaysia, China and Korea are ethnically homogenous. In China, entrepreneurial mistrust arises from political inequality, where the Communist Party exercises a political monopoly. In Korea, institutional mistrust arises from extreme economic inequality between wealthy family business groups and the working population, manifesting in complex politics. Hence, a better understanding of institutional trust in market-supporting institutions depends on intergroup social relations and different forms of inequality.

The Emergence of FBGs: Entrepreneurial Dynamism and Technology Assimilation

Family-owned and controlled business groups are vital agents of entrepreneurship and technological modernization in late industrialized Asia (Mathews, 2002). These groups emerged and matured over two decades, beginning in 1960 in Korea (Amsden, 1989) and Malaysia in the 1970s (McVey, 1992). Private FBGs emerged in China after 1989 following the collapse of the Soviet Union, when Chinese policymakers accelerated market reforms, allowing for greater private enterprise involvement in the economy (Huang, 2008). Each of these states initiated export-oriented industrial development policies to catch up to the productivity levels of firms from more advanced economies (Carney & Gedajlovic, 2003; Hobday, 1995). Asian states authorized the emergence of privately owned business group structure because they facilitate imitation and learning about technology and enables technology spillovers across affiliated firms (Amsden, 2001).

Indeed, the diffusion of groups in the region is a model of imitation, a process described by Granovetter (2005) as cross-national mimetic isomorphism. In seeking to become the first Asian industrial state, Japan looked to the German model of developmental capitalism, emulating *Konzerns* as a preferred model for big business in Japan's pre-war *Zaibatsu* (Shimotani, 1997). The patriarchs of elite family-controlled Zaibatsu imitated German structures that became standard for their reference group to appear modern and dynamic. Equally, Granovetter (2005) suggests that Korean *Chaebol* imitated Japanese business groups in the 1950s because the *Zaibatsu* were familiar in Korea from Japan's colonial rule. Similarly, British-owned and controlled business groups across Southeast Asia were a common organizational form in the colonial era (Jones & Wale, 1998). During the 1980s, the developmental state model was adopted in Southeast Asia, and each state enabled the emergence of business groups to facilitate export-led development strategies (Carney, 2008).

Relatedly, much of the technological dynamism in emerging markets stems from imitation. When domestic firms have limited technical and organizational capability, and the state encourages them to enter international markets, firms may grow much faster by importing and assimilating existing know-how from advanced countries. The primary task is to coordinate and combine knowledge flows with available capital and physical resources to invest for successful imitation because know-how already exists (Gerlach, 1997).

A critical organizational process for imitative learning is a project management capability (Amsden & Hikino, 1994) that facilitates the efficient combination of relatively generic resources to enter new industries, often unrelated to one another. The learning by imitation experience was repeated across Asia's newly industrializing economies (Mathews, 2017). In the first instance, firms acquired basic manufacturing and quality control skills in electronics and medium-tech industries (Hobday, 2000). For example, Korean firms rapidly diffused ISO 9001 quality standards. To do so, they formed a variety of inter-organizational linking mechanisms, such as performing subcontracting and original equipment manufacturing (OEM), licensing products and brands and sending technical personnel on overseas reconnaissance missions. Hobday says, 'OEM and subcontracting systems acted as a training school for (Asian) firms helping them to couple export market needs with foreign technological learning' (1995, p. 1172). As Asian firms approached the efficiency frontier, they adopted and often improved upon best practice organizational processes. For example, Korean firms adopted and improved Motorola's Six Sigma quality assurance process (Yu & Zaheer, 2010).

Corporate Governance by Personal Rule in FBGs

By corporate governance, we refer to FBG owner preferences for governance practices, accountability processes within and beyond the organization and organization structure. The Weberian distinction between traditional authority, based on the personal rule, and rational-legal authority based upon bureaucratic control and impersonal forms of authority is essential to our argument. The distinction results in differences in owners' access to financial capital, reliance upon professional managers, the selection of boards of directors, and organizational structures between FBGS and bureaucratic organizations. Consistent with the belief in the inherent superiority of rational-legal authority, World Society theorists (Meyer, 2010; Meyer et al., 1997) predict that transnational and professional agents, located primarily in Western liberal economies, will diffuse rational-legal processes to peripheral or less developed economies. The content and the transfer of these processes guide the rationalization of traditional authority. The carriers of these rationalizing logics include World Organisations such as the United Nations technical agencies, the World Bank and International Monetary Fund, and a range of actors in Professional associations in accounting, law, medicine, and management consulting. Meyer (2013) describes the carriers of rationalizing logic as 'high school mediating actors' comprised of individuals with many years of university education and the attainment of professional accreditation. Potential recipients of such institutions do not passively accept every aspect of world society rationalizing logic but hybridize and translate institutions in the form they consider practical or acceptable (Djelic & Quack, 2010).

While Asian FBGs have comprehensively adopted production technologies and processes from Japanese and Western firms, they have not, typically, fully adopted rational-legal governance prescription will. The authority structure of the archetypal Western firm tends to be relatively bureaucratic and impersonal. Resulting from the separation of ownership and control, professionally managed firms, especially those in the UK and North America, rely upon arms-length capital (equity and debt) than Asian FBGs. Arms-length investors tend to provide capital through financial intermediaries concerned with returns on their portfolios rather than any particular firm's performance. Accordingly, managers and investors will typically view their respective interests in instrumental terms. The instrumentality of depersonalized investor-management relations pervades Western firms' governance structures. For example, accountability to shareholders requires that professional managers rationalize their decisions with reference to the maximization of shareholder value. More generally, managers are subject to bureaucratic constraints consisting of codified standards of managerial conduct, performance appraisal processes, and quarterly reporting requirements that check managerial discretion (Carney, 2005).

Similarly, the primary form of organization for multi-business firms is the M-form or multidivisional structure (Williamson, 1985). The M-form structure enables business unit performance to be assessed by transparent quantitative metrics. Managers can evaluate underperforming units at market prices. Due to their transparency, underperforming business units are visible to private equity firms, and predators may seek to acquire and restructure such businesses to improve their market value.

In contrast, the entrepreneurial owners of Asian FBGs concentrate control in their own hands; an authority structure described as personal rule (Üsdiken, 2010). In these organizations, family owners govern the most critical transactions under the norms of relational contracting. Leading theories of the firm, such as transactions cost and agency theory, consider the persistence of personal rule in modern corporations as anachronistic because the progressive rationalization of the corporation is expected to depersonalize family authority. However, neither the separation of ownership and control nor the depersonalization of authority has occurred in most Asian public corporations, except for the notable exception of Japan (Claessens et al., 2000).

The concentration of authority in a family patriarch enables the dominant coalition of trusted associates to exercise control over the firm's resources and make critical strategic decisions with 'unlimited jurisdiction' (Biggart, 1998, p. 316) while retaining a 'tight grip' (Tsui-Auch, 2004, p. 718) over the direction of the firm. In a study of the top 100 Taiwanese business groups, Luo and Chung (2005) did not find a single case where the key leader (the most powerful post in the group) was not a family member.

However, FBGs make extensive use of professional management at the operational level but rarely admit professional managers into the dominant coalition's inner circle (Carney, 2013; Tsui-Auch, 2004). The admitted few are likely to have prior social ties or have demonstrated loyalty and long service to the family. Tsui-Auch distinguishes between 'family-related managers' and nonfamily managers. The former includes family members and relatives, friends, and employees who the owning family considers family members. In some cases, families use marriage or adoption to incorporate trustworthy executive talent beyond the family (Mehrotra et al., 2011).

Western corporate governance systems comprise an interconnected set of external (e.g. stock markets, credit rating agencies) and internal governance mechanisms (e.g. a board of directors, audit committees) that monitor senior management decision-making on behalf of investors. However, while Asian states have sought to establish comparable systems of governance and other market-supporting institutions, FBGs have been slow to avail themselves of these mechanisms. Either because FBGs have developed alternative internal means or because they have little institutional trust in market-supporting institutions. While many FBG list affiliates on public stock exchanges, they remain firmly under the parent's control, who typically acquire a controlling share of the firm's public equity. The ownership level required for control will depend upon the particular context. In some jurisdictions, effective control may require an absolute majority of voting stock. In other cases, dual-class shares or comments providing the family with special decision rights, such as the right to appoint a CEO or determine the board's composition, might establish control.

Internal governance mechanisms also reflect personal control. Asian state authorities advocate compliance with 'codes of best practice' that call for independent boards, separating the CEO and Board Chairperson's role (van Essen et al., 2012). While some FBGs adopt these practices and avow their commitment to high standards of corporate governance. However, there is a significant gap between de jure and de facto corporate governance practices (Khanna et al., 2004). For example, boards may appear to have many independent directors, but independence is nominal for many directors. A patriarch may appoint board members from their networks, or they are executives of group affiliated firms. Independent members may be unwilling or unable to stand up to a powerful patriarch and may exercise little influence. Boyd and Hoskisson (2010) conclude that many seemingly independent boards are little more than 'rubberstamps'.

The multidivisional organization is an efficient structure for firms diversified into multiple geographic and product markets (Chandler, 1990). Described by Williamson as the M-form, the structure separates 'operating from strategic decision-making … and … the requisite internal control apparatus has been assembled and is systematically employed' (Williamson, 1975). Despite its efficiencies, family firms around the world are typically resistant to its adoption. In the United States and Europe, family-controlled firms were slower than managerial and bank-controlled firms to adopt the M-form structure due to the requirement that family owners decentralize management control and improve accountability and transparency of the firm's performance to outsiders (Mayer & Whittington, 2004). The structure reduced the discretion of the entrepreneur to exercise control. While Asian business groups' system of vertical and horizontal relationships with affiliated firms varies enormously (Yiu et al., 2007), but very few approximate the Williamson ideal M-form organization. Advocates of good governance and transparent and formal organizations justify their arguments in terms of improved financial performance. The patriarchs of Asian FBGs resist this advice due to factors other than the desire to protect social and emotional endowments.

More recently, world society sources of governance rationalization have emerged targeting family businesses in the Asian region. These rationalizing forces include globalizing financial institutions and family management consultants and advisors. The emergence of global family offices practices provides advice and structures separating family financial wealth from the firm and applying portfolio management techniques to family wealth (Glucksberg & Burrows, 2016). Professional bodies such as the Society of Trust and Estate Planning offer customized tax and legal advice about the effective intergenerational transfer of wealth (Harrington, 2012). Other consultants focus on managing family relationships addressing problems of conflict, family dysfunction, and socializing next-generation family members into business ownership (Kuusela, 2018). Executive search firms are touting their services to help family-managed firms to identify top-level management talent. Business families in North America and Europe have become avid consumers of family business advisory services (Harrington, 2017). However, while one article suggests that 90% of Asia's business families intend to hand over the business to a family member, they rarely engage in formal succession planning (Schultz, 2015). Consequently, the extent to which the patriarchs of Asian family business groups avail themselves of the growing array of professional advice is understudied in the literature.

The Politics of Institutional Trust: Divisions Between Groups Based on Economic, Political, and Ethnic Stratification

So far, we show that Asian FBGs combine entrepreneurial and technological dynamism while retaining a conservative and personalized form of corporate organization. This section argues that with low levels of institutional trust, FBGs have resisted the financial promise of Western models of corporate governance and organizational structure. To be fully effective, these models require robust principal-agent relationships across a variety of institutional settings. For example, in stock markets, the relationship between majority and minority investments depends on institutional trust in third-party agents who uphold institutional rules and processes, such as rules protecting fraudulent expropriation of minority investors.

Such rules and processes involve multiple subsystems, such as stock market administrators who enforce laws governing IPOs, professional certification procedures for stockbroker membership, auditors who certify financial statements, and credit rating agencies who provide risk analysis about listed firms. Each of these institutional subsystems delegates authority to specific professionals. However, these subsystems' efficacy ultimately depends upon state authority vested in agents of the judiciary, officials, and financial agencies. However, employees in the subsystems are potentially fallible and capable of opportunism. If self-serving behaviour is detected and unaddressed by the state authorities, institutional trust is likely to erode or fail to develop (Bachmann et al., 2012; Fisman & Miguel, 2007).

The control and authority of particular subsystems are often concentrated among members of specific social groups. Such groups' stratification is multifaceted across different societies based on differences in ethnicity, caste, race, language, religion, economic status, and political affiliation. Social membership differences can undermine institutional trust because members of one group may make prejudicial and categorical judgments about other groups. This can occur because reliable information may not transmit to other social groups or is discredited when it does. Such processes can reinforce a perceived difference that engenders feelings of injustice or exclusion by some groups. For example, participation in Initial Public Offerings may be withheld by particular social groups when they perceive capital markets to be controlled by a rival social group (Yenkey, 2018). Thus, institutional trust depends on the social integration of distinct social groups (Evans, 1995).

However, for various political reasons reflecting fundamental inequalities, states have not adequately addressed the social integration of the rival groups. In these circumstances, mistrust between different social groups may be exacerbated, and out-groups may withhold institutional trust in state mediated institutions, including those underpinning robust principal-agent relationships. We suggest that the typical governance of Asian FBGs functions as a defence mechanism against untrusted state institutions and will likely persist so long as both FBGs and institutions develop on a path-dependent trajectory.

Political Inequality: Sources of Institutional Mistrust in China

Mao believed that China's reverence for traditional values was a significant obstacle to the realization of his Communist project. Indeed, Mao's launch of the disastrous Cultural Revolution was intended to destroy the culture of traditional authority and in particular, to disrupt traditional family values. Reliance on the family survived this assault (Greif & Tabellini, 2010), and commitment to family remains strong. One scholar observes that 'you trust your family absolutely, your friends and acquaintances to the degree that mutual dependence has been established. ...With everybody else, you make no assumptions about their goodwill' (Redding, 1990, p. 66).

Nevertheless, the Chinese state maintains a vast reach over the national economy where the Chinese Communist Party (CCP) exercises a monopoly of political control over the levers of power. The CCP is a hierarchical but profoundly secretive organization operating beyond and above the law. In contrast with the rule of law, the CPP is said to operate a 'rule by law' regime that rejects the basic premise that the rule of law exists to impose significant limits on powerful individuals. Instead, 'rule by law' refers to an instrumental conception of law in which law is merely a tool to be used as the State sees fit' (Peerenboom, 2002, p. 8). Consequently, China's legal system is somewhat underdeveloped and opaque (Huang, 2008). This is not to say that the CCP may eventually seek to achieve the ideal of the rule of law. Nevertheless, law enforcement can appear arbitrary in various aspects of the economy, such as property rights, labour rights, or intellectual property protection.

Thus, while the legal system has significant institutional voids, there is sufficient regularity to support general prosperity and high, seemingly sustainable economic growth levels. However, entrepreneurs who have responded to opaque and ambiguous property rights have resorted to guanxi relations as an insurance mechanism to support transactions. Guanxi relations are restricted to localized family and kinship ties for relatively small and medium-sized enterprises, especially for protection against predatory lower-level party cadres (Peng, 2004). However, guanxi's real value derives from ties with well-placed politicians and state bureaucrats (Ge et al., 2019). Such connections are often described as patron-client relationships, entailing an exchange of favours. The favours bestowed by the political patron can be substantial, including preferential access to economic resources, such as subsidies or bail-outs of failing ventures, information about opportunities, and bureaucratic facilitation of permits and licenses. Perhaps more important, political links to a well-placed patron of the protection from predation by lower-order officials. Ties with higher-level patrons can fuel the emergence of substantial enterprises. Chinese tech giant Huawei gains significant support from the state's 'Belt and Road' initiative, resulting in exclusive contracts to construct telecoms networks for China's diplomatic allies such as Pakistan and Iran.

However, political patrons expect reciprocity for their favours (Peck & Zhang, 2013). The compensation for political patrons is extensive, producing a new class of 'red capitalists' (Peck & Zhang, 2013) comprised of party and government officials who have converted their political power into economic wealth. While patron-client ties are mutually beneficial, they constitute low-trust relationships. The entrepreneurial client typically occupies a subordinate position to the political patron. A patron may reveal a 'grabbing hand', and the client-entrepreneur may be unable to limit the patron's claims.

Moreover, political ties are precarious, and their value is highly contingent on the patron's ongoing tenure (Sun et al., 2012). Indeed, the precarity of political ties may threaten a family's control of its enterprises. For example, Chinese state regulators abruptly postponed Alibaba's FinTech company Ant Group Co.'s initial public offering after its billionaire founder Jack Ma openly criticized the 'pawn shop' like financial system.

Thus, while political ties may compensate for institutional voids enabling the construction of large business groups, they rest upon a tenuous low-trust relationship. They inevitably leave both patron and client entrepreneurs in a state of mutual suspicion, with the diminished prospect of building a more permanent institutional trust. The current general secretary of the CPP, and president of the People's Republic of China, Xi Jinping, recently removed term limits on his presidency and endowed himself with unlimited authority. Xi is seeking to clamp down on all forms of corruption. Whether a lifelong dictatorial power can establish institutional trust remains an open question.

Korea Economic Inequality

The Korean state's role was pivotal in forming, growing, and subsequent internationalization of the Chaebol family-controlled business groups. Under President Park Chung-hee's long-term president term, from 1962 to 1979. The state developed a system of supervisory institutions designed to lead domestic industrialization to catch up with arch-rival Japan (Carney, 2008). Indeed, the state selected the particular families who would lead the industrial strategy as Alice Amsden puts it, 'a group of millionaires would be allowed to enter the central stage, thus encouraging national capitalism' (1989, p. 14). President Park envisaged the government's role as one of overseeing and disciplining the millionaires to avoid any abuse of power. The heart of the discipline was government-mediated licences, and funding was tied to the achievement of industrial goals regarding new product creation, capacity building, and ambitious export targets. The government discipline and the rise of Chaebol were interactive. Large business groups consolidated power in response to the state's performance-based incentives.

However, the Korean state's capacity to discipline the largest groups was progressively eroded by trade and financial liberalization that enabled the Chaebol to reduce the financial dependence on state by borrowing on international markets. The effect of financial liberalization was to create an increasingly independent and more powerful corporate sector with influence over the direction of liberalization. What began as state-led industrialization in the 1960s morphed into a co-equal partnership between the state and the largest Chaebol (Granovetter, 2005). Public opinion about the Chaebol is not favourable. The Chaebol suppressed wages and was perceived to exploit labour. Many viewed the Chaebol as 'immoral profiteers' benefiting from government connections. This public sentiment is deeply rooted and remains prevalent in Korea this today.

When the state began to construct market-supporting institutions, it did so incrementally and partially in a manner that increased the Chaebol's power. The consequence of the liberalizing strategy was to create and prolong the life of influential and autonomous business groups that are largely beyond the discipline state (Carney, 2008). Indeed, Chang (2006) suggests that government actions created new mechanisms to funnel foreign debts into the largest groups' coffers. Korea was a major casualty of the Asian financial crisis.

Consequently, international organizations, such as the International Monetary Fund, pressured the state to engage in a far-reaching restructuring programme on the Chaebol. The weaker groups were subject to such restructuring, but the stronger groups were able to resist. As Chang (2006) suggests, 'old habits die hard', and corporate owners and politicians sought to continue existing practices in the face of large-scale redundancies. Moreover, Chaebol embeddedness in regional communities provides a more substantial basis for identity than equity ownership (Biggart, 1998). As a result, family-owned Chaebol proved resilient (Granovetter, 2005).

Nevertheless, in the face of widespread social criticism and government attempts to curb their power, Chaebol business families tenaciously maintain ownership and control (Jun et al., 2019). The state's most recent attempts to wrest control and impose reform have targeted family ownership succession with substantial inheritance and estate taxes and prosecuting family members who evade taxes (Ortiz et al., 2020). For example, following the passing of Cho Yang, chairman of the Korean Chaebol Hanjin Group, in 2019, family heirs were liable for $175 million, which severely diluted the family's ownership stake in the group. With the recent passing of Samsung chairman Lee Kun-Hee, the family could face a $10 billion inheritance tax (*Korean Times*, 2019). Whether inheritance taxes will dilute family ownership remains an open question as families seek to evade taxes with increasingly complex legal structures (*Korea Herald*, 2019). Despite public resentment surrounding Chaebol family members' conspicuous wealth along with the suspicion of state complicity, we suggest the perceived inequity of concentrated wealth will fuel continuing levels of institutional mistrust.

Malaysian Ethnic Inequality

The basis of institutional mistrust in Malaysia stems from ethnic inequalities, which, ironically, the state has systemically sought to erase. In doing so, the state has also maintained enduring social peace among an ethnically diverse population, made up of ethnic Malays (65%), ethnic Chinese (25%), ethnic Indians (8%), and others (2%). However, the minority ethnic Chinese population constitutes a dominant capitalist class controlling some 65% of private-sector assets. The stark and enduring wealth inequality was a critical ingredient in Sino-Malay sectarian violence in 1969. The event is significant because the Malaysian state responded with a comprehensive affirmative action strategy in its New Economic Policy in 1971. Since the NEP implementation, Malaysia has attained notable social achievements, including the virtual eradication of poverty, lower levels of income inequality, and improvements in a variety of quality-of-life indicators, including life expectancy, infant mortality, and literacy. The NEP has stimulated higher economic growth levels, low unemployment, and the construction of world-class communications and transportation infrastructure.

The NEP socio-political objectives were intertwined with a developmental state strategy to create a population Malay-owned corporate enterprise. Key NEP measures mandated ethnic Malay ownership requirements in publicly listed firms and targeted funding creating wholly-owned Malay companies. However, the strategy's unintended consequences produced a widely emulated ethnic Chinese-Malay hybrid, colloquially known as the Ali Baba system. In the system, Ali being the Malay, fronting a Baba, or Chinese or Indian owned business. For example, a Malay-owned firm might receive a government contract through affirmative action programmes. However, the contract would be sub-contracted to another company for a profit, usually a non-Malay firm with greater organizational capability.

The Malaysian state subsequently engaged in a project of constructing market-supporting institutions with liberal market reforms. However, the institutions of affirmative action and liberal market reforms were combined and infused with personalized patron-client relations (Carney & Andriesse, 2014). According to Gomez (2009), the creation of the Malaysian stock exchange functioned as a mechanism for politically connected entrepreneurs to capitalize on the value of their connections. The interaction of these institutional spheres has produced a succession of short-lived business groups with a managerial ethos that provides few incentives to develop sustainable competitive advantages in the international marketplace. Ethnic Chinese entrepreneurs amassed enormous fortunes in diverse industries; luminous examples include Overseas Chinese Banking Corp. (OCBC), Oriental Holdings, and Lion Group. However, in the post-colonial period, many of these enterprises became enmeshed in patrimonial politics and absorbed 'political-bureaucratic figures' into their management (Ling, 1992). These companies' fortunes were tied up with their political patrons, whose tenure is contingent upon political developments. In documenting the rise and fall of family-controlled business groups, Gomez highlights these businesses' instability and concludes that 'What is obvious is that the companies established by a number of the foremost businessmen in the post-colonial period were not sustained into the modern period' (2009, p. 7). The rapid rise and contraction of entrepreneurially controlled business groups continue today (Gomez, 2018) (Table 10.1).

The Complicated Politics of Institutional Trust

We have argued that the effective functioning of market-supporting institutions is dependent upon high levels of institutional trust. However, we have argued that economic, political, and ethnic inequalities in these advanced Asian economies have tended to obstruct the development of institutional trust. This is because state authority ultimately underpins the impersonal authority and bureaucratic due process necessary for various organizations and institutions. Ironically, the Chinese Communist Party and the Korean and Malaysian states have established laudable political goals to increase national security, shared prosperity, and reduce economic inequalities. However, the fallibility and venality among politicians, state bureaucrats, and entrepreneurs often result in patron-client relationships. We have argued

10 Family Business Groups in Advanced ... 257

Table 10.1 Summary of three institutional mistrust in Asian economies

	China	Korean	Malaysia
Type of institutional mistrust	Political inequality inherent in patron-client relationships	Economic inequality between the working population and the powerful and autonomous FBGs	Ethnic inequality between wealthy minority and Malay population
Source of mistrust	CCP exercises a monopoly of political control and operates as a hierarchical and profoundly secretive organization	Government-mediated licences and funding were tied to the achievement of industrial goals regarding new product creation, capacity building, and ambitious export targets	Minority ethnic Chinese population constitutes a dominant capitalist class controlling some 65% of private-sector assets
FBG's response	Entrepreneurial and family BGs exchange favours with political patrons for insurance and protection	Consolidated power and gradual escape state discipline	Ethnic Chinese BGs became enmeshed in patrimonial politics and absorbed 'political-bureaucratic figures' into their management
Primary examples	Country Garden, Hengli Petrochemical, Haidilao, Winner Medical, Lens Technology	Samsung, Hyundai, LG, Hanjin	OCBC, Oriental Holdings, and Lion Group. YTL

these are ultimately low-trust relationships since they are motivated by personal gain or private protection and not anchored by an impersonal authority. Mutual mistrust can generalize to larger social groups when particular social groups categorize others as untrustworthy. So long as these social divisions persist, economic actors will seek the potential gains and protection of such relationships while retarding the creation of a comprehensive institutional trust.

To be clear, we do not condemn all business state relationships as forms of corruption or eroding institutional trust. Indeed, the concept of embedded autonomy (Evans, 1996) refers to productive collaboration between a Weberian state bureaucracy and accountable corporate and managerial elites. As a basis of information sharing, conflict avoidance and the pursuit of mutually beneficial goals, embedded autonomy entails capable bureaucrats forging trust with their corporate counterparts and can be a vital ingredient in a successful developmental state strategy. Both practitioners and academics agree on the potential mutual benefits of embedded autonomy (Puente & Schneider, 2020). Indeed, the epitome of a world society institution, the World Bank incorporates the concept of embedded autonomy in its Washington consensus prescription for the developmental state. What is not well understood by academics or practitioners is exactly what kinds of firms can contribute to collaborative business state relationships. The extent to which business families and family business groups can contribute productively to these goals remains an open question worthy of further research by family business scholars. The complicated politics of institutional trust is not limited to the advanced Asian economies discussed in this book chapter. Indeed, the global epitome of high-quality market-supporting institutions, the United States, has recently undergone an erosion of institutional trust. A legitimately elected president has fomented wide-ranging institutional mistrust in various institutions, including media, national security agencies, political parties, and the electoral system. However, the agency of the president is not sufficient to single-handedly wreak such mistrust. Instead, politicians can appeal to particular groups' underlying grievances, such as marginalized working-class workers, by disseminating distrust of capitalist elites. Similar bouts of institutional mistrust are evident in Europe and Latin America. More generally, the effectiveness of regulatory and professional institutions such as the Securities Commission, the accounting profession, and credit rating agencies depends on government leaders' willingness to support legal-rational processes that uphold their integrity. Perceived corruption is indicative of low levels of institutionalized trust.

Sociologists (e.g. Zucker, 1986) have long observed that traditional societies relying upon personal authority as a primary mechanism for governing business organizations have limited capacity to expand the scale and scope of their operation. Because personal authority relies upon familiarity and proximity, it follows that to build enterprises that can scale their businesses beyond local communities into national and international markets, firms must increasingly rely upon the structure and processes of impersonal authority. Such mechanisms rest upon accepting standardized bureaucratic procedures such as human resource recruitment, compensation, and employee evaluation. Thus the authority structures of multinational family-controlled business groups such as Korea's Samsung, Malaysia's YTL infrastructure group, and China's Shi Yong Hong business family accommodate various elements of rational-legal authority into their managerial bureaucracies. The contribution of this paper, with its focus upon deficits of institutional trust, suggests family business groups represent a hybrid organization incorporating traditional authority in their governance practices and structures and rational-legal authority in the operational and technical parts of the business. We suggest this capacity for hybridization of the family business to function in a broad range of institutionally varied jurisdictions indicates robustness and flexible organizational form, which explains their prevalence and ubiquity.

Returning now to the question of whether family business groups will become major consumers of 'world society' sources of rationalization in the form of family business consultants and advisers. We are equivocal. A fundamental relationship in capitalist economies is the fiduciary responsibility of an agent to a principal. One consequence of low institutional trust is actors' reluctance to rely upon fiduciary relationships. The fiduciary duty implies 'holding in trust'. It is attached to a wide range of specific relationships, for example, between a firm's directors and firm stakeholders, professional executives and stockholders, lawyers and trustees, and stockbrokers and their clients. The fiduciary relationship has both a legal and a moral connotation. In its legal form, the fiduciary has a duty of skill and care to employ the best professional judgement for the principal's benefit. In its moral form, the fiduciary responsibility is more akin to stewardship for multiple stakeholders or communities. The expectation is that the agent will uphold the expectation of competence, judgement, and honesty and put explicit duties of the role ahead of their own needs. We suspect that low levels of institutional trust will weaken the expectations associated with fiduciary positions. A corollary is that family business groups will perpetuate personal control and opaque governance arrangements, which may ultimately inhibit the emergence of more complex forms of capitalist organization. However, we do not underestimate Asian business families' capacity to hybridize their governance structures to meet the demands of a shifting and unpredictable institutional context.

Conclusion

In their analysis of European business groups Schneider et al. (2018) conclude that over the past 50 years, the population of business groups has significantly declined. They depict a long-term trend toward the gradual restructuring and disappearance of business groups in Belgium, Germany, Netherlands, France, Italy, and Spain. For particular reasons, they find that business groups remain prominent in just two European countries, Sweden and Portugal. We have seen a substantial decline in state involvement in the economy and an emphasis on projects to develop market-supporting institutions during this period. Our analysis suggests similar projects in Asian economies have not yet resulted in a similar decline. We conclude with a question: can institutional trust explain differential patterns of business groups' longevity across European and Asian jurisdictions? Our answer is in the affirmative. We offer the tentative conclusion that broad entrepreneurial trust in the state is necessary to restructure family business groups. Further research is warranted.

References

Amsden, A. H. (1989). *Asia's next giant: South Korea and late industrialization.* Oxford University Press.

Amsden, A. H. (2001). *The rise of "the rest": Challenges to the west from late-industrializing economies.* Oxford University Press.

Amsden, A. H., & Hikino, T. (1994). Project execution capability, organizational know-how and conglomerate corporate growth in late industrialization. *Industrial and Corporate Change, 3*(1), 111–147.

Bachmann, R., Gillespie, N., & Kramer, R. (2012). Trust in crisis: Organizational and institutional trust, failures and repair. *Organization Studies, 33*(2), 285–287.

Bachmann, R., & Inkpen, A. C. (2011). Understanding institutional-based trust building processes in inter-organizational relationships. *Organization Studies, 32*(2), 281–301.

Biggart, N. W. (1998). Deep finance: The organizational bases of South Korea's financial collapse. *Journal of Management Inquiry, 7*(4), 311–320.

Boyd, B. K., & Hoskisson, R. E. (2010). *Corporate governance of business groups.* Oxford University Press.

Boyer, R. (2005). How and why capitalisms differ. *Economy and Society, 34*(4), 509–557.

Carney, M. (2005). Corporate governance and competitive advantage in family-controlled firms. *Entrepreneurship Theory and Practice, 29*(3), 249–265.

Carney, M. (2008). *Asian business groups: Context, governance and performance.* Chandos Asian Studies Series.

Carney, M. (2013). Personally managed Asian business groups. In G. S. Drori, M. A. Höllerer, & P. Walgenbach (Eds.), *Organizations and managerial ideas: Global themes and local variations* (pp. 219–232). Routledge.

Carney, M., & Andriesse, E. (2014). Malaysia's personal capitalism. In E. Redding & M. Witt (Eds.), *The Oxford handbook of Asian capitalism* (pp 144–168). Oxford University Press.

Carney, M., & Gedajlovic, E. (2002). The co-evolution of institutional environments and organizational strategies: The rise of family business groups in the ASEAN region. *Organization Studies, 23*(1), 1–29.

Carney, M., & Gedajlovic, E. (2003). Strategic innovation and the administrative heritage of East Asian family business groups. *Asia Pacific Journal of Management, 20*(1), 5–26.

Carney, M., Gedajlovic, E., & Yang, X. (2009). Varieties of Asian capitalism: Toward an institutional theory of Asian enterprise. *Asia Pacific Journal of Management, 26*(3), 361–380.

Carney, M., Van Essen, M., Estrin, S., & Shapiro, D. (2018). Business groups reconsidered: Beyond paragons and parasites. *Academy of Management Perspectives, 32*(4), 493–516.

Chandler, A. D. (1990). The enduring logic of industrial success. *Harvard Business Review, 68*(2), 130–140.

Chang, S. J. (Ed.). (2006). *Business groups in East Asia: Financial crisis, restructuring, and new growth.* Oxford University Press.

Claessens, S., Djankov, S., & Lang, L. H. (2000). The separation of ownership and control in East Asian corporations. *Journal of Financial Economics, 58*(1–2), 81–112.

Djelic, M.-L., & Quack, S. (Eds.). (2010). *Transnational communities: Shaping global economic governance.* Cambridge University Press.

Evans, P. B. (1995). *Embedded autonomy: States and industrial transformation.* Princeton University Press.

Evans, P. (1996). Reconstructing agency in a global economy: Reflections on embedded autonomy. *Political Power and Social Theory, 10*, 333–345.

Fisman, R., & Miguel, E. (2007). Corruption, norms, and legal enforcement: Evidence from diplomatic parking tickets. *Journal of Political Economy, 115*(6), 1020–1048.

Fogel, K. (2006). Oligarchic family control, social-economic outcomes, and the quality of government. *Journal of International Business Studies, 37*(5), 603–622.

Ge, J., Carney, M., & Kellermanns, F. (2019). Who fills institutional voids? Entrepreneurs' utilization of political and family ties in emerging markets. *Entrepreneurship Theory and Practice, 43*(6), 1124–1147.

Gerlach, M. L. (1997). The organizational logic of business groups: Evidence from the Zaibatsu. *Beyond the firm: Business groups in international and historical perspective* (pp. 245–273). Oxford University Press.

Glucksberg, L., & Burrows, R. (2016). Family offices and the contemporary infrastructures of dynastic wealth. *Sociologica, 10*(2).

Gomez, E. T. (2009). The rise and fall of capital: Corporate Malaysia in historical perspective. *Journal of Contemporary Asia, 39*(3), 345–381.

Gomez, E. T. (2012). Targeting horizontal inequalities: Ethnicity, equity, and entrepreneurship in Malaysia. *Asian Economic Papers, 11*(2), 31–57.

Gomez, E. T. (2018). *Minister of finance incorporated: Ownership and control of corporate Malaysia.* Palgrave Macmillan.

Granovetter, M. (2005). Business groups and social organization. In N. Smelser & R. Swedberg (Eds.), *Handbook of economic sociology* (pp. 429–450). Princeton University Press.

Greif, A., & Tabellini, G. (2010). Cultural and institutional bifurcation: China and Europe compared. *American Economic Review, 100*(2), 135–140.

Guillén, M. F., & Capron, L. (2016). State capacity, minority shareholder protections, and stock market development. *Administrative Science Quarterly, 61*(1), 125–160.

Hallward-Driemeier, M., & Pritchett, L. (2015). How business is done in the developing world: Deals versus rules. *Journal of Economic Perspectives, 29*(3), 121–140.

Harrington, B. (2012) Trust and estate planning: The emergence of a profession and its contribution to socioeconomic inequality *Sociological Forum, 27*(4), 825–846.

Harrington, B. (2017). *Capital without borders*. Harvard University Press.

Hobday, M. (1995). East Asian latecomer firms: Learning the technology of electronics. *World Development, 23*(7), 1171–1193.

Hobday, M. (2000). East versus Southeast Asian innovation systems: Comparing OEM-and TNC-led growth in electronics. *Technology, Learning, and Innovation,* 129–169.

Hoskisson, R. E., Johnson, R. A., Tihanyi, L., & White, R. E. (2005). Diversified business groups and corporate refocusing in emerging economies. *Journal of Management, 31*(6), 941–965.

Huang, Y. (2008). *Capitalism with Chinese characteristics: Entrepreneurship and the State*. Cambridge University Press.

Jeffries, F. L., & Reed, R. (2000). Trust and adaptation in relational contracting. *Academy of Management Review, 25*(4), 873–882.

Jones, G., & Wale, J. (1998). Merchants as business groups: British trading companies in Asia before 1945. *The Business History Review,* 367–408.

Jun, I. W., Kim, K. I., & Rowley, C. (2019). Organizational culture and the tolerance of corruption: The case of South Korea. *Asia Pacific Business Review, 25*(4), 534–553.

Khanna, T., Palepu, K. G., & Srinivasan, S. (2004). Disclosure practices of foreign companies interacting with US markets. *Journal of Accounting Research, 42*(2), 475–508.

Khanna, T., Kogan, J., & Palepu, K. (2006). Globalization and similarities in corporate governance: A cross-country analysis. *Review of Economics and Statistics, 88*(1), 69–90.

Khanna, T., & Rivkin, J. W. (2001). Estimating the performance effects of business groups in emerging markets. *Strategic Management Journal, 22*(1), 45–74.

Korean Herald. (2019, April 18). High inheritance tax fuels chaebol monopoly. Jung Min- Kyumg. http://www.koreaherald.com/view.php?ud=2019041800 00688. Accessed January 21, 2021

Korea Times. (2019, April 9). *Chaebol cornered by ruinous inheritance tax*. Nam Hyun-woo. https://www.koreatimes.co.kr/www/nation/2019/04/694_266 887.html. Accessed January 21, 2021

Kuusela, H. (2018). Learning to own: Cross-generational meanings of wealth and class-making in wealthy Finnish families. *The Sociological Review, 66*(6), 1161–1176.

La Porta, R. L., Lopez-de-Silanes, F., Shleifer, A., & Vishny, R. W. (1998). Law and finance. *Journal of Political Economy, 106*(6), 1113–1155.

Liang, Z., & Carney, M. (2020). Business group persistence and institutional maturity: the role of management practices. *Industrial and Corporate Change.*

Ling, S. L. M. (1992). The transformation of Malaysian business groups. In R. T. McVey (Ed.), *Southeast Asian capitalists* (pp. 103–126). Cornell University

Luo, X., & Chung, C. N. (2005). Keeping it all in the family: The role of particular-istic relationships in business group performance during institutional transition. *Administrative Science Quarterly, 50*(3), 404–439.

Mahmood, I. P., Zhu, H., & Zajac, E. J. (2011). Where can capabilities come from? Network ties and capability acquisition in business groups. *Strategic Management Journal, 32*(8), 820–848.

Mathews, J. A. (2002). Competitive advantages of the latecomer firm: A resource-based account of industrial catch-up strategies. *Asia Pacific Journal of Management, 19*(4), 467–488.

Mathews, J. A. (2017). Dragon multinationals powered by linkage, leverage and learning: A review and development. *Asia Pacific Journal of Management, 34*(4), 769–775.

Meyer, J. W. (2010). World society, institutional theories, and the actor. *Annual Review of Sociology, 36*, 1–20.

Meyer, J. W. (2013). Empowered actors, local settings, and global rationalization. In *Global themes and local variations in organization and management* (pp. 429–440). Routledge.

Meyer, J. W., Boli, J., Thomas, G. M., & Ramirez, F. O. (1997). World society and the nation-state. *American Journal of Sociology, 103*(1), 144–181.

Mayer, M., & Whittington, R. (2004). Economics, politics and nations: Resistance to the multidivisional form in France, Germany and the United Kingdom, 1983–1993. *Journal of Management Studies, 41*(7), 1057–1082. McVey, 1992.

McVey, R. (1992). The materialization of the Southeast Asian entrepreneur. In R. H. McVey (Ed.), *Southeast Asian capitalists* (pp. 7–33). Cornell Southeast Asia Program Publications.

Mehrotra, V., Morck, R., Shim, J., & Wiwattanakantang, Y. (2011). Must love kill the family firm? Some exploratory evidence. *Entrepreneurship Theory and Practice, 35*(6), 1121–1148. Morck.

Morck, R. (2010). The riddle of the great pyramids. In A. M. Colpan, T. Hikino, & J. R. Lincoln (Eds.), *The Oxford handbook of business groups.*

Morck, R., & Tian, G. Y. (2015). Canada: The Rise and Fall, and Rise and Fall Again. In A. M. Colpan & T. Hikino (Eds.), *Business groups in the West: Origins, evolution, and resilience* (pp. 458–490). Oxford University Press.

Morck, R., Wolfenzon, D., & Yeung, B. (2005). Corporate governance, economic entrenchment, and growth. *Journal of Economic Literature, 43*(3), 655–720.

Morck, R. K., Stangeland, D. A., & Yeung, B. (1998). *Inherited wealth, corporate control and economic growth: The Canadian disease* (No. w6814). National Bureau of Economic Research.

Ortiz, M., Carney, M., Duran, P., Braun, M., & Riutort, J. (2020). Inheritance tax, shareholder protection, and the market value of family firms: A cross-country analysis. *Global Strategy Journal.*

Peck, J., & Zhang, J. (2013). A variety of capitalism… with Chinese characteristics? *Journal of Economic Geography, 13*(3), 357–396.

Peerenboom, R. (2002). *China's long march toward rule of law.* Cambridge University Press.

Peng, Y. (2004). Kinship networks and entrepreneurs in China's transitional economy. *American Journal of Sociology, 109*(5), 1045–1074.

Portes, A., & Vickstrom, E. (2011). Diversity, social capital, and cohesion. *Annual Review of Sociology, 37*, 461–479.

Puente, I., & Schneider, B. R. (2020). Business and development: How organization, ownership and networks matter. *Review of International Political Economy, 27*(6), 1354–1377.

Redding, S. G. (1990). *The spirit of Chinese capitalism.* de Gruyter.

Rousseau, D. M., Sitkin, S. B., Burt, R. S., & Camerer, C. (1998). Not so different after all: A cross-discipline view of trust. *Academy of Management Review, 23*, 393–404.

Schneider, B. R., Colpan, A. M., Wong, W., Colpan, A. M., & Hikino, T. (2018). Politics, Institutions, and Diversified Business Groups. *Business Groups in the West: Origins, Evolution and Resilience*, 70–94.

Shapiro, S. P. (1987). The social control of impersonal trust. *American Journal of Sociology, 93*(3), 623–658.

Shimotani, M. (1997). *The history and structure of business groups in Japan.* Business groups in international and historical perspective, Oxford University Press.

Schultz, A. (2015). *Asian families slow to consider succession.* http://www.barrons.com/articles/asian-families-slow-to-consider-succession-1431579049. Accessed August 20, 2021.

Sun, P., Mellahi, K., & Wright, M. (2012). The contingent value of corporate political ties. *Academy of Management Perspectives, 26*(3), 68–82.

Tsui-Auch, L. S. (2004). The professionally managed family-ruled enterprise: Ethnic Chinese business in Singapore. *Journal of Management Studies, 41*(4), 693–723.

Üsdiken, B. (2010). The kin and the professional: Top leadership in family business groups.

Üsdiken, B. (2012). The Kin and the professional: Top leadership in family business groups. In *The Oxford handbook of business groups.*

Van Van Essen, M., Oosterhout, J., & Carney, M. (2012). Corporate boards and the performance of Asian firms: A meta-analysis. *Asia-Pacific Journal of Management, 29*(4), 873–905.

Williamson, O. E. (1985). *The economic institutions of capitalism: firms, markets, relational contracting.* Free Press.

Williamson, O. E. (1975). Markets and hierarchies: analysis and antitrust implications: A study in the economics of internal organization. *University of Illinois at Urbana-Champaign's academy for entrepreneurial leadership historical research reference in entrepreneurship.*

Yenkey, C. B. (2015). Mobilizing a market: Ethnic segmentation and investor recruitment into the Nairobi Securities Exchange. *Administrative Science Quarterly, 60*(4), 561–595.

Yenkey, C. B. (2018). Fraud and market participation: Social relations as a moderator of organizational misconduct. *Administrative Science Quarterly, 63*(1), 43–84.

Yiu, D. W., Lu, Y., Bruton, G. D., & Hoskisson, R. E. (2007). Business groups: An integrated model to focus future research. *Journal of Management Studies, 44*(8), 1551–1579. Yenkey 2015.

Yu, J., & Zaheer, S. (2010). Building a process model of local adaptation of practices: A study of Six Sigma implementation in Korean and US firms. *Journal of International Business Studies, 41*(3), 475–499.

Zucker, L. G. (1986). Production of trust: Institutional sources of economic structure, 1840–1920. *Research in Organizational Behavior, 8*, 53–111.

11

Conceptualising the Governing Ownership System in a Family Business Group

Tuuli Ikäheimonen, Marita Rautiainen, and Sanjay Goel

Introduction

How can a family govern ownership in a complex family business group (hereafter FBG)? To study this question, we examine the ownership system in an FBG and explore the mechanisms of managing the boundaries between family and business systems for a better-governing family ownership. To increase understanding of the family business ownership system, it is important to understand how a family governs ownership and in what processes and methods the family is engaged when doing this. As a system, family business consists of three overlapping subsystems: family, ownership and business.

T. Ikäheimonen (✉)
LUT School of Engineering Science, LUT University, Lappeenranta, Finland
e-mail: tuuli.ikaheimonen@lut.fi

M. Rautiainen
School of Engineering Science, LUT University, Lahti, Finland
e-mail: marita.rautiainen@lut.fi

S. Goel
Nistler College of Business and Public Administration, University of North Dakota, Grand Forks, ND, USA
e-mail: sanjay.goel@und.edu

© The Author(s), under exclusive license to Springer Nature Switzerland AG 2023
M. Rautiainen et al. (eds.), *The Palgrave Handbook of Managing Family Business Groups*,
https://doi.org/10.1007/978-3-031-13206-3_11

The three-circle model presented by Tagiuri and Davis (1996), and developed further by Gersick et al. (1997), views family business as a complex system, where each subsystem has their own lifecycle and *"family companies mature through their lives from simple-owner-manager control to the more complex later-generation forms"* (Gersick et al., 1999, p. 288). Family firms have the possibility to develop via managing the size and scale of multiple businesses organised as FBGs, instead of scaling up a single business from small to large over multiple generations (Rautiainen, 2012; Rosa & Pihkala, 2019; Rosa et al., 2014). The businesses of business families thus evolve in a variety of ways over time and develop highly idiosyncratic FBGs, held together by a transgenerational, long-term vision for their future together.

Family business characteristics differentiate family businesses from other types of companies. Equally, characteristics like concentrated ownership, e.g., a family holds a large amount of voting power (e.g., Aguilera & Crespi-Cladera, 2012; Goel et al., 2012); generational aspects (Gersick et al., 1999); duality of goals (simultaneous existence of financial and family-centric goals) (Parada et al., 2019; Zellweger et al., 2013); and the existence of both family and individual goals (Rautiainen et al., 2010) also affect the necessary governance solutions (Goel et al., 2019).

There is vast literature on business groups which are defined as a collection of legally independent firms that are linked by multiple ties, i.e., transactional and contractual economic arrangements, ownership and social relationships (Granovetter, 1995; Khanna & Rivkin, 2001). FBGs, which are typical in Asia but are also found in most economies in Western countries (Morck et al., 2005; Yiu et al., 2007), contain complex connections and multiple ties combined with family relations; and through these connections, family owners coordinate to achieve mutual objectives (Beckhard & Dyer, 1983; Rautiainen et al., 2019; Yiu et al., 2007). The FBG can be seen, like family businesses in general, as a system consisting of three subsystems: the family, the business and ownership. However, an FBG with several companies along a group of different owners (family and non-family members) brings complexity to the whole system that must be manageable.

In family businesses, an essential factor is ownership, which connects the family and the business. In an FBG, ownership acts as a multi-layered thread that ties individual companies and owners to the group and defines its structure. Ownership plays a significant role in the family business context and affects governance structures in business groups (La Porta et al., 1999; Morck et al., 2005; Young et al., 2008). The way the family is organised, and proportionate to holdings, determines how ownership power is organised within the firm and among family owners (Gersick & Feliu, 2014; Olson et al.,

2003). However, because the owners are also related to each other as family members, and are socialised to acknowledge moral obligations to each other, the distribution of ownership and power (and even the understanding of these concepts) among family owners is rarely as straightforward as the proportional shareholding—creating a multi-layered and idiosyncratic notion of ownership and its rights and obligations among family owners.

The family's ownership can be manifested and made tangible in several ways, e.g., as direct governance control through family board members, indirect (and informal) control through members nominated by the family, the direct managerial control through family managers and through managers chosen by the family (Corbetta & Salvato, 2004; Pieper et al., 2008; Silva & Majluf, 2008). As families expand and the number of owners increases in subsequent generations, cohesion at the ownership level becomes crucial (Ward, 1987), so the interaction between the family and ownership needs special attention. In FBGs, this need is emphasised, as mature FBGs contain both individuals in a family and several businesses in a group with different ownership logics and motives (Pihkala et al., 2019).

When the family business reaches a point where it includes several owners and many companies, the family needs to acknowledge the added complexity in a systemic sense and create mechanisms where multiple, and often varying, goals towards business and ownership can be discussed, and a degree of workable consensus can be achieved at the family owners' level. As a complex system containing several business and ownership structures, there is a need for deliberate strategic decisions to manage family, business and ownership levels coherently and simultaneously. Different governance solutions can bring clarity to the complexity, so a specifically tailored governance system that allows FBG particularities is crucial. Mature FBGs can exhibit a wide variation of governance systems in place, ensuring and enabling the use of ownership power over related companies and the group, and achieving a workable goal congruence among different owners (Goel et al., 2019).

In this study, we start our examination from the notion of ownership that connects and influences both business and family. From the governance point of view, the points where family ownership and business meet and influence each other are the most interesting ones and are also central for the success of the family business, so the effective management and use of ownership becomes important for the success of the family business. This study presents a new concept of "*governing ownership*" to describe the intersection of ownership and governance subsystems as distinct from family and business governance, and a governance system that provides the organising framework so that both the family and business goals can be mutually acknowledged and pursued.

Ownership is governed to avoid problems that can affect both the family and the business. Anecdotal evidence shows that family owners are building a specific ownership governance by which the ownership system is ruled. From the family perspective, the objectives to pursue by governing ownership issues in family business are linked to the conflict avoidance, the wealth preservation and ensuring the family business continuity (Gersick & Feliu, 2014; Olson et al., 2003; Suess, 2014). Our research question is *How does the family govern ownership to meet the diverse goals of the family and the family's goals towards the business? More specifically, what kind of ownership governance is put into place to ensure that a workable goal congruence can be achieved and a paralysing conflict can be averted?*

Thus, the objective of this study is to explore how family owners build and enlarge goal congruence between the family goals and business goals of the family. To achieve this objective, we analyse the ownership system in a Finnish FBG and explore ownership governance practices. We present a case study of an FBG in its fourth generation, where the owning family has invested time and effort into building a comprehensive system for governing ownership in the family and business levels. The case illustrates the policies, practices and methods that the family use for governing ownership and illustrates the requirements and possibilities for an ownership governance system. We limit our examination only to those structures, processes and practices that concern the family owners as a social group and individual members.

We contribute to an overlooked area of research in the context of FBGs by presenting the concept of *"governing ownership"* and creating the framework to illustrate the purpose, elements, objectives and implementation of the effective ownership governance system in this context. We also contribute to the family business literature by providing additional knowledge about the relationship between the owning family and businesses: that is, the family governance side, as most of the studies concentrate on the business governance side of the phenomenon (Howorth & Robinson, 2020). We present governing ownership as a distinct conceptual space from family governance and business governance, each of which have their own governance systems, comprising of structures, mechanisms and processes. In the following sections of the paper, we briefly review the current literature on ownership systems and governance in family businesses. We then present outlines for the conceptualisation of governing ownership. Following this, the research methodology and results of the empirical investigation are explored. Finally, there is a general discussion of the findings and concluding remarks, including suggestions for future research.

Literature Review

Governing Ownership System in a Complex Family Business Group

The ownership system is a major defining issue in a family business, but even more significant in FBG (Almeida & Wolfenzon, 2006; Jaffe & Lane, 2004; Pihkala et al., 2019). As a research approach, the system approach concerns complex entities, which are themselves part of a greater whole, and to be composed of interrelated components that interact together and share common properties (Ashmos & Huber, 1987; Checkland, 1981). Family business is defined as a complex system with a tight connection and interaction between three subsystems: family, business and ownership (Beckhard & Dyer, 1983; Tagiuri & Davis, 1996). Each subsystem has its own life cycle, where events are not concurrent with the other subsystem. However, events always have some degree of effect on other systems.

Changes in a family subsystem are related to the development of the family as a collective (Davis & Tagiuri, 1989; Gersick et al, 1999). The family subsystem includes emotional relationships and socialised moral obligations towards other family members. This forms the family process and task systems, capturing all elements taking part in the profit-making (Davis & Stern, 1988), where the lifestyle and wealth accumulation goals can play an important role for a particular family member (Zachary, 2011). Nonetheless, individual owners are not immune to the collective FBG (Rautiainen et al., 2012); instead, they may form a strong personal identification with the group as an ongoing *"social enterprise"* to be passed on to future generations (Schneper et al., 2008).

Family business is linked to transgenerational wealth *"a continuous stream of wealth that spans generations"* (Habbershon & Pistrui, 2002, p. 223), where family owners benefit from the growth and wealth generated by the business (Morck et al., 2005). Intergenerational wealth transfer and the increase in assets being transferred from one generation to the next requires management practices and an understanding of the meaning of ownership to build the system that best fits FBG. The interplay between multiple social and financial factors is complex, so protecting the family wealth, and family business continuity, needs a particularistic array of financial solutions tailored to the family's long-term needs, but also a well-functioning governance system that responds dynamically to the family's changing needs.

Ownership subsystem is a dynamic element comprising legal, psychological and social aspects (Rautiainen et al., 2012), and it connects the family and business subsystems in a family business (Klein et al., 2005). Family business ownership is seen to develop from controlling owner to a sibling partnership, ending with a cousin consortium (Gersick et al., 1999) and family syndicate or dynasty (Jaffe & Lane, 2004; Ward, 2001). However, this evolution does not follow a well-demarcated path for all family businesses; instead, it depends on family ownership decisions or actions (Ward, 2001). The changes in an ownership subsystem occur predominantly due to succession (Sharma et al., 2003), inheritance or variation in business development (Rautiainen & Pihkala, 2019), in addition to the evolution of the "definition" of the family.

In multigenerational family businesses, ownership is generally inherited, and sometimes new owners have little understanding of what they, as owners, are committed to (Thomas, 2002). With hundreds of share owners, there may be family shareholders who view their shareholdings as an investment with claims to an income and ease of liquidation rather than as a commitment to the continuity of the family business (Thomas, 2002). In situations where the family owner needs cash, for example, the owners expect the use of the assets to be flexible, which in turn requires diversification of investments (Neubauer & Lank, 1998). This is challenging, especially in the context of FBG with multiple companies diversified into different industries with different ownership structures (Pihkala et al., 2019). Diversification of family ownership can bring greater flexibility and give more options for the family in wealth management. At the same time, diversification can also increase complexity, as the number of domains to be managed increases on a variety of dimensions (Akhter et al., 2021).

Especially, when examining the family and business functioning in an FBG context, the meaning of ownership is highlighted (Chung & Chan, 2012). Ownership can be seen as a voting power and source of control which owners have over the company (Pieper & Klein, 2007; Ward & Dolan, 1998). This perspective has led to the examination of ownership via varying governance solutions, however, by focusing mainly on the business governance and not the governance of owners.

Studies about owners can be divided further based on research on the ownership base or structures (e.g., Chung & Chan, 2012), the development of ownership (Gersick et al., 1999) or owners as individuals or a collective, namely a family (Rautiainen et al., 2010). Especially in an FBG context, the management of ownership structure, either by "pruning the family tree"

(Lambrecht & Lievens, 2008) or by creating systems to manage the diverse ownership groups, and potentially diverse goals of increasing number of owners, is a crucial, and yet understudied, topic (Pihkala et al., 2019; Goel et al., 2019). As a step towards this, scholars have emphasised the importance of the owners' shared vision, united way of actions and responsibility towards both the business and the family (e.g., Davis, 2007a; Goel et al., 2019). The systems that owners design must be able to address goal differences of various kinds, including the trade-offs between short- and long-term goals and economic and non-economic goals. Governance systems could bring balance to a complex ownership system and be the determining factor in whether the family is a net positive resource for the business (as well as the family itself), or ends up restricting the success of the FBG (Habbershon & Pistrui, 2002).

Governing family ownership involves a deliberate and tailored governance system that can produce a diverse array of solutions tailored to the family and business needs. In this sense, ownership should be seen as strategic in nature, shaping how resources are accessed and used in the pursuit of economic value for the family (Foss et al., 2021). Both aspects—ensuring the commitment of owners and anticipating future needs—need a governance system to deliberately manage the complexities of a dynamic FBG.

Elements of Governance in the Family Business Group

Governance plays a critical role in managing tensions between overlapping subsystems and conflicts potentially arising from the goal differences of owners, owner groups and businesses in an FBG (Goel et al., 2019). In the FBG, idiosyncratic elements of family businesses run through the system, but the level of complexity is higher, partly due to increased ownership and structural complexity, which itself is partly idiosyncratic and partly influenced by lower relatedness among businesses. The latter implies that FBGs are not structured purely on the basis of technical or economic synergies among businesses. The FBG form allows the family members to explore their own entrepreneurial intentions by managing individual businesses that are owned together by the family and/or non-family members, which often leads to diversification and independent (yet internal) venturing in the family business. Through this dynamic, the family business grows both in size and in complexity. This, in turn, requires a governance system that allows the requisite level of integration across the individual businesses in the group or otherwise provides a coherent and tractable way to assess the economic and non-economic value of the FBG to the owners.

Along with the business development, more owners tend to join the business either because of ownership development (Gersick et al., 1997) and/or when outside investors participate in the business (Navarro & Ansón, 2009). Group ownership creates unique needs for the FBG governance system and affects the organisation of FBG governance significantly (Colli & Colpan, 2016). Along with the varying owners and owner collectives, the diversity of the goals multiplies, increasing possible tensions raising from the goal incongruence. Consequently, the meaning of the governance system as a tool to manage the goal congruence among shareholders grows in importance in an FBG (Goel et al., 2019).

The degree of ownership concentration affects the power balance among shareholders and set demands for the governance system and its ability to ensure equitable realisation of all shareholders' interests (Colli & Colpan, 2016). Other ownership-related dimensions also influence the needs for a governance system, such as number of owners and owning families, type of owners, dispersion of ownership among families or family members, and relationships between owners. However, research on these dimensions, and their effect on the family business governance (Daspit et al., 2018), is in its early stage.

A governance system consists of governance structures, mechanisms and processes. Goel et al. (2019) divide governance structures into formal, regulation-based structures and informal structures, based more on relationships, such as trust, culture, history and specific idiosyncrasies of the family business. Both formal and informal structures are necessary and functional if they complement each other. The formal control is needed to minimise the managerial or owners' opportunism, especially in the case of controlling owners and minority shareholders (Yiu et al., 2007). Social or relational control, instead, is important for promoting social interaction and the formation of a shared vision among shareholders (e.g., Goel et al., 2019; Mustakallio et al., 2002). Governance mechanisms, rules, practices and processes direct and control firm behaviour, and support the balancing and aligning of the interests of stakeholders (Walsh & Seward, 1990). In FBGs, intra-group control and coordination devices, like equity ties, interlocking directors, resource sharing, managerial ties and social and family ties, play crucial roles (Colli & Colpan, 2016).

Most of the governance literature is about business governance, covered largely in the broader field of strategic management, finance and economics, under the term "corporate governance". However, the relationship between the family and the business leads to the need to consider the family-business-relating outcomes, e.g., ownership continuity, stakeholder benefits and satisfaction, emotional ownership, development of leadership competencies from generations to generation and intrafamily entrepreneurship (Gersick & Feliu, 2014; Goel et al., 2019). As the family evolves, the number of family owners and participating family branches tend to increase. This increases the pressure to build the family governance system to govern the relationship between the business and the family (Suess, 2014) and to manage the family participation in the business. The central purpose of the family governance is also to build commitment and cohesion among the business family, and to collect the family members' insight for the collective view of the business and the family's role within it (Gersick & Feliu, 2014).

FBG governance should be "a flexible, evolving system, which should adapt to the changing contexts and contingencies, aiming at achieving the owners' goals and ultimately sustaining entrepreneurial capability in the FBG" (Goel et al., 2019, p. 255). When functioning well, the governance "nurtures the emergence of the family's shared dream (Gersick et al., 1997; Lansberg, 1999) and structures the operationalisation of that dream in organisational practice" (Gersick & Feliu, 2014, p. 199). It is crucial that an FBG governance system fits the goals, structure and development of the owning family, and is able to delegate the management power to participating companies (e.g., Jaffe & Lane, 2004). In practice, this means that the system has to be built based on needs arising from the family, as well as ownership systems in the FBG, and it has to adapt for the changes in these FBG subsystems as they develop and change. The governance of the FBG also needs to take into account the characteristics and governance requirements of individual companies and enables simultaneous consideration and implementation of different objectives at both company and group levels.

To succeed in the governing of a complex FBG, both family governance and business governance need to be utilised effectively: the family governance should create coherence among family owners and form the shared vision of the family's goals for the business, and the business governance should enable the implementation of the owners' vision (Goel et al., 2019; Suess, 2014). However, as ownership, in the end, gives a mandate to govern the complicated wholeness, the precondition for the well-functioning governance system is built at the ownership subsystem. Thus, an additional, conceptually separate domain of governance is needed for the ownership governance system to bring family owners' goals closer to the business goals, to offer channels for discussions between the participants from the family and business subsystems, and to clarify the owners' responsibilities and rights. Also, operationalisation of the family's goals towards the business, to the business practices and operations (Gersick & Feliu, 2014), could be defined as a part of the ownership governance function. Consisting of a combination of structures, processes, mechanisms and rules, the ownership governance system enables the owners to take their role as a resource, not as a burden in their family business group (Davis, 2007b; Habbershon & Pistrui, 2002).

Drawing clear boundaries between the family and business governance, as well as business and ownership governance, is not easy. For example, family governance structures depicted in earlier literature consists of a wide variation of meeting formats to gather the family members together to discuss and decide about issues. But then, who are actually those who get the invitation? Family members? Family owners? Family owners including next generation family owners? Further, what specific goals are being discussed? Family goals as a family? Family goals for businesses? Continuity as a business family? Family participation? Ownership goals and arrangements? We address this as a conceptually distinct governance space in the next section.

Towards Conceptualising Governing Ownership

Ownership evolves over the family business group life cycle, leading to a change in ownership norms to meet the evolving challenges of the whole FBG system. Individual family owners have a legal right to govern resources invested in family business (e.g., Foss et al., 2021). This right, afforded by ownership, allows owners to deploy resources in novel ways: acquiring and selling resources, investing in them or recombining them according to the owners' unique, idiosyncratic and ultimately inalienable beliefs about paths to their goals—it is the privilege of ownership. The interplay between multiple social family and financial factors creates complexity, as goals of individuals need to be articulated, and the overlap or complementarities between these goals assessed and negotiated. Family owners have many opportunities to invest and use their capital, so dedication to financial planning and coordination of family wealth in a matured FBG is essential. This requires competence that most family owners may not have, especially when it comes to new owners, for example, following a generational change.

Competence in ownership plays an important role in creating value for family business (Foss et al., 2021). The well-functioning ownership governance system can be seen as a visible manifestation of ownership competence. An ownership governance system is often drawn up by the family office that manages and oversees the wealth management affairs related to such issues as tax, wealth transfer, fiduciary oversight, investment management, governance, estate planning, risk management, compliance, communication, financial education, among other issues (Rosplock & Welsh, 2012). Along with the process of planning ownership governance, owners are likely to develop their personal understanding towards the assets. Governing ownership also requires the building of deeper understanding about the family's goals, both at family and business levels, as well as creating structures, processes, practices and policies to implement these goals. Creation of an ownership governance system may facilitate owners to define and manage what they want to own, for what purpose, and how the owned assets can be used to create value, as well as understanding how to set goals, define strategy and build management tools to achieve wealth creation.

In Fig. 11.1, we place ownership governance in the conceptual frame of FBG governance, together with family governance and business governance, and explain the possibilities that governing ownership provides to the FBG owners, when they pursue the accomplishment of both family goals and the family's goals for business. Section A (Fig. 11.1) represents the goals of the family owners, each of whom may have slightly different goals. The goals of the individual family owners are made cohesive via the family governance system—consisting of a formal governance system, such as family council, family constitution, etc. (Parada et al., 2019; Suess, 2014), and an informal governance system, consisting of trust and positive emotional connections among family members (e.g., Mustakallio et al., 2002). While the overall congruence is a dynamic process and a moving target (depicted by variance in Section A, the congruence achieved at any point of time is represented in aggregate family goals, arrow A.

Section B represents the goals of various businesses of the family. Section B acknowledges that goals for various businesses could be different from goals of individual family members (Section A). In addition, each of the businesses may have different goals due to differences in economic opportunity in the external environment, degree of downside risk that needs to be managed and differences in individual goals of business managers. These differences are made congruent via the business governance system—consisting of a formal governance system represented by the composition and functioning of boards of directors, as well as an informal governance system, consisting of cultural norms of obligations and performance (Goel et al., 2019; Parada et al., 2019). This congruence is represented in aggregate business goals, arrow B. Again, this does not assume that complete congruence has been achieved among all the business-related goals (nor is it necessary to achieve this), but merely represents congruence at any point of time.

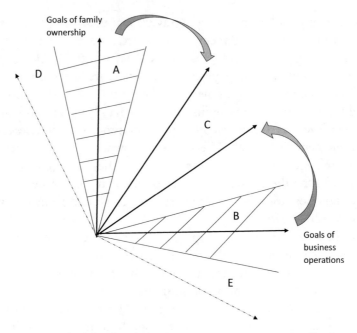

Fig. 11.1 Fan model of the family business governance conceptualisation

To emphasise, Sections A and B exhibit different directions, acknowledging the family's goals individually and collectively may be different (e.g., pursuit of "happiness") than the goals of individual businesses, as well as businesses collectively (e.g., returns to capital and satisfying internal and external stakeholders). In an FBG, the ownership governance system attempts to make these different goals congruent, as well as creating reinforcing loops so that the achievement of goals for the family owners also achieves the goals of the businesses.

Section C represents the *ownership governance system* (structures, processes, rules and policies). The effect of the ownership governance system is to increase the acknowledgement and socialisation of owners towards business goals, via developing responsible and knowledgeable owners, who are good stewards of business operations. This, in turn, increases the congruence of the family's goals towards the business goals, by making the achievement of business goals instrumental to achieving the family's goals—as represented by the movement of aggregate family goals, arrow A, towards the aggregate business goals, arrow B. In addition, and simultaneously, the ownership governance system also sets in motion the dynamic to make the business goals congruent to the family's goals, by making the achievement of goals of the family's goals (e.g., in terms of returns, risk, pursuit of businesses that interest the family, etc.) instrumental to achieving the goals of the business and its managers—as represented by the movement of aggregate business goals, arrow B, towards the aggregate family goals, arrow A. A well-functioning ownership governance system can create a functional "workable" congruence between the goals of the family owners as well as the businesses. It is also acknowledged that complete congruence may not be possible, due to philosophical and domain differences between the goals of family and businesses; but a complete congruence is not necessary for the healthy functioning of an FBG.

Finally, an ownership governance system, as represented by Section C, works best when it is in balance—providing equal space to both family and business goals to have a voice. If Section C tilts upwards towards family goals, it implies that it is designed to serve the goals of the family, and the family owners are not very well conversant about obligations of ownership and needs of businesses they own. This could result in a reduction in performance on business goals, as they may be starved of attention (e.g., capital, vision, strategy, etc.). If Section C tilts downward towards business goals, it implies that the ownership governance system is designed to serve as the goals of the business, and the family owners are forced to serve business goals. This could result in family owners abandoning their ownership to pursue their own interests.

Sections D and E represent distinct goals of specific family owners and businesses that are so different that they cannot be made congruent via the use of governance systems. Some family owners may have very distinct and idiosyncratic goals about the businesses that they would like to own, and also where they would like to deploy their personal wealth. They are represented in Section D. Similarly, some businesses may have very different goals due to their idiosyncratic characteristics and economic logic. These are represented in Section E. In both cases, the respective governance systems (family governance for Section D and business governance for Section E) would be either inadequate or prohibitively expensive to bring these voices into a semblance of congruence. For these cases, non-governance strategies would need to be adopted—e.g., a buy-out in the case of family owners representing Section D, and divestment in case of businesses representing Section E.

The governing of ownership in an FBG is important, yet we know little about how ownership is governed across generations and how the family manages the interests of its diverse and large ownership group and prepares for potential challenges in ownership. Solving such challenges is not straightforward. We argue that a long-term perspective is crucial to understand the extent and channels of governing ownership across generations. Next, we introduce a case example that suggests some guidelines to help govern family ownership.

Methodology

The Case Study Approach

The single case study method was selected to investigate how the family governs ownership in a family business group active in Finland. A case study approach allows for empirically investigating "*a contemporary phenomenon in depth and within its real-world context*" (Yin, 2018, p. 15). Major strengths of case studies are that they measure and record behaviour (Yin, 2018) and allow data collection from a variety of resources, both qualitative and quantitative (Chetty, 1996). The choice of a single case study was based on the approach of Dyer and Wilkins (1991), who argue that a single deep case is the optimum form of case study research. They highlight that "the *careful study of a single case leads researchers to see new theoretical relationships and question old ones*" (Dyes & Wilkins, 1991, p. 614). This method was valuable in this research mainly for two reasons. First, the use of the case study approach was appropriate for the study of governing ownership, since it provided in-depth contextual information on the emergence of ownership governance development embedded in the case (cf. Dyer & Wilkins, 1991). Second, it facilitated a holistic and more variegated and nuanced examination of the complex and cross-functional relationship between owners' capabilities in a case setting. This is enabled by the collection of rich, fine-grained data from multiple sources (cf. Dyer & Wilkins, 1991).

Context

There are various strategies available to guide the case selection process depending on the logic and purpose of the research, whether the researchers seek cases with unique or typical characteristics (Neergaard & Ulhøi, 2007). The researchers need to understand and describe the context of the scene in question to such a degree that they can generate a theory in relationship to that context. This means that researchers should get as close as possible to the phenomena under investigation and provide a rich description of the scene and underlying dynamics of the case (Dyer & Wilkins, 1991; Mintzberg, 1979). For this research, we followed a selection of a longitudinal case, guided by its power to explain and illuminate aspects of theory, rather than the extent to which they were typical in the field (Flyvbjerg, 2011; Silverman, 2013).

In this chapter, we will present a case of a Finnish FBG in its fourth generation. In the case, the business family has invested time and effort into building a comprehensive system for governing the family- and business-level ownership.

Data Collection

To capture the development of ownership governance, it is vital to explain and provide reasoning over time. This means conducting a process analysis on the development of the phenomenon under study (Pettigrew, 1997). Process analysis is meant to uncover how organisational and/or managerial phenomena unfold over time (including emergence and change) (Langley et al., 2013). Given the limited knowledge on the internal complexity in family business groups, we have combined theory elaboration (Lee et al., 1999) and theory building (Eisenhardt, 1989) approaches in our analysis.

The data collection process has taken place over three years (2018–2020), and mapping followed the rules defined and suggested by Rosa et al. (2019) and Rautiainen et al. (2012). The data have been collected in several stages. Two authors have visited the company several times. We processed data stage-by-stage by integrating variety of data sources over time to enhance an understanding of actors, processes and experiences within the family business group context. Our processual longitudinal approach relied on multiple unique data sources, i.e., archival material, field observations, interviews, journal/newspaper articles and contextual knowledge (see Table 11.1).

Case Description

Our case example is a Finnish family business conglomerate, founded in 1901. It has evolved to become a collection of five individual business groups, consisting of holding companies, trade and technology businesses and real estate holdings. The whole group is today privately owned by a Finnish family, having 17 owners in 4th and 5th generations. The group includes several holding companies and six operative companies, most of them having a subsidiary structure and operations both in domestic markets and abroad. Employing 3,600 employees in total, the family business group has achieved yearly sales of almost 1.5 billion in the past years, and has been one of the top ten family businesses, revenue-wise, in Finland.

Table 11.1 Description of data

Source	Type of information	Qty	Summary of content	The use in the analysis	The use in the findings
Visits at headquarters	Visits at the company between years 2018–2020	5	During the visit's familiarisation to the entrepreneurs, location and offerings	Building in-depth understanding of the case context	Backgrounding the findings, triggering and nurturing research process
Interviews	Several interviews with current head of owners' family	5	Open interviews about the longitudinal development of the company First and second interview focused on history including questions, such as how the group is developed Third and fourth interview focused on present situation, including questions related to current situation, succession processes, ownership and governance structures Fifth interview was targeted mainly to ownership governance development	Identify the owner's own narrative of the governance development and involvement in the development Confirmation of dates and facts about the actions that triggered and guided the governance structure changes and development over the years	Constructing ownership governance processes by the main owner Displaying the relationship between ownership and governance allocation Display the interplay between ownership and governance

Source	Type of information	Qty	Summary of content	The use in the analysis	The use in the findings
Newspaper and journal articles	Professional journals, regional newspaper articles, professional magazines	>10	Description of the company development due to different special events in the company history	Triangulate facts and observations about company through analysing evidence of external recognition of the company over time	Emphasising external endorsement of owner's qualities in managing and developing ownership governance
Websites	Different group company webpages	4	The company information from different business areas: car dealership, lighting electronics, audiovisual technology	To define how the company is publicly displayed and what information it provides	Case background information

284   T. Ikäheimonen et al.

In the early 2000s, the family realised that only some of their companies were profitable. In addition, it turned out, some of the group companies did not interest any of the owners, either in a business or ownership sense. A common perception among the owners was that something needed to be done fast to make the businesses healthier and to provide value for the owners. An important discussion took place between the owners—what companies should be owned in future, in what structure the companies would be organised, in what role the owners would operate in different companies and by what logic would the ownership arrangements be made. As a part of the process, boards of different companies were delegated to divide businesses for categories like "market leaders", "growth businesses" and "high-risk companies". Based partly on this division, and partly on family's and individual owners' interest in some companies, the family then determined what businesses they wanted to be involved in, and what they were willing to give up. In 2002, the FBG was reorganised based on created ownership strategy.

When the family members discussed targets of ownership, they also discussed and decided on the principles and rules to guide the family ownership of the companies. These principles encompassed, for example, the owners' expectations for the business development and financial performance, agreement about what companies the owners were ready to invest in and which business decisions the owners wanted to influence. Owners also defined limits for the authority of the group companies' boards and management, and they developed family governance policies regarding, e.g., family members' participation in the companies, the methods to collect and communicate owners' collective vision, and education and involvement of the next generation owners in the business decision-making.

In many cases, the intrafamily conflicts can form the obstacle for family business success (e.g., Olson et al., 2003). To prevents conflicts, the family invested time and effort into building a governance system to promote discussions and mutual understanding among family owners. All fourth-generation owners form the owners' council, a governance entity that meets between General Meetings and is built to collect the owners' thoughts about the ownership, different companies and the family business group development. The owners' council follows the official rules of procedures accepted by the General Meeting. Jaffe and Lane (2004) mention the owners council's role to be to form the collective insight or vision based on the family owners' varying preferences, and further, to communicate the vision to the board of directors, which in turn, interprets the owners' vision for the business objectives. This is also one of the main purposes for the case company's owners' council. The council ensures that the owners have a shared view with respect to the businesses, and that this vision is communicated to the boards of the group companies. This brings the owners ambitions and goals to the board's consciousness, and the actual board meetings can focus on business issues only.

In addition to defining the objectives for the business group ownership, the family also monitors business performance and the execution of the family vision. At the ownership level, the group companies are examined in the spring, when the family owners meet to discuss business matters, and their appropriateness and attraction from the perspective of the group and ownership. There are only owners in this meeting. After the meeting, the chairs of all operative parent companies receive information about the discussions and the results, including, e.g., notions about the issues that the family thinks need special attention or development in the near future. After this, the fourth-generation notions are communicated to the fifth generation during the summer.

In complex FBGs, often in later generations with an increasing number of owners, one way to consult owners and/or family members in company matters is to organise regular family meetings (Jaffe & Lane, 2004). In the case company, the family has a family owners' meeting twice a year. The first is organised in the spring, about a month before the General Meeting. In this meeting, the CEO and the chairs of each operative company also attend, and chairs go through the previous year's activities and performance. The second meeting, in the autumn, focuses on strategy, and its purpose is to present the updated strategy to the family owners.

Suess (2014) notes that family meetings are often arranged to advance the relationship between the family and the board of directors. In our case, the family meetings are arranged to provide for the wider group of family owners a possibility to get to know and discuss business issues. Acute issues, that are demanding owners' immediate attention, are mainly handled at holding-level ownership entities. The family also uses a "three-document practice" to follow the performance of the group companies, and to get and share information with the chairs and top management of the companies. The three documents include information about the current situation and future prospects of the company, the performance evaluated by using previously defined key performance indicators, and an estimation of leadership potential of the personnel for future development purposes. Owners go through all the documents in late autumn. The results of this annual seminar will be brought to the attention of all board members and top management to guide the strategy work in group companies.

In family and owners' meetings, the family discusses business issues and meets chairs and CEOs of the family group companies as a collective. However, family members represent the family also as individuals. The family has drawn up the owners' policy to direct family owners' participation and responsibilities in family-owned companies. When drafting the owners' policy, the family has agreed that the policy must be clear and concise and clearly distinguish those issues that are under the owners' consideration from those that belong to the companies' management or the board. Based on the owners' policy, the company management and the board are responsible in operative matters, the company strategies within the scope of current business fields, acquisitions and sales of companies and operations belonging to the line of business, as well as the appointment of an operative management. As such, the family's owners' policy is close to the owner constitution that often addresses issues regarding the governance and family's participation in the company (Suess, 2014).

Since 1914, family members have primarily carried out their responsibilities for the companies through board membership. The family has established principles for forming the boards at each level of the group (Table 11.2). At the group level, non-family board members from separate group companies interlock to some extent, and the family encourage them to meet from time to time to foster the knowledge sharing about group-level activities among board members. Family members with board membership also participate in knowledge sharing; they are expected to transmit (within the limits of confidentiality) knowledge of the individual businesses and their performance to other family owners.

The chairs of each of the companies compile the agenda for board meetings but ensure from the owners that the agenda is appropriate. The owners' insight about the company direction plays a significant role in board meetings, too: if the board wants to get the owners' opinions for the issues, and owners representing the family in a meeting are not able to give it, the issue

Table 11.2 Principles guiding the composition of the board at different levels of the FBG

	Holding level	Operative company level	Subsidiary level
The board consists of...	owners	two owners and outsider members	mostly outsiders
The chair is...	one of the owners	an outsider	outsiders
The deputy chair is...	one of the owners	one of the owners	an outsider

is drawn away from the agenda and brought back after the owners have discussed and formed a shared insight about it.

We summarise the findings from the case to be as follows. The case illustrates how the owner family of a complex FBG manages the family, business and ownership in a way that enables all relevant issues to be addressed, and further, maintains a balance between them. As a way to do this, the family has developed the governance system consisting of the family, the business and ownership governance systems. The separation of spaces between the family, the business and ownership governance provides strategic attention of the family to each of these areas, and at the same time binds them together coherently, so that no one domain has a chance to dominate or overpower the other domains.

The case shows that family governance establishes the value of collectivity for each family member. Family governance structures and processes allow the development of shared goals while retaining for each family member the possibility to also pursue individual goals. Business governance functions as both a channel to share and a way to monitor the implementation of the family vision regarding FBG development. In addition, the business governance enables the family members' direct participation in business decision-making and in the education of future competent owners in a real business environment.

The family sees ownership to be the glue connecting family business subsystems, and owners have put remarkable efforts into developing the ownership governance system to be a deliberate and separate construction to specifically discuss the aspect of ownership objectives like ownership distribution, changes in ownership, goals of ownership (both financial and non-financial) and for creating collective goals and evaluating performance on ownership goals and development. These discussions increase the appreciation and understanding of owners about the business objectives that they can take back to other family members and family governance, and also the value of family ownership, that they can take back to business governance.

Discussion—Governing Ownership in a Family Business Group

The case illustrates how the family manages with the issues arising from three family business subsystems in a complex FBG, and how they manage to do it deliberately and consciously, so that relevant issues in each subsystem are provided adequate structure and due process. Next, we discuss the implications of the case to our conceptualisation of governing ownership by focusing on Sections A, B and C (Fig. 11.1), as Section D and E did not come up in interviews. We show that although family governance and business governance are important parts of FBG governance, they are not enough without an emphasis on ownership and its governance. We argue instead that effective governing of ownership, and the well-structured ownership governance system, is the key to keep an FBG functioning, and to sustain its possibilities for stability, continuity and growth. By doing this, we contribute to the FBG literature by presenting the concept *governing ownership*, and outlining elements, objectives and the implementation of an ownership governance system.

The conflicts between family members may harm the success of the family business considerably. On the other hand, a shared vision has been found to have a significant positive impact on business performance, as it guides participating actors in their efforts to achieve an agreed future state (Alvarado-Alvarez et al., 2021). Ensuring the family unity, enabling the creation of a collective vision of the family goals and the family's goals for business, and fostering the goal congruence among family owners seems to be crucial for the success of the FBG (Goel et al., 2019). In this case, the family actively discussed family-related issues to achieve the consensus on goals, and to create a shared vision of expectations towards businesses. The family also put effort into figuring out the target of interests of individual owners. As forums for discussions, located in the family governance system (Section A in Fig. 11.1), the family used regular family meetings.

In addition to the topic discussed by the case family, many other topics relating to the family and the family's well-being can be discussed or taken into account in the frame of family governance. (Gersick & Feliu, 2014; Suess, 2014). Issues like balance between the family's economic and non-economic goals, management of the family's relationships to each other, overall family strategy, plans for developing the family's competencies and capabilities over generations, processes to address conflicts and disagreements, socialisation of new family members (e.g., spouses) in the family system, collective events, ceremonies and rituals, are all targets to clarify the family's vision about themselves as a business family, and to create cohesion among family members.

Especially in the FBG context, with potentially many family members and family branches, the existence of the family governance system is crucial for the family happiness and coherence. It should also take into account the whole family, including both owning family members and those without ownership, and retired and upcoming generations. If the family governance fails in these tasks, the influence may also reflect the business goals (Olson et al., 2003; Suess, 2014).

Based on our case, we can infer that, in Section A of our conceptualisation, the drivers for the discussions are well-being of the family and decisions about the family's (and individuals') goals. This may lead to the contradiction between the business and family objectives, and it may create tension between varying owner groups. If so, it is important to recognise that the family governance system is not able to create goal congruence and cohesion between different owner groups having differing goals.

Business governance ensures the legitimacy of the business operations but is also utilised to articulate the owners' goals for the management, to turn goals into strategic directions, to ensure that there are resources needed, and finally, to monitor the accomplishment of goals (Goel et al., 2019). In this case, the business governance ensures representation of relevant competencies for each business (via space for outsiders), as well as the family's voice, via the presence of its representatives, to ensure that the business' individual interests do not undercut the FBG's overall objectives (e.g., in terms of risk profile and values). It also provides for family members to gain experience in governance and to develop their long-term competence to be a responsible owner.

A business governance system, in our conceptualisation in Section B, is driven by the business goals. It aims to ensure the effectiveness and productivity of the business operation and balance between the needs of different ownership groups. In Section B, the goals of different group companies are also discussed and a suitable level of goal congruence created between them. However, business governance, based on the principle of equal treatment of shareholders, and the "business first" ideology, must not prioritise or take family owners' expectations and goals into action directly without the proper process to operationalise the family vision into business operations and results. This, again, may create tension between the family and business goals.

Both the family governance system and the business governance system are capable of fulfilling their roles in their own sections, either in Section A or Section B. However, there is a need for the governance system to bridge the gap between different goals and purposes the family and business subsystems have (Section C in Fig. 11.1). In addition, ownership issues vary in their time frame from, e.g., operative issues, and this creates the need for the forum to adapt longer-term family and ownership issues into shorter-term business issues. These needs are highlighted in the FBGs with multiple companies, multiple owners and complex ownership structures, requiring the multiple-level coordination and control to manage the complexity of the FBG. In many cases, the only common denominator in the complexity is ownership.

To manage the complexity of the FBG, the family built the ownership governance system consisting of structures, mechanisms, processes, practices and owners' policy (Table 11.3). The purpose of the ownership governance system is to increase goal congruence between the family and business goals, to foster the creation of coherence about the shared vision and strategic directions of the FBG among the owners and to implement good ownership as a business family in group companies.

In the case company, the owners' office serves the owners by creating a functioning interface between the operative and holding companies, arranging the corporate governance of the holding companies and by organising communication between the owners and the holding companies. The Owners' Office does not deal with the family matters. Other important structures in the family's ownership governance system are the Owners' council, which collects both 4th-generation owners and representatives of the 5th generation to discuss ownership and business, and the boards of directors of the holding companies. In the holding company boards, the owners make central decisions concerning ownership and the future of the FBG companies.

There are also processes and practices in the ownership governance system. The purpose of these practices and processes is to provide forums for delivering the owners' visions further to the boards and top management of the companies, and to support discussions between the family owners, the company management and the chairs of the operative companies. As different

Table 11.3 Ownership governance system in the case company

Structures	Processes and practices	Rules and principles: Owners' policy
Owners' office Owners' council Board of directors of holding companies	Family owners' meetings with owners, company chairs, and CEOs Practice of "three documents" Owners' annual seminar of business issues	Family owners' participation in board of directors Training procedures for next generation board membership Control of ownership issues in board meetings Rules about family owners' participation in operational management

companies are represented in the same meetings, these meetings work also as channels for intra-group knowledge sharing. The three-document practice and the owners' annual seminar of business issues provide the family the possibility to share their vision about the business development directly with the business actors, and also to monitor the accomplishment of their vision at the business level.

Finally, the important part of the ownership governance system is governing family members and family owners' participation in the business decision-making and business operations. Rules and principles regarding these, as well as the training of the next generation family members in governance, are written into the owners' policy.

Based on the notions from the case company, the ownership governance system has to be a two-way system. Its important function is to act in the middle, as a mediator, between the family and the business. To fulfil this function, the ownership governance system consists of structure, processes, practices and rules to govern the owners' participation in business operations and business decision-making, and at the same time, to monitor the accomplishment of the family vision in the group companies. Organising the information flow from the owners to the businesses and back is the central purpose of the ownership governance. In addition, the elements of ownership governance have to be built so that they facilitate connecting ownership to the business governance functions, and the family governance functions to the ownership.

The creation of the ownership governance system has had several significant outcomes for the functionality of the FBG and the experienced well-being/happiness of the family owners. At first, the ownership governance system provides the arena to bring the family and business goals closer to each other. This is implemented by providing suitable structures for family owners to meet and discuss their aims and goals, but also providing possibilities for the owners to meet and have deep conversations about the business issues together with the companies' chairs and CEOs. As such, the ownership governance system facilitates management of complexity due to the multiplicity of owners and businesses, as the number of them increases, and this increases cohesion and reduces conflicts among family owners.

The other dimension of family well-being and cohesion relates to the family owners' experiences of fairness. Mutually agreed policy regarding the owners' roles and participation ensures the fairness of practices and implementation of the procedural justice (e.g., Frank et al., 2011). That is, the owners can trust in their right to use their voices in decision-making,

292 T. Ikäheimonen et al.

neutrality and transparency, as well as equality and the equity of decision-making. Increasing family cohesion is a desirable goal in preserving business as a family business.

The ownership governance system maintains and develops the continuity of ownership and ensures that ownership decisions are based on shared values and approved so that they can also be implemented in business operations. With an effective ownership governance system, the family seeks to ensure that both the flexibility and the objectivity of business decision-making are not compromised.

The earlier discussion on risk management in family businesses has mostly concentrated on the examination of the risk-oriented behaviour (or lack of it) of family businesses and the relation between risk-taking and family business performance (e.g., Zahra, 2005). The individual-level examinations, or non-financial side of risk management, and their objectives have seldomly been explored in family business group literature. Ownership governance enables the discussions about the balance between business and ownership risks, i.e., owners are aware of the extent to which ownership can be used in a variety of critical situations and are aware of the extent of risks that can affect either the business, ownership or both. This, in turn, ensures business continuity as well the implementation of wealth creation.

Conclusions and Suggestions for Future Research

In this chapter, we presented a descriptive case about a FBG in its fourth generation and reflected the findings to the literature of family business ownership management, family business governance, family governance and FBG governance literature to form the suggestion of the conceptualisation for governing ownership in family business groups. This also forms the contribution of the chapter.

The system to govern ownership is the holistic entity, comprising of three separate and interdependent systems—the family, the business and the ownership governance. The overall objective of the larger system could be to ensure the business success and continuity, the family well-being (both financial and mental) and objective decision-making in business issues. The family business group context may benefit the development of this kind of system to provide governance clarity and manage the complexity that develops over time in a family business group—in family, business and ownership structure, with more family members, multiple businesses (some without any relationship with other businesses in the group), more owners (including non-family owners) with congruent or incongruent objectives. At the same time, the distinct domains of governance in the FBG structure, as evidenced in our case, enable effective risk management, encourage dialogue and collaboration among different owners and different generations, and foster implementation of the family's entrepreneurial intentions over generations.

We also suggest some possibilities for future studies. In the family case company, there was a governance leader almost exclusively dedicated to developing the ownership and ownership-related part of the governance system. This, in turn, ensured the establishment of the governance system. It is well known that, for example, in family business renewal, the role of a strong family member in promoting change is crucial (e.g., Salvato et al., 2010; Sievinen et al., 2020). It could be fruitful to study performance differences of having this kind of so-called family "ownership champion" in the development and implementation of the effective ownership governance system. As the family follows the processes set within the governance system, the system is expected to become institutionalised, as subsequent family leaders accept it as a given and work largely within its boundaries. It is an empirical question as to whether subsequent leaders that emerge from within the system are also interested in preserving the system. In addition, the development of the rules regarding governing ownership could be an interesting topic for closer examination. For example, how do the intrafamily rules for the use of ownership develop through time and generations? When there are inherited rules regarding ownership, how flexible do these rules need to be to account for variations in family ownership evolution, and how are these dynamic rules themselves institutionalised over time?

In our case, the family developed multifaceted mechanisms and structures to control risks relating to business operations, the family wealth, and the risk to compromise the family unity and the owners' objectivity in decision-making. The different risk perspectives have not been considered earlier simultaneously in the same framework. Instead, they are fragmented across different topics, e.g., family conflicts, succession risks, business stagnations and irrelevance due to lack of innovation, etc. The combined view of different risk management perspectives in an FBG context could result in a deeper understanding of conflict among owners, as well as performance differences among family business groups, including their disintegration.

References

Aguilera, R. V., & Crespi-Cladera, R. (2012). Firm family firms: Current debates of corporate governance in family firms. *Journal of Family Business Strategy, 3*(2), 66–69.

Akhter, N., Rautiainen, M., Pihkala, T. & Ikäheimonen, T. (2021). The risk that became true: Case study of a Pakistani family business portfolio diversification. In H. D. Yan & F. L. T. Yu (Eds.), *The Routledge companion to Asian family business* (pp. 478–493). Routledge.

Almeida, H., & Wolfenzon, D. (2006). A theory of pyramidal ownership and family business groups. *The Journal of Finance, 61*(6), 2637–2680.

Alvarado-Alvarez, C., Armadans, I., Parada, M. J., & Anguera, M. T. (2021). Unraveling the role of shared vision and trust in constructive conflict management of family firms. An empirical study from a mixed methods approach. *Frontiers in psychology,* 12.

Ashmos, D. P., & Huber, G. P. (1987). The systems paradigm in organization theory: Correcting the record and suggesting the future. *Academy of Management Review, 12*(4), 607–621.

Beckhard, R., & Dyer, W. G., Jr. (1983). Managing continuity in the family-owned business. *Organizational Dynamics, 12*(1), 5–12.

Checkland, P, B. (1981). *System thinking, system practice.* Chichester.

Chetty, S. (1996). The case study method for research in small-and medium-sized firms. *International Small Business Journal, 15*(1), 73–85.

Chung, H. M., & Chan, S. T. (2012). Ownership structure, family leadership, and performance of affiliate firms in large family business groups. *Asia Pacific Journal of Management, 29*(2), 303–329.

Colli, A., & Colpan, A. M. (2016). Business groups and corporate governance: Review, synthesis, and extension. *Corporate Governance: An International Review, 24*(3), 274–302.

Corbetta, G., & Salvato, C. A. (2004). The board of directors in family firms: One size fits all? *Family Business Review, 17*(2), 119–134.

Daspit, J. J., Chrisman, J. J., Sharma, P., Pearson, A. W., & Mahto, R. V. (2018). Governance as a source of family firm heterogeneity. *Journal of Business Research, 84,* 293–300.

Davis, J. A. (2007a). Assessing and enhancing individual power in the family business system. *Harvard Business School Publishing.* Note, 808-026.

Davis, J. A. (2007b). Governance of the family business owners. *Harvard Business School, 9-807*(21), 1–7.

Davis, P., & Stern, D. (1988). Adaptation, survival, and growth of the family business: An integrated systems perspective. *Family Business Review, 1*(1), 69–84.

Davis, J., & Tagiuri, R. (1989). The influence of life stage on father-son work relationships in family companies. *Family Business Review, 2*(1), 47–74.

Dyer, W. G., Jr., & Wilkins, A. L. (1991). Better stories, not better constructs, to generate better theory: A rejoinder to Eisenhardt. *Academy of Management Review, 16*(3), 613–619.

Eisenhardt, K. M. (1989). Building theories from case study research. *Academy of Management Review, 14*(4), 532–550.

Flyvbjerg, B. (2011). Case study. In N. K. Denzin & Y. S. Lincoln (Eds.), *The Sage handbook of qualitative research* (4th ed., pp. 301–316). Sage.

Foss, N. J., Klein, P. G., Lien, L. B., Zellweger, T., & Zenger, T. (2021). Ownership competence. *Strategic Management Journal, 42*, 302–328.

Frank, H., Kessler, A., Nosé, L., & Suchy, D. (2011). Conflicts in family firms: State of the art and perspectives for future research. *Journal of Family Business Management, 1*(2), 130–153.

Gersick, K. E., Davis, J. A., Hampton, M. M., & Lansberg, I. (1997). *Generation to generation, life cycles of the family business.* Harward Business School Press.

Gersick, K. E., & Feliu, N. (2014). Governing the family enterprise: Practices, performance, and research. In L. Melin, M. Nordqvist & P. Sharma (Eds.), *The Sage handbook of family business*, 196–225.

Gersick, K. E., Lansberg, I., Desjardins, M., & Dunn, B. (1999). Staging and transitions: Managing change in the family business. *Family Business Review, 12*(4), 287–297.

Goel, S., Ikäheimonen, T., & Rautiainen, M. (2019). Governance in family business groups: Resolving multiple contingencies to sustain entrepreneurial capability. In M. Rautiainen, P. Rosa, T. Pihkala, M. J. Parada, & A. Discua Cruz (Eds.), *The family business group phenomenon* (pp. 253–283). Palgrave Macmillan.

Goel, S., Mazzola, P., Phan, P. H., Pieper, T. M., & Zachary, R. K. (2012). Strategy, ownership, governance, and socio-psychological perspectives on family businesses from around the world. *Journal of Family Business Strategy, 3*(2), 54–65.

Granovetter, M. (1995). Coase revisited: Business groups in a modern economy. *Industrial and Corporate Change, 4*, 93–140.

Habbershon, T., & Pistrui, J. (2002). Enterprising families domain: Family-influenced ownership groups in pursuit of transgenerational wealth. *Family Business Review, 15*(3), 223–237.

Howorth, C., & Robinson, N. (2020). *Family business.* Routledge.

Jaffe, D. T., & Lane, S. H. (2004). Sustaining a family dynasty: Key issues facing complex multigenerational business-and investment-owning families. *Family Business Review, 17*(1), 81–98.

Khanna, T., & Rivkin, J. W. (2001). Estimating the performance effects of business groups in emerging markets. *Strategic Management Journal, 22*, 45–74.

Klein, S. B., Astrachan, J. H., & Smyrnios, K. X. (2005). The F-PEC scale of family influence: Construction, validation, and further implication for theory. *Entrepreneurship: Theory & Practice, 29*(3), 321–338.

Lambrecht, J., & Lievens, J. (2008). Pruning the family tree: An unexplored path to family business continuity and family harmony. *Family Business Review, 21*(4), 295–313.

Langley, A. N. N., Smallman, C., Tsoukas, H., & Van de Ven, A. H. (2013). Process studies of change in organization and management: Unveiling temporality, activity, and flow. *Academy of Management Journal, 56*(1), 1–13.

Lansberg, I. (1999). *Succeeding generations: Realizing the dream of families in business.* Harvard Business Review Press.

La Porta, R., Lopez-de-Silanes, F., Shleifer, A., & Vishny, R. (1999). The quality of government. *Journal of Law, Economics, and Organization, 54*(2), 471–517.

Lee, T. W., Mitchell, T. R., & Sablynski, C. J. (1999). Qualitative research in organizational and vocational psychology, 1979–1999. *Journal of Vocational Behavior, 55*(2), 161–187.

Mintzberg, H. (1979). An emerging strategy of "direct" research. *Administrative Science Quarterly, 24*(4), 582–589.

Morck, R., Wolfenzon, D., & Yeung, B. (2005). Corporate governance, economic entrenchment, and growth. *Journal of Economic Literature, 43*, 655–720.

Mustakallio, M., Autio, E., & Zahra, S. A. (2002). Relational and contractual governance in family firms: Effects on strategic decision making. *Family Business Review, 15*(3), 205–222.

Navarro, M. S., & Ansón, S. G. (2009). Do families shape corporate governance structures? *Journal of Management & Organization, 15*(3), 327–345.

Neergaard, H., & Ulhøi, J. P. (Eds.). (2007). *Handbook of qualitative research methods in entrepreneurship.* Edward Elgar.

Neubauer, F., & Lank, A. G. (1998). *The family business: Its governance and sustainability.* Macmillan Business.

Olson, P. D., Zuiker, V. S., Danes, S. M., Stafford, K., Heck, R. K., & Duncan, K. A. (2003). The impact of the family and the business on family business sustainability. *Journal of Business Venturing, 18*(5), 639–666.

Parada, M. J., Akhter, N., Basco, R., Discua Cruz, A. & Fitz-Koch, S. (2019). Understanding the dynamics of business group development: A transgenerational perspective. In M. Rautiainen, P. Rosa, T. Pihkala, M. J. Parada, & A. Discua Cruz (Eds.), *The family business group phenomenon* (pp. 201–222). Palgrave Macmillan.

Pettigrew, A. M. (1997). What is a processual analysis? *Scandinavian Journal of Management, 13*(4), 337–348.

Pieper, T. M., & Klein, S. B. (2007). The bulleye: A systems approach to modeling family firms. *Family Business Review, 20*(4), 301–319.

Pieper, T. M., Klein, S. B., & Jaskiewicz, P. (2008). The impact of goal alignment on board existence and top management team composition: Evidence from family-influenced businesses. *Journal of Small Business Management, 46*(3), 372–394.

Pihkala, T., Goel, S., Rautiainen, M., Mukherjee, K., & Ikävalko, M. (2019). Deciphering ownership of family business groups. In M. Rautiainen, P. Rosa, T. Pihkala, M. J. Parada, & A. Discua Cruz (Eds.), *The family business group phenomenon* (pp. 223–252). Palgrave Macmillan.

Rautiainen, M. (2012). *Dynamic ownership in family business systems—A portfolio approach.* Acta universitatis Lappeenrantaensis 485, Lappeenranta University of

Technology978-952-265-292-8, ISBN 978-952-265-293-5 (PDF), ISSN 1456-4491 (Dissertation).

Rautiainen, M., & Pihkala, T. (2019). The emergence of a family business group: The role of portfolio entrepreneurship. In M. Rautiainen, P. Rosa, T. Pihkala, M. J. Parada, & A. Discua Cruz (Eds.), *The family business group phenomenon* (pp. 65–87). Palgrave Macmillan.

Rautiainen, M., Pihkala, T., & Ikävalko, M. (2010). Family business in family ownership portfolios. *International Journal of Entrepreneurial Venturing, 1*(4), 398–413.

Rautiainen, M., Pihkala, T., & Ikävalko, M. (2012). Family business system models—a case study and some implications of open systems perspective. *Journal of Small Business & Entrepreneurship, 25*(2), 155–168.

Rautiainen, M., Rosa, P., Pihkala, T., Parada, M. J., & Discua Cruz, A. (2019a). *The family business group phenomenon.* Palgrave Macmillan.

Rosa, P., Howarth, C., & Discua-Cruz, A. (2014). Habitual and portfolio entrepreneurship and the family business. In L. Melin, M. Nordqvist, & P. Sharma (Eds.), *The Sage handbook of family business* (pp. 364–383). Sage.

Rosa, P., & Pihkala, T. (2019). Theoretical insight into the nature, diversity and persistence of business groups. In M. Rautiainen, P. Rosa, T. Pihkala, M.-J. Parada, & A. Discua Cruz (Eds.), *The family business group phenomenon* (pp. 17–35). Palgrave Macmillan.

Rosa, P., Rautiainen, M., & Pihkala, T. (2019). The methodological challenges of researching family-owned business groups. In M. Rautiainen, P. Rosa, T. Pihkala, M. J. Parada, & A. Discua Cruz (Eds.), *The family business group phenomenon* (pp. 37–62). Palgrave Macmillan.

Rosplock, K., & Welsh, D. H. B. (2012). Sustaining family wealth: The impact of the family office on the family enterprise. In A. I. Carsrud & M. Brännback (Eds.), *Understanding family businesses, undiscovered approaches, unique perspectives, and neglected topics* (pp. 289–312). Springer.

Salvato, C., Chirico, F., & Sharma, P. (2010). A farewell to the business: Championing exit and continuity in entrepreneurial family firms. *Entrepreneurship & Regional Development, 22*(3–4), 321–348.

Schneper, W. D., Celo, S., & Jain, N. K. (2008). Agents, altruism, and corporate governance: The impact of family ownership on non-executive compensation and training. *Proceedings of ASBBS, 15*(1), 1340–1352.

Sharma, P., Chrisman, J. J., & Chua, J. H. (2003). Succession planning as planned behavior: Some empirical results. *Family Business Review, 16*(1), 1–15.

Sievinen, H. M., Ikäheimonen, T., & Pihkala, T. (2020). Strategic renewal in a mature family-owned company—A resource role of the owners. *Long Range Planning, 53*(2), 101864.

Silva, F., & Majluf, N. (2008). Does family ownership shape performance outcomes? *Journal of Business Research, 61*(6), 609–614.

Silverman, D. (2013). *Doing qualitative research: A practical handbook.* Sage.

Suess, J. (2014). Family governance–Literature review and the development of a conceptual model. *Journal of Family Business Strategy, 5*(2), 138–155.

Tagiuri, R., & Davis, J. (1996). Bivalent attributes of the family firm. *Family Business Review, 9*(2), 199–208.

Thomas, J. (2002). Freeing the shackles of family business ownership. *Family Business Review, 15*(4), 321–336.

Ward, J., & Dolan, C. (1998). Defining and describing family business ownership configurations. *Family Business Review, 11*(4), 305–310.

Yin, R. K. (2018). *Case study research and applications.* Sage.

Yiu, D., Lu, Y., Bruton, G. D., & Hoskisson, R. E. (2007). Business groups: An integrated model to focus future research. *Journal of Management Studies, 44,* 1551–1579.

Young, M. N., Peng, M. W., Ahlstrom, D., Bruton, G. D., & Jiang, Y. (2008). Corporate governance in emerging economies: A review for the principal-principal perspective. *Journal of Management Studies, 45,* 196–220.

Walsh, J. P., & Seward, J. K. (1990). On the efficiency of internal and external corporate control mechanisms. *Academy of Management Review, 15*(3), 421–458.

Ward, J. L. (1987). *Keeping the family business healthy: How to plan for continuing growth, profitability and family leadership.* Jossey-Bass.

Ward, J. L. (2001). Developing effective ownership in the family controlled business. *National Association of Corporate Directors, 25*(7), 1–9.

Zachary, R. K. (2011). The importance of the family system in family business. *Journal of Family Business Management, 1*(1), 26–36.

Zahra, S. A. (2005). Entrepreneurial risk taking in family firms. *Family Business Review, 18*(1), 23–40.

Zellweger, T. M., Nason, R. S., Nordqvist, M., & Brush, C. G. (2013). Why do family firms strive for nonfinancial goals? An organizational identity perspective. *Entrepreneurship Theory and Practice, 37*(2), 229–248.

12

Informal Governance Practices in Family Business Groups: A Framework and Suggestions for Research

Tom Liljeström, Tuuli Ikäheimonen, and Timo Pihkala

Introduction

Managing within formal corporate governance in family business groups is guided by codes and regulations that determine rather clearly the roles and tasks for participating actors: owners, the board, and the management. It is surprising that very little attention has been given to the informal practices surrounding the formal ones, although the informal practices can form a decisive part of governance and internal efficiencies of family business groups. Several important questions deserve closer attention. How are informal governance practices born? How long do they last? Finally, and maybe most decisively, are they considered a legitimate way to use power?

Governance holds a different content depending on the definition used. The purpose of governance is defined as, for example, exercising power and control over the organization and its entities creating value and serving (Åberg

---

T. Liljeström (✉) · T. Ikäheimonen · T. Pihkala
School of Engineering Science, LUT University, Lahti, Finland
e-mail: Tom.Liljestrom@student.lut.fi

T. Ikäheimonen
e-mail: tuuli.ikaheimonen@lut.fi

T. Pihkala
e-mail: timo.pihkala@lut.fi

© The Author(s), under exclusive license to Springer Nature
Switzerland AG 2023
M. Rautianen et al. (eds.), *The Palgrave Handbook of Managing Family Business Groups*,
https://doi.org/10.1007/978-3-031-13206-3_12

299

et al., 2019; Haalien & Huse, 2005; Huse et al., 2005); organizing resource allocation (e.g., Chen et al., 2018; Daily et al., 2003a); and solving problems arising from the varying goals of the participating actors (Daily et al., 2003b; Oehmichen et al., 2017; Zahra et al., 2000). Hambrick et al. (2008) referred to corporate governance as the formal structures, informal structures, and processes that exist as part of roles and responsibilities in the corporate context. Regardless of the chosen definition, the concept tends to include actors, descriptions of the interactions between actors, and the purpose and added value of governance (Schönning et al., 2019; Voordeckers et al., 2014). Actors can be labeled simply as owners, shareholders, the board, management (Jocovic et al., 2015), and stakeholders (Huse & Rindova, 2001), or as coalitions of internal and external actors (Haalien & Huse, 2005).

In this chapter, we suggest that informal governance behavior represents a response to governance effectiveness in situations where formal governance does not suffice or would be considered too rigid, slow, or exclusive. Furthermore, we suggest that informal governance practices can be analyzed through three dimensions: duration, transparency, and legitimacy. Of particular interest for this chapter is what distinctions can be identified regarding informal governance practices, especially from the perspective of family business groups.

This chapter contributes to our understanding of governance in family business groups in three ways. First, we highlight the importance of surrounding informal governance practices as a prerequisite for effective formal practices in family business groups. Second, we propose a framework where the informal governance practices relate by duration, transparency, and legitimacy to the formal governance practices. Third, we point out the continuum and the dynamic, developing nature of informal governance practices in order to increase flexibility and effectiveness of management and governance in family business groups. We conclude by acknowledging the high demands set on methodological implications in future empirical research.

Literature Review

Features of Informal Governance

Formal governance captures the interactions between governance actors and those tasks that have been described for them either by law, codes, or regulations, or else in good governance recommendations. Time used for governance in annual general meetings and board meetings is increasingly filled with necessary governance matters like risk management and regulatory requirements. The ability to react quickly is especially needed in times of rapid change and in relation to disruptive business fields, and formal governance mechanisms and ways of work can fail to fill this need. It seems that companies need more flexible and faster working methods to cover areas like implementation of strategy (Beer & Eisenstat, 2000; Candido & Santos, 2015) or evolution and the use of agile methods (Baskerville & Pries-Heje, 2011; Katayama & Bennett, 1999). In parallel with external needs, the behavioral perspective on governance (e.g., Hambrick et al., 2008; van Ees et al., 2009) seeks to clarify the internal sources and mechanisms of actual board and governance behavior. Hambrick et al. (2008) divide the behavioral process within an organization into an inward aspect, revealing how decision-making processes may be biased, and an outward behavioral process of understanding how symbols and language can address normative compliance with societal norms and values. Van Ees et al. (2009) also distinguish between internal and external processes, with the former interactions including both collaboration and conflict, political bargaining, power and trust, conflict and emotions, and the latter involving coordination and cooptation, such as societal networks and director interlocks, social elites, and social movements.

While it seems that the phenomenon of informal governance grows out of an organization's needs to respond to internal or external necessities, informal governance research has not been very clear about its underlying assumptions regarding the phenomenon. In other words, prior studies have assumed that

- there is no clear duration for informal practices,
- there are no differences in the transparency of informal governance practices, and
- all informal governance practices are equally legitimate.

Nevertheless, multiple studies refer to the specific nature of informal governance practices. For example, Taylor (2001) refers to the ad-hoc nature of informal governance practices, suggesting that companies both large and small must be agile and able to respond quickly to fast-moving markets to succeed in today's unpredictable world. This, according to Taylor, means building decentralized structures and delegating real power to boards of subsidiaries, various divisions, and joint ventures. On the other hand, Roberts et al. (2005) suggest that less formal, off-board meetings with non-executives serve as a vital hidden space where background concerns can begin to be shared and discussed among the non-executives, and if appropriate, the chief executive. Bankewitz (2015) stresses that it is important to create a setting where board members apply their knowledge. From the standpoint of finding best practices through knowledge transfer, results presented by Machold et al. (2011) show how certain board working structures and process-oriented boardroom dynamics deserve further research efforts. They also say that a potentially fruitful line of inquiry may be to link research on the board process tradition with that of literature on team and entrepreneurial learning to shed further light on how well and how quickly new knowledge is transferred and used.

The Origin of Informal Practices

How are informal governance practices born? We suggest that in conducting research on informal governance, understanding the origin of the practices is vital (Chrisman et al., 2018). While the separation between external and internal sources has been well identified (Chrisman et al., 2018; Huse, 2005b), we suggest that a more organizational perspective should be adopted. Ocasio (1997) discussed delegated and emerged structures, in which context they are initiated and by whom. In delegated structures, the practices are created as managerial decisions by the owner, the board, or the CEO. These practices can also be identified as concrete decisions. On the other hand, the emerged structures are not intentionally induced but rather grow out of the routinization of daily operations (Concannon & Nordberg, 2018; Ocasio, 1997). Thus, we can identify a continuum with one end consisting of a clearly delegated managerial decision given to some persons to start a new way of work and the other of a situation where a new way of work has emerged.

Prior research on informal governance has remained rather silent on the origin of informal governance. The inherent assumption seems to be that informal governance mechanisms emerge as a type of self-organizing process. For example, Hambrick et al. (2008) argue that as corporations and societal norms evolve, so too do the boundaries of what constitutes governance. Similarly, Stevenson and Radin (2015) discuss the effects of informal networks on board members. They suggest that these networks emerge from the board members' need to influence each other, and thus, the emerged network relationships serve as tools for the use of power on boards.

On the other hand, informal governance mechanisms have also been presented as intentional decisions to, for example, advance the need for agility, change management, and strategy implementation (Beer & Eisenstat, 2000; Taylor, 2001). One of the key reasons for using informal practices is the inability of formal processes to respond to emerging problems. Beer and Eisenstat (2000) followed a company where the decision to shift from producing standardized, technically excellent products to integrated, tailored solutions created a cold war between those advocating the old way of doing business and those advocating the new strategy. As silent killers of strategy, they identified ineffective management and communication within the governance chain, thus leaving conflicting priorities, with the result being poor coordination. Since management avoided engaging in the conflict, matters had to be handled outside formal processes (Beer & Eisenstat, 2000). On the other hand, the challenge of agility has been investigated from the standpoint of optimal ways of organizing companies, challenging traditional hierarchical organizational models with models made up of teams responsible for decisions. Laloux (2014) approaches this notion from the angle of self-directed teams, and McChrystal et al. (2015) describes agility formed by empowered cross-sectional teams, "war rooms," where decisions are made faster than in a normal hierarchical management process. The focus in these studies has been on minimizing time and enhancing quality in steering activities.

The Temporality of Informal Practices

The duration of informal governance practices is decisive for research on informal governance. Hendry and Kiel (2004) distinguished between continuous and occasional practices. They suggested that in strategy processes, boards may assume the role of strategic control, that is, "exerting a continuous process of formal and informal influence over management, beginning early in strategy development and involving iterative consultation from development through to implementation and evaluation" (2004, p. 511). Later, Hendry et al. (2010) studied strategizing by the board of one company and identified an "episodic-continuous" dichotomy at work.

The temporary nature of informal governance practices has most typically been related to temporary organizations (Burke & Morley, 2016), project organizations (Turner & Müller, 2003), and networks (Jones et al., 1997). However, such practices have also been identified in long-lived organizational contexts, where temporary informal governance practices are introduced to respond to unexpected situations. For example, Concannon and Nordberg (2018) studied the liminal spaces in governance and suggested that "In liminal spaces, logics are suspended along with hierarchies and rules, which can be seen as inducing at least temporary deinstitutionalization. Using liminal spaces can be a mechanism of responding to an external jolt or as a means of provoking change in anticipation of, or absent, such a jolt" (p. 72).

Corporate governance is strongly guided by institutional pressures (DiMaggio & Powell, 1983; Parada et al., 2010). The external expectations for corporate governance direct businesses to communicate about formal and durable governance practices. Informal and temporary practices, on the other hand, do not serve external communication needs, but rather the needs of internal effectiveness. For example, McNulty and Pettigrew (1999) suggest that the strategic contribution of non-executives can be considerably enhanced by informal interim dialogue between board meetings. These arrangements are likely to be temporary, though, put in place only for the development of strategy.

The temporary nature of governance practices is closely related to their legitimacy. That is to say, should the introduced mechanisms be considered temporary, they may be better tolerated without the need to institutionalize and formalize them in the company rules. On the other hand, continuous informal governance practices may face increasing pressures of illegitimacy and end up being formalized or ended. Lawrence et al. (2011) studied the effects of episodic power on governance practices and reported that the use of episodic power was often associated with centralized decision-making practices and that the use of such practices disrupted the assumption of good governance.

The Accountability of Informal Practices

One of the key tasks of governance is to create accountability (Huse, 2005b). In this regard, informal governance practices cause doubts about the legitimate use of power (Anderson et al., 2007; Roberts et al., 2005). Stone (2013) says that informal power consists of the ability to obtain desirable outcomes within an organization, at some cost, by going outside normal channels. Wenstöp (2009) interestingly points out three dimensions of power: structure influencing, opinion shaping, and dimension making.

In their study on new directions for governance, Hambrick et al. (2008) take up the discussion of hidden versus open structures. Informal governance activities can be open and known to all in the governance chain of owners, board, and top management team and be a part of the company culture. Alternatively, the activities can be hidden and not known to anyone other than the participants. The hidden forms of informal governance have some obvious positive characteristics. For example, based on a wide range of related research, Noble (1999) concludes that the interaction and communication between managers and coalitions of managers is perhaps the most significant informal process within most organizations. In the family business context,

Calabro and Mussolino (2013) suggest that the existence of unwritten rules shared by family members (and by non-family members) reduces deviations from goals and interests.

However, hidden forms of governance—as effective as they may be for the organization—may create mistrust. Roberts et al. (2005) point out that conflict between investors and executives arises "not from an inherent conflict of interest between investors and executives, but rather from a tension between what serves actual effectiveness and what supports distant perceptions of effectiveness" (p. 21). Should the conflict over effective governance be severe, it may lead to parallel systems of governance: official, formal governance and unofficial, real and hidden governance. Concannon and Nordberg (2018) recognize risks in the use of less formal governance practices. They suggest that even if informal discussions create value for the company, less formal practices raise risks related to transparency and accountability.

Informal Governance in FBGs

Hidden or Open Informal Governance

The transparency of informal governance practices is related to three main issues: first, the participants may want to keep them secret because it could be regarded as an illegitimate form of influence or power by others participating in the governance chain; second, keeping things in a closed circle may encourage the participants to engage in more open communication; and third, it may be used to avoid personally or socially embarrassing or worrying situations from becoming widely known.

The informal governance practices may be applied due to disagreements. Corporate governance highlights the importance of upholding a constructive cognitive conflict. Yet very little research exists on the tools needed to go from differing views to board decisions. An atmosphere of open and constructive discussion, with a willingness to re-evaluate previous opinions does not necessarily exist. A lack of a process for resolution of different views can cause issues to be discussed in smaller settings without others knowing about them. If this continues, an open board discussion might cease, and other ways of resolving are needed. For example, should communication be impossible otherwise, an outsider could act as a mediator between the parties (Gabrielsson & Huse, 2005). Furthermore, the conflicting parties may not want to fight openly in the presence of an outsider, thus leaving space for decision-making. As an example, the owners of a family business group might engage an outside professional to lead some of the company's board meetings in especially demanding situations, e.g., if the board members have lost trust in each other and have difficulties in communicating with each other because of different views regarding the company. The informal board leader's task then is to rebuild trust between the board members by creating a shared situational picture regarding the direction in which to steer the company. Problems among the owners can be delicate family issues that the family members do not want to become generally known. As is typical with family business groups, the family ownership system may affect the business system directly and lead to difficulties in managing the company (Gabrielsson et al., 2016; Goel et al., 2019; Rautiainen & Pihkala, 2019).

If the participants of informal governance are only company owners, the arrangement is not about gaining excessive power from the official governance chain (Roberts et al., 2005). On the other hand, in a family business group the decision-making power can be used to adjust the governance structure rather freely. E.g., Parada et al. (2020) point out that *"there is evidence that family businesses that have adopted these governance mechanisms still resort to informal means to make decisions, such as making decisions at-the-dinner-table or through informal conversations between family members."*

Aquilera and Crespi-Cladera (2016) have pointed out that ownership structure is a powerful force in explaining the observed governance of companies. However, it is evident that due to informal arrangements, the formal governance processes—e.g., board meeting minutes, do not necessarily fully reflect the true nature of the situations. In that sense, informality may cause problems in terms of the accountability of governance practices (Concannon & Nordberg, 2018). Paradoxically, the stakeholders' decision to apply informal practices would be a sign of their joint interest in securing decision-making power despite eventual problems. These arrangements may be hidden from the rest of the organization for different reasons.

The decision to conduct informal governance practices openly may depend on several factors as well. While transparent informal governance may be a way for the stakeholders to signal its legitimacy, it can also serve as a means for intervening in the organization. That is, by communicating about the sharing of information in the governance chain, it is possible to affect the culture of the family business group and to signal expected ways of working within the organization. Furthermore, open communication about informal practices may be an attempt to reduce suspicion of management and governance within the group. Intentional intervention in the governance chain can affect the group simultaneously in several ways. First, it supports an active search for competitiveness through open discussion and effective leadership in the organization (Zhang & Bartol, 2010). This may be crucial if the information chains have become inflexible or slow to adjust. Second, it supports the development of networks and communities of practice among the participants in the governance chain, which enables more efficient and agile knowledge processes (Foss, 2007; Foss et al., 2010). This is important especially within family business groups, that may struggle with developing internal synergies, innovations, and use of groups resources. Open communication of informal practices is needed also if the owners' or management's intent is to initiate a cultural shift in the governance chain and create more interactive processes in the governance structure. Third, the mechanism may create a space where the participants can share and discuss different background concerns related to ongoing decision-making (Roberts et al., 2005). Roberts et al. (2005) have suggested that these liminal spaces may be hidden, but as we have described they can be intentionally organized as open and transparent.

Temporary or Continuous Informal Governance

Informal governance practices have mostly been considered as responses to sudden changes in the business environment. In this sense, the informal practices would in general be considered temporary (Concannon & Nordberg, 2018) or episodic (Hendry et al., 2010). However, several informal practices can be used constantly and in multiple ways. Classic theory of the firm (March & Simon, 1993) recognizes that satisficing often takes place instead of looking for optimal solutions. This explains why several, potentially overlapping practices, can take place at the same time, and go on for the time being. Practices develop as needed, and are not necessarily coordinated or pre-planned.

The continuity of informal practices is related to growing needs of companies in the family business group to involve certain stakeholders. If the management has concluded that the business environment has changed permanently and now requires fast and agile responses one natural way is to employ informal practices to address this need. Huse (2005a) suggests that in environments characterized by dynamism and rapid changes, fast decision-making may be needed, and board members may be needed who can rapidly understand a situation and ratify suggestions presented by the management. These practices can be organized on a constant basis to provide each member involved in the governance chain with a good shared situational picture of the company and its market. This is supported by Brunninge et al. (2007), who suggested that expanding the circle of people involved helps strategic change. In a family business group, the owners involved in the governance can be equally involved in strategic change, independent of their position in the governance chain. This may lead to changes in the governance structures as the governance chain develops into a governance circle—allowing each participant to be involved in information sharing and operative management. For example, financial reporting can be sent directly from the CFO to the owners instead of going through the board, and new board members or owners can be taken along to visit important clients or join the company's stand in important fares. In large family business groups, these structural changes may be critical for the sustained efficiency of the FBG.

For members involved in the governance structure, the continuous practices may seem more legitimate than occasional practices (Westphal & Zajac, 2013) as they become routinized, and the use of continuous methods is less demanding for the governance chain since tasks, reporting, and communication are agreed upon only once. Furthermore, the use of informal governance creates social capital embedded in the relationships, and the management may want to preserve that social capital (Mustakallio et al., 2002). Subsequently, different informal practices created for occasional use may prove their necessity as long-lived arrangements.

FBG decision-makers can show an interest in organizing their informal practices on a continuous basis for different reasons. For example, a family business group can arrange informal occasions for owners, boards of the FBG companies, and top management to form a shared culture, to share information, and learn to know each other as persons. The chairman of the board can establish informal contacts with the CEO between board meetings to share information and ideas and stimulate a culture of openness. This enhances a culture where dialogue is not restricted to structure. This pattern is in line with an earlier study by Garg and Eisenhardt (2017), who suggested that dyadic discussions between the CEO and board members are essential for an effective strategy-making process.

Delegated Versus Emerged Informal Governance Practices

In constant pursuit of effectiveness, family business groups are facing trade-offs between formal and informal governance practices. A family business group often has a significant overlap of roles between owners, board, and management. Because of this it is quite natural that formal board decisions are not necessarily the starting point for informal practices. If the idea for a new practice emerges with influential persons present, this can be enough for a launch. Later the practice can be ratified by the board, but can also continue unratified as a reflection the evolving culture of communication in the FBG.

While informal practices may have perks regarding flexibility, speed, and communication, the lack of a formal backbone structure may cause problems for the whole group. This can be especially prevalent in groups dominated by the founder. The founder's active and informal operative role that typically emerges during the early stages of the group's formation can later begin to limit the freedom of the group companies' boards and top management teams considerably. This can be surfaced with an evaluation of the group's boards and top management teams. There is a risk that the founder micromanages the group as in the early years after foundation. The appropriate role of the founder can be worth to evaluate. It can be a good idea to discuss if the founder would create more value to the group by focusing on his own area of expertise and ease of the governance tasks of the group.

When focusing on boards, Huse (1998) suggests that the interactions between the board and management may be conscious or unconscious and may result in the adoption of new techniques to improve board performance. The founder's role in the group can be unconscious and strongly related to the founder's personality and position as owner in the group (Gnan et al., 2015). A repositioning of the founder's role might give place for other owners and group company board members to contribute more within their area of expertise. This could be a way for increasing agility within the FBG (Baskerville & Pries-Heje, 2011; Katayama & Bennett, 1999).

Conclusions and Implications

Informal governance has remained an elusive topic. The difficulties in defining the phenomenon have consequences for theory formation, methodologies, and knowledge accumulation on informal governance. The conceptual vagueness of informal governance leads to low validity of the research instruments and low comparability of research results. In this chapter, we focused on the dimensions of informal governance that have major implications for the governance of family business groups.

This chapter makes three major contributions. First, we highlight that formal corporate governance in family business groups tends to be embedded in informal governance practices, and the effectiveness of the formal governance might be severely hampered without surrounding informal practices. As a consequence, it is worthwhile to evaluate the governance as a whole. Formal governance can gain much from a surrounding framework of informal practices. Second, we have proposed a conceptual set of informal governance practices building on the aspects of *duration, transparency, and legitimacy.* Third, we highlight that although earlier research has agreed that informal governance has arisen from the need to secure the effectiveness of corporate governance, studies have made surprisingly little effort at understanding informal governance practices as forms of organizing. In this chapter, we consider informal governance practices as a wide field of organizational activities aiming for the effectiveness of management and governance. Within this field of practices, these activities may differ from each other in several ways. For example, there is a big difference between a practice that is hidden, episodic, and emergent and a practice that is generally known, long term, and intentionally created. For the conceptual and theoretical development of informal governance, recognizing and defining these forms separately could be a way to advance our understanding of an effective governance structure in family business groups.

Avenues for Future Research

Understanding the nature of different forms of informal governance in FBGs leads to a set of questions for future research. First, the difference between emerged and delegated informal governance practices is a decisive one: while delegated practices are likely to be easiest to identify, they are also very close to being "formal." That is, the question regarding the origin of governance practices tests the boundaries between formal and informal governance and is likely to reveal a long continuum of formality instead of a binary-type distinction between formal–informal practices. In FBGs that typically have concentrated ownership and multiple separate businesses are likely to be pulled to both directions simultaneously: increasing formality increases the FBG's and its businesses' legitimacy and credibility and thereby even informal governance practices need to be clearly delegated and governed. At the same time, the constant search for synergies within the FBG is bound to create emergent forms of informal governance.

Second, we suggest that informal governance practices may develop from one form to another. Further research focusing on the evolution of informal governance practices from emergent to delegated, from episodic to continuous, and from hidden to visible would contribute to understanding the dynamics of informal governance. Furthermore, FBGs are likely to have different developmental governance processes in the various separate businesses as well in the ownership level of the system. Due to the processual nature of the research topic, these research targets would benefit from qualitative, longitudinal research methodologies.

Third, the different forms of informal governance can be seen as organizational responses to (1) the need for governance effectiveness and (2) need for creating new synergies among the FBG businesses. These motives raise questions about decision-making practices related to governance. What are the governance actors' logics regarding whether to keep things hidden or visible? How do decision-makers choose between episodic and continuous informal governance practices? Once detected, can emerged informal governance practices become formalized? What idiosyncratic features of family business groups have to be considered? Finally, how to the different choices made on the informal governance relate to the motives for using them—do they create increased governance effectiveness or increased possibilities for synergy?

Fourth, our framework suggests methodological implications. The aspects of duration, transparency, and legitimacy set high demands for future empirical research. That is, for empirical research an analysis of the delegated, continuous, and visible practices would be rather easy to depict. However, informal governance in an organization may also include practices that are hidden from general knowledge, emergent by origin, and episodic. With respect to data gathering, these characteristics present a challenge: How do you ask about things that are hidden? The challenge requires us to make decisions regarding the informants and their ability to perceive and reflect on their governance behavior. That is, we assume that the selected informants would be aware of possible informal governance practices even if they are hidden from the main organization. In addition, we would assume that these decision-makers would be able to recognize, label, and reflect upon these unspoken practices. These issues are crucial to an understanding of informal governance, and we encourage future research to focus on these questions.

Fifth, we suggest that the distinction between episodic and continuous informal governance practices needs to be accounted for in the analysis of governance effectiveness. That is, the decision to make short-term arrangements to aid in the governance process may contain clear expectations about the effectiveness of such arrangements. On the other hand, it is rather likely that continuous informal governance practices have remained durable because of their ability to make an impact. From this perspective, the effectiveness of informal governance practices cannot be estimated by their duration. However, studying episodic and continuous practices in the same study would pose a serious challenge for research methodologies. We suggest that these aspects need to be considered in future research, otherwise such a study would likely draw biased conclusions. These characteristics set high demands for empirical research, especially regarding structured research instruments.

References

Åberg, C., Bankewitz, M., & Knockaert, M. (2019). Service tasks of board of directors: A literature review and research agenda in an era of new governance practices. *European Management Journal, 37*, 648–663. https://doi.org/10.1016/j.emj.2019.04.006

Anderson, D. W., Melanson, S. J., & Maly, J. (2007). The evolution of corporate governance: Power redistribution brings boards to life. *Corporate Governance: An International Review, 15*, 7780–7797. https://doi.org/10.1111/j.1467-8683.2007.00608.x

Aquilera, R. V., & Crespi-Cladera, R. (2016). Global corporate governance: On the relevance of firm's ownership structure. *Journal of World Business, 51*, 50–57. https://doi.org/10.1016/j.jwb.2015.10.003

Bankewitz, M. (2015). Boards' different advisory tasks—What makes board members use their knowledge? *American Journal of Management, 16*, 54–69. https://ezproxy.cc.lut.fi/scholarly-journals/boards-different-advisory-tasks-what-makes-board/docview/1829021160/se-2?accountid=27292

Baskerville, R., & Pries-Heje, J. (2011). Post-agility: What follows a decade of agility? *Information and Software Technology, 53*, 543–555. https://doi.org/10.1016/j.infsof.2010.10.010

Beer, M., & Eisenstat, R. A. (2000). The silent killers of strategy implementation and learning. *MIT Sloan Management Review, 41*, 29–40.

Brunninge, O., Nordqvist, M., & Wiklund, J. (2007). Corporate governance and strategic change in SMEs: The effects of ownership, board composition and top management teams. *Small Business Economics, 29*, 295–308. https://doi.org/10.1007/s11187-006-9021-2

Burke, C. M., & Morley, M. J. (2016). On temporary organizations: A review, synthesis and research agenda. *Human Relations, 69*, 1235–1258. https://doi.org/10.1177/0018726715610809

Calabro, A., & Mussolino, D. (2013). How do boards of directors contribute to family SME export intensity? The role of formal and informal governance mechanisms. *Journal of Management & Governance, 17*, 363–403. https://doi.org/10.1007/s10997-011-9180-7

Candido, C., & Santos, S. (2015). Strategy implementation: What is the failure rate? *Journal of Management & Organization, 21*, 237–262. https://doi.org/10.1017/jmo.2014.77

Chen, X., Huang, J., Li, X., & Zhang, T. (2018). Corporate governance and resource allocation efficiency: Evidence from IPO regulation in China. *Journal of International Accounting Research, 17*, 43–67. https://doi.org/10.2308/jiar-52104

Chrisman, J. J., Chua, J. H., Le Breton-Miller, I., Miller, D., & Steier, L. P. (2018). Governance mechanisms and family firms. *Entrepreneurship Theory and Practice, 42*, 171–186. https://doi.org/10.1177/1042258717748650

Concannon, M., & Nordberg, D. (2018). Boards strategizing in liminal spaces: Process and practice, formal and informal. *European Management Journal, 36*, 71–82. https://doi.org/10.1016/j.emj.2017.03.008

Daily, C. M., Dalton, D. R., & Cannella, A. A., Jr. (2003a). Corporate governance: Decades of dialogue and data. *Academy of Management Review, 28*, 371–382. https://doi.org/10.5465/amr.2003.10196703

Daily, C. M., Dalton, D. R., & Rajagopalan, N. (2003b). Governance through ownership: Centuries of practice, decades of research. *Academy of Management Journal, 46*, 151–158. https://doi.org/10.5465/30040611

Dimaggio, P. J., & Powell, W. W. (1983). The iron cage revisited: Institutional isomorphism and collective rationality in organizational fields. *American Sociological Review, 48*, 147–160. https://doi.org/10.2307/2095101

Foss, N. J. (2007). The emerging knowledge governance approach: Challenges and characteristics. *Organization, 14*, 29–52. https://doi.org/10.1177/2F1350508407071859

Foss, N. J., Husted, K., & Michailova, S. (2010). Governing knowledge sharing in organizations: Levels of analysis, governance mechanisms, and research directions. *Journal of Management Studies, 47*, 455–482. https://doi.org/10.1111/j.1467-6486.2009.00870.x

Gabrielsson, J., Calabrò, A., & Huse, M. (2016). Boards and value creation in family firms. In R. Leblanc (Ed.), *The handbook of board governance* (pp. 748–762). Wiley. https://doi.org/10.1002/9781119245445.ch37

Gabrielsson, J., & Huse, M. (2005). "Outside" directors in SME boards: A call for theoretical reflections. *Corporate Board: Role, Duties & Composition, 1*, 28–37. https://doi.org/10.22495/cbv1i1art3

Garg, S., & Eisenhardt, K. (2017). Unpacking the CEO-board relationship: How strategy making happens in entrepreneurial firms. *Academy of Management Journal, 60*, 1828–1858. https://doi.org/10.5465/amj.2014.0599

Gnan, L., Montemerlo, D., & Huse, M. (2015). Governance systems in family SMEs: The substitution effects between family councils and corporate governance mechanisms. *Journal of Small Business Management, 53*, 355–381. https://doi.org/10.1111/jsbm.12070

Goel, S., Ikäheimonen, T., & Rautiainen, M. (2019). Governance in family business groups: Resolving multiple contingencies to sustain entrepreneurial capability. In M. Rautiainen, P. Rosa, T. Pihkala, M. J. Parada, & A. Discua Cruz (Eds.), *The family business group phenomenon*. Palgrave Macmillan. ISBN: 978-3-319-98542-8.

Haalien, L., & Huse, M. (2005). *Board of directors in Norwegian family businesses: Results from the value creating board surveys* (Research Report 7/2005). Norwegian School of Management BI. http://hdl.handle.net/11250/94089

314   T. Liljeström et al.

Hambrick, D. C., Werder, A. v., & Zajac, E. J. (2008). New directions in corporate governance research. *Organization Science, 19*, 381–385. https://doi.org/10.1287/orsc.1080.0361

Hendry, K. P., & Kiel, G. C. (2004). The role of the board in firm strategy: Integrating agency and organizational control perspectives. *Corporate Governance: An International Review, 12*, 500–520. https://doi.org/10.1111/j.1467-8683.2004.00390.x

Hendry, K. P., Kiel, G. C., & Nicholson, G. (2010). How boards strategise: A strategy as practice view. *Long Range Planning, 43*, 33–56. https://doi.org/10.1016/j.lrp.2009.09.005

Huse, M. (1998). Researching the dynamics of board—Stakeholder Relations. *Long Range Planning, 31*, 218–226. https://doi.org/10.1016/S0024-6301(98)00006-5

Huse, M. (2005a). Corporate governance: Understanding important contingencies. *Corporate Ownership & Control, 2*, 41–50. https://doi.org/10.22495/cocv2i4p3

Huse, M. (2005b). Accountability and creating accountability: A framework for exploring behavioural perspectives of corporate governance. *British Journal of Management, 16*, 65–79. https://doi.org/10.1111/j.1467-8551.2005.00448.x

Huse, M., Minichilli, A., & Schöning, M. (2005). Corporate boards as assets for operating in the new Europe: The value of process-oriented boardroom dynamics. *Organizational Dynamics, 34*, 285–297. https://doi.org/10.1016/j.orgdyn.2005.06.007

Huse, M., & Rindova, V. (2001). Stakeholders' expectations of board roles: The case of subsidiary boards. *Journal of Management & Governance, 5*, 153–178. https://doi.org/10.1023/A:1013017909067

Jocovic, M., Milovic, N., & Lojpur, A. (2015). Changes in management role in the corporate governance system—Example of Montenegro. *Journal of Contemporary Management Issues, 20*, 149–161. https://hrcak.srce.hr/150572

Jones, C., Hesterly, W. S., & Borgatti, S. P. (1997). A general theory of network governance: Exchange conditions and social mechanisms. *Academy of Management Review, 22*, 911–945. https://doi.org/10.5465/amr.1997.9711022109

Katayama, H., & Bennett, D. (1999). Agility, adaptability and leanness: A comparison of concepts and a study of practice. *International Journal of Production Economics, 60–61*, 43–51. https://doi.org/10.1016/S0925-5273(98)00129-7

Laloux, F. (2014). *Reinventing organizations: A guide to creating organizations inspired by the next stage in human consciousness*. Nelson Parker.

Lawrence, T., Suddaby, R., & Leca, B. (2011). Institutional work: Refocusing institutional studies of organization. *Journal of Management Inquiry, 20*, 52–58. https://doi.org/10.1177/1056492610387222

Machold, S., Huse, M., Minichilli, A., & Nordqvist, M. (2011). Board leadership and strategy involvement in small firms: A team production approach. *Corporate Governance: An International Review, 19*, 368–383. https://nbn-resolving.org/urn:nbn:de:0168-ssoar-267331

March, J., & Simon, H. (1993). *Organizations*. Blackwell.

McChrystal, S., Collins, T., Silvermann, D., & Fussell, C. (2015). *Team of teams: New rules of engagement for a complex word*. Penguin Publishing Group.

McNulty, T., & Pettigrew, A. (1999). Strategists on the board. *Organization Studies, 20*, 47–74. https://doi.org/10.1177/0170840699201003

Mustakallio, M., Autio, E., & Zahra, S. A. (2002). Relational and contractual governance in family firms: Effects on strategic decision making. *Family Business Review, 15*, 205–222. https://doi.org/10.1111/j.1741-6248.2002.00205.x

Noble, C. H. (1999). The eclectic roots of strategy implementation research. *Journal of Business Research, 45*, 119–134. https://doi.org/10.1016/S0148-2963(97)00231-2

Ocasio, W. (1997). Towards an attention-based view of the firm. *Strategic Management Journal, 18*, 187–206. https://doi.org/10.1002/(SICI)1097-0266(199707)18:1+%3c187::AID-SMJ936%3e3.0.CO;2-K

Oehmichen, J., Heyden, M. L. M., Georgakakis, D., & Volberda, H. W. (2017). Boards of directors and organizational ambidexterity in knowledge-intensive firms. *International Journal of Human Resource Management, 28*, 283–306. https://doi.org/10.1080/09585192.2016.1244904

Parada, M. J., Gimeno, A., Samara, G., & Saris, W. (2020). The adoption of governance mechanisms in family businesses: An institutional lens. *Journal of Family Business Management*. ISSN: 2043-6238.

Parada, M. J., Nordqvist, M., & Gimeno, A. (2010). Institutionalizing the family business: The role of professional associations in fostering a change of values. *Family Business Review, 23*, 355–372. https://doi.org/10.1177/0894486510381756

Rautiainen, M., & Pihkala, T. (2019). The emergence of a family business group: The role of portfolio entrepreneurship. In M. Rautiainen, P. Rosa, T. Pihkala, M. J. Parada, & A. Discua Cruz (Eds.), *The family business group phenomenon*. Palgrave Macmillan.

Roberts, J., McNulty, T., & Stiles, P. (2005). Beyond agency conceptions of the work of the non-executive director: Creating accountability in the boardroom. *British Journal of Management, 16*, 5–26. https://doi.org/10.1111/j.1467-8551.2005.00444.x

Schönning, A., Walther, A., Machold, S., & Huse, M. (2019). The effects of directors' explorative, Transformative and exploitative learning on boards' strategic involvement: An absorptive capacity perspective. *European Management Review, 16*, 683–698. https://doi.org/10.1111/emre.12186

Stevenson, W. B., & Radin, R. F. (2015). The minds of the board of directors: The effects of formal position and informal networks among board members on influence and decision making. *Journal of Management and Governance, 19*, 421–460. https://doi.org/10.1007/s10997-014-9286-9

Stone, R. W. (2013). Informal governance in international organizations: Introduction to the special issue. *The Review of International Organizations, 8*, 121–136. https://doi.org/10.1007/s11558-013-9168-y

Taylor, B. (2001). From corporate governance to corporate entrepreneurship. *Journal of Change Management, 2*, 128–147. https://doi.org/10.1080/714042492

Turner, J. R., & Müller, R. (2003). On the nature of the project as a temporary organization. *International Journal of Project Management, 21*, 1–8. https://doi.org/10.1016/S0263-7863(02)00020-0

van Ees, H., Gabrielsson, J., & Huse, M. (2009). Toward a behavioral theory of boards and corporate governance. *Corporate Governance: An International Review, 17*, 307–319. https://doi.org/10.1111/j.1467-8683.2009.00741.x

Voordeckers, W., Van Gils, A., Gabrielsson, J., Politis, D., & Huse, M. (2014). Board structures and board behaviour: A cross-country comparison of privately held SMEs in Belgium, The Netherlands and Norway. *International Journal of Business Governance and Ethics, 9*, 197–219. https://doi.org/10.1504/IJBGE.2014.063279

Wenstöp, P. Z. (2009). Consequences of board power. In M. Huse (Ed.), *The value creating board*. Routledge.

Westphal, J. D., & Zajac, E. J. (2013). A behavioral theory of corporate governance: Explicating the mechanisms of socially situated and socially constituted agency. *The Academy of Management Annals, 7*, 607–661. https://doi.org/10.5465/19416520.2013.783669

Zahra, S. A., Neubaum, D. O., & Huse, M. (2000). Entrepreneurship in medium-size companies: Exploring the effects of ownership and governance systems. *Journal of Management, 26*, 947–976. https://doi.org/10.1016/S0149-2063(00)00064-7

Zhang, X., & Bartol, K. M. (2010). Linking empowering leadership and employee creativity: The influence of psychological empowerment, intrinsic motivation, and creative process engagement. *Academy of Management Journal, 53*, 107–128. https://doi.org/10.5465/amj.2010.48037118

13

Territoriality in Family Business Groups: The Impact of Ownership in Sharing Territories

Noora Heino❿, Marita Rautiainen❿, and Tuuli Ikäheimonen

Introduction

Brown et al. (2005) state that '*Life in organizations is fundamentally territorial*' (p. 577). That is, organisations are favourable contexts for establishing territorial boundaries and manifesting territoriality, as they entail settings characterised by power and politics, with the motives for ownership often guided by the desire to hold claim to several objects, thus triggering territorial behaviour (Brown, 2009). In a family business, the business and the ownership are shared with other actors within the same domain. Besides having the legal-economic rights to possess business entities and objects, family owners exhibit deep psychological and social attachment towards their possessions. Thus, the family owners both as individuals and as a collective group aim to construct, communicate, maintain and restore proprietary attachment to objects permanently or temporarily, and they are sensitive to the property

---

N. Heino (✉) · M. Rautiainen · T. Ikäheimonen
School of Engineering Science, LUT University, Lahti, Finland
e-mail: noora.heino@lut.fi

M. Rautiainen
e-mail: marita.rautiainen@lut.fi

T. Ikäheimonen
e-mail: tuuli.ikaheimonen@lut.fi

© The Author(s), under exclusive license to Springer Nature
Switzerland AG 2023
M. Rautianen et al. (eds.), *The Palgrave Handbook of Managing Family Business Groups*,
https://doi.org/10.1007/978-3-031-13206-3_13

lines that define the boundaries of their various owned targets (Brown et al., 2005). Hence, there is a need for family owners to maintain power and authority and to protect one's or a group's territories.

Despite the increased interest in human behaviour in business organisations, territories, territorial boundaries and territorial behaviours are rather unexplored areas of research in the context of family businesses. Most existing studies view territories only as static geographic places or physical environments/spaces and focus on the surrounding territories (local contexts) in which family firms operate as well on the relationships and effects they have on one another (Bau et al., 2019; Del Baldo, 2012; Garmendia-Lazcano et al., 2020; Martínez-Sanchis et al., 2020; Nordqvist & Melin, 2010). Furthermore, the tendency to examine how legal, social and political power are manifested within family firms rather than focus on territories causes researchers to refer overly much to legal and social family system boundaries (Distelberg & Blow, 2011). Moreover, territorial behaviour has mainly been investigated among non-family employees (Atalay & Özler, 2013; Sieger et al., 2011), with researchers focusing on how psychological ownership affects their work attitudes and behaviours while making few references to family members and owners. However, as Rantanen and Jussila (2011) note, families in business, like any other groups, have territorial motivations and are constantly searching for whatever territorial gratification the possessions can provide them.

Additionally, although current research on territoriality in organisations has focused on such topics as social systems (Brown, 1987), social processes (Porteus, 1976), marking and defending (Brown et al., 2005), and control and power relations (Sassen, 2013), studies examining territoriality predominantly underline only the psychological and social aspects of the phenomenon. However, a business, which operates not only as a social system but also as an entity, is composed of a variety of material and immaterial elements that can be legally, psychologically and socially seen as different personal territories. As territorial behaviours also manifest themselves in private spaces and towards those objects over which individuals and groups hold legal ownership rights, all three dimensions of ownership, legal-economic, psychological and social, should be taken into account when examining territories and territoriality in business organisations and among business owners.

In this study, we extend the territoriality research streams to levels of ownership and analyse how different dimensions of ownership affect territorial behaviour and the territorial division of family business groups during and after critical events. We analyse how the two types of territoriality, marking and defending, take shape during such events and highlight the factors in family ownership and in those critical incidents that influence them. Thus, our research question is as follows: '*How does ownership affect the division of territory and territorial behaviour during critical events impacting family business groups?*' We use a qualitative approach consisting of multiple case analyses, with the cases being purposively selected. We also conducted semi-structured interviews with family business group owners.

By using qualitative research methods and introducing the concept of territoriality into family business group research, we can investigate this phenomenon in more depth and contribute to an understanding territory-related behaviour by family business group owners that might appear irrational or unusual. Indeed, we are able to demonstrate how ownership and feelings of ownership influence family business group owners' motives, attitudes and behaviours. As a result, our contribution is twofold. First, our study advances the theoretical understanding of owners' territorial behaviour in family business groups. We underline that when looking at territories and territoriality from an owner's perspective, besides taking the psychological and social aspects of the phenomenon into account, the legal-economical point of view also needs to be considered. This is particularly evident with respect to the critical events impacting family business groups when major changes in ownership or at a generational stage occur. Second, we contribute to territoriality research by extending the territoriality discussion from the individual level to a collective level by showing that the family unit has collective motives for retaining, altering and protecting its possessions (territories) and that it exercises group territoriality. Third, we extend the examination of territoriality from that of an individual organisation to family business groups, i.e. how territoriality concerns many businesses simultaneously. We also highlight that both legal-economic as well as psychological and social attachments create a setting for negotiating territorial boundaries between the actors involved in the business, where the different actors may claim their share of the family business group.

The paper is structured as follows. First, we introduce the theoretical foundations of our study and discuss ownership in general and family businesses and family business groups in particular. Second, we introduce the concepts of territory and territoriality, while also discussing their links to the concept and dimensions of ownership. By doing so, we set the stage for our contribution, as our empirical work advances each of these discussions. Before moving on to our analysis and findings, we introduce our cases and outline the research process as well as the choices of methods. Towards the end of the paper, we focus on the novel ideas and leads that arise from our analysis,

320 N. Heino et al.

specify how our findings extend existing knowledge and discuss their utility for future research as well as practice.

Literature

Ownership in Business Organisations

Ownership is always a social construct (see Berger & Luckmann, 1966) linking items of property to one or more people and defining social relations among persons (Stein, 1976). As a relationship between people and ownable things, the concept can be defined in multiple ways. Typically, in business organisations the concept encompasses three dimensions: legal-economic, psychological and social (i.e. socio-psychological and socio-symbolic). Legal-economic ownership is defined as follows: '*the total body of rights to use and enjoy a property, to pass it on to someone else as an inheritance, or to convey it by sale. Ownership implies the right to possess property*' (Webster's New Word Law Dictionary, 2006). It can be seen as a system of rules and principles relating to coordinating property and as the most fundamental element for claiming and holding possessions since it addresses a question concerning people's normative standing, meaning the legal rights and duties held against one another with respect to an object (Dorfman, 2010). In general, the legal ownership of an asset consists of three elements: the right to use the asset, the right to appropriate the returns from the asset and the right to change its form, substance and location (Libecap, 2002). In business organisations, legal ownership establishes the right of people to exert an influence in managing the firm and have a seat on the board of directors. Although legal-economic ownership is socially constructed (see Berger & Luckmann, 1966), it is based on institutionalised and social agreements, such as laws and other formal regulations, and it is recognised by society (Rautiainen, 2012).

However, Etzioni (1991) notes that ownership is a '*dual creation, part attitude, part object, part in mind, part real*' (p. 466). The other two forms of ownership, psychological and social ownership, are based on emotions and can exist without legal-economic ownership (Pierce et al., 2001; Sieger, 2011); they can also operate separately from each other (Atalay & Özler, 2013; Shu & Peck, 2011). Accordingly, psychological ownership is defined as '*the feeling of possessiveness and of being psychologically tied to an object*' (Pierce et al., 2001, p. 299). It is a psychological state referring to feelings of possessiveness and attachment where an individual (or a group) perceives that an object is 'theirs' (e.g. *'This family firm is OURS and belongs to US'*). Feelings of ownership emerge because people are motivated to be effective and competent in altering their possessions (e.g. Deci & Ryan, 1985; Furby, 1978; White, 1959), to use the possessions to define themselves and the groups they belong to (i.e. to answer the question *'Who am I and where do I belong?'*; e.g. Dittmar, 1992; Mead, 1934; Porteus, 1976), to assume the possessions as a place in which to dwell and feel at home (e.g. Altman, 1975; Ardrey, 1966; Duncan, 1981), and to seek stimulation through the possessions because they meet their arousal requirements (Duncan, 1981; Kamptner, 1989; Porteus, 1976).

Social ownership entails two dimensions, socio-psychological and socio-symbolic ownership, and it is internalised through a process of interaction. Socio-symbolic ownership is based on a status, a role or an identity, whereas socio-psychological ownership refers more to possessing something through affective and collectivistic emotions. In both instances, possessions are experienced as extensions of the self (Dittmar, 1992). Social ownership extends the meaning of the concept beyond its general legal, financial and structural definition, as it is constructed by possessions and social agreements between individuals and groups (Nordqvist, 2005). It also highlights ownership as shared and collective phenomenon; individuals become members of a social group through collective possessions and a collective identity.

Ownership in Family Businesses and Family Business Groups

In a family business, ownership is unique, multifaced and mostly shared among others. That is, in most cases the owner is not an individual person but a collective, a specific social group labelled a family (e.g. Gersick et al., 1999; Tagiuri & Davis, 1996). While economic and strategy researchers (Anderson & Reeb, 2003; Burkart et al., 2003; La Porta et al., 1999) refer to legal-economic ownership as the main distinguishing factor, psychological and social ownership also significantly affect family businesses since elements of all three are typically intertwined. In other words, when looking at a family's level of engagement in the firm and behavioural issues, for instance, besides its legal status (Hall, 2005), emotional attachments based on the shared values, culture and history of the family and the business become important factors in ownership (Rau et al., 2018). Family owners are likely to form a strong personal identification with and devotion to their businesses (Bernhard & O'Driscoll, 2011). Additionally, social ownership is related to both forms of ownership and takes place in family firms during social interaction, including negotiations regarding ownership, and it results in mutual agreements regarding the targets of ownership (Brundin et al., 2014). It also highlights the collective nature of family ownership when family members make agreements with each other or the family as a social and structured group makes contracts with others.

As ownership in family business groups entails dealing with multiple businesses simultaneously, it is often seen as highly complex (Almeida & Wolfenzon, 2006; Jaffe & Lane, 2004), but also as flexible, loose and persistent as well as rather tolerant of the pressures arising from the family dynamics (Mäkimattila et al., 2016). The ownership structures of family business groups can be organised in a number of ways: for instance, the businesses may be owned by the founder or leading person of the family, several family members may own businesses within the group (but not involving the whole family), some businesses may be owned through another company or companies (e.g. pyramid structures, holding companies) and some businesses may even involve non-family owners. Accordingly, some businesses may have multiple series of shares with differential voting rights, thus leading to different positions of power and control. The owners may also value various businesses and parts of the business differently, and their businesses may have different objectives, resources, positions in the market and links to other businesses inside or outside the group (Pihkala et al., 2019). Since collecting several businesses within a business group may provide the owners with opportunities to follow self-deserving interests, their possessive feelings and emotional attachment towards different businesses may vary (across generations, too). That is to say, typically the level of psychological ownership determines the owner's level of interest in and expectations for the businesses (Pihkala et al., 2019).

Territories and Territoriality

Territories and territoriality comprise two different categories. Typically, territories refer to spaces '*where the accumulation of economic actions and common values takes place*' (Pallares-Barber et al., 2004, p. 638), as they play an important role in the activities of the people living there. Territoriality, on the other hand, refers to the exclusive right of space (Sack, 1983), the psychological possession of a space by an individual or group (Altman, 1975) and the behaviours of individuals and groups (Brown et al., 2005). According to Sack (1983), territoriality is best understood as '*a spatial strategy to affect, influence* or control resources and people, by controlling area; and, as a strategy, territoriality can be turned on and off. In geographical terms, it is a form of spatial behavior' and fundamentally 'a human strategy to affect, influence and control' (pp. 1–2). Hence, it is a behavioural expression of ownership of an object that emerge when social actors occupy or try to occupy a shared social space or a target of ownership.

It is rather noteworthy that in recent years the concept of territory has assumed a more 'holistic' meaning as it has evolved from the notion of a (static) place, with a predominant geographic and object connotation, to having a more dynamic and complex meaning and comprising system involving tangible and intangible elements that give a sense of place to a network of actors (Del Baldo, 2012). In other words, the concept of territory can be used to describe 'a stretch of land, an idea, a function, or anything else that holds a person's fancy to such a degree that he [or she] seeks to own it' (Bakker & Bakker-Rabdau, 1973, p. 271). Accordingly, besides physical objects like businesses, homes, automobiles, tools, machines and office rooms (e.g. Beaglehole, 1932; Belk, 1988; Dittmar, 1992; Prelinger, 1959), many targets within the social structure of entities (e.g. people, groups, units, departments, their practices and the relationships between social entities) have been referred to as potential targets of a personal sense of possession (e.g. Dirks et al., 1996; Dittmar, 1992; Kostova, 1998; Peters & Austin, 1985) as well as objects that are abstract in nature (e.g. rhymes, songs, other artistic creations, words, ideas and privileges) (e.g. Beaglehole, 1932; Heider, 1958; Isaacs, 1933; James, 1890).

Brighenti (2006) thus notes that 'relationship, rather than space, is ... at the conceptual core of territory, so that spatial and non-spatial territories can be seen as superimposed one onto the other and endowed with multiple connections, according to different scales and degrees of visibility' (p. 65). He continues by saying that territory is regarded as 'an activity of boundary-drawing and as a process which creates pre-assigned relational positions — actors who, by building and shaping their social relationships draw different types of boundaries' (Brighenti, 2006, p. 65). When people create territories, they create boundaries that both unite and divide space along with everything it contains (Penrose, 2002). Boundaries demarcate spaces for their possessions (Malmberg, 1980).

As social constructions, territories only come into being when they are produced through social interactions among relevant parties driven by psychological mechanisms (see Pierce & White, 1999). Indeed, 'instead of thinking of places as areas with boundaries around, (places) can be imaged and articulated moments in networks of social relations and understandings' (Massey,

1993, p. 58). Interacting actors produce territories, but territories as such also shape the actors, including their rationality (Crevoisier, 2014). Through communication, learning and memory, individuals and groups participate in the social construction of territories; they for instance learn to negotiate with other potential owners of the same territory and to adapt their behaviour to fit the surrounding social structures (see Ardrey, 1966).

Territories and territoriality are interconnected, with the notion of territories logically preceding territoriality and territorial actions. However, it is only via these actions that territories and territorial boundaries are defined and created (Elden, 2010). Accordingly, Brown et al. (2005) note that territories come into existence through the territorial behaviours of individuals and groups, and hence, they define territoriality as '*an individual's behavioural expression of his or her feelings of ownership toward a physical or social object*' (p. 578), adding that '*territoriality reflects the social meanings of actions regarding claiming and protecting objects as they are negotiated in a given social context*' (p. 579). Due to the socially constructed nature of territories (see Dittmar, 1992), they are not absolute or permanent (Raffestin, 2012); rather, they are constantly de-constructed, re-constructed, de-functionalised and re-functionalised through the interactions of social actors.

Since territoriality conveys the idea of psychologically possessing a place or an object (Altman, 1975), it is closely linked to the concept of psychological ownership (Brown et al., 2005). Psychological ownership is similar to the idea of proprietary attachment in territoriality research, meaning that both concepts complement and build on one another. However, the greatest distinction between the two concepts is that whereas psychological ownership is a psychological state referring to feelings of possessiveness and attachment towards an object, territoriality is a social behavioural concept, referring to behaviours that emanate from a sense of psychological ownership for the purposes of constructing, communicating, maintaining and restoring one's attachment to an object (Brown et al., 2005).

Territoriality literature suggests that people occupy territories, use them, invest in them and familiarise themselves with them because territories make them feel efficacious (e.g. Thrasher, 1936; Yablonsky, 1962), allow them to distinguish themselves from others (e.g. Hatch & Cunliffe, 2006; Richards & Dobyns, 1957), provide them with (physical) security and (psychological) safety (Brown, 1987; Porteus, 1976), and serve as a source of stimulation (e.g. Duncan, 1981; Kamptner, 1989). It is via these actions—(1) control over a target of possession, (2) interdependent investment (of energy, time, intellect, skills and physical resources) into the target and (3) inter-subjective familiarisation (knowledge processing) with the target and personalisation of that target—that a sense of ownership of a territory develops. Scholars have also suggested that the degree of territorial behaviour is linked to the degree of proprietary attachment (Brown, 1987; Csikszentmihalyi & Rochberg-Halton, 1981; Ley & Cybriwsky, 1974). For instance, Altman (1975) distinguishes different levels of territory (primary, secondary and public) and states that the more people have a psychological interest in and feel a sense of satisfaction with the territory in question, the more control they will claim over those territories.

Although scholars like Sommer (1974) have suggested that territoriality should be distinguished from legally owned objects, such as organisation, properties and so forth, others, like Soja (1971), note that territoriality affects human behaviour at all social activity levels and that the concept is constructed from the Western idea of private ownership. A business is not only as a social system, but also an entity, meaning it is comprised of a variety of material and immaterial elements that can be legally, psychologically and socially seen as different personal territories. As territorial behaviours also manifest themselves in private spaces and with respect to the objects over which individuals and groups hold legal ownership rights, we argue that all three dimensions of ownership, legal-economic, psychological and social, should be taken into account when examining territories and territoriality in business organisations. Besides feelings of attachment and social contracts, the drawing of territorial boundaries and territorial behaviour are in many cases based on legal-economic ownership, which encompasses the rights to control and exercise jurisdiction over the territory and resources within it (Simmons, 2001).

Territorial Behaviours of Marking and Defending

The objectivation of territoriality comprises two distinct behaviour sets, marking and defending, both of which can further be divided into two subcategories: marking occurs either as *control-oriented* or as *identity-oriented* territoriality and defending occurs as *anticipatory* or *reactionary* territoriality (Brown et al., 2005). Marking refers to those behaviours that construct and communicate an individual's or a group's proprietary attachment to particular objects. Marking, which makes use of either physical symbols (e.g. nameplates on doors, labelled group spaces, pictures of family owners on websites, family name or logo on a letterhead) or social symbols (e.g. titles used by certain people, social rituals that convey belonging and access, public pronouncements) as discursive or visual expressions of ownership, is a way to make others aware of one's territory and begin the process of negotiating acceptance of one's territorial claim in the social environment. Defending, on the other hand, appears as forceful territorial actions when an individual or a group feels the need to defend or restore its territory. It serves as a response to a perceived or potential invasion of an established territory and manifests itself in such actions as locking doors or using receptionists to prevent entry or access to certain spaces or people, establishing passwords for files and computers, discrediting the outgroup's understanding of information, acquiring new, higher-quality information, seeking informal support from others or making formal complaints (Brown et al., 2005).

In more detail, identity-oriented marking involves marking an object or territory with symbols that reflect one's own or a group's identity (Brown et al., 2005; Sundstrom & Sundstrom, 1986), while control-oriented marking refers to markers that are not personalised but that instead communicate the boundaries of a territory and who has psychological ownership over it (Altman, 1975; Becker & Mayo, 1971; Smith et al., 1983). Once territorial boundaries are defined or modified, individuals and groups may begin personalising their space. As Pratt and Rafaeli (2001) observe, territoriality represents a form of personalisation that expresses an individual's personal and professional identity. Identity-oriented marking enables individuals and groups to distinguish themselves from others, to construct and express a variety of facets of their identities to themselves and to others (Brown et al., 2005). Whereas identity-oriented marking involves marking an object to express an identity or self, control-oriented marking is used to control access to or use of the object in question (Brown & Altman, 1981, 1983). It organises and brings meaning to spaces, roles and other objects that serve as personal territories. Control-oriented marking of territories is likely to manifest itself especially when new actors (individuals or groups) flow into the space and reality, and/or when new constructs are formed (e.g. when a new function is introduced to the organisation).

Since territorial boundaries are socially constructed norms or psychological contracts, they often come into conscious awareness only when or after they are being violated (Brown & Robinson, 2011). This indifference or disagreement of ownership of the target, which manifests itself in encroaching on another individual's or group's territory, is defined as 'an infringement' (e.g. Brown et al., 2005; Lyman & Scott, 1967). Accordingly, it threatens proprietary claims over a territory, and thus, threatens a loss of the benefits derived from controlling that territory (Brown & Robinson, 2011). Fear of infringement has the potential to induce territorial anticipatory and reactionary defences with the first occurring prior to and the latter after an infringement (Brown et al., 2005). Anticipatory defences manifest themselves in such actions as holding information, locking doors, setting passwords on computers, hiding files or even planting useless ideas to prevent illegitimate entry into or theft of those targets. Importantly, compared to control-oriented marking, anticipatory defences are not communicative actions in nature; rather, they prevent any attempted infringement on a territory by ensuring the actual attempt fails (Brown et al., 2005).

Despite fierce attempts to mark territories and establish anticipatory defences, territorial infringements may still occur. Reactionary defences are behavioural reactions to a perceived infringement (see Brown & Robinson, 2011). They are mostly based on immediate emotional responses (Zajonc, 1984) that occur when someone threatens an individual's or a group's territory, for instance by using or taking something without permission (Brown, 1987; Brown et al., 2005; Wollman et al., 1994). Different ways of perceiving an infringement have led to different kinds of reactions; the greater the anger caused by the infringement, the greater the reactionary defence (Brown & Robinson, 2011). Reactionary defences may manifest themselves in such actions as complaining, shouting, slamming doors, glaring or otherwise expressing and showing physical discomfort in response to a violated territory.

Territories and Territoriality in Family Businesses and Family Business Groups

While territories have received scholarly attention, territoriality is rather unexplored area of research in a family business context. Recently, Basco and Suwala (2020) have provided an extensive overview of family business studies exploring topics related to space and searched for a fertile ground between family business studies and regional studies. Although they identify several types of spatial entities in the literature, it seems that most studies examining family business territories have adopted the rather narrow view and notion of territories as only static geographic places or physical environments/spaces. That is to say, much research has focused on the surrounding territories (local contexts) into which such businesses are inserted as well on the relationships and effects they have on one another (Basco, 2018; Bau et al., 2019; Del Baldo, 2012; Garmendia-Lazcano et al., 2020; Kahn & Henderson, 1992; Martínez-Sanchis et al., 2020; Seaman, 2015). When examining the manifestations of legal, social and political power inside family firms, researchers likewise refer to legal and social family system boundaries rather than territories (Distelberg & Blow, 2011). Such boundaries are typically constituted, though, through personal contacts, social networks, knowledge and identification with certain territories. For instance, James (1999) notes that '*one way to minimize the potential for continuous and disruptive squabbling is for family members to be strategically separated and given different territories or areas of responsibilities'* (p. 52).

Family businesses are territorially embedded and have historical roots in certain places. For family members, the actual territories where their firms are located represent places where they grew up and have lived together and where meaningful life experiences take or have taken place (Kalantaridis & Bika, 2006). In other words, territories create a strong 'sense of place' and roots for family firms. For instance, Björnberg and Nicholson (2012), as well as Martínez-Sanchis et al. (2020), have suggested that territorial factors enhance family members' sense of emotional ownership. The emotional connection stemming from family their attachment to and identifying with a given space becomes closely tied to organisational identity (Shrivastava & Kennelly, 2013) and is reflected also in their behaviour and actions (Pallares-Barbera et al., 2004; Miller et al., 2011; Zellweger & Nason, 2008). That is to say, family firms experience a high level of territorial embeddedness, i.e. an embodiment of geographic and social proximity with their immediate surroundings based on a sense of belonging and territorial identity (Amato et al., 2020; Martínez-Sanchis et al., 2020). They exhibit greater concern for the welfare of their employees, are less likely to downsize than other types of firms (Amato et al., 2020) and intend to stay where they dwell (belong) even during difficult times like financial crises (Zhou et al., 2017). In this sense, family firms stabilise geographical proximity and spatial structures across generations. As Astrachan (1988) notes, space can act as an integrative factor in the family firm's success *'while firms that are acquired and managed in harmony with the local culture will have a higher level of morale and long-run productivity'* (p. 165).

Territoriality research on family firms has mainly focused on the effects of psychological ownership on the work-related attitudes and behaviours of non-family employees (Atalay & Özler, 2013; Bernhard & O'Driscoll, 2011), while prior studies make few references to family business members and owners. Rantanen and Jussila (2011) have discussed how family firms, just like any other firm, have territorial motivations and actively search for whatever territorial gratification the possession can provide them. Also, Heino et al. (2019) have discussed the shared territories of family members and proposed that a family's shared collective psychological ownership can aid in the family business succession process by reducing negative territorial behaviours (e.g. reluctance to share or let go of control and authority) and by increasing positive (caring and protective) territorial behaviours with respect to the business. However, empirical evidence on these issues and other links to territories and territorial behaviour are still lacking.

Methodology

To best address our research question, we selected a multiple case study method to investigate the territoriality phenomenon in family business groups. Multiple cases increase the methodological rigour and strengthen the precision, validity and stability of the findings (Miles & Huberman, 1994), and also the evidence from multiple cases is considered more compelling (Yin, 2013). The major strengths of case studies are that they measure and record behaviour (Yin, 2013) while also making it possible to empirically investigate *a contemporary phenomenon in depth and within its real-world context* (Yin, 2013, p. 15). In this study, the case study method provided in-depth contextual information on the changes in family business groups and the phenomenon of territory behaviour embedded in the specific case during critical events. It also facilitated a holistic examination of the complex and cross-functional relationship between territoriality and change processes in a family business group setting, which is a task that requires the collection of rich data from multiple sources of evidence (see Dyer & Wilkins, 1991).

Case Selection

Several different strategies are available to guide the case selection process, depending on the logic and purpose of the research and whether the researchers seek cases with unique or typical characteristics (Neergaard, 2007). The cases discussed in this study were selected using criterion-based selection methods (LeCompte & Preissle, 1993; Patton, 1990). Such methods permit a sample to be constructed that fits a predefined profile, that is, researchers always use specific criteria based on the questions guiding the study. This method was valuable in this research for two primary reasons. First, the multiple case method enhanced the interpretive status of the evidence. The criterion was met in part by the complementarity of interviewing family members combined with other data sources, such as observation. Second, the case needed to have been in the group expansion stage long enough for us to best assess what determines an owner's territories during each expansion phase. This criterion provided us with an opportunity to look at critical incidents that occurred during the development of the company. To be eligible for selection, each company also had to be in the form of a family

330 N. Heino et al.

business group. To maintain anonymity, the real names of these firms are not disclosed.

Data Collection

Data on critical events can be collected in many ways, e.g. through interviews (Edvardsson, 1992), creating hypothetical situations (Bitner, 1990) or using traditional questionnaires (Johnston, 1995). In this study, the data collection process followed recommendations for case study analysis (e.g. Eisenhardt, 1989; Yin, 2013), meaning we combined preliminary unstructured interviews with formal semi-structured interviews and extensive archival documents, i.e. company reports, company brochures, newspapers, company webpages, company videos and published books, as well as informal talks (see Table 13.1).

The interviews helped us improve our understanding not only of the three cases, but also of territoriality in the family business group in general. The interviews lasted from one to two hours and followed an interview protocol that continually evolved throughout all three cases (Strauss & Corbin, 2015; Turner, 2010). The topics covered during the interviews ranged from the personal interests of general family owners in the family business group to relationships among family owners, the processes and procedures followed, decision-making dynamics and the governance structure. In addition to the interviews, we reviewed an extensive amount of archival data, as each case has a long history.

Data Analysis

The data analysis process consisted of looking at critical events in the three cases and the possible reactions of the owners with respect to territorial boundaries and control of possessions being changed. The critical incidents technique was first developed by Flanagan (1954) to capture data showing both negative and positive critical incidents of human behaviour in solving practical problems. Critical incidents have also been used extensively in management literature (Edvardsson & Roos, 2001). The critical incident technique is well suited to a qualitative research approach since it offers a practical step-by-step approach to collecting and analysing information on human activities and their significance for the people involved (Edvardsson & Roos, 2001; Hughes, 2008). Each of the three cases were different in relation to the business group structure, the ownership structure, generational

13 Territoriality in Family Business Groups: The Impact ...

Table 13.1 Data sources and case characteristics

Type of data		Case 1	Case 2	Case 3
Number of interviews	With founder	1	2	
	With family owners	3	1	5
	With non-family owners		1	2
Archival materials	Company presentations	3		1
	Newspaper articles	> 20	> 10	> 10
	Company webpages	3	2	4
	Company books	2	3	
	Video material	> 20		
Number and character of observed companies	Separate groups	2	2	6
	Separate companies in different groups	> 40	> 10	> 40
	Structural form	Ltd. holdings and separate companies	Plc. holdings, Ltd. holdings and separate companies, foundation	Ltd. holdings and separate companies
Time perspective	Founding year	1965	1871	1901
	Number of companies during the company's history	> 60	> 100	> 50
	Reviewed generation	1st, 2nd, 3rd	4th, 5th	4th, 5th

(continued)

stage and role of the owners. At first stage of data analysis, we treated each case separately with the aim of identifying critical incidents that had impacted territorial behaviour and led to new boundary divisions, and therefore, resulted in changes to the business group and ownership structure. For each case, we used theory-driven questions and pinpointed recurring topics using simple, guiding research questions: What were the main challenges faced by the owners in the group? Who had the most power to define the expected outcomes? How was the group structure organised? This phase

Table 13.1 (continued)

Type of data		Case 1	Case 2	Case 3
Ownership	Structural form	Partial sibling partnership	Partial sibling partnership	Cousin consortium
	Number of family owners	11	6	22
	Family ownership	100%	Plc. 15%, Ltd. 100%	100%
Turnover	Total	€239 mn.	€81 mn.	€1.4 bn.
Employees	Total	1,900	220	3,600
Industries		Steel construction, private equity activities	Logistics, energy, events Private equity activities	Multi-industry group (5 different industries)

was useful for exploring emerging patterns and identifying similarities and differences in the way the sense of territoriality developed within the family business group and how the owners managed the changes in development. The specific research questions regarding the phenomenon were as follows: *How and when did the major changes in the company occur? How have the different changes within the family business group been managed? What critical elements have played a key role in the change and in which phases?* The central issues at stake involved what problems arose, how they developed and what their outcome was in relation to territorial boundary changes.

To understand the emergence, development and regeneration of the incidents, it is important to account for the role of time and history. According to Brown et al. (2005), members in organisations develop, maintain and defend relationships with many aspects of organisational life. From a relationship perspective, a lengthy process exists between an owner perceiving and reacting to a critical situation and ultimately making a decision to exit. Time and history have the role of detaching an owner from a critical incident. Our processual, longitudinal approach to archival data mapping followed the rules defined and suggested by Rosa et al. (2019) and Rautiainen (2012). We processed the data on a stage-by-stage basis by integrating a variety of data sources over time to enhance an understanding of actors, processes and experiences within the family business group context. The analysis of archived materials covers the development of a family business group from its inception until the present day. Although the archival data is not free of all potential bias, it enabled us to observe and analyse the development of the family business group over an extended period. The discontinuous nature of the family business group's development profile facilitated the research approach, meaning we were able to focus our initial attention on archive material for specific years and combine this information with the points raised in the interviews.

Brief Description of the Cases

Case 1 is a family business founded in 1965. The family business group currently has 11 owners spanning three generations. The transition of this family business into a family business group began from early on, as the founder was quite active in converting his family business into a large family-owned and managed business group. At first, when there was only one company, ownership was shared with two non-family members. When the business started to develop, the founder bought out the interests of the other partners; since he was very good at identifying different business opportunities, the family holdings grew rapidly into a diversified portfolio consisting of several companies. Between the years 1965 and 2003, the founder established several business start-ups and orchestrated a number of company takeovers, joint ventures, business investments, company divisions and company closures, and during that time, he likewise developed an impressive business portfolio. In the portfolio, some of the businesses were directly owned by the entrepreneur, while others were owned through other companies. The group formation did not follow a systematic strategy; instead, the business growth has been opportunity driven. In the 1980s, the next generation was incorporated into the business through various ownership arrangements.

When the actual business succession process started in 2003, the family had a complex structure of different companies, some of which were legally separate and connected only by the founder. The second-generation family members found this arrangement too complex to understand and manage. This led the founder and the second generation (three members) to organise the companies both in the interests of the owners and for financial reasons. Some of the companies were sold, and the proceeds were transferred to the new family investment companies. The remaining companies were moved into a holding structure that clarified the complexity in terms of both the management of different companies and the use of resources. After a few years, it became evident that the second-generation owners had different views and interests regarding how to develop the group. One of the siblings was quite entrepreneurial and interested in growth. He wanted to focus on developing and growing the successful businesses in the group. For this reason, arrangements were continued such that the recently formed holding structure was demolished and the companies were divided amongst each owner based on their individual interests, leading to a new division of tasks among the owners. This resulted in two different holdings, the first concentrating on wealth management (pyramidal) and the other on growth business (pyramidal), thereby continuing the original business idea started by the founder. This structural arrangement of businesses was complex and required setting up new companies.

The third generation (seven members) participated in the family business throughout the ownership changes in 2012. The ownership of the one group was divided between one second-generation member and seven third-generation members through two different companies. The second-generation member retained majority voting power. However, due to the need to balance the value differences between the businesses in the group, equal ownership was sought through various cross-ownership arrangements among all family members. The changes have resulted in a highly complex web of ownership relationships. As the family business is moving further towards the cousin consortium stage, ownership has been divided among several generations of extended family members. This in turn has meant that new companies were set up to take care of ownership arrangements. Due to a change in ownership, the family business group is moving again towards an increasing number of businesses.

Case 2 is a family business founded in 1871 spanning five generations. At present, the family maintains ownership interest in two large business entities: a public company, partly owned by the family, and a private company, fully owned by the family. The development of the family business group has taken some 145 years. During this process, approximately one hundred different companies have been involved, and the number of different operations (start-ups, acquisitions, exits and buy-outs) has reached nearly two hundred. As of 2021, the core corporation included a public company with several subsidiaries and a private, family-owned company with a few subsidiaries. Ownership in the public company is shared with non-family members (mainly investment companies); the family owns more than a 50% share through other businesses and through private ownership, while non-family companies own the rest. The private family company with subsidiaries is 100% owned by the family. The family has invested in other private companies through the family company and privately; this has been done to capture new business opportunities in other fields.

The development of the family business group and the transfer of ownership has taken place for four generations from father to son. Ownership has been kept simple and in possession of only a few owners (i.e. the father and the son). In 2006, the business group was in a holding model with several subsidiaries; in addition, the family had a foundation as well as various legally separate individual businesses. The holding company had an efficient board of directors that constantly monitored new companies to be acquired and took care of the sale or liquidation of dormant companies. During the years 2000–2006, there were many changes in the number of companies and gradually the holding structure became too cumbersome to manage. In addition, some of the companies under the holding required large financial investments. The holding company's board suggested that the family sell several companies and focus only on the most productive ones. The family had to clarify their ownership policy and make decisions about what businesses they wanted to continue to be involved in. Relying on the family's long history, the family wanted to retain companies that represented family identity to them. As a result, the holding structure was dismantled, and the companies were divided into two different structures. The key business functions were moved to a publicly listed holding and important businesses for the family remained in a privately owned holding.

Case 3 is a family business conglomerate founded in 1901 spanning in five generations, now a collection of six holdings privately owned by the family. The holdings are divided into three different categories: three trading holdings, two real property holdings and three multinational technology holdings. All holdings are privately owned by fourth- and fifth-generation family members, with eight fourth-generation owners and nine fifth-generation owners. The family business group include six operating companies, all of which are held as subsidiaries of industrial holding companies. This particular family business group is one of the top ten family businesses, revenue wise, in the country. Nonetheless, at the beginning of the twenty-first century the family made the rather alarming discovery that the business itself did not bring any results. All profits came from reals estate. The businesses were also arranged in a cumbersome structure, and the family noted that some of them did not bring knowledge-based added value or ownership value. The owners had to make decisions about how to structure the different companies, the role in which the owners would operate in the different companies and the logic by which the ownership arrangements would be made. The division of companies also took place on the basis of the ranking of the business: market leaders, growth business and high-risk companies. According to this division, the family determined what businesses they wanted to be involved in and what they were willing to give up. Consequently, the family sold several

336 N. Heino et al.

companies that were not suitable to the family business group. The ownership was divided between the cousins, and at the same time, they set terms and conditions regarding what businesses each owner individually wanted to be involved in. The family also drew up a list of principles that needed to be agreed upon when owning the company together. As a result of these arrangements, separate industrial holding companies were established, and structures put in place to hold the different operating businesses.

Analysis

The purpose of this study is to gain a better understanding of the family business group owners' behaviour in relation to their territorial possessions during and after critical events. To answer the research question *How does ownership affect the division of territory division and territorial behaviour during critical events impacting family business groups?*, a thorough analysis of the three case studies was undertaken. Through a combined analysis of empirical observations and the theoretical framework, we identified a set of dimensions that help us understand how critical incidents in a family business group are related to different forms of ownership and to an owner's marking and defending behaviour. Table 13.2 offers a summary description of the critical incidents in three different cases and how these incidents impact an owner's territorial behaviour, with legal, social and psychological ownership as background factors. A key insight from our findings is that owners can define, maintain, modify and distribute business territories as desired, both within the group and in relation to outsiders based on the control, identity and legitimacy gained through their ownership.

We view territories as any material or immaterial targets within the social structure of entities that can be seen as potential targets of a personal sense of possession and follow Brown and colleagues' (2005) definition of territoriality as owners' behavioural expression of their feelings of ownership towards a physical or social object over which they feel a proprietary attachment. According to our analysis, territories in family business groups include both physical spaces and other tangible objects as well as a number of intangible objects, such as activities, roles, issues, ideas and information relating to owning, managing and/or governing the businesses. We found that the conditions of change are likely to trigger marking behaviour as the family members both as individuals and as a collective aim to re-build a mutual understanding of territories in relation to roles, spaces, relationships and

Table 13.2 Family owners' actions and behaviour during and after critical events

Critical incident	Demand to change	Actions/what was done	How territory division/territoriality occurred	Form of territorial behaviour
Case 1: Succession from founder to second-generation members	Demand for increasing professionalisation and clearer company structure Demand for clearer ownership structure that would enable control over the business group	Founder gave up/diminished his ownership, and the organisation was adapted to fit a new ownership structure and its demands	New family members entered the founder's territory, old territories were de-constructed, and new ones were established. These were marked to indicate each family member's control	Control-oriented marking Identity-oriented marking
Case 1: Structural arrangement of businesses for two holdings: one for wealth management and the other for growth businesses	Owners' personal interests and goals for the businesses differed from each other, demand for further structural re-arrangements	New ownership arrangements were made, including re-organising companies as holdings and establishing an asset balancing company. Legal ownership was divided between second-generation owners	Dividing businesses into two holdings, created new territories and ensured total decision-making power over companies for both owners. New territorial boundaries were expressed	Control-oriented marking Identity-oriented marking

(continued)

Table 13.2 (continued)

Critical incident	Demand to change	Actions/what was done	How territory division/territoriality occurred	Form of territorial behaviour
Case 1: Inclusion of the third-generation in ownership, ownership succession	New generation was joining the business, changes in ownership increased the need to defend some family members' decision-making power, demand for new ownership arrangements	New ownership arrangements were made, re-organising ownership and establishing a new company in order to include the third generation in the business. Introduction of dual-class shares	New territories were created for new family members in order to prevent new members from having control over the old territories and to prevent the old territories from being de-constructed and re-constructed. Control over territories as well as family identity were expressed	Control-oriented marking; Identity-oriented marking
Case 2: Re-organising both the structure and the ownership of the group companies	Cumbersome group structure was difficult to manage, demand for clearer company structure and for external funding to make new investments	Division of the companies into publicly owned and privately owned holdings and individual companies. Opening some companies to outside investors/owners. Ownership policy was clarified	The family created a structure that enabled outsiders to join the business and enter some territories but kept control of the companies and those territories supporting their identity	Control-oriented marking; Identity-oriented marking; Anticipatory defending

Critical incident	Demand to change	Actions/what was done	How territory division/territoriality occurred	Form of territorial behaviour
Case 3: Re-organising the group structure	Unproductive/performing companies in the business group, demand for business development; what to keep and what to sell?	Selling some companies. Organising the companies into new holding structures. Defining new roles for family members	Some territories were let go and new ones created. Underperforming businesses were given up, and new rules, social agreements and processes were created to protect the owners' control over those companies and territories that hold special value to them. Those territories were marked, and family and personal identities expressed ('cousin companies')	Control-oriented marking; Identity-oriented marking
Case 3: Organising the ownership under a family office and creating a wealth management system	Need for building a new management system to preserve and create wealth	Creating the family office structure. Enabling simultaneous wealth preservation and wealth creation	The family built a 'nest' and created an owners' council for family governance structures. They formed unified rules on how to manage their ownership and territories. These rules were marked to express family control	Control-oriented marking

objects (Brown et al., 2005). In other words, since shared social understandings of territorial boundaries exist and change involves shifts in social structures (Hatch & Cunliffe, 2006; Katz & Kahn, 1978), critical change events threaten the family's sense of ownership over their territories in the existing organisational structure and system. We found that family owners use both marking and defending strategies and behaviours to express and secure their ownership, control and identities in those territories where they hold legal ownership rights and feel a sense of attachment. That is to say, their territorial behaviours are designed to reflect, communicate, preserve and restore the family's psychological ownership of its territory. According to our analysis, in the case of family business groups, territoriality improves organisational functioning while it, in part, actively constructs both the physical and social structures of these organisations. Territoriality is likely to strengthen the family's identity and commitment to the business and territories.

The Effect of Different Dimensions of Ownership on Territorial Behaviour and Territory Division

Our analysis shows that in all cases, the three different forms of ownership, psychological, legal-economic and social, affected the actions of the family, the changes made in business operations, ownership and management, and the division, marking and defending of territories. First, the family owners expressed strong feelings towards their possessions. The analysis supports the observation that based on feelings of possessiveness and attachment, family owners are motivated to be effective and competent in altering their possessions (Deci & Ryan, 1985; Furby, 1978). Actions undertaken by family members either as individuals or as a group were designed to reflect, communicate, preserve or restore the family's psychological ownership of its valued territories. The need for action stemmed from the need to respect and reaffirm the identity, efficacy and security of the family within the businesses. That is to say, the family owners use their possessions to define themselves and the family as a group that they belong to and as a safe place where they feel at home.

Moreover, in all three cases the motivation for action often appeared to be collective and family-related; the motives to mark and defend, alter possessions and/or define and occupy territories were strongly related to the desire to preserve the family's control and socio-emotional wealth as well as their social family identity, which had become an integral part of the family members' personal identity and history. In other words, the family owners see their businesses as part of their extended self and seek to personalise them.

Accordingly, territorial behaviour serves the family owners' need to establish, develop and safeguard a concept of themselves within the business—both individual and group identity. Hence, the families had a need to establish and maintain a sense of efficacy in business-relevant domains. The identification and protection of the territories helped the family to identify the goals they aspired to achieve. The families are also well acquainted with their targets of ownership (territories), they exert control over them and invest time, energy and resources into them, all of which reinforce their sense of ownership. This in turn is reflected in their behaviour.

Second, with respect to legal ownership, territories were de-constructed and re-constructed, new territories established and the boundaries of those territories marked to express the family's control and identity. Legal ownership offered family members the opportunity to impose themselves on the group or parts of it, and thereby, it promoted the emergence of ownership as a psychological state. Legal ownership also gave the family owners the ability to organise and perform the activities necessary to achieve desired goals. Different legal ownership structures were built to fulfil ownership wishes from both collective and individual points of view. In all cases, legal-economic ownership manifested the change in ownership and supported an increasing number of family members becoming involved in ownership through succession. Legal control over the businesses provided owners with the ability to control the territories and changes, to organise their relationships between the separate businesses and to exit certain businesses when desired. It also provided them with the power to alter both ownership and positions and to invite or not invite family members and outsiders into the businesses and certain territories.

However, these ownership arrangements also had their downsides—an increasing number of owners as well as companies adopting different structures pose challenges to management by both family owners and a family business group. Interestingly, in all three cases family owners are seemingly able to discuss family ownership values, indicating that these values are made explicit among family owners. Although in all cases the interweaving between family and different companies is complex, little evidence exists of serious conflicts. Low levels of conflict in ownership may speak to the fact that family values tend to dominate. It is noteworthy that since the families hold legal ownership rights to their possessions, actual infringements or violations from those outside the business group did not manifest themselves in our cases. Hence, reactionary defending was not needed.

The family members defined the territorial boundaries of the group among themselves. They did this because a territory cannot be shared unless there is a mutual understanding of what is being shared. Importantly, since the family members have legal ownership to define the boundaries of their possessions, there was less indifference or disagreement among the ownership of the targets. Due to aspects of legal ownership, social agreements on the boundaries of these territories may also have been more easily established, as they would be in cases where only psychological and social ownership would have been present.

Third, social ownership gave the family owners the legitimacy to act and modify territorial boundaries. Family status, the family owners' roles in the businesses and their collective identity created social benefits. That is to say, social recognition of the owners, their territories and identities by others reinforced the justification for their legal ownership and actions taken during and after critical events. The interviews also revealed that besides viewing group ownership as an economic asset, it also reflected each family's social, cultural and symbolic inheritance, which were reflected in their identities. Accordingly, besides the fact that territoriality is a manifestation of both social and political power (Sack, 1983; Storey, 2012), it also contains cultural and historical elements (Storey, 2012). The cultural component linking identity and a sense of place was very much present in the context of the family business groups. Since the family and the business, as well the narratives related to both, are interrelated and overlapping, they help strengthen the firm's territorial roots and family history.

Territory Division and Territoriality in Critical Incidents

In case 1, three critical points can be identified where actions are taken to re-organise business territories and territorial behaviour. The first critical situation arose during the first generational change. The founder had to give up most of the companies he had set up and adapt to the new and more professionally managed corporate structure. He also had to adapt to new ownership arrangements whereby his decision-making power was radically reduced when the second generation joined the business. Two members from the next generation entered the founder's territory to share both ownership and decision-making power in managing the new corporate structure. They both used markers to establish new territories for themselves, to make others aware of their territories and to indicate their control. In this way, they could begin the process of negotiating acceptance of their territorial claim in the social environment. Accordingly, the founder used markers to indicate his power over those targets of ownership that he remained partly in control of. The need for this control-oriented marking of territories was necessary when new family members joined the business, new territorial boundaries were drawn and new functions were introduced to the group. As new family members assumed new ownership and management roles within the group, besides expressing their control, their identities were also needed to communicate to others through identity-oriented marking. For instance, their pictures, titles and professions were added to the group website and new arrangements were announced both internally and publicly.

The second critical situation occurred when, based on the different interests of the second-generation members, the family business group structure had to be further developed. The personal interests of the two successors in business differed substantially: one was more interested in wealth management, while the other was more interested in business growth. As a result, the holding structure was dismantled to legally separate the companies. Importantly, both successors retained ownership in both companies, but control and management of the companies was assigned to each owner according to their target of interest. In other words, with this arrangement the second generation delimited clear territories between different business functions in terms of management and leadership. As they described it, now both had their own 'sandboxes' in which to play. Again, the family owners expressed their new territorial boundaries, their identities and their control using multiple markers. That is to say, with control-oriented marking they were able to communicate the boundaries of the established territories: who has control and psychological ownership over them (as both had legal ownership). Since each owner acted as the figurehead for one company, identity-oriented marking represented a form of personalisation that expressed both their personal and professional identities.

The third critical point appeared due to the inclusion of the third generation in the business. Third-generation ownership was decentralised with respect to both second-generation corporate entities. As a result, the family built a dual-class share structure with different voting rights to ensure the legitimacy of the decision-making process and the retention of power in the hands of the second generation. At the same time, a new company was established for the third generation, and part of the ownership of this new company was also distributed to the original founder of the family business group. That is to say, new ownership territories were created for new family members in order to prevent them from having ownership and control over the old territories and to avoid the old territories from being de-constructed and re-constructed at that time. The fact that the second generation remained in control of the old territories was expressed to others again by using control- and identity-oriented marking.

In case 2, as presented earlier in the case description, the business operations and ownership were transferred from father to son according to the rule drawn up by the founder, so each generation included only one major family owner and other heirs were bought out when the generational change took place. Additionally, a certain family heirloom item was given to the successor as a symbolic expression of the transfer of control. Since only one descendant had been given the opportunity to have major ownership and control over the company, there had been no actual need for territory division, territory disputes or territorial behaviour among owners in the past (besides that which may have appeared between the incumbent and descendant). It is worth mentioning that the latest owner had broken this code and given ownership rights to all his children, though again, only one heir took responsibility for the companies, while the others remained in more passive roles.

The first critical incident occurred at a point when the group's holding structure was becoming too complicated to handle and some of the companies required large financial investments outside the family. The group's professional management wanted the family to give up some of the companies and open investment opportunities and ownership to non-family members. The family ended up in a situation where, from the standpoint of family values and identity, important companies would have been sold to outsiders, thus giving control to outsiders. Also, there would have been a serious loss of family identity. The family experienced this as a threat of infringement on their territory. However, the situation was critical since the continuation of the group's businesses depended on additional investments, so something had to be done. With infringement seeming inevitable, the family made the choice to use anticipatory defending to limit outsider control only to territories of their choosing. By choosing what territories to share with others and what to keep exclusively within the family, they would be able to maintain as much family control and identity as possible. The family owners evaluated potential threats related to their territories and then engaged in anticipatory defending to maintain their ownership over the shared territory to which they felt an emotional attachment. To best retain their family's status and power, they kept key information to themselves.

A solution was reached in which the companies were divided into separate holding structures so that those companies that held special emotional and identity value for the family remained fully in their control. Those companies that the family was not attached to and that needed outside funding the most were transformed into public companies. The motives for these changes were not communicated to outsiders, and the actions were taken with the purpose of thwarting infringement actions taken by outsiders. By building another holding only for family owners, the family prevented non-family owners from entering their territory (Brown & Robinson, 2011). That is to say, the family used marking and defending to discourage outgroup members from even attempting to access their territories, and it sought to restrict territorial access to family members alone. Hence, the family had a strong shared identity and a desire to express their family identity to themselves as well as to others. As a result of such territoriality, the collective family identity within the group was strengthened further and the locus of self-conceptualisation was reinforced more from the standpoint of 'we' than 'I' (on collective identity, see Brewer & Gardner, 1996).

In case 3, two critical points can be identified where new boundary creation and territoriality took place. The first significant critical incident, which took place in the early 2000s, resulted in major changes in both business operations and ownership. Underperforming companies in the group were sold and the remaining companies were organised into new holding structures. As a result of these changes, the property lines that define the boundaries of the family's various owned targets were re-created. The new division of territories was based on each owner's personal interest. However, by creating a strong shared collective vision of both group issues and family ownership goals, family unity resulted, and the goals of individual family members were aligned. All businesses were now managed separately under separate leadership, with new roles and tasks being designated to each family member. Some of the territories were shared among other family members, while others remained under the exclusive control of only one family member/owner. During the social construction of shared territories, family members also negotiated their individual spaces within the jointly owned spaces and objects. Here again, the family used control- and identity-oriented marking to construct and communicate the family's control, identity and proprietary attachments.

The second critical incident occurred when new arrangements had to be made for family ownership in the group. The family needed to form unified rules on how to best manage and control their ownership and territories. A family council was arranged to manage ownership, which included the task of building processes as well as tools for wealth management. The idea behind integrating management processes for family owners was to ensure both wealth preservation and wealth creation. That is to say, the family built a strong family governance system that helped it manage collective ownership and give individual owners the freedom to make decisions about their own privately owned entities and territories. These targets of ownership were marked to express the family's control.

Discussion and Conclusions

In this study, we have shown how territoriality emerges and how business territories are shared during critical events impacting family business groups. We have noted that all three dimensions of ownership (legal-economic, psychological and social) and critical points of a family business group strongly impact the territorial behaviours of the owners, thus shaping the group's ownership structures and processes. Families with business groups and large ownership portfolios are usually long-term investors with substantial wealth and a desire to maintain their possessions and eventually pass the firm on to the next generation. Infringement or the fear of infringement into a family's territory is likely to trigger protective and defensive territorial behaviour aimed towards outsiders. As suggested by Heino et al. (2019), a family with a strong sense of possession may feel threatened and try to protect their 'turf' when change is externally imposed. However, in our cases the need for changes in ownership, business boundaries and territories originated mostly from inside the family business group, based on the initiative and needs of the owners and business themselves. That is to say, although the family owners aim to maintain control of their possessions instead of always prohibiting others from entering the territory, territoriality may also be intended to facilitate interactions and/or processes. Legal ownership offers family business group owners ways to provide for themselves, with the ability to carry out their individual interests, to develop relationships between the family members and outsiders, and to modify their possessions and territorial boundaries. At the same time, feelings of ownership, emotional attachments and social agreements provide motivations and the basis for making such changes.

We have shown that both planned and unplanned changes in the businesses (e.g. succession, decisions and the process of buying, selling or re-organising part of the business portfolio) can be viewed as critical events that shape the family business group's ownership and leadership structures and territorial boundaries. These changes typically include social and highly emotional processes, as they involve several human actors interacting with one another and in relation to the business in a dynamic context. Thereby, territorial behaviour is likely to manifest itself in these types of events. We have demonstrated that the desire to maintain power and authority and to protect one's or a group's territory is as much present in family businesses and family business groups as in any other organisation. Both spatial and social boundary defences and strategies to secure ownership and resources are visible in family business groups. Just like with the management of (state) borders, business owners do not merely draw lines around their holdings but also establish connections between actors and spaces.

Since territorial behaviour emerges from feelings of ownership and appears as social behaviour, we found that the concept of territoriality helps us to understand the critical incidents and dynamics witnessed in family business groups. Besides various psychological and social aspects, we have also taken the legal-economic dimension of ownership into account when examining territory sharing and territoriality in our cases, as it gives the family business group owners the right to act and shape both the processes and the results of these events. We have shown that psychological ownership acts as a motive for action and change, that actions are implemented via legal ownership and that social ownership gives legitimacy to the act.

We have noted that by bringing more attention to the issue of territoriality in family businesses, we are able to help researchers and practitioners better understand the behavioural impact of it on social business environments. This makes a valuable addition to current knowledge of social and behavioural dynamics in business organisations. Thereby, our study has both theoretical and practical implications.

As noted previously, little theoretical and/or empirical work has thus far examined the issue of territoriality (e.g. Altman, 1975) in a family business context and especially from the perspective of business owners. By investigating the phenomenon among business owners in the family business groups, we have thus offered revelatory insights (Corley & Gioia, 2011) and contributed to both the research on territoriality (e.g. Alok, 2014; Axelsson & Axelsson, 2009; Baer & Brown, 2012; Brown & Robinson, 2011; Brown et al., 2005; Brown & Zhu, 2016) and family businesses spatial issues (Amato et al., 2020; Basco, 2018; Bau et al., 2019; Del Baldo, 2012; Garmendia-Lazcano et al., 2020; Kahn & Henderson, 1992; Martínez-Sanchis et al., 2020; Seaman, 2015). Moreover, we have provided tools for understanding the dynamics of the family business groups on a deeper level (Rautiainen et al., 2019).

First, our research contributes to discussions on the concept of territories and the targets of territorial behaviour. While most previous studies have treated family business territories only as static geographic places and physical environments/spaces in which firms operate as well as their relationships with one and other (Bau et al., 2019; Backman & Palmberg, 2015; Kahn & Henderson, 1992; Martínez-Sanchis et al., 2020), we have suggested a more dynamic and complex meaning of territories by highlighting their socially constructed nature and constantly changing features in a family business group context. We have shown that the ownership targets to which the family owners feel a sense of attachment are diverse in nature (i.e. both material and immaterial objects) and are both legally and socially constructed as territories through the drafting of formal contracts, negotiating to whom they belong and determining their boundaries. Accordingly, and contrary to Brown et al. (2005), who discuss territoriality in relation to smaller objects/pieces of ownership, we have demonstrated that in family business groups, the targets of ownership and territories that family owners mark and defend as their own can also be enormous entities, such as entire corporations.

Second, our research contributes to territoriality research (e.g. Brown et al., 2005) by suggesting that all dimensions of ownership, social, psychological and legal-economic, affect territorial behaviour and boundary sharing in business organisations and should be taken into account since they are likely to influence the territorial behaviour of the owners of family business groups. Our study highlights that territoriality cannot be distinguished from legally owned objects, as territorial behaviours manifest themselves also in these private spaces and towards objects over which individuals and groups hold legal ownership rights. We have shown how ownership, in particular its psychological and legal dimensions, gives the owners both the motives and the right to exercise power over other individuals and groups in relation to territorial marking and defending. In more detail, we also demonstrated that by the control gained through legal ownership, family owners can define, maintain, modify and distribute territories as desired, both within the group and in relation to outsiders. In addition to legal ownership, the motives and routes associated with psychological ownership (e.g. efficacy, identity, control, self-investment, knowledge, protection of family history, culture and values) strongly influence what territories are desired and how such territories are defined, maintained, shaped and divided based on an owner's individual and collective interests and needs. Thereby, our findings support earlier studies suggesting that when family members have mutual shared interests, they are likely to develop a collective sense of ownership towards the firms and businesses they already legally own. In addition to the legal aspects of ownership, emotional and social dimensions become important factors in ownership (Rau et al., 2018). We also confirmed that family business owners, as with any other individuals and groups, have territorial motivations and search for whatever territorial satisfaction their possession may provide to them (Rantanen & Jussila, 2011).

Third, we extended territoriality analyses to the collective level by demonstrating that much of the territorial behaviour evident in family businesses appears at the group level and manifests itself between groups (in-groups and out-groups). By presenting collective motives as important factors impacting the phenomenon of territorial behaviour (i.e. motives are shared to a certain extent), we advanced scholarly understandings of collective constructs and how they emerge (see Morgeson & Hofmann, 1999). Although the primary focus of analysis in human territoriality studies has been on the individual level, the idea of territorial collectives and territories shared by collectives is not new. Previous research has contributed to our understanding of collective proprietary attachment and associated states, such as a 'sense of community' (e.g. Goemans, 2005; Suttles, 1972; Whyte, 1943), 'group awareness' (e.g. Calsyn, 1976; Yablonsky, 1962), shared intimate knowledge of a territory (e.g. Moore et al., 1983; Suttles, 1968) as well as exclusive ownership and valiant defense of the collective territory (e.g. Brown, 1987; Efran & Cheyne, 1973; Malmberg, 1980; Vasquez, 1995). Individuals are dependent on and interrelated with other individuals, and this mutual dependence creates a context for their actions and interactions (see Malmberg, 1980; Morgeson & Hofmann, 1999) when trying to construct, communicate, maintain and restore those territories to which they feel a proprietary attachment. This is particularly evident in family businesses and family business groups since, according to our analysis, the family as a collective makes decisions about desired possessions and shares the targets of ownership (territories). Hence, family members undertake territorial actions both together as a group and together as individuals (sometimes also on behalf of the group).

We have also contributed to research on territoriality by extending the territoriality discussion within an individual organisation to family business groups in general, i.e. to discussions concerning many businesses simultaneously. We have also shown that while the number of owners grow with the transfer of entities to successive generations, the challenge for family business owners is to provide for the competing demands of owners with a range of interests. We confirmed that family members develop a group identity (Ledgerwood et al., 2007) that consists of the features that each group member wants the group to possess with respect to the target (e.g. certain business or a particular element of family culture) (see Goemans, 2005); likewise, they collectively define crucial aspects of the group both for themselves and to communicate this family identity to others. Thereby, by moving from individual social identity to shared group-level identity (see Brewer & Gardner, 1996), the collective ownership (territory) approach helps define 'who we are', allowing the family to distinguish itself and its possessions from other groups and their possessions.

Moreover, our analysis has shown that consistent with Iacobucci and Rosa (2010), by establishing new company structures, the ownership can be shared with outsiders without having to share the ownership of other entrepreneur's businesses. Family business groups prefer to de-construct and re-construct territories when determining who will head their businesses, even though this may cause more complexity for managing ownership and for the business group as a whole. Although boundary division threatens to disrupt existing territories and individual positions within them, family owners are willing to negotiate and change territorial boundaries to secure continuity. We find that ownership is a tool that provides both the legal means to determine who owns what and psychological motives that affect the decisions made by the owners. Thereby, ownership is an important factor in shaping the territorial behaviour of owners in family business groups and the division of territories. Accordingly, territorial behaviours of marking and defending modify the family business group structure.

Fourth, as territories and territoriality are rather unexplored areas of research in a family business context, our study contributes to the family business literature by examining family business owners' territorial behaviour. Since previous studies have mainly investigated territoriality among non-family employees (Atalay & Özler, 2013; Bernhard et al., 2011) and focused on how psychological ownership affects their work attitudes and behaviours (Ramos et al., 2014; Sieger et al., 2011), we provide the owner's viewpoint with respect to the territoriality discussion. Our results are consistent with previous studies done by Pallares-Barber et al. (2004), Miller et al. (2011) and Zellweger and Nason (2008), all highlighting that the organisational and family identity created through an emotional connection stemming from the family members' attachment to territory is reflected in their behaviour. That is to say, our research lays an important foundation for better understanding territorial behaviour in family businesses; the results reveal that besides legal ownership, psychological and social ownership are likely to also strongly influence family owners' territorial behaviour.

Our findings are also consistent with previous studies suggesting that a family member's shared psychological ownership motives can increase caring and protective territorial behaviours towards the business (Heino et al., 2019). In other words, family business group owners desire to maintain power and authority and protect their territories. Based on collective motivations and identity, the family owners use control-oriented and identity-oriented marking behaviours to personalise their possessions and to draw boundaries around given spaces and objects. Through marking behaviour, the family owners in our cases constructed and communicated to others their proprietary attachment to particular possessions and established enduring boundaries and proprietary control of those territories (Brown et al., 2005, 2014; Brown & Robinson, 2011) based on their feelings of attachment

(Brown et al., 2005). They also used some anticipatory defences to prevent possible infringements that would have threatened their control over those territories that they value the most. They evaluated potential threats related to their ownership (territories) and then used anticipatory defences to maintain and shape their status, ownership and control of their territories. These actions (and the motives behind them) were not communicated per se to outsiders.

Finally, our research has implications for policy makers. By understanding the phenomenon and the effects of ownership on territorial behaviour, business owners and managers can broaden their insights to better comprehend the dynamics and tensions related to inter-group and intra-group behaviour within family business organisations. That is to say, we can better understand family business group owners' behaviour that might initially appear irrational or unusual but is in fact related to their notion of territories and territoriality. Indeed, we have demonstrated how a sense of ownership and ownership feelings influence family business group owners' motives, attitudes and behaviours. Our study should encourage additional theoretical and empirical research on the subject, not only on marking and defending behaviour, but also more generally on ownership and territoriality in family businesses.

References

Almeida, H. V., & Wolfenzon, D. (2006). A theory of pyramidal ownership and family business groups. *The Journal of Finance, 61*(6), 2637–2680.

Alok, K. (2014). Authentic leadership and psychological ownership: Investigation of interrelations. *Leadership & Organization Development Journal, 35*, 266–285.

Altman, I. (1975). *The environment and social behavior: Privacy, personal space, territory, and crowding.* Brooks/Cole Publishing.

Amato, S., Patuelli, A., Basco, R., & Lattanzi, N. (2020). Family firms amidst the global financial crisis: A territorial embeddedness perspective on downsizing. *Journal of Business Ethics.* https://doi.org/10.1007/s10551-021-04930-0

Anderson, R. C., & Reeb, D. M. (2003). Founding-family ownership and firm performance: Evidence from the S&P 500. *Journal of Finance, 58*(3), 1301–1328.

Ardrey, R. (1966). *The territorial imperative.* Atheneum.

Astrachan, J. H. (1988). Family firm and community culture. *Family Business Review, 1*(2), 165–189.

Atalay, C. G., & Özler, D. E. (2013). A research to determine the relationship between organizational justice and psychological ownership among non-family employees in a family business. *Procedia—Social and Behavioral Sciences, 99,* 247–256.

Axelsson, S. B., & Axelsson, R. (2009). From territoriality to altruism in inter-professional collaboration and leadership. *Journal of Interprofessional Care, 23*(4), 320–330.

Backman, M., & Palmberg, J. (2015). Contextualizing small family firms: How does the urban–rural context affect firm employment growth? *Journal of Family Business Strategy, 6*(4), 247–258.

Baer, M., & Brown, G. (2012). Blind in one eye: How psychological ownership of ideas affects the types of suggestions people adopt. *Organizational Behavior and Human Decision Processes, 118*(1), 60–71.

Bakker, C. B., & Bakker-Rabdau, M. K. (1973). *No trespassing! Explorations in human territoriality.* Chandler and Sharp.

Basco, R. (2018). Family business in emerging markets. In R. Grosse & K. E. Meyer (Eds.), *The Oxford handbook of management in emerging markets* (pp. 527–545). Oxford University Press.

Basco, R., & Suwala, L. (2020). *Spatial familiness: A bridge between family business and economic geography.* Edward Elgar Publishing.

Bau, M., Chirico, F., Pittino, D., Backman, M., & Klaesson, J. (2019). Roots to grow: Family firms and local embeddedness in rural and urban contexts. *Entrepreneurship Theory and Practice, 43*(2), 360–365.

Beaglehole, E. (1932). *Property: A study in social psychology.* Macmillan.

Becker, F. D., & Mayo, C. (1971). Delineating personal distance and territoriality. *Environment and Behavior, 3*(4), 375.

Belk, R. W. (1988). Possessions and the extended self. *Journal of Consumer Research, 15,* 139–168.

Berger, P. L., & Luckmann, T. (1966). *The social construction of reality: A treatise in sociology of knowledge.* Penguin.

Bernhard, F., & O'Driscoll, M. P. (2011). Psychological ownership in small family-owned businesses: Leadership style and nonfamily-employees' work attitudes and behaviors. *Group & Organization Management, 36*(3), 345–384.

Bitner, M. J. (1990). Evaluating service encounters: The effects of physical surroundings and employee responses. *Journal of Marketing, 54,* 69–82.

Björnberg, Å., & Nicholson, N. (2012). Emotional ownership: The next generation's relationship with the family firm. *Family Business Review, 25*(4), 374–390.

Brewer, M. B., & Gardner, W. (1996). Who is this "we"? Levels of collective identity and self representations. *Journal of Personality and Social Psychology, 71*(1), 83.

Brighenti, A. M. (2006). On territory as relationship and law as territory. *Canadian Journal of Law and Society, 21*(2), 65–86.

Brown, B. (1987). Territoriality. In D. Stokols & I. Altman (Eds.), *Handbook of environmental psychology* (Vol. 2, pp. 505–531). Wiley.

Brown, B. B., & Altman, I. (1981). Territoriality and residential crime: A conceptual framework. *Environmental Criminology, 1,* 55–76.

Brown, B. B., & Altman, I. (1983). Territoriality, defensible space and residential burglary: An environmental analysis. *Journal of Environmental Psychology, 3*(3), 203–220.

Brown, G. (2009). Claiming a corner at work: Measuring employee territoriality in their workspaces. *Journal of Environmental Psychology, 29*, 44–54.

Brown, G., Crossley, C., & Robinson, S. L. (2014). Psychological ownership, territorial behavior, and being perceived as a team contributor: The critical role of trust in the work environment. Personnel psychology, 67(2), 463-485.

Brown, G., Lawrence, T. B., & Robinson, S. L. (2005). Territoriality in organizations. *Academy of Management Review, 30*(3), 577–594.

Brown, G., & Robinson, S. (2011). Reactions to territorial infringement. *Organization Science, 22*, 210–224.

Brown, G., & Zhu, H. (2016). 'My workspace, not yours': The impact of psychological ownership and territoriality in organizations. *Journal of Environmental Psychology, 48*, 54–64.

Brundin, E., Samuelsson, E. F., & Melin, L. (2014). Family ownership logic: Framing the core characteristics of family businesses. *Journal of Management & Organization, 20*(1), 6–37.

Burkart, M., Panunzi, F., & Shleifer, A. (2003). Family firms. *Journal of Finance, 58*(5), 2167–2202.

Calsyn, R. J. (1976). Group responses to territorial intrusion. *The Journal of Social Psychology, 400*, 51–58.

Corley, K. G., & Gioia, D. A. (2011). Building theory about theory building: What constitutes a theoretical contribution? *Academy of Management Review, 36*(1), 12–32.

Crevoisier, O. (2014). Beyond territorial innovation models: The pertinence of the territorial approach. *Regional Studies, 48*(3), 551–561.

Csikszentmihalyi, M., & Rochberg-Halton, E. (1981). *The meaning of things: Domestic symbols and the self*. Cambridge University Press.

Deci, E. L., & Ryan, R. M. (1985). The general causality orientations scale: Self-determination in personality. *Journal of Research in Personality, 19*(2), 109–134.

Del Baldo, M. (2012). Family and territory values for a sustainable entrepreneurship: The experience of Loccioni Group and Varnelli Distillery in Italy. *Journal of Marketing Development and Competitiveness, 6*(3), 120–139.

Dirks, K. T., Cummings, L. L., & Pierce, J. L. (1996). Psychological ownership in organizations: Conditions under which individuals promote and resist change. In R. W. Woodman & W. A. Pasmore (Eds.), *Research in organizational change and development* (Vol. 9, pp. 1–23). JAI Press.

Distelberg, B. J., & Blow, A. (2011). Variations in family system boundaries. *Family Business Review, 24*(1), 28–46.

Dittmar, H. (1992). *The social psychology of material possessions: To have is to be*. St. Martin's Press.

Dorfman, A. (2010). Private ownership. *Legal Theory, 16*(1), 12–16.

Duncan, N. G. (1981). Home ownership and social theory. In I. S. Duncan (Ed.), *Housing and identity: Cross-cultural perspectives* (pp. 98–134). Croom Helm.

Dyer, W. G., Jr., & Wilkins, A. L. (1991). Better stories, not better constructs, to generate better theory: A rejoinder to Eisenhardt. *Academy of Management Review, 16*(3), 613–619.

Edvardsson, B. (1992). Service breakdowns, a study of critical incidents in an airline. *International Journal of Service Industry Management, 3*(4), 17–29.

Edvardsson, B., & Roos, I. (2001). Critical incident techniques—Towards a framework for analysing the criticality of critical incidents. *International Journal of Service Industry Management, 12*(3), 251–268.

Efran, M. G., & Cheyne, J. A. (1973). Shared space: The co-operative control of spatial areas by two interacting individuals. *Canadian Journal of Behavioral Science, 5*, 201–210.

Eisenhardt, K. M. (1989). Building theories from case study research. *Academy of Management Review, 14*, 532–550.

Elden, S. (2010). Land, terrain, territory. *Progress in Human Geography, 34*(6), 799–817.

Etzioni, A. (1991). The socio-economics of property. *Journal of Social Behavior and Personality, 6*(6), 465–468.

Flanagan, J. C. (1954). The critical incident technique. *Psychological Bulletin, 51*(4), 327–358.

Furby, L. (1978). Possession in humans: An exploratory study of its meaning and motivation. *Social Behaviour and Personality, 6*(1), 49–65.

Garmendia-Lazcano, A., Iturrioz-Landart, C., & Aragon-Amonarriz, C. (2020). Identifying territory-linked family business groups: A methodological proposal. *Journal of Family Business Management, 12*(1), 120–135.

Gersick, K. E., Lansberg, I., Desjardins, M., & Dunn, B. (1999). Stages and transitions: Managing change in the family business. *Family Business Review, 12*(4), 287–297.

Goemans, H. E. (2005). Bounded communities: Territoriality, territorial attachment, and conflict. In M. Kahrer & B. Walter (Eds.), *Territoriality and conflict in an era of globalization* (pp. 25–61). Cambridge University Press.

Hall, A. (2005*). Beyond the legal: Psychological ownership and responsibility in the family business*. Paper presented at the FBN 16th Annual World Conference, Brussels, Belgium.

Hatch, M. J. & Cunliffe, A. L. (2006). *Organization theory: Modern, symbolic and postmodern perspectives* (2nd ed.). Oxford University Press.

Heider, F. (1958). *The psychology of interpersonal relations*. Wiley.

Heino, N., Tuominen, P., Tuominen, T., & Jussila, I. (2019). The socio-psychological challenges of succession in family firms: The implications of collective psychological ownership. In *The Palgrave handbook of heterogeneity among family firms* (pp. 715–746). Palgrave Macmillan.

Hughes, H. (2008). Critical incident technique. In S. Lipu, A. Lloyd, & K. Williamson (Eds.), *Exploring methods in information literacy research* (pp. 49–66). Centre for Information Studies, Charles Sturt University.

Iacobucci, D., & Rosa, P. (2010). The growth of business groups by habitual entrepreneurs: The role of entrepreneurial teams. *Entrepreneurship Theory and Practice, 34*(2), 351–377.

Isaacs, S. (1933). *Social development in young children*. Routledge and Kegan Paul.

Jaffe, D. T., & Lane, S. H. (2004). Sustaining a family dynasty: Key issues facing complex multigenerational business- and investment-owning families. *Family Business Review, 17*(1), 81–98.

James, H. S. (1999). Owner as manager, extended horizons and the family firm. *International Journal of the Economics of Business, 6*(1), 41–55.

James, W. (1890). *The principles of psychology*. Holt.

Johnston, B. (1995). The determinants of service quality: Satisfiers and dissatisfiers. *International Journal of Service Industry Management, 6*(5), 53–71.

Kahn, J. A., & Henderson, D. A. (1992). Location preferences of family firms: Strategic decision making or "home sweet home"? *Family Business Review, 5*(3), 271–282.

Kalantaridis, C., & Bika, Z. (2006). Local embeddedness and rural entrepreneurship: Case-study evidence from Cumbria, England. *Environment and Planning A, 38*(8), 1561–1579.

Kamptner, N. L. (1989). Personal possessions and their meanings in old age. In S. Oskamp & S. Spacapan (Eds.), *The social psychology of aging* (pp. 165–196). Sage.

Katz, D., & Kahn, R. L. (1978). Organizations and the system concept. *Classics of Organization Theory, 80*, 480.

Kostova, T. (1998). *The quality of inter-unit relationships of the MNE as a course of competitive advantage* (Unpublished doctoral dissertation). University of Minnesota, Carlson School of Management, Minneapolis, MN.

La Porta, R., Lopez-De-Silanes, F., & Shleifer, A. (1999). Corporate ownership around the world. *Journal of Finance, 54*(2), 471–518.

LeCompte, M., & Preissle, J. (1993). *Ethnography and qualitative design in educational research* (2nd ed.). Academic Press.

Ledgerwood, A., Liviatan, I., & Carnevale, P. J. (2007). Group-identity completion and the symbolic value of property. *Psychological Science, 18*(10), 873–878.

Ley, D., & Cybriwsky, R. (1974). Urban graffiti as territorial markers. *Annals of the Association of American Geographers, 64*, 491–505.

Libecap, G. (2002). A transaction costs approach to the analysis of property rights. In *The economics of contracts: Theory and applications* (pp. 140–156). Cambridge University Press.

Lyman, S. M., & Scott, M. B. (1967). Territoriality: A neglected sociological dimension. *Social Problems, 15*, 236–249.

Mäkimattila, M., Rautiainen, M., & Pihkala, T. (2016). Systemic innovation in complex business portfolios—A case study. *International Journal of Business Innovation and Research, 10,* 363–379.

Malmberg, T. (1980). *Human territoriality.* Mouton.

Martínez-Sanchis, P., Aragón-Amonarriz, C., & Iturrioz-Landart, C. (2020). How does the territory impact on entrepreneurial family embeddedness? *Journal of Enterprising Communities: People and Places in the Global Economy, 16*(2), 196–217.

Massey, D. (1993). Power-geometry and a progressive sense of place. In J. Bird, B. Curtis, T. Putnam, G. Robertson, & L. Tickner (Eds.), *Mapping the future: Local cultures and global change* (pp. 59–69). Routledge.

Mead, G. H. (1934). *Mind, self and society.* University of Chicago Press.

Miles, M. B., & Huberman, A. M. (1994). *Qualitative data analysis: An expanded sourcebook.* Sage.

Miller, D., Breton-Miller, I. L., & Lester, R. H. (2011). Family and lone founder ownership and strategic behaviour: Social context, identity, and institutional logics. *Journal of Management Studies, 48*(1), 1–25.

Moore, J., Vigil, D., & Garcia, R. (1983). Residence and territoriality in Chicano gangs. *Social Problems, 31,* 182–194.

Morgeson, F. P., & Hofmann, D. A. (1999). The structure and function of collective constructs: Implications for multilevel research and theory development. *Academy of Management Review, 24,* 249–265.

Neergaard, H. (2007). 10 sampling in entrepreneurial settings. In *Handbook of qualitative research methods in entrepreneurship* (p. 253). Edward Elgar Publishing.

Nordqvist, M. (2005). *Understanding the role of ownership in strategizing: A study of family firms* (Doctoral dissertation). Internationella Handelshögskolan.

Nordqvist, M., & Melin, L. (2010). Entrepreneurial families and family firms. *Entrepreneurship & Regional Development, 22*(3–4), 211–239.

Pallares-Barber, M., Tulla, A., & Vera, A. (2004). Spatial loyalty and territorial embeddedness in the multi-sector clustering of the Berguedà region in Catalonia (Spain). *Geoforum, 35*(5), 635–649.

Patton, M. (1990). *Qualitative evaluation and research methods* (2nd ed.). Sage.

Penrose, J. (2002). Nations, states and homelands: Territory and territoriality in nationalist thought. *Nations and Nationalism, 8*(3), 277–297.

Peters, T., & Austin, N. (1985). *A passion for excellence.* Random House.

Pierce, B., & White, R. (1999). The evolution of social structure: Why biology matters. *Academy of Management Review, 24,* 4.

Pierce, J. L., Kostova, T., & Dirks, K. T. (2001). Toward a theory of psychological ownership in organizations. *Academy of Management Review, 26*(2), 298–310.

Pihkala, T., Goel, S., Rautiainen, M., Mukherjee, K., & Ikävalko, M. (2019). Deciphering ownership of family business groups. In M. Rautiainen, P. Rosa, T. Pihkala, M.-J. Parada, & A. Discua Cruz (Eds.), *The family business group phenomenon—Emergence and complexities.* Palgrave Macmillan.

Porteus, J. D. (1976). Home: The territorial core. *Geographical Review, 66*, 383–390.

Pratt, M. G., & Rafaeli, A. (2001). Symbols as a language of organizational relationships. *Research in Organizational Behavior, 23*, 93–132.

Prelinger, E. (1959). Extension and structure of the self. *The Journal of Psychology, 47*(1), 13–23.

Raffestin, C. (2012). Space, territory, and territoriality. *Environment and Planning D: Society and Space, 30*(1), 121–141.

Ramos, H. M., Man, T. W. Y., Mustafa, M., & Ng, Z. Z. (2014). Psychological ownership in small family firms: Family and non-family employees' work attitudes and behaviours. *Journal of Family Business Strategy, 5*(3), 300–311.

Rantanen, N., & Jussila, I. (2011). F-CPO: A collective psychological ownership approach to capturing realized family influence on business. *Journal of Family Business Strategy, 2*(3), 139–150.

Rau, S. B., Werner, A., & Schell, S. (2018). Psychological ownership as a driving factor of innovation in older family firms. *Journal of Family Business Strategy, 10*(4), 100246.

Rautiainen, M. (2012*). Dynamic ownership in family business systems—A portfolio approach* (Dissertation). Acta universitatis Lappeenrantaensis 485, Lappeenranta University of Technology.

Rautiainen, M., Rosa, P., Pihkala, T., Parada, M. J., & Cruz, A. D. (2019). *The family business group phenomenon*. Springer International Publishing.

Richards, C., & Dobyns, H. (1957). Topography and culture: The case of changing cage. *Human Origin, 16*(1), 16–50.

Rosa, P., Rautiainen, M., & Pihkala, T. (2019). The methodological challenges of researching family-owned business groups. In *The family business group phenomenon* (pp. 37–62). Palgrave Macmillan.

Sack, R. D. (1983). Human territoriality: A theory. *Annals of the Association of American Geographers, 73*, 55–74.

Sassen, S. (2013). When territory deborders territoriality. *Territory, Politics, Governance, 1*(1), 21–45.

Seaman, C. (2015). Creating space for the business family: Networks, social capital & family businesses in rural development. *Journal of Family Business Management, 5*(2), 182–191.

Shrivastava, P., & Kennelly, J. J. (2013). Sustainability and place-based enterprise. *Organization & Environment, 26*(1), 83–101.

Shu, S., & Peck, J. (2011). Psychological ownership and affective reaction: Emotional attachment process variables and the endowment effect. *Journal of Consumer Psychology, 21*(4), 439–452.

Sieger, P. (2011). *Long-term success of family firms: Investigating specific aspects of firm-level entrepreneurship and individual-level antecedents* (Dissertation). University of St. Gallen, Switzerland.

Sieger, P., Bernhard, F., & Frey, U. (2011). Affective commitment and job satisfaction among non-family employees: Investigating the roles of justice perceptions and psychological ownership. *Journal of Family Business Strategy, 2*(2), 78–89.

Simmons, A. J. (2001). On the territorial rights of states. *Philosophical Issues, 11,* 300–326.

Smith, C. A., Organ, D. W., & Near, J. P. (1983). Organizational citizenship behavior: Its nature and antecedents. *Journal of Applied Psychology, 68,* 653–663.

Soja, E. W. (1971). *The political organization of space.* Commission on College Geography Resource Paper 8, Association of American Geographers, Washington, DC, pp. 1–54.

Sommer, R. (1974). *Tight spaces: Hard architecture and how to humanize it.* Prentice-Hall.

Stein, B. A. (1976). Collective ownership, property rights, and control of the corporation. *Journal of Economic Issues, 10*(2), 298–313.

Storey, D. (2012). *Territory: The claiming of space.* Prentice Hall/Pearson Education.

Strauss, A., & Corbin, J. (2015). *Basics of qualitative research: Procedures and techniques for developing grounded theory* (4th ed.). Sage.

Sundstrom, E., & Sundstrom, M. G. (1986). *Work places: The psychology of the physical environment in offices and factories.* Cambridge University Press.

Suttles, G. D. (1968). *The social order of the slum.* University of Chicago Press.

Suttles, G. D. (1972). *The social construction of communities.* University of Chicago Press.

Tagiuri, R., & Davis, J. (1996). Bivalent attributes of the family firm. *Family Business Review, 9*(2), 199–208.

Thrasher, F. M. (1936). *The gang: A study of 1,313 gangs in Chicago* (2nd revised ed.). University of Chicago Press.

Turner, D. W. (2010). Qualitative interview design: A practical guide for novice researcher. *The Qualitative Report, 15*(3), 754–760.

Vasquez, J. A. (1995). Why do neighbors fight? Proximity, interaction or territoriality. *Journal of Peace Research, 32,* 277–293.

White, R. W. (1959). Motivation reconsidered: The concept of competence. *Psychological Review, 66*(5), 297–333.

Whyte, W. F. (1943). *Street corner society.* University of Chicago Press.

Wollman, N., Kelly, B. M., & Bordens, K. S. (1994). Environmental and intrapersonal predictors of reactions to potential territorial intrusions in the workplace. *Environmental and Behavior, 26*(2), 179–194.

Yablonsky, L. (1962). *The violent gang.* Macmillan.

Yin, R. K. (2013). *Case study research: Design and methods.* Sage.

Zajonc, R. B. (1984). On the primacy of affect. *American Psychologist, 39,* 117–123.

Zellweger, T. M., & Nason, R. S. (2008). A stakeholder perspective on family firm performance. *Family Business Review, 21*(3), 203–216.

Zhou, H., He, F., & Wang, Y. (2017). Did family firms perform better during the financial crisis? New insights from the S&P 500 firms. *Global Finance Journal, 33,* 88–103.

Part III

Innovation Strategies in Family Business Groups

14

The Temporal Evolution of Innovation Management in a Family Business Group

Timo Pihkala, Marita Rautiainen⊙, and Naveed Akhter

Introduction

This study is about the temporal evolution of innovation management in family business groups. It highlights the process of how family business owners adopt new ways to manage innovation in their business groups. Family firms are often portrayed as conservative (La Porta et al., 1999; Pittino et al., 2016; Sharma et al., 1997) and resistant to change (Hall et al., 2001; Ward, 1997). Family involvement is also seen as a negative aspect related to innovation (Naldi et al., 2007). The family agenda may influence the strategic decisions of a family business (Miller et al., 2011) by impacting on the decisions related to innovation. Owners' interest to protect family wealth and control may determine the extent of innovation efforts and results they achieve (Nieto et al., 2015). These central attributes lead to the view that

---

T. Pihkala (✉) · M. Rautiainen
School of Engineering Science, LUT University, Lahti, Finland
e-mail: timo.pihkala@lut.fi

M. Rautiainen
e-mail: marita.rautiainen@lut.fi

N. Akhter
Jönköping International Business School (JIBS), Jönköping, Sweden
e-mail: naveed.akhter@ju.se

© The Author(s), under exclusive license to Springer Nature
Switzerland AG 2023
M. Rautiainen et al. (eds.), *The Palgrave Handbook of Managing Family Business Groups*,
https://doi.org/10.1007/978-3-031-13206-3_14

compared to non-family businesses there is less willingness in family firms to invest in innovation. However—at the same time current research (e.g., Feranita et al., 2017; Nieto et al., 2015) states that there is a paradox in the discussion of innovation when it comes to family businesses' ability to innovate. That is, earlier research has observed that family firms are less innovative in terms of inputs (e.g., R&D) but more innovative in terms of outputs (e.g., patents) (De Massis et al., 2013; Kammerlander et al., 2015). The question, therefore, is not simply whether family firms innovate more or less than non-family firms, but how they approach the innovation itself (Nieto et al., 2015; Rondi et al., 2019), what are their innovation sourcing mechanisms (Rautiainen et al., 2020) and the results they achieve.

In their recent review of the innovation studies in family firms, Calabrò et al. (2019) concluded that the evolution of innovation in family firms has not been focused in any study. They suggest that so far the research has offered a rather static view of the family influence on the innovation (Calabrò et al., 2019). Mäkimattila et al. (2016) studied the innovation processes in family businesses from the perspective of systems theory. Mäkimattila et al. (2016) suggested that innovation practices in family businesses' are likely to change along with the owners' influence, generational changes, ownership changes, or changes in the business context. Additionally, as the business grows in complexity, it creates internal—systemic—needs for changes (Mäkimattila et al., 2016). In this study, we take the temporal perspective of innovation management in family business groups which we define as the temporal tracking of an organization's decision on key issues linked to innovation in the business: "what" type of innovation, "how" to embark on the innovation journey, and "when", i.e., timing perspective (Afuah, 2003, 2020). Indeed, the temporal is at the heart of innovation management as the core challenge organizations face when dealing with innovation (Dodgson et al., 2014), drawing on past experiences, current resources, and priorities with a plan for future possibilities (Ellwood & Horner, 2020). A business group is a collection of legally independent firms that are bound by ties that are economic (such as ownership, financial, and commercial) and social (such as family, kinship, and friendship) (Yiu et al., 2005, p. 183). Family business groups are interesting research targets for several reasons. First, Hsieh et al. (2010) noted that firms that are in a group structure innovate better than their unaffiliated counterparts. A business group acts as a platform among affiliated firms i.e., for the exchange and integration of resources supporting and cultivating the continuous inputs of tangible and intangible resources. Guzzini and Iacobucci (2014) pointed out that the firms' level of innovation in business groups depends on the position in the group structure. Second, family business groups have been found to operate with parallel innovation strategies, thus making the evolution of innovation management more transparent (Rautiainen et al., 2020). Its underlying premise is that acquiring parallel innovation strategies depends on the firm's ability to use resources and the level of risk inherent in the decision of innovating, factors that make an influential characteristic in innovation processes. Third, the focus on a whole family business group system will enable the analysis of the temporal changes in the innovation management better than in single stable family businesses.

The purpose of this paper is to uncover the temporal evolution of innovation management in a family business group. Our research question is, how the family business owners change their innovation management practices along with the development of the family business group?

The contribution of the study is threefold: first, we bring evidence of the temporal development of innovation management in a family business group. The analysis shows that the evolution of innovation management is characterized by the adoption of new guidelines created by the business group owners. These guidelines emerge along with new needs that are created by the innovation processes in the business group, and they seem long-lasting rules for the innovation activities in the family business group. Second, by adding to the earlier literature discussing the owners' influence on innovation in family businesses. Our study confirms the earlier conception of the owners' central role in innovation processes. In addition, based on our findings, we suggest that a large share of the innovation activities in the business group could have been difficult or even impossible for non-owning managers. From this perspective, our results underline the owners' importance for the development of family business groups. Finally, our study contributes to the literature of family business innovation, and especially to the research targeting the innovation activities in family businesses by introducing the innovation management framework for analyzing the owners' innovation activities. We suggest that the perspective of innovation management provides a fruitful view on the wide range of innovation practices conducted within a family business group.

The paper is structured as follows. In the second section we introduce the innovation management framework. In the third section the methodology of the study is discussed. In the fourth section we present the empirical analysis, and we conclude the paper with a discussion about the central results of the study.

Innovation Management in Family Business Groups

Innovation management captures the organization's decision-making on the central issues of innovation in the business: the type of innovation, buy or make, timing, finance, and resource allocation (Afuah, 2003). These issues are intertwined in many ways and they are likely to change during the evolution of the business (Calabrò et al., 2019). Guzzini and Iacobucci (2014) note that in the literature there is a common assumption that the heads of the business groups are coordinating the innovation activities in the affiliated firms. From this perspective, it is reasonable to assume that the business group innovation management concerns the whole business group system.

The type of innovation is probably the most typical way to characterize the decision-making on innovations. That is, innovations may be radical or incremental, and their implementation may consider a start-up of a new business (Pittino et al., 2013; Rothwell & Dodgson, 1991) or it takes place as a gradual addition to the present technologies or products (De Massis et al., 2015; Nieto et al., 2015). The radical innovation is closely related to the willingness to take risks and to the strong commitment to financing the R&D and the other innovation processes (De Massis et al., 2015; Nieto et al., 2015). In the family business context, Naldi et al. (2007), among others, have suggested that family businesses are risk-averse and that could be one of the factors explaining their low R&D expenditure. However, the case of family business groups may divert from the stand-alone family businesses. In their study of the innovation incentives in Italian business groups, Guzzini and Iacobucci (2014) reported that the R&D intensity depends on the ownership of the controlled firms and that the R&D expenditure is higher in the head and intermediate firms in the business groups than it is in stand-alone firms or firms at the bottom of business groups.

Make or buy concerns the decision, of whether to conduct the innovation process internally or to use external sources of innovation (Afuah, 2003; Kogut & Zander, 1992; Pittino et al., 2013). In this sense, multiple approaches have been identified; The literature on family business has suggested that family-owned businesses seem less likely to invest in internal innovation processes (Brinkerink & Bammens, 2018; McConaughy et al., 2001; Nieto et al., 2015), while other studies have provided evidence of family businesses' use of external sources of innovation (e.g., Feranita et al., 2017; Pittino et al., 2013; Rautiainen et al., 2020). In family business groups, however, it is likely that several parallel strategies are applied for innovation. That is, the family business group may simultaneously carry out internal innovation processes, actively seek external innovations to add into the business agglomeration and carry out collaborative innovation (Rautiainen et al., 2020). The use of external sources to innovation may be linked to internal incentives such as access to resources (Feranita et al., 2017; Sirmon & Hitt, 2003) or the ability to learn from external innovations and absorb them into internal innovation processes (Kogut & Zander, 1992). Finally, Rothwell and Dodgson (1991) point out that large firms may employ small firms as "windows" for new technologies.

Timing of innovation deals with the market entry strategy. That is, the business may seek to introduce innovations first in the market, second in the market, or as a late entrant (Chandy & Tellis, 2000; Mitchell, 1989). It is generally assumed that an early entry would be associated with better performance than a late entry (Afuah, 2003; Chandy & Tellis, 2000). In business groups the decisions on timing may depend on different factors. First, business groups form an innovation infrastructure (Mahmood & Mitchell, 2004) that supports the first in the market-strategy. Second, business groups have a possibility of creating new product or technology combinations by bringing together existing assets in the affiliate firms (Lechner & Leyronas, 2009). Third, early entry may be a result of the opportunism of the family business owners (Levie & Lerner, 2009).

Financing innovation concerns the question, whether the innovation is financed internally or externally (Belenzon & Berkovitz, 2010; Guzzini & Iacobucci, 2014; Komera et al., 2016). The decision to pursue innovation is expensive and requires solutions on the financing. In their study, Belenzon and Berkovitz (2010) found that business groups foster innovation via internal capital markets. That is, they use internal funding to finance the innovation processes in the business group affiliates. This strategy has several benefits: first, the business group can develop better internal capabilities for using knowledge spillovers from the innovation processes (Belenzon & Berkovitz, 2010; Kogut & Zander, 1992); second, the decision-making for the financing is likely to be faster than for external financing; and third, the business group can benefit from the insider information of the R&D projects (Guzzini & Iacobucci, 2014).

Resource management seeks to ascertain the effective use of the firm's resources. Sirmon and Hitt (2003) suggested three elementary components for a resource management model: the resource inventory, resource bundling, and leveraging resource bundles. For innovation activities in family firms, knowing the resources and being able to organize them into effective combinations and use them flexibly are crucial factors. Without the ability to manage the resource base, the family firm cannot make use of the "innovation infrastructure" (Mahmood & Mitchell, 2004; Soh et al., 2004) or secure the full potential of the innovations. Kogut and Zander (1992) suggested that firms are bound by path dependency, that is, what a firm has done before tends to predict what it can do in the future. In this sense, for family business groups the different businesses, innovation processes, and capabilities are the accumulated resources that restrict the family business group's next steps. Mäkimattila et al. (2016) suggested that along with the growth of the complexity of the business group, the way the resource bundles are organized or leveraged for further use will also change.

Methodology

The Case Study Approach

To address our research question, the single case study method was selected to investigate how the owner managers in family business groups manage innovation activities. We adopted a longitudinal single-case study approach based on the revelatory nature of the case. The use of a single-case study approach offers the opportunity for rich insights and findings relevant to our research question (Stake, 2010). A case study approach allows to empirically investigate *"a contemporary phenomenon in depth and within its real-world context"* (Yin, 2009, p. 15). Particularly this is useful in the research of small and medium size businesses (Chetty, 1996). The choice of a single-case study was based on the approach of Dyer Jr. and Wilkins (1991) who argue that a single deep case is the optimum form of case study research. They highlight that "the *careful study of a single case leads researchers to see new theoretical relationships and question old ones*" (Dyer Jr. & Wilkins, 1991, p. 614). This method was valuable in this research for two reasons. First, the use of the case study approach was appropriate for the study of family business groups since it provided in-depth contextual information on the emergence of innovation phenomena embedded in the case (cf. Dyer Jr. & Wilkins, 1991). Second, it facilitated the holistic examination of the complex and cross-functional relationship between owner manager and innovation activity setting, which is a task that requires the collection of rich data from multiple sources of evidence (cf. Dyer Jr. & Wilkins, 1991).

Case Selection

There are various strategies available to guide the case selection process depending on the logic and purpose of the research, whether the researchers seek cases with unique or typical characteristics (Neergaard, 2007). The researchers need to understand and describe the context of the scene in question to such a degree that they can generate a theory in relation to that context. This means that researchers must go as close as possible to the phenomena under investigation and provide a rich description of the scene and underlying dynamics of the case (Dyer Jr. & Wilkins, 1991; Mintzberg, 1979). For the purpose of this research, we followed a selection of a longitudinal case, guided by its power to explain and illuminate aspects of theory, rather than the extent to which they were typical in the field (Silverman, 1998, 2013). We studied a Finnish family business group founded in 1965. Currently there are 11 owners spanning three generations. The transition of this family business into a family business group started in the early years, as the founder was quite active and eager to convert his family business into a large family-owned and managed business group.

There were three key criteria determining the selection of the case in this study. The first was to find a case which provided a theoretically relevant setting of the family business group that shows a useful variation on the dimensions of theoretical interest. The second was that the story of the case must be a convincing and representative sample of how owners are managing innovation activity and there is a causal inference in demonstrating owner's role in guiding the decisions. The third criterion was to find a case containing rich and abundant data with clear examples of new relationships that current theoretical perspectives have not yet captured.

Data Collection

This study involved several types of data, including archival records, accounting reports, websites, and interviews (see Table 14.1). One of the authors interviewed the firm's founder and owners and collected data through archival records between 2016 and 2017. The substantial secondary data (i.e., company history books and newspaper articles) were collected to shed light on the historical context within which the firm was founded. The use of archival records allows framing of real event descriptions to their relevant context (Welch, 2000). The secondary data was used in our interview to improve respondents' recall of past events (Huber & Power, 1985).

Table 14.1 Data collection and analysis

Source	Type of information	Qty	The use in the analysis
Websites	Different company web pages (Peikko group, Peikko Finland) Wikipedia	3	To define how the company is publicly displayed and what information it provides
Interviews	First interview 4.5 hour with founder, Second interview 1.5 hour with second generation member (son 1), Third interview 1 hour with second generation member (son 1), and Fourth interview 1.40 hour with a second generation member (son 2)	4	Discussions about the development of the group i.e., how different companies in the group were found, why the founder wanted to be in the business and what was the life cycle of the company in the group. Second interview opened the development of the current situation, succession and ownership Based on these discussions the company table (Table 14.2) was developed Third and fourth interviews were made to deepen the knowledge of the division of roles and responsibilities of the second generation members. In addition, information was obtained from the third-generation succession process

Source	Type of information	Qty	The use in the analysis
Newspaper and journal articles	Professional journals, regional newspaper articles, professional magazines	10	To identify different special events in the company history that attracted media attention, these events were connected to Table 14.2
Videos	Company's YouTube videos, The Story of Peikko, several product demonstration videos, technology development videos, innovation and internationalization videos	20	To gather information about ownership, entrepreneurship, growth and innovation on different occasions. The development of technology, different products and internationalization. Information was connected to Table 14.2
Presentations	Peikko Group ownership power-point presentations given by the second-generation members	3	Presentations contain important information about the current family and company ownership structures
Books	History book on the career of the founder Family business group book, a chapter about the emergence of this case	2	A longitudinal group development path was drawn based on the story. Figure was sent to the founder and second-generation members. When they were acquainted with the map, deeper interviews were done to discuss about the backgrounds of each company

Table 14.2 Innovation activities in the Case FBG

Company	Time	Operation	Type of innovation	Strategic role	Level of integration	Timing	Make or buy	Financing	Owner's role Typology about innovation management
Peikko Group Ltd.	1965	Start-up, the creation of a new business	Metal structure for construction	Creation of a new business area	Basis for a business group	First in the market	Make	Owners own financing	Entrepreneur
Makron Ltd.	1966–1999	Start-up, the creation of a new business, restructuring, exit	Research-based innovation, license bought, new product, unrelated	Access, new products, new technology	No integration, basis for a business group	First in the market	Producing new types of machines for creating different products	cash flow from Peikko	Entrepreneur
Ansasrauta Ltd.	1968	Acquisition	Metal structure for construction	New products, new competence	Full merger in Peikko Group	Buying a competitor	Buy	Owners own financing	Strategic decisionmaker
Leiron Ltd.	1979–1982	Acquisition, exit	Piles and rock tips	New competence	Full use in Peikko Group	Buying a product close to Peikko	Buy	Financing from owners' other companies	Strategic decisionmaker

Company	Time	Operation	Type of innovation	Strategic role	Level of integration	Timing	Make or buy	Financing	Owner's role Typology about innovation management
Proplast Ltd.	1984–1994	Start-up, innovation, exit	IPRs related to plastics	Access to IPR	Synergy with Pexep in Makron Group	first in the market	Make	Financing from owners' other companies	Strategic decisionmaker
Pexep Ltd.	1984–1994	Start-up, production company, exit	Plastic products	New product	Synergy with Proplast	first in the market	Make	Financing from owners' other companies	Strategic decisionmaker
Fixtron Ltd.	1985–1996	Start-up, the creation of a new business, exit	Wooden construction, related	New product	No integration, business sold to Makron	first in the market	Make	Financing from owners' other companies	Innovator

(continued)

Table 14.2 (continued)

Company	Time	Operation	Type of innovation	Strategic role	Level of integration	Timing	Make or buy	Financing	Owner's role Typology about innovation management
Nostera Ltd.	1985–1997	Acquisition, exit	New technology solution, new business field, unrelated	New product	No integration, positioned in Makron	New technological solution for the existing market	Buy	Financing from Makron	Innovator
Ventipress Ltd.	1985–1991	Acquisition, entry in different industry, exit	Health care technological product, new business field, unrelated	New product	No integration, positioned in Makron	New technological solution for the existing market	Buy	Financing from Makron	Innovator
Plytec Ltd.	1986–2001	Acquisition, name changed, exit	Plywood boards, new business field, unrelated	New product, new competence	No integration, positioned in Makron	New technological solution for the existing market	Buy	Financing from Makron	Initiator for joint venture, created the investor group

Company	Time	Operation	Type of innovation	Strategic role	Level of integration	Timing	Make or buy	Financing	Owner's role Typology about innovation management
Skanveir Ltd.	1985	Acquisition, exit	Magnetic cranes, trademarks acquired, widening product range	New product, new competence	Partial integration, positioned in Makron	Late entry	Buy	Financing from Makron	Strategic decisionmaker, opportunist
Eimo Plc.	1985–2003	Acquisition, public listing, exit	Mobile phone shells, new business field	New product, new competence	No integration, basis for a business group	Second in the market	Buy	Owners own financing, from owners' other companies and other exits	Investor, later strategic decision maker, after public listing a key shareholder and decision maker
M.J. Paasikivi Ltd.	1987–1997	Acquisition, exit	Casting letters for gravestones, new business field	New product, new competence	No integration, positioned in Makron	Generating cash flow for other businesses	Buy	Financing from Makron	Strategic decision maker

(continued)

Table 14.2 (continued)

Company	Time	Operation	Type of innovation	Strategic role	Level of integration	Timing	Make or buy	Financing	Owner's role Typology about innovation management
Lahden Teräteos Ltd.	1987–1996	Acquisition, exit	Log machines, developing new technology	Access, new product	Technology was applied in Makron	use for technology development	Buy	Financing from Makron	Strategic decision maker
MJV-Sähkö Ltd.	1988–2004	Spin-off (MBO), exit	Electronics assembly business, related	New organization	Outsourced from the Makron electronics dept.	Separated to grow independently	Co-operation	MBO	Strategic decision maker, decided about separating the business and exit
Protim Ltd.	1989–1993	Acquisition, exit	Plywood products, new products, unrelated	Access, new product	No integration, positioned in Makron	New product category	Buy	Financing from Makron	Opportunist

Company	Time	Operation	Type of innovation	Strategic role	Level of integration	Timing	Make or buy	Financing	Owner's role Typology about innovation management
Deltatek Ltd.	1989–2002	Start-up, merger	Metal structure for construction, a major innovation, related	New product	Full integration into Peikko	First in the market	Make	Start-up as a joint venture, located in Makron, later moved to Peikko	Initiated joint venture, later orchestrated the full use of innovation
Felpimet Ltd.	1989	Acquisition, merger	Increasing tool capacity, investment in resources	Access to technology capacity	Merger to Eimo	Use for technology development	Buy	Financing from Eimo	Strategic decision maker
Tasoplast Ltd.	1989	Acquisition, merger	Plastic products, investment in resources	Access to technology capacity	Merger to Eimo	Use for technology development	Buy	Financing from Eimo	Strategic decision maker

(continued)

Table 14.2 (continued)

Company	Time	Operation	Type of innovation	Strategic role	Level of integration	Timing	Make or buy	Financing	Owner's role Typology about innovation management
Fickert & Winterlind Ltd.	1993–1999	Start-up, controlled bankruptcy	Stone machines, investment in resources	Access, new product	No integration, positioned in Makron	Use for technology development	Make	Financing from Makron	Strategic decision maker
Aliko Ltd.	1995–2002	Acquisition, exit	Plate cutters and disk breakers, new products	Access, new product	Partial integration, positioned in Makron	Participation in innovation development	Buy	Financing from Makron, partial ownership	Strategic decision maker
Triple S Plastic Plc.	2001	Acquisition	New production method, new skills for mobile phone production	New product, new competence	Merger to Eimo	Buying market share, capacity, technology, products	Buy	Financing from Eimo, share exchange	First and second generation as Strategic decision makers

Company	Time	Operation	Type of innovation	Strategic role	Level of integration	Timing	Make or buy	Financing	Owner's role Typology about innovation management
Cim Precision Ltd.	2001	Acquisition	New production method, new skills for mobile phone production	new competence	Merger to Eimo	Use for technology development	Buy	Financing from Eimo	First and second generation as Strategic decision makers
Wiser Ltd.	2005	Acquisition new business field, exit	Patents and innovations, new product development	Access	No integration, kept separate	new technology	Buy	Owner's personal financing	Owner as an opportunist
Lahti Levy Ltd.	2007	Start-up	Nail plates, new product development	New product	No integration, kept separate	Late entrant	Make	Owner's personal financing	Owner as an opportunist

As all interviews were one-to-one, in-depth interviews spread over a considerable period, it allowed the interviewees the opportunity to reflect as well as make sense of their experience and decisions. Such a retrospective sensemaking (Weick, 1995) allows insights into how and why people construct certain realities and with what effects. Persons selected for an interview are the key owners and have been in key positions during the period of changes in the group. Interviews were used to deepen the understanding of the distinct changes in business and ownership. The themes of the interviews allowed participants talk openly about questions like the start-up of the family business, the first steps, reasons to grow, reasons to diversify over time, etc. Interviewees provided unrestricted accounts of the approach and rationale of the innovation management. Owners were contacted several times afterwards to check details or contradictions in the case. This procedure was important to improve the overall quality of the data analysis (Reay, 2014) and has been used previously to understand the development of diversified family firms over a long period (Roscoe et al., 2013).

Data Analysis

An analysis was made of the archived materials and interviews with the main owners covering the development of the company starting from 1965 through to 2010. One important benefit in archival data is that, while the data cannot be assumed to be free of all bias, it has not been distorted further by our study. The data was analyzed in a three-stage process. At the first stage, the case study data was organized into an event-based, chronological order by the emergence of different companies in the family business group (see Table 14.2) which has allowed us to identify and track the events and milestones in the innovation management practices (Langley et al., 2013). At the second stage, the motivations and roles of the key actors were tracked in the formation of different companies by integrating the secondary data with key insights drawn from the interviews. We engaged in in-depth within case analysis during these two steps and later compared different businesses and key actors' roles for common insights linked to innovation management to emerge from the data. The family business group's evolution over time was examined with particular attention to the nature of the innovation sourcing in the different companies. In the final stage, the built theory frame and empirical data were matched by mapping different companies in Table 14.2 based on their innovation nature and related to the literature on family business innovation research and to our research question. Interpretive approach was utilized to analyze our empirical material. Interpretive approach

Case Description

The family business was founded in 1965 when the founder established Peikko Ltd. The development of the family business into a family business group has taken place at different stages. At the first stage, the founder built a portfolio of companies through various arrangements i.e., start-ups, joint ventures, and business acquisitions. The ownership of companies was either solely by the founder or shared with the non-family business owners. Some of the companies also formed a pyramidal ownership structure. The portfolio structure facilitated the use of resources and reorganizations between companies. In the mid '90s the founder had a large business portfolio where most of the companies were based on innovation. When the generational change began the founder had an extensive group with over 20 different businesses in several industries. The second stage was during succession, with the process of generational change, the number of companies was reduced, and the structure was simplified into a holding model. With this, ownership was transferred entirely to the family which helped both the management of companies and ownership. At the third stage the holding was dismantled, to clarify the division of tasks and individual interests between the second-generation members. With this structural change, owners improved the management and the division of tasks within the family business group.

The family business has gone through major shifts from a single business in 1965 to a business group structure. Peikko group, with over 30 subsidiaries in 32 countries, focuses on the global construction business and supplies a large selection of concrete connections and composite beams for both precast and cast-in-situ solutions for a wide variety of applications. Peikko group's turnover is over $200 million, and it employs more than 1,800 employees. The second group, Troll Capital, takes care of the family's wealth preservation in capital investments as well as makes VC investments to innovative start-ups or growth companies. Troll Capital has been involved in growing hundreds of innovative companies in the past 20 years.

In the founding stage there was one family owner who identified a lot of opportunities for new business ventures and thus started to develop the

380   T. Pihkala et al.

company portfolio. Through the succession process the number of owners increased from one to four in two generations. New companies were established to enable the ownership succession while the third generation entered the family business and was connected with ownership permutations to the existing groups. Currently, the family business group is in the second generation with 11 owners.

Analysis

In this family business group, the owners' participation has been a characterizing factor for all strategic decisions (see Table 14.2). Table 14.2 shows that the owners have been major decision-makers for the innovation management in the business. From this perspective, the case is a typical family-owned business group in which there is no clear separation between ownership and control, and the owners' decision-making has concerned the whole group (Guzzini & Iacobucci, 2014; Iacobucci & Rosa, 2010). The issues linked to time and temporality are fundamental to understanding an organization's dynamics in innovation management and especially in family business groups (Ellwood & Horner, 2020). The development of the business group is strongly reflecting the temporal evolution of innovation management by the business group owners (Calabrò et al., 2019) due to the involvement of multiple owners, businesses, and generations. For instance, innovations managing practices can be introduced by various owners for different businesses and at a different point in time. Furthermore, along with innovations in the business group, the owners have adopted new methods and guidelines for managing and organizing the innovations. These practices seem to be rather long-lived—that is, once adopted, they have lasted till today. Thus, the time perspective of innovation management allows tracking the traces of innovation management practices over a period (Ellwood & Horner, 2020).

As decision-makers, the owners have shown that they are able to conduct a high variety of varying innovation paths for the businesses. The first two companies were clearly based on internal innovations (see Table 14.2). In this sense, the start-up of the family business was based on Schumpeterian (1934) idea of an entrepreneurial venture. The first business focused on an innovation aimed at the construction industry. The solution was a real novelty and followed the first in the market-strategy. The innovation created the basis for many forthcoming businesses in the growing business group. The second company, a start-up as well, was originally a research-based innovation that was transformed into a manufacturing company to produce new types of machines for the construction company. Despite the strong synergies between the two businesses, the owner decided to keep them as separate companies. This decision can be regarded as the creation of the emerging business group (Iacobucci & Rosa, 2010). After the start-ups of the first two companies, the owner acquired two companies to introduce new products in the group (see Table 14.2). The Ansasrauta acquisition was to buy a competitor from the business and to add new products and competencies into the construction products business. The acquisition was totally integrated with the existing company. Furthermore, the Leiron acquisition was to bring complementing products and competencies in the construction business. These two acquisitions clearly speeded up the innovation process for the evolving business—the original innovations were not general enough to be offered to customers—instead, more variety was needed. In this sense, the owner operated as a strategic decision-maker as he actively sought to widen the product range through external innovation (Rautiainen et al., 2020; Rothwell & Dodgson, 1991). At this stage, another permanent pattern emerged. The owner started using internal financing for innovative acquisitions (Belenzon & Berkovitz, 2010; Guzzini & Iacobucci, 2014). Doing this, the owner has been able to use his central position in the group. The use of internal finance makes it possible to engage into diversifying strategies, lower the price of finance (Belenzon & Berkovitz, 2010), create strategic links between the companies in the business group, and grasp opportunities faster (Guzzini & Iacobucci, 2014). It seems that since the Leiron acquisition, internal finance has been the dominant form of finance almost without exceptions in the business group (see Table 14.2).

During 1984–1985 the owner implemented eight business arrangements—three start-ups and five acquisitions (see Table 14.2). The three start-ups were all based on the introduction of new products in the market and could have been included in the already functioning businesses. However, the owner remained consistent with his idea of building a business group. The start-ups were closely related to the earlier businesses in the emerging business group and benefited from the synergies and financing from them. This pattern is yet another long-lived innovation strategy for the owner—the start-ups are almost without exception closely related to the earlier business domains, representing the business group's internal innovation processes. Nieto et al. (2015) suggested that family firms' risk aversion might lead to lower innovation effort, lower use of external sources of innovation, and more incremental innovations. The present business group seems to contradict Nieto et al. (2015) as the owner seems willing to take risks, and the business group follows two parallel innovation strategies (Rautiainen et al.,

2020) simultaneously—it seems to produce related innovations internally, but the external innovation acquisitions mostly represent unrelated diversification. All five acquired businesses in 1984–1985 were related to introduction of new products as well as introduction of new technology in the business group (Rothwell & Dodgson, 1991). Iacobucci and Rosa (2010) noted that for SME business groups, scale and scope are more important than the individual companies. At this stage, the emerging business group seems like a portfolio that the owner can use for innovative activities in diversified businesses. One of the acquired businesses, Eimo, turned out to be a huge success (see Table 14.2). Producing plastic coverings for cellular phones, the company grew along with the world's largest mobile phone manufacturers, went public, and was finally sold to a major player in Japan in 2003.

After two years of absorbing the acquisitions, the owner launched another set of business arrangements. During 1987–1989 he conducted seven operations, of which five were acquisitions, one was a spin-off, and one was a start-up (see Table 14.2). Most of the acquisitions concerned introduction of new products in the business group, two of them also representing a major increase in production capacity, whereas the spin-off was separated from one of the main businesses and later sold out in 2004. The start-up concerned one of the most striking innovations in the business group. The innovation was a result of the business group's internal innovation processes. It was launched as a start-up but as it turned out to be a strategic innovation, it was later merged with the main company in the business group. Earlier research has discussed the innovation drivers in business groups (e.g., Belenzon & Berkovitz, 2010; Guzzini & Iacobucci, 2014). Belenzon and Berkovitz (2010) suggested that knowledge spillover is not the main driver for innovation in business groups as separate companies are unlikely to cite each other's patents. Our study elucidates the spillover problem. It seems that in family-owned business groups the spillover innovations can be organized into separate start-ups and this pattern of organization seems more related to the business group strategy and innovation practices than the use of IPRs. The innovation concerned a new type of metal structure that is currently a central element of the business group strategy.

Altogether, these arrangements in 1987–1989 (see Table 14.2) represent a new stage for the business group development as five of them concerned the creation of resource bundles within the business group (Sirmon & Hitt, 2003). That is, the acquisitions were related to the emerging core companies in the business group, their technologies were absorbed in a wider use and, through leveraging the resource bundles (Sirmon & Hitt, 2003), the owner made sure that the innovation effect was exploited in full.

During 1993–1995 the owner conducted only two innovation operations (see Table 14.2). In 1993 he initiated a start-up of a new unrelated business focusing on stone machines. This move was an exception from the earlier strategy of the owning family to startup only related innovations. Quite soon the risks involved in a diversifying start-up were realized and the business turned out to be unsuccessful. The company was terminated in a bankruptcy in 1999. In 1996 the owner acquired another business that brought a set of new products to the business group, again broadening the line of businesses they were actively participating (Sirmon & Hitt, 2003). Parts of the business were later integrated in the main company and the rest of the business was sold in 2002.

In 2001, the large-scale Triple S acquisition added products, production skills and competences, and a market share in Eimo (see Table 14.2). At the time of acquisition, the acquired company was larger than Eimo and after the acquisition, it was fully merged with Eimo. Similarly, in 2001, the owner also acquired The Cim Precision which was equally merged with Eimo. The company brought new production methods, new competencies, and technology development to the business group. These acquisitions clearly followed the same resource bundling strategy, simultaneously carrying important tasks of including external innovations into the business group (Sirmon & Hitt, 2003).

Discussion and Conclusions

In family business groups, innovation means more than single innovations, more than single businesses and more than internal R&D activities. In this study we have presented an analysis of a family business group that has grown from single innovations to a diversified business complex, having adopted several practices for innovation management during its development. The findings in our study suggest three main contributions to the current literature on family business innovation.

First, our study provides evidence of the temporal development of the innovation management practices in a family business group (Calabrò et al., 2019). In the case, the family business owner formed a set of guidelines to manage the innovation practices and hence, the development of the business group. That is, the owner started with the decision to keep different innovations in separate companies, thereby creating the basis for the business group development. Next, he chose to finance the innovation activities internally. Conducting internal and external innovation in parallel, he separated internal and external innovations by the type of innovation. The internally developed innovations considered related diversification almost without exception while the external acquisitions were about unrelated diversification. Finally, the owner turned to support the development of resource bundles in the business groups through external innovation acquisitions. We suggest that the adoption of guidelines takes place as the new innovations are carried out, thus, they are not created in advance but for the exact need. Interestingly, once created, they seem to be very long-lived. For instance, in this case all the identified guidelines have been preserved in the innovation management of the business group till the present day.

Second, our study brings more information about the central role of the owner guiding the innovation in the family business group. Earlier studies (Guzzini & Iacobucci, 2013; Iacobucci & Rosa, 2010) have suggested that there is no separation between ownership and control in family-owned businesses. Our study findings concur, and we further suggest that for hired management many of the innovation activities could have been very difficult or even impossible, as both internal and external innovation activities often concerned the ownership arrangements that would have gone beyond the mandate of a hired manager. In other words, should a hired manager seek to carry out a similar innovation process, he/she would need to constantly secure the approval from the business owners, which would slow down the organizational processes. It is also viable to suggest that the owner of the business group has assumed the role of the adventurer (Rondi et al., 2019), who is willing to take reasonably high risks and is only modestly tied to family business traditions. This posture to innovation is a long-lasting characteristic.

Finally, the literature on family business innovation has centered on the input and output of innovation (De Massis et al., 2013). Only recently, some studies have pointed out the need to study the activities of innovation (Feranita et al., 2017). In this study we approached the family business group innovation activities from the perspective of innovation management. Based on our findings, this perspective seems fruitful for understanding the innovation dynamics within the business group over a long-time frame. We suggest that the perspective of innovation management helps capturing the large variance of innovation activities in a business group. For example, should innovation be studied at the CEO level, the results would be biased toward those activities that do not require ownership arrangements. Similarly, the focus on R&D spending would provide an extensive view on the internal innovations activities but leave the external innovation activities (acquisitions, collaborations) unnoticed.

Our study raises possibilities for further research. First, based on our findings, the innovation management guidelines seem long-lasting and even difficult to replace. In the case analysis, indications of large shifts in the innovation management guidelines were not found. It is however likely that in other business groups they may have taken place. Further research is warranted on the reasons, decision-making and outcomes of such changes. Second, it seems evident, that the different innovation management dimensions are intertwined. Yet, they are introduced at different stages during the development of the business group. We suggest that more research is needed to uncover the interdependencies between the different innovation management choices. We would assume that even if the innovation management decisions take place over a very long time, they are path-dependent, and the earlier choices are in fact dictating the coming choices.

References

Afuah, A. (2003). Redefining firm boundaries in the face of the internet: Are firms really shrinking? *Academy of Management Review, 28*(1), 34–53.

Afuah, A. (2020). *Innovation management-strategies, implementation, and profits.* Oxford University Press.

Belenzon, S., & Berkovitz, T. (2010). Innovation in business groups. *Management Science, 56*(3), 519–535.

Brinkerink, J., & Bammens, Y. (2018). Family influence and R&D spending in Dutch manufacturing SMEs: The role of identity and socioemotional decision considerations. *Journal of Product Innovation Management, 35*(4), 588–608.

Burrell, G., & Morgan, G. (2017). *Sociological paradigms and organisational analysis: Elements of the sociology of corporate life.* Routledge.

Calabrò, A., Vecchiarini, M., Gast, J., Campopiano, G., De Massis, A., & Kraus, S. (2019). Innovation in family firms: A systematic literature review and guidance for future research. *International Journal of Management Reviews, 21*(3), 317–355.

Chandy, R. K., & Tellis, G. J. (2000). The incumbent's curse? Incumbency, size, and radical product innovation. *Journal of Marketing, 64*(3), 1–17.

Chetty, S. (1996). The case study method for research in small- and medium-sized firms. *International Small Business Journal, 15*(1), 73–85.

De Massis, A., Frattini, F., & Lichtenthaler, U. (2013). Research on technological innovation in family firms: Present debates and future directions. *Family Business Review, 26*(1), 10–31. https://doi.org/10.1177/0894486512466258.

De Massis, A., Frattini, F., Pizzurno, E., & Cassia, L. (2015). Product innovation in family versus nonfamily firms: An exploratory analysis. *Journal of Small Business Management, 53*(1), 1–36.

Dodgson, M., Gann, D. M., & Phillips, N. (2014). Perspectives on innovation management. In *The Oxford handbook of innovation management* (pp. 3–25). Oxford University Press.

Dyer, W. G., Jr., & Wilkins, A. L. (1991). Better stories, not better constructs, to generate better theory: A rejoinder to Eisenhardt. *Academy of Management Review, 16*(3), 613–619.

Ellwood, P., & Horner, S. (2020). In search of lost time: The temporal construction of innovation management. *R&D Management, 50*(3), 364–379.

Feranita, F., Kotlar, J., & De Massis, A. (2017). Collaborative innovation in family firms: Past research, current debates and agenda for future research. *Journal of Family Business Strategy, 8*(3), 137–156.

Guzzini, E., & Iacobucci, D. (2014). Ownership as R&D incentive in business groups. *Small Business Economics, 43*(1), 119–135.

Hall, A., Melin, L., & Nordqvist, M. (2001). Entrepreneurship as radical change in the family business: Exploring the role of cultural patterns. *Family Business Review, 14*(3), 193–208.

Hsieh, T.-J., Yeh, R.-S., & Chen, Y.-J. (2010). Business group characteristics and affiliated firm innovation: The case of Taiwan. *Industrial Marketing Management, 39*(4), 560–570.

Huber, G. P., & Power, D. J. (1985). Retrospective reports of strategic-level managers: Guidelines for increasing their accuracy. *Strategic Management Journal, 6*(2), 171–180.

Iacobucci, D., & Rosa, P. (2010). The growth of business groups by habitual entrepreneurs: The role of entrepreneurial teams. *Entrepreneurship Theory and Practice, 34*(2), 351–377.

Kammerlander, N., Dessi, C., Bird, M., Floris, M., & Murru, A. (2015). The impact of shared stories on family firm innovation: A multi-case study. *Family Business Review, 28*, 332–354.

Kogut, B., & Zander, U. (1992). Knowledge of the firm, combinative capabilities, and the replication of technology. *Organization Science, 3*(3), 383–397.

Komera, S., Lukose, P. J., & Sasidharan, S. (2016). Business group affiliation and innovation in medium and high-technology industries in India. In *Technology* (pp. 43–56). Springer.

Langley, A., Smallman, C., Tsoukas, H., & Van de Ven, A. H. (2013). Process studies of change in organization and management: Unveiling temporality, activity, and flow. *Academy of Management Journal, 56*(1), 1–13.

La Porta, R., Lopez-de-Silanes, F., & Shleifer, A. (1999). Corporate ownership around the world. *The Journal of Finance, 54*(2), 471–517.

Lechner, C., & Leyronas, C. (2009). Small-business group formation as an entrepreneurial development model. *Entrepreneurship Theory and Practice, 33*(3), 645–667.

Levie, J., & Lerner, M. (2009). Resource mobilization and performance in family and nonfamily businesses in the United Kingdom. *Family Business Review, 22*(1), 25–38.

Mahmood, I. P., & Mitchell, W. (2004). Two faces: Effects of business groups on innovation in emerging economies. *Management Science, 50*(10), 1348–1365.

Mäkimattila, M., Rautiainen, M., & Pihkala, T. (2016). Systemic innovation in complex business portfolios—A case study. *International Journal of Business Innovation and Research, 10*(2–3), 363–379.

McConaughy, D. L., Matthews, C. H., & Fialko, A. S. (2001). Founding family controlled firms: Performance, risk, and value. *Journal of Small Business Management, 39*(1), 31–49.

Miller, D., Breton-Miller, L., & Lester, R. H. (2011). Family and lone founder ownership and strategic behaviour: Social context, identity, and institutional logics. *Journal of Management Studies, 48*(1), 1–25.

Mintzberg, H. (1979). An emerging strategy of "direct" research. *Administrative Science Quarterly, 24*, 582–589.

Mitchell, W. (1989). Whether and when? Probability and timing of incumbents' entry into emerging industrial subfields. *Administrative Science Quarterly, 34*, 208–230.

Naldi, L., Nordqvist, M., Sjöberg, K., & Wiklund, J. (2007). Entrepreneurial orientation, risk taking, and performance in family firms. *Family Business Review, 20*(1), 33–47.

Neergaard, H. (2007). 10 Sampling in entrepreneurial settings. In *Handbook of qualitative research methods in entrepreneurship* (p. 253). Edward Elgar.

Nieto, M. J., Santamaria, L., & Fernandez, Z. (2015). Understanding the innovation behavior of family firms. *Journal of Small Business Management, 53*(2), 382–399.

Pittino, D., Visintin, F., Baù, M., & Mazzurana, P. (2013). Collaborative technology strategies and innovation in family firms. *International Journal of Entrepreneurship and Innovation Management, 17*(1–3), 8–27.

Pittino, D., Visintin, F., Lenger, T., & Sternad, D. (2016). Are high performance work practices really necessary in family SMEs? An analysis of the impact on employee retention. *Journal of Family Business Strategy, 7*(2), 75–89.

Rautiainen, M., Konsti-Laakso, S., & Pihkala, T. (2020). *Innovation in family business groups: Going beyond an RD perspective*. Edward Elgar.

Reay, T. (2014). *Publishing qualitative research*. Sage.

Rondi, E., De Massis, A., & Kotlar, J. (2019). Unlocking innovation potential: A typology of family business innovation postures and the critical role of the family system. *Journal of Family Business Strategy, 10*(4), 100236.

Roscoe, P., Discua Cruz, A., & Howorth, C. (2013). How does an old firm learn new tricks? A material account of entrepreneurial opportunity. *Business History, 55*(1), 53–72.

Rothwell, R., & Dodgson, M. (1991). External linkages and innovation in small and medium-sized enterprises. *R&D Management, 21*(2), 125–138.

Schumpeter, J. (1934). *The theory of economic development: An inquiry into profits, capital, credit, interest, and the business cycle*. Harvard University Press.

Sharma, P., Chrisman, J. J., & Chua, J. H. (1997). Strategic management of the family business: Past research and future challenges. *Family Business Review, 10*(1), 1–35.

Silverman, D. (1998). Qualitative research: Meanings or practices? *Information Systems Journal, 8*(1), 3–20.

Silverman, D. (2013). *Doing qualitative research: A practical handbook.* Sage.

Sirmon, D. G., & Hitt, M. A. (2003). Managing resources: Linking unique resources, management, and wealth creation in family firms. *Entrepreneurship Theory and Practice, 27*(4), 339–358.

Soh, P.-H., Mahmood, I. P., & Mitchell, W. (2004). Dynamic inducements in R&D investment: Market signals and network locations. *Academy of Management Journal, 47*(6), 907–917.

Stake, R. E. (2010). *Qualitative research: Studying how things work.* Guilford Press.

Ward, J. L. (1997). Growing the family business: Special challenges and best practices. *Family Business Review, 10*(4), 323–337.

Weick, K. E. (1995). *Sensemaking in organizations* (Vol. 3). Sage.

Welch, C. (2000). The archaeology of business networks: The use of archival records in case study research. *Journal of Strategic Marketing, 8*(2), 197–208.

Yin, R. K. (2009). *Case study research: Design and methods.* Sage.

Yiu, D., Bruton, G. D., & Lu, Y. (2005). Understanding business group performance in an emerging economy: Acquiring resources and capabilities in order to prosper. *Journal of Management Studies, 42*(1), 183–206.

15

Open Innovation and Family Business Groups: Anomalies Arising from the Context?

Suvi Konsti-Laakso, Tuomo Uotila, and Martti Mäkimattila

Introduction

Recently, there has been a growing interest in studying innovation activities in the family firm context. As a research topic, a family firm's innovation activities are at the crossroads of two different research domains: family business research and innovation research. Whereas family business research has increasingly investigated innovation in family businesses, innovation research—particularly open innovation research—has remained focused on innovation in light of firm size, age and industry.

Recent research on innovation in family firms has yielded interesting findings: it seems that family firms invest less in innovation activities than non-family firms, yet they are more effective in generating innovations (Calabró et al., 2019). In addition, according to a review conducted by

---

S. Konsti-Laakso (✉) · T. Uotila
LUT School of Engineering Science, LUT University, Lahti, Finland
e-mail: suvi.konsti-laakso@lut.fi

T. Uotila
e-mail: Tuomo.uotila@lut.fi

M. Mäkimattila
LAB University of Applied Sciences, Lahti, Finland
e-mail: martti.makimattila@lab.fi

© The Author(s), under exclusive license to Springer Nature Switzerland AG 2023
M. Rautianen et al. (eds.), *The Palgrave Handbook of Managing Family Business Groups*,
https://doi.org/10.1007/978-3-031-13206-3_15

Gjergji et al. (2019), family firms are less open compared with non-family firms. This means that despite family firm's social capital, they seem to rely less on external knowledge collaboration in their innovation activities than non-family firms. The reasons behind these results are not yet clear, but they indicate that something interesting is taking place in family firms. However, relatively little is known about how family firms, as well as enterprising families, manage their innovation activities.

Open innovation research builds on the assumption that firms are single, independent actors in their innovation activities (Bigliardi et al., 2020; Torchia & Calabró, 2019). Because these companies utilise external knowledge in varying levels of intensity, some open and family business innovation scholars have begun to wonder where the companies' boundaries actually lay. West and Bogers (2017) concluded that the most profound insights for open innovation research can be derived from the nature and role of the firm. Feranita et al. (2017) identified family-controlled business portfolios as an unearthed issue in collaborative innovation. Despite these initial explorations into the topic, amongst open innovation research, there are no literature reviews that explicitly identify the firm's organisational characteristics or design as a future research avenue. In general, open innovation research focuses on firm size, industry and innovation type (Bigliardi et al., 2020; Torchia & Calabró, 2019). For family firms, studies concerning small- and medium-sized companies are relevant and close (Calabró et al., 2019). Family firms represent a certain type of 'firm nature' because they are characterised by mixed goals between business and family. For this reason, family firms and businesses constitute an interesting research area.

In the current paper, we introduce family business groups (FBGs) as an underlying structural variable for open innovation research, as well as family business research. We take a closer look at the current research findings or anomalies concerning innovation in family firms, proposing alternative perspectives from the FBG point of view. The research question is as follows: How does the FBG setting challenge open innovation research? Our aim is to highlight the underlying assumption of a single, autonomous firm in (open) innovation research and discuss situations where a single company can be an instrumental entity in a larger constellation. As a result, more fine-grained views and research are needed to provide explanations for these anomalies. At the same time, innovation research is lacking an understanding of how firms utilise outbound open innovation and organisational variables like firm identity or group affiliations.

This chapter is organised as follows: first, open innovation and its two main streams—namely inbound and outbound innovation—are discussed.

Then, we continue by explaining the family effect of innovation and introduce FBGs as a context for innovation. We underline our main arguments with an illustration. A discussion and conclusion finalise this chapter.

Literature

Open Innovation

'Innovation is widely considered as the life blood of corporate survival and growth' (Zahra & Covin, 1994, p. 183). Innovation is the multistage process whereby organisations transform ideas into new and/or improved products, services or processes to advance, compete and differentiate themselves successfully in their marketplace (Baregeheh et al., 2009).

Open innovation refers to the active, intentional and strategic use of knowledge residing outside organisation's boundaries (Chesbrough, 2003). Open innovation takes many forms, such as acquiring or selling ready innovations, technical inventions or knowledge, ideas, market knowledge, components or other useful information (Bogers & West, 2012). Cassiman and Valentini (2016) described these 'outside-in' and 'inside-out' processes as 'buying and selling knowledge'.

Open innovation reflects the paradigm shift from closed systems to open ones and is in line with the development of information and communication technologies and globally dispersed knowledge. Despite the shortcomings in addressing previous research findings and the overly dichotomous approach to openness (Trott & Hartmann, 2009), open innovation has become one of the most thriving research streams in innovation studies. The strength of the open innovation framework is that it is an innovation-specific framework, unlike, for example, the actor–resources–activities (ARA) model (Håkansson & Johansson, 1992), which aims to explain why firms collaborate in general. Open innovation builds on previous theoretical concepts from strategy and networking, such as the ARA model, but as a distinction, open innovation attempts to describe purely innovation-related activities, leaving out any other field of business. As such, despite its critiques, it is noted to be successfully in combining previously separated research streams from product development, networking and strategic management.

Open innovation can be seen as an innovation strategy; thus, openness refers to the degree of an organisation's choice regarding whether to follow an open or closed strategy for knowledge search (Laursen & Salter, 2006). Laursen and Salter (2006) distinguished four types of openness:

sourcing, acquiring, selling and revealing. The search for knowledge outside firm boundaries connects firms to different stakeholders and actors, such as existing and potential customers, suppliers, competitors, research institutes and universities (Brunswicker et al., 2015). Brunswicker et al. (2015) showed that amongst small- and medium-sized companies, different types of openness profiles can be identified that characterise SME's knowledge sourcing. These are (1) a minimal searcher, (2) a supply chain searcher, (3) a technology-oriented searcher, (4) an application-oriented searcher and (5) a full-scope searcher. However, it is only seldom brought up that openness is not static; it varies in time. Mäkimattila et al. (2013) investigated openness in a networked innovation process, which lasted more than 10 years; they showed how firm's openness decreased as the innovation process evolved and matured. As the business opportunity became clearer and timely closer, firm's openness declined. Thus, openness was moderated by the proximity of a new business opportunity.

For open innovation research, these final stages of the innovation process seem to be a problematic area, and these later stages, that is, commercialisation, are poorly understood in the literature. According to West et al. (2014), open innovation research should focus on the outbound type of open innovation. Limited research on this matter has concluded that companies tend to prefer knowledge search, that is, the 'outside-in' type, but they rarely utilise the inside-out type (Huizing, 2011). In addition, according to Huizing (2011), outbound innovation is not widely utilised in companies compared with inbound innovation. Companies are reluctant to sell their ideas and IP because they are afraid of losing possible new business opportunities.

One reason for the obsolete research on outbound innovation may be that this line of research goes beyond the scope of traditional innovation management research, which focuses on a firm's organisation of R&D and innovation management processes, practices and their relation to performance. Gentile-Lüdecke et al. (2020) showed that there is a positive relationship between centralisation and outbound activities, implying that decision-making authority is crucial for the outbound type of activity. Thus, outbound innovation relates closely to strategic decisions regarding whether to pursue certain business opportunities, and those decisions belong to the board and owners. As family owners often play multiple owner and manager roles in their firm, family firms are interesting arena for outbound innovation.

The Family Effect on Innovation

Family firms are typically characterised by an intergenerational orientation, willingness to ensure firm survival and preservation of prosperity and family wealth (Calabró et al., 2019). These characteristics shape innovation in family firms either positively or negatively. Family ownership is likely to foster innovation because of the long-term orientation of family owners (Dyer Jr, 2003), which increases the propensity to bear the risk of investing in innovation (Sciascia et al., 2015). Thus, family ownership encourages family firms to provide the resources necessary for innovation (Zahra, 2005). On the other hand, because of intergenerational orientation and securing firm survival, it seems that family firms are more hesitant to take the risk associated with innovation activities than non-family firms (Calabró et al., 2019). Research indicates that sometimes changes in family ownership are needed to pursue more innovative strategies (Lambrecht et al., 2017).

Family influence on innovation can be condensed into three aspects: ownership, management and governance (Matzler et al., 2015). These aspects give family owners the discretion to determine the goals and strategic options of the firm (Lambrecht et al., 2017). Family owners make decisions and retreat from radical and progressive innovations, whereas incremental innovations may be left to the hands of the managers (Bergfeld & Weber, 2011). Matzler et al. (2015) results show that family participation in management and governance has a negative impact on innovation inputs and a positive influence on innovation outputs. This suggests that family members are risk-averse and reluctant to invest in innovation, but at the same time, they invest in innovation more effectively. Matzler et al. (2015) also concluded that family managers and directors have a positive impact on a firm's innovation output and that family board members have an important role in innovation output.

Research has indicated that family-managed firms are efficient in the utilisation of employed inputs and, hence, can obtain greater innovation output than non-family-managed firms from their usually restricted innovation input pool (Duran et al., 2016). It is also suggested that the founder's role particularly shapes the family firm's innovation. Kammerlander et al. (2015) found that although a strong founder focus in shared stories is negatively associated with innovation in family firms, a strong family focus in shared stories is positively associated with innovation in family firms.

Family business research acknowledges that family firms are heterogeneous in terms of their size, governance and age (Chua et al., 2012) but also in terms of how innovative and entrepreneurial they are. Innovation research

394　S. Konsti-Laakso et al.

and family firm research tend to share the same assumptions and, perhaps, definition; that is, they understand family firms as single, independent and autonomous firms. FBG differs from a single firm as a context for innovation, and next we elaborate this context further.

Family Business Groups as a Context for Innovation

According to Bergfeld and Weber (2011), "Successful families strive to secure their wealth long-term by applying radical and progressive innovation as mechanisms to diversify the orientation of their holdings and assure the future-proofness of their firms." FBGs can be considered a network of legally independent firms that are operating in diverse industries, with a common dominant family owner(s) and that are coordinated through multiple formal and informal ties (Carney et al., 2011). In general, business groups are found to be a fruitful environment for innovation because of their resource pool and internal capital market (Hsieh et al., 2010). They typically emerge as a response to new business opportunities (Belenzon & Berkovitz, 2010); thus, they emphasise active family influence (Maury, 2006) and enterprising families (Feranita et al., 2017; Riar et al., 2021). Rautiainen et al. (2020) have suggested that innovation in the emergence of FBGs may not necessarily lie in internal R&D but rather in the active utilisation of sourcing, acquisitions and venturing. FBGs, however, may prefer full control instead of other collaborative forms (Rautiainen et al., 2020). For innovation, the FBG provides at least the following perspectives:

Resource pool: Instead of a single, family-governed firm, a family business group forms a system in which active entrepreneurial family owner-managers may operate. FBGs can constitute an effective innovation system of their own. Mäkimattila et al. (2016) proposed that it is conceivable that businesses within a group together constitute an effective innovation system with the required critical mass for innovative processes or that the organisations would be expected to take part in an innovation process because of their joint ownership background. For enterprising families, business groups can be seen as a resource pool in which the knowledge is available for all firms and orchestrated by active, entrepreneurial owners. The most skilful teams may be shifted from one company to another inside the FBG.

Nature of firm: FBGs set the boundaries of the firm in a different way; thus, the nature of the firm is different than that of a standalone firm. This is illustrated in Fig. 15.1. For the entrepreneurial family, the boundaries cover the entire FBG system instead of a single firm. The permeability of the firm boundary can be different depending on the firm's position in the FBG. Here, multiple companies may be established for a single innovation (Rautiainen et al., 2020). Previous research has noted that a firm belonging to a business group may exist for specific dedicated purposes, such as conducting R&D or manufacturing or holding patents (Rautiainen et al., 2020). Thus, the FBG structure may be dynamic and changing, depending on the entrepreneurial family's strategic vision, actions and speed of innovation process.

Triggering effect of multiple drivers: Mäkimattila et al. (2016) suggested that innovation in a family business group is powered by social, business and individual drivers. Like any other entrepreneurial firms, family firms' innovation is also affected by the business driver: the development needs that emerge from the competitive situation and environment of the distinct businesses or whole group. Social drivers accrue from the ownership—and in the case of family business—from the familiness and relationships between the family members. Individual drivers, such as family members' individual interests in certain industries and entrepreneurial activities, affect the need to establish new companies. Innovation may be triggered by non-economic goals (Diaz-Moriana et al., 2020). Because the drivers may independently move innovation forward, the innovation process may require all of them to be fulfilled.

Systemic driver: Changes in family relationships, individual interests, rising conflicts and internal competition might reshape the groups and initiate innovations. This adaptation to external forces fosters innovation, which is called the systemic driver (Mäkimattila et al., 2016). As the FBG becomes large enough, the system itself will create a constant need to develop it further. The internal complexity, heterogeneity, dynamism, differing time frames of the distinct businesses and varying expectations towards different businesses may lead to the emergence of a systemic driver. At the same time, there is a tendency for the business to shift towards the multifaceted development of diversified portfolios with individually and socially-driven innovation.

Openness of a firm: Mäkimattila et al. (2013) showed that the openness of a firm is not a static feature; instead, it varies in the different phases of an innovation process. Thus, the openness of a firm belonging to the FBG may depend on the maturity of innovation. Besides this temporal dimension in openness, FBGs provide another dimension in studying openness: the structural dimension, that is, openness towards other companies belonging or not belonging to the same FBG.

To sum up, we can extract the inconsistencies or 'anomalies' that derive from current research on open innovation and innovation in family firms.

They can be condensed into two different topics: (1) family firms' innovation efficiency and input/output ratio and (2) differences in openness. Our main argument is that because open innovation and family business research tend to use a single, independent firm as a unit of analysis, firms' position in the family business group may somewhat explain these inconsistent findings—or at least play a role in finding these explanations. Because the focus is changed from a single firm to a family business group, some interesting alternative perspectives for these anomalies can be discussed. We use a generative illustration (Fig. 15.1) to illustrate our main argument.

Instead of managing one firm, family owners operate multiple companies belonging to a group. The group itself is not static but dynamic and changing because of the active ownership and systemic drivers. The firms inside the FBG are positioned on different layers (illustrated as numbers 1–4 in Fig. 15.1), here depending on the maturity of the innovation, related business opportunities and the firm's strategic importance for its owners. This importance is triggered and facilitated by the social, business and individual drivers (Mäkimattila et al., 2016). The layers represent the different positions the company may have as a part of a business group. The most important businesses are at the top of the pyramid, close to the owners (layer 4 in Fig. 15.1). As the businesses or companies develop and mature, they move from different layers to another (e.g., from layer 1 to layer 2). These companies may shift closer to the owners because of the changes in drivers: social

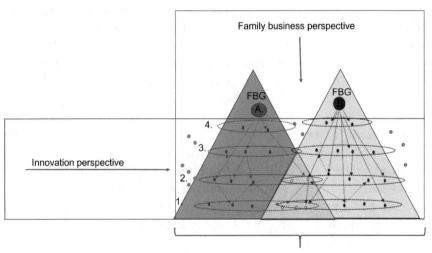

Fig. 15.1 FBG as an underlying variable for innovation perspectives

drivers as the family relations change or business drivers as a response to emerging business opportunities or changes in markets.

Proposition 1. Firms in FBG are positioned depending on the maturity of the innovation, related business opportunities and the firm's strategic importance for its owners.

Proposition 2. The dynamism of FBG is driven by the presence of a systemic driver.

The layers are constructed in line with the innovation life cycle. Typically, the life cycle starts with the explorative phase (layer 1), during which technology is emerging and development contains a high level of uncertainty. These highly speculative ventures may be established to explore promising future opportunities; they may be joint ventures together with other enterprising families and active owners of other FBGs, research institutes or ecosystem members.

As the potential future opportunity is starting to take shape in terms of business logic, some decisions are made regarding whether to pursue the opportunity or exit the venture. Levels 2 and 3 present the companies that are driving forward these promising new businesses. Some ventures are merged tighter to FBG, kept as a 'hobby company' or sold to other parties, depending on the owner's interests, values and needs. Layer 4 represents companies in a business group that are 'near and dear' to the owners. These companies are typically mature and traditional companies in terms of their functions and may be the historical family firm, hence depicting the family owner's interests. As such, the FBG structure allows family firms to renew themselves, despite the imprint generated by longevity and traditions. Concerning new venture development, Riar et al. (2021) studied entrepreneurial family (EF) member entrepreneurial activity; they identified the motives for EF members to start new ventures, such as preserving the entrepreneurial mindset, sustaining family harmony, finding family fit, succession-related motives and emancipation from the family firm. These ventures may be characterised by uncertainty and different search strategies. Thus, the following research proposition is set:

Proposition 3. FBG structure enables the exploration and exploitation of novel innovations whilst maintaining core business.

As indicated in Fig. 15.1, from an open innovation perspective, a firm's affiliation to an FBG may often remain invisible; that is, a firm's interdependencies are not visible. In the FBG setting, there can be different kinds of collaboration between firms, for instance, staff relocations. Firms may be established with a dedicated purpose and then merged or closed down after they have accomplished their mission. This may cause distortion in research results concerning efficiency: A single company may appear as a failure, even though it has accomplished its mission from the viewpoint of the FBG. Thus, the firms are *instrumental*, tool-like entities or instruments for active and entrepreneurial owners who are mostly concerned about the group and its performance related to multiple goals. The firms belonging to the FBG may seem to be independent—and legally they are—but they are controlled by a family entity (illustrated as A or B in Fig. 15.1). This relates particularly to the lack of outbound type of open innovation research as the innovations can be developed in another and commercialised in another firm owned by the same owner. We condense this to the following research proposition:

Proposition 4. Innovation can develop into a business through many individual companies within FBG.

The presented situation includes different types of openness. Openness can be directed at other companies in the FBG, at other FBGs and at non-FBG companies. However, in many cases, this openness may not be easy to detect. FBG can be more open in exploring new technologies in collaborative manner and joint ventures may take place at the intersection between two FBGs. However, as indicated by Rautiainen et al. (2020), the preferred innovation sourcing mechanisms were those that gave the family entrepreneur full control. Therefore, it is likely that along the way, full control is preferred if the emerging business is perceived interesting. If an innovating firm is actually a part of an FBG, the results may 'disappear' elsewhere in the group because the decisions on how to exploit possible future business opportunities are in the hands of owners and the board. Therefore, for outbound innovation research, the FBG setting is particularly important because it may cause the innovation to go out of sight of one firm but remain under the control of the family. To sum up, we suggest the following research proposition.

Proposition 5. Firm's level, direction and nature of openness are affected by FBG affiliation.

Discussion and Conclusion

Miles et al. (2010) stated that traditional organisational forms will not be able to respond effectively to future opportunities and challenges. This is true for family firms as well; therefore, FBGs are one way to tackle future opportunities and the related risks and challenges in family firms. However, it is not known how prevalent the structure of FBGs actually is. Despite this, FBGs are under-researched, poorly identified and understood phenomena, but they provide an interesting arena to study open innovation and notable underlying variable to study family firm innovation.

Concerning family business innovation anomalies, the current study proposes the following outcomes: First, innovation inputs and outputs may take place in different firms. This means that innovation inputs and outputs are more difficult to measure. In the FBG setting, a single firm may have a limited but dedicated, instrument-like role in a family-owned and -controlled group. Although FBGs consist of legally independent firms, the decision power, resources and innovation outputs do not necessarily reside inside the boundaries of a single firm: they reside inside group boundaries. Thus, the nature and boundaries of a firm are set based on ownership.

Second, in FBGs, 'openness' has many faces. Openness may be internal between firms that are under the control of owners. Openness may be external to other firms or even between FBGs. Internal openness refers to the fact that family members as managers and directors may be in a position to better use those resources controlled by the entire FBG and/or the family, and they can orchestrate the system to achieve innovation. In the emergence of the FBG, external openness may be more relevant, but as the FBG matures, it is capable of generating innovations as a single system (Mäkimattila et al., 2016). Therefore, it is important to recognise the temporal phase of the family business group and single firms belonging to the FBG. There is a difference whether the company is a 'still in the garage' or whether it is a firm with multiple generations.

The FBG setting is particularly important for studies focusing on outbound innovation. As Matzler et al. (2015) pointed out, innovation cannot be understood without taking owners into consideration, and this especially applies to outbound innovation. The existence of FBGs may be a vehicle for family firms or EF members to exploit those opportunities generated by R&D capabilities in the group.

Limitations and Further Research

As the current paper has speculated about scenarios for open innovation research in FBGs, there are some limitations that need to be acknowledged. Because business ownership and FBGs are difficult to detect statistically, we do not know the magnitude of this phenomenon. Therefore, the presented framework should be cautiously applied. Thus, further research should investigate the population of these companies and the prevalent phenomenon of FBGs. FBG research has identified multiple methodological challenges (Rautiainen & Pihkala, 2019), including, amongst others, definitional challenges, a lack of available and accurate data and access to data. For example, quantitative data, such as the Community Innovation Survey (CIS), include a variable concerning affiliation to a business group but do not include a variable concerning family affiliation. The development of new variables that would capture family and ownership relations would advance this matter.

Following Feranita et al., (2017), research should go beyond single-firm boundaries, studying how enterprising families organise their businesses. How do different firms under family control and ownership collaborate, and how does the FBG structure enable innovation in its different stages? One line of research is to empirically validate the presented framework. Longitudinal, qualitative case study research could provide evidence of the dynamics of the FBG. This requires access to informants who have a timewise sufficient perspective to cover the essential parts of the innovation process and the roles of different entities in the process. From this perspective, research should pay attention to firm interdependencies and study the FBG system formed by different actors, resources and activities. In line with this, the ARA model could be one suitable framework.

References

Baregheh, A., Rowley, J., & Sambrook, S. (2009). Towards a multidisciplinary definition of innovation. *Management Decision, 47*(8), 1323–1339.

Belenzon, S., & Berkovitz, T. (2010). Innovation in business groups. *Management Science, 56*(3), 519–535.

Bergfeld, M. M. H., & Weber, F. M. (2011). Dynasties of innovation: Highly performing German family firms and the owners' role for innovation. *International Journal of Entrepreneurship and Innovation Management, 13*(1), 80–94.

Bigliardi, B., Ferraro, G., Filippelli, S., & Galati, F. (2020). The past, present and future of open innovation. *European Journal of Innovation Management, 24*(4), 1130–1161.

Bogers, M., & West, J. (2012). Managing distributed innovation: Strategic utilization of open and user innovation. *Creativity and Innovation Management, 21*(1), 61–75.

Brunswicker, S., & Vanhaverbeke, W. (2015). Open innovation in small and medium-sized enterprises (SMEs): External knowledge sourcing strategies and internal organizational facilitators. *Journal of Small Business Management, 53*(4), 1241–1263.

Calabrò, A., Vecchiarini, M., Gast, J., Campopiano, G., De Massis, A., & Kraus, S. (2019). Innovation in family firms: A systematic literature review and guidance for future research. *International Journal of Management Reviews, 21*(3), 317–355.

Carney, M., Gedajlovic, E. R., Heugens, P. P., Van Essen, M., & Van Oosterhout, J. (2011). Business group affiliation, performance, context, and strategy: A meta-analysis. *Academy of Management Journal, 54*(3), 437–460.

Cassiman, B., & Valentini, G. (2016). Open innovation: Are inbound and outbound knowledge flows really complementary? *Strategic Management Journal, 37*(6), 1034–1046.

Chesbrough, H. W. (2003). *Open innovation: The new imperative for creating and profiting from technology*. Harvard Business Press.

Chua, J. H., Chrisman, J. J., Steier, L. P., & Rau, S. B. (2012). Sources of heterogeneity in family firms: An introduction. *Entrepreneurship Theory and Practice, 36*(6), 1103–1113. https://doi.org/10.1111/j.1540-6520.2012.00540.x

Diaz-Moriana, V., Clinton, E., Kammerlander, N., Lumpkin, G. T., & Craig, J. B. (2020). Innovation motives in family firms: A transgenerational view. *Entrepreneurship Theory and Practice, 44*(2), 256–287.

Duran, P., Kammerlander, N., Van Essen, M., & Zellweger, T. (2016). Doing more with less: Innovation input and output in family firms. *Academy of Management Journal, 59*(4), 1224–1264.

Dyer, W. G., Jr. (2003). The family: The missing variable in organizational research. *Entrepreneurship Theory and Practice, 27*(4), 401–416.

Feranita, F., Kotlar, J., & De Massis, A. (2017). Collaborative innovation in family firms: Past research, current debates and agenda for future research. *Journal of Family Business Strategy, 8*(3), 137–156.

Gentile-Lüdecke, S., de Oliveira, R. T., & Paul, J. (2020). Does organizational structure facilitate inbound and outbound open innovation in SMEs? *Small Business Economics, 55*(4), 1091–1112.

Gjergji, R., Lazzarotti, V., Visconti, F., & García-Marco, T. (2019). Open innovation in family firms: A systematic literature review. *Management Research: Journal of the Iberoamerican Academy of Management, 17*(3), 204–332.

Håkansson, H., & Johanson, J. (1992). A Model of Industrial Networks. In B. Axelsson & G. Easton (Eds.), *Industrial Networks: A New View of Reality* (pp. 28–34). Routledge.

Hsieh, T. J., Yeh, R. S., & Chen, Y. J. (2010). Business group characteristics and affiliated firm innovation: The case of Taiwan. *Industrial Marketing Management, 39*(4), 560–570.

Huizingh, E. K. (2011). Open innovation: State of the art and future perspectives. *Technovation, 31*(1), 2–9.

Kammerlander, N., Dessi, C., Bird, M., Floris, M., & Murru, A. (2015). The impact of shared stories on family firm XE "family:Family firm" innovation: A multicase study. *Family Business Review, 28*(4), 332–354.

Lambrechts, F., Voordeckers, W., Roijakkers, N., & Vanhaverbeke, W. (2017). Exploring open innovation in entrepreneurial private family firms in low-and medium-technology industries. *Organizational Dynamics, 46*(4), 244–261.

Laursen, K., & Salter, A. (2006). Open for innovation: The role of openness in explaining innovation performance among UK manufacturing firms. *Strategic Management Journal, 27*(2), 131–150.

Mäkimattila, M., Melkas, H., & Uotila, T. (2013). Dynamics of openness in innovation processes—A case study in the Finnish food industry. *Knowledge and Process Management, 20*(4), 243–255.

Mäkimattila, M., Rautiainen, M., & Pihkala, T. (2016). Systemic innovation in complex business portfolios: A case study. *International Journal of Business Innovation and Research, 10*(2–3), 363–379.

Matzler, K., Veider, V., Hautz, J., & Stadler, C. (2015). The impact of family ownership, management, and governance on innovation. *Journal of Product Innovation Management, 32*(3), 319–333.

Maury, B. (2006). Family ownership and firm performance: Empirical evidence from Western European corporations. *Journal of Corporate Finance, 12*, 321–341.

Miles, R., Snow, C., Fjeldstad, Ø., & Miles, G. (2010). Designing organizations to meet 21st-century opportunities and challenges. *Organizational Dynamics, 39*(2), 93–103.

Rautiainen, M., Konsti-Laakso, S., & Pihkala, T. (2020). Innovation in family business groups: Going beyond an R&D perspective. In A. Calabrò (Ed.), *A research agenda for family business: A way ahead for the field* (pp. 231–246). Edward Elgar Publishing. Cheltenham.

Riar, F. J., Wiedeler, C., Kammerlander, N., & Kellermanns, F. W. (2021). Venturing motives and venturing types in entrepreneurial families: A corporate entrepreneurship perspective. *Entrepreneurship Theory and Practice, 46*(1), 44–81.

Sciascia, S., Nordqvist, M., Mazzola, P., & De Massis, A. (2015). Family ownership and R&D intensity in small-and medium-sized firms. *Journal of Product Innovation Management, 32*(3), 349–360.

Torchia, M., & Calabrò, A. (2019). Open innovation in SMEs: A systematic literature review. *Journal of Enterprising Culture, 27*(02), 201–228.

Trott, P., & Hartmann, D. A. (2009). Why'open innovation'is old wine in new bottles. *International journal of innovation management, 13*(04), 715–736.

West, J., Salter, A., Vanhaverbeke, W., & Chesbrough, H. (2014). Open innovation: The next decade. *Research policy, 43*(5), 805–811.

West, J., & Bogers, M. (2017). Open innovation: Current status and research opportunities. *Innovation, 19*(1), 43–50.

Zahra, S. A. (2005). Entrepreneurial risk taking in family firms. *Family Business Review, 18*(1), 23–40.

Zahra, S. A., & Covin, J. G. (1994). The financial implications of fit between competitive strategy and innovation types and sources. *The Journal of High Technology Management Research, 5*(2), 183–211.

16

Innovation in Family Business Groups

Sabyasachi Sinha and Vinod Thakur

Introduction

Business groups are a collection of legally independent but interconnected firms, generally prevalent in emerging economies (Khanna & Rivkin, 2001). Business groups provide many benefits due to economies of scale and scope and preferential access to resources (Khanna & Yafeh, 2007; Purkayastha et al., 2018). Due to institutional infrastructure and financial wherewithal, business groups are considered to be better positioned to facilitate innovation across group firms (Belenzon & Berkovitz, 2010; Chang et al., 2006; Mahmood & Mitchell, 2004). In a family business group (FBG), the family controls various group firms through several intermediaries (Ashwin et al., 2015; Mahmood et al., 2011; Morck & Yeung, 2003). Della Piana (2012) defines FBG as "a set of legally separate firms under the strategic guidance of a family and its trusted intermediaries, which are bound together by both shareholdings and personal ties" (Della Piana et al., 2012: 177).

S. Sinha (✉)
Strategic Management Group, Indian Institute of Management, Lucknow, India
e-mail: sabyasachi@iiml.ac.in

V. Thakur
Strategic Management, Fore School of Management, New Delhi, India
e-mail: vinod.thakur@fsm.ac.in

© The Author(s), under exclusive license to Springer Nature
Switzerland AG 2023

403

M. Rautianen et al. (eds.), *The Palgrave Handbook of Managing Family Business Groups*,
https://doi.org/10.1007/978-3-031-13206-3_16

Due to globalization, hypercompetition, and shortened product lifecycle, firms engage in innovation to increase their financial performance (Cardinal, 2001; Duran et al., 2016; Lavie et al., 2010). Extant literature has highlighted that though family firms are reluctant but engage in innovation to grow, overcome financial and economic challenges, and most importantly enhance their competitive advantage (De Massis et al., 2013). Family business groups especially those operating in emerging markets are competing in industries which are facing significant technology disruptions. Unless family business groups reorient themselves to proactively engage in innovation activities, their survival, growth, and sustenance will be at risk. Though there is some discussion on the family firm and innovation (Block et al., 2013; De Massis et al., 2013; Kosmidou & Ahuja, 2019), we have a limited studies to analyze how family business groups organize and manage innovation across various group companies (Lodh et al., 2014). Through this chapter, we try to narrow this gap by examining the innovation across companies associated with a family business group and role of the family business group in facilitating innovation efforts in the affiliated companies. Hence research question for this study is as follows: How do family business groups manage and organize innovation activities?

Through an analysis of innovation-related activities in four prominent family business groups located in India (Kant, 2016), this study throws light on the influence of family business groups on innovation across various group companies. The chapter explains the various initiatives taken at the centralized and decentralized level by these large family business groups to sustain innovation. Our study makes exciting contributions to family business literature. First, we highlight that family business groups' aspirations to be globally competitive and top management teams—including the family business group (FBG) board—that support innovation-lead-growth are the primary triggers for enhanced innovation across various group companies of the FBG. Second, we found that family business groups support innovation through building and enabling structure and context at both group level and affiliated firm level. Such support includes shared group resources, building inter-organizational and intra-organizational knowledge exchange mechanisms, and institutionalizing an innovation culture. The findings are divergent from the existing paradigm on innovation in family firms. They suggest that, unlike standalone family firms, family business groups, especially in emerging market contexts, are amenable to innovation. In the family business groups, innovation infrastructures such as technology, capital, and skilled resources across affiliated firms, can be utilized to perform innovative activities.

The chapter is organized as follows. A brief literature review on innovation in family business groups is provided, followed by a discussion on the innovation process in family business groups. Then, innovation-related activities adopted by the FBGs are explained by drawing from the case studies of Indian family business groups. In the end, we suggest directions for future research and conclude the discussion.

Family Business Groups and Innovation

Business groups are defined as "collections of publicly traded firms in a wide variety of industries, with a significant amount of common ownership and control" (Khanna & Palepu, 2000). Affiliated firms within the group frequently coordinate with each other in terms of resources, strategies, and behavior (Chang et al., 2006). These internal transactions reduce cost, enhance efficiency, and facilitate innovation across group companies (Mahmood & Mitchell, 2004). FBGs are characterized by family ownership and control over the business operations (Della Piana et al., 2012; Gedajlovic et al., 2012). Family business groups (FBGs) are an important part of the economic landscape across the world (La Porta et al., 1999; Peng & Delios, 2007; Yabushita & Suehiro, 2014). Cross-holdings among firms, director interlock, pyramidal ownership structures, and family ties distinguish FBGs from other firms (Ashwin et al., 2015; Khanna & Rivkin, 2001; Purkayastha et al., 2018; Sarkar & Sarkar, 2000). FBGs consist of multiple companies (Claessens et al., 2000; Khanna & Palepu, 2000), which may be different legal entities headed by various family members, having separate financial statements and governance mechanisms (Young et al., 2008). FBGs provide an internal capital market for group companies to operate efficiently (Cuervo-Cazurra, 2006), especially in countries with high institutional voids (Khanna & Yafeh, 2007). *Keiretsu* in Japan, *chaebol* in South Korea, *business houses* in India, *groupos economico* in Latin America, and *family holding* in Turkey are different manifestations of family business groups across the world (Mahmood & Mitchell, 2004; Peng et al., 2018; Ward, 2000).

Firms need to innovate to stay relevant (Tether, 1998; Capelleras & Greene, 2008). Innovation encompasses identifying new opportunities, converting them into reality, and capturing value. In a highly competitive environment prevalent across industries with a shorter product life cycle, innovation is regarded as a source of competitive advantage (Barney, 1991; Craig & Dibrell, 2006; Duran et al., 2016). There are mixed findings regarding the innovative behavior of family firms due to variation in socioemotional preferences, firm-level heterogeneity, and various country-level factors (Chrisman & Patel, 2012; De Massis et al., 2013; Duran et al., 2016; Miller et al., 2015). Family firms are known to be risk-averse (Gomez-Mejia et al., 2014), which results in a lower preference for innovation (Block et al., 2013; De Massis et al., 2013). On the other hand, family firms are considered effective innovators due to reduced agency problems (Cassia et al., 2012; Craig et al., 2006; De Massis et al., 2013). Moreover, firms associated with family business groups, when operating in an industry with high technological opportunities, promote innovation within group companies and ensure the success and survival of the firm (Ashwin et al., 2015; Lodh et al., 2014; Miller et al., 2008). Due to the presence of group companies across multiple industries, investment in innovative efforts enhances FBG's capability to exploit growth opportunities in multiple product markets (Choi et al., 2015; McGrath & Nerkar, 2004). FBGs have huge incentives to support innovation as a source of long-term growth, survival, and competitiveness (Astrachan, 2010; Chrisman & Patel, 2012; Greve, 2008; Sirmon & Hitt, 2003), prompting them to invest in innovative efforts to create wealth for the future generations (Craig et al., 2006; Zahra, 2005). Drawing from the existing literature on innovation in family firms, we argue that FBGs can spur innovation-related efforts in affiliated firms in the following ways:

- Family control across group firms can help in setting up an innovation-related initiative across different lines of business which are separate legal entities (Nieto et al., 2015). Family control in the form of ownership and management ensures that bureaucratic processes should not jeopardize a firm's chance to develop new technologies in an effective manner (Astrachan, 2010; Della Piana et al., 2012; Liang et al., 2013).
- It is relatively easier for a large and diversified business group with economies of scale and scope coupled with internal financing options to facilitate the innovation process (Carney & Gedajlovic, 2003; Ward, 2000). FBGs can internally finance innovative activities across various affiliates. Innovative affiliates stand more chance of getting easy access to capital within the group than a standalone firm (Ashwin et al., 2015; Mahmood & Mitchell, 2004). Diversification also reduces the uncertainty in terms of the outcome of the innovation process (Khanna & Yafeh, 2007).
- In FBGs, cross-fertilization of ideas and sharing best practices across different affiliates can spur innovative activities (Ashwin et al., 2015; Khanna & Palepu, 2000). Further, sharing of knowledge and human capital between diverse group-related firms due to close family ties and

unique family culture is relatively easier, which leads to an effective innovation process (De Massis et al., 2015; Mahmood et al., 2011; Yabushita & Suehiro, 2014).

- Foreign technology partners prefer to collaborate with firms affiliated with business groups due to the preferential access of group companies to critical resources compared to standalone firms (Ashwin et al., 2015; Lester & Cannella, 2006; Mahmood et al., 2011). Further, the high social capital of family business groups facilitates collaboration with other firms to support innovative activities (Arregle et al., 2007; Kammerlander & van Essen, 2017).
- Due to their long-term orientation (Zahra, 2005), FBGs respond to customer's current and future needs in a proactive manner (Beck et al., 2011), which leads to significant investments in innovative activities to launch products and services in the existing and new markets (Michael Carney & Gedajlovic, 2003; Cassia et al., 2012; Craig et al., 2006; Zahra, 2005).

Innovation Process in Family Business Groups

Though family firms spend less on innovation compared to non-family firms, however they are found to be more efficient in their innovation process (Carney, 2005; Duran et al., 2016). This is because family principals are well informed about the industry dynamics due to the significant amount of time spent in the business. Moreover, family involvement in the management of the business makes sure that the money is invested in the right projects and that resources available are utilized in the most efficient manner (Duran et al., 2016; Kammerlander & van Essen, 2017). The innovation process of FBGs can be defined in terms of innovation input, activity stage, and innovation output stage (De Massis et al., 2013; Duran et al., 2016; Lumpkin, 2011).

- Input stage—This stage consists of assigning resources available within the group firms for innovation. These resources could also be skills and capabilities of family and non-family members and family social capital (Kammerlander & van Essen, 2017; Mahmood et al., 2011). Further, these resources could be the entrepreneurial spirit of family founders, the firm's management practices, and the trust and communication among family members (Block et al., 2013; Chrisman et al., 2005). The interaction between family systems and family members, also known as familiness, provides a potential advantage in terms of a unique bundle of resources (Habbershon et al., 2003).

- Activity stage—This stage consists of organizing and deploying resources to create an economic value across affiliated firms (Craig & Dibrell, 2006). This stage analyzes the family's role in hiring and allocation of resources, streamlinig processes, improving skills and capabilities, and the decision-making process within the group firms to improve the innovation (De Massis et al., 2013).
- Output stage—Competitive advantage, number of new products and patents, productivity, long-term business growth, and creation of social capital are important aspects under this stage of innovation in family business groups (De Massis et al., 2013; Duran et al., 2016; Thieme, 2007)

The existing literature on innovation in family firms is restricted to exploring innovation in a single family firm (Block et al., 2013; De Massis et al., 2013). Despite the prevalence of FBGs in all parts of the world, limited research happened to understand efforts of FBGs toward enhancing innovative activities across group firms (Lodh et al., 2014). This makes it important to understand how innovation activities are managed and organized in family business groups.

Methodology

We wanted to have an in-depth understanding of innovation activities conducted in family business groups. The case study method is considered an ideal method for generating relevant knowledge in the management domain (Eisenhardt, 1989). Moreover, it allows in-depth examination of a complex phenomenon happening in the real world (De Massis & Kotlar, 2014). A qualitative research design was more suitable to understand the innovation in family business groups. Accordingly, our study was based on a series of multiple case studies (Yin, 2014). We applied theoretical sampling to choose our sample in order to understand the innovation activities across affiliated firms (Miles et al., 2014). More specifically, we chose the following four leading family business groups based in India to understand their innovation efforts: Tata group, Reliance group, Aditya Birla group, and Mahindra group. The data was collected through secondary sources such as scanning websites of various companies associated with these groups, media reports, and other online sources (Chittoor & Das, 2007; Roy & Karna, 2015).

16 Innovation in Family Business Groups 409

Cross case analysis was also conducted to analyze findings across various family business groups (Eisenhardt, 1989; Yin, 2014). We chose to study innovation in Indian family business groups for three reasons. First, in India, a vast majority of listed firms are family businesses (Ray et al., 2018), and most of them are family business groups, i.e., controlled by families (Sarkar & Sarkar, 2000). Second, due to economic liberalization in the early 1990s, innovation investments increased manifold in Indian family business groups (Ashwin et al., 2015). Third, due to institutional voids, in emerging markets like India (Khanna & Palepu, 2000), business groups provide access to group companies in terms of technology through centralized research and development (R&D) operations, finances, and skilled manpower to enhance innovative efforts (Mahmood & Mitchell, 2004).

Cases of Innovation in Family Business Groups

Tata Group

Tata Group was founded by Jamshetji Tata in 1868, majorly controlled by the Tata clan. It had a revenue of USD 106 billion in 2019–20, with over 7,50,000 employees across group companies (Tata Group, 2020). The group's business spanned across various industries such as information technology, automotive, defence, consumer retail, and airlines. Twenty-eight companies of its portfolio were listed in the Indian stock market. Tata group had been pioneering new initiatives since its inception. Its steel business was the first Indian company to raise capital in India. The group had incorporated India's first airline company in 1932 and the first information technology (IT) company in 1968. The automotive company of the group made India's first home-built light commercial vehicle in 1986, and the group chairman's pet project to build a lowest-cost car—Tata Nano—was a renowned case study (Kumar, 2012). Innovation in the Tata group was managed through group-wide efforts leveraging the learning across different group companies. Individual businesses also had separate innovation management setups (Tata Group, 2020).

Centralized Management of Innovation

To support respective companies in their innovation journeys, Tata Group Innovation Forum (TGIF) was set up in 2007. It consisted of the CEOs, CXOs, and innovation champions of different group companies. The forum's objective was to foster a culture of innovation within the group companies. The strategy adopted was to create a supportive environment, build a network of innovation evangelists within the Tata group, and advise group companies on how to improve their innovation capability. Global innovation experts and thinkers were also regularly invited to deliver talks to stimulate innovative thinking among managers in the Tata group.

Tata business excellence group—a pre-existing centralized unit to drive business excellence in group companies—was identified as the implementation arm of the TGIF. The group's training center—Tata Management Training Centre (TMTC)—continuously organized programs to build people capabilities to drive innovation. TMTC also published articles in their in-house journal to narrate the stories of innovation in group companies. The group conceptualized Tata Innovista—an annual event to reward and recognize innovation across affiliated firms. Through this process, innovation projects in group companies were judged by internationally acclaimed external jurors and awarded by the group chairman.

In 2010, TGIF initiated a platform—Tata ideas—to allow group companies to list out challenging problems, which people across the group could solve, comment, and vote, and the best idea could be chosen for implementation. This program later transformed into another experiment—"challenges worth solving." The winning idea was awarded in the Tata Innovista event. Another platform was initiated to ensure winning ideas were implemented (Gopalkrishnan, 2019).

Innovation initiatives were used to build a competitive advantage for the group companies. The Group Chief Technology Officer stated, "We want to provide intellectual property-based differentiation in products and services. This will enable us to go to places where no one else can follow quickly" (*The Economic Times*, 2015). Joint projects initiated by employees from different group companies were sponsored centrally through TGIF.

Business Level Innovation Management

Tata chemicals innovation center, Tata steel Europe research development and technology, Tata motors European technical center, and TCS innovation labs were some of the business-level innovation management structures set by the company to manage research, development, and innovation in the group managed at the business unit level (Tata Chemicals, 2020). Tata Chemicals was chosen as one of India's top 25 most innovative companies in 2020 by the Confederation of Indian Industry. The company's innovation investments were not limited to the applied business but also in basic sciences such as Chemistry, Agro Sciences, Nutritional Sciences, Material Sciences, and Energy Sciences. The chief executive officer (CEO) of the company mentioned:

> We strongly believe that innovation powers Excellence in whatever we do. We will continue to drive value through innovation, digitalization, and sustainability across our various business units…our commitment to be a leading sustainable, innovative, science-led chemistry company. (Tata Chemicals, 2020).

Tata Motors launched an automobility collaboration network 2.0 (TACnet 2.0) in 2019—a platform to orchestrate innovation for new technologies and business models. The platform also allowed Tata Motors to engage with start-ups. The President of the electric mobility business and corporate strategy, Tata Motors Ltd, mentioned: "TACNet enables us to connect with the outside world for innovation and collaboration opportunities. We are looking forward to unlocking the potential of India's finest start-ups and technology and solution-based companies (Economic Times Brand Equity, 2019)."

In 2011, this business of Tata group received two prestigious awards: (a) most innovative in high-tech corporate category; (b) an award from the Indian government recognizing them for generating the highest number of patents for an Indian-owned private business in the preceding five years. Multiple other pieces of evidence on the input and output side showcase the commitment of Tata Steel—a group company—to innovation. Tata Steel also initiated a platform for triggering crowdsourcing new ideas for the steel business, and it mentioned: "We want to collaborate with innovative people and organizations to help develop solutions to our current challenges and create new opportunities for the future. To do this, we want to explore new ways of working with others and identify the best ideas and technologies, wherever they may be."

Reliance Group

Reliance group was the biggest private sector business group in India, with an annual turnover of USD 94 billion and a profit after tax of approximately USD 6 billion (Reliance Industries Limited, 2020). The family business group was founded by Late Dhirubhai Ambani in 1973 and was now being managed by his son Mukesh Ambani who was the chairman. The group had a market capitalization of over $200 billion (KP, 2020) and ranked as one of the top 50 most valued companies globally. Reliance had an employee count of 1,95,618. Apart from its core business of oil and gas, the group had a leading presence in retail, telecommunication, digital services, media, and entertainment.

Innovation at Reliance

The group spent \$362 million on research and development efforts in the financial year 2020. More than 900 scientists worked with various group companies to spearhead innovation and research. The group had also been granted 140 patents in the year 2020 (Reliance Industries limited, 2020). The group believed in "Integrated innovation-led exponential growth." The group managed its innovation charter through the Reliance Innovation Council (RIC), which consisted of Nobel laureates, global thought leaders, and scientists with a vision of making Reliance one of the most innovative business groups in the world. The council was taking innovative initiatives through several programs and initiatives (Reliance Industries Limited, 2017)—(a) LEAP, (b) Seven innovation habits, (c) Beyonders, (d) D4 (Define, Discover, Develop, and Demonstrate), and (e) Mission Kurukshetra (Reliance Industries Limited, 2017).

- Leap—The objective of the leap was to connect Reliance with global thought and innovation leaders through frequent and interactive sessions. The group had organized 39 leap interactions so far.
- Seven innovation habits—This program was developed for entry and middle-level employees to develop specific innovation skills and capabilities.
- Beyonders—The aim of this program was to create innovation leaders across the group through training in innovative approaches. The participants were provided opportunities to lead innovative projects across group companies.
- D4 (Define, Discover, Develop, and Demonstrate)—This was an action-oriented program that encouraged participants to identify innovative opportunities in day-to-day business operations.
- Mission Kurukshetra (MK)—Mukesh Ambani launched "Mission Kuruskehtra" (MK), an innovation platform to make Reliance one of the most innovative business groups in the world (RIL News, 2017). As per the group, the aim of the program was to democratize innovative activities across group companies (Reliance Innovation Council India, 2017) Under this initiative, employees across group companies were encouraged to collaborate and develop innovative ideas that can be pursued

further to explore big opportunities for future growth (John, 2017). The consolidated annual report of the group for the financial year 2020 stated:

> MK aims at democratizing creativity and innovation by empowering everyone to innovate. It is a digital platform via which all ideas are submitted, brought to logical conclusions, and executed for impact. Through MK, employees put creative problem-solving into practice and reskill themselves in ideation.

For the year 2020, the group received more than 29,000 ideas on the MK innovation platform, 26% more than the previous year. Reliance had assigned more than 750 domain experts as idea champions. These idea champions took decisions on the potential of ideas and worked with both ideators and implementers on ideas that could bring growth opportunities.

The group had launched the Reliance innovation awards (RIA), which included the game-changer award for the most innovative project, the path-breaker award for innovation leaders, and lifetime innovation leadership award for the senior management to recognize innovative efforts across group companies (Reliance Innovation Council India. (2017)). The group also initiated a start-up accelerator program JioGenNext to advise and mentor people with bright ideas to launch their ventures in the Jio ecosystem (JioGenNext, 2020). The idea behind these engagements was to leverage innovative solutions being built by start-ups. The accelerator had also forged tie-ups with several technology companies such as Microsoft and venture capital firms.

Aditya Birla Group

Aditya Birla Group (ABG) was one of the leading family business groups in India, with annual revenue of USD 46 billion (Aditya Birla Group, 2020). The group had 120,000 employees of 42 different nationalities across various group companies in 36 countries. The group headquarter was based out of India's financial capital, Mumbai. ABG had a presence in 12 different industries like metals, cement, fibers, carbon black, chemicals, and telecommunications, to name a few. In most industries, the group was one of the leading players nationally as well as internationally.

In 2012, ABG decided to centralize the R&D activities of different group companies by launching a company named Aditya Birla Science & Technology Company (ABSTC) in Mumbai (Mazumdar, 2012). An initial investment of $40 million was made for this state-of-the-art R&D hub. The company had been mandated to work in material science, metallurgy, fibers, engineering, and simulation technology (The Aditya Birla Science and Technology Company Private Limited, 2012). These areas were aligned with the company's core operations and industries. The group took inspiration from the innovation process followed by US-based General Electric, which had a dedicated R&D center to spur innovation across group companies. ABG had become the second group to launch a corporate R&D center in India after Tata group. As per management, the centralized efforts helped explore future growth areas for different companies. Group had filed for 60 patents so far, and the ABSTC was working on 50 projects for various group companies. As per experts, this move was helpful in assimilating in-house and foreign technology across various group companies. So far, the centralized innovation efforts turned out to be successful for ABG. In 2018, the group chairman Kumar Mangalam Birla stated:

> The business payoffs of the R&D efforts have already started to kick in. The most obvious ones include innovative designs and control systems to increase yield, improve quality, achieve higher efficiency and raise capacities. (The Hindu Business Line, 2018).

ABG had also launched Aditya Birla Bizlabs in 2015, a platform to collaborate with start-ups, students, and incubators to explore open source innovation in machine learning, artificial intelligence, cloud computing, big data analytics, and intelligent solutions (YourStory, 2019). The group President of corporate strategy and business development, Umesh Adhikary, mentioned:

> The genesis of Bizlabs was primarily to look at how we can collaborate with the start-up ecosystem, which is coming up with disruptive ideas and solutions to address most of the pain points being faced by businesses today.

The company had made a strategic collaboration with 20 start-ups to further its digital and technological agenda (YourStory, 2019). The company had also started an initiative Reinforcing Engineering Pride & Recognizing Innovative Seamless Manufacturing (REPRISM), in 2017 to bring together employees from different companies to bring innovative ideas in engineering and manufacturing to achieve global excellence through innovation and productivity (YouTube, 2019). The initiatives had turned out to be successful, and the company had relaunched it in 2019 to give a fillip to share innovative practices across group companies (people matters).

Mahindra Group

Mahindra group was USD 19.4 billion group having a presence in 22 different industries ranging from automobile, information technology, real estate, and finance to hospitality and aerospace. The group was established in the year 1945 and employed 2,50,000 people across 100 countries in 2021. The group had 72 manufacturing facilities across the world. Mahindra group was a firm believer in innovation and created a group strategy office to drive innovation across various group companies. Different firms were encouraged to collaborate and promote best practices. The company believed in "innovate more with less, innovate together, and innovate for all (Mahindra Group, 2020)." In 2019, the company launched #NurtureYourCuriosity campaign around innovation. The group's chief market officer stated:

> Solutions to the world's problems can only emerge when one asks the right questions. Only the curious ask these questions and challenge the status quo. To make the world a better place, we must nurture this curiosity and seek meaningful innovations. Our aim with this campaign is to encourage individuals to nurture their curiosity while showcasing how this is leading to innovations and the leveraging of new-age technologies at Mahindra. This is yet another way by which we are enabling and encouraging people to Rise. (Mahindra, 2019)

The family business group also launched innovation awards to encourage new ideas suggested by employees from different companies and created a platform where these ideas could be recorded and propagated as learning for different businesses (Mahindra, 2019). Group executive chairman Mr. Anand Mahindra stated:

> In order to institutionalize the culture of innovation, number one the leadership has to send the signal very clearly that the innovation is critical. So I see my job to use every opportunity to tell people that innovation is critical. We give 'rise' awards for innovation. We even have 'rise' awards for failed innovation, the best-failed innovation. These are signals about why innovation is important. Second, you need to support a culture of innovation in your company. Your performance measurement system must include innovation as a criterion for recognition for compensation. Like this, you have to populate your entire ecosystem with signals and signs that innovation is critical. (YouTube, 2019)

Mahindra had initiated a venture capital arm for the group—Mahindra partners—to invest in technology start-ups (Mahindra Partners, 2020). The group was initiating new events and activities to engage more actively to become an active partner in the Indian and global start-up ecosystem, especially in the mobility services sector, through events such as Catapult (Mahindra, 2021).

Discussion

Family business scholars highlighted the reluctance of family firms to invest in innovation (De Massis et al., 2013; Duran et al., 2016; Gomez-Mejia et al., 2014). Four cases discussed in this chapter rather showcase a contrary narrative and highlight that family business groups have a strong pro-innovation orientation. Our analysis of the four Indian family business groups—Tata, Reliance, Aditya Birla, and Mahindra—rather reiterates the findings of Ashwin et al. (2015), Cassia et al. (2011), Craig and Moores (2006), and Lodh et al. (2014). All four FBGs have portfolio companies with high technological opportunities. The findings highlight that owner(s) leading top management team in a family business group encourage innovation in affiliated firms in order to make the group globally competitive.

FBGs take various initiatives at the corporate level, i.e., headquarter level, and at the firm level, to enable innovation across the group companies. For instance, it has been highlighted that innovation programs are coordinated through a group-level council—Reliance Innovation Council or Tata group innovation forum, or Aditya Birla Science & Technology Company. Also, group Chairmen—who happen to be from the family running the family business group—pay special attention to initiating such units and subsequently overseeing the progress of the central innovation chartering unit. One of the important activities of these units is to shape the innovation culture across group firms, re-orient the senior executive mindset to promote entrepreneurship and innovation, allocate resources based on a standard operating procedure, and enhance the exploratory skill of the executives. Further, the central innovation chartering unit plays a crucial role in cross-fertilizing ideas, sharing best practices, and exchanging knowledge resources and human capital across different affiliates. This unit also celebrates the success of innovation projects within group firms and acts as a broker to source innovation best practices globally and diffuses the same across group firms. These findings are aligned with existing literature highlighting the role of a group-level R&D center in providing economies of scope in terms of innovative efforts of a business group (Chang & Hong, 2000) (Fig. 16.1).

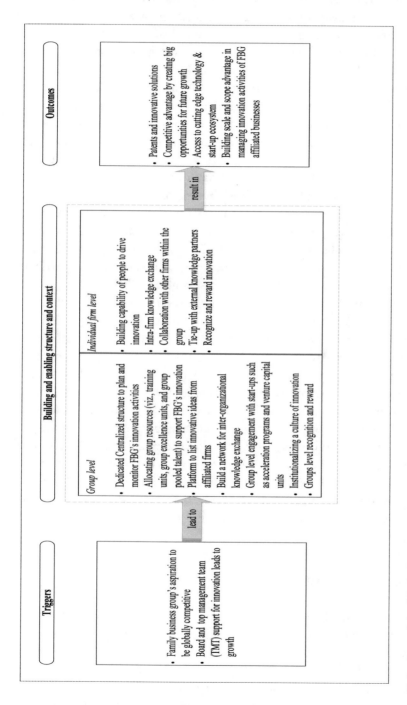

Fig. 16.1 A model of FBGs innovation activities

Findings also mention the role of group in creating a common platform to share innovative ideas and facilitating knowledge exchange across group companies. Further ideas are recognized and rewarded on a group level to develop the culture of innovation across group companies. FBGs therefore provide an innovation infrastructure in the form of technology, skilled human resources, and finances to affiliated firms to conduct innovative activities (Mahmood & Mitchell, 2004). Another interesting observation is the adoption of new models of managing innovation and entrepreneurship, which are gaining traction globally—disruptive innovation, open innovation, design thinking, and engaging with technology start-ups. Tata Group's TCS COIN program and TACnet, Aditya Birla group's Bizlabs, Reliance group's JioGenNext, and Mahindra group's Mahindra partners all strongly suggest that family business groups are geared to compete with the non-family businesses conglomerates in rapid scaling up innovation and entrepreneurship management capabilities (Mazzelli et al., 2018)—including the latest trend of powering entrepreneurship and innovation through engaging with the start-up ecosystem (Adner, 2017; Zahra & Nambisan, 2012).

Further, the study highlights that the push toward innovation at the group leads to an increase in innovation efforts at the firm level as well. Affiliated firms start exchanging ideas with each other or collaborate with other firms outside the group to sustain innovation. For instance, the Tata Swatch initiative in the Tata Group. Tata Swatch—originally innovated in TCS (software business)—was later exploited by Tata chemicals with an active corporation of Titan (the watch business). The opportunity leveraging was coordinated and derived by the group innovation team. Similar group-level driving and leveraging of opportunities across the portfolio companies were evident in all four FBGs. Finally, FBG gains from innovation in terms of high patents and access to the latest technology, which the portfolio companies can leverage to build innovative solutions. Moreover, innovation helps the group in staying competitive in different product markets and provides opportunities for the future growth.

Direction for Future Research

Our discussions highlighted that contrary to some earlier findings that family businesses are risk-averse, our case analysis of Indian family business groups suggests that they have not only invested in innovation, but they had also adopted the latest global best practices in managing innovation and entrepreneurship. Future research may try to investigate the following on which extant studies seem to be silent or where results are contradictory, or where the progress of practice demands that theory needs to be advanced to match with the advances in practice.

1. Under what contexts do business groups exhibit higher pro-innovation and pro-risk-taking behavior?
2. Do emerging economy business groups exhibit higher pro-innovation behavior versus their developed country counterparts?
3. How do the inter-organizational relations influence transfer of innovation across affiliate companies in family business groups?
4. How does the adoption of new-age innovation management practices such as open innovation, design thinking, and disruptive innovation get diffused in family business group firms, and how has that affected the family business group performance?
5. How does engaging with the national and global start-up ecosystem reshape the business portfolio and group innovation capability portfolio of family business groups?

Conclusion

FBGs are prevalent across all parts of the world (La Porta et al., 1999). Therefore, it is important to understand the influence of family business groups on innovation. There have been limited studies exploring innovation in family business groups (Mahmood & Mitchell, 2004). This article aims to understand how family business groups are managing innovation in their affiliate firms to increase efficiency and explore new growth opportunities. Drawing on case studies from Indian family business groups (Manikutty, 2000), we highlighted that family business groups consider innovation as an important strategic effort and are inclined to invest in innovation.

Further, family business groups work on innovative efforts both at centralized and at the level of portfolio companies. FBGs create a dedicated council or a unit to spur innovation across various companies affiliated with the group. Also, cross-fertilization of ideas is encouraged by organizing various programs, which provide a platform for employees across group companies to interact and discuss the merit of ideas. The role of the central team is to take the worthy ideas forward and explore if new business opportunities can emerge from these ideas. Similarly, good innovative practices are shared across group companies to increase overall efficiency. FBGs have also created platforms to engage with various start-ups to explore emerging business ideas.

We hope that our effort may be helpful for both academicians and practitioners. For practitioners, our research highlights best practices adopted by family business groups in managing innovative efforts within group companies and accessing external knowledge through continuous engagement with start-ups. For academicians, our study has provided potential avenues for future research to further look into this line of inquiry.

References

About Us | Tata group. (2020). Tata.Com. https://www.tata.com/about-us

Aditya Birla Group. (2020). Aditya Birla Group PowerPoint presentation. Retrieved from https://www.adityabirla.com/about-us/downloads/Group-presen tation-Dec-2020.pdf

Adner, R. (2017). Ecosystem as structure: An actionable construct for strategy. *Journal of Management, 43*(1), 39–58.

Areas of expertise—The Aditya Birla Science and Technology Company Private Limited. (2020). Adityabirlascienceandtechnology.Com. http://www.adityabirlascienceand technology.com/areas_of_expertise/index.html

Arregle, J.-L., Hitt, M. A., Sirmon, D. G., & Very, P. (2007). The development of organizational social capital: Attributes of family firms. *Journal of Management Studies, 44*(1), 73–95.

Ashwin, A. S., Krishnan, R. T., & George, R. (2015). Family firms in India: Family involvement, innovation and agency and stewardship behaviors. *Asia Pacific Journal of Management, 32*(4), 869–900.

Astrachan, J. H. (2010). Strategy in family business: Toward a multidimensional research agenda. *Journal of Family Business Strategy, 1*(1), 6–14.

Barney, J. (1991). Firm resources and sustained competitive advantage. *Journal of Management, 17*(1), 99–120.

Beck, L., Janssens, W., Debruyne, M., & Lommelen, T. (2011). A study of the relationships between generation, market orientation, and innovation in family firms. *Family Business Review, 24*(3), 252–272.

Belenzon, S., & Berkovitz, T. (2010). Innovation in business groups. *Management Science, 56*(3), 519–535.

Block, J., Miller, D., Jaskiewicz, P., & Spiegel, F. (2013). Economic and technological Importance of innovations in large family and founder firms: An analysis of patent data. *Family Business Review, 26*(2), 180–199.

Capelleras, J-L., & Greene, F. J. (2008). The determinants and growth implications of venture creation speed. *Entrepreneurship & Regional Development, 20*(4), 317–343.

Cardinal, L. B. (2001). Technological innovation in the pharmaceutical industry: The use of organizational control in managing research and development. *Organization Science, 12*(1), 19–36.

Carney, M. (2005). Corporate governance and competitive advantage in family-controlled firms. *Entrepreneurship Theory and Practice, 29*(3), 249–265.

Carney, M., & Gedajlovic, E. (2003). Strategic innovation and the administrative heritage of East Asian family business groups. *Asia Pacific Journal of Management, 20*(1), 5–26.

Cassia, L., De Massis, A., & Pizzurno, E. (2011). An exploratory investigation on NPD in small family businesses from Northern Italy. *The International Journal of Business and Management, 2*, 1–14.

Cassia, L., De Massis, A., & Pizzurno, E. (2012). Strategic innovation and new product development in family firms: An empirically grounded theoretical framework. *International Journal of Entrepreneurial Behavior & Research, 18*(2), 198–232.

Catapult—A Platform For Start-Ups To Rise. (2021, January 27). Mahindra.Com. https://www.mahindra.com/news-room/knowledge-centre/impact-stories/cat apult-a-platform-for-start-ups-to-rise

Chang, S.-J., Chung, C.-N., & Mahmood, I. P. (2006). When and how does business group affiliation promote firm innovation? A tale of two emerging economies. *Organization Science, 17*(5), 637–656.

Chang, S. J., & Hong, J. (2000). Economic performance of group-affiliated companies in Korea: Intragroup resource sharing and internal business transactions. *Academy of Management Journal, 43*(3), 429–448.

Chittoor, R., & Das, R. (2007). Professionalization of management and succession performance—A vital linkage. *Family Business Review, 20*(1), 65–79.

Choi, Y. R., Zahra, S. A., Yoshikawa, T., & Han, B. H. (2015). Family ownership and R&D investment: The role of growth opportunities and business group membership. *Journal of Business Research, 68*(5), 1053–1061.

Chrisman, J. J., McMullan, E., & Hall, J. (2005). The influence of guided preparation on the long-tenn perfonnance of new ventures. *Journal of Business Venturing, 20*(6), 769–791.

Chrisman, J. J., & Patel, P. C. (2012). Variations in r&d investments of family and nonfamily firms: Behavioral agency and myopic loss aversion perspectives. *Academy of Management Journal, 55*(4), 976–997.

Claessens, S., Djankov, S., & Lang, L. H. P. (2000). The separation of ownership and control in East Asian Corporations. *Journal of Financial Economics, 58*(1–2), 81–112.

Craig, J., & Dibrell, C. (2006). The natural environment, innovation, and firm performance: A comparative study. *Family Business Review, 19*(4), 275–288.

Craig, J. B. L., Moores, K., & Cassar, G. (2006). A 10-year longitudinal investigation of strategy, systems, and environment on innovation in family firms (vol 19, pg 1, 2006). *Family Business Review, 19*(2), 169–169.

Cuervo-Cazurra, A. (2006). Business groups and their types. *Asia Pacific Journal of Management, 23*(4), 419–437.

De Massis, A., Frattini, F., & Lichtenthaler, U. (2013). Research on technological innovation in family firms: Present debates and future directions. *Family Business Review, 26*(1), 10–31.

De Massis, A., Frattini, F., Pizzurno, E., & Cassia, L. (2015). Product innovation in family versus nonfamily firms: An exploratory analysis. *Journal of Small Business Management, 53*(1), 1–36.

De Massis, A., & Kotlar, J. (2014). The case study method in family business research: Guidelines for qualitative scholarship. *Journal of Family Business Strategy, 5*(1), 15–29.

Della Piana, B., Vecchi, A., & Cacia, C. (2012). Towards a better understanding of family business groups and their key dimensions. *Journal of Family Business Strategy, 3*(3), 174–192.

Duran, P., Kammerlander, N., van Essen, M., & Zellweger, T. 2016. Doing more with less: innovation input and output in family firms. *Academy of Management Journal, 59*(4), 1224–1264.

Eisenhardt, K. M. (1989). Agency Theory: An assessment and review. *The Academy of Management Review, 14*(1), 57–74.

First Leadership Talk by Shri. Anand bgbfh, Chairman, Mahindra Group. (2019, January 10). YouTube. https://www.youtube.com/watch?v=kgOwIdWZZ2w

Gedajlovic, E., Carney, M., Chrisman, J. J., & Kellermanns, F. W. (2012). The adolescence of family firm research: Taking stock and planning for the future. *Journal of Management, 38*(4), 1010–1037.

Gomez-Mejia, L. R., Campbell, J. T., Martin, G., Hoskisson, R. E., Makri, M., et al. (2014). Socioemotional wealth as a mixed gamble: Revisiting family firm R&D investments with the behavioral agency model. *Entrepreneurship Theory and Practice, 38*(6), 1351–1374.

Gopalkrishnan, R. (2019, July 30). Creating an innovation ecosystem. *Hindustan Times*.

Greve, H. R. (2008). A behavioral theory of firm growth: Sequential attention to size and performance goals. *Academy of Management Journal, 51*(3), 476–494.

Habbershon, T. G., Williams, M., & MacMillan, I. C. (2003). A unified systems perspective of family firm performance. *Journal of Business Venturing, 18*(4), 451–465.

How Aditya Birla Bizlabs is connecting with innovative startups. (2019, September 26). YourStory.Com. https://yourstory.com/2019/09/how-aditya-birla-bizlabs-connects-innovative-startups/amp

How Tata Group is trying to embed innovation in its DNA. (2015, August 7). *The Economic Times.* https://economictimes.indiatimes.com/how-tata-group-is-trying-to-embed-innovation-in-its-dna/articleshow/48372888.cms?from=mdr

Innovation—About Us. (2020). Tata Chemicals Limited.

Innovation | Tata group. (2020). https://www.Tata.Com. https://www.tata.com/about-us/innovation

Innovation through collaboration: Tata Motors launches TACNet 2.0. (2019, September 18). ETBrandEquity.Com.https://brandequity.economictimes.indiat imes.com/news/business-of-brands/innovation-through-collaboration-tata-mot ors-launches-tacnet-2-0/71184515

JioGenNext. (2020). Jiogennext.Com. https://www.jiogennext.com/

John, S. (2017, August 6). With groundbreaking Ideas, Mukesh Ambani wants to make Reliance the most innovative company. *The Economic Times.* https:// economictimes.indiatimes.com/news/company/corporate-trends/with-groundbre aking-ideas-mukesh-ambani-wants-to-make-reliance-the-most-innovative-com pany/articleshow/59933559.cms

Kammerlander, N., & van Essen, M. 2017. *Research: Family firms are more innovative than other companies,* 5.

Kant, K. (2016, August 18). *In India, 15 of the top 20 business groups are family-owned!* Rediff. Retrieved February 10, 2018, from https://www.rediff. com/money/report/special-in-india-15-of-the-top-20-business-groups-are-family-owned/20160818.htm

Khanna, T., & Palepu, K. (2000). The future of business groups in emerging markets: Long-run evidence from Chile. *Academy of Management Journal, 43*(3), 268–285.

Khanna, T., & Rivkin, J. W. (2001). Estimating the performance effects of business groups in emerging markets. *Strategic Management Journal, 22*(1), 45–74.

Khanna, T., & Yafeh, Y. (2007). Business groups in emerging markets: Paragons or parasites? *Journal of Economic Literature, 45*(2), 331–372.

Kosmidou, V., & Ahuja, M. K. (2019). A Configurational approach to family firm innovation. *Family Business Review, 32*(2), 154–173.

Kp, Y. (2020, September 16). *RIL now bigger than all PSUs combined; Mukesh Ambani firm's Market-Cap more than Rs 15 lakh crore* [Press release]. https://www.financialexpress.com/market/reliance-industries-market-cap italisation-now-bigger-than-all-psus-put-together/2084018/

Kumar, A. (2012, December 27). *Thriving on frugal innovation. Business standard.* https://doi.org/www.Business-Standard.Com. https://www.business-standard. com/article/companies/thriving-on-frugal-innovation-112122700125_1.html

La Porta, R., Lopez-De-Silanes, F., & Shleifer, A. (1999). Corporate ownership around the world. *The Journal of Finance, 54*(2), 471–517.

Lavie, D., Stettner, U., & Tushman, M. L. (2010). Exploration and exploitation within and across organizations. *Academy of Management Annals, 4,* 109–155.

Lester, R. H., & Cannella, A. A. (2006). Interorganizational familiness: How family firms use interlocking directorates to build community-level social capital. *Entrepreneurship Theory and Practice, 30*(6), 755–775.

Liang, Q., Li, X., Yang, X., Lin, D., & Zheng, D. (2013). How does family involve-ment affect innovation in China? *Asia Pacific Journal of Management, 30*(3), 677–695.

Lodh, S., Nandy, M., & Chen, J. (2014). Innovation and family ownership: Empirical evidence from India. *Corporate Governance-an International Review, 22*(1), 4–23.

Lumpkin, G. T. (2011). From legitimacy to impact: Moving the field forward by asking how entrepreneurship informs life. *Strategic Entrepreneurship Journal, 5*(1), 3–9.

Mahindra Group. (2020). 2019–2020 Mahindra group Powerpoint presentation. Retrieved from https://www.mahindra.com/resources/pdf/about-us/mahindra-group-presentation-FY19-20-arial.pdf

Mahindra Partners has successfully helped grow and take to maturity new businesses and investments of the $20 billion Mahindra Group. (2020). Mahindrapartners.Com. https://www.mahindrapartners.com/

Mahindra Innovation Awards. (2020). Innovation.Mahindra.Com. https://innovation.mahindra.com/home

Mahmood, I. P., & Mitchell, W. (2004). Two faces: Effects of business groups on innovation in emerging economies. *Management Science, 50*(10), 1348–1365.

Mahmood, I. P., Zhu, H., & Zajac, E. J. (2011). Where can capabilities come from? Network ties and capability acquisition in business groups. *Strategic Management Journal, 32*(8), 820–848.

Manikutty, S. (2000). Family business groups in India: A resource-based view of the emerging trends. *Family Business Review, 13*(4), 279–292.

Mazumdar, R. (2012, March 7). Kumar Mangalam Birla unifies group's R&D activities, launches Aditya Birla Science & Technology Company. *The Economic Times.* https://economictimes.indiatimes.com/tech/ites/kumar-mangalam-birla-unifies-groups-rd-activities-launches-aditya-birla-science-technology-company/articleshow/12169578.cms

Mazzelli, A., Kotlar, J., & De Massis, A. (2018). Blending in while standing out: Selective conformity and new product introduction in family firms. *Entrepreneurship Theory and Practice, 42*(2), 206–230.

McGrath, R. G., & Nerkar, A. (2004). Real options reasoning and a new look at the R&D investment strategies of pharmaceutical firms. *Strategic Management Journal, 25*(1), 1–21.

Miles, M. B., Huberman, A. M., & Saldana, J. (2014). *Qualitative data analysis: A methods sourcebook (Third).* Sage.

Miller, D., Breton-Miller, I. L., & Scholnick, B. (2008). Stewardship vs. Stagnation: An empirical comparison of small family and non-family businesses. *Journal of Management Studies, 45*(1): 51–78.

Miller, D., Wright, M., Breton-Miller, I. L., & Scholes, L. (2015). Resources and innovation in family businesses: The Janus-Face of socioemotional preferences. *California Management Review, 58*(1), 20–40.

Mukesh Ambani to Challenge Employees to Come Up with Innovative Ideas. (2017, August 11). RIL News. https://rilnews.wordpress.com/2017/08/11/mukesh-ambani-to-challenge-employees-to-come-up-with-innovative-ideas/

Morck, R., & Yeung, B. (2003). Agency problems in large family business groups. *Entrepreneurship Theory and Practice, 27*(4), 367–382.

Nieto, M. J., Santamaria, L., & Fernandez, Z. (2015). Understanding the innovation behavior of family firms. *Journal of Small Business Management, 53*(2), 382–399.

Peng, M. W., & Delios, A. (2007). What determines the scope of the firm over time and around the world? An Asia Pacific perspective. *Asia Pacific Journal of Management, 23*(4), 385–405.

Peng, M. W., Sun, W., Vlas, C., Minichilli, A., & Corbetta, G. (2018). An institution-based view of large family firms: A recap and overview. *Entrepreneurship Theory and Practice, 42*(2), 187–205.

Purkayastha, S., Manolova, T. S., & Edelman, L. F. (2018). Business group effects on the R&D intensity-internationalization relationship: Empirical evidence from India. *Journal of World Business, 53*(2), 104–117.

Ray, S., Mondal, A., & Ramachandran, K. (2018). How does family involvement affect a firm's internationalization? An investigation of Indian family firms. *Global Strategy Journal, 8*(1), 73–105.

Reliance Innovation Council India. (2020). Ril.Com. https://www.ril.com/Innovation-R-D/Innovation.asp

Reliance Industries limited. (2017). 2016–2017 Annual report of Reliance Industries Limited. Retrieved from https:// https://www.ril.com/ar2016-17/people-and-innovation.html

Reliance Industries limited. (2020). 2019–2020 Annual report of Reliance Industries Limited. Retrieved from https://www.ril.com/getattachment/299caec5-2e8a-43b7-8f70-d633a150d07e/AnnualReport_2019-20.aspx

Reprism 2019—Curtain Raiser. (2019, April 1). YouTube. https://www.youtube.com/watch?v=kn7b6ej6NNI

Roy, K., & Karna, A. 2015. Doing social good on a sustainable basis: Competitive advantage of social businesses. *Management Decision.*

Sarkar, J., & Sarkar, S. (2000). Large shareholder activism in corporate governance in developing countries: Evidence from India. *International Review of Finance, 1*(3), 161–194.

Sirmon, D. G., & Hitt, M. A. (2003). Managing resources: Linking unique resources, management, and wealth creation in family firms. *Entrepreneurship Theory and Practice, 27*(4), 339–358.

Spark innovation with curiosity. (2019, July 3). Mahindra.Com. https://www.mahindra.com/news-room/press-release/spark-innovation-with-curiosity

Tata Chemicals recognised amongst India's top 25 most innovative companies by CII for the second time in a row. (2020, December 9). www.Tatachemicals.Com. https://www.tatachemicals.com/Asia/News-room/Press-release/tata-Chemicals-recognised-amongst-indias-top-25-most-innovative-companies-by-cii-for-the-second-time-in-a-row

Tether, B. S. (1998). Small and large firms: Sources of unequal innovations? *Research Policy, 27*(7), 725–745.

The Hindu BusinessLine. (2018, March 12). *R&D efforts paying off, says Kumar Mangalam Birla*. https://www.thehindubusinessline.com/companies/rampd-eff orts-paying-off-says-kumar-mangalam-birla/article20404681.ece1

Thieme, J. (2007). Perspective: The world's top innovation management scholars and their social capital. *Journal of Product Innovation Management, 24*(3), 214–229.

Ward, J. L. (2000). Reflections on Indian family groups. *Family Business Review, 13*(4), 271–278.

Yabushita, N. W., & Suehiro, A. (2014). Family business groups in Thailand: Coping with management critical points. *Asia Pacific Journal of Management, 31*(4), 997–1018.

Yin, R. K. (2014). *Case Study Research: Design and Methods (fifth)*. Sage Publications.

Zahra, S. A. (2005). Entrepreneurial risk taking in family firms. *Family Business Review, 18*(1), 23–40.

Zahra, S. A., & Nambisan, S. (2012). Entrepreneurship and strategic thinking in business ecosystems. *Business Horizons, 55*(3), 219–229.

Part IV

Sustainability, Identity, Values and Beyond

17

Business Groups Owned by Family and Sustainability Embeddedness: Understanding the Family Sustainability Spectrum

Marcela Ramírez-Pasillas⊙, Ulla A. Saari, and Hans Lundberg

Introduction

Increased awareness about the climate emergency, social and environmental inequalities, and environmental degradation influence the adoption of sustainability by business groups worldwide, including business groups owned by family. Business groups owned by family enhance the complexities of goals, scales, and forms of business groups when families are involved in the business (Rautiainen et al., 2019). Family motivations, involvement, and

---

M. Ramírez-Pasillas (✉)
Center for Family Entrepreneurship and Ownership (CeFEO), Media,
Management and Transformation Center (MMTC), Jönköping International
Business School, Jönköping University, Jönköping, Sweden
e-mail: Marcela.Ramirez-Pasillas@ju.se

U. A. Saari
Center for Innovation and Technology Research (CITER), Unit of Industrial
Engineering and Management, Faculty of Management and Business, Tampere
University, Tampere, Finland
e-mail: ulla.saari@tuni.fi

H. Lundberg
School of Business and Economics, Linnaeus University, Växjö, Sweden
e-mail: hans.lundberg@lnu.se

© The Author(s), under exclusive license to Springer Nature
Switzerland AG 2023
M. Rautianen et al. (eds.), *The Palgrave Handbook of Managing Family Business Groups*,
https://doi.org/10.1007/978-3-031-13206-3_17

429

ownership broaden the scope of these complexities. In addition, the rise and development of business groups owned by family are an increasingly relevant phenomenon, influencing economies and wealth distribution in the world (i.e., Rautiainen, 2012; Discua et al., 2012; Scott & Rosa, 1999), thereby adding to the reasons why sustainability is an increasing priority for business groups owned by family.

On the macro level, the introduction of the United Nations' 2030 Agenda and its Sustainable Development Goals (SDGs) originated out of concern for social and planetary crises (Raworth, 2017; Rockström et al., 2009a, 2009b). The SDGs triggered an increased interest and engagement by business groups owned by family in contributing to sustainable development. This interest for and engagement in social and ecological sustainability will probably grow more due to the partnership between the United Nations' Conference on Trade and Development (UNCTAD) and the Family Business Network (FBN), *Family Business for Sustainable Development (UN FBSD)*.

When becoming signatories to the *UN FBSD,* the families, their businesses, and the broader business family ecosystems commit to developing a business model in line with the SDGs and reporting periodically on their progress. Examples of signatories to the *UN FBSD* include the Burg Groep B.V. (Switzerland, owned by the Bakker and Surendok), Corporación Empresarial Pascual (Spain, owned by the Pascual family), and the Sasser Family Companies (USA, owned by the Sasser family).

All in all, we argue that the context of business groups owned by family offers a relevant setting to investigate corporate sustainability concerning the family's unique contribution to businesses, society, and nature.

Family values (Masques et al., 2014), the founder's participation (Bingham et al., 2011), the CEO's choices (Block & Wagner, 2014), the socioemotional wealth (Ernst et al., 2022; Berrone et al., 2010), and family involvement (Memili et al., 2018), are significant aspects that influence the family's engagement with social and/or ecological sustainability in the family business. Literature on family business highlights that family and non-family firms follow different social and/or ecological sustainability practices (Miroshnychenko & De Massis, 2022; Van Gils et al., 2014; Berrone et al., 2010; Dyer & Whetten, 2006). However, currently, we lack research on how social and ecological sustainability are embedded in the business practices of business groups owned by family. We argue that this is important since literature signals varying levels of adoption of social and ecological sustainability practices by family businesses (e.g., Campopiano & De Massis, 2015; Cruz et al., 2014; Miroshnychenko et al., 2022).

Sustainability in family businesses has been researched mostly from social and economic aspects of the success and functionality of a family business (Campopiano et al., 2014; Fitzgerald et al., 2010). Gradually more research has started considering ecological aspects (Berrone et al., 2010; Miroshnychenko & De Massis, 2022; Neubaum et al., 2012) as well as generational perspectives regarding family businesses' sustainability practices (Delmas & Gergaud, 2014). There are different levels of sustainability adoption within and across family businesses (Clauß et al., 2022; Cruz et al., 2014; Memili et al., 2018). Specifically, the business groups owned by family require a close examination of sustainability embeddedness due to the owning family's values, socioemotional wealth, and stewardship (Ernst et al., 2022; Le Breton-Miller & Miller, 2016; Van Gils et al., 2014). Sharma and Sharma (2019, 2021) call for research regarding the influence of commitment, control, and continuity of the business families in their sustainability aspirations and how such aspects help introduce a sustainability purpose in the business groups.

In parallel, literature on corporate sustainability has been growing over the last decade without regard to business groups owned by family. The business group level case for sustainability indicates that corporate sustainability generates benefits such as cost savings, operational efficiencies, improved reputations, and increased competitiveness through sustainability (Laudrum, 2018). Increased awareness about the effects of the climate emergency, biodiversity loss, land use, overproduction of certain chemicals, and environmental degradation influence engagement in corporate sustainability (Härtel & Pearman, 2010; Ripple et al., 2019). In particular, climate change, the rate of biodiversity loss, interferences with nitrogen cycles, and freshwater use are global priorities (Wang-Erlandsson et al., 2022; Röckström et al., 2009a,b) for operating in a safe and fair space (Raworth, 2017; Röckström et al., 2009a). The SDGs promote sustainability work among business groups on these problems and other grand societal challenges.

As the owning family develops its sustainability ambitions in the business group, tensions in working with different SDGs, multiple stakeholders, and regions might take place. Still, the owning family is developing awareness and strategies to pursue ecological, social, and ethical challenges and opportunities (Ramírez-Pasillas & Nordqvist, 2021). Research at the interface of family, business groups, and sustainability is important to advance our understanding of the owning family's influence on the sustainability approaches of its business group. Therefore, this chapter develops a conceptual framework that examines the commitment, control, and continuity of the owning family to global corporate sustainability of its business group (Sharma & Sharma, 2021).

The chapter contributes to research on family business groups in two ways. Firstly, our proposed framework on sustainability embeddedness merges literature on family businesses, corporate sustainability (Landrum, 2017, 2018), and sustainability science (Röckström et al. 2009a, 2009b). Can help better understand the engagement of the owning family as a distinct context for variety in the family's sustainability approach in the business group. Secondly, our conceptual framework adopts a focus on the owning family as a potential control mechanism regulating the relationship between sustainability embeddedness and the business group (Aguilera et al., 2021).

An Introduction to Corporate Sustainability

Sustainable development has been introduced to corporate sustainability literature as a response to the climate crisis and increased inequalities around the world. According to the Brundtland Commission Report, *Our Common Future* (World Commission on Environment & Development, 1987), sustainable development corresponds to development that meets the needs of the present without compromising the future generations' ability to meet their own needs in consideration of issues of environmental conservation and societal justice. Sustainable development requires the government and organisations to address measures, policies, and processes to promote the conservation, restoration, and regeneration of the biosphere as well as the stimulation of economic and societal progress.

Specifically, corporate sustainability as a concept emerged at the beginning of the 2000s when more ethical and transparent business practices were called for both in academia and society (Van Marrewijk, 2003). At that point, multiple frameworks emerged, including corporate sustainability, corporate social responsibility, corporate citizenship or the so-called corporate philanthropy, corporate governance, business ethics, and even sustainable entrepreneurship and inclusive business (Reficco & Ogliastri, 2009). Corporate sustainability focuses on the interface of three dimensions (social, ecological, and financial). In the 2020s, corporate sustainability is still relevant in the context of assessing business practices and their degree of sustainability (van Zanten & van Tulder, 2021). This is especially highlighted in the context of the SDGs that are referred to as major sustainable development goals globally, which are derived out of concerns for social and planetary boundaries (Raworth, 2017; Rockström et al., 2009a). The SDGs advocate that companies incorporate social and ecological sustainability in their strategies, operations, and collaborations to meet societal challenges (e.g., van Zanten & van Tulder, 2018).

Sustainable development acknowledges multifaceted problems in economic, ecological, and social dimensions that require companies' deep understanding and interest in the natural environment, social issues, and the global economy. Van Zanten and van Tulder (2021) suggest that the linkages between corporate strategies and the SDGs are a critical measure for the success of corporate sustainability targets. Thus, companies that create more positive impacts on the three corporate sustainability dimensions with reference to the SDGs are more sustainable as compared to other companies.

In the context of the family business literature, corporate social responsibility (CSR) has been a more commonly adopted framework. It is explained with the concepts of familiness and socioemotional wealth, which are two important characteristics of family businesses (Randerson, 2022). Familiness has been defined as the unique set of resources of a family firm that are formed as a result of interactions at various levels that take place in the family, among the family members, and in the business that they operate (Habbershon & Williams, 1999). The concept of socioemotional wealth is an overarching one explaining family business behaviour and its environmental dimensions (Berrone et al., 2012). Socioemotional wealth has been used for explaining why family firms are willing to accept higher financial risks for maintaining a good reputation, ensuring a positive trans-generational succession, and engaging in environmental issues (Gomez-Mejía et al., 2007).

In some family businesses, the social and ecological dimensions of sustainability are the focus of the companies' philanthropical initiatives. CSR and philanthropy can be related to similar causes and are considered together via independent foundations (Ramírez-Pasillas & Lundberg, 2019). However, recent research indicates that in some cases, CEOs may attempt to make up for shortfalls in their companies' CSR activities by joining a board of a non-profit foundation or supporting individual initiatives, which could result in differing priorities in the causes that the company and the foundation focus on (Lungeanu & Weber, 2021). Nevertheless, in the case of family firms, there have been more signs of philanthropy, especially during the COVID-19 pandemic, which have been actualised as active CSR-related collaborations locally in diverse areas (Rivo-López et al., 2021). Furthermore, the family's business orientation focuses on the well-being of the communities in which they operate, and their socioemotional values impact their strategies and business model development (Baù et al., 2021).

Yet, sustainability is a future-oriented concept that concerns ecological and social issues that should also be considered from the perspective of different generations (Brunninge et al., 2020). This is demonstrated, for example, by the way family firms are making strategic efforts towards a transition to the circular economy (e.g., Spanish food retail leader Mercadona) (Núñez-Cacho et al., 2018).

CSR activities can have a strong influence on strategic and investment decisions for family businesses. In a study of family business activities in the Indonesian Stock Exchange (IDX) during 2016–2018, it was found that family businesses were cautious about how they invested and tended to avoid risks related to decisions that could bring growth in economic wealth, but that could have a negative impact on the family's socioemotional wealth; this indicates that family businesses are concerned about their reputation more than their economic growth (Erawati et al., 2021). There is some indication in strategic management literature that as the percentage of family ownership increases in the family business, the number of employees and focus on environmental issues decrease, while the number of diversity-related CSR issues increases (Lamb et al., 2017). Yet, the diversity of composition in ownership results in contrasting practices (e.g., Miroshnychenko & Di Massis, 2022; Samara et al., 2018).

Business groups have a central role to play in nurturing sustainability. The annual list of wealthiest families in America gathers 1.3 trillion US dollars (*Fortune*, 2021), which signals the financial viability and potential contribution that can be made to corporate sustainability by engaging more in pro-social and pro-environmental endeavours. Pro-social behaviour can be seen as an important family business value with a significant impact on the way the family demonstrates citizenship behaviour and engages in civic wealth creation through its business activities (Lumpkin & Bacq, forthcoming; Campopiano et al., 2014). Recent research indicates that in the family firms' business performance, there are also purpose-driven goals that are not focused on financial profit; these goals include the demonstration of family orientation, its pro-social behaviour, and its moral obligation to behave as good citizens (Pratono & Han, 2021).

The COVID-19 pandemic has transformed the way CSR activities are linked to the core business in family firms in emergencies. Literature indicates that family businesses are more likely to adopt strategies that drive more ethical behaviour, thus creating new perspectives for developing their CSR activities (Rivo- López et al., 2021).

Based on a study of Chinese family-owned firms, another tendency among family businesses can also be seen: environmental misconduct can be compensated for by philanthropic activities for distracting public attention from this harmful behaviour, which indicates that philanthropy can sometimes be motivated by environmental misconduct (Du, 2015). In India, family-owned companies have an important role in promoting and planning CSR activities in the local community and economy (Panicker, 2017). In Europe, for example in Poland, family firms have a significant role in driving sustainable social development and it has been found that family businesses share the family wealth with those in need and their CSR activities can also have an impact on the cross-generational sustainability of companies when transitioning the younger successors (Bielawska, 2021).

However, paradoxes exist in literature calling for further research (Van Gils et al., 2014). In a global study of listed family businesses in 45 countries, family businesses engaged less in pollution prevention, green supply chain, and green product development as compared to non-family businesses (Miroshnychenko & De Massis, 2022). In contrast, in another study of firms in 29 countries, family-controlled firms showed a higher level of CSR performance and they balanced internal and external stakeholders' demands better (García-Sánchez et al., 2021). In another international study of family businesses in 20 countries, family ownership had an economic impact on CSR issues, showing greater social and ethical commitment by family businesses as compared to non-familybusinesses (Martínez-Ferrero et al., 2016). These authors also found that the higher the level of managerial discretion in a company, the stronger its commitment to CSR, but CSR could also be employed as a self-defence mechanism for distracting stakeholders. Yet, the ethical orientation of family owners and their CSR priorities was intended to satisfy CSR stakeholders' demands.

When working with corporate sustainability, family and non-family managers need to deal with complex issues that have high levels of ambiguity, including the impact of their decisions on their organisations and the external environment (Hahn et al., 2014). For instance, corporate reporting can give a positive appearance of the degree of corporate sustainability to selected stakeholders (Campopiano et al., 2014; Hahn and Lüffs, 2014). But in practical terms, how far the sustainability practices have actually been implemented in every part of the organisation and its ecosystem is something that needs to be assessed case by case (e.g., Laudrum, 2018). Thus, the degree to which corporate sustainability has been embedded can differ according to the owning family, the industrial sector, and the country. We, therefore, discuss the different degrees or levels of corporate sustainability *as* corporate sustainability embeddedness next.

Corporate Sustainability Embeddedness

Corporate sustainability embeddedness represents the sustainability approach that a corporation adopts. It denotes worldviews, interpretations, mindsets, types, or phases (Landrum, 2017). Hence, sustainability embeddedness in a corporation indicates a level of awareness, understanding, and operationalisation of ecological and social sustainability. It also helps to understand how a corporation chooses to relate and work with the SDGs.

Compared to our previous understanding of corporate sustainability anchored solely on ecological economics and environmental management (cf., Miroshnychenko & De Massis, 2022), in this chapter, we adopt sustainability embeddedness to broaden the concept of corporate sustainability to include concerns for societal issues. In line with Landrum (2018), we integrate the micro-level company perspective with a broader macro-level perspective of the sustainability challenges at the societal level. The macro-level corporate sustainability assessment presents the highest-level target of an economic dimension embedded within the natural ecosystem's boundaries with an understanding of the limited natural resources on the planet (e.g., Whiteman et al., 2013). This also sets the bar higher when studying how companies embed sustainability to minimise the negative impacts on the environment, maximise societal benefits, and restore nature.

Thus, the development of a sustainability approach is considered an embeddedness process for reaching higher levels of corporate sustainability in three dimensions—ecological, social, and economic. To understand the level of sustainability embeddedness, the strategy, impacts, and linkages between all three dimensions need to be considered internally and externally, with the company's stakeholders as also concerning the state of the natural environment (Baumgartner & Ebner, 2010) and relations to society. Hence, corporate sustainability embeddedness varies depending on the company's commitment to sustainability in relation to its strategy, leadership, practices, and investments in innovations, people, communities, and the natural environment (e.g., Sukitsch et al., 2015).

Even though there is clear scientific evidence of more sustainability embeddedness due to the climate emergency, environmental degradation, biodiversity loss, and inequalities (Ripple et al., 2019; Rockström et al., 2009a, 2009b), in some companies, corporate sustainability embeddedness is still related to incremental strategic improvements and not as radical action required for ensuring sustainability transitions. Therefore, Landrum (2018) proposes distinguishing a spectrum from weak to strong sustainability. Weak sustainability is observed in those companies that do not yet comprehend the urgency of the requirements for a deeper level of sustainability embeddedness and tend to focus on financial feasibility and business perspectives in their sustainability goals (Dyllick & Muff, 2016). In other cases, the relevance of corporate sustainability embeddedness has often been made with the business case, that is, relating corporate sustainability to a higher value in stock prices, cost savings, operational efficiencies, an increase in competitive advantage, and reputational perspectives (Dyllick & Muff, 2016). This also corresponds to weak and moderately weak sustainability embeddedness.

Companies operating at weak levels of sustainability embeddedness still primarily focus on profit and growth, which is defined from a pure business economic dimension which places little attention on the social and ecological dimensions of sustainability (Landrum, 2018).

In contrast, companies that have been forerunners in the adoption of sustainability policies have proactively developed their businesses, reaching higher levels of corporate sustainability embeddedness and economic performance in the stock markets and in financial accounting (i.e., Eccles et al., 2014). These companies exhibit strong sustainability. In these companies, shareholder activism can drive the corporate sustainability strategy with a long-term vision (Yang et al., 2018). In particular, when activists drive change regarding corporate sustainability, they help make sustainability more accepted and embedded in a corporation and in society.

There are various approaches to corporate sustainability embeddedness termed in a continuum or a 'sustainability spectrum' (Landrum, 2017). The level of sustainability embeddedness considers the degree of weak and strong sustainability guiding corporate decisions and practices in a business journey (Landrum, 2017). Literature on the sustainability spectrum associates labels ranging from three (e.g., Aggerholm & Trapp, 2014) to seven (e.g., Maon et al., 2010). The most well-known reference to corporate sustainability embeddedness goes back to Dunphy et al. (2003) who defined six phases that companies pass through when working towards sustainability (rejection, non-responsiveness, compliance, efficiency, strategic proactivity, and sustaining corporation). Dunphy et al. (2003) argue that each phase builds a foundation for the next phase. However, the phases do not indicate that the organisations have moved in a linear manner; they can go back and forth between phases (Dunphy et al., 2007).

This chapter adopts the sustainability spectrum developed by Landrum (2017, 2018). Thus, the embeddedness of corporate sustainability evolves from a weak to a very strong degree of sustainability, with the following labels: non-participatory, compliance, business-centred, systemic, regenerative, and co-evolutionary (Landrum, 2017). Sustainability embeddedness in compliance, business-centred and systemic logics is very economic science-oriented and solely business-oriented, while the orientation of the regenerative and co-evolutionary logics are ecological science and natural ecology oriented. The level of knowledge about sustainability ranges from meeting the compliance requirements to a more profound understanding of the need to repair the damages to the systems and perceiving humans to be in a relationship with the natural ecosystem (Landrum, 2018). Stronger sustainability embeddedness will enable companies to move from implementing only incremental improvements to more regenerative systemic business development.

A co-evolutionary logic implies that companies operate in balance and are synchronised with nature. At stronger sustainability levels, companies introduce, assess, and transition their business strategies and practices in a way that the enterprising activities contribute to achieving sustainable development (van Zanten & van Tulder, 2018).

The spectrum of sustainability embeddedness provides an important conceptual tool for examining the strategic approaches of business groups owned by family. In business groups owned by family, the family becomes a key shareholder who pushes or pulls sustainability embeddedness in various directions given the levels of family involvement in the business' ownership and management. Investigating the connection between sustainability embeddedness and family involvement in business groups can help understand the influence of the owning family in shaping corporations that depend on and affect natural resources, communities, and regions worldwide for creating prosperity. We elaborate on this in the next section.

Corporate Sustainability in Business Groups Owned by Family

Business groups increase the complexities when working with sustainability. For instance, the structure is a key feature of business groups. Various organisations are integrated into a business group, thus constituting a portfolio of businesses distributed in several industry sectors, or specialised within an industry (e.g., Rautiainen et al., 2019). Another aspect is the legal disposition of the business groups. Some business groups favour a parent company as a legal, fiscal, and strategic controlling mechanism across organisations, while other groups are managed through a controlling foundation (Rey-Garcia & Puig-Raposo, 2013). A group structure can be used for blurring shortcomings in sustainability work thus reducing accountability and transparency.

For example, business groups commonly choose to prepare a consolidated global sustainability report without encouraging the development of individual reports for every organisation in the business group. A business group can also be employed to sustain irresponsible endeavours like the painkiller OxyContin, a medicine that induces addiction. Purdue Pharma, a company owned and managed by the Sackler family, manufactured the pills.

Hence, the structure of a business group can also be used for influencing a stronger view of sustainability in organisations across regions. For example, IKEA's vision, '*creating a better everyday life for many people*,' does not differ much from many other purposefully crafted visions. The myriad ways in which IKEA's vision is operationalised and practised establishes clear guidelines and ambitions across the company's subsidiaries and franchises in different countries to foster prosperity for all. However, literature on family business agrees that the family's involvement in ownership and management results in varying degrees of adoption of sustainability practices (i.e., Berrone et al., 2010; Cruz et al., 2014; Memili et al., 2018). The owning family actively monitors the managers, reducing the risk of misusing CSR as entrenchment (Martínez-Ferrero et al., 2016).

Specifically, Sharma and Sharma (2021) propose that corporate sustainability in business families depends on: *commitment, control*, and *continuity*. We review family business literature by relating to these three aspects.

Commitment: Commitment to corporate sustainability means '*core values to use the family business as a force of good for society*' (Sharma & Sharma, 2021:6). Commitment to corporate sustainability is anchored in business families' values and goals. Le Breton-Miller and Miller (2016) show that the family business' values spread to its stakeholders and help balance ecological concerns with stakeholders' concerns (Neubaum et al., 2012). Family businesses are also recognised for their non-economic goals (Campopiano & De Massis, 2015; Cabrera-Suárez et al., 2014). Family-centred values and goals include economic and non-economic goals resulting from overlapping the family, ownership, and business systems (Kotlar & De Massis, 2013; Raitis et al., 2021). Thus, the commitment to corporate sustainability manifests in unique approaches followed by the owning family due to its values and goals that define the family's involvement in the business and its relationship with the community, including commitment to the community, community support, sense of community (Niehm et al., 2008), and the natural environment (Neubaum et al., 2012). Family members and their businesses build their businesses strongly embedded in their communities (Basco, 2015; Baù et al., 2019) to meet sustainability challenges.

Further, the philanthropic or pro-social behaviour of family businesses is also influenced by family ownership and family management (Lumpkin and Bacq, forthcoming), including charitable programmes and volunteerism (Campopiano et al., 2014; Cruz et al., 2014). Family values and goals also affect how a family business relates to employees, customers, and suppliers while pursuing sustainability (e.g., García-Sánchez et al., 2021; Uhlaner et al., 2004). For instance, Cruz et al. (2014) found that family businesses can be responsible and irresponsible and engage in responsible practices towards external stakeholders while acting less responsibly towards internal stakeholders. Memili et al. (2018) found a negative relationship between family involvement and sustainability practices (cf., also Miroshnychenko & De Massis, 2022), and Huang et al. (2009) show that, for instance, the age of a family business influences the introduction of green innovations.

Control: Corporate sustainability is connected to the control exercised by the owning family to '*implement strategic decisions and resources in the family business*' (Sharma & Sharma, 2021: 6). Family businesses adopt different approaches for working with social and environmental issues (Berrone et al., 2010; Marques et al., 2014) and this approach is influenced by the control exercised by the owning family and its involvement in the business' management (García-Sánchez et al., 2021). In this regard, there are contrasting views since family involvement impacts corporate sustainability (e.g., Block & Wagner, 2014; Huang et al., 2009; Samara et al., 2018). Family businesses tend to have a person responsible for CSR and the existence of such a position implies that the family business conducts sustainability assessments and implements sustainability initiatives (Marques et al., 2014).

Another aspect is that family businesses rely on reports and codes of ethics and also have a dedicated section on CSR on companies' websites (Campopiano & De Massis, 2015). These authors find that family businesses' corporate sustainability reports bring in environmental and philanthropic issues since they are concerned about protecting their socioemotional wealth by responding to environmental pressures.

Continuity: Continuity for corporate sustainability is connected to the owning family and its businesses' long-term orientation (Sharma & Sharma, 2019) going '*beyond the tenure of the incumbent generations*' (Sharma & Sharma, 2021: 6). It emphasises the family business' futurity and preservation (Brigham et al., 2014). A long-term orientation implies that the owning family exercises care for the long-run regarding investments, stewardship, and lengthy tenures (Le Breton-Miller & Miller, 2005). Combinations of 100 per cent family ownership, first-generation leadership, and family presence in management or the board catalyse social and environmental performance

(Samara et al., 2018). Hence, continuity manifests in a specific social or economic purpose that is persevered with over the long-term (Miller & Le Breton-Miller, 2005). While a long-term orientation allows the owning families to realise long-term investments, it also fosters the adoption of sustainable business practices (Memili et al., 2018). A long-term orientation also carries the formation, protection, and transfer of a legacy (Hirigoyen & Poulain-Rehm, 2014). It also brings in considerations for the family's past, present, and future, including the next generation's jobs, income, and careers (Miller & Le Breton-Miller, 2005). Because of a family business' long-term orientation, policies are created for selecting and developing family managers (Le Breton-Miller & Miller, 2016). Such policies are important since family businesses tend to select family members more than non-family members for these positions (Campopiano & De Massis, 2015). Also, the next-generation members can be very influential stakeholders in decisions related to eco-certification to improve product quality and positioning of products as eco-friendly when intending to take over the business (Delmas & Gergaud, 2014).

To sum up, family business literature approaches corporate sustainability as a result of addressing social, ecological, and economic aspects in varying degrees (Sharma & Sharma, 2019). Thus, sustainability by family businesses calls for research on these different approaches and practices (Le Breton-Miller & Miller, 2016), or put more technically, we need to better understand business groups' sustainability spectrum. We conceptualise this next.

Sustainability Embeddedness of Business Groups Owned by Family

We argue that investigating sustainability embeddedness of business groups owned by family requires a closer examination of the owning family's involvement in the business group. In our mind, sustainability embeddedness comprises diverse approaches representing ecological, social, and economic aspirations, expectations, and responsibilities linked to the owning family's involvement in the family business. Such approaches influence and are influenced by the business group's structure, collective capabilities, interactions, and collaborations with multiple global and local stakeholders, including CEOs/managers, partners, communities, and the natural environment.

We examine the interlink between the owning family's involvement and corporate sustainability, shaping the sustainability embeddedness of a business group as portrayed in Fig. 17.1. We argue that the resulting sustainability embeddedness is moulded by the family's involvement adopted in its commitment, control, and continuity in relation to corporate sustainability. In business groups, the owning family can be a sole or majority shareholder regulating corporate sustainability through the parent company or the controlling foundation due to its socioemotional wealth. Socioemotional wealth influences the pursuit of non-economic goals for satisfying the owning family's preferences (Berrone et al., 2012). The owning family's values and goals permeate the business group affecting its relationship with nature and communities resulting in a socially driven business group, a socially and ecologically driven business group, or a flourishing business group (see Fig. 17.1).

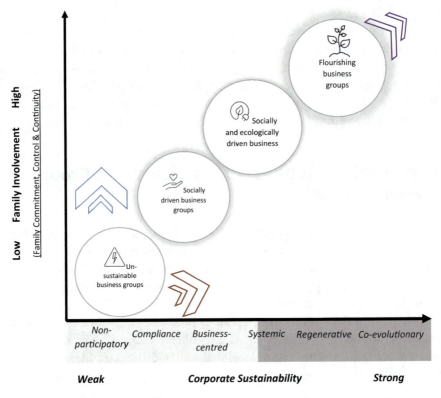

Fig. 17.1 Sustainability embeddedness of business groups owned by family

A socially driven group owned by a family will prioritise the relationship with its communities and civic wealth creation (in line with Lumpkin and Bacq, forthcoming). A socially and ecologically driven business group owned by a family will address social and environmental concerns. A flourishing business group owned by a family will focus on both social and ecological concerns internally and externally and will invest in giving back to society and nature (e.g., García-Sánchez et al., 2021).

In this manner, sustainability embeddedness sets the foundation of how the owning family strives to create value alignment—or not—with the resilience of ecological, social, and economic contextual aspects of the planet (Rockström et al., 2009a, 2009b).

Adopting the sustainability embeddedness spectrum (Laudrum, 2017; 2018) in business groups owned by family, we contextualise the sustainability embeddedness spectrum according to the family's involvement (family commitment, control, and continuity). We relate the spectrum to family business literature and provide an illustrative example of a business group owned by a family.

Non-participatory: A non-participatory owning family's approach is that of being disconnected from a broad sustainability view in the business group (that is, without any concern for social and ecological issues); thus, the family's commitment, control, and continuity regarding sustainability practices are guided by a purely economic logic or profit maximisation. The owning family can support or remain silent on the business group's lack of sustainability practices. Thus, commitment, control, and continuity are anchored in concerns for societal problems and the natural environment. An example of this very weak level of sustainability embeddedness in the family's involvement is the Sackler family and its Purdue Pharma. Two Sackler brothers purchased Purdue Pharma in 1952 developing it with a focus on pain management and relying on aggressive marketing strategies. The Sackler family developed a reputation as a key philanthropic donor in the United States. It was also recognised for being 'extravagant' in art philanthropy, for instance, the Sackler Trust has donated up to 202 m Euros to art institutions only in Britain since 2009 (O'Hagan, 2022). The family incorporated Purdue Pharma as a privately held company in 1991 and the company had been financially successful when the OxyContin scandal emerged. Patrick Radden Keefe exposed the family, the business, and the public health tragedy in his article *The family that built an empire of pain* in *the New Yorker* (Radden Keefe, 2017). However, the company had been under scrutiny even before this scandal broke out.

Despite being aware of the problems with OxyContin, the Sackler family did not try to apologise and compensate for its transgressions. Instead, it engaged in a lawsuit to be approved of bankruptcy and released from liability for the harm caused by OxyContin (Mann, 2021). In 2022, Purdue Pharma and the Sackler family reached a settlement to the lawsuits filed by a group of states, the District of Columbia, *The New York Times*, and other media outlets to pay $5.5 billion to $6 billion to a trust that will be employed to pay victims of addition, hospitals, municipalities, and states. The money will fund addiction treatment programmes and the family will lose control of Purdue Pharma. In Fig. 17.1, this approach to sustainability embeddedness is illustrated with the circle 'unsustainable business groups.'

Compliance: In this approach, the owning family aims to merely observe the regulations and standards of the countries in which it operates. Corporate sustainability is, thus, perceived as an obligation (Laudrum, 2017, 2018). Respect for laws, regulations, and industry-standards guides the family's commitment, control, and continuity regarding sustainability practices. The owning family exercises its control by employing certification and reporting practices for corporate sustainability (e.g., Campopiano & De Massis, 2015). If expected by the community, philanthropic activities can be carried out by the owning family and its business group (e.g., Campopiano et al., 2014). For example, supporting communities includes caring for the disadvantaged, engaging in charity initiatives, and sharing wealth for society's development (Le-Bretton Miller & Miller, 2016). Yet, ecological concerns do not have a central role in the family's commitment; thus, these are only addressed to avoid breaking regulations.

A compliance approach can explain the emergence of varied sustainability approaches with internal and external stakeholders (e.g., Cruz et al., 2014) and across the group's businesses. The owning family's continuity will imply that complying with the law is an instrument for sustaining the licence to operate so as to transfer the business group to the next generation. Sustainability embeddedness represents a slightly to moderately weak approach. In Fig. 17.1, this approach to sustainability embeddedness is illustrated with the circle 'socially driven business groups.' One example of such a group is the Swedish family Andersson, owners of Mellby Gård, a business group integrating 19 companies in its portfolio. The owning family believes in active corporate governance, long-term orientation, and partnerships (Mellby Gård, 2022). The owning family focuses on preserving the entrepreneurial spirit of its companies while remaining the largest shareholders and assuming the responsibility for business development (Mellby Gård, 2022). The companies follow regulations and standard practices in the countries in which they operate. The owning family strives to minimise the use of resources and present accidental pollution, and avoid the use of conflict minerals. The owning family performs philanthropic activities through its businesses by donating funds to programmes supporting children, providing health service access, internet access, and entrepreneurship in certain developing countries.

Business-centred: The owning family adopts a business-centred approach to pursuing sustainability as a business case. The family's commitment, control, and continuity regarding sustainability strives to develop operational efficiencies, obtain cost savings, and develop environmentally friendly products to increase the group's competitiveness (i.e., Maon et al., 2010). The owning family's commitment to sustainability moves to a moderate position, thus sustainability drives the business group's development. The owning family do not react as a response to external pressures (e.g., Neubaum et al., 2012). Instead, the owning family matches family and the business continuity with a broader understanding of sustainability. Sustainability practices help improve the financial performance and vary according to firm types, industry sector, and country (e.g., Memili et al., 2018). Different economic, social, and ecological performance goals can be set based on current business development (Sharma & Sharma, 2021). Sustainability practices and policies can also affect the recruitment of personnel and job satisfaction (e.g., Pittino et al., 2016), which in turn improves the efficiency of operations and the company's productivity.

A business-centred approach can explain the emergence of different sustainability approaches with internal and external stakeholders and across the group's businesses. Family control starts building a more robust sustainability capacity and relies on social/sustainability innovations for becoming more efficient. The owning family's philanthropic endeavours are meant to improve the business' competitiveness. In Fig. 17.1, this approach to sustainability embeddedness is illustrated with the circle 'socially and ecologically driven business groups.' One example of such a group is the Bennet family. Carl Bennet owns 100 per cent of the group Carl Bennet AB, having six international companies. While Carl Bennet is the president of the board, his spouse, Nina Bennet and their son-in-law, Dan Frohm are board members. Dan Frohm, who has been pointed out as a potential successor is married to Carl Bennet's only daughter Anna Bennet (Svensson, 2021). Carl Bennet adopts a long-term orientation and strong responsibility, which is infused in the parent company and its portfolio of businesses. Social, ecological, and economic sustainability issues are considered important conditions for the long-term sustainability of the businesses. Thus, sustainability is part of the value creation of business operations and board discussions. Carl Bennet collaborates and donates money to academia and research institutions via the parent company with the purpose of developing good financial conditions by building competitive and sustainable operations. In line with this business-centric approach, Carl Bennet collaborates with social enterprises in developing countries to help improve children's education and supporting awards and competitions fostering sustainability in Sweden. This example represents a moderate level of sustainability embeddedness.

Systemic: The systemic approach denotes owning families that pursue a sustainable transformation of their business groups at a system level. Hence, the owning family's commitment, control, and continuity manifest in adopting agendas that aim for the common good. The long-term orientation of the business and the planet are matched (Whiteman et al., 2013). Because of the owning family's long-term orientation, its business groups invest strategically in sustainability (e.g., Memili et al., 2018). Social and ecological sustainability are incorporated into the long-term orientation of the business group. The owning family's commitment to sustainability prioritises a broader view on sustainability as the most important direction for the business group. The owning family's control manifests in allowing and supporting business development locally and globally. For instance, the owning family supports collaborations with stakeholders that help create a positive future outlook for the businesses (Le-Bretton Miller & Miller, 2016). Thus, the owning family promotes collaborative partnerships for sustainability. While sustainability embeddedness is strong, in this approach, '*there is no mention of environmental carrying capacity as a motivation or consideration*' (Laudrum, 2017: 298) nor consideration of planetary boundaries (Whiteman et al., 2013). In Fig. 17.1, the systemic approach to sustainability embeddedness is illustrated with the circle 'flourishing business groups.' An example of the owning family operating at a systemic level is the Swedish Kamprad family and its Inter IKEA Group. Since its creation, founder, Ingvar Kamprad, has adopted a commitment to an inclusive agenda, resulting in the democratisation of design and furniture in its companies. IKEA's sustainability strategy aspires to create a positive impact on people, society, and the planet, understanding the resource limitations of the world (Inter IKEA, 2022). Further, the Kamprad family has also launched The Kamprad Foundation to stimulate and reward education and scientific research on entrepreneurship, the environment, health, and social development (Familjen Kamprads Stiftelse, 2022). In line with its hands-on approach, the foundation gives grants to education and research that benefit people as soon as possible and with cost-effectiveness (Familjen Kamprads Stiftelse, 2022).

Regenerative: The owning family' regenerative approach highlights a very strong commitment to sustainability, comprising repairing, restoring, and regenerating nature. The family's commitment, control, and continuity manifest in economic and non-economic goals avoiding any harm to the biosphere while contributing to a regenerative society. A strong sense of social and ecological responsibility guides the owning family's commitment, control, and continuity; thus, the family commits to restoring nature as a necessary condition for societal prosperity. For example, the next generation's commitment displays strong concern and willingness to continuously find ways of improving sustainability practices in the business group (e.g., Delmas & Gergaud, 2014). The resulting control goes beyond certification efforts and is concentrated on radical innovations through collaborations to give back to both society and nature. The owning family is concerned and works at addressing and sustaining the environmental carrying capacity of the planet. The socioemotional wealth assures the ecological behaviour of the business group (Berrone et al., 2010). There is a strong sustainability alignment and collaboration between the business group's internal and external stakeholders. In Fig. 17.1, this approach to sustainability embeddedness is illustrated with the circle 'flourishing business group.' An example of a business aspiring to become regenerative is the US privately held company Patagonia founded by Yvon Chouinard. The company is managed by first- and second-generation members. Patagonia is not a business group yet, but it is an example of a privately owned business embracing a regeneration approach. The founder's commitment, control, and continuity have prioritised sustainability since the creation of the company. His commitment is captured by his environmental philosophy: 'Lead an examined life; Clean up our own life; Do our penance; Support civil democracy; and Influence other companies' (Chouinard, 2005: 160). Despite challenges in the transformation of supply chains and products, the long-term orientation of the owning family continues to push forward sustainability. For instance, currently, Patagonia is developing regenerative organic certified pilot programmes to develop agricultural systems in collaboration with farmers, concerned businesses, and experts that build a healthy soil, draw carbon back into the ground, and improve the farmers' life quality (Patagonia, 2022).

Co-evolutionary: The co-evolutionary approach proposes that the owning family concentrates their efforts on sustaining sustainability practices in an absolute balance with nature and society. In Fig. 17.1, this approach to sustainability embeddedness is illustrated with the circle 'flourishing business groups.' The family's commitment, control, and continuity adopt a transformative view of the human–environment relationship regarding power structures. Thus, the owning family sees that its business group operates in harmony with the natural environment. The owning family creates power structures that allow the parent business or controlling foundation to support and interact with the natural environment. The owning family's role is safeguarding nature and society through the activities of the business group and related foundations. The charity foundations support creativity for building a culture of radical innovations benefiting nature and society. Since this is the strongest sustainability embeddedness level that the owning family can have, it represents an ideal type.

*To sum up, w*hen relating the owning family's involvement with the corporate sustainability spectrum, the resulting sustainability embeddedness of a family business group is influenced by the family's ambition and contribution to sustainable development via its business group. Further, we posit that different logics emerge when relating family involvement to corporate sustainability. Such logics represent the ways in which the owning family realises the values and goals through the parent company or the controlling foundation. As illustrated in Fig. 17.1, the business groups owned by families adopting a systemic, regenerative, and co-evolutionary approach operate sustainably (marked with a dark colour grey line), while the remaining approaches do not yet operate fully sustainably (marked with a light colour grey line).

Theoretical Implications

This chapter contributes to emerging literature on family business groups by connecting the owning family's involvement with sustainability embeddedness. Sustainability embeddedness derives from six approaches (Laudrum, 2017, 2018). Each approach defines how the owning family considers and relates to sustainable development influencing the development of their business groups. We introduce family involvement as a central dimension (that is, family commitment, control, and continuity) in shaping a business group's sustainability embeddedness, exercising influence through the parent company or the controlling foundation. Thus, our conceptual framework focuses on the owning family as a potential control mechanism regulating the relationship between sustainability embeddedness and the business group (Aguilera et al., 2021). Thus, a strong sustainability orientation crafted through family involvement indicates that the owning family believes in creating good through businesses, philanthropic activities, and connections with nature (i.e., Raworth, 2017). In contrast, a weak sustainability orientation promotes a profitable business without regard for our planet's carrying capacity.

We also contribute to the rapidly emerging literature on family businesses' sustainability practices. Our sustainability embeddedness spectrum adds to an understanding of the limited environmental performance of family businesses (e.g., Miroshnychenko & De Massis, 2022; Miroshnychenko et al., 2022) or strong sustainability performance (Samara et al., 2018). The spectrum allows an examination of business groups owned by family engaged in sustainable development. Sustainability implies collaborating with internal and external stakeholders and building capabilities for radical innovation. Thus, we suggest that there can be an alignment or misalignment in sustainability embeddedness within a business group because of the paradoxes of the owning family when working with sustainability. When operating in several regions and industry sectors, the owning family (often) faces conflicting goals, expectations, and obligations generated by different institutional frameworks. Tensions can result from the role of the natural environment in their sustainability agenda or the stakeholders' goals and capabilities. For instance, the owning family can choose to prioritise certain SDGs in the business group, which can impact the goals and needs of certain stakeholders. Also, the owning family experiences tensions when addressing social, technical, collaborative, and ecological challenges of the business group. We suggest that our proposed sustainability embeddedness framework allows analysing such diversity within and between business groups owned by family.

Future Research

Sustainability research in family business is gradually becoming popular. Our analytical framework on the family sustainability spectrum proposes several significant ways forward for examining business groups owned by family. Future research can use our framework to investigate the role of family in meeting social challenges and addressing the conservation, restoration, and regeneration of nature through business groups. In particular, understanding practices, processes, and strategies to embed social and ecological sustainability in the business groups owned by family is necessary to avoid crossing other planetary boundaries thus preventing disasters (e.g., Wang-Erlandsson et al., 2022). Research can help develop more specific models based on empirical data on the different levels of sustainability embeddedness.

Another way forward for future research is a focus on the micro-level daily business practices and values of the owning family across generations in their engagement regarding new sustainable business opportunities. This focus will provide a better understanding of the varying contexts and levels of adoption of social and ecological approaches of the owning family across generations actualised in the operations of the business group. Another way forward for future research is studying how the family's commitment, control, and continuity of the business group to sustainability are reflected in strategies, and the business group's impact on preventing crossing further planetary boundaries. For this, the meso- and macro levels can consider the inclusion of stakeholders where society and nature are considered key stakeholders. In addition, researchers can examine similarities and differences in the family's involvement and levels of sustainability embeddedness across businesses within a group, as also in different countries and regions.

Given the influence and economic power of business groups owned by family, research on sustainability is not only a necessity but a priority for examining and understanding the resilience and transformation of business models.

References

Aggerholm, H., & Trapp, N. (2014). Three tiers of CSR: An instructive means of understanding and guiding contemporary company approaches to CSR? *Business Ethics: A European Review, 23*, 235–247.

Aguilera, R. V., Aragon-Correa, J. A., Marano, V., & Tashman, P. A. (2021). The corporate governance of environmental sustainability: A review and proposal for more integrated research. *Journal of Management, 47*(6), 1468–1497.

Arregle, J.-L., Hitt, M. A., Sirmon, D. G., & Very, P. (2007). The development of organizational social capital: Attributes of family firms. *Journal of Management Studies, 44*(1), 73–95.

Basco, R. (2015). Family business and regional development—A theoretical model of regional familiness. *Journal of Family Business Strategy, 6*(4), 259–271.

Baù, M., Block, J., Discua Cruz, A., & Naldi, L. (2021). Bridging locality and internationalization—A research agenda on the sustainable development of family firms. *Entrepreneurship and Regional Development, 33*(7–8), 477–492.

Baù, M., Chirico, F., Pittino, D., Backman, M., & Klaesson, J. (2019). Roots to grow: Family firms and local embeddedness in rural and urban contexts. *Entrepreneurship Theory and Practice, 43*(2), 360–385.

Baumgartner, R. J., & Ebner, D. (2010). Corporate sustainability strategies: Sustainability profiles and maturity levels. *Sustainable Development, 18*(2), 76–89.

Bennet, Carl (2022). *Sustainability. Carl Bennet AB*. Accessed January 22, 2022, at: https://www.carlbennetab.se/sv/kort-om-cbab.

Berrone, P., Cruz, C., & Gomez-Mejia, L. (2012). Socioemotional wealth in family firms: Theoretical dimensions, assessment approaches, and agenda for future research. *Family Business Review, 25*(3), 258–279.

Berrone, P., Cruz, C., Gomez-Mejia, L. R., & Larraza-Kintana, M. (2010). Socioemotional wealth and corporate responses to institutional pressures: Do family-controlled firms pollute less? *Administrative Science Quarterly, 55*(1), 82–113.

Bielawska, A. (2021). Social involvement of polish family businesses. *Sustainability, 13*(17), 9484.

Bingham, J. B., Dyer, W. G., Jr., Smith, I., & Adams, G. L. (2011). A stakeholder identity orientation approach to corporate social performance in family firms. *Journal of Business Ethics, 99*(4), 565–585.

Block, J. H., & Wagner, M. (2014). The effect of family ownership on different dimensions of corporate social responsibility: Evidence from large US firms. *Business Strategy and the Environment, 23*(7), 475–492.

Brigham, K. H., Lumpkin, G. T., Payne, G. T., & Zachary, M. A. (2014). Researching long-term orientation: A validation study and recommendations for future research. *Family Business Review, 27*, 72–88.

Brunninge, O., Plate, M. and Ramírez-Pasillas, M. (2020). Family business social responsibility: Is CSR different in family firms? In Härtel, C., Zerbe, W. J. and Ashkanasy, N. M. (Eds.), *Emotions and Service in the Digital Age. Research in Emotions in Organizations Vol. 16* (217–246). UK: Emerald Publishing.

Cabeza-García, L., Sacristán-Navarro, M., & Gómez-Ansón, S. (2017). Family involvement and corporate social responsibility disclosure. *Journal of Family Business Strategy, 8*(2), 109–122.

Cabrera-Suárez, M. K., Déniz-Déniz, M. D. L. C., & Martín-Santana, J. D. (2014). The setting of non-financial goals in the family firm: The influence of family climate and identification. *Journal of Family Business Strategy, 5*(3), 289–299.

Campopiano, G., & De Massis, A. (2015). Corporate social responsibility reporting: A content analysis of family and non-family firms. *Journal of Business Ethics, 129*(3), 511–534.

Campopiano, G., De Massis, A., & Chirico, F. (2014). Firm philanthropy in small and medium-sized family firms: The effects of family involvement in ownership and management. *Family Business Review, 27*(3), 244–258.

Carroll, A., & Buchholtz, A. (2014). *Business and society: Ethics, sustainability, and stakeholder management.* Cengage Learning.

Chouinard, Y. (2005). *Let My People Go Surfing.* Penguin.

Clauß, T., Kraus, S., & Jones, P. (2022). Sustainability in family business: Mechanisms, technologies and business models for achieving economic prosperity, environmental quality and social equity. *Technological Forecasting and Social Change, 176*, 121450.

Cruz, C., Larraza-Kintana, M., Garcés-Galdeano, L., & Berrone, P. (2014). Are family firms really more socially responsible? *Entrepreneurship Theory and Practice, 38*(6), 1295–1316.

De Mendonca, T., & Zhou, Y. (2019). What does targeting ecological sustainability mean for company financial performance? *Business Strategy and the Environment, 28*(8), 1583–1593.

Delmas, M., & Gergaud, O. (2014). Sustainable certification for future generations: The case of family business. *Family Business Review, 27*(3), 228–243.

Discua Cruz, A., Hamilton, E. & Jack, S. L. (2012). Understanding entrepreneurial cultures in family businesses: A study of family entrepreneurial teams in Honduras. *Journal of Family Business Strategy, 3*(3), 147–161.

Dolan, K. A. (2015). *Billion-Dollar bloodlines: America's richest families 2015.* FORBES. Accessed April 27, 2021, at: https://www.forbes.com/family-business/.

Du, X. (2015). Is corporate philanthropy used as environmental misconduct dressing: Evidence from Chinese family-owned firms. *Journal of Business Ethics, 129*(2), 341–361.

Dunphy, D. C., Griffiths, A., & Benn, S. (2003). *Organizational change for corporate sustainability.* Routledge.

Dyer, W. G., & Whetten, D. A. (2006). Family firms and social responsibility: Preliminary evidence from the SandP 500. *Entrepreneurship Theory and Practice, 30*(6), 785–802.

Dyllick, T., & Muff, K. (2016). Clarifying the meaning of sustainable business: Introducing a typology from business-as-usual to true business sustainability. *Organization and Environment, 29*(2), 156–174.

Eccles, R. G., Ioannou, I., & Serafeim, G. (2014). The impact of corporate sustainability on organizational processes and performance. *Management Science, 60*(11), 2835–2857.

Erawati, N. M. A., Hariadi, B., & Saraswati, E. (2021). The role of corporate social responsibility in the investment efficiency: Is it important? *The Journal of Asian Finance, Economics, and Business, 8*(1), 169–178.

Ernst, R-A., Gerken, M., Hack, A. & Hülsbeck, M. (2022). Family firms as agents of sustainable development: A normative perspective. *Technological Forecasting & Social Change, 174*, 121135.

Familjen Kamprads Stiftelse (2022). *Om Familjen Kamprads stiftelse.* Accessed, January 22, 2022, at: https://familjenkampradsstiftelse.se/om-stiftelsen/.

García-Sánchez, I. M., Martín-Moreno, J., Khan, S. A., & Hussain, N. (2021). Socio-emotional wealth and corporate responses to environmental hostility: Are family firms more stakeholder oriented? *Business Strategy Environment, 30*(2), 1003–1018.

Mellby Gård (2022). *Mellby Gård in Brief.* Company Website. Accessed January 22, 2022, at: https://mellby-gaard.se/en/

Gómez-Mejía, L. R., Haynes, K. T., Núnez-Nickel, M., Jacobson, K. J., & Moyano-Fuentes, J. (2007). Socioemotional wealth and business risks in family-controlled firms: Evidence from Spanish olive oil mills. *Administrative Science Quarterly, 52*(1), 106–137.

Habbershon, T. G., & Williams, M. (1999). A resource-based framework for assessing the strategic advantages of family firms. *Family Business Review, 12*(1), 1–25.

Hahn, R., & Lülfs, R. (2014). Legitimizing negative aspects in GRI-oriented sustainability reporting: A qualitative analysis of corporate disclosure strategies. *Journal of Business Ethics, 123*(3), 401–420.

Hahn, T., Preuss, L., Pinkse, J., & Figge, F. (2014). Cognitive frames in corporate sustainability: Managerial sensemaking with paradoxical and business case frames. *Academy of Management Review, 39*(4), 463–487.

Härtel, C., & Pearman, G. I. (2010). Understanding and responding to the climate change issue: Towards a whole-of-science research agenda. *Journal of Management and Organization, 16*(1), 16–47.

Hirigoyen, G., & Poulain-Rehm, T. (2014). The corporate social responsibility of family businesses: An international approach. *International Journal of Financial Studies, 2*(3), 240–265.

Huang, Y.-C., Ding, H.-B., & Kao, M.-R. (2009). Salient stakeholder voices: Family business and green innovation adoption. *Journal of Management and Organization, 15*(3), 309–326.

Inter IKEA (2022). *This is Inter IKEA Group.* Accessed January 22, 2022, at: https://www.inter.ikea.com/en/this-is-inter-ikea-group.

Kallmuenzer, A., Nikolakis, W., Peters, M., & Zanon, J. (2017). Trade-offs between dimensions of sustainability: Exploratory evidence from family firms in rural tourism regions. *Journal of Sustainable Tourism, 26*(7), 1204–1221.

Khanna, T. (2000). Business groups and social welfare in emerging markets: Existing evidence and unanswered questions. *European Economic Review, 44*(4), 748–761.

Kotlar, J., & De Massis, A. (2013). Goal setting in family firms: Goal diversity, social interactions, and collective commitment to family-centered goals. *Entrepreneurship Theory and Practice, 37*(6), 1263–1288.

Lamb, N. H., Butler, F., & Roundy, P. (2017). Family firms and corporate social responsibility: Exploring "concerns." *Journal of Strategy and Management, 10*(4), 469–487.

Landrum, N. E. (2017). Stages of corporate sustainability: Integrating the strong sustainability worldview. *Organization and Environment, 31*(4), 287–313.

Landrum, N. E., & Ohsowski, B. (2018). Identifying worldviews on corporate sustainability: A content analysis of corporate sustainability reports. *Business Strategy and the Environment, 27*(1), 128–151.

Le Breton-Miller, I., & Miller, D. (2006). Why do some family businesses out-compete? Governance, long-term orientations, and sustainable capability. *Entrepreneurship Theory and Practice, 30*(6), 731–746.

Le Breton-Miller, I., & Miller, D. (2016). Family firms and practices of sustainability: A contingency view. *Journal of Family Business Strategy, 7*(1), 26–33.

Lumpkin, G. T. and Bacq, S. (forthcoming). Family business, community embeddedness, and civic wealth creation. *Journal of Family Business Strategy, 13*(2), 100469.

Lungeanu, R., & Weber, K. (2021). Social responsibility beyond the corporate: Executive mental accounting across sectoral and issue domains. *Organization Science, 32*(6), 1473–1491.

Mann, B. and NPR (2021). *The sacklers, who made billions from oxycontin, win immunity from opioid lawsuits.* Accessed January 22, 2022, at: https://www.npr.org/2021/09/01/1031053251/sackler-family-immunity-purdue-pharma-oxycontin-opioid-epidemic?t=1642868833099.

Maon, F., Lindgreen, A., & Swaen, V. (2010). Organizational stages and cultural phases: A critical review and a consolidative model of corporate social responsibility development. *International Journal of Management Reviews, 12*(1), 20–38.

Marques, P., Presas, P., & Simon, A. (2014). The heterogeneity of family firms in CSR engagement: The role of values. *Family Business Review, 27*(3), 206–227.

Martínez-Ferrero, J., Rodríguez-Ariza, L., & García-Sanchez, I. M. (2016). Corporate social responsibility as an entrenchment strategy, with a focus on the implications of family ownership. *Journal of Cleaner Production, 135*, 760–770.

Memili, E., Fang, H. C., Koç, B., Yildirim-Öktem, Ö., & Sonmez, S. (2018). Sustainability practices of family firms: The interplay between family ownership and long-term orientation. *Journal of Sustainable Tourism, 26*(1), 9–28.

Miller, D., & Le Breton-Miller, I. (2005). Management insights from great and struggling family businesses. *Long Range Planning, 38*(6), 517–530.

Miroshnychenko, I., & De Massis, A. (2022). Sustainability practices of family and nonfamily firms: A worldwide study. *Technological Forecasting and Social Change, 174*, 121079.

Miroshnychenko, I., De Massis, A., Barontini, R., & Testa, F. (2022). Family firms and environmental performance: A meta-analytic review. *Family Business Review, 35*(1), 1–23.

Neubauer, F., & Lank, A. (1998). *The family business. Its governance for sustainability.* Macmillan Press.

Neubaum, D. O., Dibrell, C. C., & Craig, J. B. (2012). Balancing natural environmental concerns of internal and external stakeholders in family and non-family businesses. *Journal of Family Business Strategy, 3*(1), 28–37.

Neubaum, D. O., & Micelotta, E. (2021). WANTED–Theoretical contributions: An editorial on the pitfalls and pathways in family business research. *Family Business Review, 34*(3), 242–250.

Neumeyer, X., & Santos, S. C. (2018). Sustainable business models, venture typologies, and entrepreneurial ecosystems: A social network perspective. *Journal of Cleaner Production, 172*, 4565–4579.

Niehm, L. S., Swinney, J., & Miller, N. J. (2008). Community social responsibility and its consequences for family business performance. *Journal of Small Business Management, 46*(3), 331–350.

Núñez-Cacho, P., Molina-Moreno, V., Corpas-Iglesias, F. A., & Cortés-García, F. J. (2018). Family businesses transitioning to a circular economy model: The case of "Mercadona". *Sustainability, 10*(2), 538.

O'Hagan, S. (2022). *Patrick Radden Keefe on exposing the Sackler family's links to the opioid crisis.* Accessed February 29, 2022.

Panicker, V. S. (2017). Ownership and corporate social responsibility in Indian firms. *Social Responsibility Journal, 13*(4), 714–727.

Patagonia (2022). *Regenerative organic certification.* Accessed at January 22, 2022, at: https://www.patagonia.com/our-footprint/regenerative-organic-certifica tion.html.

Pittino, D., Visintin, F., Lenger, T., & Sternad, D. (2016). Are high performance work practices really necessary in family SMEs? An analysis of the impact on employee retention. *Journal of Family Business Strategy, 7*(2), 75–89.

Pratono, A. H., & Han, L. (2021). From family business orientation to organisational citizenship behaviour: Prosocial behaviour in family business performance. *Journal of Family Business Management.* https://doi.org/print.doi:10.1108/JFBM-02-2021-0014

Radden Keefe, P. (2017). *The family that built an empire of pain: The sackler dynasty's ruthless marketing of painkillers has generated billions of dollars—and millions of addicts.* Accessed January 22, 2022: https://www.newyorker.com/magazine/2017/10/30/the-family-that-built-an-empire-of-pain.

Raitis, J., Sasaki, I., & Kotlar, J. (2021). System-spanning values work and entrepreneurial growth in family firms. *Journal of Management Studies, 58*(1), 104–134.

Ramirez-Pasillas, M. and Lundberg, H. (2019). Corporate social venturing: An agenda for researching the social dimension of corporate venturing by family-owned businesses. In: J. M. Saiz-Alvarez and J. M. Palma Ruiz (Ed.), *Handbook of research on entrepreneurial leadership and competitive strategy in family business* (173–192). Hershey: IGI Global.

Ramírez-Pasillas, M. and Nordqvist, M. (2021). Because family cares: Building engagement for family entrepreneurship through sustainability. In Allen, M. and Gartner, W. (Eds.), *Family entrepreneurship: Insights from leading experts on successful multi-generational entrepreneurial families* (315–329). Switzerland: Springer Nature.

Randerson, K. (2022). Conceptualizing family business social responsibility. *Technological Forecasting and Social Change, 174*, 121225.

Rautiainen, M. (2012). *Dynamic ownership in family business systems—A portfolio approach.* Dissertation, Acta universitatis Lappeenrantaensis 485, Lappeenranta University of Technology.

Rautiainen, M., Rosa, P., Pihkala, T., Parada, M. J., and Cruz, A. D. (2019). The family business group phenomenon. *Sl]: Springer International Publishing*.

Raworth, K. (2017). *Doughnut economics: 7 ways to think like a 21st-Century economist.* Chelsea Green Publishing.

Rees, W., & Rodionova, T. (2015). The influence of family ownership on corporate social responsibility: An international analysis of publicly listed companies. *Corporate Governance: An International Review, 23*(3), 184–202.

Reficco, E. A., & Ogliastri, E. (2009). Business and Society in Latin America: An Introduction (Empresa y Sociedad en América Latina). *Academia Revista Latinoamericana De Administración, 43*, 1–25.

Ripple, W., Wolf, C., Newsome, T., Barnard, P., Moomaw, W., & Grandcolas, P. (2019). World scientists' warning of a climate emergency. *BioScience, 70*(1), 8–12.

Rivo-López, E., Villanueva-Villar, M., Michinel-Álvarez, M., & Reyes-Santías, F. (2021). Corporate social responsibility and family business in the time of COVID-19: Changing strategy? *Sustainability, 13*(4), 2041.

Rockström, J., Steffen, W., Noone, K., Persson, Å., Chapin, F. S., III., Lambin, E. F., et al. (2009a). A safe operating space for humanity. *Nature, 461*, 472–475.

Rockström, J., Steffen, W., Noone, K., Persson, Å., Chapin, F.S., Lambin, E.F., Lenton, T.M., Scheffer, M., Folke, C., Schellnhuber, H.J., Nykvist, B., de Wit, C.A., Hughes, T., van der Leeuw, S., Rodhe, H., Sörlin, S., Snyder, P.K., Costanza, R., Svedin, U., Falkenmark, M., Karlberg, L., Corell, R.W., Fabry, V.J., Hansen, J., Walker, B., Liverman, D., Richardson, K., Crutzen, P., Foley, J.A.(2009b): A safe operating space for humanity. *Nature, 461*. 7263. 472–475. https://doi.org/10.1038/461472a.

Samara, G., Sierra, V., & Parada, M. (2018). Who are the best performers? The environmental social performance of family firms. *Journal of Family Business Strategy, 9*(1), 33–43.

Scott, M., & Rosa, P. (1999). Entrepreneurial diversification business cluster formation and growth. *Environment and Planning C, 17*(5), 527–547.

Sharma, P., & Sharma, S. (2019). The role of family firms in corporate sustainability. In A. Sturdy, S. Heusinkveld, T. Reay, & D. Strang (Eds.), *The Oxford Handbook of Management Ideas* (pp. 1–18). Oxford University Press.

Sharma, P., & Sharma, S. (2021). Pioneering business families committed to sustainable development. In P. Sharma & S. Sharma (Eds.), *Pioneering Family Firms' Sustainable Development Strategies* (pp. 1–50). Edward Elgar Publishing.

Sukitsch, M., Engert, S., & Baumgartner, R. J. (2015). The implementation of corporate sustainability in the European automotive industry: An analysis of sustainability reports. *Sustainability, 7*(9), 11504–11531.

Svensson, A. (2021). *Finansklanerna—Bennet*. Accessed January 22, 2022, at: https://15familjer.zaramis.se/2021/05/08/finansklanerna-bennet/#:~:text= Dan%20Frohm%2C%20gift%20med%20Anna,%C3%A4r%20bosatta%20i% 20New%20York.andtext=Tankesmedjan%20Katalys%20har%20uppskattat% 20det,f%C3%B6rm%C3%B6genhet%20till%20omkring%2060%20miljarder.

Uhlaner, L. M., Van Goor-Balk, H. J. M., & Masurel, E. (2004). Family business and corporate social responsibility in a sample of Dutch firms. *Journal of Small Business and Enterprise Development, 11*(2), 186–194.

Van Gils, A., Dibrell, C., Neubaum, D. O., & Craig, J. B. (2014). Social issues in the family enterprise. *Family Business Review, 27*(3), 193–205.

Van Marrewijk, M. (2003). Concepts and definitions of CSR and corporate sustainability: Between agency and communion. *Journal of Business Ethics, 44*(2), 95–105.

van Zanten, J. A., & van Tulder, R. (2018). Multinational enterprises and the sustainable development goals: An institutional approach to corporate engagement. *Journal of International Business Policy, 1*(3–4), 208–233.

van Zanten, J. A., & van Tulder, R. (2021). Analyzing companies' interactions with the Sustainable Development Goals through network analysis: Four corporate sustainability imperatives. *Business Strategy and the Environment, 30*(5), 2396–2420.

Wang-Erlandsson, L., Tobian, A., van der Ent, R. J., et al. (2022). A planetary boundary for green water. *Nature Reviews Earth & Environment*. https://doi.org/10.1038/s43017-022-00287-8

Whiteman, G., Walker, B., & Perego, P. (2013). Planetary boundaries: Ecological foundations for corporate sustainability. *Journal of Management Studies, 50*(2), 207–336.

World Commission on Environment and Development. (1987). *Our Common Future*. Oxford University Press.

Yang, A., Uysal, N., & Taylor, M. (2018). Unleashing the power of networks: Shareholder activism, sustainable development and corporate environmental policy. *Business Strategy and the Environment, 27*(6), 712–727.

18

Socioemotional Wealth and the Development of Family Business Group

Dony Abdul Chalid and Mira Kartika Dewi Djunaedi

Introduction

Through diversification, a Family Business Group might be seen as a collection of minor businesses. However, little is known about how an FBG emerges and develops. An FBG is made up of numerous different types of businesses that are owned by the same family (Granovetter, 2010; Mukherjee et al., 2019). The purpose of FBGs is to maximize founder goals while maintaining long-term profitability (Piana et al., 2012). Such objectives are set by the founders and serve as the foundation for the creation of an FBG and its strategic decisions and behaviors. The founders' ideals, vision, and experience during their entrepreneurship might be the aims that will be passed down to future generations.

The concept of socioemotional wealth (SEW) can be used to track the emergence and evolution of an FBG. SEW is defined as a family's "affective endowment" (Gómez-Mejia et al., 2011, p. 654), that is, the non-economic,

---

D. A. Chalid
Faculty of Economics and Business, Universitas Indonesia, Depok, Indonesia

M. K. D. Djunaedi (✉)
Faculty of Economics and Business, Universitas Esa Unggul, Jakarta, Indonesia
e-mail: mira.kartika@esaunggul.ac.id

© The Author(s), under exclusive license to Springer Nature Switzerland AG 2023
M. Rautianen et al. (eds.), *The Palgrave Handbook of Managing Family Business Groups*, https://doi.org/10.1007/978-3-031-13206-3_18

affective utilities or values that a family derives from its ownership position in a particular firm (Berrone et al., 2012; Gómez-Mejia et al., 2007, 2010). SEW is anchored at a deep psychological level among family owners whose identities are inextricably linked to the organization (Berrone et al., 2010, p. 87). As a result an FBG's SEW and its priorities can be derived from its founder's life experiences and values. SEW of FBGs varies (Daspit et al., 2021), with various priorities (Debicki et al., 2016). In the family business literature, the SEW approach has been identified as a possible dominant paradigm (Berrone et al., 2012). SEW is a concept that summarizes a family's affective value gained from a firm (Berrone et al., 2010, p. 82; Gómez-Mejia et al., 2010) rather than just economic ones (Gómez-Mejia et al., 2010; Jones et al., 2008).

Berrone et al. (2012) proposed a theoretical dimension of SEW called "FIBER dimensions," which is derived from the SEW model of Gómez-Mejia et al. (2007), considering that many researchers use this dimension framework to generate empirical evidence in their publications.

An FBG can emerge and evolve in a variety of ways. Rautiainen and Pihkala (2019), for example, believe that an FBG can arise and evolve from portfolio entrepreneurship. An entrepreneur creates, owns, and manages multiple businesses at the same time. Portfolio entrepreneurship is a way to lower business risk (Rautiainen & Pihkala, 2019). We propose in this chapter that the creation and development of an FBG can be influenced by the founders' experiences, critical events, and past, which shape their SEW and priorities. Although numerous studies on SEW in family businesses have been conducted, research on SEW in FBG is still limited.

The purpose of this study is to examine the dynamics of SEW in FBG and how SEW impacts the strategy decisions and development of family firms into medium-sized business groups. None has examined the evolution of FBG in connection with SEW. First, we wish to investigate how family experience shapes their SEW and classify it according to the FIBER dimension for two medium-sized FBGs. We are specifically comparing the SEW and its importance between generations of the two families based on their FIBER dimensions. Research on SEW across time is still limited. For example, Cleary et al. (2019) investigated the presence of the SEW dimension using FIBER on corporate disclosure using longitudinal content analysis. They found that FIBER dimensions are present in the chairman's statement of two Irish family breweries and change over time. Importantly, SEW develops within next-generation family members, and they desire to preserve and protect it, as it influences decisions that they make in life (Murphy et al., 2019). The influences of next-generation family members' life paths will influence the strategic and business decisions they make in the FBG. One issue has been raised in search of the SEW dimension. The issue is the derivation of SEW from several sources and its origin (Kalm & Gómez-Mejia, 2016; Murphy et al., 2019) including cross-country differences of the origin and development of SEW (Jaskiewicz & Dyer, 2017; Murphy et al., 2019).

Second, we would like to examine the heterogeneity of FBG in SEW that serve as a reference point for the development of FBGs. Numerous studies have examined how a family's condition or dynamics affect the heterogeneity of FBG (see, for example, Bertrand et al., 2008; Karaevli & Yurtoglu, 2018; Terlaak et al., 2018). In developing the SEW approach, numerous researchers have used the SEW framework to explain the heterogeneity of FBGs. We would like to examine whether family firms with different SEW conditions have different approaches to the development of FBGs.

Although family businesses are prevalent in Asia, research on family businesses using data from Asian countries is still limited in comparison to other regions, such as the United States or Europe (Teixeira et al., 2020). In addition, our data are considered valuable and rich because information about FBG is difficult to obtain, particularly in Indonesia's private, closed FBGs. We conducted interviews with two medium-sized Chinese family businesses in Indonesia. We interviewed founders and subsequent generations about their family experiences, including their desire to own and run the FBG. We employed a narrative approach to examine SEW and its effect on the development of FBGs. The remainder of the chapter is organized as follows. We begin with a review of the literature, focusing on SEW and their relationship to the FBG. Next, the chapter explains the two FBGs that we used as the cases for this study, and our findings are presented using a narrative approach. The discussion is then built around the findings, and we conclude with concluding remarks.

FBG and Socioemotional Wealth

Most literature assumes that FBG evolvement is due to diversification. However, how small family firms or entrepreneurship grow into medium-sized or large FBG is unknown. An FBG can vary from one sector to another, from a larger to a smaller one (Rosa et al., 2019), and from dominant ownership to disperse ownership and types of generations that owned the FBGs. FBGs are always assumed to be similar with regard to their preferences for pursuing SEW (Daspit et al., 2021; Prügl, 2019). Examining the variation of

SEW across FBG is limited and challenging (Daspit et al., 2021). Furthermore, an understanding of how SEWs are related to FBG emergence and evolvement across generations is lacking. Previous research on family businesses, such as Filser et al. (2018), Schepers et al. (2014), and Goel et al. (2013), showed that SEW varies among family businesses.

The understanding of FBGs and their emergence and development, including their heterogeneity and priorities across generations, can be viewed from the SEW perspective. One of the most significant developments in the family business literature is the concept of SEW, which is primarily founded on the seminal work of Gómez-Mejia et al. (2007). As SEW is founded at a deep psychological level in family members (Berrone et al., 2012; Murphy et al., 2019) and influences firm behavior (Debicki et al., 2016), we should recognize that SEW can emerge from the founders' life history in establishing the family firms that shape the family business's affective value, non-economic goals, and even the psychological states that serve as the reference point for the family business decision under risk (Jiang et al., 2018).

Existing research has indicated that family businesses accept lower stock valuations in exchange for retaining family control during initial public offerings (Leitterstorf & Rau, 2014), and that family businesses avoid acquisitions that jeopardize family control, routines, and values (Miller et al., 2010). According to Gómez-Mejia et al. (2007), family firms seek to protect elements central to their SEW, such as reputation, relationships, and social capital, and these preferences can be expressed through family owners' investment decisions. Gu et al. (2019) examined how controlling owners' family considerations affect their new industry entry decisions in FBGs in emerging economies using a sample of 101 distinct Taiwanese business groups over a 20-year period (1980–2000). They discovered that although the exercise of family influence (a representative of the focused SEW) has a negative effect on controlling owners' likelihood of entering new industries, the pursuit of new industry entry has a positive effect on the succession of the family dynasty (a typical form of the broad SEW). In addition, they discovered that the effects of SEW preservation on such decisions are generational dependent, with the effects being stronger when the founder generation is in control. Moreover, according to Naldi et al. (2013), preserving SEW is either an asset or a liability in family-controlled businesses. They discovered that it is an asset in business contexts, such as industrial districts, where tacit rules and social norms take precedence, but is a potential liability in contexts, such as stock exchange markets, where formal regulations and transparency principles take precedence.

Berrone et al.'s (2012) paper on FIBER dimensions is widely regarded in the family business literature. However, one of the proposed FIBER's shortcomings is its inability to quantify the SEW associated with its construct. From the family influence and control dimension, the family ownership construct is the simplest to quantify. Furthermore, latent variables are required to quantify the remaining FIBER dimensions' constructs. Unresolved issues regarding the relationship between multidimensional FIBER dimension constructs also occur (Brigham & Payne, 2019). Debicki et al. (2016) contributed to the field of family business literature by emphasizing the importance of SEW constructs. Debicki et al. (2016) demonstrated how differences in SEW importance can result in disparate strategic behaviors among family firms. Different families have a wide range of goals and aspirations, both short-term and long-term. According to Debicki et al. (2016), discernible differences should occur among family firms in terms of the importance of SEW in relation to the FBG's strategic decisions regarding diversification.

Case Studies

Both FBGs are medium-sized businesses that operate in Indonesia. The founders of both families are Chinese descendants who migrated to Indonesia. In-depth interviews with open-ended questions were conducted in 2013. After Mr. Pan's passing, we held interviews for the second generation of Mr. Pan in January 2020. However, following Mr. Fan's death, we were unable to interview his family. The founders and their second generation are among the participants. For the case study analysis, we used two case studies with narrative approaches (Hamilton et al., 2017).

Case 1: Mr. Pan FBG

In 1957, the Pan siblings founded a small trade chemical company in Surabaya. In 1973, Mr. Pan joined this company and acquired a minor stake in the business. Mr. Pan was in charge of the Jakarta branch and was successful in expanding it. In 1982, however, his older brother decided to leave the business by selling all of its assets and dividing the proceeds among his siblings. Mr. Pan was unhappy with the disaggregation of the company. After this happened, Mr. Pan still worked with his brother, but they had many fights with him (Fig. 18.1).

Due to a series of disappointing experiences and his dire financial circumstances, Mr. Pan decided it was time to leave his brother's company for good and launch his own chemical industry business in 1988. Mr. Pan secured his bank loans with his entire estate, including his home. After working hard for two years, he was able to get his house back and use a warehouse he had bought as collateral instead.

Mr. Pan suffers from an incurable illness that affects his health and hinders his ability to run the business. He required a survival plan for the family business. Due to his illness, Mr. Pan decided in 1983 to purchase land, apartments, and warehouses for his family and use them as the capital for future business expansion. Mr. Pan meticulously plans all of these investments to ensure the future well-being and wealth of his descendants, avoid the disregard of others, and, of course, enhance the family name and his own reputation. He saw future opportunities for land acquisition. The most secure and low-risk way for him to invest his money is in land and property. Even if the land's value doesn't go up very much in the future, he won't lose any money.

Mr. Pan established their new permanent and official headquarters in the heart of Jakarta in 2013 and plans to construct warehouses for rent on his several hectares of land. Mr. Pan also owns several additional hectares of land, which he plans to leave to his son for development. In addition to his chemical business, Mr. Pan's land and real estate investments during his time in office will become the Pan property family business.

During the second generation, they emphasized the reputation of their founder. The second generation claims they have no reason to compete with their cousins because they are not engaged in any conflict. The second generation, on the other hand, asserts that they must preserve and grow the family business in order to avoid the disgrace of other families toward their family and to earn the respect of others through positive impacts. The Pan family owned 100 percent of their chemical and logistics businesses but only a minority stake in their heavy equipment company, which was a joint venture with a second-generation family friend.

Following the death of the company's founder in 2018 and under the direction of the second generation, the company diversified beyond the chemical industry. The family's chemical business has expanded to include industrial chemicals and personal care products in addition to general chemicals. The logistics division of the chemical company has been spun off into a separate entity that owns trucks able to transport chemicals and provide services in PLB. A PLB is a warehouse where goods from other countries

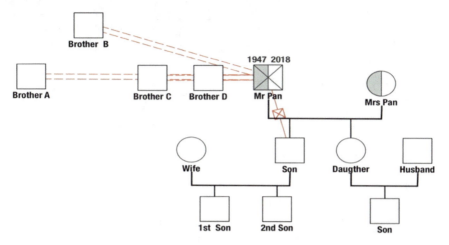

Fig. 18.1 Pan family genogram (*Note* The Genogram of the Pan Family illustrates the Pans' primary family tree and the emotional bonds between Pan's siblings during their formative years. The red dashes represent sibling rivalry. Conflicts between Pan's siblings began when Brother B decided to leave the family businesses founded by Pan's brothers. There were no conflicts with Pan's sister because they were not affiliated with the family businesses. Mr. Pan exercised indirect control over his son as CEO for the duration of his life to ensure that his son's decisions regarding the family business did not significantly increase the firm's survival risk. Mrs. Pan inherited the majority of the company after Mr. Pan's death, but she had no influence in how her son ran the family businesses

that come from a certain area regulated by the government and are subject to certain import tariffs are kept (Fig. 18.2).

The warehouses are the result of Mr. Pan's lifetime of real estate investment. PLB receives warehouse space, import tax clearance, and transportation services from the logistics company. When the owners of the heavy equipment company decide to construct PLB warehouses, heavy equipment is required to support the PLB warehouses. However, the second generation believed that it was more cost-effective to purchase heavy equipment from wholesalers. In 2016, the second generation decides to enter the heavy equipment industry in partnership with friends. The second generation will establish a holding company in Singapore in the future. This was the intention of the company's founder, and the second generation recognized the tax advantages. The plan also depends on the fact that the Indonesian government wants investment from other countries.

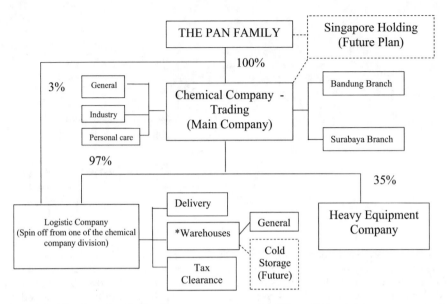

Fig. 18.2 The Pan family business group structure (*Note* *Warehouses are part of the real estate industry. The majority of the shares are owned by the father [Mr. Pan]. The founder held a 3% stake in the logistics company prior to his passing. It is now in the son's possession. Two friends own the remaining 65% of Heavy Equipment Company, with each owning 35% and 30%. Following Mr. Pan's demise, the majority of the shares pass to his widow. It is not permitted for in-laws to own stock)

Case 2: Mr. Fan FBG

Mr. Fan was an expert at spotting opportunities when it came to expanding his business and believes that timing is everything. Prior to establishing his first business, Mr. Fan foresaw the possibility of renting cranes to ships so they could move their cargo and anchor in a harbor. He successfully rents the crane from his friend, who owns it, to the ship captain. The profits are split between him and his companion. Mr. Fan uses his earnings to purchase a Bemo, a small transport vehicle (autorickshaw). He earns money by operating the Bemo with his wife's assistance. Consequently, he views the demand for wood in the construction industry as an opportunity. Due to the island's prohibition on wood cutting, Mr. Fan traveled to Borneo to sell his Bemo in order to ship wood to the island. This is where Mr. Fan became wealthy. Mr. Fan then grows his business by buying wood and starting a construction company (Fig. 18.3).

Mr. Fan believes he can generate revenue for the family business by utilizing his stewardship behavior. In 1971, he began expanding the company's customer base by assisting struggling business owners in regaining

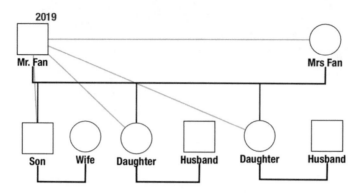

Fig. 18.3 Fan family genogram (*Note* The Fan family did not experience any intrafamily conflict. Throughout our interviews, the family attempted to align the vision of the family business with stewardship values)

their footing, regardless of profit. Mr. Fan has always prioritized giving back to the community when it comes to real estate. Mr. Fan constructs gardens, whereas others with such a large parcel of land construct hotels for profit. Mr. Fan also owns a company that manages two expansive gardens that serve as wedding, corporate, and special event venues. Mr. Fan, a plant and nature enthusiast with a conservationist heart, envisioned the gardens in 2008. Mr. Fan established an international training and development center in 2013 to provide professional training to disadvantaged individuals who are unable to continue their education. Mr. Fan wants to train people on the beautiful island where he lives to be competitive so that they can take care of the island's natural resources, cultural heritage, and history in the future.

The majority of Mr. Fan's family businesses were under his control, but he was never involved in their management. On the basis of trust, he hired professionals for public and trusted companies and gave them the authority to set their own compensation and manage the business. Mr. Fan has always stated that he is unconcerned with the profitability of his company and prefers to leave business operations to the experts. Before Mr. Fan receives his share of the company's profits, he shares them with the professionals. Additionally, Mr. Fan is prudent with his employees. Always concerned with the welfare of his employees, he ensures that their salaries are sufficient to support their families. If not, Mr. Fan will increase their pay. In return, his employees feel more loyalty and a sense of belonging, which makes them work harder and, indirectly, brings in more money.

Mr. Fan was initially unaware that his company had the potential to become quite large. However, Mr. Fan occasionally considers what he hopes to discover in this life. His wife also questions the meaning of his existence.

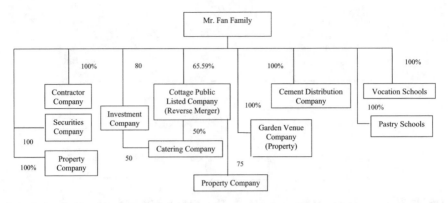

Fig. 18.4 Mr. Fan family business group structure (*Notes* The ownership of Cottage public company is as per 2012. There is a dilution of Fan family ownership after 2012, but the Fan family is still the ultimate shareholder. We suspect there is more than one company under Mr. Fan Business Group. Due to a lack of information, the picture of the family business group is based on interviews done before the founder died and documents.)

He decided to invest his wealth via private banking. Despite this, he incurs losses. Then, Mr. Fan decided to invest in lands and properties. Since he is a civil engineer and his wife is an architect, he will be able to construct and design on the lands he has purchased in his retirement. Thankfully, properties and lands investing have become wildly profitable. Its value skyrockets. The purpose of his life at the time was not to make money, but to enjoy a peaceful retirement.

He then expanded his business into real estate, cement distribution (1980), training centers, and public listed companies via backdoor listing in 2011, including villas, catering, and city services (Fig. 18.4). The majority of Mr. Fan's businesses have been taken over by professionals, and he has retired while remaining a passive owner. He wields considerable influence over the strategic decisions of the family business. Additionally, he created two beautiful gardens for himself and the community.

Findings

Socioemotional Wealth Heterogeneity

Both families come from impoverished backgrounds, but their experiences in establishing the family business differ greatly. SEW may be better able to account for the diversity of family businesses (Swab et al., 2020). Family history, significant occurrences, and family values all contribute to the SEW distinctions between the two families. SEW distinctions between two families extend to the next generation's experience and significant events during their leadership, as well as to their own family values (Distelberg & Sorenson, 2009). Furthermore, the differences in SEW between the two families influence their decision to diversify as part of their FBG development strategy. We wish to investigate how family experience influences the SEW of two medium-sized FBGs and classify it according to the FIBER dimension.

Family Control and Influence

The first dimension of FIBER is the family control and influence dimension. Even if the firm's performance was jeopardized, the family maintained family control and influence. This may be seen in the two cases when a family member owns the majority of the company. Although the founder or family members prefer to keep their ownership, distinctions in how they control the business are noted.

In the case of Mr. Pan, the founder believes that majority stake is critical because it signifies not only his control over the company but also his authority over his children. Mr. Pan used majority ownership to intervene in the company's critical decisions and to ensure the company's survival. Some of Mr. Pan's ownership and managerial positions were passed down to his children. Family members with limited shares and their positions at the top of management may not accurately reflect the true family control and influence dimension. Although their position in top management enables them to influence family firms' strategic decisions, their influence is limited if those decisions are not in line with the founder's vision, particularly when the company's stability is threatened. Mr. Pan's control is intended to safeguard the family business's existence.

> Mr. Pan: Until I die, I will retain control of the majority of the shares. I have made a will. To ensure the company's survival, I own the majority of the stock. I am retaining the majority of the shares for a variety of reasons. They are unaware of their parents' hardship in establishing a family business. I was extremely poor and have difficulty earning money. It is important for me to maintain the company, as we cannot afford to be poor and are unable to combat poverty in the manner in which I once did. Additionally, due to my health condition, it is physically impossible for me to repeat the process. Second, while some children are exceptionally obedient, others are not. Nowadays, they outnumber the former significantly.

Mr. Pan's concern is about his children's obedience to him and his wife. Mr. Pan is concerned that once his children have taken over the control of the family business, they will be unconcerned with their parents' well-being.

> Mr. Pan: I've heard stories about parents selling their possessions to pay for their children's international education. When children achieve success, they demonstrate little concern for the well-being of their parents. Another example is a wealthy father who transfers the majority of his company's stock to his children. Finally, the father must rely on the income generated by the children, but the children who have successfully run the firm do not provide enough income to support the father. I do not wish to transfer all of my shares to my son. It is acceptable for me to release my share if my son is obedient, but I would prefer to retain the shares until my death if he is disobedient to us. To ensure my wife's security as a parent, I intend to leave the majority of my ownership to her and the remainder to my children when I die.

Mr. Pan has communicated to his children that their son is not permitted to leave the company, but their daughter may, if she desires. If the daughter wishes to exit the business, she cannot take the majority of the shares. She is only permitted to acquire a small percentage of the company's stock. Mr. Pan also stipulates that if the daughter leaves the company, the son is responsible for ensuring that his sister does not suffer impoverishment but may miss out on privileges she enjoyed when she joined the company.

Mr. Pan had drafted a will specifying the distribution of his estate to his wife and children. His will outline in detail and with care who would receive his inheritance if one of the family members died first. It states that each family member receives a certain percentage of their wealth in their will. Mr. Pan controlled the majority share of the company. Mr. Pan is pleased to hand over the chemicals and, eventually, the property business to the children once they have gained sufficient experience.

A different situation was found in the second case. Mr. Fan, as a founder, also dominantly controlled the family firm's ownership, but the ownership was to fulfill and maintain his stewardship behavior. Although Mr. Fan dominantly holds ownership, he delegates the management of the company to professionals. He does not concern himself about the firms' performance and will treat company losses according to God's will. Mr. Fan still owned majority ownership because he is concerned about the value that he has in the company. Mr. Fan has a more significant affective value or non-economic objective than the family control and influence dimension of SEW. With control, he is able to influence the employee's value and action.

Mr. Fan: I was raised Catholic and believe that God bestows wealth and fortune on us. If I am defrauded by others, I will pray to God and accept the loss as God's will. And if I am trusted with a business opportunity, I will act in accordance with God's will. I truly believe that God has predetermined whether we will be successful or not, aside from the fact that we must exert effort and work. Profit is not my primary objective when conducting business. What matters is how we conduct business properly. And my first priority is to assist those in need and to foster community. I am overjoyed if I am required by another. Finally, I have my own philosophy: I want to live a meaningful life and help others live meaningful lives.

Mr. Fan hired professionals for public and trust companies on the basis of trust and empowered them to set their own compensation and manage the business. Mr. Fan has always stated that he is unconcerned about his company's profit and prefers to leave business operations to professionals. Mr. Fan even shared the company's profits with the professionals. Mr. Fan is always concerned about his employees' well-being and ensures that their wages are sufficient to support their families. If not, Mr. Fan will raise their pay. In exchange, his employees develop a sense of loyalty and belonging, which results in increased employee productivity and, indirectly, increased profits.

The professional: Mr. Fan believes in a principle of 'you reap what you sow.' He is convinced that God will look after him. If he suffers a loss in one location, he will profit in another business opportunity.

Identification of Family Members with the Firm

The second aspect of the FIBER dimension is the identification of family firms with the firm, where the two families saw the success of the family firms as their self-reflection or achievement. The accomplishments of the family business are the accomplishments of the founders.

Mr. Pan's life journey in building and preserving his family business is the driving force behind his desire to continue expanding his family business assets. Mr. Pan's reputation serves to compensate for his negative emotions. Mr. Pan established his reputation by successfully establishing his own family businesses and increasing his family net assets through diversification of his businesses. The image of success is used to demonstrate himself and increase his confidence (Haslam & Ellemers, 2005). Mr. Pan wanted to show that he could achieve the same level of success as his brothers and earn their respect.

Mr. Pan: I was mentally exhausted, recalling how I expanded the Jakarta branch beyond the Surabaya office, establishing it as the business's headquarters. However, I was willing to assist my brothers once more, believing that brothers should assist one another. However, they disappointed me for the second time. My brothers are constantly interfering with my decisions. And I am rewarded with the tiniest shards of wealth. I feel unappreciated and treated unfairly.

Through his experience, Mr. Pan has a point of view involving his family members. The family members see the family firm as their sources of living for the family, in which they need to preserve the family firm's survivability through the growth of the family business group. The reputation of the Pan family is impacted by the family business group's capacity to survive. Others can't label them as a poor family.

Mr. Pan's daughter: For the legacy, my father brainwashed us into believing that this company originated from his empty hands, so do not squander it. It is an honor that this business will be passed on to the next generation. We must maintain the business, but as directed by our father, we must expand it. This is the primary objective, but the secondary objective is to ensure the welfare of others. Although our business is small, we have begun to provide benefits to our employees, such as education and employee loans. Thirdly, there is the issue of our third generation. If the business is merely a trading company, our children may be hesitant to return and work for the family business. They may prefer to work somewhere else that offers better pay and benefits. We need something to entice the children to return, and the business must evolve into something that will attract the third generation to join.

Nevertheless, the second generation is motivated differently than the first generation in terms of growing their family businesses. While the second generation continues to grow their family businesses, they strive to make a positive impact on the lives of others through their family businesses. For instance, recruiting additional employees enables employers to provide for their employees' welfare. This is one of the reasons they need to expand the firm to secure the resources necessary to sustain such a positive impact. Mr. Pan's son has considered how to persuade the third generation to join the family business after they graduate. He asserted that the family needs to do something to entice the third generation to join the family business, which is to grow it beyond a simple and small trading company.

Similarly, Mr. Fan also thinks the performance of the firm is the reflection of his self-performance. However, Mr. Fan emphasized reputation as the most important factor within family and his FBG. Mr. Fan also wanted to show his philanthropist side.

> Mr. Fan: My reputation is non-negotiable. As human beings, we require principles in our lives. The critical point is that we must believe in God. We must live according to God's will. If it is not within our rights, then do not touch it, especially if it is within the rights of another. We must also be fair in business. I will not accept a business plan that is not suitable. For instance, I was offered the opportunity to profit from the construction of a hospital. I decline the opportunity, knowing that the purpose of building a hospital is not for profit.

Mr. Fan has always placed an emphasis on giving back to society, which identifies him as a steward, for instance, in the management of a company's real estate. While others with such a large piece of land constructed hotels for profit, Mr. Fan constructed gardens in 2008. His philanthropist behavior is shared by his employees and professionals.

> "The professionals: Mr. Fan owns a sizable piece of land surrounded by hotels. Others may believe that Mr. Fan should profit from the land property by developing hotels. Rather than that, he constructed two massive gardens that serve as event and wedding venues. Mr. Fan informed me that he had no reason to construct a hotel. He stated that there would be no differences between him and other hotel owners. If I build a hotel, I am just another ordinary businessman with an ordinary view. When he built the gardens, Mr. Fan designed and purchased all of the trees, gazebos, and other features. Until now, the garden's revenue from renting the venue does not cover the cost of maintenance, as he is not in it for the money, but for the enjoyment of his hobby. However, I now understand that the land value will increase significantly, even if the gardens lose money."

Binding Social Ties

The third dimension of FIBER is binding social ties. Between the two FBGs are considerable variances. In Case 1, Mr. Pan is more concerned with the growth and survival of his family business than with stakeholders. Although this does not rule out the possibility of Mr. Pan's family business having social ties to the communities or stakeholders, Mr. Pan did not prioritize social ties as one of their FBG achievements. As previously stated, Mr. Pan focused on growing the family business to improve the welfare of his internal family members.

Mr. Pan's children will continue his father's vision but have a different set of goals. According to Mr. Pan's daughters, although the son shares the founder's vision of expanding and growing the family business, he has slightly different goals based on his Christian values. For the son, maximizing his ability enables him to pursue his own objectives and ideas.

Mr. Pan's daughter: My brother is not competing against others, but against himself. He is putting himself under duress. He is testing himself because he is aware of our father's expectations. As a result, he is pushing himself to live up to the expectations. He is competing against his own capability and his ability to achieve beyond it. My brother is aware of his potential and wishes to maximize it. This is how he can earn his satisfaction, which is consistent with his religious values. Christian doctrine teaches that you were created for a specific purpose and that God provides us with the means to accomplish that purpose. As a result, my brother's hypothesis is that if my father has provided me with such enormous funds and capital, what can I do with it in the future? As a result, he is opposing that notion. It is as if he wishes to maximize his talent and ability in order to ensure that he is not here in vain. Additionally, we have our own Christian value, which is that the means to an end should not be justified. My brother wishes to make a positive impact on others by demonstrating that a family business can be successful without resorting to bribery, cheating, or other practices that are not permitted in the Christian way. If we wish to grow, we should abstain from such practices. If the family business succeeds, it is a source of pride for the family members to have had a positive impact on others. In other words, set a good example for others to follow.

In Case 2, Mr. Fan's family business places a higher priority on both internal and external stakeholders than the Pan family business does. The Fan family's stewardship actions have had a significant effect on stakeholders, society, and the community. In addition, the Fan family's emphasis on strong social ties influences the type of business in which the family invests and diversifies. For instance, they selected a troubled business to assist and restore its health to its normal condition.

In the founder stage, Mr. Fan has extended his stewardship behavior toward his employees, customers, community, and society at large. The stewardship value, as a manifestation of binding social ties (Kuttner et al., 2021), becomes the family SEW that Mr. Fan preserves and passes on to the next generation. Mr. Fan believes that by utilizing his stewardship behavior, he can generate revenue for his family business. In 1971, he became the president and director of one company, where he increased the company's customer base by assisting weak entrepreneurs in regaining their business without regard to profit.

> Mr. Fan: Every aspect of life is a choice. My mother taught me to care for the poor, and my father taught me to be disciplined. There was a time when my mother purchased an excessive number of broom sticks, and I inquired as to why. She stated this so the broom vendor would not have to carry an excessive amount of weight. My mother will distribute the broomsticks among her friends. And when she encountered a beggar, she instructed me to bring him home and provide him with clothing and food. And if she meets a sewer cleaner, she will cook for them. My mother always told me that if I became a successful businessman, I should take an interest in and care for the very poor and in need. Since then, I have continued to spread my mother's message. When I moved to an island and met my future wife, we began making monthly donations to more than 17 foundations.

Mr. Fan established an international training and development center in 2013 to provide professional training to the poor who are unable to continue their studies. Mr. Fan wants to raise the human capital of the island where he lives to a competitive level so that it can preserve its natural assets, history, and culture in the future.

> Mr. Fan: I established a training center to assist children who have dropped out of school. The training center is unprofitable. I fund the training center entirely out of my own pocket. I did not charge a rental fee for the use of the training center for a surgery colloquium. And my children begin to whine. They want to create an international school in addition to a training center in order to earn a profit and cover the cost of the building and operations. And I have no objection to my children realizing it.

Emotional Attachment

The fourth dimension of FIBER is emotional attachment. In our case, emotions reflect past experiences that converge to influence and shape the family members' decisions on family business. These personal experiences and the journey toward establishing his family business became the founder's experience, which he will never forget and is inextricably linked to his emotional attachment to his family business.

In Case 1, Mr. Pan showed his emotional experience of struggling to build his family business and still experiencing this negative emotion, sibling conflict, and unfair treatment. Mr. Pan endures two events throughout the family firm's history that serve as turning points in his family firm's decision. However, the first event, and most pertinent to our topic, occurs when internal conflict between Mr. Pan and his siblings generates negative emotions, which in turn influences Mr. Pan's motivations for running his family business. Pelled et al. (1999) asserted that negative emotions associated with family conflicts (Levinson, 1971) can have a detrimental effect on the group's process and dynamics. However, for Mr. Pan, negative emotions were the driving force behind the establishment of his family business. His emotional attachment pervades the family business and fuels his desire to build and expand it through the connection between his past and present selves (Berrone et al., 2012; Kleine et al., 1995). According to Berrone et al. (2012), emotions are not static; however, in Mr. Pan's situation, the negative emotions he experienced remained static. According to his daughter, Mr. Pan was unable to recover from his past experiences. Below is the part where Mr. Pan uses all his energy to build his family business while being driven by his negative emotions:

Mr. Pan: To build this company, I must rely on my capability and intelligence. I am required to borrow money from banks and pledge all of my assets, including my home, as collateral. After two years of tireless effort, I was able to reclaim our home and replace it with a warehouse that I purchased. I worked extremely hard just to keep up with bank interest payments. My health has deteriorated in the four years since I founded my company. I have incurable diseases. My activity has been restricted due to my health conditions, as I cannot afford to be exhausted. I need to devise a strategy for keeping my business afloat, as my wife has no experience running a business. With improved financial circumstances, I decided to scale back the business and wait for my children to continue and expand it after graduating from university. In the meantime, I need to protect and grow my net asset value so that my son, when he is ready, will have sufficient capital to continue growing the family business.

With his illness, the second event, Mr. Pan decided to diversify his family business into a property business by purchasing lands, apartments, and warehouses for his family and to use as capital for future business expansion. Mr. Pan carefully plans all of these investments to ensure the future life and wealth of his descendants, avoid the disregard of others, and, of course, enhance the family name and Mr. Pan's reputation. This is due to the negative emotions that Mr. Pan suffers that drive all the investment decisions that formed the Pan's FBG.

Mr. Pan: I was considering a way out, a way to protect and expand my assets. My wife lacks the experience necessary to run the business. It's challenging for me to run and grow the business in the background. I must consider how to increase the value of my assets until my son and daughter are prepared to take over the business. It is critical for me to grow my assets and business in order to provide a better life for my children. When we are wealthy, it is much easier to ask for assistance than when we are poor. Given the incurability of my illness, the first thing I decided to do was acquire land and property, such as warehouses. I noticed that purchasing a good piece of land could potentially double the value of my asset in the future. I saw future opportunities for land acquisition. Investing in land and property is the most secure and low-risk way for me to invest my money. That is safest route in which I will not lose money, even if the land value does not increase significantly in the future. The second decision I made was to engage in a high-risk investment known as foreign exchange trading. Profits from foreign exchange trading have enabled me to acquire a number of properties.

In Case 2, Mr. Fan has no negative emotional experiences; rather, he views himself as an emotional person who is compassionate toward others. Mr. Fan establishes his own business, the contractor company that he is so passionate about. However, prior to establishing his own business, Mr. Fan was an expert at spotting opportunities and believed in timing when it came to expanding his business. That is also how he accumulated wealth and expanded his family business.

Mr. Fan: If our customers' businesses fail, we must safeguard them. We assist them in overcoming their difficulties and provide funding until their business is restored to health. I will even increase an employee's salary if they believe it is insufficient to support their economic life. And when it comes to professionals, I always allow them to set their own salaries and never reject them. And as a result of my actions, they develop a greater sense of loyalty, honesty, and belonging to family businesses.

Mr. Fan's decisions in running a business are heavily influenced by his stewardship aspect. These include decisions related to behavior toward business partners. This is also known by the professional managers he recruited.

"The Professionals: There is one company that controls the distribution of one cement brand in East Indonesia," the non-family CEO explained. I am astounded to learn that they can send their children to school and improve their lives by selling the cement brand. When Mr. Fan discovers that the agents are having difficulty paying their debts, he does not compel them to pay on time. Rather than that, the company guides these agents and assists them in re-establishing the business's health. The company supplied the products and provided financial assistance to help them reclaim their business. Finally, the agents achieve success. Additionally, the company pays these agents a share of the cement company's profits every six months. Outside of the profits earned by the agents selling the cement, the cement company can transfer millions of rupiah to the agent. Eventually, these agents develop a bond with the cement company. They will promote the company's cement brand over competing brands.

Renewal of Family Bonds Through Dynasty Succession

The fifth dimension of FIBER is the renewal of family bonds through dynasty succession. Both families placed importance on the continuation of the family business. In both cases, we learned during our interviews that the second generation has begun to become involved in the family business. A part of Chinese culture is that the family business is passed down to the children, particularly the first-born son.

In Case 1, Mr. Pan as the founder controlled the majority share of the company. Mr. Pan is pleased to hand over the chemicals and, eventually, the property business to the children once they have gained sufficient experience.

> Mr. Pan: I will eventually release my share. My generation will own the business. As such, it is my intention to plan for my succession to the company. I have relinquished control of the company's operations and empowered my son to lead it and make his own decisions. However, he will not flee from my watchful eye as the company's adviser. And I will retain the majority share of the company's stock. I remain the primary decision maker. And if he makes a decision that jeopardizes the continuation of the family business, I will intervene, and he must follow my decision.

In Mr. Pan's case, he decided to plan his succession earlier due to his illness to preserve the family firms for the sake of his own family's future. Mr. Pan's primary consideration in selecting his heir and transferring ownership is based on Confucian values in China (Yan & Sorenson, 2006). Although the Chinese have migrated overseas and are assimilated into the host country's culture, overseas Chinese families continue to value Confucianism as a source of family values (Yan & Sorenson, 2006). In general, Mr. Pan prioritized the succession of family businesses next to family control and influence. The continuation of the family firm ensures his family's life, wealth, and well-being.

18 Socioemotional Wealth and the Development of ...   479

According to Mr. Pan's daughter, the children were aware of their father's ordeal. In Mr. Pan's entire life, he only recalls negative experiences and fails to see the positive aspects of those experiences that inspired him to become a successful man by overcoming his family's economic hardships by growing his net assets. According to the daughter, the reason for her continued emphasis on increasing net asset value is that, with a sizable net asset, the family can use it as security or collateral for debt expansion.

> Mr. Pan's daughter: My father wishes for the security of his descendants. According to my father, a large company indicates that the business is progressing and that we will not be underestimated by others. My father compares the chemical family business to a bowl of rice that can be used to feed the family. It is the family's cash cow and cannot be destroyed.

Mr. Pan's children agreed that the family has only one goal: to enlarge the family business, which will be passed on to the next generations. Mr. Pan's children have to safeguard the interest of their founder toward their FBG. The family members also have to be united to support their interests. Through unity, family-member conflicts can easily ease.

> Mr. Pan's daughter: We believe that we have a single primary objective: our business must expand, and all family members must remain united. And the reason our business must expand is to increase our family assets. And our score and the family's interest are established. And it is not in my self-interest to pursue my own family welfare. I believe that we have an adequate amount of privilege. The majority of parents desire greater wealth for their children. However, there is no point of satisfaction. And the business will not grow if we continue to embezzle funds for our family's welfare. We must expand our business if we wish to increase our income. This is what I mean by value of responsibility. When the business is profitable, we can pay dividends.

After years of conducting the initial interview with the founder and his children, Mr. Pan passed away in 2018 due to complications with his illness. His wife and two children inherited the family business. However, the majority of the company's shares are owned by his wife, who serves as President Commissioner. However, she lacks discretion over business decisions due to her lack of understanding of the family business's operations. The son has the discretion and authority to direct the family business's future directions.

> The Second Generation (following Mr. Pan's demise): My father is an extremely well-organized individual. He writes the will in such a way that the majority of

the shares end up in the hands of my mother. He has made provisions in his will for share transfers in the event of the death of one or more family members in order to ensure that the company shares remain in the family. However, we do not argue over who will receive how many shares. My father has his own will and discretion regarding the transfer of shares, which we will respect.

The family legacy has been to grow the business and increase family assets. Mr. Pan's motivation is to ensure that his descendants do not suffer or become impoverished, do not waste what he has built in the family business, and must survive to succeeding generations. For the second generation, they will carry on the family legacy by increasing family assets annually and sustaining the family business for future generations. However, avoiding generations of suffering and impoverishment is no longer a reason for the second generation to expand the family business. The second generation believes that they have sufficient resources to support their families. Their daughter claims that they are educated not to be consumptive individuals and are not required to live a very wealthy lifestyle.

In Case 1, the founder lets his son learn how to run his family business independently before transferring ownership to him. This is different from what is happening in Case 2. Mr. Fan wants to ensure that his son is capable and knowledgeable about the family business. As a result, Mr. Fan enlisted their children's help in the family business, allowing them to gain experience and learn how to run it.

The generation gap between Mr. Fan and his children is the inability of his children to follow his vision. According to Mr. Fan, the generation gap occurs because he is more emotional, whereas the second generation is more realistic. The reason for this is that Mr. Fan builds his business and family wealth from nothing into something. Further, he also sees a lot of other people's weaknesses and intends to help them. Such an intention is bigger than thinking about his business profits. In other words, helping others is more important than just looking for profit.

> Mr. Fan: In my opinion, my children is being realistic, but I am more of an emotional type of person. Because I have start from nothing, I grow and I developed. I used to be an activist and see a lot of people's weaknesses. And I have the intention to help them. My intention to help the needy is bigger than my business. I want to fix future generations. This is my importance rather than looking for a profit.

Mr. Fan's succession was still unplanned at the time of our interview. Mr. Fan has not yet decided on his successors, even though he has incorporated his son and daughters into the family business. The second generation struggled to live up to Mr. Fan's philanthropic reputation. In particular, the second generation struggles to adhere to Mr. Fan's principle of ideal or pure stewardship.

> Second generation: Profitability is always a secondary concern for our business. My father's principle is that money will find us if we follow societal and religious norms. When we want to accomplish something, the objective must be sound. It developed into the family firm's value. For example, my father built a training facility that will drain our finances just to keep running. We will not rent the training facility to another party if the other party's purpose is not appropriate. We would rather incur such losses. And, to this day, I am unable to quantify our family business's success using the value of our family firm. Even if we incur losses, as long as the purpose is sound, it can be considered a success for the business. And I continue to struggle with replicating my father's stewardship behavior. I am battling to be an obedient steward. I believe that being a steward must be financially supported. Otherwise, our money will dwindle and we will be unable to support ourselves.

Following their graduation and return to assist Mr. Fan's business, the entire family has agreed to establish its stewardship vision. The visions are as follows: (1) continuing the family legacy through transformation, (2) synergizing family members to fulfill our destiny, (3) developing character through empowerment and leading by example, and (4) adding value. The Fan family business's primary vision is to give back to society and to bless others through value addition. Additionally, givers must be genuine (honest and sincere), influential, visionary, powerful, and socially responsible. These visions will be the Fan family business guidelines.

Socioemotional Wealth and FBG Development

Using the FIBER dimension to analyze SEW conditions in both cases revealed FBG heterogeneity. There is heterogeneity between FBG and SEW dimensions, and this heterogeneity may evolve over time within FBG. There may be differences in values and attitudes between the founding generation and succeeding generations. These differences result from each generation's preferences, self-beliefs, experiences, opinions, and behaviors (Mendez, 2008), which determine the SEW differences and significance between the founder and second generation. The second generation of new SEW may be an extension of the founder's SEW. When a founder is still alive, they exert a strong influence over their generation, frequently overshadowing their SEW to their second generation (Davis & Harveston, 1999), which will serve as the legacy for the following generation to carry on. Significantly, SEW is transferred from the founder stage to the next generation of family members, who are motivated to preserve and protect it because it influences the decisions they make for the family business group in their personal lives. While the SEW between the founder and subsequent generations may remain constant, the drivers of the SEW may vary (Ruf et al., 2020). After a succession transition and the death of the founder, it is up to the succeeding generation to decide whether or not to continue the family business group's SEW.

Diversifying their primary business is motivated by a desire to reduce risk in order to preserve the primary family business (Kim et al., 2004). When it comes to diversification and investment opportunity decisions, SEW has been a point of reference for family businesses (Gu et al., 2019). Family influence and control, as well as the duty to perpetuate the family dynasty, are the SEW dimensions that have prompted family firms to adopt a conservative investment strategy, avoiding uncertain long-term investments but diversifying their primary business to avoid sibling power competition in an equal inheritance situation (Gu et al., 2019). The requirement for debt and outside expertise, which can jeopardize the family's control, is one reason family businesses diversify less than non-family businesses (Gómez-Mejia et al., 2010). Gu et al. (2019) and Gómez-Mejia et al. (2010) are contradicted by both of our examples.

Several SEW dimensions influence the family firm's decision to diversify in relation to the development of the FBG, including the type of business they wish to enter. As demonstrated in Case 1, the effect of SEW on family business development groups depends on the occurrence of an event that threatens the continuation of the family business, thereby indirectly affecting the family's income and wealth. When the founder experiences health issues, he opts for a strategy of diversification. By initiating an early succession plan, this is meant to ensure that the business remains in the family's hands. Through diversification, the founder attempts to mitigate family business risk, preserve family ownership, and amass capital and assets to support the second generation's expansion of the family business. Mr. Pan must diversify in order to safeguard family ownership and guarantee the continuation of the family business into the second generation. Thus, through a critical event, family influence and control, as well as the renewal of family bonds through dynasty succession, influence the Pan FBG's diversification decisions (Fig. 18.5).

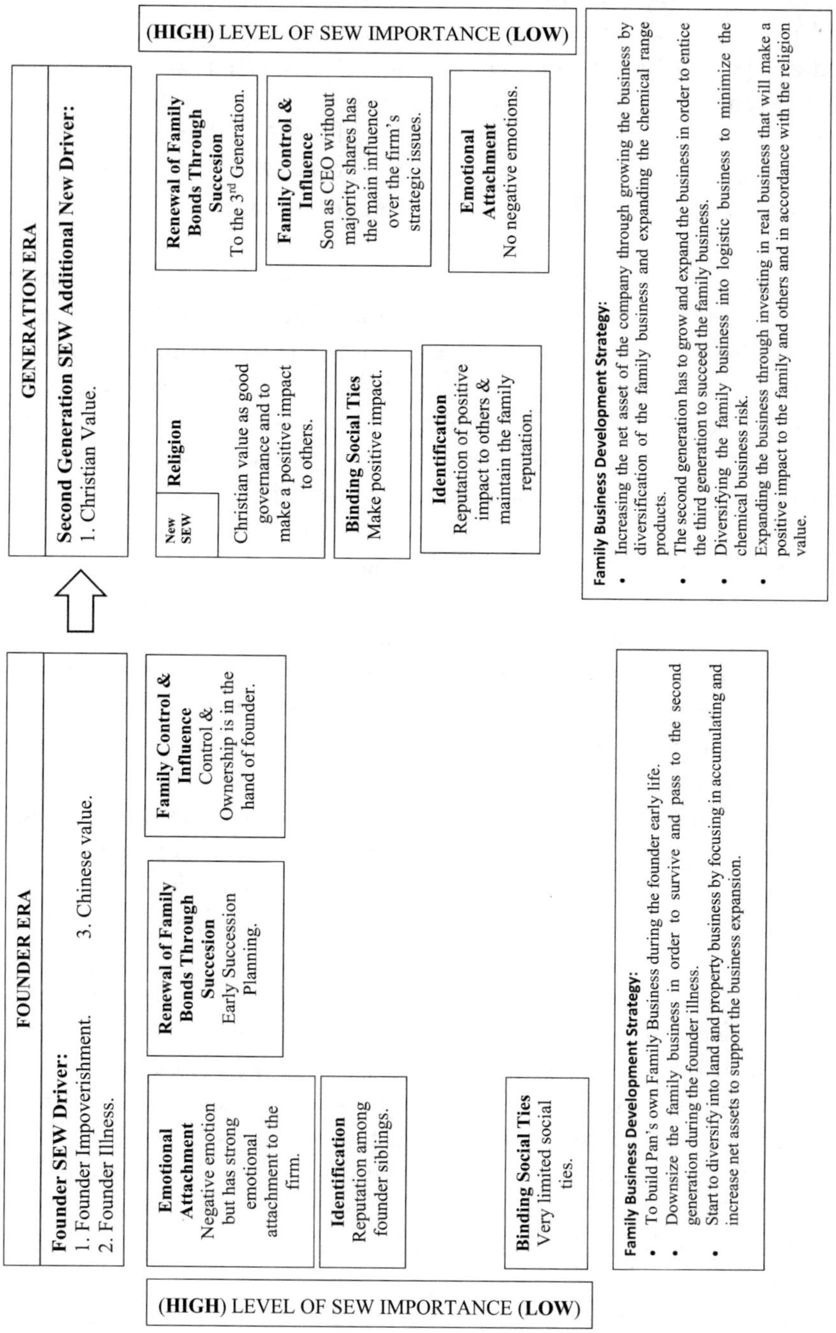

(HIGH) LEVEL OF SEW IMPORTANCE (LOW)

GENERATION ERA

Second Generation SEW Additional New Driver:
1. Christian Value.

Renewal of Family Bonds Through Succesion
To the 3rd Generation.

Family Control & Influence
Son as CEO without majority shares has the main influence over the firm's strategic issues.

Emotional Attachment
No negative emotions.

New SEW — Religion
Christian value as good governance and to make a positive impact to others.

Binding Social Ties
Make positive impact.

Identification
Reputation of positive impact to others & maintain the family reputation.

Family Business Development Strategy:
- Increasing the net asset of the company through growing the business by diversification of the family business and expanding the chemical range products.
- The second generation has to grow and expand the business in order to entice the third generation to succeed the family business.
- Diversifying the family business into logistic business to minimize the chemical business risk.
- Expanding the business through investing in real business that will make a positive impact to the family and others and in accordance with the religion value.

FOUNDER ERA

Founder SEW Driver:
1. Founder Impoverishment.
2. Founder Illness.
3. Chinese value.

Family Control & Influence
Control & Ownership is in the hand of founder.

Renewal of Family Bonds Through Succesion
Early Succession Planning.

Emotional Attachment
Negative emotion but has strong emotional attachment to the firm.

Identification
Reputation among founder siblings.

Binding Social Ties
Very limited social ties.

Family Business Development Strategy:
- To build Pan's own Family Business during the founder early life.
- Downsize the family business in order to survive and pass to the second generation during the founder illness.
- Start to diversify into land and property business by focusing in accumulating and increase net assets to support the business expansion.

(HIGH) LEVEL OF SEW IMPORTANCE (LOW)

Fig. 18.5 The Pan family firm socioemotional wealth

Berrone et al. (2012) demonstrated that family businesses can influence and shape current activities, events, and relationships by utilizing family involvement in the business, a longer history, and knowledge of shared experiences and past events. Families' emotions can range from positive to negative, and they emerge and change in response to more or less crucial events in each family's business system (Berrone et al., 2012). Emotions permeate family businesses and influence their strategic decision-making (Baron, 2008; Berrone et al., 2012). The intensity of emotions varies depending on the generation stage of the controlling owner (Gu et al., 2019).

Mr. Pan's negative emotions in the early stages of his business serve as a pivotal point of reference for him to utilize all of his abilities, strength, and knowledge in establishing and expanding his own family business. In this instance, Mr. Pan's negative emotions motivate him to establish and expand the family business. When a family business expands and diversifies, as measured by an increase in business or family assets, a reputation is earned. Mr. Pan's negative emotions continue to exist and will be remembered forever. To counteract negative emotions, the Pan family businesses must be large and prosperous, as this will establish their reputation among their brothers. Here, negative emotions play a major role in the growth of the family business and its reputation. Therefore, a good reputation is the result of a successful family business that grows or transforms, with emotions serving as moderator.

The second generation will continue the family business's tradition of increasing the value of its assets through diversification and increased product expansion. However, the drivers of business expansion are distinct, and this will influence the FBG's business entry decisions. The second generation demonstrates filial piety to their parents by continuing the family business dynasty. In other words, the second generation is responsible for caring for and supporting their parents. However, the behavior of the subsequent family generation is changing. Filial piety may become less significant, resulting in succession issues for the FBG, which is too small to attract a younger generation to run the FBG. The second generation of the Pan family is aware of this and has determined that their family business must be large and appealing for the third generation to join. In order to recognize the significance of renewal bonds through succession, Pan's family business has begun diversifying into a logistics company, expanding the property business, and expanding the range of chemical products in the primary business. In addition, the family business has a joint venture with its close business partners.

In addition, during the second generation, the relationship between SEW's significance and the growth of the family business shifted. Religion serves as a point of reference for the second generation in determining the type of business in which to invest and in diversifying and expanding the business for the benefit of its stakeholders. Religion plays a significant role in the second generation's business investment decisions. Bonding social ties, despite its lack of significance, serves as one of the SEWs for the second generation of the Pan family in expanding their family business. Lastly, the second generation does not experience negative emotions as did the founder. Consequently, negative emotions within the second generation do not contribute to the development of the FBG. Figure 18.5 depicts the relationship between the SEW and family business development strategy of Pan FBG.

Mr. Fan believes that, of all the SEW dimensions, binding social ties are the most important (Fig. 18.6). He influences the nature of the business and its investment decisions through his philanthropic and stewardship actions toward the environment, society, and employees. Mr. Fan favors troubled businesses regardless of their profitability or loss. His goal is to assist the business in regaining profitability. This includes the cement distribution company. One major event in the region caused the economy to suffer and freeze in all sectors. There are no customers interested in purchasing the product. Mr. Fan chose to deliver his goods to sand and rock dealers without immediate payment. He educates all of his customers and assists those who are unable to pay without regard to profit. From there, the cement distribution company expands. Under Mr. Fan's leadership, customers receive bonuses and a share of the company's profits. This strengthens customer loyalty to the company's products and increases revenue.

Regarding the focus of his businesses, Mr. Fan focuses on environmental and green construction that does not harm the surrounding environment or community. For instance, establishing an educational institution or training center to assist students who are unable to continue their education in higher education without profit, instead subsidizing their education, and constructing real estate based on the concept of green building.

Mr. Fan's stewardship and philanthropic values became the family legacy of the second generation. Throughout the second generation, the strategy for developing the FBG has remained consistent. Prior to this point, the second generation has prioritized environmental sustainability and social values when expanding the business, particularly in the real estate industry. For example, the second generation is aware of the region's narrow roads and parking lots shortages at many destinations. In this instance, the second generation enlarges roadways and simplifies parking lots while preserving trees and promoting sustainable practices. Figure 18.6 depicts the Fan family's SEW and family business development strategy.

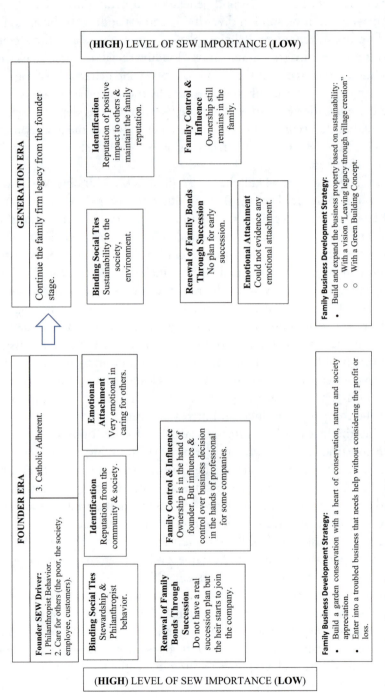

Fig. 18.6 The Fan family firm socioemotional wealth

Conclusions and Implications

Conclusions

Using cases of two medium-sized FBGs in Indonesia, one of the big economy countries in Asia, we deal with the family experiences, which form the family firm SEW as a source of FBG's heterogeneity and importantly how such SEW impacts and becomes the reference point for the development of the family firms into a business group. We find that the importance of SEW depends on family values, critical events, and founder experience, which form the FBG's SEW and are embedded in the FBG. Furthermore, SEW constructs do not always serve as the influencing factors of FBG development strategy. Instead, it can be the outcome of a FBG strategy (i.e., reputation). Furthermore, SEW constructs, such as emotional value, can serve as a moderator between reputation as a family identity with a firm construct and FBG development.

Furthermore, we also find that although a construct of SEW is preserved, such constructs experience a different point of view among generations: for example, reputation toward extended families in the founder stage versus reputation toward stakeholders in the generation stage. Another example is that under the founder stage, ownership has to remain dominant in every layer of business diversification; under the generation stage, ownership does not have to be dominant in every layer of business diversification but remains dominant in the main family business. We can conclude that SEW contributes to the heterogeneity of FBG. Different families have distinct SEWs and their importance, which influences the FBG development strategy. Our results agree with those of Debicki et al. (2016), where the importance of SEW influences the strategic behaviors of FBG and how such variations in the importance of SEW lead to heterogeneous strategic behavior among FBG.

This study provides preliminary evidence, in addition to Debicki et al.'s (2016) paper, by demonstrating the generational shift in the importance of SEW and how such changes affect an FBG's strategy. In addition, we demonstrate that SEW is consistent across generations despite differences in its perceived importance. We discovered that family experience, critical events, and founders' values all contribute to the importance of SEW and thus to the FBG's group heterogeneity issues that affect FBG development strategy. We also discovered that SEW can evolve through the emergence of new SEW across generations, with the founder's SEW serving as the FBG's SEW foundation. Apart from our preliminary evidence, we provide insights into how

SEW is formed at the family firm level by the individual-level construct of the founder's value and experience.

Limitations and Future Research

Our approach and analysis are not without limitations. First, we acknowledge that limited information exists regarding the two FBGs that we use as case studies. For example, our analysis of Mr. Fan's stewardship and philanthropic behavior is based on the companies that directly experienced the effect via the Fan family firm's narrative. We are able to convince ourselves, however, through articles, that the second generation is continuing the Fan family vision and stewardship behavior in expanding the family business. Another example is the fact that, as this investigation came to a close, we were unable to confirm any changes to the family SEW in relation to the FBG development with Mr. Pan after our initial interview because he had passed away.

Second, the findings of this study are limited in their ability to explain what happens in family businesses in general, as they are based solely on what was discovered in the two companies studied. However, the heterogeneity of SEW in family businesses is intriguing and warrants additional empirical research, such as the factors that influence the development of SEW in family businesses. Third, unlike Brigham and Payne (2019) and Swab et al. (2020), we do not focus on SEW constructs across generations of family firms.

Concerns about the broad applications of SEW to family business topics have been noted (Swab et al., 2020). Our research demonstrates that SEW varies across FBGs and generations. Additional research is required to ascertain the diversity of SEW among FBGs. Moreover, FBGs need to be clustered by region, culture, ethnicity, family experiences, and generation. Second, not all SEWs have an effect on the strategic decisions of FBGs. Further research is required to determine the significance of SEW for family firms operating in the same region, with different culture, and family experiences. Finally, how each of the SEW dimensions relates to each other in FBG strategic decisions should be studied.

Based on our findings, we offer a number of issues for additional research (Table 18.1) that come up in our two cases and can contribute to the body of literature between SEW and FBG. Additionally, our issues for each SEW dimensions can be explored separately and applied to family businesses besides FBGs.

Table 18.1 SEW and FBG

SEW elements	Case 1	Case 2	Further exploration of SEW in FBGs
Family control and influence	• "To ensure the company's survival, I am retaining the majority of the shares until I die" • "To ensure my wife's security as a parent, I intend to leave the majority of my ownership to her and the remainder to my children when I die" • "Majority shares will remain in the family" • "I have relinquished control of the company's operations and empowered my son to lead it and make his own decisions. However, he will not flee from my watchful eye as the company's adviser. And I will retain the majority share of the company's stock. I remain the primary decision maker"	• "I owned the majority of his family's businesses but was never involved in their daily management"	• There is a need to differentiate between ownership and control measurement. Having a controlling interest in FBG does not mean having a dominant ownership. Control authorization is in the hand of the dominant founder • Diversification decisions, either joint venture or independent business, depend on the portion of ownership held by the family • The magnitude of shares indicates who decides FBG strategically • Family involvement with limited shares as long as the main heir is appointed has great influence in making FBG decisions • Ownership and inheritance depend on a family's culture and ethnicity

(continued)

Table 18.1 (continued)

SEW elements	Case 1	Case 2	Further exploration of SEW in FBGs
Identification of family members with the firm	• "The company originated from his empty hands, so do not squander it" • "It is an honour that this business will be passed on to the next generation" • "We must maintain the business, but as directed by our father, we must expand it" • "We cannot be seen as Pan's poor family"	• "My reputation is not-negotiable" • "As a human being, we require principles in our lives" • "We must also be fair in business"	• Identification plays a role in deciding the FBG's development • A large family business group means self-achievement and reputation • Reputation and identification play a role in deciding the types of new business • There is an interconnection between: the identification of family members and social ties; Identification of family members with emotional attachment; identification of family members with renewal family bonds through dynasty successions

SEW elements	Case 1	Case 2	Further exploration of SEW in FBGs
Binding social ties	• If the family business succeeds, it is a source of pride for the family members to have had a positive impact on others • "To make a positive impact on others by demonstrating that a family business can be successful without resorting to bribery, cheating, or other practices that are not permitted in the Christian way"	• "I want to live a meaningful life and help others live meaningful lives" • "What matters is how we conduct business properly" • "My first priority is to assist those in need and to foster community"	• How FBG is concerned with its community and social ties depends on the founder's perspective and his values • Concern for social ties to stakeholders and the community is limited when FBG is more focused on family wealth • The importance of FBG social ties will also depend on the type of generation
Emotional attachment	• "I was mentally exhausted... I feel disappointed for the second time. I decided to run my own family business and do not wish to be poor anymore" • "...to protect and expand my assets" "Our business must expand, and all family members must remain united"	• "...compassionate toward others" • "We must develop a greater sense of loyalty, honesty, and belonging to family businesses"	• Emotions can be negative or positive and can remain static • FBG can grow as a result of negative emotions • Emotional experiences shape the level of attachment to the founders and next generations • The founder's emotional attachment shapes the direction of the future FBG and becomes the vision of its next generation

(continued)

Table 18.1 (continued)

SEW elements	Case 1	Case 2	Further exploration of SEW in FBGs
Renewal of family bonds through Dynasty succession	• "It is my intention to plan for my succession to the company" • "My father has his own will and discretion regarding the transfer of shares, which we will respect" • "My son, which carry my first name, will be the leader of the FBG. But majority of the ownership will be in the hand of my wives when I die" • "I trained my son to work in the family business during his college holidays since he is the competent one"	• "I want to fix future generations" • And I continue to struggle with replicating my father's stewardship behavior. I am battling to be an obedient steward. I believe that being a steward must be financially supported. Otherwise, our money will dwindle and we will be unable to support ourselves"	• Succession will be the importance to family business groups • Ownership inheritance: The children's obedience to their parents • Heir: Either the first-born son or the competent one • Each FBG has a different succession strategy • Chosen heirs have a different perspective on FGB development

References

Baron, R. A. (2008). The role of affect in the entrepreneurial process. *Academy of Management Review, 33*, 328–240.

Berrone, P., Cruz, C., & Gómez-Mejia, L. R. (2012). Socioemotional wealth in family firms: Theoretical dimensions, assessment approaches, and agenda for future research. *Family Business Review, 25*(3), 258–279.

Berrone, P., Cruz, C., Gómez-Mejía, L., & Larraza-Kintana, M. (2010). Socioemotional wealth and corporate responses to institutional pressures. *Administrative Science Quarterly, 55*(1), 82–113.

Bertrand, M., Johnson, S., Samphantharak, K., & Schoar, A. (2008). Mixing family with business: A study of Thai business groups and the families behind them. *Journal of Financial Economics, 88*(3), 466–498.

Brigham, K. H., & Payne, G. T. (2019). Socioemotional wealth (SEW): Questions on construct validity. *Family Business Review, 32*(4), 326–329.

Cleary, P., Quinn, M., & Moreno, A. (2019). Socioemotional wealth in family firms: A longitudinal content analysis of corporate disclosures. *Journal of Family Business Strategy, 10*, 119–132. https://doi.org/10.1016/j.jfbs.2018.11.002

Daspit, J, J., Chrisman, J. J., Ashton, T., Evangelopoulos, N. (2021). Family firm heterogeneity: A definition, common themes, scholarly progress, and directions forward. *Family Business Review, 34*(3), 1–27.

Davis, P. S., & Harveston, P. D. (1999). In the founder's shadow: Conflict in the family firm. *Family Business Review, 12*(4), 311–323.

Debicki, B. J., Kellermanns, F. W., Chrisman, J. J., Pearson, A. W., & Spencer, B. A. (2016). Development of a socioemotional wealth importance (SEWi) scale for family firm research. *Journal of Family Business Strategy, 7*(1), 47–57.

Distelberg, B., & Sorenson, R. L. (2009). A focus on values, resource flows and adaptability. *Family Business Review, 22*, 65–81.

Filser, M., De Massis, A., Gast, J., Kraus, S., & Niemand, T. (2018). Tracing the roots of innovativeness in family SMEs: The effect of family functionality and socioemotional wealth. *Journal of Product Innovation Management, 35*(4), 609–628. https://doi.org/10.1111/jpim.12433

Goel, S., Voordeckers, W., Van Gils, A., & Van Den Heuvel, J. (2013). CEO's empathy and salience of socioemotional wealth in family SMEs—The moderating role of external directors. *Entrepreneurship & Regional Development, 25*(3–4), 111–134. https://doi.org/10.1080/08985626.2012.710262

Gómez-Mejia, L. R., Haynes, K. T., Núñez-Nickel, M., & Jacobson, K. J. L. (2007). Socioemotional wealth and business risks in family-controlled firms: Evidence from Spanish olive oil mills. *Administrative Science Quarterly, 52*(1), 106–137.

Gómez-Mejia, L. R., Makri, M., & Kintana, M. L. (2010). Diversification decisions in family-controlled firms. *Journal of Management Studies, 47*(2), 223–252.

Gomez-Mejia, L.R., Cruz, C., Pascual, B., & De Castro, J.(2011). The bind that ties: socioemotional wealth preservation in family firms. *The Academy of*

Management Annals, 5(1), 653–707. https://doi.org/10.1080/19416520.2011. 593320

Granovetter, M. (2010). Business groups and social organizations. In N. Smelser & R. Swedberg (Eds.), *The handbook of economic sociology* (pp. 429–450). Sage.

Gu, Q., Lu, J. W., & Chung, C. N. (2019). Incentive or disincentive? A socioemotional wealth explanation of new industry entry in family business groups. *Journal of Management, 45*(2), 645–672.

Hamilton, E., Cruz, A. D., & Jack, S. (2017). Re-framing the status of narrative in family business research: Towards an understanding of families in business. *Journal of Family Business Strategy, 8,* 3–12.

Haslam, S. A., & Ellemers, N. (2005). Sociel identity in industrial and organizational psychology: Concepts, controversies and contributions. In G. P. Hodgkinson & J. K. Ford (Eds.), *International review of industrial and organizational psychology* (pp. 39–118). Wiley.

Jaskiewicz, P., & Dyer, W. G. (2017). Addressing the elephant in the room: Disentagling family heterogeneity to advance family business research. *Family Business Review, 30*(20), 111–118.

Jiang, D. S., Kellermanns, F. W., Munyon, T. P., & Morris, M. L. (2018). More than meets the eye: A review and future directions for the social psychology of socioemotional wealth. *Family Business Review, 31*(1), 125–157.

Jones, C. D., Makri, M., & Gómez-Mejia, L. R. (2008). Affiliate directors and perceived risk bearing inpublicly traded, family controlled firms: The case of diversification. *Entrepreneurship Theory and Practice, 32,* 1007–1026.

Kalm, M., & Gómez-Mejia, L. R. (2016). Socioemotional wealth preservation in family firms. *Revista de Administracao, 51,* 409-411

Karaevli, A., & Yurtoglu, B. B. (2018). Founding family effects on business group growth: Longitudinal evidence from Turkey (1925–2012). *Long Range Planning, 51*(6), 831–864.

Kim, D., Kandemir, D., & Cavusgil, S. T. (2004). The role of family conglomerates in emerging markets: What Western companies should know. *Thunderbird International Business Review, 46,* 13–38.

Kleine, S. S., Kleine, R. E., III., & Allen, C. T. (1995). How is a possession "me" or "not me"? Characterizing types and an antecedent of material possession attachment. *Journal of Consumer Research, 22,* 327–343.

Kuttner, M., Feldbauer-Durstmüller, B., & Mitter, C. (2021). Corporate social responsibility in Austrian family firms: Socioemotional wealth and stewardship insights from a qualitative approach. *Journal of Family Business Management, 11*(2), 238–253.

Leitterstorf, M. P., & Rau, S. B. (2014). Socioemotional wealth and IPO underpricing of family firms. *Strategic Management Journal, 35*(5), 751–760.

Levinson, H. (1971). Conflicts that plague family businesses. *Harvard Business Review, 49*(2), 90–98.

Mendez, N. (2008). Generation gap. In S. J. Loue & M. Sajatovic (Eds.), *Encyclopedia of aging and public health.* Springer.

Miller, D., Le Breton-Miller, I., & Lester, R. H. (2010). Family ownership and acquisition behavior in publicly-traded companies. *Strategic Management Journal, 31*(2), 201–223.

Mukherjee, K., Rautiainen, M., Pikhala, T., Rosa. P. (2019). The dynamics and complexity of family business groups. In *The family business group phenomenon* (pp. 177–197). Palgrave Macmillan.

Murphy, L., Huybrechts, J., & Lambrechts, F. (2019). The origins and development of socioemotional wealth within next-generation family members: An interpretive grounded theory study. *Family Business Review, 32*(4), 396–424.

Naldi, L., Cennamo, C., Corbetta, G., & Gómez-Mejia, L. (2013). Preserving socioemotional wealth in family firms: Asset or liability? The moderating role of business context. *Entrepreneurship Theory and Practice, 37*(6), 1341–1360.

Pelled, L. H., Eisenhardt, K. M., & Xin, K. R. (1999). Exploring the black box: An analysis of work group diversity, conflict, and performance. *Administrative Science Quarterly, 44*(1), 1–28. Sage.

Piana, B. D., Vecchi, A., & Cacia, C. (2012). Toward a better understanding of family business groups and their key dimensions. *Journal of Family Business Strategy, 3*, 174–192. https://doi.org/10.1016/j.jfbs.2012.05.004

Prügl, R. (2019). Capturing the heterogeneity of family firms: Reviewing scales to directly measure socioemotional wealth. In E. Memili & C. Dibrell (Eds.), *The Palgrave handbook of heterogeneity among family firms* (pp. 461–484). Palgrave Macmillan. https://doi.org/10.1007/978-3-319-77676-7_17

Rautiainen, M., & Pihkala, T. (2019). The emergence of a family business group: The role of portfolio entrepreneurship. In *The family business group phenomenon* (pp. 65–87). Palgrave Macmillan.

Rosa, P., Rautiainen, M., & Pihkala, T. (2019). The methodological challenges of researching family-owned business groups. In *The family business group phenomenon* (pp. 37–62). Palgrave Macmillan.

Ruf, P. J., Moog, P. M., & Rius, I. B. (2020). Values as antecedents of socio-emotional wealth behaviour in family firms. *International of Journal Entrepreneurship and Small Business, 40*(1), 83–113.

Schepers, J., Voordeckers, W., Steijvers, T., & Laveren, E. (2014). The entrepreneurial orientation–performance relationship in private family firms: The moderating role of socioemotional wealth. *Small Business Economics, 43*, 39–55. https://doi.org/10.1007/s11187-013-9533-5

Swab, R. G., Sherlock, C., Markin, E., & Dibrell, C. (2020). "SEW" what do we know and where do we go? A review of socioemotional wealth and a way forward. *Family Business Review, 33*(4), 424–445.

Teixeira, S., Veiga, P. M., Figueiredo, R., Fernandes, C., Ferreira, J. J., & Raposo, M. (2020). A systematic literature review on family business: Insights from an Asian context. *Journal of Family Business Management, 10*(4), 329–348.

Terlaak, A., Kim, S., & Roh, T. (2018). Not good, not bad: The effect of family control on environmental performance disclosure by business group firms. *Journal of Business Ethics, 153*(4), 977–996.

Yan, J., & Sorenson, R. (2006). The effect of Confucian values on succession in family business. *Family Business Review, 19*(3), 235–250.

Dony Abdul Chalid is a lecturer at Universitas Indonesia's Faculty of Economics and Business. He earned his Ph.D. in 2013 from the University of Bologna. His research focuses on finance, corporate governance, and family business. Recent publications include the Review of Accounting and Finance, Journal of Economic Studies and the Review of Behavioral Finance.

Mira Kartika Dewi Djunaedi is a lecturer at Universitas Esa Unggul, Faculty of Economics and Business in Indonesia. She earned her doctoral degree from the University of Indonesia in 2020. She is the second generation of her father's family business, having witnessed its growth and decline. She has a strong interest for research in the broad areas of family business, finance, and corporate governance.

19

Explaining FBGs' Influence and Actions via a Sensemaking Lens

Sanjay Goel, Marita Rautiainen[iD], Tuuli Ikäheimonen[iD], and Hikari Akizawa

Introduction

Family business groups (here after FBGs) evolve in many different ways to accommodate the goals and interests of the family members. A common element of these goals is the enduring survival and longevity of the FBG as a going concern. FBGs may shed businesses, and even family owners, in an attempt to achieve these goals. The nature and core of the relevant family may change as a result, or cause, of the decisions shaping the FBG. These decisions are taken in the context of embeddedness in their institutional context.

S. Goel (✉)
Nistler College of Business and Public Administration, University of North Dakota, Grand Forks, ND, USA
e-mail: sanjay.goel@und.edu

M. Rautiainen
School of Engineering Science, LUT University, Lahti, Finland
e-mail: marita.rautiainen@lut.fi

T. Ikäheimonen
LUT School of Engineering Science, LUT University, Lappeenranta, Finland
e-mail: tuuli.ikaheimonen@lut.fi

H. Akizawa
Oikos Research GK, Tokyo, Japan

© The Author(s), under exclusive license to Springer Nature Switzerland AG 2023
M. Rautianen et al. (eds.), *The Palgrave Handbook of Managing Family Business Groups*,
https://doi.org/10.1007/978-3-031-13206-3_19

498 S. Goel et al.

The surrounding environmental context is deployed to shape and pursue the entrepreneurial opportunities and risks that family members and the family sees. Viewed from this perspective, the presence of FBGs all over the world at any point of time is the result of evolutionary forces in their internal (family) and external environment.

In this chapter, we further the understanding of FBGs via the ontological lens of subjectivism. Instead of assuming an objective external environment to which FBGs react or respond, we assume that FBGs receive and construct their external environment subjectively and idiosyncratically via sensemaking and sensegiving processes. The process of retrospective sensemaking and sensegiving, driven by the controlling coalition of the FBG at any point of time, leads to an organizing and connecting narrative for the structure and portfolio of the FBG.

Our perspective maps on to the phenomenon of FBGs in three specific ways. First, it reifies that owning families are not powerless actors and do not receive their external environment as mandates or constraints (Carney & Gedajlovic, 2002). Instead, they are powerful actors in their own right, and have the power to not just influence their environment, but also force their subjective construction of their environment on other, less powerful actors. Second, we provide preliminary insights into when and how FBGs use agency to incorporate tumult and upheaval (which we term "epochal events") in their external environment to construct an entrepreneurial narrative that leads them to accumulate resources for action. This in turn rewards them with resilience, longevity, and family cohesion, via a dynamic evolution of FBG structure that allows them to profit from the external tumult—in other words, it allows them to control their external environment. Finally, it sheds light on how and why FBGs play a more than a selfish and self-serving role in the construction of a national identity and psyche—even while FBGs become global via continued entrepreneurial actions leading to expansion beyond their national geographic boundaries, unlike multinational companies with diverse shareholding, they also become deeply embedded in the identity and psyche of their countries of origin. By representing "grounded" capital that does not flee or move around based primarily on economic returns, FBGs may play a constructive role in multi-faceted development of their home country when it is most needed.

Because of the genesis of FBGs in entrepreneurial behavior, owning families may be adept at constructing and using their external environment to both create and mine entrepreneurial opportunities to meet their economic and non-economic goals, but also to preserve their legacy assets constituting of assets of tradeable economic value, as well as those of non-tradeable symbolic and emotional value. Research on entrepreneurship that focuses on constructionist approaches discusses how entrepreneurs manipulate and develop tangible resources via constructing and changing the linguistic boundary around tangible outcomes they want to create (Clark & Jennings, 1997).

The internal dynamics of the family itself affects whose voice, whose language takes precedence in the construction of opportunities attributed to the owning family as a group. Relationships among family members are suffused with both emotions and moral obligations. Unlike economic contracts, familial relations cannot terminate unequivocally, and may fester in various stages of engagement and disengagement for many generations. In turn, these dynamics may have an effect on the ownership and management of the FBG as ownership and employment in FBG may be used as a currency to placate discordant voices and determine participation in the economic and social wealth and opportunities that such engagement may bring. Powerful owners may also disenfranchise some family owners, by buying their ownership out, even at the expense of degrading their familial relationship. The ownership structure thus may change via changes in legal ownership, which itself reflects the internal tensions and changes in power, harmony, and conflict among different family members. The owners of the FBG impose their vision and their linguistically constructed opportunities on the rest of the group, and define boundaries of legitimate entrepreneurial action in the FBG via sensemaking processes. Differences in perception lead to differences in opportunities that are perceived/constructed (Dorado, 2005).

Sensemaking and Sensegiving as a Process of Reality Construction

Extant research has provided insights to sensemaking and sensegiving in organization development and change processes e.g., large group interventions regarding strategy, emotion, and sensemaking (Bartunek et al., 2011), change management and the way middle managers make sense of senior management initiatives (Balogun, 2006), and how moderators of leadership affect sensegiving during organizational change (Kraft et al., 2015) to name a few. Sensemaking and sensegiving are cognitive processes that are activated by actors when they are faced with equivocality and uncertainty to make sense of and give sense to what is happening and has happened (Gioia & Chittipeddi, 1991). Sensemaking is an active process of constructing reality in situations that are confusing, surprising, and ambiguous (Gioia & Thomas,

1996; Weick, 1993, 1995) and has been recognized as a central activity in organizations, and a building block of organizing (Maitlis & Christianson, 2014) whereas sensegiving draws attention to the *act* which makes reality (Mininni & Manuti, 2017). Sensemaking is based on the ontological assumption of subjectivity, which holds that reality and meaning is created socially, actively, and linguistically, rather than being an innate part of an objective environment awaiting discovery (Berger & Luckmann, 1966; Boyce, 1995; Cornelissen, 2012; Hill & Levenhagen, 1995; O'Leary & Chia, 2007). As a derivative, sensemaking is a process via which individuals, and groups, construct an understanding of issues and events that are novel, non-routine, ambiguous, and potentially disruptive. The relationship between secular changes in the external environment and sensemaking is recursive. When powerful actors (e.g., leaders) are successful in influencing the sensemaking of organizational members, these individuals are motivated to make changes in their own roles and practices; they are also able to help others by explaining the vision and co-constructing ways of working that are consistent with it (Maitlis & Christianson, 2014). This is because sensemaking provides a coherent and absorbable narrative that relevant actors can understand and subscribe to, empowering them to act within their own sphere consistent with the mandates of the narrative.

A related concept to sensemaking is sensegiving. Sensegiving has been defined as to "a process of attempting to influence the sensemaking and meaning construction of others toward a preferred redefinition of organizational reality" (Gioia & Chittipeddi, 1991: 442). Gioia and Chittipeddi (1991) defined the term "sensegiving" as a critical process that attempts to influence on how the construction of meaning evolves and through which issues are constructed and interpreted in organizations. It is an interpretive process where actors influence each other through persuasive or evocative language (Dunford & Jones, 2000) used by leaders and stakeholders of organization (Corley & Gioia, 2004; Gioia & Chittipeddi, 1991).

Sensegiving is critically important and a key leadership activity particularly in times of change (Maitlis & Lawrence, 2007; Smirchich & Morgan, 1982; Weick, 1995). The change can fail when organizational ambiguity and sensemaking gaps occur among members of an organization and if leaders cannot communicate the underlying sense of the change to employees (Kraft et al., 2015; Maitlis & Lawrence, 2007). It follows that when change is of a very high magnitude (e.g., paradigmatic, or once in a lifetime (epochal), the degree of tumult and upheaval in the external environment can paralyze relevant actors in an organization. Stories that involve sensegiving and sensemaking can be a way to analyze the workings of power and the creation of knowledge during change (Brown et al., 2008). Researchers (Kraft et al., 2015; Maitlis & Christianson, 2014; Sandberg & Tsoukas, 2015) state that in the research of sensegiving, there is a lack of explicit account of context (Kraft et al., 2015). Sensegiving is embedded in a social and organizational context affected by organizational and individual factors (Maitlis & Lawrence, 2007). These factors in turn create variation in the degree to which change initiatives are successful. Managed or led, sensemaking processes that do not adequately take into account these factors run the risk of failure, as evidenced by the high number of unsuccessful change initiatives (Burnes & Jackson, 2011; Kraft et al., 2015).

Collective sensemaking refers to the construction of a reality that a group can share and accept—editing out the differences between individual realities via selective memory, imposition via use of power, and/or appeal to a shared identity. This may occur through the production and retelling of "accounts"—discursive constructions of reality that interpret or explain (Antaki, 1994; Balogun, 2003; Balogun & Johnson, 2004, 2005; Rouleau, 2005; Rouleau & Balogun, 2011). In this context, Weber and Glynn (2006) reviewed that the dominant view has been that institutions are cognitive constraints on sensemaking. However, as they propose, this is a restrictive view because it minimizes the role of agency and differences in the "sensemakers"—i.e., "how individual agency can strategically decouple symbolic sensegiving from action (Suchman, 1995; Westphal & Zajac, 2001), while others have argued that many institutions may be most critical in inducing problems and setting agendas, but less constraining in generating the solutions to address these issues (Swidler, 2002). Institutions are thus likely to play a broader role in sensemaking than making some things unthinkable and unsensible. "We believe that this agent-driven sensemaking perspective is particularly relevant to understand FBGs, as they pursue their own goals, and are powerful actors who can reify their 'sense-made' institutions for other actors."

Sensemaking and sensegiving is a collective process, in which cues for constructing a new meaning of information are generated and communicated. Developing the logic of going to different businesses, to increase their group size is aided by entrepreneurial actors in the family who give sense to environmental change by borrowing and incorporating specific "facts" from the change—"facts" being snippets of reality around which there is reasonable agreement. Family as a collective group may have been able to develop ways to develop coherence from the dispersed and diverse information among members and engage in cooperative information exchange. As such, cognitive ability is an important factor in the motivated information

502   S. Goel et al.

processing among family owners and other stakeholders. Family owners need not share the same values, but they may have equivalent or overlapping values. However, collectivistic values provide a foundation for effective performance in interdependent settings. If family members/owners do not feel that their meanings and values had been understood and acknowledged, they might not accept sensemakers' sensegiving. Instead, they are persisted in trying to have their meanings and accompanying values recognized. The pivot from sensemaking to sensegiving occurs when the sensemaker develops a plausible account helping family as a collective to constructive engagement in a variety of sensegiving interactions with multiple stakeholders.

Sensemaking taps into the historical, social, and cultural context of business families—a variety of communication genre (including verbal and non-verbal communication that itself is deeply embedded social and cultural practices and norms), a continuous effort to link the constructed past to the future, and a deliberative process to create a shared meaning to delineate the boundaries of the business family and maintain a workable internal cohesion. FBGs show widely different paths of evolution. They have complex ownership structures with varying components of family and non-family ownership in its different constituent groups. There is also the possibility of having multiple heads at the top with different parts of the FBG run by different branches of the owning family. In addition, within a FBG, there is an acceptance of changes and turnover in their business portfolio for family or economic reasons. For this reason, they may be less susceptible to being tied to their "legacy" and "legacy businesses" unlike a family business—rather FBGs may be more concerned about incorporating institutional elements in their narrative to maintain their relevance, and to ensure their survival.

Thus, businesses in an FBG that may have started for idiosyncratic, non-rational, non-economic, and non-strategic reasons (e.g., to maintain harmony and avoid conflict, to allow for ownership discretion as part of ownership rights, to repay or gain favors, or as a result of persuasion by an overly persuasive and passionate family member, etc.) at a preceding point of time, become connected formally to the FBG via a coherent economic and strategic logic that is constructed later by the family or the family leader—i.e., the logic *succeeds*, rather than *precedes* entry into new businesses. In the process, the "creators" use the family *as well as* the external context as sources of raw material, picking and choosing those aspects and snippets of data, information, and sub-narratives that enable them to write a coherent narrative of their own for their FBG. In the process of developing this narrative, they also "construct" the enabling economic and strategic logic of keeping the businesses together (e.g., via finding profitable ways to share resources and competencies, modifying product features or services, bundling products, and finding economies of scope) which makes the resultant FBG pay off economically for all owners. FBGs also need to construct a logic of continuity in the face of major changes in their institutional environment due to big historic events—e.g., wars, decolonization, globalization, etc. These aspects speak to the embodied and sociomaterial nature of sensemaking (Maitlis & Christianson, 2014), broadening its understanding as a largely cognitive and discursive process (Cunliffe & Coupland, 2012; Stigliani & Ravasi, 2012; Whiteman & Cooper, 2011).

FBGs integrate the external environment in their own stories and narratives for the following reasons:

1. To prevent discontinuity and construct continuity for the family as well as the external environment. The resultant continuity reduces uncertainty by allowing them to legitimize the FBG as part of the environment, making the FBG a communal or national asset. It allows the FBG to develop a reinforcing solidity, presence, permanence, and resilience over time.
2. To construct a connecting logic and motivation among family members to have workable harmony and avoid conflict, especially relative to the FBG core—thereby yielding family synergies.
3. To cultivate institutional resources and construct a proactive logic to orchestrate ownership and leadership of entrepreneurial opportunities in their external environment. In particular, sensemaking helps them manage the tumult and chaos in their external environment, providing them with a narrative and logic to continue their businesses, and even find new entrepreneurial opportunities from the tumult.

A conceptual framework for layers of sensemaking that are embedded in the FBG context is depicted in Fig. 19.1. Individual sense making of the external environment becomes the input to collective negotiated sensemaking at the family level. The family is the entrepreneurial actor that deploys its negotiated sense of the external environment in constructing the FBG. In turn, the FBG operations and family dynamics themselves provide the inputs, in addition to the external environment, to dynamically "sensemake" the narratives for future actions.

We promote the perspective that FBGs are constructed over time by enterprising families via sensemaking using cues from their external environments. The owning family of the FBG is hardly a powerless social actor from this perspective, operating within the constraints of its institutional environment and buffeted by winds of institutional change. Social position affects actors'

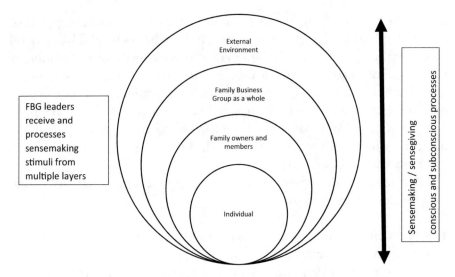

Fig. 19.1 Layers of sensemaking in FBGs relative to the external environment

perception (Dorado, 2005). Therefore, as a relatively powerful social actor, FBG's perceptions and constructions of its institutional environments may in fact be imposed on other, less powerful actors.

This perspective is valuable because it allows for the construction of genuinely new and imaginative strategic resources and competencies, as well as economic and non-economic synergies that may otherwise not be visible via following a purely rational and deliberative process. It taps more meaningfully, energetically, comprehensively, and creatively, into the idiosyncratic features and characteristics of families, and ties these features more directly into explaining not just the existence, but also the success and endurance of FBGs—the process of constructing coherence as well as revising the narrative across multiple generations becomes one of the owning family's core strengths. Importantly, by focusing on family's idiosyncratic aspects and particularly its competencies in weaving a narrative via sensemaking and sensegiving, this approach is a counter-weight to attempts to over-homogenize family business research which aim to construct theories focusing on what is common among families and family businesses. Finally, a related argument in this perspective's favor is that it incorporates more of the phenomenon in developing abstractions, allowing for more realism in theory building, which itself is a valuable epistemological goal. We illustrate this aspect of FBG development via detailed abstractions from three illustrative case studies.

Illustrative Cases

Three illustrative case studies of sensemaking opportunities via incorporating external developments in the institutional environment to construct a logic and impetus for environmental action.

Toyoda Family Business House of Japan

The Toyoda Family Business House of Japan. The case illustrates how a prominent leader of the FBG, Taizo Ishida was handed the baton at the right time to develop and transform the FBG and prepare it for its post-WW II dominance in world economy using both economic logic and legitimacy by incorporating narrative elements both from its internal and external environment. The case has been constructed via various public resources, including published biographies of the company's founders and managers.

Toyoda Family Business Group (TFBG) got its start from an automatic loom business. The founder and inventor, Sakichi Toyoda, was regarded as a contributor of industrializing in Japan and has been socially respected. Toyota Moter Corporation was established in 1937 by Kiichiro and his brother-in-law, Risaburo. After World War II (WW II), however, they both left the company to bear the responsibility of its financial failure and to resolve the dispute with the labor union. Taizo Ishida took the baton when asked by Kichiro and Riaburo to be the president in 1950. He was already 62 years old, but by chance recognized in public as *Oh-Banto* (senior, respected person in a merchant house). Taizo was influenced by the social values of Ohmi merchants: e.g., doing business with care about local community (sanpo-yoshi); right deed first, profit next (sengi-kori); and do good things modestly and quietly (intoku-zenji). These values were perfect for transformation of TFBG, and also fit the urgency with which Japan wanted to recover its economic might and national pride after (WW II). As Taizo got socialized in these values, they became the latent internal grist to sensemaking, along with contemporary external developments in Japan and the world.

For reenergizing family business, President, Taizo Ishida, did four things; solved imminent labor problem, developed own distinctive financial scheme to make company grow, and trained hopeful successor Eiji. Observing from the broader perspective, what moved *Oh-Banto* Taizo might be the social mission of the founder Sakichi for industrialization in Japan that he consistently and enthusiastically had. In the following, the process described chronologically focusing on the influence of Sakichi. Taizo incorporated

506　　S. Goel et al.

the founder's social mission along with the nationalistic desire for industrialization and reconstruction of Japanese industrial strength, as well as self-confidence, which was shattered by the end of WW II.

When Taizo took the baton from Kiichiro, he increased capital using booming, and started to invest boldly in the plant and equipment of the five-year production plan in 1951 and the new automobile factory in 1958. This new factory became the field of establishing Toyota Production Method and the company history (1987) evaluated that this investment was the bedrock of later success of the company. The same company history introduced Taizo's theory, "The primary condition of business is to keep the financial discretion". It resonated in the new "reconstruction, rebuild, and restore" mindset that post-war Japan was infused with. The militaristic narratives that were promoted by the leaders were replaced by "catching up with industrialization" and "restoring the national strength and pride" imperatives. In this light, Taizo's actions and Sakichi's guidance were well placed—"You are the merchant..."

In concluding his autobiography—when he had just invested in the new factory—Taizo stated about the future prospect of the company having cited Sakichi's words:

> So far, the performance and price of American automobiles are much better than us. Still, however, as Volkswagen succeeded, we can find different customer needs like I could find in India and ultimately develop world-level quality cars by ourselves. We have a good exemplar. Sakichi once said, 'I will develop the loom for you other than imported ones,' and after making great efforts, he finally developed the world-level automatic loom.

It was the hard time when the company started to invest largely in the new automobile factory in 1957, but trial export exposed the problems of performance and quality in 1958. The spirit of "rebuilding and restoring Japanese image in peace-time industries" and the formation of Ministry of International Trade and Industry (MITI) were used to spur improvements in quality to international standards.

For Taizo the desire to save a family business as Oh-banto may be to save the dream of the founder Sakichi. Social values of Ohmi merchant might essentially resonate with the self-help sprit—diligence, independence, honesty, and frugality—in Smiles' book, which inspired young Sakichi. These values also helped the company connect with the epochal developments in its external environment, and develop a narrative for action that resonated both internally among its employees, and externally among the Japanese consumers, government, and more generally with the country's psyche.

The Tata Family Business House of India

The case illustrates how the Tata family of India constructed its FBG and gave it both economic logic and legitimacy by incorporating narrative elements both from its internal and external environment. The illustrative summary below bases on the book "The Tatas: How a Family Built a Business and a Nation" (Kuber, 2019).

The history of India's Tata business group is an illustration of how the Tata family entwined the narrative of their entrepreneurial endeavors and business aspirations with contemporaneous events in their environment to construct one of the largest FBGs. Jamsetji Nusserwanji Tata laid the foundation of Tata group in 1868—by then a 29 year old who had learned the ropes of business while working in his father's banking firm—when he established a trading company in Bombay. The Tata family themselves were immigrants to India—they were Parsis, an ethnoreligious group in India, emigrated from Iran. They assimilated in the Indian subcontinent, so much so that their businesses are considered an integral contributors of building India as a nation.

Jamsetji Tata is described by the group as "a visionary entrepreneur, an avowed nationalist and a committed philanthropist, [who] helped pave the path to industrialization in India by seeding pioneering businesses in sectors such as steel, energy, textiles and hospitality." The group's business and philanthropic endeavors played well with the nationalist sentiment of the Indian socio-political context, as it struggled to find a voice and develop a nationalist discourse to take the country back from British rule. One of the most spectacular and symbolic businesses that Tata group entered into under Jamsetji Tata's leadership is the Taj Mahal Hotel in Mumbai in 1903. According to the group's history, Jamsetji Tata "set his mind on building it after being denied entry into one of the city's fancy hotels for being an Indian." This further endeared the group to India's domestic socio-political context and positioned the group to enter into new industries after India achieved its independence from the British rule in 1947. Each generation of the family invested not only in the expansion of its own business interests but also in nation building. Today, the Tata group is a $110-billion global enterprise, headquartered in India, comprising over 100 independent operating companies. When the Indian government began liberalizing the economy in the 1990s, Tata Group incorporated international expansion in their own narrative and set out an aggressive plan to internationalize. The group now operates in more than 100 countries across six continents and employs over 695,000 people.

The John Nurminen Family Business from Finland

Nurminen family has been very entrepreneurial over the years, both individually and as a group. In the last couple of decades of twentieth century, the Nurminen family faced globalization, and especially the epochal event of European integration as a political and monetary union. The break-up of Soviet Union expanded the EU further. This implied removal of intra-European borders, mobility of labor, and easy of developing pan-European global companies. The illustrative summary below is derived from the teaching case "John Nurminen Family: Ownership Strategy Enabling Business Portfolio Development" (Rautiainen & Goel, 2018).

Nurminen family business was founded in 1871 when founder Johan Nurminen established a business in the timber industry, capitalizing on Finland's rich forestry resources. The company grew rapidly because the family as a whole was very entrepreneurial. By 1945, it had become a well-established FBG with multiple businesses within the group. At the time of writing, the Nurminen FBG has two main business entities—Nurminen Logistics, which is a public company organized into six businesses that is 75% owned by the family, and John Nurminen Ltd., which is a private company wholly owned by the family. The businesses collectively provide a comprehensive set of high-quality logistics services, such as those in railway transport, terminal facilities, freight forwarding, special and heavy transports, project logistics, and related value-added services. The Nurminen Logistics main market areas are Finland and Russia and other neighboring countries. In addition to Finland, Nurminen also has offices in the Baltic countries (Estonia, Latvia, and Lithuania) and Russia.

Over many generations, Nurminen family members have exhibited remarkable entrepreneurial inclination and skill for constructing opportunities, taking risks, and even going against the family's dominant logic. The family in turn created a strong center that keeps the risk for the whole group within reasonable bounds. Family members are free to start their own businesses with advice and intangible support from the group, but the group may not risk any family capital. When the family member has grown any business to a reasonable size and ensured its viability, the Nurminen FBG then buys the company and makes it part of its portfolio. Any business that is on the block for divestment from the group is first offered to the family in case any family member wishes to run it independently.

The group grew rapidly by positioning itself in the mainstream of epochal events in its external environment. The end of WW II and the need for reconstruction in Europe made logistics and Finnish natural resources important assets that Nurminen family could provide. Many businesses were started around the logistics capability, specialized around different industries and modes of transportation. In addition, the integration of EU provided further narrative raw material to the family to position itself as fulfilling EU's ambition of being a legitimate and powerful economic union and developing pan-European companies bringing in material and people from all of Europe. The break up of Soviet Union and the creation of EU-10 countries provided further opportunities to bring in the Baltic countries in the fold to promote their economic development and further the family's entrepreneurial ambitions. The mobility of people within Europe and later the rapid growth of global travel led one of the family members to start a travel agency, that was then brought in the group as one of the group companies. Overall, the group entered or exited more than 60 businesses over more than five decades, as the narrative of entering some of the businesses changed due to changes in the external environment. When apparel industry largely moved out of Europe to Asia, the group exited that business, for example. In each of their entries and exits, Nurminen FBG allowed family members to first construct the logic of entry based on opportunity, assessed the risk to the overall portfolio, and made decisions accordingly. The family members could work as part of the group or independently, which allowed multiple levels of sensemaking to thrive, and a collective sensemaking to develop and co-exist (as opposed to subsume or overpower individual sensemaking). This allowed the group, and family members to build resilience even when there were no visible economic synergies.

Discussion

From the illustrative cases above, we elicited common themes in sensemaking and sensegiving by FBGs that allowed the latter to both control the uncertainties imposed by the environments they faced, and also construct their own entrepreneurial narrative and actions by incorporating the dominant themes from the tumult they faced in their environment. Table 19.1 shows the context of the three cases, as well as common themes that were extracted from them. Each of the three illustrative FBGs faced an epochal event—an event characterized by upheaval, tumult, and a high degree of uncertainty in the external environment. Each FBG incorporated the dominant theme from the event in order to provide a coherent narrative for its own actions. This narrative had a ready audience in the external environment—there was perfect resonance with the dominant understanding of the "need of the hour." Thus,

FBGs in our illustrations were able to garner additional tangible and intangible resources from their external environment. In addition, they were able to create an inspiring narrative that held their family together, by providing them an empowering and optimistic view of the future of the group, that in turn drove further entrepreneurial actions.

As FBGs evolve over generations, they add layers of complexity in their structure. Deploying a complexity perspective, it would be fruitful to study the kinds of overlapping and intersectional issues with amplifying or dampening effects that occur during implementation of change. In particular, as FBGs develop in power and influence by incorporating elements of the epochal environment they face, they also increase their influence, and their voice becomes more authoritative in the external environment. Do FBGs use their influence predominantly to further their own interests or develop synergies between their own interests and the needs of the external stakeholders? What FBG characteristics explain the variance in the use of their influence?

Future research can also study the process of negotiation in collective sensemaking among family members. Whose are the central and peripheral voices and who manages the process? Does the process benefit by unfolding at its own pace, or via a leader inserting the missing pieces in the narrative? This could explain the differences between intended and realized strategy for example, and the relative power of individual owners vs. family as a collective owner.

Future research can also further study the pattern of activities, relationships, and resultant narratives that fuel further actions, especially those that in turn let the FBG influence the external environment and external stakeholders. We have argued that an essential aspect of the process of sensemaking in FBGs is that enduring FBGs use the process to empower themselves, and accumulate a variety of resources, for further entrepreneurial action. It is not necessarily that FBGs "exploit" the power vacuum in in their external environment (Morck & Yeung, 2003)—rather they develop an actionable narrative that provides them legitimacy and other resources to act entrepreneurially and ensure their longevity.

While our cases above are illustrative to anchor our conceptual ideas, in-depth case studies about inter-generational sensemaking process, especially in the context of high tumult and uncertainty in the environment, may provide more insights about the agency and power of FBGs to influence and entrepreneurially "deploy" environmental events to further their continuity and longevity; what are the critical events in environment, how the narrative develops along generations, and how the narrative is edited in future as it evolves from a "story" to a "legend" passed on to the family as well as

19 Explaining FBGs' Influence and Actions via a Sensemaking Lens

Table 19.1 Key elements in constructing an entrepreneurial narrative and action via sense making in illustrative cases

FBG → Key elements	Toyoda (Japan)	Tatas (India)	Nurminen (Finland)	Common theme
Epochal event	Japan's surrender in World War II	Indian independence from British rule	Progressive integration of European countries into a political and monetary union	A significant, world-changing event that disrupts extant institutions and changes the value of extant resources of all kinds
Imported event construction	Restoring Japan's infrastructure and a sense of dignity and pride	Indian self-reliance—charting the nation's future without relying on others	Unleashing the economic benefits of border-free trade and labor mobility	The FBG borrows or incorporates pieces of the event's common narrative and amplifies it
Entrepreneurial narrative for external stakeholders	Partnering with public resources and Japanese talent to rebuild Japan and restore Japan's pride via use of technology and industry in peace time industries FBG output quality as tied to national reputation	Deploying resources in both core infrastructure and high visibility "pride" businesses as Indian businesses for Indians	Helping European companies develop a pan-European footprint, exploit the continent's diversity, and build European companies of global scale	Collaborators in achieving a broader mission, sharing the group identity with others

(continued)

Table 19.1 (continued)

FBG → Key elements	Toyoda (Japan)	Tatas (India)	Nurminen (Finland)	Common theme
Entrepreneurial action	Focusing on industries where reliability and quality were valuable. Deployment of frugality and attention to detail as differentiation	Diversification into a wide variety of industrial and consumer products and services as a national company	Entering into a wide array of businesses around logistics, transportation management, and travel in Finland and neighboring countries	Rapid deployment of group's capabilities, including family members' individual passions and risk management at the group level
Illustrative resources attracted and orchestrated	Guiding public investment in education and technology, developing long-term partnership with suppliers, mission-driven zeal. Reputation as a national icon	Public resources, public's trust. Reputation as a national icon. Brand building and longevity	Inclusion as an European champion and an European asset	Legitimacy, inclusion via identification with a higher entity (nation, government, peoples)
Internal benefits to the FBG	Coherence around a mission, rapid development, and redeployment of extant resources and personnel	Coherence around a mission, reduced conflict via FBG structure as entrepreneurial family members and managers could be rapidly deployed throughout the group	Entrepreneurial opportunities to a large number of independent-minded and entrepreneurial family members, FBG cohesion	Group stability, risk management, pipeline of well-trained family members or non-family managers for succession, and well-defined group identity

to external stakeholders. The early stages of the process also raise interesting questions. For example, what is the driving force that starts the process? Is the process started consciously or does the new narrative just emerge (in the beginning)? If consciously, how and by whom is the consciousness about the need and process created? Is sensemaking the mechanisms for the family or the business to survive—by using other words, is the new narrative needed to collect the family together first, and only after that, to save the business?

Conclusion

Via this chapter, we aim to start a broader conversation on the topic of sensemaking by FBGs as they develop a narrative that resonates with different stakeholders and establishes the basis for FBGs entrepreneurial actions. As we depict in this chapter, there are multiple layers of sensemaking embedded in an FBG. Individual family members have both legal ownership and moral claims over the FBG. The family also develops a collective sensemaking via contributions of individual discourse. The FBG adds another layer as owners become more diverse and operating managers of businesses may contribute their own perspective. Finally, external environment provides secular events and other raw material, as well as other stakeholders that may have a voice in FBG's sensemaking that constructs their world and a fitting narrative. Our illustrative case studies show that FBGs from different countries used sensemaking perspective to control, and even harness, epochal events in their environment to increase their reach and become "one" with the emerging mission or needs of the environment. This allowed them to increase their centrality and influence in their relevant environment, and also allowed them to increase internal cohesion. We hope that our perspective spawns several conversations and carefully crafted empirical studies to advance knowledge around these topics.

References

Antaki, C. (1994). *Explaining and arguing: The social organization of accounts.*

Balogun, J. (2003). From blaming the middle to harnessing its potential: Creating change intermediaries. *British Journal of Management, 14*(1), 69–83.

Balogun, J. (2006). Managing change: Steering a course between intended strategies and unanticipated outcomes. *Long Range Planning, 39*(1), 29–49.

Balogun, J., & Johnson, G. (2004). Organizational restructuring and middle manager sensemaking. *Academy of Management Journal, 47*(4), 523–549.

Balogun, J., & Johnson, G. (2005). From intended strategies to unintended outcomes: The impact of change recipient sensemaking. *Organization Studies, 26*(11), 1573–1601.

Bartunek, J. M., Balogun, J., & Do, B. (2011). Considering planned change anew: Stretching large group interventions strategically, emotionally, and meaningfully. *The Academy of Management Annals, 5*(1), 1–52.

Berger Peter, L., & Luckmann, T. (1966). *The social construction of reality: A treatise in the sociology of knowledge.*

Boyce, M. E. (1995). Collective centring and collective sense-making in the stories and storytelling of one organization. *Organization Studies, 16*(1), 107–137.

Brown, A. D., Stacey, P., & Nandhakumar, J. (2008). Making sense of sensemaking narratives. *Human Relations, 61*(8), 1035–1062.

Burnes, B., & Jackson, P. (2011). Success and failure in organizational change: An exploration of the role of values. *Journal of Change Management, 11*(2), 133–162.

Carney, M., & Gedajlovic, E. (2002). The co-evolution of institutional environments and organizational strategies: The rise of Family Business Groups in the ASEAN region. *Organization Studies, 23*(1), 1–32.

Clark, V., & Jennings, P. D. (1997). Talking about the natural environment: A means for deinstitutionalization. *American Behavioral Scientist, 40*(4), 454–464.

Corley, K. G., & Gioia, D. A. (2004). Identity ambiguity and change in the wake of a corporate spin-off. *Administrative Science Quarterly, 49*, 173–208.

Cornelissen, J. P. (2012). Sensemaking under pressure: The influence of professional roles and social accountability on the creation of sense. *Organization Science, 23*(1), 118–137.

Cunliffe, A., & Coupland, C. (2012). From hero to villain to hero: Making experience sensible through embodied narrative sensemaking. *Human Relations, 65*(1), 63–88.

Dorado, S. (2005). Institutional entrepreneurship, partaking, and convening. *Organization Studies, 26*(3), 385–414.

Dunford, R., & Jones, D. (2000). Narrative in strategic change. *Human Relations, 53*, 1207–1226.

Gioia, D. A., & Chittipeddi, K. (1991). Sensemaking and sensegiving in strategic change initiation. *Strategic Management Journal, 12*, 433–448.

Gioia, D. A., & Thomas, J. B. (1996). Identity, image and issue interpretation: Sensemaking during strategic change in academia. *Administrative Science Quarterly, 41*, 370–403.

Hill, R. C., & Levenhagen, M. (1995). Metaphors and mental models: Sensemaking and sensegiving in innovative and entrepreneurial activities. *Journal of Management, 21*(6), 1057–1074.

Kraft, A., Sparr, J. L., & Peus, C. (2015). The critical role of moderators in leader sensegiving: A literature review. *Journal of Change Management, 15*(4), 308–331.

Kuber, G. (2019). *The Tatas: How a family built a business and a nation.* Harper Business.

Maitlis, S., & Christianson, M. (2014). Sensemaking in organizations: Taking stock and moving forward. *Academy of Management Annals, 8*, 57–125.

Maitlis, S., & Lawrence, T. B. (2007). Triggers and enablers of sensegiving in organizations. *Academy of Management Journal, 50*(1), 57–84.

Mininni, G., & Manuti, A. (2017). A rose is more than a rose … the diatextual constitution of subjects and objects. *Text & Talk, 37*, 243–263.

Morck, R., & Yeung, B. (2003). Agency problems in large family business groups. *Entrepreneurship Theory and Practice, 27*(3), 367–382.

O'Leary, M., & Chia, R. (2007). Epistemes and structures of sensemaking in organizational life. *Journal of Management Inquiry, 16*(4), 392–406.

Rautiainen, M., & Goel, S. (2018). John Nurminen family: Ownership strategy enabling business portfolio development. In *SAGE business cases.* SAGE Business Cases Originals.

Rouleau, L. (2005). Micro-practices of strategic sensemaking and sensegiving: How middle managers interpret and sell change every day. *Journal of Management Studies, 42*(7), 1413–1441.

Rouleau, L., & Balogun, J. (2011). Middle managers, strategic sensemaking, and discursive competence. *Journal of Management Studies, 48*(5), 953–983.

Sandberg, J., & Tsoukas, H. (2015). Making sense of the sensemaking perspective: Its constituents, limitations, and opportunities for further development. *Journal of Organizational Behavior, 36*(S1), S6–S32.

Smircich, L., & Morgan, G. (1982). Leadership: The management of meaning. *Journal of Applied Psychology, 18*, 257–273.

Stigliani, I., & Ravasi, D. (2012). Organizing thoughts and connecting brains: Material practices and the transition from individual to group-level prospective sensemaking. *Academy of Management Journal, 55*(5), 1232–1259.

Suchman, M. C. (1995). Managing legitimacy: Strategic and institutional approaches. *Academy of Management Review, 20*(3), 571–610.

Swidler, A. (2002). Saving the self: Endowment versus depletion in American institutions. *Meaning and modernity: Religion, polity, and self*, 41–55.

Weber, K., & Glynn, M. A. (2006). Making sense with institutions: Context, thought and action in Karl Weick's theory. *Organization Studies, 27*(11), 1639–1660.

Weick, K. E. (1993). The collapse of sensemaking in organizations: The Mann Gulch disaster. *Administrative Science Quarterly, 38*, 628–652.

Weick, K. E. (1995). *Sensemaking in organizations*. Sage.

Westphal, J. D., & Zajac, E. J. (2001). Decoupling policy from practice: The case of stock repurchase programs. *Administrative Science Quarterly, 46*(2), 202–228.

Whiteman, G., & Cooper, W. H. (2011). Ecological sensemaking. *Academy of Management Journal, 54*(5), 889–911.

20

Intergenerational Flourishing: Sharing Knowledge from Generation to Generation in Mexican Family Business Groups

Fernando Sandoval-Arzaga, María F. Fonseca,
and Maria José Parada🆔

Introduction

Family Business Groups (FBGs) show a strong ability to survive across generations when they are able to develop their own resources and capabilities, that in turn allow them to develop a "business portfolio" resulting in transgenerational entrepreneurship (Parada et al., 2019; Zellweger et al., 2012), increase their survival rates by mitigating conflicts (Cruz et al., 2013), or provide opportunities for new generations to protect the family legacy (Sieger et al., 2011). Knowledge seems to be a critical dimension to achieving such transgenerational continuity, yet there is still a dearth of understanding of how knowledge is shared and integrated among generations. Furthermore, business families do not use their full potential when it comes to their collective

---

F. Sandoval-Arzaga (✉) · M. F. Fonseca
Business School, Tecnologico de Monterrey, Monterrey, Mexico
e-mail: fsandoval@tec.mx

M. F. Fonseca
e-mail: maria.fonseca@tec.mx

M. J. Parada
Department of Strategy and General Management, ESADE Business School, Sant Cugat del Vallès, Spain
e-mail: mariajose.parada@esade.edu

© The Author(s), under exclusive license to Springer Nature
Switzerland AG 2023

M. Rautianen et al. (eds.), *The Palgrave Handbook of Managing Family Business Groups*,
https://doi.org/10.1007/978-3-031-13206-3_20

517

knowledge base and do "not assign top priority to knowledge management" (Döring & Witt, 2020); even though various studies demonstrate the importance of sharing knowledge as essential to obtain a competitive advantage (Lo & Tian, 2020; Singh et al., 2020; Than et al., 2019;), "due to its importance, it is worth to further investigate knowledge sharing" (Lo et al., 2021, p. 2163).

Sharing and integrating knowledge among generations is essential because it contributes to the continuity of FBGs. First, help to build an identity and culture in the business family, FBGs are usually complex to achieve this due to their large number of members and generations; second, it allows fostering innovation and the creation of new products that contribute to the creation of the FBGs business portfolio; third, encourage governance and learning mechanisms for the new FBGs leaders; and fourth, contribute to generate the economic, family, and social legacy of FBGs by socializing knowledge in the business family. However, this impact of knowledge on FBGs is a gap in FBGs literature that has not been sufficiently investigated.

Given the practical implications of this topic have for FBGs and the critical gap in the literature (Döring & Witt, 2020, Lo & Tian, 2020; Singh et al., 2020; Than et al., 2019), we aim to explore the impact of *sharing knowledge mechanisms* among generations in FBGs that allow them to flourish intergenerationally.

We understand intergenerational flourishing as a dynamic process of the enterprising family to create value and transform positively across generations. Intergenerational flourishing is measured through satisfaction with the succession process (Sharma et al., 2003), with the creation of entrepreneurship opportunities for the next generations (Habbershon et al., 2010; Jaskiewicks et al., 2015; Nordqvist & Zellweger, 2010) and with the construction of a family legacy (Hammond et al., 2016).

We believe that sharing and integrating knowledge among generations (Cabrera-Suárez et al., 2001; Cohen & Sharma, 2016; Sandoval-Arzaga et al., 2011) is crucial to enhancing intergenerational flourishing in the family business. As the authors would describe it, intergenerational flourishing implies that human flourishing is where the transformation is expected to occur. Professor VanderWeele, from Harvard University, has conducted robust and comprehensive research to identify the outcomes for human flourishing; he has highlighted that there are four fundamental pathways (domains) for humankind to attain some identified outcomes of human flourishing. The pathways are family, work, education, and community involvement; and the outcomes: happiness and life satisfaction, physical and mental health, meaning and purpose, character and virtue, and close social relationship (VanderWeele, 2017). Intergenerational flourishing implies interaction among individuals, and it considers the importance of learning for knowledge to be generated and integrated, therefore as a virtuous cycle.

Knowledge is not a commodity located "out there"; rather, it is a product of what happens "in- between" (Wood, 2002). This means that knowledge is shared, recombined, and advanced when members of a business communicate with one another or work together. This occurs because knowledge is tacit (Polanyi, 1966). When knowledge is deployed as people converse or work jointly, knowledge integration is approached as a "dynamic capability" (Eisenhardt & Martin, 2000; Teece et al., 1997). For this reason, the main questions we want to explore include: *What are the practices and mechanisms necessary for sharing the knowledge flow in a FBG? How do these knowledge-sharing mechanisms impact intergenerational flourishing in a FBG?*

To answer these questions, we use exploratory research based on a qualitative case study methodology (Miles & Huberman, 1994; Stake, 2000; Yin, 1994). We identify three relevant Mexican FBGs, which are an example of intergenerational flourishing, from at least three generations, from different industries, and with different complexities of business and family, that allow us to do cross-case analysis.

This study makes several contributions. On the one hand, exploring knowledge-sharing mechanisms and intergenerational flourishing in FBGs sheds light on an underexplored topic in FBGs literature, thereby increasing our knowledge of one of the main current phenomena in business families, as is FBGs and their long-term survivability (Rautiainen et al., 2018). On the other hand, we extend current knowledge about knowledge sharing among generations (Boyd et al., 2015), a topic widely mentioned in the literature but still with important gaps in relation to how they allow family business groups to thrive over time.

At a practical level, our work has important implications for business owners and for, educators and consultants. For business owners, our work could help family business leaders and owners to understand the mechanisms and develop strategic decisions that are necessary to share and integrate knowledge across generations as part of their knowledge management strategy. For educators and consultants, this work contributes to developing insights and robust frameworks to understand and help business families to achieve flourishing intergenerational through sharing knowledge in FBGs.

The remaining of the chapter develops as follows. In the next section, we present the literature about knowledge sharing. We introduce the methodology and we continue with the findings. We finish our chapter with conclusions, implications, and further research.

Literature Review

Knowledge-Sharing Mechanisms in FBGs

FBGs are a "collection of separate ideas, resources, technologies, and businesses held by the same governing enterprising family" (Rautiainen et al., 2020, p. 232). An enterprising family "share a focus on preserving and growing wealth as a family" (Berent-Braun & Uhlaner, 2012, p. 105). In this sense, FBGs are a space where knowledge is deployed for enterprising families to achieve their purposes.

One of the most valuable resources for organizations is knowledge. Knowledge is essential in order to generate competitive advantages, innovate, solve complex problems, and contribute to achieving maximum value in knowledge assets (Barney, 1991; Boisot, 1995; Von Krogh et al., 2000; Lawson & Lorenz, 1999; Leonard & Sensiper, 1998; Nonaka & Takeuchi, 1995; Spender, 1998). Additionally, knowledge is an essential element in the construction of their dynamic capabilities (Eisenhardt & Martin, 2000; Teece et al., 1997).

Organizations exploit knowledge through knowledge management (KM) in different contexts and inter-organizational relationships; specific studies in these inter-organizational contexts have increased rapidly in the last two decades (Agostini et al., 2020). This means the internal benefit of knowledge that flows from relationships with partners, clients, strategic alliances, or academics that open innovation provides is achieved through the development of skills to manage knowledge within the organization (Brunswicker & Vanhaverbeke, 2015).

To develop these skills within the organization, knowledge management researchers have created models to create and manage knowledge (Boisot et al., 2007; Nonaka & Takeuchi, 1995), and others have described it in different processes such as: creating, acquiring, sharing, transfer, apply, or protect knowledge (Davenport & Al Ahbabi et al., 2019; Costa & Monteiro, 2016; Prusak, 1995). Within these processes, "sharing was the most frequent process studied by scholars" (Lo et al., 2021. p. 9). Knowledge sharing means disseminating or making the knowledge of individuals available to others in activities of a particular process (Al-Erman et al., 2018; Camelo-Ordaz et al., 2011).

For enterprising families, knowledge allows them to obtain competitive advantages (Boyd et al., 2015) as a primary issue of their strategic management (Barros-Contreras et al., 2020) and their innovation capacity (De Massis et al., 2016; Letonja & Duh, 2016). Moreover, accumulating knowledge across generations (Chirico, 2008), transferring and building that knowledge in the succession process between the incumbent and potential successors (Boyd et al., 2015; Cabrera-Suárez et al., 2018), and sharing and integrating it (Chirico & Salvato, 2008, Cohen & Sharma, 2016; Sandoval-Arzaga et al., 2011) in the different stages of evolution of the family and the family business are a source for their longevity and sustainability across generations.

FBGs must share and integrate knowledge as a sustainable strategy to develop their own capabilities and have a better knowledge management strategy. Zahra et al. (2020) define knowledge integration as "an organizational capability for creating novel combinations of different strands of knowledge, [...] from within and beyond the organization, and across time, and which derive from individual and group contributions, facilitated by both formal and social processes" (p. 163).

Integrating knowledge implies identifying the different mechanisms for sharing knowledge at different levels (personal, group and organizational) and in its different types. There are two main types of knowledge: "know that" and "know how" (Ryle, 1949). "Know that" is linked to learning theories or theorizing itself, while "know how" is linked to intelligent practice, recognizing how to do something to the performance of an activity. Different authors of organizational knowledge have subsequently taken up this distinction: declarative vs procedural knowledge (Grant, 1996); information vs know how (Kogut & Zander, 1992); explicit vs tacit (Nelson & Winter, 1982; Nonaka & Takeuchi, 1995).

"Know that" (declarative, information, or explicit) is codifiable and therefore easy to communicate and imitate, while "know how" (procedural) is the opposite, so it is tacit, semiconscious, or unconscious in nature and as the philosopher Polanyi (1966) tells us: "we know more than we can tell" (p. 6). Tacit knowledge cannot be articulated or verbalized; it is only acquired through physical or cognitive practice and incorporated into human skills (Nelson & Winter, 1982). But it is precisely the tacit knowledge, because of its low ability to be imitated, which allows the development of unique resources to family businesses, their "familiness" (Chrisman et al., 2005; Habbershon & Williams, 1999) and which also works better in certain environments, such as those of high uncertainty or innovation context (Le Breton-Miller & Miller, 2015). Thus, tacit knowledge is potent because it allows for anticipating problems, proposing innovative solutions, visualizing opportunities, guiding or validating practices, and clarifying complex phenomena (Sandoval-Arzaga, 2005).

Both explicit and tacit knowledge are actually part of the same thing, where one (tacit) is assimilated by paying attention to, performing or understanding the meaning of the other (explicit), and both form a joint entity (Polanyi, 1966). Thus, knowledge is in a spectrum (Leonard & Sensiper, 1998) between the purely explicit ("know that") and the purely tacit ("know how"), so it is a matter of degrees of competencies. We don't necessarily have to "know that" to "know how" to do it and vice versa (Ryle, 1949); for example, you can learn to play a musical instrument by watching someone else play it without knowing the musical notes.

For FBGs, in which transgenerational continuity depends on the ability to build their capabilities for the development of a business portfolio, the achievement of transgenerational entrepreneurship and providing opportunities for new generations, having mechanisms for sharing tacit knowledge is key to their flourishing intergenerational process.

In order to integrate knowledge and identify its sharing mechanisms, it is also necessary to identify the different levels or dimensions in which it is applied. These levels are the individual and the social (group or cultural). Spender (1996a, 1996b) makes a matrix which combines explicit and implicit knowledge with individual and social levels. Thus, we have four types of knowledge: (a) conscious (individual-explicit); (b) objectified (social-explicit); (c) automatic (individual-implicit); and d) collective (social-implicit). Objective knowledge is what we understand as scientific, which is explicit, decontextualized, empirically tested, and validated. "It is objective and independent of the knower" (Spender, 1996b, p. 57). The other three types of knowledge (conscious, collective, and automatic) are tacit and more difficult to understand. For this research, we will be interested, in addition to the objective, in the conscious and collective.

Conscious knowledge is that possessed by an expert who, for example, uses his specific knowledge in a consciously way to solve problems. This type of knowledge can be tacit depending on the context in which it is used; it is not private knowledge but applied in a specific context. Thus, an executive in a non-family business may be very successful, but when hired by a family business he may fail or lose his expertise because he is in a different context. This is what Craig and Moores (2017) call "Learning our Family Business" because in order to know how to lead one must learn the unique particularities of the own family business.

Collective knowledge is that which is immersed in the social context, many of the social norms that are in people's unconscious, the knowledge we take for granted and acquire in our education and development. It is part of "a collective body of knowledge" (Spender, 1996b, p. 62). It is part of social-situated learning in which a learner learns the sociocultural practices of a community, in which they observe the relationships and interconnections, the formation of identities, the participation in activities, the use of artifacts, and the knowledge provided by the community (Lave & Wenger, 1991). In organizational terms, it is the type of knowledge that is embedded in the organization's culture as well as in its organizational routines and habits (Nelson & Winter, 1982).

Thus, starting from the different types of knowledge that occur in different dimensions, we have identified the various mechanisms for sharing knowledge that can be observed and integrated into the FBGs. We have grouped them into three different types: 1. knowing that 2. knowing how, and 3. collective knowing.

The mechanisms of *knowing that* are those related to objectified knowledge, which is explicit-social knowledge. In family businesses this knowledge can be learned by reflecting (Cohen & Sharma, 2016), where family members can learn how to think independently through disciplined thinking. Formal education, reading books, attending conferences or workshops, and family businesses or industry-related aspects are part of these mechanisms (Sandoval-Arzaga et al., 2011). Part of this category of knowledge is the set of formal documents regarding the company and the family. For example, processes, policies, family constitution, annual reports, etc.

Knowing how mechanisms are those related to expert knowledge that is individual and explicit. It is part of the tacit knowledge that can only be manifested or displayed when we do something (Tsoukas, 2003). In entrepreneurial families, this knowledge is learning by working and learning by creating (Cohen & Sharma, 2016), either by working inside or outside the family business and in the creation of new businesses or by innovating or expanding existing ones. The mechanisms that we have identified as good practices in family businesses can be developed at different stages of the development of family members (Sandoval-Arzaga et al., 2011), including: working outside the family business, working inside the family business, informal visits to the family business, temporary-summer jobs in the family business, challenging projects (with little guidance) within the family business, own entrepreneurship projects related or unrelated to the family core business, and personal development experiences.

Finally, *Collective Knowing mechanisms* are those related to collective knowledge, which is social-implicit and means known to be part of a community. They are mechanisms related to knowledge located in the business family and in its connection with the environment, linked to being part of a community of practitioners (Brown & Duguid, 1991) outside the family business or within it, and which generates identity with the family business (Parada & Dawson, 2017) and social leadership (Fonseca & Sandoval-Arzaga, 2018). This is knowledge also of a tacit nature that to be shared requires the use of creative language, such as stories, metaphors, or narratives (Czarniawska, 1997; Nonaka & Takeuchi, 1995; Spender, 1996b); master-apprentice relationships (Lave & Wenger, 1991; Nonaka & Takeucho, 1995, Spender, 1996b) or learning the routines of the organization (Nelson & Winter, 1982). In family business it is obtained through learning by absorbing, interacting, or engaging personal advisors (Cohen & Sharma, 2016). Absorbing through imitation and observation, interacting through exploration, asking questions or listening to stories, and having guidance and advice from referents and mentors. It is a socialization process that takes place within the company and the entrepreneurial family in which there can be formal and informal spaces to share this type of knowledge. The mechanisms that we have identified as good practices (Sandoval-Arzaga et al., 2011) are: family stories, rituals, traditions and narratives (business family culture), leading by example (by observing), role models (from inside and outside the enterprising family), master-apprentice relationships (ancestor-successor, non-family members, experts-novices), mentoring relationships, contact networks and belonging to communities (social capital) whether family, business or social (foundations, philanthropic, or government) and routines and habits of the enterprising family (family trips, meetings or councils).

Table 20.1 shows the mechanisms for sharing knowledge.

Methodology

This study aims to increase our understanding of the mechanisms for knowledge sharing in FBGs. Moreover, in particular the main questions are: *What are the practices and mechanisms necessary for the flow of knowledge in a FBG? How do these mechanisms of knowledge impact the intergenerational flourishing of a FBG?*

Table 20.1 Sharing knowledge mechanisms in FBGs

Knowing that	Knowing how	Collective knowing
• Formal education, book reading, lectures or workshops • Formal family and company documents	• Working outside the family business • Working inside the family business • Informal visits to the family business • Temporary jobs in the family business • Challenging projects (let-do-little guidance) within the family business • Own entrepreneurial projects • Personal development experiences	• Family stories, rituals, traditions and narratives • Leading by example (by observing) - Role Models • Teacher-apprentice relationships • Mentoring relationships • Networking and community membership (family, business, social) • Routines and habits of the entrepreneurial family

Source Own elaboration

To answer these questions, we use exploratory research based on a qualitative case study methodology (Miles & Huberman, 1994; Stake, 2000; Yin, 1994). The case study method is a tool used to analyze and interpret reality, which should contribute to the knowledge of an individual, organizational, social, or political phenomenon (Yin, 1994). The case study method is a process that researches a phenomenon and is the product of that research, that should include a variety of contexts are included within which there is a series of sections, groups, and times. This variation allows a holistic view of the phenomenon (Stake, 2000).

We followed a purposeful sampling approach for data collection in order to identify and select cases that would provide us with rich information (Patton, 2002) about the topic at hand. Our key variables for such a choice included the need to be a transgenerational family business, with at least one generational transition, to observe knowledge sharing across generations and intergenerational flourishing. We also looked for business groups, defined as "a group of related, and/or unrelated, businesses owned and controlled by members of one or more families" (Mukherjee et al., 2019. p. 3) from different industries to avoid possible effects from industry with regard to knowledge sharing, and we purposefully looked for family businesses that showed different complexities of business and family in order to observe if knowledge sharing can be present in different types of FBGs.

With these criteria in mind, we selected three relevant Mexican FBGs, which are an example of intergenerational flourishing, they are in the third

526 F. Sandoval-Arzaga et al.

generation or beyond, and they display different complexities and belong to different industries, as shown in the table below.

We interviewed a leader from each of the FBGs who met the criteria of being an owner of the company, having a position in one of the governing bodies or a management position and being part of the intermediate generation. This last characteristic is important because it allows them to have a bridge vision between the previous generations that led the company and the new generations that are in the process of development. The characteristics of the FBGs are shown in Table 20.2.

All these FBGs were analyzed from a historical perspective of at least five years, given their relationship with the Family Enterprise Institute for Mexico

Table 20.2 FBGs Characteristics

FBG	Business Portfolio	Year of foundation	Number of employees	Family Characteristics	Interviewed Characteristics
ALFA	• Mobility Platform • Agribusiness Platform • Strategic Investments	1956	13,000	G4 Nine Branches	Family Council Member Active member of the Family Foundation Top Management Team G3 member
DELTA	• Optical retails • Optometric specialization • Ophthalmology Clinics • Wholesale of optical products	1936	4,000	G4 Four Branches	Family Council President Board member Experience & Personal VP G3 member
EPSILON	• Retail • Consumer Credit • Banking • Real State	1941	100,000	G4 Seven Branches	Family Member of the Corporate Board Coordinator of the Family Council President of the Family Foundation G3 member

Source Own Elaboration

and Latin America of the Tecnologico de Monterrey (IFEM), through which it was possible to have contact formally and informally with the family group (in addition to in-depth interviews with their leaders), on different occasions either by accessing documents or in their participation in academic events, linking family businesses or in the production of audiovisual material for the dissemination of different family members. The following Table 20.3 shows this relationship with each FBG.

In order to analyze our data derived from in-depth interviews and the historical perspective, we followed an interpretive approach (Alvesson & Sköldberg, 2000; Burrell & Morgan, 1979). We build a sharing knowledge mechanisms codes for each type of knowledge (knowing that, knowing how, and collective knowing) based on the literature review and described in the previous table, and then we codify the data to obtain the relevant information. An example of the quotations obtained is shown in Table 20.4.

We went back and forth from our theoretical underpinnings to our data to build new insights about knowledge sharing and intergenerational flourishing. Two of the authors ran the interviews and independently analyzed the transcriptions of each case in order to identify patterns and themes. The following themes emerged that matched our theoretical underpinnings.

Findings—Case Description

Our findings highlight interesting insights about the sharing knowledge mechanisms that emerge in the FBG as a consequence of the interaction among generations. Below we explain how each case supports the three mechanisms we draw from the literature.

Knowing that Mechanisms

Knowing that mechanisms emerge from objective knowledge which is explicit, decontextualized and independent of the knower (Spender, 1996b). In other words, this knowledge is learned through formal education (Sandoval-Arzaga et al., 2011), often wise, allowing to incorporate of new knowledge into the family business.

The formal education history of each of the interviewees from the Alfa, Delta, and Epsilon Family Business Groups is an example of the *knowing that* they have accumulated over the years.

Jorge Alfa studied his professional career in marketing at Michigan State, studied in Mexico for an Executive MBA at a prestigious university,

528   F. Sandoval-Arzaga et al.

Table 20.3 Formal and informal contact in the last five years

FBG	Documents	Academic events	Family business events	Audiovisual content
ALFA	• Journalistic articles • Company history book • Business reports	• Family Business lesson speaker • Main speaker in entrepreneurial students' competition • Main speaker in the closing ceremony of family business program	• Inc. Family Forum	• Testimonial video interviews
DELTA	• Case study • Business reports • Journalistic articles	• Family Business lesson speaker • Family business webinar • Lecturer at the IFEM consultant training program	• Inc. Family Forum • Family Business industrial day conference • Family Business Panel	• IFEM Podcast
EPSILON	• Case study • Business reports • Journalistic articles	• Family Business lesson speaker • Training partner in the educational model XXI at Tec de Monterrey	• Inc. Family Forum • Family Business Panel	• IFEM Podcast • Testimonial video interviews

Source Own Elaboration

in addition to studying seminars and conferences at different universities, particularly on business and family governance issues.

Gonzalo Delta also studied two professional careers in administration and marketing in Denver and later also his Master's degree in International

Table 20.4 Quotations examples

Sharing Knowledge Mechanisms in FBGs			
	Knowing that	**Knowing how**	**Collective knowing**
ALFA	"I understood my business family because I was studying a set of seminars on family governance at various universities"	"All of these different roles that I played (in the company) were like studying a micro master but in practice. [...] For me this is a competitive advantage of family businesses"	"My grandparents were my inspiration. From my paternal grandfather I inherited the idea and the taste to continue developing one of the companies"
DELTA	"I studied family business issues through organizations such as the Family Firm Institute and Wealth Advising"	"I ran an office of one of the family company's business units in Los Angeles, California. After 2 years I returned to Mexico and rotate through different positions within the FBG"	"People sometimes only wanted me to be in certain groups because of my last name but not because of the person I am [...] I prefer to belong more to professional groups related to family businesses and personnel development which bring more value to the business family"
EPSILON	"I studied family business issues in Mexico through some universities and law firms specialized in the subject"	"I was a listener & observer of the board of directors and after one year I became a board member representing my family branch"	"My uncle and FBG President, created spaces to mentor me and two of my cousins to be prepared to join FBG. I admire the leadership style of my uncle"

Source Own Elaboration

Business in the United States. He studied family business issues through organizations such as the Family Firm Institute and Wealth Advising. Since then, he has regularly participated in seminars and conferences related to the family business and management issues.

Sofia Epsilon studied her professional career in management in Mexico and later her Master's degree in Organizational Development at Pepperdine

University in the United States. She studied family business issues in Mexico through universities and law firms specialized in the subject.

All of the family leaders interviewed have gone abroad to gain knowledge to later incorporate this new knowledge within the family business in the form of new practices, new business ideas, and professionalization of the family business.

In all cases, the family protocol is a document from which they have learned the general topics of the family business, and the rules of the same have given them the knowledge of what they must comply with to develop within the Family Group. On the other hand, the policies, procedures, and reports generated by their different companies have given them explicit knowledge of the FBG industry to which each one belongs all of them being knowledge-sharing mechanisms (Sandoval-Arzaga et al., 2011) that trigger explicit knowledge and collective knowledge.

Knowing How Mechanisms

The family members interviewed displayed a high level of tacit knowledge manifested in the different activities they got involved in (Tsoukas, 2003). We observe their capacity to learn by working in different places outside the family businesses, or when they worked within the family business, and as they created new ideas or businesses or even processes (Cohen & Sharma, 2016).

Jorge Alfa acquired his "know-how" by working outside the family group for four years, both in investment banking and in the cement industry. Later he joined one of the companies of his own family branch, where he exercised leadership with his brother. After that, he started a venture in the automotive industry, which was incorporated as one of the companies of his family branch.

In the field of corporate governance, Jorge Alfa entered the FBG management consulting program and completed all of its phases: first as a listener on the Board, then as a developing director, and finally, he became a graduate director. He perfected this know-how by implementing corporate governance in his family's companies. He developed his know-how as a responsible shareholder by being part of the family council and the foundation of FBG. As an executive, he continues to operate within the companies of his family branch. Jorge says:

All of these different roles that I played were like studying a micro master but in practice. I developed skills: human talent, strategic planning and corporate governance. For me, this is a competitive advantage of family businesses.

Gonzalo Delta worked outside the family business for five years in the United States in a company in the same line of business as FBG,

It was a pride for me to show that I could enter a company following the entire process and be selected for the position in a company in the same sector of my family business.

He joined FBG when he was commissioned with the project of starting and opening an office of one of the company's lines of business in Los Angeles, California. After two years, he returned to Mexico and was invited to join FBG and rotate through different positions within the company. He was Brand Manager, Training Manager, and is currently Vice President of Experience and Personnel.

Gonzalo Delta acquired the development of know-how in corporate governance, first as a listener on the Board of Directors and later as a member of the Board. His training in family businesses led him to assume the position of Chairman of the Family Council and to develop specific skills to incorporate good practices, separate emotions, and not take matters as personal issues.

Sofia Epsilon joined FBG by doing the one-year training program of one of the companies of the Epsilon Family Group. Subsequently, she formally joined one of the companies for two years, "*Those years for me was like studying a master's degree in retail and logistics,*" and she learned in practice about the family business. After that she became part of the management team in the area of personnel management.

Like her colleagues, Sofia Epsilon was a listener on the Board of Directors and later became a board member representing her family branch. In addition, her background in family business issues has led her to become President of the Family Council. She has also been invited to be President of the FBG Foundation.

Collective Knowing

Collective knowing has been developed in a natural way in the family business groups interviewed, given the joint work done by two or three generations working together within the specific social context developed in a family business, as knowledge is embedded in the culture of the organization, and by interacting with the different members within the family business allows to learn routines and habits (Nelson & Winter, 1982). Moreover, narratives have played an important role in transmitting collective knowing in the family, as values and identity have been transferred in this process (Parada & Dawson, 2017),

Jorge Alfa's grandparents have been a constant inspiration in his development. From his paternal grandfather, he inherited the idea and the taste to continue developing one of the companies of his family branch; as a child, he did not live with him so much, but when he observed him, he identified his discipline, orderly work and structured way of thinking; however, when he grew up, he lived with him more and had a very enriching relationship with him. From his maternal grandfather, he learned more about the entrepreneurial sense, "he was daring and intelligent to capture value." His father was also an important figure in developing an entrepreneurial spirit and forging his own path, of which he remembers different stories that marked his formation. His father used to tell him:

I want to be the owner of my time and build something of my own.

For Jorge Alfa, business is an art, and he realized in his growth, with his family relationships, that it is necessary to complement the skills of innovation and strategy:

I admire entrepreneurs but also those who are orderly or structured.

In his inspiration, he looks, in addition to his grandparents and his father, to his uncles and aunts as the people who have instilled in his knowledge and allowed him to develop.

This implicit social knowledge also leads him to a relationship with his generation, with his siblings, in which he states that respect and complementarity are fundamental, while at the same time emphasizing that his mother is a *Chief Emotional Officer*, a hidden CEO who "*ties up the whole process.*"

Alfa FBG has created a calendar of activities to foster both the good relationship among its members and to awaken the love for the BFG. For the corporate and business sphere, its main activities are: an open office where family members who so choose can go and dialogue with the directors of the various FBG companies, an annual visit to the factories to learn about operations, new projects, and interact with employees.

To promote harmony and interaction with family members, the following activities are carried out: one family retreat per year; on Sundays Grandma's house is open and all members can go ("*52 Sundays when you can meet another family member*"); a Christmas gathering attended by more than 100 family members; development of campaigns to promote values in which a specific value is promoted once a month; they also have a family intranet.

The spaces where all this planning of activities, socialization and acquiring awareness and identity as part of the entrepreneurial family takes place are the family council and the training and communication and events committees. In the family council, where the process of elaboration and revision of the family protocol is enjoyment and an opportunity to interact, Jorge Alfa says:

The journey to the destination and its return is also part of the trip.

The training committee is in charge of attending to the family members of the different branches in order to train them as good shareholders. In the meetings, Jorge always seeks to nurture each member and thank them all for what they have and are building.

The training committee is a space to attend to the needs of the family members of each branch to develop as responsible shareholders, while the communication and events committee is responsible for promoting the values and philosophy of FBG.

All this collective knowing that Jorge Alfa has developed leads him to declare that his main desires are to achieve and ensure the continuity of the FBG legacy, that "*the following generations fall in love with the project.*"

For **Gonzalo Delta**, his father has been a source of training and inspiration that gave him the identity and love for the family business. He recalls that since he was a child, family trips consisted of visiting the different points of sale and telling him the stories of how each one of them was opened; after school, he would go to the office to be close to his father, where he understood the value of work and of creating. She says:

My dad taught me that the business family was a club, one that I always wanted to belong to.

He also learned from his father the value of humility, as he remembers how he always taught him to be part of the team when he saw him arrive at a hotel with the regional managers, and his father always carried their bags and did not let anyone else do it, they did not understand how a CEO carried the bags of others. Another value that was transmitted to him from his father is effort, discipline, and work. His responsibilities since he was a child were always very clear.

Gonzalo Delta emphasizes that he has also learned a lot from his grandparents, cousins, and siblings. Especially from those who have been his bosses and from whom he has learned many things. He remembers the lessons that each one of them has left him:

- Brother A: *"Trust but validate."*
- Brother B: *"Only if you see yourself as part of the problem can you be part of the solution."*
- Cousin A: *"Empower but demand"*, *"Trust their abilities first and then demand compliance."*
- Father: *"Keep up the good work."*
- Aunt A: *"Great, not just huge."*
- Uncle B: *"Innovate and transcend with the times. What got us here will not get us where we want to go."*

Forming social capital and having a network of contacts has also been important in Gonzalo Delta's social learning. He also understood that people sometimes only wanted him to be in certain groups because of his last name but not because of the person he was, which has always been a challenge for him, and that is why he has preferred to belong more to professional groups related to family businesses and personnel development, which bring more value to the business family.

The activities and routines that Delta FBG has created to foster and share knowledge are varied. Its approach is open and based on trust. For example, to start new businesses, everyone knows they can do it, and if the idea will contribute to FBGs growth, it is usually supported from within the Group's formal business structures. They have a significant budget that they designate for each family member of the leading generation to strengthen their knowledge as long as the courses they take contribute to the growth of the business family. They hold an annual family assembly and a Christmas dinner attended by the family members of the different branches.

Another important area is the Family Council, which seeks to ensure the harmony and socialization of the business family. Within this body, they seek to promote the development and care of NextGen. For this purpose, they carry out the necessary actions to promote and share knowledge: (a) They are paid for university, Master's degree and a vocational workshop. (b) From the age of 18, they can be listeners to both the shareholders' meeting, Board of Directors, and family council, and after the meeting, they get together in a space for feedback. (c) They created the NextGen committee to address the issues that the next generation is interested in and where, for example, they meet informally in a restaurant for the *"happy hour next-gen"* in which the family protocol is made known, and at the same time dialogue and interaction is created with them.

Gonzalo Delta shows his collective knowing when describing his wishes for the future of the entrepreneurial family:

To leave a mark, to have done the right things and to look forward to the harmony, evolution and complexity of FBG.

In **Sofia Epsilon's** case, her Uncle A, FBG President, created the spaces to mentor her and two other G3 members to be prepared to join FBG. Sofia admires her Uncle A's leadership style and the way he has handled change. Her grandmothers have also shaped her development: from her paternal grandmother, she says, they have learned to be very practical. When she was a child, on family trips when visiting grandma, they would take her to the warehouses of the family business to assemble their own bicycles. She also remembers family trips as a child on a cruise ship where they developed family harmony. Her father would take her to the office, and when she was greeted, she commented:

I felt a lot of pride and interest in the business.

For the following generations, they have carried out different activities that foster love for the family business. For example, a rally in the stores: tours of the stores and picking up bicycles in the warehouse, children under 13 were put to work in the warehouses for 1 or 2 days packing and loading a truck, tours of the offices to interact with the managers of the different areas and even one of the little ones discovered that she wanted to study marketing.

Formally everyone has had to go through the Epsilon FBG training, where they must work in the different areas of the family business. They also offer the benefit to newly graduated family members to work for the FBG for six months and grow their resumes while they find another job outside the family business. The spaces from where they promote and share knowledge are the family council and the Board of Directors. Also, the Family Office promotes entrepreneurship both inside and outside the FBG.

The collective knowing is reflected in the identity she has developed with FBG: "*I am very proud to belong to the business family*" she thinks a lot about doing things well, leaving a legacy and "generating good things for the country." She wants the new generations to incorporate values into their lifestyle, "*money doesn't define you*," she says. Reinventing himself as FBG is one of her main concerns.

Intergenerational Flourishing

As we have described, flourishing is a process and not an outcome. The three FBGs in our research have identified the transformation of their different stages of their lives by knowing what their families have allowed them to understand and to love in the developing of their purpose as a family but including their purposes as individual human beings.

Jorge Alfa has a clear vision of the family project, and he has been able to transfer it into his own present and future. **Gonzalo Delta** has recognized the legacy of leadership by co-creating and making space for all in the family with love, respect, and joy. **Sofia Epsilon** as well, has shared that many activities in different moments of her life have contributed to the person she is now, and she can also anticipate that there are more possibilities in front of you when you know your needs and search for answers in your own family set of values.

Conclusions and Discussion

Knowledge Flow in an FBG

One of the questions answered by this study is in relation to identifying the practices or mechanisms that are necessary in order to allow knowledge to flow in a FBG. The different mechanisms described in the findings previously allow us to see some characteristics that could be particular to FBGs. Usually, the study of knowledge in family businesses has been focused on different processes such as succession (Boyd et al., 2015; Cabrera-Suárez et al., 2018), innovation (De Massis et al., 2016; Letonja & Duh, 2016), socialization (Chirico & Salvato, 2008, Cohen & Sharma, 2016), or even in small family businesses (Bracci & Vagnon, 2011) but not in FBGs.

In the mechanisms of *knowing that* the high level of education and their training abroad is a pattern that is repeated in the three cases described but also shared with other family members of the current generation. The best educational preparation is improved from one generation to the next as it progresses thanks to the strategies that the FBGs can develop due to their economic capacity, such as, in this case, sufficient funds to pay for the education of the following generations.

Although in the three cases, we can distinguish different degrees of institutionalization, they all have well-established family and corporate governance bodies. This plays in favor of the development of the three types of mechanisms: the *knowing that* by being able to share formal documents created in the different councils, the *knowing how* by having positions in which family members can actively participate, and the *collective knowing* by encouraging from these bodies the observation of how they work, setting an example and fostering mentoring relationships through them.

Both the economic wealth and the level of institutionalization of the FBGs allow them to have competitive advantages (Boyd et al., 2015) and a more developed *familiness* (Habbershon & Williams, 1999) compared to other types of family businesses that are a form of heterogeneity among family firms (Memili & Dibrell, 2019).

In the *knowing-how* mechanisms, in Alfa and Delta cases, the work outside the family business before formally joining a position within the company is highlighted. In order to develop the "know-how" of the management in Delta and Epsilon cases, it is shown that they have rotated through different positions in the family business before assuming management or vice-presidency of the Group. All three cases share a process of training to become good management directors, from being a listener to developing the ability to be a good executive director. That means, in FBGs, acquiring knowing how is given through a formal process of care and development of the successors (LeBreton-Miller et al., 2004) and specific learning about my own family business (Carig & Moores, 2017) as a critical success factor in the succession and formation of family leaders.

It is interesting to note that in two of the cases, the capacity for entrepreneurship occurs more within the FBG in related business and not as a creation of new businesses, start-ups, or business model innovation, but in the Alfa case, the not related entrepreneurship occurs more in the companies of the family branch than inside the FBG. This can be understood as something that generally concerns large corporations and the slow pace they show in generating new businesses and managing dual business models (Markides, 2000). In all three cases, the "knowing-how" of family governance has been acquired in the exercise of the formal family council position, but it was developed due to: the trust of the enterprising family members, the formal knowledge that they have acquired on the subject of family businesses, and the business family commitment that has been instilled from the collective knowing. This reinforces the importance of having good institutions to teach family business around the world (Salvato et al., 2015).

In all three cases, the mechanisms of *collective knowing* show greater intensity, perhaps because the other two mechanisms tend to be colder (such as knowing that) or more pragmatic (such as knowing how); that is, collective

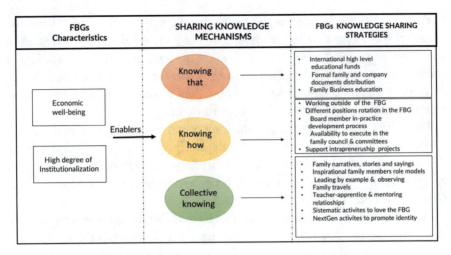

Fig. 20.1 FBGs Knowledge-sharing strategies (*Source* Own elaboration)

knowing is what gives the human and face of enterprising families because is rooted in an ethical behavior (Astrachan et al., 2020; Cruz et al., 2014). Undoubtedly, the example and role models of previous generations are an essential mechanism to feel part of the entrepreneurial family. Stories, sayings and narratives, as well as family trips stand out as identity creators from an early age. The different activities to foster love for the family and the development of skills of the next generations are a common denominator, some more formal than others, but it has been a glue of all three FBGs. The integration of knowledge as organizational capability (Zahara et al., 2020) in family firms could be possible only with collective knowing.

The following chart shows a summary of the strategies for knowledge sharing in FBGs (Fig. 20.1).

Flourishing of Enterprising Families—A Framework of 4C's to Attain a Sense of Purpose

When it comes to describing what a business family is considered to succeed, we have to admit that there is no single answer. Indeed, each family might have its own definition of success, and it will still be valid. We begin by offering a definition of a business family; a business family is a family that "has founded and continues to control at least one established and successful family business, plans to continue to have family members involved in business venturing, and regards the management of long-term family wealth rather than of any one business as the focal objective" (Le Breton-Miller &

Miller, 2018). Thus, family wealth objective requires that families strategize and plan to maintain alignment and long-term commitment, achieving financial and non-financial goals.

The ultimate motivation of a business family might be associated with the notion of continuity, but not necessarily of a particular business unit. Therefore, it is important to better understand why and how a family business group evolves for generations: their idiosyncratic goals in the family business, the resources and capabilities to create value, and their governance structures within and around in order to thrive (Kammerlander et al., 2015). We believe in the importance of developing certain competencies to thrive and flourish in the long term, overcoming challenges, and understanding differences between individuals in order to attain a sense of purpose.

We define Flourishing of Enterprising Families as a dynamic process that consists of knowing and understanding the needs of family members in order to enhance their capabilities in such a way that allow them to achieve their goals and their legacy, ensuring integrity, inclusion and flourishing of each member of the family and their relationship with others, and with society. In order to attain a sense of purpose, we argue that families might fulfill four sets of competencies as they evolve in life: Governance and Leadership, Family Entrepreneurship, Intergenerational Culture, and Ownership and Legacy.

Governance and Leadership

These are the capabilities of the enterprising family to ensure competent leadership that orchestrates the family and the company, not only from the strategy perspective but also reaching an emotional balance. This set of competencies involves the creation and management of the governing bodies of the system that enhance the decision-making process.

Family Entrepreneurship

These are the capabilities of the enterprising family to reinvent itself through the innovation of its business models and the creation of new ventures or business units. These competencies include the mechanisms and funding structures that families put in place to promote transgenerational entrepreneurship and the mindset of searching for new business opportunities aligned with technological trends and digital transformation.

Intergenerational Culture

These are the capabilities of the enterprising family to work together, foster family alignment, and develop synergies among its members. These competencies are to advocate the existence and development of deep dialogue, knowledge sharing, and education within and across generations.

Ownership and Legacy

These are the capabilities of the enterprising family to create wealth and social impact. This is responsible ownership. To become a conscious enterprising family generation by generation.

Flourishing must be identified with prosperity, doing well and developing in a harmonious way to better impact society; family members as individuals are in charge of knowing those competencies, and by practicing the knowing-how as a group or as a family, they are expected to develop their mindsets which would allow them to become a conscious and responsible enterprising family across generations. As Craig and Newbert (2020) have suggested, business-owning families may balance their desire for private gain with their moral obligation to protect and promote the interests of those on whom their businesses depend; thus, the process of flourishing when families are developing their competencies is becoming an important aspect of the decision making in the evolution of enterprising families.

The second question this study answer is about the impact of knowledge mechanisms on the intergenerational flourishing of a FBG. Intergenerational flourishing is the dynamic process by which family entrepreneurs achieve their goals their legacy and ensure the integrity of each member of the family; and to achieve it, they must develop four sets of competencies as they evolve in life: Governance and Leadership, Family Entrepreneurship, Intergenerational Culture, and Ownership and Legacy.

In this study, we can observe the impact of knowledge-sharing mechanisms and their strategies in each of these four competencies. We can clearly observe that in the Governance and Leadership competency, the mechanisms of knowing how play preponderant roles in the development of this competency since they all focus on the know-how of management and corporate and family governance. The same happens with the mechanisms of knowing that go more to a formal business and family business education.

For the family entrepreneurship competency, we can observe a much lower intensity in the mechanisms for knowledge sharing as it only shows the possibility of supporting BFG related ventures and not in a broader strategy to foster entrepreneurship in the new generations.

For intergenerational culture competencies, as well as ownership and legacy, the mechanisms of collective knowing are preponderant. Both the formation of identity with the entrepreneurial family and teaching how to be good owners who contribute to society are part of the stories, narratives, and inspirational models of entrepreneurial families.

The following matrix shows this impact (Fig. 20.2).

We think that this project is relevant because it increases our knowledge of one of the main current phenomena in business families such as FBGs (Rautiainen et al., 2018) and because it also helps complement previous understanding of knowledge sharing and integration among generations (Boyd et al., 2015; Chirico & Salvato, 2008). At a practical level, our work has important implications for business owners and for educators and consultants. For business owners, our work could help family business leaders and owners to understand the mechanisms and develop strategic decisions that are necessary to share and integrate knowledge across generations. For educators and consultants, this work contributes to developing insights

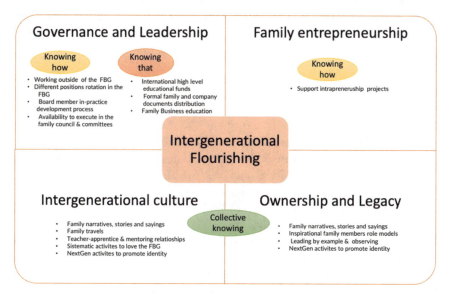

Fig. 20.2 Impact of the FBGs knowledge-sharing strategies in the intergenerational flourishing competencies (*Source* Own elaboration)

and robust frameworks to understand and advise business families to achieve intergenerational flourishing through sharing knowledge in FBGs.

Limitations and Further Research

Our study, while drawing interesting conclusions, is not without limitations. Although three relevant family members were interviewed for this exploratory stage, it would be desirable to inquire into more family members of the three FBGs in order to have a complete interpretation and analysis of the flows and mechanisms of knowledge sharing. The inclusion of more interviewees would allow us to capture the different or similar perceptions about knowledge sharing and its role in the intergenerational flourishing

Our study has focused on the Mexican context, which limits the possibilities of understanding knowledge-sharing flows in other cultures. Finally, we suggest that future research on this topic could be a focus on the specific impact that each of the described knowledge mechanisms (knowing that, knowing how, and collective knowing) would have on the performance of the FBG. It is also possible to inquire whether in different cultures the shared practices or strategies for each mechanism of knowledge change in the FBG. Go deep into empirical research regarding intergenerational flourishing as a process to develop competent business families that ensure generational continuity for FBGs opens a whole path for research for the benefit of enterprising families.

References

Agostini, L., Nosella, A., Sarala, R., Spender, J. C., & Wegner, D. (2020). Tracing the evolution of the literature on knowledge management in inter-organizational contexts: a bibliometric analysis. *Journal of Knowledge Management*.

Akhter, N. (2016). Portfolio entrepreneurship in family firms: Taking stock and moving forward. In F. Kellermanns & F. Hoy (Eds.), *The Routledge companion to family business*. Taylor & Francis Ltd.

Al Ahbabi, S. A., Singh, S. K., Balasubramanian, S., & Gaur, S. S. (2019).Employee perception of impact of knowledge management processes on public sector performance. *Journal of Knowledge Management, 23*(2), 351–373.

Al-Emran, M., Mezhuyev, V., Kamaludin, A. and ALSinani, M. (2018). Development of M-learning application based on knowledge management processes. In *Proceedings of the 2018 7th International Conference on Software and Computer Applications* (pp. 248–253).

Alvesson, M., & Skoldberg, K. (2000). *Reflexive methodology*. Sage.

Astrachan, J. H., Binz Astrachan, C., Campopiano, G., & Baù, M. (2020). Values, spirituality and religion: Family business and the roots of sustainable ethical behavior. *Journal of Business Ethics, 163*(4), 637–645. https://doi.org/10.1007/s10551-019-04392-5

Barney, J. (1991). Firm resources and sustained competitive advantage. *Journal of Management, 17*(1), 99-120.

Barros-Contreras, I., Basco, R., Martín-Cruz, N., & Hernangómez, J. (2020). Strategic management in family business. The missing concept of the familiness learning mechanism. *Journal of Family Business Management*.

Berent-Braun, M. M., & Uhlaner, L. M. (2012). Family governance practices and teambuilding: Paradox of the enterprising family. *Small Business Economics, 38*(1), 103–119.

Boisot, M. H. (1995). Is your firm a creative destroyer? Competitive learning and knowledge flows in the technological strategies of firms. *Research Policy, 24*(4), 489–506. ISO 690

Boisot, M., MacMillan, I. C., & Han, K. S. (Eds.). (2007). *Explorations in information space: Knowledge, agents, and organization*. Oxford University Press.

Boyd, B., Royer, S., Pei, R., & Zhang, X. (2015). Knowledge transfer in family business successions. *Journal of Family Business Management, 5*(1), 17–37.

Bracci, E., & Vagnoni, E. (2011). Understanding small family business succession in a knowledge management perspective. *IUP Journal of Knowledge Management, 9*(1), 7.

Brown, J. S., & Duguid, P. (1991) Organizational learning and communities-of-practice: Toward a unified view or working, learning and innovation. *Organization Science, 2*(1), 40–57.

Brunswicker, S., & Vanhaverbeke, W. (2015). Open innovation in small and medium-sized enterprises (SMEs): External knowledge sourcing strategies and internal organizational facilitators. *Journal of Small Business Management, 53*(4), 1241–1263.

Burrell, W. G., & Morgan, G. (1979). *Sociological paradigms and organizational analysis*. Heinemann.

Cabrera-Suárez, K., De Saá-Pérez, P., & García-Almeida, D. (2001). The succession process from a resource- and knowledge-based view of the family firm. *Family Business Review, 14*(1), 37–46.

Cabrera-Suárez, M. K., García-Almeida, D. J., & De Saá-Pérez, P. (2018). A dynamic network model of the successor's knowledge construction from the resource-and knowledge-based view of the family firm. *Family Business Review, 31*(2), 178–197.

Camelo-Ordaz, C., Garcia-Cruz, J., Sousa-Ginel, E., & Valle-Cabrera, R. (2011). The influence of human resource management on knowledge sharing and innovation in Spain: the mediating role of affective commitment. *The International Journal of Human Resource Management, 22*(7), 1442–1463.

Chirico, F. (2008). Knowledge accumulation in family firms: Evidence from four case studies. *International Small Business Journal, 26*(4), 433–462.

Chirico, F., & Salvato, C. (2008). Knowledge integration and dynamic organizational adaptation in family firms. *Family Business Review, 21*(2), 169–181.

Chrisman, J. J., Chua, J. H., & Steier, L. (2005). Sources and consequences of distinctive familiness: An introduction. *Entrepreneurship Theory and Practice, 29*(3), 237–247.

Cohen, A. R., & Sharma, P. (2016). *Entrepreneurs in every generation: How successful family businesses develop their next leaders.* Berrett-Koehler.

Costa, V., & Monteiro, S. (2016). Key knowledge management processes for innovation: A systematic literature review. *VINE Journal of Information and Knowledge Management Systems, 46*(3), 386–410.

Craig, J. B., & Moores, K. (2017). *Leading a family business: Best practices for long-term stewardship.* ABC-CLIO.

Craig, J. B., & Newbert, S. L. (2020). Reconsidering socioemotional wealth: A Smithian-inspired socio-economic theory of decision-making in the family firm. *Journal of Family Business Strategy, 11*, 1–14.

Cruz, A., Howorth, C., & Hamilton, E. (2013). Intrafamily entrepreneurship: The formation and membership of family entrepreneurial teams. *Entrepreneurship Theory and Practice, 37*(1), 17–46.

Cruz, C., Larraza-Kintana, M., Garcés-Galdeano, L., & Berrone, P. (2014). Are family firms really more socially responsible? *Entrepreneurship Theory and Practice, 38*(6), 1295–1316.

Czarniawska, B. (Ed.). (1997). *A narrative approach to organization studies* (Vol. 43). Sage Publications.

Davenport, T. H., & Prusak, L. (1995). *Working knowledge. How organizations manage what they know.* Harvard Business School Press.

De Massis, A., Frattini, F., Kotlar, J., Petruzzelli, A. M., & Wright, M. (2016). Innovation through tradition: Lessons from innovative family businesses and directions for future research. *Academy of Management Perspectives, 30*(1), 93–116.

Döring, H., & Witt, P. (2020). Knowledge management in family businesses-Empirical evidence from Germany. *Knowledge Management Research & Practice, 18*(2), 175–187.

Eisenhardt, K., & Martin, J. (2000). Dynamic capabilities: What are they? *Strategic Management Journal, 21*, 1105–1121.

Fonseca, M., & Sandoval-Arzaga, F. (2018) Mexico: The essence of leadership in Mexico. In S. Western & É. J. Garcia (Eds.), *Global leadership perspectives.*

Grant, R. M. (1996). Toward a knowledge-based theory of the firm. *Strategic Management Journal, 17*(S2), 109–122.

Habbershon, Timothy G., Nordqvist, M., & Zellweger, T. (2010). Transgenerational entrepreneurship. In *Transgenerational entrepreneurship: Exploring growth and performance in family firms across generations* (pp. 1–38).

Habbershon, T. G., & Williams, M. L. (1999). A resource-based framework for assessing the strategic advantages of family firms. *Family Business Review, 12*(1), 1–22.

Hammond, N. L., Pearson, A. W., & Holt, D. T. (2016). The Quagmire of legacy in family firms: Definition and implications of family and family firm legacy orientations. *Entrepreneurship Theory and Practice, 40*, 1209–1231.

Jaskiewicz, P., Combs, J. G., & Rau, S. B. (2015). Entrepreneurial legacy: Toward a theory of how some family firms nurture transgenerational entrepreneurship. *Journal of Business Venturing, 30*(1), 29–49.

Kammerlander, N., Sieger, P., Voordeckers, W., & Zellweger, T. (2015). Value creation in family firms: A model of fit. *Journal of Family Business Strategy, 6*, 63–72.

Kogut, B., & Zander, U. (1992). Knowledge of the firm, combinative capabilities, and the replication of technology. *Organization Science, 3*(3), 383–397.

Lawson, C., & Lorenz, E. (1999). Collective learning, tacit knowledge and regional innovative capacity. *Regional studies, 33*(4), 305–317.

Lave, J., & Wenger, E. (1991). *Situated learning: Legitimate peripheral participation.* Cambridge University Press.

Le Breton-Miller, I., & Miller, D. (2015). The arts and family business: Linking family-related resources to the market environment. In *Academy of Management Proceedings* (Vol. 2015, No. 1, p. 13248). Academy of Management.

Le Breton-Miller, I., & Miller, D. (2018). Beyond the firm: Business families as entrepreneurs. *Entrepreneurship Theory and Practice, 42*(4), 527–539.

Le Breton-Miller, I., Miller, D., & Steier, L. P. (2004). Toward an integrative model of effective FOB succession. *Entrepreneurship Theory and Practice, 28*(4), 305–328.

Leonard, D., & Sensiper, S. (1998). The role of tacit knowledge in group innovation. *California Management Review, 40*(3), 112–132.

Letonja, M., & Duh, M. (2016). Knowledge transfer in family businesses and its effects on the innovativeness of the next family generation. *Knowledge Management Research & Practice, 14*(2), 213–224.

Lo, M. F., Tian, F., & Ng, P. M. L. (2021). Top management support and knowledge sharing: The strategic role of affiliation and trust in an academic environment. *Journal of Knowledge Management.*

Lo, M. F., & Tian, F. (2020). Enhancing competitive advantage in Hong Kong higher education: Linking knowledge sharing, absorptive capacity and innovation capability. *Higher Education Quarterly, 74*(4), 426–441.

Markides, C. (2000). *All the right moves: A guide to crafting breakthrough strategy.* Harvard Business Press.

Memili, E., & Dibrell, C. (Eds.). (2019). *The Palgrave handbook of heterogeneity among family firms.* Palgrave Macmillan.

Miles, M. B., & Huberman, M. (1994). *Qualitative data analysis: An expanded sourcebook* (2nd ed.). Sage.

Mukherjee K., Rautiainen M., Pihkala T., Rosa P. (2019) The dynamics and complexity of family business groups. In M. Rautiainen, P. Rosa, T. Pihkala, M. Parada, & A. Cruz (Eds.), *The family business group phenomenon*. Palgrave Macmillan.

Nelson, R., & Winter, S. (1982). *An evolutionary theory of economic change*. The Belknap Press of Harvard University Press.

Nonaka, I., & Takeuchi, H. (1995). *The knowledge-creating company: How Japanese companies create the dynamics of innovation*. Oxford university press.

Nordqvist, M., & Zellweger, T. (Eds.). (2010). Transgenerational entrepreneurship: Exploring growth and performance. In *Family firms across generations*. Edward Elgar.

Parada, M. J., & Dawson, A. (2017). Building family business identity through transgenerational narratives. *Journal of Organizational Change Management*.

Parada, M. J., Akhter, N., Basco, R., Discua Cruz, A., & Fitz-Koch, S. (2019). Understanding the dynamics of business group development: A transgenerational perspective. In M. Rautiainen, P. Rosa, T. Pihkala, M. Parada, & A. Cruz (Eds.), *The family business group phenomenon*. Palgrave Macmillan.

Patton, M. Q. (2002). *Qualitative research & evaluation methods* (3rd ed.). Sage Publications, Inc.

Polanyi, M. (1966). *The tacit dimension*. Doubleday.

Rautiainen, M., Konsti-Laakso, S., & Pihkala, T. (2020). Innovation in family business groups: Going beyond an R&D perspective. In A. Calabro (Ed.), *A research agenda for family business a way ahead for the field* (pp. 231–246).

Rautiainen, M., Rosa, P., Pihkala, T., Parada, M. J., & Cruz, A. D. (Eds.). (2018). *The family business group phenomenon: Emergence and complexities*. Springer.

Ryle, G. (1949). *The concept of mind*. University of Chicago Press.

Salvato, C., Sharma, P., & Wright, M. (2015). *From the guest editors: learning patterns and approaches to family business education around the world—Issues, insights, and research agenda*.

Sandoval-Arzaga, F. (2005). *El conocimiento tácito en los procesos de aprendizaje en equipos de trabajo* (Doctoral dissertation, Tesis Doctoral, 2.005, Universidad Ramón Llull).

Sandoval-Arzaga, F., Ramírez-Pasillas, M., & Fonseca-Paredes, M. (2011). Knowledge integration in Latin American family firms. In *Understanding entrepreneurial family businesses in uncertain environments opportunities and resources in Latin America* (pp. 181–202).

Sharma, P., Chrisman, J. J., & Chua, J. H. (2003). Predictors of satisfaction with the succession process in family firms. *Journal of Business Venturing, 18*(5), 667–687.

Sieger, P., Zellweger, T., Nason, R. S., & Clinton, E. (2011). Portfolio entrepreneurship in family firms: A resource-based perspective. *Strategic Entrepreneurship Journal, 5*(4), 327–351.

Singh, A. K., Verma, J., & Verma, R. (2020). Understanding role of market-orientated IT competence and knowledge sharing mechanism in gaining competitive advantage. *Global Business Review, 21*(2), 418–435.

Spender, J.-C. (1996a). Making knowledge the basis of a dynamic theory of the firm. *Strategic Management Journal, 17*(S2), 45–62.
clearpage

Spender, J.-C. (1996b). Competitive advantage from tacit knowledge? Unpacking the concept and its strategic implications. In B. Moingeon & A. Edmondson (Eds.), *Organizational learning and competitive advantage* (pp. 56–73). Sage.

Spender, J.-C. (1998). The dynamics of individual and organizational knowledge. In C. Eden & J.-C. Spender (Eds.), *Managerial and organizational cognition: Theory, methods and research* (pp. 13–39). Sage Publications, Inc.

Stake, R. E. (2000). Case studies. In N. K. Denzin & Y. S. Lincoln (Eds.), *The handbook of qualitative research* (2nd ed., pp. 435–454). Sage.

Teece, D. J., Pisano, G., & Shuen, A. (1997). Dynamic capabilities and strategic management. *Strategic Management Journal, 18*, 509–533.

Than, S. T., Nguyen, C. H., Tran, T. Q., & Le, P. B. (2019). Building competitive advantage for Vietnamese firms: The roles of knowledge sharing and innovation. *International Journal of Business Administration, 10*(4), 1–12.

Tsoukas, H. (2003). Do we really understand tacit knowledge? In M. Easterby-Smith, MA Lyles (Eds.), *Handbook of organizational learning and knowledge.*

VanderWeele, T. J. (2017). On the promotion of human flourishing. *Proceedings of the National Academy of Sciences, 114*(31), 8148–8156.

Von Krogh, G., Ichijo, K., & Nonaka, I. (2000). *Enabling knowledge creation: How to unlock the mystery of tacit knowledge and release the power of innovation.* Oxford University Press on Demand.

Wood, M. (2002).Mind the gap? A processual reconsideration of organizational knowledge. *Organization, 9*, 151–171.

Yin, R. K. (1994). *Case study research* (2nd ed.). Sage.

Zahra, S. A., Neubaum, D. O., & Hayton, J. (2020). What do we know about knowledge integration: Fusing micro-and macro-organizational perspectives. *Academy of Management Annals, 14*(1), 160–194.

Zellweger, T., Nason, R. S., & Nordqvist, M. (2012). From longevity of firms to transgenerational entrepreneurship of families introducing family entrepreneurial orientation. *Family Business Review, 25*(2), 136–155.

21

Transition from Family Business to Business Family: Managing Paradoxical Tensions in Organizational Identities and Portfolio Entrepreneurship

Jeremy Cheng and Roger King

Introduction

Most family business groups experience the transition from family business to business family. An emerging body of literature has examined this transition (Habbershon & Pistrui, 2002; Le Breton-Miller & Miller, 2018; Michael-Tsabari et al., 2014; Steier et al., 2015), mostly from the theoretical perspectives of organizational identity or portfolio entrepreneurship. In this study, we define "family business" as an operating business where ownership by a single family results in effective control of leadership and operations by that family and a clear intent exists to pass this ownership or control on to the next generation. Informed by Steier et al. (2015) and Davis (2020), we conceptualize "business family" as a family (i) bounded by a shared ownership identity *and* (ii) owning a shared portfolio of companies and other assets, with the intent to preserve and grow the portfolio value across generations.

J. Cheng (✉)
The Chinese University of Hong Kong, Hong Kong, China
e-mail: jeremycheng@link.cuhk.edu.hk

R. King
The Hong Kong University of Science and Technology, Hong Kong, China
e-mail: rking@ust.hk

© The Author(s), under exclusive license to Springer Nature Switzerland AG 2023
M. Rautianen et al. (eds.), *The Palgrave Handbook of Managing Family Business Groups*,
https://doi.org/10.1007/978-3-031-13206-3_21

Organizational identity theory can explain how family business and business family as two identity archetypes may result in different entrepreneurial strategies to respond to change and disruptions (e.g., Brinkerink et al., 2020; Prügl & Spitzley, 2021). While a strong identification of family members with the family business can raise the socioemotional wealth of the owning family (Gomez-Mejia et al., 2011), fixating on the legacy business identity may slow down the family's response to entrepreneurial opportunities (Shepherd & Haynie, 2009), suppressing the propensity to build new ventures. Existing studies have also used the lens of portfolio entrepreneurship to examine the motivations and processes of developing a business portfolio by families-in-business (e.g., Carter & Ram, 2003; Sieger et al., 2011). Availability and timely deployment of familiness (i.e., the family-controlled pool of resources and capabilities) predict diversification and/or corporate venturing activities, while families-in-business build a portfolio of businesses for economic and socioemotional motives. Business families may organize their portfolio as a multi-business corporation or as a business group, potentially managed by a family office and/or a holding company (Steier et al., 2015), as a planned act or/and as part of the effectuation process (Fitz-Koch et al., 2019).

Positioning the formation of business family and family business groups at the nexus of the organizational identity and portfolio entrepreneurship literature reveals a chicken-and-egg puzzle: do families-in-business build a business family identity first, which eventually guides the venturing behavior as the traditional organizational identity theory may argue (Albert & Whetten, 1985)? Or do families-in-business unfold multiple ventures first as the effectuation approach may suggest (Sarasvathy, 2001) and gradually evolve a stronger business family identity at a later stage? This begs a deeper understanding of the underlying changes and their dynamics in the transition. Another interesting phenomenon is: why do some family businesses become business families, while others stay as family businesses, especially when financial resources are not a limiting factor? This begs the question of what triggers and/or catalyzes the transition. Even though organizational identity and portfolio entrepreneurship have been powerful lenses to understand the transition, they fail to comprehend the complex multidimensional evolution in entirety.

In this exploratory study, we analyze the understudied phenomenon of the transition from family business to business family, examining the changes and triggers of the transition. Applying a paradox lens (Schad et al., 2016; Smith & Lewis, 2011) to analyze our multi-case data, we argue that families-in-business need to resolve underlying paradoxical tensions related to organizational identity (i.e., being a family owner/governor versus a family operator; minimizing intra-family faultlines for a shared ownership identity versus preserving the faultlines for control and command) and portfolio entrepreneurship (i.e., investing in new ventures versus in the legacy business; smart harvesting versus holding onto existing assets; and liberating personal wealth versus tying personal assets to business ownership) in the transition. Instead of propounding that the business family identity drives portfolio strategy, we posit that paradoxical tensions of both dimensions are inherent and embedded in the family enterprise system (Schuman et al., 2010). Certain paradoxes may become more salient, when families-in-business experience disruptions or when they face decisions as to whether to exit from the legacy business.

The contributions of this study are threefold. *First*, it is novel to position the transition from family business to business family as resolving paradoxical tensions related to organizational identity and portfolio entrepreneurship. Recognizing that families-in-business may exist in different dynamic equilibria of multiple paradoxical tensions opens new avenues for researching strategic and entrepreneurial behavior. The application also offers interesting insights into the theory of paradox (Schad et al., 2016; Smith & Lewis, 2011). *Second*, we ground our definition of business family on the concepts of organizational identity and portfolio entrepreneurship and unfold the discussion using business family as a unit of entrepreneurial analysis, thereby addressing the call of Neubaum and Payne (2021) to advance the centrality of family in family business research. In particular, we enrich the conversation to remove the broad-brushed assumption of one-family-one-business and explain how business families shape a multi-business portfolio (De Massis et al., 2021), which is important for understanding the formation and evolution of family business group. *Third*, we expand the discussion of family firm heterogeneity (Neubaum et al., 2019) by treating business family as a unique form of families-in-business in terms of its organizational logic and entrepreneurial strategies. We advance the notion that family heterogeneity is an underestimated source of family firm heterogeneity (Frank et al., 2019; Jaskiewicz & Dyer, 2017).

Theoretical Background

Business Family as a Unit of Entrepreneurial Analysis

The use of "business family" as a unit of analysis has gained traction over the past two decades (e.g., Habbershon & Pistrui, 2002; Zellweger et al., 2012). Yet, it is important to differentiate the use of the term "business family" from "family-in-business" before we unfold the discussion. In this chapter, we use "family-in-business" as an umbrella term to cover any family which is engaged in a business(es) as a collective. From a shared narrative perspective, Hamilton et al. (2017) argued that families-in-business "form circles of attachment which relate to future generations taking up a position in the family and business realms to engage in continuing a family legacy, rather than being merely a link in inheriting a running business, property or assets" (p. 8). The clarity which Hamilton et al. (2017) brought in is how shared narratives shape and reflect the connections between family and business(es) and how they guide the formation and renewal of collective identity within and across generations. Variations in the family-business connection and the generativity of the shared identity may contribute to different forms or types of families-in-business. Here, business family is a subset of family-in-business. Table 21.1 shows how some prior studies defined "business family" and other similar terms such as "enterprising family," "entrepreneuring family," and "entrepreneurial family" (for a more detailed typology based on family habitual entrepreneurship, see Rosa, Howorth, and Discua Cruz (2014)).

From this brief list of definitions, we distill several anchoring features of business family, mostly derived in comparison with family business. *First*, the value of the portfolio owned by the business family is the key, not the mere existence and continuity of a business per se (Le Breton-Miller & Miller, 2018). Davis (2020) asserted that a business family should exercise emotional calmness in judging the contribution of an underlying asset to the portfolio value. *Second*, a business family should be able to embrace the "family-as-investors mindset" (Habbershon & Pistrui, 2002) or "owner's mindset" (Davis, 2020), which is different from the "family-in-business mindset" (Habbershon & Pistrui, 2002) or "operator's mindset" (Davis, 2020) beheld by a family business. *Third*, transgenerational entrepreneurship is at the core of business family to keep reinventing the portfolio over time, especially amid ongoing internal and external disruptions. *Finally*, shared identity and shared wealth are the glue that keep the business family together. While family business is also connected by their shared identity and wealth (Hamilton et al., 2017), what constitutes their shared identity and wealth may be different.

Term	Definition	Anchoring Feature(s)	Source
Enterprising family	'Enterprising families...are not simply families in business or enterprise. An enterprising family is a particular type of family–a family who is "enterprising." Enterprising families have a family-as-investor mindset and entrepreneurial-strategy methods.' (p.228)	Investor mindset Entrepreneurial methods Mindset-method coupling	Habbershon and Pistrui (2002)
Entrepreneuring/enterprising family	"...we define business-owning families as two or more family members who own a firm together... in keeping with our more general definition of entrepreneurship as related to value creation and growth orientation, we define the entrepreneuring or enterprising family as a business-owning family that is focused on growing family wealth and protecting shared wealth together by way of business value creation." (p.104)	Shared wealth Value creation	Berent-Braun and Uhlaner (2012)

(continued)

Table 21.1 (continued)

Term	Definition	Anchoring Feature(s)	Source
Business family	"...we count as business families those that have founded and continue to control at least one established and successful family business, plan to continue to have family members involved in business venturing, and *regard the management of long-term family wealth rather than of any one business as the focal objective*" (p. 528)	Transgenerational entrepreneurship Continuity of family wealth (and not single business per se)	Le Breton-Miller and Miller (2018)
Business family	"...we categorize incumbent family firms archetypically as either family businesses–in which organizational identity is largely defined by the operational activities performed–or business families–where the operational activities are less central to the family firm' organizational identity..." (p.2)	Reduced centrality of operational activities in the business family identity	Brinkerink et al. (2020)

Term	Definition	Anchoring Feature(s)	Source
Entrepreneurial family	"We define an entrepreneurial family as a group of individuals related by kinship, adoption, or affinity (by marriage or other relationship) who jointly own and/or manage multiple assets, following a shared vision for how such assets should collectively create value across generations." (p. 360)	Shared ownership Transgenerational value creation	De Massis et al. (2021)

Transition as Managing Paradoxical Tensions

Family business and business family are embedded in paradoxes. Paradoxes are "persistent contradictions between interdependent elements" (Schad et al., 2016, p. 5). While seemingly distinct and oppositional, these elements are mutually constitutive and supportive. As hybrid systems combining the conflicting realms of the socialistic "family" and the capitalistic "business" (Schuman et al., 2010), both family business and business family are prone to the inherent paradoxes. Based on the core activities and elements of organizations, Smith and Lewis (2011) catalogued four paradoxes, namely (i) *belonging* (tensions of competing identities, values, roles, and memberships), (ii) *organizing* (tensions of competing organizational structures and processes), (iii) *learning* (clashes of tradition and change), and (iv) *performing* (tensions of competing goals and strategies). Building on the work of Steier et al. (2015) and King and Cheng (2020), we postulate that family business and business family differ on these dimensions (see Table 21.2) and that the transition from family business to business family may involve identifying and managing tensions related to these paradoxical dimensions.

Regarding the *belonging* paradox, family business and business family may rest on competing identities, values, and roles. Family business hinges more on the operator's mindset, which stresses on operational excellence and control. This may be achieved at the expense of the financial return, contradicting with the owner's mindset of business family (Davis, 2020; Habbershon & Pistrui, 2002). Yet, as the situation requires, a business family may have to put on its operator's hat, especially when the family's engagement in the newly acquired business can enhance the value of the venture and hence that of the portfolio. Considering the *organizing* paradox, managing and leading a single business versus a multi-business portfolio may require a different organizational structure and leadership: family business stresses more on control through a more hierarchical design and centralized leadership while business family on flexibility in resource deployment and collaboration among portfolio companies, via the coordination of a family office or a holding company (Steier et al., 2015). Yet, control and collaboration are both important to govern the business family in the long run, especially considering the opportunistic acts of members with divergent interests (Sundaramurthy & Lewis, 2003). On *learning*, family business may prefer acquiring knowledge to enhance the existing operation where preserving the tradition and respecting wisdom of the prior family leaders are crucial, while business family may orient more toward learning groundbreaking and potentially disruptive ideas with the hope to nurture new

Table 21.2 Differences between family business and business family

	Family business	Business family
Definition (Family-business relationship)	An operating business where ownership by a single family results in effective control of leadership and operations by that family and a clear intent exists to pass this ownership or control on to the next generation	A family (i) bounded by a shared ownership identity and (ii) owning a shared portfolio of companies and other assets (which may change over time), with the intent to preserve and grow the portfolio value across generations
Belonging (identities, values, roles, and membership)	"Family-in-business mindset" or "operator's mindset"—focusing on operational control and operational excellence	"Family-as-investors mindset" or "owner's mindset"—focusing on value maximization (or optimization) of the portfolio
Organizing (structuring and leading)	Usually a functional structure under one business organization; likely more hierarchical; usually with a single leader with superior ability to operate the business	Likely organized as a multi-business corporation or business group, potentially managed by a family office and/or holding company; distributed leadership is encouraged to provide the diverse talents required in managing the portfolio
Learning (tradition and change)	Preference to learn and innovate the existing business; preserving tradition and wisdom from the prior generations of leaders is important	A stronger orientation to change, innovate, and nurture new ventures; tradition is not unchangeable to create and embrace a new future

(continued)

Table 21.2 (continued)

	Family business	Business family
Performing (goals and strategies)	Value creation from within the existing business; perpetuation of the business as an important goal; strong emotional attachment to the legacy business, even though it may be non-performing or under-performing	Value creation from acquiring and nurturing new ventures and divesting of non-performing assets; each business in the portfolio should benefit from the family's involvement or else should be sold or restructured

ventures and inspire a new future. Yet, without acknowledging the tradition, it is arguably hard for the business family to innovate for the future (e.g., De Massis et al., 2016). On *performing*, family business may emphasize more on value creation from within the existing business, but the strong emotional attachment to this business may at times drive sub-optimal decisions. Business family, on the other hand, creates value by acquiring and nurturing new ventures and divesting assets at the right time. Each business in the portfolio should benefit from the family's involvement or else should be sold or restructured (Steier et al., 2015). But to successfully transition from family business to business family, the latter must be able to accommodate the socioemotional needs, especially the identity loss post-sale of the legacy business.

Identifying the Paradoxical Tensions

While adopting the paradox lens to meta-theorize the transition appears to be grounded, co-existence of multiple paradoxical tensions and their interactions can be daunting in terms of developing a coherent and fundamental understanding of the transition. We pick *belonging* and *organizing* to "zoom in" as this pair of paradoxical dimensions meaningfully differentiates between family business and business family. The choice is also guided by the extant literature on organizational identity—converging with *belonging* paradox— and portfolio entrepreneurship—informing the *organizing* paradox.

Belonging: Shifting Organizational Identities

Organizational identity captures elements of an organization that are the most central, distinctive, and enduring (Albert & Whetten, 1985). Habbershon and Pistrui (2002) contrasted between "family-in-business" and "family-as-investors" as separate identities. "Family-in-business" emphasizes operational decision-making of a particular business and managerial efforts that drive a family "to think of itself as a particular type of a family (e.g., a 'brewery family' or a 'manufacturing family'), which in turn locks it into path-dependent corporate strategies and family traditions that dictate its capital asset strategies" (Habbershon & Pistrui, 2002, p. 231). The family-as-investors mindset, on the other hand, encourages the stewardship of wealth-creating resources and capabilities and by pursuing active capital allocation strategies, these families preserve and grow transgenerational wealth, which does not bound to "a particular business entity or legacy asset" (Habbershon & Pistrui, 2002, p. 231). They asserted that "family-as-investors" has a different "mindset" and pursue different entrepreneurial "methods."

Organizational identity addresses "who we are" (being), which subsequently guides "what we do" (doing). Yet, the traditional view of being-to-doing has been challenged. Kreiner et al. (2015) developed the notion of identity elasticity, "the tensions that simultaneously stretch, while holding together, social constructions of identity" (p. 981). Brinkerink et al. (2020) applied this concept to explain how heterogeneous organizational identities can affect, and get affected by, strategic decisions. They anchored two identity archetypes at the ends of an identity elasticity continuum, with "family business" at the inelastic end (representing a tight overlap between being and doing) and "business family" at the elastic end (a loose overlap between being and doing). Brinkerink et al. (2020) argued that business family with a more elastic organizational identity is more likely to frame disruptive innovation earlier and treat it more as opportunities rather than threats when compared to family business. Building on the organizational identity framework of Fotea and Fotea (2020), Widz and Parada (2020) argued that the mismatch between family, business, and legacy business identities would require realignment to reflect the nature of the current portfolio. Through sensemaking and storytelling, families could develop a collective family-business identity, which would be signaled to internal and external stakeholders, thereby raising the awareness of the identification of business family.

Organizing: from Single Business to Portfolio of Companies

Portfolio entrepreneurship is defined as simultaneous ownership of multiple ventures by a single ultimate owner (Sieger et al., 2011). Westhead and Wright (1998) described a portfolio founder as one who "retains his/her original business and inherits, establishes, and/or purchases another business" (p. 176). Moving from individual entrepreneurs to entrepreneurial families, Rosa et al. (2014) examined different forms of family habitual entrepreneurship. Compared to individual owners or wealth creators, business families serving as a portfolio owner may have a distinct set of rubrics governing their portfolio decisions (Carter & Ram, 2003; Le Breton-Miller & Miller, 2018; Steier et al., 2015). Theories based on agentic and institutional considerations tend to see business group formation as a rational strategy to optimize overall business performance and to fill institutional voids. From the effectuation perspective (Sarasvathy, 2001), however, portfolio development can be conceptualized quite differently. Rather than being rigorously planned from pre-set goals, a business group is formed as "the end result of an emerging process of entrepreneurial venturing over time" (Fitz-Koch et al., 2019, p. 356). The business group may be the result of a business family pursuing different business opportunities based on interests of the family and individual members rather than on planned business objectives. It is particularly salient that multigenerational families seek to maintain shared family control of their highly diversified financial and business assets through portfolio development (Jaffe & Lane, 2004). Here, alignment of what constitutes value to members of the business family appears critical to engage in portfolio entrepreneurship. The portfolio value can be broadened to cover not only financial capital but also non-financial capital such as human, spiritual, relational, and structural capital (Cheng et al., 2021). This echoes the discussion of why financial and socioemotional goals influence the emergence of portfolio entrepreneurship.

Even though organizational identity and portfolio entrepreneurship are key anchors to examine the transition, it has been far from clear what paradoxical tensions families-in-business experience in terms of identity shifts and portfolio development. The ongoing challenges to the notion of being-to-doing and the paradigm of rational planning sharpen the chicken-and-egg puzzle: do families-in-business build a business family identity first, which eventually guides the venturing behavior, as the organizational identity theory may argue? Or as the effectuation approach may suggest, do families-in-business unfold multiple ventures first and grow a strong business family identity later? Identifying the paradoxical tensions of *belonging* and *organizing* appears to be the first step to advance the understanding of this puzzle. This gives rise to our first research question: ***What are the paradoxical tensions embedded in the transition from family business to business family?***

The Transition Trigger: Raising the Paradoxical Cognition

Organizational paradoxes often remain latent, but they may become more salient under three conditions namely (i) plurality, i.e., when a multiplicity of competing views arises with power diffusion, (ii) scarcity, i.e., when scarcity demands reallocation of resources, or (iii) change, i.e., when environmental change reopens sensemaking and reprioritizes needs (Smith & Lewis, 2011). Naturally, as families-in-business move from the second generation to the third and subsequent ones, ownership becomes more dispersed, and the new leadership may not enjoy the same power as their patriarch or matriarch in the founding generation. The incoming leader may have to negotiate and renew the vision, missions, and values of the family and the business, so that the growingly diverse interests of members from different branches can be realigned (Jaffe & Lane, 2004). At the same time, they may also have to cater for the growing financial needs of the bigger family, by diversifying their business and their investments (Jaffe & Lane, 2004). Over time, families-in-business may also experience a major liquidity event, where the core legacy business may be sold. Whether the exit is planned or not, the loss of legacy business removes the identity glue to gel all family members together. Instead, they must reconstruct a new identity, and this may give rise to the business family. In addition to these internal triggers, King and Cheng (2018) have posited that the emergence of wide-ranging disruptive technologies fast suppresses the business cycle and put the families-in-business in developmental pressure, thereby advancing the transition. Other external disruptions such as the COVID-19 pandemic may also have a similar effect on families-in-business (Calabrò et al., 2021). As Quinn and Cameron (1988) noted, paradoxes are perceived more frequently in turbulent times.

An interesting phenomenon arises as these triggers appear to be "out there" and should influence most if not all families-in-business: why do some family businesses become business families, while others stay as family businesses, especially when financial resources are not the limiting factor? How families-in-business perceive these triggers and their subsequent transition as a planned act or as a natural evolution may be relevant. On the one hand, Habbershon and Pistrui (2002) tended to see the transition more as a planned act: "This is not to say that an a priori commitment to a family-as-investor mindset or sustainable wealth creation comes naturally to families. It takes a continuous effort to generate it and sustain it" (p. 232). The planned act may heighten cognition of paradoxical tensions embedded in the system. On the other hand, taking more a natural evolution perspective, Michael-Tsabari et al. (2014) argued that factors such as multiplicity of views across generations and scarcity of resources may facilitate the evolution beyond the legacy business and the development of a multi-business portfolio. Yet, the debate on the divergent nature of the transition is far from conclusive, and it is eminent to understand the relations between the triggers and the transitions. This drives our second research question: ***What triggers and/or catalyzes the transition from family business to business family?***

Methods

Given the limited understanding of the multidimensional transition from family business to business family, we adopted an exploratory multi-case setup to analyze our research questions, informed by the positivistic approach (Eisenhardt, 1989; Leppäaho et al., 2016). A case presents a holistic description and analysis of a person, an institution, or a bounded system (Yin, 2009). Multiple cases afford a replication logic, with each case serving to (dis)confirm inferences drawn from the others, thereby raising the ability to yield more robust and generalizable theories than single case studies (Eisenhardt, 1989; Yin, 2009). Inductive case research helps early stage theory development and identifies processes which enable "researchers to get closer to the action" (Steier, 2007, p. 1101). This empirical setup is particularly useful to understand the complexity of description of "the actual human interactions, meanings, and processes that constitute real-life organizational settings" (Eisenhardt & Graebner, 2007, p. 25).

We applied theoretical sampling and selected three business families, each of which owned a large business group and with family members identifying themselves as a business family. We chose large family groups to make sure that financial resources were not a major limitation for portfolio development. To minimize external variation beyond the phenomenon of interest (Eisenhardt, 1989), the participating families were all ethnic Chinese, with their culture largely informed by Confucian collectivism. This culture stressed on maintaining a strong family business identity and family control (Gupta & Levenburg, 2010), factors that might affect the transition. The legacy businesses of the participating families were all in manufacturing. We knew these families for an extended period, from five to over 10 years. These families had participated in the prior studies (Cheng & Au, 2014; Cheng & King,

2021; King & Cheng, 2018; King et al., 2017), which afforded us a much deeper understanding of their developmental trajectory. To counteract potential biases due to familiarity with the families, a third researcher who did not take part in the prior studies participated in the interviews. This researcher sought clarifications and challenged implicit assumptions held by us in the data collection and interpretation.

The bulk of the data was collected through semi-structured interviews with members of these business families. Before starting primary data collection, secondary data was gathered (e.g., books related to the family business groups and/or the owning families, company websites, and newspaper clips). These secondary data was important for understanding the development trajectory of the family business groups, and aided the data collection by providing updated information to shape the interview questions. We also triangulated the secondary data with some of the accounts provided by the participants. All interviews were recorded and transcribed verbatim by Otter, an automated transcription service. All transcripts were checked to ensure their accuracy. The average interview time was 102 minutes; the duration of the longest interview was about two hours. The multi-method approach allowed us to capture changes in identity narratives and portfolio development over an extensive period.

We took a three-pronged approach for data analysis. In the first step, we engaged in open coding of interview data for triggers of the transition as well as the underlying changes in the transition. We kept the coding process open at this stage to record the terms, concepts, and observations that informants used. We read the transcripts line by line and assigned a code to illustrate the content without imposing our own interpretations or that from the literature. This process was iterative, and it produced a list of primary codes. In the second step, we compared the primary codes and known constructs from the literature to develop secondary codes as "knowledgeable agents" (Gioia et al., 2013). Our coding in this step was relatively open in that we actively sought secondary codes that captured the essence of numerous but conceptually overlapping primary codes. We thoroughly analyzed all secondary codes and their potential relations within cases. In this step, we asked how these secondary codes might relate to each other in addressing our research question. Extant literature related to organizational identity and portfolio entrepreneurship was unfolded as insights were developed (Eisenhardt, 1989). In the third phase, after completing the within-case analysis, we moved on to the cross-case analysis. The intention was not only to draw similarities between cases, but also to look for differences and explore meaningful contingencies.

Findings and Propositions

In this section, we describe the three cases in brief, sharing necessary background to understand their transition, such as the portfolio owned by the family and their perceived identity (i.e., whether they see themselves more as a family business or business family). We then present the data structure and explain each dimension with selective case evidence. We also draw propositions as appropriate.

The Business Family Cases

Case 1. The Lee Family and Lee Kum Kee Group

Established in 1888, Lee Kum Kee was among the few ethnic Chinese family businesses that have passed the century mark. The Lee family's legacy business has continued to generate appreciable wealth by manufacturing the renowned oyster sauce and over 100 other condiments. As the third-generation patriarch, Lee Man Tat bought out his siblings in a family feud. The fourth generation and the fifth one comprised of only Man Tat's children and grandchildren respectively. The family began to diversify into other businesses, thanks to their unique value of "constant entrepreneurship." In 1992, the family ventured into traditional Chinese health products and built "Infinitus" as a multi-billion brand, which had outgrown the sauce business. They also went into property and other financial investments. In 2019, the family released their 1,000-year business vision statement: "Guided by the principles of *Si Li Ji Ren* (which means considering the interest of all before taking any action), constant entrepreneurship and autopilot leadership, we strive to be the most trusted enterprise for a healthier and happier world beyond 1,000 years." As the family and the business were navigating the different stages through this 1,000 year journey together, the family members constantly checked in with their current standing to better understand how to improve. Sammy Lee, a fourth-generation member and Executive Chairman of the Lee Kum Kee Group, noted: "I do not think we are there yet [sic: being a business family]. At the moment, we are still a family business." Andrea Lee, a fifth-generation member, saw that the transition was in place: "Taking a step back and tracking our progress and growth, I believe we are still very much a family business now, but we are making that transition to a business family."

Case 2. The Tan Family and Luen Thai Group

Founded by Dr Tan Siu-lin in 1965, Luen Thai had grown from a garment company into a global conglomerate. Dr Tan, together with his eldest son Dr Henry Tan and five other second-generation members, ventured into different businesses under three umbrella companies: (i) Luen Thai Holdings, (ii) Luen Thai Enterprises Ltd., and (iii) Tan Holdings Corporation. As the legacy business, the garment-manufacturer Luen Thai Holdings was listed on the Stock Exchange of Hong Kong in 2004. Luen Thai Enterprises was a holding company with wide-ranging business interests, particularly retail, in China, the United States, Micronesia, and Southeast Asia. Tan Holdings Corporation represented the family's interest in Micronesia, which the Tans considered as their second home. While the family naturally developed a business portfolio over the years, they were more inclined to see it as a family enterprise, with resources primarily focused on Luen Thai Holdings. The transition happened after the family's sale of majority stake of Luen Thai Holdings in 2017. Henry Tan restructured the portfolio into six major divisions, namely (i) retail, (ii) tourism, (iii) fishery, (iv) real estate, (v) Micronesia and the Pacific, and (vi) investments. The tourism business, S.A.I. Leisure Group, got listed in 2019. He saw the concept of portfolio management grew stronger: "I think we are in the transition, and today we are more business family than family business."

Case 3. The Kuvinichkul Family and Metta Group

A third-generation member of her family's legacy business Alumet in Thailand, Juthasree "June" Kuvinichkul knew that the aluminum manufacturer had limited room for further upside in face of disruptive technologies. She chose to evolve her Thai Chinese family business into a business family by initiating and leading corporate restructuring to set up Metta Group, a family holding company under which a growing portfolio of regional game-changing tech and contemporary non-tech businesses and investments operate alongside the original endeavor. The Metta Group included Metta Tech (e.g., Grab), Metta Finance (the multi-family "club" of 159 Capitals and YouTech as a fintech company), Metta Green (e.g., Prabkaya Solution as a recycling company), Metta Aluminum (e.g., Alumet), and other investments that the group helps groom. June Kuvinichkul and her two siblings remained connected to the family in this new structure. Her parents felt great attachment to the aluminum business, but agreed that the family should exit in the recent years. Seeking alignment at the top level that the family did not have to pass onto any business, June Kuvinichkul saw themselves more as a business family: "Now we have Metta Group (which builds, invests, incubates, and operates businesses), the family office (which takes care of financial investments, family assets, and family welfare) and the original family business. We probably think of ourselves as a business family rather than family business."

Table 21.3 summarizes key facts of the three business families and the participants.

The structure and ordering of the data are shown in Fig. 21.1. The more specific first-order categories based on the terminologies the participants used appear on the left; the researcher-induced second-order themes stand in the middle; and the aggregate dimensions appear on the right. We will explain all these with necessary power quotes below.

Shifting Organizational Identities

The first part of the data centers around the paradoxical tensions embedded in the transition, which were aggregated under "shifting organizational identities" and "embracing portfolio entrepreneurship." For the organizational identity dimension, we discovered two major themes, i.e., (i) the family-business relationships and (ii) the diminishing intra-family faultlines, which are described below.

Family-Business Relationships

Organizational identity is about "who we are." In our study, the business families growingly differentiated between the identity of "family owner," "family governor," and "family operator." Given the extensive portfolio, these business families were under pressure to engage external talents to manage the operating businesses. Growingly, the role of the business families was to structure and oversee the portfolio. Our observation was that the transition was accompanied by resolving the identity paradox, moving from the "operator" identity to "owner" and/or "governor" identity, even though the families would have to balance between the multiple identities in certain contingencies.

Family owner/governor: Business families positioning themselves as an owner or investor adopted a different mentality. The Lee family apparently embedded their owner's mentality in their core values. As Sammy Lee of Lee

21 Transition from Family Business ...   567

Table 21.3 Participants and key facts of their business families and business groups

	The Lee Family Lee Kum Kee Group	The Tan Family Luen Thai Group	The Kuvinichkul Family Metta Group
Headquarter	Hong Kong	Hong Kong	Thailand
Year of Establishment	1888	1965	1980
Legacy Business	Sauce	Textile	Aluminum
Major Businesses in the Portfolio	• Sauce • Health products • Property investment • Traditional Chinese medicine materials • Venture capital	• Retail • Tourism • Fishery • Real estate • Micronesia and the Pacific • Investments	• Technology • Finance • Environment • Aluminum • Investments
Perceived Identity	• G4: More like a family business • G5: Transitioning to business family	Transitioning to business family	More like a business family
Ethnicity	Chinese	Chinese	Thai Chinese
Generational engagement	• G3: Spiritual leader (Mr Lee Man Tat passed away at the age of 91 in July 2021) • G4: Active owner-governor; few also took executive role in the group • G5: Active contributors to the family governance system; mostly not serving the group	• G1: Spiritual leader • G2: Active management of the group and/or the underlying operating business • G3: Some took executive positions in the group or in the operating businesses	• G2: Active management of the legacy business and overseer of the group • G3: Active management of the group or its operating businesses
Participants, and their roles and generation represented	• Sammy Lee, Executive Chairman of the Lee Kum Kee Group (G4) • Andrea Lee (G5), chair of family office • Brian Lee (G5) • Jamie Lee (G5)	• Henry Tan, CEO of the family group (G2) • Connie Hui, senior family office director (non-family member)	• June Kuvinichkul, CEO of the family group (G3)

(continued)

Table 21.3 (continued)

	The Lee Family Lee Kum Kee Group	The Tan Family Luen Thai Group	The Kuvinichkul Family Metta Group
Interview duration	120 minutes	122 minutes	65 minutes

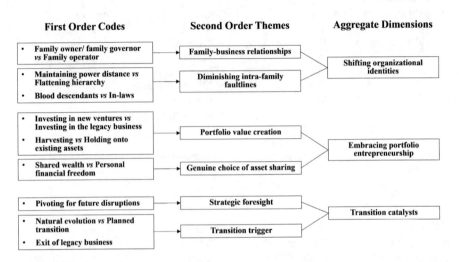

Fig. 21.1 Data structure

Kum Kee Group described their "Autopilot Leadership Model," it was clear that the family wanted to stay away from the operator role:

> Autopilot Leadership is about empowerment. Whenever we tackle a problem or a task, I prefer to step back as the Chairman and support the CEO in their own decision making, leadership, and execution. This approach helps unlock our talents' potential and creates a win-win situation for everyone. (Sammy Lee)

At a deeper level, wearing the owner's hat, June Kuvinichkul of Metta Group saw no obligation to pass on the legacy business:

> We do not mean that we have to pass on any business or even the Metta Group. Market mechanisms work best but if we can, we have control over wealth and all the assets. We can take care of them, take care of people, and have family banks to provide family members starting resources to build their own path. (June Kuvinichkul)

While all business families in our study had a respectable family governance system, the "family governor" identity was only mentioned in the Lee family case. How the Lees structured their governance system to detach family members from operating businesses and engage them in different governance capacities might explain this:

> We currently have two family members each taking care of the sauce business and the health products business. In parallel, we have other roles in the family council, family office, family investment, and family learning and development that encourages contribution from other family members. We all take up different roles and sometimes we rotate through different positions. Everyone is welcome to contribute, and we don't discriminate against family members who are less involved with the business. We are all stewards in our own ways. (Sammy Lee)

Appreciably, this governor role was contrasted with the operator identity:

> The way you structure your governance system is crucial to shaping how everything works. How you balance governing and operating roles determines the mechanisms, values, and stewardship that you want to encourage in the family and in the business. There aren't any right or wrong answers as this comes down to preference and collective alignment. What's more important is how you make these big decisions together as a team. (Andrea Lee)

Family operator: While all three business families still maintained their operating businesses, they attached themselves more to their owner or governor identity. June Kuvinichkul stressed on why her family did not encourage the operator identity in the legacy business:

> When we are forced to do something out of responsibility, when we do not work on what we are truly passionate about, there is no way in which it can be rewarding. We cannot pay back as much compared to if we get to do what we are passionate about. So, we do not believe in passing on any business. We can quit. We can exit at any time that is good. (June Kuvinichkul)

Yet, Henry Tan of Luen Thai Group pointed out that the need for balancing between the owner identity and the operator one at times: "Just in some of the businesses, you still need family presence in operation." He cited the example of sending a family representative to officiate the launch of a new shop. When the shopping mall knew that a family representative would attend the ceremony, they would appreciate the relationship more and go the extra mile.

570 J. Cheng and R. King

Given all these, we propose that families-in-business resolving the identity paradox, gradually shifting from the "operator" identity to the "owner" or "governor" identity, can stand a better chance to transform into business families. This leads to our first proposition:

> Proposition 1: Shifting the organizational identity from being an "operator" to an "owner" and/or "governor" can advance the transition from family business to business family.

Diminishing Intra-Family Faultlines

Another observation related to organizational identity was whether family members could converge on the same identity. Faultlines, which "divide a group's members on the basis of one or more attributes" (Lau & Murnighan, 1998, p. 325), appeared to be relevant. While intra-family faultlines were natural, identity-based faultlines might weaken the propensity of the business family to translate their entrepreneurial orientation to their desired entrepreneurial outcomes (Calabrò et al., 2021). Families-in-business which found ways to minimize such faultlines might be readier for the transition from family business to business family. In our study, we recognized two sources of differences that might create identity-based faultlines, namely (i) maintaining power distance versus flattening hierarchy and (ii) blood descendants versus in-laws.

Maintaining power distance versus flattening hierarchy: Power distance can be seen as "the extent to which the less powerful members of organizations and institutions (like the family) accept and expect that power is distributed unequally" (Hofstede, 2011, p. 9). Business families that aspired to diminish the generational power distance apparently could make better collective ownership decisions. Jamie Lee, a fifth-generation member of the Lee family and daughter of Sammy Lee, commented:

> Our family and our business have evolved so much throughout the generations. The theme in our family right now is leveling the playing field and flattening the hierarchy while we are constantly developing our team to continue our enterprise. While I still felt a bit of distance from my grandfather, I now feel that the distance between my generation and my dad's is narrowing as we are working together. One key ingredient to the success of teamwork is appreciating diversity in terms of age, gender, where we were educated, how we were brought up... As we are working on openly and respectfully communicating with each other, I can respect my dad as my dad, but I can also respect him as a team member because we make decisions together. (Jamie Lee)

Blood descendants versus in-laws: Another faultline in business families was whether in-laws were seen as part of the family and could serve as owners. When asked about in-laws' engagement in the future portfolio, June Kuvinichkul clearly stuck to the owner's identity and emphasized the importance of interest alignment among owners and not making decisions out of family membership differences (i.e., being a blood descendant or being an in-law):

> Hopefully by then we will have exited the other two aluminum businesses, and it will be new businesses only. Now, because we do not believe in passing on any businesses and for family members who are not involved in the businesses, they do not have shares. If anyone would like to be involved, we are going to treat them just like partners. You have to buy the shares. As long as we can align the interest, we are not saying it has to be family members. I think this has changed. If you were to ask me this like ten years ago, it would be a different story because we did not have a conclusion to exit the legacy businesses then. (June Kuvinichkul)

Actively reducing intra-family differences could minimize intra-family faultlines, thus maintaining a strong and coherent owner's identity within members. This can be conducive to making collective decision required by business families. This drives our second proposition:

> Proposition 2: Diminishing intra-family faultlines facilitates the development of a coherent owner's identity within the family, thereby raising the odd of transitioning from family business to business family.

Embracing Portfolio Entrepreneurship

Portfolio entrepreneurship was another aggregate dimension that captured the changes in the transition from family business to business family. We identified two themes, namely (i) portfolio value creation and (ii) shared wealth orientation.

Portfolio Value Creation

Business families in our study emphasized more on portfolio value creation rather than preserving the legacy business. They managed to invest in new ventures instead of sticking to the old rule of predominantly investing in the legacy business. They were in a better position to exercise wise harvests instead of holding onto their existing assets.

Investing in new ventures versus in the legacy business: Business families were dedicated to diversifying their portfolio by investing in new ventures. The Lee family explained their portfolio strategy as follows:

> We have another concept called 70-20-10. At a point, we agreed that we would invest 70% into the core business, 20% into related businesses, and 10% into totally unrelated businesses. This is a reflection of how we want to embrace our constant entrepreneurial spirit. Luckily, the two core businesses are well established and do not require us to invest much money into them. So, this frees up a lot of resources for us to explore other ventures. The 10% is where we push the envelope and why we started our venture capital fund. Through this business unit, we push ourselves to go out and look for something completely different. It is where we see the most pioneering technology and the most innovative trends for the future. Taking this risk widens our horizons to how the world is changing and helps the larger enterprise decode the future. (Sammy Lee)

Harvesting versus holding onto existing assets: Families-in-business tend to focus their investment on their legacy business and hold onto their existing assets (Davis, 2020). But business families in our study embraced smart harvesting or divesting to enhance their portfolio value. When asked her family's experience divesting from their investment in Grab, June Kuvinichkul explained:

> We exited a couple of times, and we still have shares in it. That is also an example of extracting value from the Metta side into the family office. The first time we sold our shares, the proceeds were partially recycled into YouTrip (a multi-currency mobile wallet that allowed users to pay in over 150 currencies with no fees) to grow Metta Group further and also partially injected into the family office to invest. Then the second time, we transferred some shares into a unicorn tech fund to diversify across regional tech companies... So you can see how from the first tranche, we got like, 30x, 100x, and then 600x or sometimes 2-5x after the first exit depending on investment goals and performance, and then you can average up. (June Kuvinichkul)

The portfolio concept was applied to managing both new and existing investments in business families, treating value creation as their primary goal. This leads to our third proposition:

Proposition 3: The focus on portfolio value creation by (i) balancing investments in the legacy business and new ventures and (ii) exercising necessary harvesting instead of holding onto existing assets can advance the transition from family business to business family.

Genuine Choice of Asset Sharing

In the transition, business families saw the purpose and benefits of holding a collective portfolio. Yet this shared wealth orientation did not preclude personal wealth development. Business families could afford members a genuine choice, balancing between personal financial freedom and bigger familial interests. Family members should be financially independent, before they could be fully motivated to manage the family portfolio. The Tan family showed how the shared wealth orientation evolved. In a meeting discussing the ownership succession issue, the second-generation members chose to stay together and split up the shares of the group rather than dividing along the business line. Learning from other families who were "paper rich, cash poor," the Tans set a 30% payout ratio, and reinvested the rest of the profit. This allowed family members to maintain a reasonably comfortable lifestyle, while discouraging extravagant life that was against the family values. Henry Tan commented:

> In the old days, most of us, including myself, did not have much personal saving. Everything was in the family business. Since dividends and bonuses have been declared, we started to have personal wealth. I think this is the start of trying to run the business professionally. (Henry Tan)

However, Henry Tan foresaw that the rising-generation members might have different investment preferences and might prefer to opt out in the future, which is natural to many enduring business families. The existing exit mechanism charged high discount to preserve the business' liquidity. To avoid having unhappy shareholders, he thought about how to make the exit mechanism easier: "We just have to buy them out nicely and professionally, and present a fair price and process." Instead of tying personal wealth to business ownership in the context of family business, the transition into business family should be facilitated by liberating personal wealth, so that members can have a genuine choice to own assets together. This drives us to our fourth proposition:

Transition Catalysts

The second part of the data addresses the question of what triggers or catalyzes the transition from family business to business family. In addition to the discussion of natural evolution versus planned transition and the exit of legacy business in the literature (together we frame them as "transition trigger"), we found that business families exhibited strong strategic foresight, particularly in response to the future disruptions. Pivoting was a key to this strategic foresight.

Strategic Foresight: Pivoting for Disruptions

The business families in our study exhibited a strong awareness of how external disruptions could influence the going concern of their legacy business. This awareness might keep families-in-business alerted and prepare them for business and/or portfolio restructuring. June Kuvinichkul commented:

> I think business family is having a bunch of entrepreneurs and the ability to pivot and adjust as time goes by and not holding on to any business. Many families probably tie their legacy to the businesses that were created in the past. I think that is a major pitfall because as time goes by, everything changes…We look into the future and that influence how we structure everything. (June Kuvinichkul)

When asked whether the business family identity could help weather the COVID-19 pandemic, June Kuvinichkul strengthened how a business family could pivot:

> If we think in terms of having the flexibility to pivot all the time, it definitely helps. If this is a family business, it means that you will have to hold onto certain things, and you cannot pivot and change as the situation changes. This is very disruptive. But if I am being a business family, I can act like entrepreneurs and pivot like in start-ups or new businesses. (June Kuvinichkul)

Technological disruptions have fast suppressed business cycles (King & Cheng, 2018). Henry Tan foresaw how these disruptions might change the future of the business, and adopting the portfolio concept can prepare the family ahead of the curve:

> I think 30, 40 years is harder to say. But the next 10, 20 years we will probably remain as a business family and may grow into different businesses because the business cycle is going too short. Now we just have to know what to get in and what to get out, and when to get in and when to get out...I think the business will continue, but what composes the portfolio will be different. (Henry Tan)

Transition Trigger

Natural evolution versus planned transition: Our data suggested that the traditional view dichotomizing the trigger as natural versus planned might mask holistic nature of the transition. As shown in our cases, the transition carried both natural and planned elements. Seeing the transition from the natural evolution perspective may help families-in-business incorporate their histories and traditions (Ge et al., 2021) and advance their responses to various lifecycle changes such as increasing generational complexities (e.g., Gersick et al., 1997). Taking the planning perspective might help families see their future. For instance, the Lee family showed extensive planning in the family, business, and ownership systems to reap benefits of the natural evolution. The following quote echoed that the transition was both natural and planned:

> Oyster sauce was a happy accidental invention, which we continued to build on for over 100 years. In the earlier days, we had never diversified. But as the company grew, it was natural for us to do so when all the siblings were working in the company. It is great to have a big team, but sometimes there can be too many cooks in the kitchen, which naturally pushed us to try something new together and empower each other to branch out. As the youngest in my generation, I had the luxury of learning from my older siblings. I figured I wanted to try something new, so overall I think diversifying was a mixture of being a planned decision as well as a spontaneous one. (Sammy Lee)

Exit of the legacy business: Among the three business families, only the Tans had a major exit from the legacy textile business (even though they retained a non-controlling stake in it). As Henry Tan presented the proposal from a state-owned enterprise to acquire the legacy business, the family's responses were quite split. To the second- and third-generation members, the exit offered the much-needed capital to grasp opportunities in other businesses. Yet to the patriarch, it was a hard decision to relinquish control of his life creation. Emotion came in as the patriarch attached his personal identity to the success of the legacy business. Showing the psychological calmness as the portfolio architect, Henry Tan recalled how he convinced his father:

> My father did not like the idea of selling the textile business. He saw that as the family's root and it was the family's only listed company. Yet I told him that the business was only making a profit of about 2% of the turnover. If the business went down, that 2% would go away very quickly. (Henry Tan)
>
> Think about other tycoon families. If they had stayed in their original businesses, they would have never made their fortune today. As a private company, we have limited capital. The entire supply chain of the garment manufacturing industry has been experiencing many changes that require capital investment. If opportunities with better return exist, they will compete for capital with the garment business. For the benefits of the business, it is better for Luen Thai Holdings to be owned by a state-owned enterprise, with easier access of capital at a lower cost. It makes economic sense to exit.(Henry Tan)

While the legacy business could no longer serve as the identity glue after the exit, the Tans retained the "Luen Thai" brand, which has continued to gel family members and most ventures in the portfolio together. The sales proceedings incentivized the restructuring of the existing portfolio. In June Kuvinichkul's case, the family "had a discussion on this [sic: legacy business exit], and managed to convince our parents to actually let go of the aluminium businesses. So, it is just a matter of timing and we did some already." Seemingly, the intention to exit and such an alignment at the top level could also catalyze the transition.

The strategic foresight to pivot for disruptions appeared to keep activating the latent paradoxical tensions in the system, but not sufficient to surface these tensions. Recognizing the transition as containing both natural and planned elements can raise the cognition of these tensions. The *exit intention* may render the tensions more salient by reorienting the family toward the portfolio value while the *actual exit* may fund the implementation of the portfolio strategies. All these lead to our last two propositions:

> Proposition 5: Strong strategic foresight to pivot, when combined with the recognition of both the natural and planned aspects of the transition, can raise the cognition of the paradoxical tensions in families-in-business.

> Proposition 6: Exit or intention to exit from the legacy business can render the paradoxical tensions more salient.

Discussion

This study examined the transition from family business to business family, a process which most family business groups should have experienced. We conceptualized the transition as resolving paradoxical tensions, and we focused on two defining paradoxical tensions associated with organizational identity and portfolio entrepreneurship. In terms of organizational identity, we found that the ability to shift from the "operator" identity to the "owner" and/or "governor" identity could potentially advance the transition from family business to business family. Diminishing intra-family faultlines could also facilitate the development of a more coherent owner's identity within the family, thereby raising the odd of the transition. In terms of portfolio entrepreneurship, families-in-business, which could emphasize on portfolio value creation by balancing investments in the legacy business and new ventures and by exercising wise harvesting instead of holding onto existing underperforming assets, stood a better chance for the transition. In addition, the transition could be advanced if families-in-business could provide a genuine choice of asset sharing to their members and liberating their personal wealth. We also ventured into the triggers of the transition, and discovered that business families demonstrated a strong strategic foresight, which, when combined with the recognition of both the natural and planned aspects of the transition, could raise the cognition of the paradoxical tensions in families-in-business. Exit or intention to exit from the legacy business could render the paradoxical tensions more salient. Figure 21.2 summarizes the paradoxical tensions and triggers embedded in the transition as observed in this study.

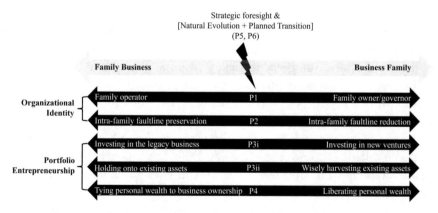

Fig. 21.2 Paradoxical tensions embedded in the transition

Shifting Identity or Building a Portfolio First?

The traditional organizational identity theory (Albert & Whetten, 1985) and the effectuation theory (Sarasvathy, 2001) tend to predict a different sequence of business family identity and portfolio development. Organizational identity theory argues that families-in-business will build their business family identity first while the effectuation theory tends to see entrepreneurs create new ventures, without having to change their own identity or that of their families. Our findings inclined to argue that families-in-business engaged in portfolio development first before gaining full awareness of their business family identity: the fourth-generation leaders of the Lees driving the portfolio expansion still saw themselves more as a family business while their fifth-generation members began to see the trait of a business family. The Tans of Luen Thai leveraged on different opportunities to build their conglomerate for decades, but the second-generation leader only reckoned the transition lately. The Kuvinichkuls of Metta Group diversified as the third-generation leader restructured the group and began the discussion of the business family strategy. Yet, from our existing interview data, we could not exclude the possibility of presence of a subconscious business family identity that might affect portfolio decisions.

The paradox theory offers an alternative approach to reconcile the contradictory predictions and fill the gap. Moving away from the simplistic discussion of the chicken-and-egg issue, the paradox theory focuses on the dynamic interplay of paradoxical tensions embedded in the family enterprise system. It assumes presence of latent tensions including but not limited to those associated with organizational identity and portfolio development. There are occasions where tensions of organizational identity and/or portfolio entrepreneurship are being triggered. It is about embracing and resolving paradoxical tensions that are rendered salient (Smith & Lewis, 2011). While less discussed above, the paradox theory assumes that the transition is not a linear process. Rather, oscillations happen across time or as contingency arises (Smith & Lewis, 2011). For instance, even though the Tans embraced their owner identity, they clearly acknowledged the importance of their operator role in occasions such as a new shop launch. As a process moving from eventual oscillations to norming, the transition is ultimately not only about whether to shape the business family identity or to build a portfolio of ventures first but to achieve a dynamic equilibrium leaning toward being a business family that secures long-term success (Smith & Lewis, 2011), defined as preserving and creating portfolio value covering both economic and socioemotional wealth.

Not All Will Become Business Families?

The paradox theory also addresses the phenomenon of why some family businesses become business families while some do not. All families-in-business live in the paradoxical tensions underlying the transition as these tensions are the inherited features of the hybrid institution comprising both the family and the business (Schuman et al., 2010). As shown, the transition requires that the families-in-business experience the necessary triggers that render latent tensions salient, and individuals should share the paradoxical cognition. The next step is for the families-in-business to embrace the tensions, re-shape the way they perceive and organize their ventures, and work through the identity shift. From oscillating between the two poles of each of the defining paradoxes (i.e., organizational identity and portfolio entrepreneurship) to norming, the paradoxical tensions can be seen as resolved, driving sustainability in the system. This echoes what Habbershon and Pistrui (2002) proposed: enterprising families bearing the family-as-investor mindset and entrepreneurial strategy methods will earn superior returns over the long run. This can also explain why family business groups may not always show a superior performance: the paradoxical tensions are not completely resolved if their portfolio strategy is not backed by a coupling business family identity, and vice versa.

Theoretical Contributions

We contributed to the literature by advancing the understanding of business families—and indirectly that of family business groups—in three ways. *First*, it is novel to position the transition from family business to business family as managing paradoxical tensions. The paradox theory is an under-utilized tool that can help meta-theorize long-term changes, but as shown, it is well positioned to explain various phenomena in family businesses and/or business families as a hybrid institution. Recognizing that families-in-business may exist in different dynamic equilibria of multiple paradoxical tensions opens new avenues for researching strategic and entrepreneurial behavior. The application also offers interesting insights into the paradox theory, by showcasing how multiple categories of paradoxes (*belonging* and *organizing* in this study but can be extended to cover the categories of *learning* and *performing*) existing in different subsystems of an institution can explain changes, which may go beyond generations.

Second, we adopted business family as a unit of entrepreneurial analysis, thereby addressing the call of Neubaum and Payne (2021) to advance the centrality of family in family business research. We went beyond the broad-brushed assumption of one-family-one-business (De Massis et al., 2021) and explained how families-in-business may shape a multi-business port-folio. Instead of taking a more intuitive approach to define business families, we anchored our definition in the theoretical perspectives of organizational identity and portfolio entrepreneurship. We are among the few studies that deep dive into defining the term "business family" when this can mean a vastly different thing to stakeholders in the family business community. Like Eskimos having a rich variety of words to denote different types of snow which arguably advance their cognition of snow in the physical world, family business scholars should rethink their use of terms such as "business family," "family-in-business," "enterprising family," and "entrepreneurial family," thereby advancing the identification and analyses of strategic and entrepreneurial issues.

Third, we expanded the discussion of family heterogeneity (Jaskiewicz & Dyer, 2017) and family firm heterogeneity by treating business family as a special form of families-in-business in terms of organizational identity and portfolio strategies. The transition is heterogeneous for each family: Families-in-business may begin their transition from a different equilibrium of the paradoxical tensions; they may have different thresholds to see the tensions as salient; and they may adopt different approaches to address the para-doxical tensions. Impacts of this source of family heterogeneity could have been underestimated and might be covered as family firm heterogeneity (Neubaum et al., 2019). Given this, we partly addressed the call to generate "an understanding of what makes successful portfolio systems in business families successful in various contexts" (Rosa et al., 2019, p. 395). The rule of thumb is that it depends on where the families-in-business are situated in the spectrum of paradoxical tensions.

Practical Implications

Family businesses and business families live in paradoxes. Our study inspires families-in-business and their advisors to rethink the transition from family business to business family as a developmental strategy. By assessing their mentalities and capabilities to manage the paradoxical tensions in shifting to the business family identity and embracing portfolio entrepreneurship, families-in-business can potentially see how the natural evolution can be blended with planned transition to honor the past while steering for the future. They should also be aware that a business family is not merely a portfolio of companies. The families must develop a corresponding business family identity to reap the benefits of the portfolio setup. In line with Schuman et al. (2010), we believe that managing paradoxes requires novel thinking, not prescriptions, since each family-in-business may have her own path to become a business family. While we did not cover the details in this chapter, we observed that business families in this study built structures such as family offices and family banks to support the transition.

Limitations and Future Research

There are several limitations in this study, pointing to future research opportunities. In terms of content, a key area for further research is on how other categories of paradoxes, i.e., *learning* and *performing*, may be part of the transition and how they interact with the *belonging* and *organizing* paradoxes. The omission was intended in this study as we were more interested in identifying the tensions that define a business family. But our rough observation is that *learning* and *performing* paradoxes are relevant. The *learning* paradox can illustrate how families-in-business address the tensions over time, individually and collectively. The *performing* paradox can advance the understanding of positive and negative outcomes in the transition. Studying these paradoxes can offer a more holistic picture of the transition.

The research design and methodology of our study also have inherent limitations. *First*, all three case studies were on ethnic Chinese family business groups, and generalization of the findings to other ethnic groups should be taken with caution. Gupta and Levenburg (2010) argued that Confucian Asian have a strong focus on business reputation and the family may be exploited to maintain this reputation in the community they operate in. The stress on business reputation might make family and business identities appeared as one and might potentially hide tensions underneath. *Second*, even though we knew the participating families for an extended period and were familiar with their development, this could not fully compensate for the need for studying the transition by a longitudinal setup. The longitudinal study might help capture more subtle, lifecycle-specific changes, and might help determine the interaction between organizational identity and portfolio entrepreneurship. *Third*, given the exploratory nature of this study, we did not go deep into each of the paradoxical tensions related to organizational identities and portfolio entrepreneurship. It can be useful to examine how resolving a specific identity-based paradoxical tension could affect tensions related to portfolio entrepreneurship, and vice versa. Researching this can help strengthen the theoretical linkage between organizational identity and portfolio entrepreneurship.

Conclusion

In this chapter, we explored the understudied phenomenon of the transition from family business to business family, examining the paradoxical tensions and triggers through the paradox lens. We found that families-in-business resolved underlying paradoxical tensions related to organizational identity and portfolio development in the transition. The use of paradox theory to analyze long-term changes in complex hybrid family institutions appears promising, and we encourage future research on this.

Acknowledgements We would like to thank the kind contribution of Pauline Yeung in this study, and we greatly benefited from her comments on the earlier version of the manuscript. All errors are our own.

References

Albert, S., & Whetten, D. A. (1985). Organizational identity. In B. M. Staw & L. L. Cummings (Eds.), *Research in organizational behavior* (pp. 263–295). JAI Press.

Berent-Braun, M. M., & Uhlaner, L. M. (2012). Family governance practices and teambuilding: Paradox of the enterprising family. *Small Business Economics, 38*(1), 103–119. https://doi.org/10.1007/s11187-010-9269-4

Brinkerink, J., Rondi, E., Benedetti, C., & Arzubiaga, U. (2020). Family business or business family? Organizational identity elasticity and strategic responses to disruptive innovation. *Journal of Family Business Strategy, 11*(4), 100360. https://doi.org/10.1016/j.jfbs.2020.100360

Calabrò, A., Frank, H., Minichilli, A., & Suess-Reyes, J. (2021a). Business families in times of crises: The backbone of family firm resilience and continuity. *Journal of Family Business Strategy, 12*(2), 100442. https://doi.org/10.1016/j.jfbs.2021.100442

Calabrò, A., Santulli, R., Torchia, M., & Gallucci, C. (2021b). Entrepreneurial orientation and family firm performance: The moderating role of TMT identity-based and knowledge-based faultlines. *Entrepreneurship Theory and Practice, 45*(4), 838–866. https://doi.org/10.1177/1042258720973997

Carter, S., & Ram, M. (2003). Reassessing portfolio entrepreneurship. *Small Business Economics, 21*, 371–380. https://doi.org/10.1023/A:1026115121083

Cheng, C. Y. J., & Au, K. (2014). *Luen Thai: Governance for the Tans' shared future*. Coutts & Co. & The Chinese University of Hong Kong.

Cheng, C. Y. J., Au, K., & Jen, M. (2021). Death smiles at us all: Changing demographics and succession-induced portfolio entrepreneurship. In T.F.-L. Yu & H.-D. Yan (Eds.), *The Routledge companion to Asian family business: Governance, succession, and challenges in the age of digital disruption* (pp. 239–260). Routledge.

Cheng, C. Y. J., & King, R. (2021). Industry 4.0 and Asian family entrepreneurship: A career perspective. In T. F.-L. Yu & H.-D. Yan (Eds.), *The Routledge companion to Asian family business: Governance, succession, and challenges in the age of digital disruption* (pp. 37–62). Routledge.

Davis, J. A. (2020). What makes a family business last? *Harvard Business Review*. Retrieved on 15 February 2020. https://hbr.org/2020/02/what-makes-a-family-business-last

De Massis, A., Frattini, F., Kotlar, J., Petruzzelli, A. M., & Wright, M. (2016). Innovation through tradition: Lessons from innovative family businesses and directions for future research. *Academy of Management Perspectives, 30*(1), 93–116. https://doi.org/10.5465/amp.2015.0017

De Massis, A., Kotlar, J., & Manelli, L. (2021). Family firms, family boundary organizations, and the family-related organizational ecosystem. *Family Business Review, 34*(4), 350–364. https://doi.org/10.1177/08944865211052195

Eisenhardt, K. M. (1989). Building theories from case study research. *Academy of Management Review, 14*, 532–550. https://doi.org/10.2307/258557

Eisenhardt, K. M., & Graebner, M. E. (2007). Theory building from cases: Opportunities and challenges. *Academy of Management Journal, 50*(1), 25–32. https://doi.org/10.5465/AMJ.2007.24160888

Fitz-Koch, S., Cooper, S., & Discua Cruz, A. (2019). Entrepreneurship and rural family identity: Understanding portfolio development in a family farm business. In M. Rautiainen, P. Rosa, T. Pihkala, M.J. Parada, & A. Discua Cruz (Eds.), *The family business group phenomenon: Emergence and complexities* (pp. 353–383). Springer International Publishing. https://doi.org/10.1007/978-3-319-98542-8_14

Fotea, S. L., & Fotea, I. S. (2020). Exploring the family identity as a unique competitive advantage to family businesses in developing a relationship marketing orientation. In S. L. Fotea, I. S. Fotea, & S. Văduva (Eds.), *Challenges and opportunities to develop organizations through creativity, technology and ethics* (pp.331–347). Springer. https://doi.org/10.1007/978-3-030-43449-6_19

Frank, H., Suess-Reyes, J., Fuetsch, E., & Kessler, A. (2019). Introducing the enterpriseness of business families: A research agenda. In E. Memili & C. Dibrell (Eds.), *The Palgrave handbook of heterogeneity among family firms* (pp. 263–296). Palgrave Macmillan. https://doi.org/10.1007/978-3-319-77676-7_11

Ge, B., De Massis, A., & Kotlar, J. (2021). Mining the past: History scripting strategies and competitive advantage in a family business. *Entrepreneurship Theory and Practice*. https://doi.org/10.1177/10422587211046547

Gersick, K. E., Davis, J. A., Hampton, M. M., & Lansberg, I. (1997). *Generation to generation: Life cycles of the family business*. Harvard Business School Press.

Gioia, D. A., Corley, K. G., & Hamilton, A. L. (2013). Seeking qualitative rigor in inductive research notes on the Gioia methodology. *Organizational Research Methods, 16*(1), 15–31. https://doi.org/10.1177/1094428112452151

Gomez-Mejia, L. R., Cruz, C., Berrone, P., & De Castro, J. (2011). The bind that ties: Socioemotional wealth preservation in family firms. *Academy of Management Annals, 5*(1), 653–707. https://doi.org/10.5465/19416520.2011.593320

Gupta, V., & Levenburg, N. (2010). A thematic analysis of cultural variations in family businesses: The CASE project. *Family Business Review, 23*(2), 155–169. https://doi.org/10.1177/089448651002300205

Habbershon, T. G., & Pistrui, J. (2002). Enterprising families domain: Family-influenced ownership groups in pursuit of transgenerational wealth. *Family Business Review, 15*(3), 223–237. https://doi.org/10.1111/j.1741-6248.2002.00223.x

Hamilton, E., Discua Cruz, A., & Jack, S. (2017). Re-framing the status of narrative in family business research: Towards an understanding of families in business. *Journal of Family Business Strategy, 8*(1), 3–12. https://doi.org/10.1016/j.jfbs.2016.11.001

Hofstede, G. (2011). Dimensionalizing cultures: The Hofstede model in context. *Online Readings in Psychology and Culture, Unit 2*. Retrieved from http://scholarworks.gvsu.edu/orpc/vol2/iss1/8

Jaffe, D. T., & Lane, S. H. (2004). Sustaining a family dynasty: Key issues facing complex multigenerational business- and investment-owning families. *Family Business Review, 17*(1), 81–98. https://doi.org/10.1111/j.1741-6248.2004.00006.x

Jaskiewicz, P., & Dyer, W. G. (2017). Addressing the elephant in the room: Disentangling family heterogeneity to advance family business research. *Family Business Review, 30*(2), 111–118. https://doi.org/10.1177/0894486517700469

King, R., & Cheng, J. (2018). *Where technological disruptors meet Asian family businesses: Rethinking next-generation leadership and career*. Lombard Odier & The Hong Kong University of Science and Technology.

King, R., & Cheng, J. (2020). Reframing succession in a disruptive era: A business family perspective. *International Family Offices Journal, 5*(2), 6–11.

King, R., Peng, Q. P., & Dowejko, M. K. (2017). *Lee Kum Kee: Female succession in family business*. HBS No. ST18-PDF-ENG. https://hbsp.harvard.edu/product/ST18-PDF-ENG

Kreiner, G. E., Hollensbe, E., Sheep, M. L., Smith, B. R., & Kataria, N. (2015). Elasticity and the dialectic tensions of organizational identity: How can we hold together while we are pulling apart? *Academy of Management Journal, 58*(4), 981–1011. https://doi.org/10.5465/amj.2012.0462

Lau, D. C., & Murnighan, J. K. (1998). Demographic diversity and faultlines: The compositional dynamics of organizational groups. *Academy of Management Review, 23*(2), 325–340. https://doi.org/10.2307/259377

Leppäaho, T., Plakoyiannaki, E., & Dimitratos, P. (2016). The case study in family business: An analysis of current research practices and recommendations. *Family Business Review, 29*(2), 159–173. https://doi.org/10.1177/0894486515614157

Le Breton-Miller, I., & Miller, D. (2018). Beyond the firm: Business families as entrepreneurs. *Entrepreneurship Theory and Practice, 42*(4), 527–536. https://doi.org/10.1177/1042258717739004

Michael-Tsabari, N., Labaki, R., & Zachary, R.K. (2014). Toward the cluster model: The family firm's entrepreneurial behavior over generations. *Family Business Review, 27*(2), 161–185. https://doi.org/10.1177/0894486514525803

Neubaum, D. O., Kammerlander, N., & Brigham, K. H. (2019). Capturing family firm heterogeneity: How taxonomies and typologies can help the field move forward. *Family Business Review, 32*(2), 106–130. https://doi.org/10.1177%2F0894486519848512

Neubaum, D. O., & Payne, G. T. (2021). The centrality of family. *Family Business Review, 34*(1), 6–11. https://doi.org/10.1177/0894486521995268

Prügl, R., & Spitzley, D. I. (2021). Responding to digital transformation by external corporate venturing: An enterprising family identity and communication patterns perspective. *Journal of Management Studies, 58*(1), 135–164. https://doi.org/10.1111/joms.12578

Quinn, R. E., & Cameron, K. S. (Eds.). (1988). *Paradox and transformation: Toward a theory of change in organization and management.* Ballinger.

Rosa, P., Howorth, C., & Discua Cruz, A. (2014). Habitual and portfolio entrepreneurship and the family in business. In L. Melin, M. Nordqvist, & P. Sharma (Eds.), *The SAGE handbook of family business* (pp. 364–382). Sage. https://doi.org/10.4135/9781446247556.n18

Rosa, P., Rautiainen, M., Pihkala, T., Parada, M. J., & Discua Cruz, A. D. (2019). Conclusions: Researching family business groups: Lessons learned and avenues for further research. In M. Rautiainen, P. Rosa, T. Pihkala, M. Parada, & A. Discua Cruz (Eds.), *The family business group phenomenon: Emergence and complexities* (pp. 387–395). Palgrave Macmillan. https://doi.org/10.1007/978-3-319-98542-8_15

Sarasvathy, S. D. (2001). Causation and effectuation: Toward a theoretical shift from economic inevitability to entrepreneurial contingency. *Academy of Management Review, 26*(2), 243–263. https://doi.org/10.2307/259121

Schad, J., Lewis, M. W., Raisch, S., & Smith, W. K. (2016). Paradox research in management science: Looking back to move forward. *Academy of Management Annals, 10*(1), 5–64. https://doi.org/10.1080/19416520.2016.1162422

Schuman, A., Stutz, S., & Ward, J. L. (2010). *Family business as paradox.* Palgrave Macmillan.

Shepherd, D., & Haynie, J. M. (2009). Family business, identity conflict, and an expedited entrepreneurial process: A process of resolving identity conflict. *Entrepreneurship Theory and Practice, 33*(6), 1245–1264. https://doi.org/10.1111/j.1540-6520.2009.00344.x

Sieger, P., Zellweger, T., Nason, R. S., & Clinton, E. (2011). Portfolio entrepreneurship in family firms: A resource-based perspective. *Strategic Entrepreneurship Journal, 5*, 327–351. https://doi.org/10.1002/sej.120

Smith, W. K., & Lewis, M. W. (2011). Toward a theory of paradox: A dynamic equilibrium model of organizing. *Academy of Management Review, 36*(2), 381–403. https://doi.org/10.5465/amr.2009.0223

Steier, L. (2007). New venture creation and organization: A familial sub-narrative. *Journal of Business Research, 60*(10), 1099–1107. https://doi.org/10.1016/j.jbusres.2006.12.017

Steier, L. P., Chrisman, J. J., & Chua, J. H. (2015). Governance challenges in family businesses and business families. *Entrepreneurship Theory and Practice, 39*(6), 1265–1280. https://doi.org/10.1111%2Fetap.12180

Sundaramurthy, C., & Lewis, M. (2003). Control and collaboration: Paradoxes of governance. *Academy of Management Review, 28*(3), 397–415. https://doi.org/10.5465/amr.2003.10196737

Westhead, P., & Wright, M. (1998). Novice, portfolio, and serial founders in rural and urban areas. *Entrepreneurship Theory and Practice, 22*(4), 63–100. https://doi.org/10.1177/104225879802200404

Widz, M., & Parada, M. J. (2020, October 28). *From family in business to business family: The blind spot of family identity* [Conference presentation]. Family Firm Institute Global Conference 2020, virtual.

Yin, R. (2009). *Case study research: Design and methods.* Sage.

Zellweger, T. M., Nason, R. S., & Nordqvist, M. (2012). From longevity of firms to transgenerational entrepreneurship of families: Introducing family entrepreneurial orientation. *Family Business Review, 25*(2), 136–155. https://doi.org/10.1177/0894486511423531

22

From Founder Identity to Family Business Group (FBG) Meta-Identity: Identity Development in the Journey from a Founder's Firm to an Entrepreneurial Family with a Portfolio of Businesses

Marta Widz and Maria José Parada ⓘ

Introduction

Family businesses—important actors in the economic landscape—are unique organizations. This uniqueness stems from the interaction of the family system with the ownership and management systems (Gersick et al., 1997), which is captured in the famous three-circle model (Taguiri & Davis, 1992). Concentrated family ownership, as well as family values and principles, influence the governance and strategic direction of the company. Further to this, family members are commonly involved in the governance and/or management, the cultivation of the vision, and the intention to hand over the business to the next generation (Chua et al., 1999). Interestingly, business families usually identify strongly with their businesses (Cannella et al., 2015), and vice versa; family businesses exhibit a strong organizational identity that

---

M. Widz (✉)
Family Office Research, Wealth Management Institute (WMI), Singapore, Singapore
e-mail: martawidz@wmi.edu.sg

M. J. Parada
Department of Strategy and General Management, ESADE Business School, Sant Cugat del Vallès, Spain
e-mail: mariajose.parada@esade.edu

© The Author(s), under exclusive license to Springer Nature Switzerland AG 2023
M. Rautianen et al. (eds.), *The Palgrave Handbook of Managing Family Business Groups*,
https://doi.org/10.1007/978-3-031-13206-3_22

reflects the family's identity. This is because the two systems—the family system and firm system—are interrelated, which enables the diffusion of the identity between the two of them. This diffusion is very evident in the family businesses with a visible presence of the founders and/or owning family, who in turn imbue their values, i.e., their identity across the whole organization (Miller et al., 2011).

But what is *identity*? Identity emerges from the contemplation of commonly asked questions—*who we are* (Albert & Whetten, 1985) and w*here we belong*, making the social context (Tajfel & Turner, 1979) an important nesting ground for the process of identity development. For example, the firms' founders usually identify strongly with their firms (Boivie et al., 2011), resulting in the phenomenon, wherein the firms become an extension of the founders themselves (Wasserman, 2006). The underlying reason for this is a perceptible and complete overlap of the attributes that define a person and those that define an organization (Dutton et al., 1994, p. 29).

The family business identity is, however, not a constant phenomenon. It evolves over time and reflects the events that take place on the firm's side and the family's side. In the initial phase of its evolution, the identity of the firm's founder is "tightly linked to that of the organization and its innovative endeavors" (Dobrev & Barnett, 2005, p. 435). Therefore, a firm's founder brings an entrepreneurial drive to an organization by transmitting his/her entrepreneurial identity to the firm's identity (Miller et al., 2011). As both the family and business grow over time, the individual identity of a firm founder may evolve into a collective identity of the enterprising family (Parada & Dawson, 2017). The enterprising family identity is usually of a more nurturing and familial nature (Millet et al., 2011) compared to the lone-founder identity because it is shaped by various events on the family side. These include succession that often sparks intra-family conflicts, and complex family relationships that, in turn, are shaped by different interests, visions, and values of the many descendants of the firm's founder. Given the involvement of family members in simultaneous commitments, a collective business family identity tends to emerge as a co-narrative of multiple individuals' narratives (Brown, 2006). To be more precise, the identity of a business family is developed by a constant process of formulation, edition, appreciation, or rejection of some elements of the narrative that is being shaped (Czarniawska-Joerges, 1994).

In this time-consuming process of reconfiguration of individual identities into a collective identity, the family reaches out to the founder's entrepreneurial identity that is usually ingrained in the legacy business, i.e. the one the family as a business family started with, and the one the established business family wishes to cultivate over generations. Hence, the common phenomenon of family members referring to themselves as *brewers* (if the legacy business is a brewery), *bakers* (if their legacy business is a bakery), *publishers* (if the legacy business is a publishing house), etc. This is especially true for the business families who are the owners of a single, legacy operational company.

In reality, however, enterprising families often hold, on average, three to four operational companies in their portfolio (Zellweger et al., 2012) at any point in time. It is a fact recognized by the family business field that some family businesses develop into a portfolio of businesses over time. Some scholars have taken cognizance of this and shifted toward "describing a family that owns more than one firm" (Michael-Tsabari et al., 2014, p. 162) by offering an extension of the three-circle model, namely the "cluster model" (Michael-Tsabari et al., 2014). Others have investigated the process of portfolio evolution by an entrepreneurial family, namely the Family Business Groups (FBGs) via acquisitions, mergers, internationalization, organic growth, and disinvestments (c.f. Mendoza et al., in this book; Rautiainen et al., 2019).

The cognition that family businesses are evolving beyond the legacy business is important to the study of identities, as the reconfiguration of the business portfolio affects the development of various identities: The individual family member identity, the collective family identity, and the organizational identity.

Unlike the more linear development of single-business family identity, identity development in the context of FBGs is more complex. In particular, as the portfolio of businesses becomes more dynamic, the owning family transitions into an investing family. This is followed by a transition in the collective family identity, from *owner identity* through *investor identity* (Thomsen & Pedersen, 2000) to an *FBG identity*. Such a transition often includes identity conflicts and identity negotiations. This process, often triggered by external stakeholders' expectations, is necessary to move away from the identity anchored in the legacy business toward a renewed identity that encompasses multiple businesses. Therefore, the question that arises is:

What Does the Process of FBG Identity Development Look Like?

Using theoretical underpinnings of identity (e.g. Burke, 2001), social identity (e.g. Tajfel & Turner, 1979), and organizational identity (e.g. Albert & Whetten, 1985) and applying them in the FBGs' context, we propose a theoretical model that shows the dynamic evolution of the firm's founder's individual identity to an FBG identity that reflects the whole business portfolio. We illustrate the proposed model with a case study of the Pentland Group. In particular, we describe how Pentland owners, the Rubin family, developed from a founders' firm into an FBG and how that was linked to the consecutive evolution of the internal and external narratives and thus identities.

Pentland Group is a family business that in 2016 employed more than 20,500 people worldwide and generated about £2.9 billion in sales. Its roots date back to 1932 when Berko and Minnie Rubin - immigrants from Eastern Europe - set up the Liverpool Shoe Company, a small fashion footwear business. From their humble beginnings as shoe retailers, the family owners built a portfolio of sports and fashion brands (Speedo, Berghaus, Canterbury, Mitre, KangaROO). In 2004, the Rubin family purchased a 57% controlling stake in the publicly listed JD Sports Fashion, a chain of over 1,300 retail shops. Even though JD Sports Fashion constituted 80% of the Pentland Group business portfolio in 2016, the Rubin family continued to identify itself with its legacy brands business. The family stood firmly behind Pentland Brands' purpose, which included many elements of "familiness": Building a family of brands for the world to love, generation after generation.[1]

By broadening the understanding of identity development in a family business and enterprising families' context, we contribute to the family business and identity literature. Previous studies have shown that the lone-founder identity impacts the organizational identity by imprinting the founder's entrepreneurial drive onto the organizational identity (e.g. Cannella et al., 2015), and how the founder's identity evolves into a more familial identity in enterprising families (Miller et al., 2011) or even a meta-identity (Shepherd & Haynie, 2009). Our work expands on these studies by explaining how the family collective identity and portfolio of businesses organizational identity arrives at the FBG identity, triggered by the incongruence between the narratives about identity and the reality of a complex business structure. In particular, we present the role that narratives play in shaping and conveying multiple identities (Brown, 2006; Dawson & Parada, 2017). We also illustrate that the transition from a founder-centric identity to an FBG identity is

---

[1] The Pentland story is based on the FBN case study written by M. Widz: Widz, M. (2017). Pentland Group. Building a Family of Brands for the World to Love, Generation after Generation, Family Business Network Polaris Report, the IMD Business school article by B. Leleux and M. Widz in 2017: Leleux, B., Widz, M. (2017) Pentland Group: A family of Brands. Lessons from the winner of the 2017 IMD Global Family Business Award. Tomorrow's Challenges. IMD, as well as the IMD Business school case studies: Leleux, B. & Widz, M. (2018) Pentland Group: A Family of Brands, IMD- IMD-7-1937, Kenyon-Rouvinez, D. & Widz, M. (2019) Pentland Brands: Succession Dilemma (A), IMD- IMD-7-2052, Kenyon-Rouvinez, D. & Widz, M. (2019) Pentland Brands: Succession Dilemma (B), IMD- IMD-7-2053.

a journey that entails overcoming the legacy and the founder's heroic narrative, in a process that involves identity conflict (Shepherd & Haynie, 2009). We conclude that this process is a natural evolution and is necessary to develop the FBG identity.

Our chapter is structured as follows. We present theoretical foundations of identity first, followed by a detailed explanation of the forces that shape the identities of an enterprising family and its firm(s) as it transitions from a single-business family and founder's firm to FBG. Our chapter concludes with a discussion, followed by limitations and recommendations for further research.

Identity Development in Family Business Groups

Identity and Family Business

Identity is a topic of interest for many scholars. On the individual level, the *social identity theory* (Tajfel & Turner, 1979, 1986) describes how persons define their identity based on the social context in which they are embedded (Burke, 2003; Fiske & Taylor, 1991). This process is based on their similarity to other social group members and anchored in mimicking their behaviors and attributes (Cantor & Mischel, 1979; Fiske & Taylor, 1991). In large part, these are the norms and customs ascribed by the broader social context in which the individual is situated (Stryker & Burke, 2000; Stryker & Statham, 1985) that define the behavioral expectations of any given group member. The repeated behavior of a social group's members, in turn, leads to the emergence of the social categorization, with which group members strongly identify and where group-specific attributes and expected behavior are clearly observable (Shepherd & Haynie, 2009).

While an *individual identity* is related to the self and is considered to be enduring, distinctive, and central (Albert & Whetten, 1985), the *collective identity* is an accumulation of individual identities of all group members and may evolve (Brown, 2006; Parada & Dawson, 2017). In particular, *identity development* has been widely studied in *organizational identity theory*, where scholars affirm that a specific type of collective identity—organizational identity—may change over time (Nag et al., 2007). Similar to individual identity, organizational identity is related to "who we are" as an organization (Albert & Whetten, 1985) and is also socially constructed (Corley & Gioia, 2004; Ravasi & Schultz, 2006). Furthermore, organizational identity is supposed to be relatively stable over time because it refers to the key characteristics of the organization (Corley & Gioia, 2004; Ravasi & Schultz, 2006). But, according to Corley and Gioia (2004), organizational identity is more dynamic and more relational compared to individual identity. In the long term, organizational identity actively evolves, and necessitates an interchange among all organizational stakeholders, wherein "an organization's self" is continuously socially constructed from the interchange between internal and external definitions of the organization" (Hatch & Schultz, 2002, p. 1004).

Individual and collective identities and their development are complex phenomena, especially in the context of family business because of the interaction of the family system with the business system (Gersick et al, 1997). While identities are described usually within the boundaries of a single social category, in the case of a family business, the enterprising family members develop multiple identities (Ashforth et al., 2000). This is because they belong to multiple social systems, captured in the three-circle model (Taguiri & Davis, 1992), and face the specific behavioral expectations associated with each of these roles. For example, they can be both business managers and the owning family members at the same time, and hence represent three distinct socially defined identities, i.e., of a businessperson, family member, and the owner, at the same time. However, the identity of every social group is different, which leads to identity tensions. For example, previous studies have shown that family identity does not fully overlap with the business owner identity, and have emphasized the role conflict that arises from these two social systems (c.f. Shepherd & Haynie, 2009).

In our book chapter, we propose a model of identity development in an FBG. It goes one step beyond the three-circle model (Taguiri & Davis, 1992), which tacitly assumes there is only one business in the hands of a family. We propose that an FBG is composed of multiple businesses and multiple family members and theorize that the development of the FBG identity is triggered by the identity conflicts, that emerge from the evolution of two main social systems drivers: the business system that grows and becomes a vibrant, ever-changing portfolio of businesses, and the family system, whose complexity increases as a family grows and new generations come on board.

Founder's Firm and Founder's Identity

The dominant characteristic of a founder's firm is the huge intersection of the business and the founder's social systems, and consequently, the overlap between the founder's and founder's firm's identities. The founder is the soul of the business, who imprints his/her values and his/her individual identity across the whole organization (Miller et al., 2011). In the founding stage, organizational identity is the expression of the founder's identity, and very often the founder's values are the same as the organizational values. A founder's identity is intimately linked to their firm via the strategic decisions that are made and will ultimately influence how their organization works and expands (Fauchart & Gruber, 2011). As a result, there is a close congruence between the founder's strategy and the firm's strategy, as well as a very strong identification of the founder-owners with their businesses (Boivie, et al., 2011). According to Wasserman (2006), the firm becomes the extension of the founder and vice versa, and the individual founder's identity is the extension of the firm's organizational identity and vice versa. In other words, there is no clear boundary between organizational identity and founder identity, which puts the two identities in a competing mode (Danes & Olson, 2003).

The same can be observed in the founder's family businesses, i.e. those businesses which were founded with a clear intention of being passed on to the next generation (Chua et al., 1999, 2004). In this set-up, nurturing the family identity would become the secondary priority compared to nurturing the entrepreneurial drive (Miller et al., 2011) and growth orientation (Wasserman, 2006), characterized by independence, discretion, and profit-earning orientation (Cannella et al., 2015).

Founder's firms are therefore characterized by the cohesiveness of the founder's self-narrative and the external narrative (see Fig. 22.1). This congruence is anchored in the business founder's entrepreneurial journey—usually a history of sacrifice and success of a founder—and that of his/her nuclear family around the core legacy business. Both narratives send signals about the identity of the entrepreneur and his/her nuclear family (in the case of a family business), and about the legacy business, which is "tightly linked to that of the organization and to its innovative endeavors" (Dobrev & Barnett, 2005, p. 435).

Case Illustration—Vignette 1: Setting Sail: The First Glimpse of Rubin Family

In 1932, Berko and Minnie Rubin, two immigrants from two Eastern European countries, arrived on ships to the city of Liverpool, England to start a new life. The pair's to-be company, Pentland, started with a business venture typical of immigrants. Under the name "Liverpool Shoe Company", the family conceived and started a small-scale wholesale shoe business, which was set up with just over £100 after the Midland bank failed to approve a loan of £500. The family was relentless in its efforts to succeed and make a name for itself.

As a "family in shoe business" the Rubin family was proud of its values which were based on courage, respectability, and hard work. Berko Rubin was the ninth son in a family of ten, a well-liked and respected leader, who was cordial but not always adept at asserting his authority. Minnie Rubin, a businesswoman with a strong will and an equally strong work ethic, perfectly complemented her husband's personality. She remained active in the family business long after Berko's death in 1969 as she tirelessly ran the family shoe business for the next three decades.

Spurred by the success of their wholesale shoe business, the Rubin family decided to expand their business. It was this entrepreneurial and familial spirit that grew to define the family's identity and that of the firm. Post-World War II, Berko and Minnie purchased Merrywell Shoes Ltd, a shoe factory that would allow local production and would boost their manufacturing operations. This was the first step of their expansion journey. The factory was located in London, the heart of England, and the founders soon realized that the city lay at the fashion industry's core. This prompted a move of manufacturing operations from Liverpool to the capital in 1964, and the family went on to invest in seven other shoe factories. The listing of the company on the London Stock Exchange the same year helped them raise additional funds, and made these ventures possible.

In the initial days of the business, the Rubin family was a small one. Berko and Minnie's only son Stephen was born in 1937 and the family's entrepreneurial mindset and resourcefulness were instilled in him from a very young age. When Berko died in 1969, Stephen, then 31 years old, took over the reins of the business and pioneered outsourcing to Asia, moving manufacturing and sourcing operations to Hong Kong and closing down domestic production. Stephen turned out to be a natural entrepreneur, and branched out in many other businesses, heavily diversifying the portfolio. The Rubin family's legacy continued, and the newly shaped business took on the name of Pentland Group.

The journey of the first-generation Rubin family is a classic example of the entrepreneurial journey, wherein the founder's entrepreneurial identity overlaps fully with the founder's firm's identity, and in which the founder's self-narrative is aligned with the external narrative (see Fig. 22.1). The fact that Minnie Rubin continued working in the legacy business for about 30 years even after the death of her husband, Berko Rubin, is a very visible illustration of the founder's entrepreneurial identity anchored in the founder's firm, which was the shoe shop in the case of Pentland Group. Despite the movement down the value stream, i.e., from retail to manufacturing, undertaken by the first generation, it was only the second generation of the Rubin family, Stephen Rubin, who initiated the venturing out with the family

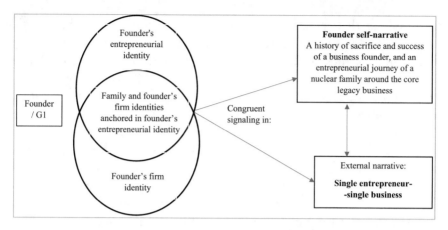

Fig. 22.1 Family and founder's firm identities anchored in founder's entrepreneurial identity

capital on a larger scale and diversified the initial portfolio, going beyond the shoe business.

Identity Conflicts: Collective Family-Owners Identity Versus Organizational Identity

As the family grows and moves to the next natural stage in its development—from Controlling Owner to Sibling Partnership (Gersick et al., 1997)—the family relationships become more complex. As the family base gets larger, the diversity in values, interests, goals, visions, and roles increases, and family interactions become more complex. The ultimate test for the family is the succession process, which naturally magnifies various family members' roles—owner-manager, family shareholder, family CEO, etc. captured in the famous three-circle model (Tagiuri & Davis, 1992)—as well as amplifies the intra-family role-driven conflicts. For example, generational transitions may cause "disagreements over growth targets, succession, product offerings, or even from seemingly mundane issues like hours of operation" (Shepherd & Haynie, 2009, p. 1245).

In the process of learning how to manage the variety of roles and needs of individual family members, and how to solve diverse conflicts and incongruences, a new *family collective identity* is formed. The development of the collective identity is always a dynamic process, based on social interactions and communications between members of the social group (Brown, 2006). In the end, collective identity is felt as the cognitive, normative, and emotional connection experienced by individual members of a social group as a result of their perceived common status with other members of that social group (Miller et al., 2011). Family collective identity is usually more familial in its nature (Miller et al., 2011) compared with the founder's identity. It also encompasses "nurturing (Giordano, 2003), caregiving (Lechner, 1993), protection (Goldberg et al., 1999), commitment and loyalty to family members (Knoester et al., 2007), and a collective gain/loss orientation (Berger & Janoff-Bulman, 2006)" (Shepherd & Haynie, 2009, p. 1251).

However, as the family collective identity emerges, it inevitably clashes with the strong founder's entrepreneurial identity, and a few members of the family may strongly identify with that entrepreneurial identity. In particular, the young third-generation family members may over-rely on the entrepreneurial identity of the founder because of the perceived attractiveness of his/her omnipresent heroic narratives, rather than develop their own entrepreneurial identity (Parada & Viladàs, 2010). The direct descendants of the founder may also retain the identity of a founder-centric business family and often refer to themselves as *brewers* (if the legacy business is a brewery), *bakers* (if their legacy business is a bakery), *publishers* (if their legacy business is a publishing house), etc. This is particularly true for business families, who are the owners of a single operational company—the founder's firm and the legacy business. They would also usually have a "one family–one business" system with simple overall governance, where ownership is concentrated in one family, and management is centralized around family members (inspired by Dieleman, 2019; Michael-Tsabari et al., 2014; Tagiuri & Davis, 1992).

However, enterprising families hold, on average, three to four operational companies in their portfolio (Zellweger et al., 2012) at any point in time. That is why scholars began to investigate enterprising families that own more than one firm (Michael-Tsabari et al., 2014, p. 162), proposed a "cluster model" (Michael-Tsabari et al., 2014), and came to the realization that it is important to study identities in businesses evolving beyond the legacy business because the reconfiguration of the business portfolio affects the development of various identities. First, the *organizational identity* (an accumulation of individual identities) evolves (Brown, 2006; Parada & Dawson, 2017) in congruence with the evolution of the family's identification with every business in the portfolio. For example, if family owners and family managers, who naturally form strong personal identification with their legacy business, view it as an ongoing "social enterprise" to be passed on to future generations (Schneper et al., 2008), then the organizational identity may reflect this view. On the other hand, if the family owners do not personally identify with other businesses in the portfolio, the organizational identity of this specific business may not encompass the family succession. Second, apart from the individual business level organizational identities, the portfolio of businesses held by a family also develops a distinctive *organizational identity at the business portfolio level*. For example, the intention to pass the business to the next generation (Chua et al., 1999), can also be seen at the family holding level, or a corporate holding level, or family office level, depending on the governance structure of the portfolio of businesses. Third, the portfolio of businesses' organizational identity is as dynamic as the portfolio itself and reflects the multiple business events such as acquisitions, mergers, internationalization, organic growth, and exits.

It's no wonder that given the complexity of organizational identities in the "portfolio of businesses", there is usually a disparity between the organization's identity and the family's collective identity. The reconciliation of both identities requires time, along with the *identity conflict* triggered by the stakeholders' expectations. Initially, there is an incongruence in signaling the identities. The family maintains the founder-centric family self-narrative, i.e. the history of sacrifice and success of a business founder, and the entrepreneurial journey of a nuclear family around the core legacy business. At the same time, the collective external narrative sends signals about the multigenerational entrepreneurial family through the organizational identity of portfolio of businesses. This is fruitful ground for identity conflicts because they arise when one internalizes only a specific identity and subsequently acts in a way inconsistent with the expectations from that role (Shepherd & Haynie, 2009). Thus, the identity conflicts of a family versus a portfolio of businesses refer to the circumstances where the founder-centric family identity and the organizational identity of a portfolio of businesses are activated together. Family owners acting in line with one identity find themselves trapped in actions inconsistent with the other identity (inspired by Shepherd & Haynie, 2009). As a result, external stakeholders are confronted with inconsistent narratives,[2] which are difficult to reconcile and send feedback to the family-business system about it. Because identity is a social construct that is constantly modified based on the interchange between internal and external definitions offered by all system stakeholders (Hatch & Schultz, 2002), an identity conflict leads to identity reformulation. *Family identity negotiations* take place in the form of ongoing conversations that "bring into existence a social reality that did not exist before their utterance" (Ford & Ford, 1995, p. 544), and which may be viewed as constitutive of system realities (Boje, 1998, p. 1). They result in a merger of individual co-narratives into

---

[2] Narratives that create identities in organizations are stories that individuals construct to make sense of the collective identity with which they identify. Identities are therefore formed by multiple narratives, by different participants, of many different types (Brown, 2006).

one collective narrative (Brown, 2006), an enmeshment of family members in simultaneous commitments as *family business owners*—the only dual role common to all family shareholders.

Owner identity is typically developed by so-called *strategic owners* (Thomsen & Pedersen, 2000)—controlling shareholders or blockholders, also referred to as large owners—who have a significant jurisdiction over the firm's operating and strategic direction. While identity determines the preferences and goals of the shareholders, the ownership concentration determines shareholders' power and incentives to enforce these preferences and goals (Thomsen & Pedersen, 2000). As soon as there is a unified commitment among family owners toward the portfolio of businesses, the multiple identities of family business owners coalesce into a family-owners' collective identity anchored in the legacy business and reflecting the portfolio of businesses.

Case Illustration—Vignette 2: Family Business? Or a Business Family?

Second Generation: Stephen Rubin

Stephen Rubin, the only son of immigrant entrepreneurs, Berko and Minnie Rubin, took the helm of the Liverpool Shoe Company in 1969. He brought to the business not only his great entrepreneurial sense but also his deep commitment to the family's values of hard work and respectability. Stephen knew that the company needed to regenerate itself as part of its change-making legacy. This entailed restructuring the shoe company's business practices for profitability while retaining its family business identity. In line with this, Stephen closed domestic production, which weighed heavily on the company's performance, and pioneered outsourcing to Asia by moving the company's manufacturing and sourcing operations to Hong Kong. The Rubin family soon became one of the biggest European importers of footwear from Asia.

Stephen also displayed a natural flair for making entrepreneurial deals. He made investments in consumer products, electrical goods, and even the construction industry. Though he continued to support the family's long-running shoe business, the portfolio of businesses began to include a broad spectrum of businesses in various geographies driven by a growing number of acquisitions in other, often unrelated, industries. The Liverpool Shoe Company was rebranded as the Pentland Group in 1973 to better reflect its new diversification trajectory. The name was borrowed from the recently acquired cargo handling company called Pentland Maritime Ship Brokers Ltd.

1974 was a watershed year for the company and Stephen when he inked his first spectacular deal, one of the many to follow. He bought a 51% stake in Unican, a company producing concentrates for homebrewed wine and beer kits, *for £51, which he went on to sell for £1,000,000 four years later. This first large-scale liquidity event enabled Pentland to launch its first own brand, Airborne, under which it sold skateboards, shoes, handbags, luggage, and sportswear. Additionally, it fueled Pentland's expansion into sportswear and brands. One of these brands was Reebok. It began as a small US distributor of athletic footwear produced in the UK. In 1981 Stephen bought a 60% stake in this American start-up venture for $77,500, unaware that this investment would generate returns worth $782,500,000 in less than 10 years, an investment multiplier of 10,000 + and the stuff of legends. Such phenomenal returns were possible because of several reasons. As a chairman of Reebok USA from 1981 to 1984, Stephen ensured that Reebok profited from Pentland's systems, be it warehousing, distribution, international trading, or sourcing from the Far East platforms. He also led innovations in marketing and fashion technology at Reebok by, for example, launching colored sports shoes (sports shoes were traditionally black or white), and garment leather for shoe production (until then only used for gloves or handbags). Pentland's creditworthiness was a factor that ensured continuous financing for the growing Reebok operations, and so was its floatation on NASDAQ in the US in 1985.*

Following Pentland's two-stage divestment of its Reebok stock that was initiated in 1991, the family faced another huge liquidity event. "We were sitting on a big pile of cash, and we talked about what we wanted to do with it", recalled Andy Rubin, Stephen's son, and third-generation family member. "We set our strategy on building a portfolio of brands that we could own or license", he added. That same year, Pentland added Pony International Inc, a global shoe and sportswear subsidiary of adidas AG, to its portfolio and acquired a 20% stake in BTF (Bernard Tapie Finance) GmbH, which just had bought a 95% interest in adidas, along with a "right of first refusal on further changes in ownership." Pentland exercised this right a year later, in 1992, and agreed to acquire the remaining 80% from Bernard Tapie. However, the firm's exclusive deal fell through because of several humble blocks related to the fact that the Pentland Group was a public company listed on the London Stock Exchange at the time. Stephen Rubin commented: "Honestly, if we had been private, I am pretty sure we would have completed the deal, and the story would have been different ever after!". Pentland ultimately ended up selling its 20% stake for £47 million and carried forth on its journey of building a family of reputable sporting and fashion brands on a global scale. Berghaus (UK's leading outdoor brand), Ellesse (an Italian brand of tennis and ski apparel), Mitre International (a soccer ball-maker company), Red or Dead (designer clothing label), Boxfresh (street fashion specialist), Canterbury (rugby brand), Speedo (swimwear brand), KicKers (a French children's footwear brand), Ted Baker (partnership for global footwear), and Lacoste shoes (serving as a global licensee) soon became the part of the Pentland family of brands either in the form of outright purchases, purchases of controlling stakes, or partnerships.

Third Generation

The growing success of the "family of brands" also allowed Pentland to divest some of its consumer product businesses. It turned its focus towards developing the necessary joint-ventures, distribution networks, and other infrastructure to forge expansion into the brands business by taking it across international waters. Pentland goods were now sold across the globe in countries like South Korea, China, Vietnam, Singapore, Malaysia, Indonesia, Argentina, and India. The acquisition strategy increasingly focused on brands and deals involving brands outnumbered those in other industries. The Rubin family remained on the lookout for good investments. A promising one was Speedo, the swimwear brand, and the family acquired an 80% stake in its European arm in 1990. Andy Rubin of the third generation was tasked with gaining complete ownership of Speedo International and Speedo Australia. He spent the summer between his first and second year at Harvard Business School, in Australia, running valuations, negotiating, and ultimately presenting the deal to the Pentland board. Remarkably, he received full empowerment from his father before actually joining the family business!

In 1991, a year later, Andy joined the business fresh from business school. It was again a watershed year for the family because they just experienced the second liquidity event due to the monetization of the Reebok stake. Since coming on board, Andy had actively co-shaped the business portfolio of brands and had been heavily involved in business operations. The same was the case with Carrie, the oldest of the four siblings, who had joined the company at 19 and worked her way up to become the President of the American affiliate's board. In 1995, Andy Rubin joined the company board as group marketing director and in 1998, he assumed the role of CEO for Pentland Brands while his father continued to serve as the Chairman of the Pentland Group.

It was a historic moment because Stephen consciously decided to leave the legacy brands business in the hands of the next generation, and to shift his focus on the investment business, a quasi-family office, which he would later expand. He also distanced himself physically by moving the office of Pentland Group and its handful of employees to Central London, while the much larger headquarters of Pentland Brands, employing hundreds of people, operated from a different location.

The quasi-family office, the Investment Division of Pentland Brands, was an embodiment of Stephen's entrepreneurial drive and acted as the investment arm of the family, and ventured into businesses within and outside the core businesses. Further businesses were constantly fueling the Pentland Group's portfolio, such as

22 From Founder Identity to Family Business Group ...   601

Body Armor (an American soft-drinks business based on coconut water), an e-commerce fashion platform Zalando, Heidi Klein (a boutique beachwear brand founded by friends Heidi Gosman and Penny Klein) wherein Pentland Group's held 60% shares. At the same time, other businesses found their way out of the portfolio, such as the iconic rubber boots brand, Hunter. As part of a larger consortium, Pentland held a 49% stake in the brand till it was sold to private equity investors, with Pentland retaining a much smaller stake. Unlike the private equity investors, however, Pentland Group tended to hold investments in their portfolio for as long as 20 to 30 years, or sometimes potentially forever. As the investment division's primary goal was the diversification of the family's wealth and bringing strong returns, the overall number of investments ran to a three-digit figure, with dozens of investments in businesses and many more in fund-type investments, all contributing to the dynamism of the Rubin family's business portfolio.

The year 2004 proved to be a significant turning point for the Pentland Group. Andy received a call from the founders of JD Sports Fashion—a sport and fashion goods retailer—and soon acquired an 11% stake in the business for £10 million. By the next year, Pentland had raised its stake in JD Sports Fashion to 57% which also marked the firm's venture into the retail business as part of its new core business legacy. For the Pentland Group, the decision to invest in JD Sports was key to maintaining their brands' operations, as that would allow them to leverage its third-party platform. Run as a publicly listed company, JD Sports had grown massively to solidify its place in the sports fashion market in the UK and beyond. With Pentland's investment, the retail channel expanded from 300 shops in 2005 in the UK to around 1,300 shops in 12 countries in 2018, and its market capitalization increased from around £100 million to over £3 billion!

By 2016, the whole Pentland Group generated £2.9 billion in sales worldwide > Sales from JD Sports accounted for 79% (£2.3 billion), while the core Pentland Brands generated just over £0.6 billion. That same year, Andy joined JD Sports Group's board as a non-executive director. By 2021, JD Sports boasted revenue of £6.167 billion with Pentland as its majority stakeholder (55% of the shares), and in turn, JD Sports constantly reaffirmed itself as the most significant holding in the overall portfolio of the Rubin family.

On the family side, among the four third-generation children, only Andy and Carrie had built their long-term careers with Pentland. When Pentland Group was again privatized in 1999, more family members, including Stephen's wife and his two daughters, joined the board. Along with the second generation, Andy and Carrie played a significant role in the family by ensuring a long-lasting relationship between its members, developing a family charter, and encouraging frequent communication to maintain family cohesion. The "familiness" of the Rubin family could easily be traced in many aspects of … the legacy business, Pentland Brands. Its overall purpose was defined as: Building a family of brands for the world to love, generation after generation. The Pentland Brands' values were visualized as the tree, and the word "family" was depicted as the tree's roots. The Rubin family personally recognized the outstanding achievements of the Pentland Brand's employees with Chairman's Awards, Values Awards, and Long-Service Awards in a special ceremony held over a three-course lunch hosted by the members of the Rubin family.

A portfolio of businesses emerges from the desire and capacity of a family to act entrepreneurially by constantly investing and de-investing in various companies. In the Rubin family, it was the second-generation family leader, Stephen Rubin, who turned out to be a savvy entrepreneur, and who enjoyed making deals. He might have been the one who took the company and the family business portfolio on a new trajectory of growth aided by the two liquidity events arising from the investments in Unican and Reebok. But it was the whole family who stood firmly behind the new strategic direction of building the portfolio of sports and fashion brands, which eventually resulted in the creation of a diversified group, borne out of the family's desire to perpetuate the legacy of entrepreneurship (Parada et al., 2019). Yet, such efforts to diversify the company's portfolio also meant that the original shoe retail business, founded by Berko and Minnie, no longer operated as the family's core legacy business. It was a fact that the original Liverpool Shoe Company's name had been replaced by the Pentland name, and the family historical narrative as a "family in shoe business", had been replaced by a new one—"family in sports and fashion brands business". The family-owners' collective identity, however, remained anchored in the legacy business, and just extended to the brands.

As the company continued to regenerate itself by adding one brand after another to its "family of brands", the division of the two main activities of the family became clearer when Andy took over the position of the CEO of Petland Brands, while his father, Stephen, continued at the Investment Division of Pentland Group in the capacity of its chairman. With the Pentland Brands business being relegated to the new firm's and family's DNA, the actions and collective identity of the family-owners fully supported the family-like corporate culture of the Pentland Brands. Many measures were taken for the Pentland Brand organization identity to continue to reflect the family's long-standing values, such as the visualization of the values with the word "family" in its roots, the overall purpose defined as *Building a family of brands for the world to love, generation after generation,* as well as the personal recognition of Pentland Brands employees by the Rubin family members.

With the acquisition of JD Sports and its expansion into other brands, Pentland solidified its position as a leader in the global retail market. History had come full circle. The Rubin family, which started its entrepreneurial journey in the shoe retail business with the Liverpool Shoe Company, and later went on to build a portfolio of brands at Pentland Brands, had finally come back to the retail business again with JD Sports. While the venture into retail with JD Sports signaled a divergence from B2B brand business, it was Pentland Brands that remained the main reference point for the family-owner collective identity for many years to come and continued to be upheld as its statement of purpose which was *Building a family of brands for the world to love, generation after generation*. The family's identification with the brands business still carried a history of sacrifice and success of the business founder, as well as the entrepreneurial journey of a nuclear family around the core legacy business.

However, the external stakeholders identified the Rubin family with the larger Pentland Group's portfolio, including the publicly listed JD Sports Fashion. It was many years after the integration of JD Sports into Pentland Group that Andy Rubin finally joined its board. The fact that JD Sports formed the bulk of the Rubin family's portfolio, also raised expectations from stakeholders about a new family collective identity and a new organizational identity, that would better reflect its current portfolio of businesses, and ultimately lead to family identity negotiations (see Fig. 22.2).

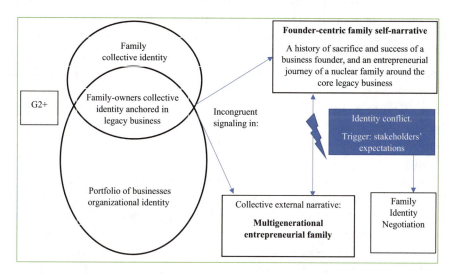

Fig. 22.2 Family-owners collective identity anchored in legacy business

FBG Identity Development

As the portfolio expands and changes its composition, the revenues generated by the core legacy business might get diluted, as the new businesses in the portfolio become the major sources of income for the entire group. As suggested by the organizational identity theory and affirmed by scholars, organizational identity can indeed be changed (Nag et al., 2007; Whetten & Godfrey, 1998), and it is the collective portfolio of businesses' identity that is adjusted to FBG identity first. This process is initiated when people share the perception that the current identity is unformulated or nebulous due to the multiple interpretations of such an identity (Corley & Gioia, 2004). Often, the trigger for change is the feeling that the identity is threatened (Ravasi & Schultz, 2006) because of business events such as mergers and acquisitions (Chreim, 2007; Empson, 2004), or spin-offs (Corley & Gioia, 2004).

Even though the organizational identity evolves toward an FBG, the family collective identity still carries the imprint of the legacy business created by the founder. Therefore, the evolution of the organizational and family identities does not occur simultaneously. This is where the crucial role of narratives as a tool for signaling and conveying multiple identities comes into play (Brown, 2006; Dawson & Parada, 2017). In particular, self-narratives are used for signaling the family narrative, and external narratives are used for signaling the organizational identity. The former still carries the founder-centric family self-narrative while the latter carries the FBG identity, i.e., the identity of the multigenerational entrepreneurial family as owners of the portfolio of businesses. Because the recipients of the signals, i.e., the various internal and external stakeholders, receive incongruent signals about family collective and organizational identities, they create incongruent images of the FBG. When the members of the FBG receive feedback about this distorted picture, it leads to an identity conflict within them. This, in turn, creates a balancing loop because identity conflicts are resolved when the enterprising family enters a family identity negotiation, and finally arrives at the coherent collective FBG identity.

In this process, many questions must be answered, such as *who we are* (Albert & Whetten, 1985) and w*here we belong* (Tajfel & Turner, 1979), as the number of co-narratives of various identities increases with the arrival of new family members and the departure of some other family members. As the family base increases, family members are enmeshed in multiple simultaneous roles and commitments (Brown, 2006; Tagiuri & Davis, 1992), creating interdependencies and interconnections. Building a coherent FBG identity—a collective family-business identity—cannot be hurried because it takes time for the enterprising family to navigate away from the omnipresent heroic narrative of the business founder.

This also involves integrating the *owner's identity* first, followed by the *investor's identity* into their *collective FBG identity*. Investor identity is particularly visible among minority shareholders, as their chief interest is to maximize the financial value of their investment and family owners may focus on developing it for the businesses in which they hold just a minority stake. Integrating investor identity into a family-owner-investor's collective identity can also constitute a challenge because owner and investor identities are very distinctive. Historically, owners and investors have displayed heterogeneous aspirations, targets, risk exposures, competencies, non-ownership ties, and capital allocation strategies (Thomsen & Pedersen, 2000). "These […] affect the way they exercise their ownership rights and therefore have important consequences for firm behavior and performance" (Thomsen & Pedersen, 2000, p. 29). For example, investor-owned companies are more likely to undertake ambitious investment programs to exploit economies of scale. Owner-governed companies, on the other hand, often pursue niche strategies related to flexibility or differentiation (Thomsen & Pedersen, 2000, p. 3334). When it comes to enterprising families who traditionally consider their family businesses a part of themselves (Canella et al., 2015), almost like their "babies", but who also intend to keep and manage a diverse business portfolio, it means a radical shift in the source of their self-identity and involves identity conflicts (Shepherd & Haynie, 2009) and identity negotiations. The ability of the business family to resolve the conflicts of identity lies in their capacity to change the narrative and develop a new collective *family-owner-investor identity* that naturally connects with the current portfolio of businesses. For some, this implies divesting the legacy business, while for others, it means keeping it in the portfolio as an "artefact" of the heroic beginning of the family's entrepreneurial success over generations.

Though the path to identity evolution is not straightforward, its steps are natural and necessary for the development of the *FBG identity*, which is a specific form of a *family-business meta-identity*. FBG meta-identity represents a higher-level identity that serves to inform "who we are as a business family" in a way that represents the intersection of multiple identities, such as *the family identity, the owner's identity, the investor identity, the multiple business identities, the family holding organizational identity, the family office identity, the family foundation identity*, etc. The FBG meta-identity is thus a higher-order awareness that not only is a reflection of their own identity but can also be embedded in the complex governance system that is understood to be a "means of stewarding the multigenerational family organization" (Goldbart & DiFuria, 2009, p. 7). For the enterprising family with a portfolio of businesses, FBG meta-identity becomes the main reference point and is reflected in the "overarching purpose that makes continuing the family business worth the strife" (Ward, 2016, p. 24). It serves to answer questions like "Why are we doing this?", "Why are we working so hard?", and "Why are we exerting so much energy to prepare for the future?" (Ward, 2016, p. 24).

Developing the FBG meta-identity is the first building block of the governance model embracing *dynamic durability* that is supported by the three processes that entrepreneurial families engage in to nurture it: (i) Sensemaking, (ii) Storytelling, and (iii) Family Learning & Development (Cheng et al., 2021). After all, the business family system is in constant flux as e changes inevitably occur in the business system and the family system. Examples of events on the family side may include marriages, births, deaths and relocations in the family, and on the business side, may include liquidity events, changes in governance, ownership successions and changes in the portfolio composition because of various investments and de-investments, etc. Because the FBG-meta identity is developed as a result of experiences the involving multiple and dynamic events that take place in both systems— the family system and the business system—the FBGs undergo a process of constant identity adjustments. The families that overcome identity conflicts quickly and without damage, naturally engage in storytelling, sensemaking and learning, which makes them well equipped to navigate the external changes with its dynamic and durable governance model.

Case Illustration—Vignette 3: The Future of "Family"

The future values of the Pentland Group will most likely mirror the family's long-standing values of entrepreneurism and Berko and Minnie Rubin's legacy that began with the Liverpool Shoe Company and has been the bedrock of the legacy business' practices for almost a century. The family values were easily transposed on the Pentland Brands' values of Passion, Courage, Creativity, and Always Learning, and the employees identified with them widely, even though the chain of family operational leadership at Pentland Brands had been broken. In 2015, Andy Rubin promoted Andy Long to become the first-ever non-family CEO of Pentland Brands. Andy Long had been with Pentland for a decade and had assumed increasing responsibility for the business over time. Andy Rubin took on the role of chairman of Pentland Brands and retained his old physical office at Pentland Brands HQ, but was not part of the newly created executive team. The transition was seamless, and Pentland Brands remained the "favorite child in the portfolio". This legacy business resonated with the family identity; it was also the

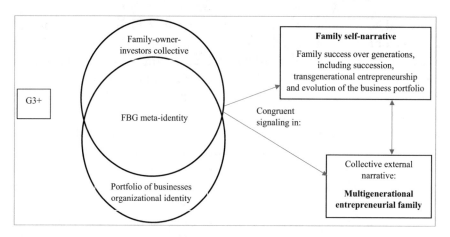

Fig. 22.3 Family Business Group (FBG) meta-identity

glue that bound the family to one another. This togetherness was especially visible during the Olympics, when the whole family would go together to watch events.

Back in 2017, Stephen was still involved in the operations of the Investment Division. He and his wife were both on the holding board of the Pentland Group, with Stephen as the chairman of the whole group. They continued to cultivate the tradition of Friday evening family dinners, which undoubtedly fostered family cohesion, not only amongst their children but also among their grandchildren—the cousins of the fourth generation, who by that time had entered their teenage and young adulthood years.

However, with most of the family portfolio's revenue coming from the retail business, JD Sports, the business family would require an extensive negotiation regarding its identity to reconcile its family collective identity with its current portfolio of businesses to arrive at the FBG meta-identity (see Fig. 22.3). *Who knows, this might become a key role for future generations of the Rubin family who have the ultimate responsibility of furthering the Pentland Group legacy. After all, known approaches to regeneration in business, long upheld by the family, have had to adapt to the growing popularity of social media, digitization, and customization. All modern business practices touted by the younger generations...*

Discussion and Conclusions

This chapter illustrates a process that facilitates a better understanding of how business families evolve their identity over time, from a founder's and founder's firm's identity to an FBG identity. This evolution occurs as the business expands and the family grows. Thus, business families enlarge and diversify their portfolio of businesses and arrive at an FBG while they advance in generational stages from Owner Firm to Cousin Consortium (Gersick et al., 1997), and at the same time, take up multiple roles as illustrated in the three-circle model (Tagiuri & Davis, 1992). This inevitably results in a transition from a lone-founder identity (Miller et al., 2011) to a collective identity (Parada & Dawson, 2017) both on the organization side and the family side. The interplay between individual and organizational identity has been a subject of study for a long time. Previous research shows how the presence of the family has a powerful influence on organizational behavior as well as how family identity is interlinked with the organizational identity (c.f. Canella et al., 2015; Miller et al., 2011; Shepherd & Haynie, 2009).

The Rubin family case perfectly showcases the strong identification of the founders with the business (Canella et al., 2015). It is natural for a founder's firm to reflect the values and operational style of the owner-manager and cultivate his/her vision and intention to give continuity to the business across generations (Chua et al., 1999).

At the founding stage there is a quasi-complete symbiosis between the founder identity and the organizational identity (see Fig. 22.1), which has a clear entrepreneurial spirit with its unique leadership style, but above all, is characterized by a complete overlap of the attributes that define a person and those that define an organization (Dutton et al., 1994).

While it could be concluded that the first-generation family business possesses, by default, the founder identity, we observe that the subsequently developed family business identity results from a dynamic process. As new generations come on board, identity development occurs by asking questions such as *who we are* (Albert & Whetten, 1985) and w*here we belong* (Tajfel & Turner, 1979), redefining the social context in which family business owners are embedded. This process portrays the different events that take place in both contexts, the family context, and the business context. The arrival of new family members and the departure of some other family members, results in the emergence of a collective identity (Parada & Dawson, 2017) of an enterprising family. But the evolution toward the new identity is not necessarily a smooth process, because it requires the family collective identity to be in conflict with the identity of the business (Shepherd & Haynie, 2009). This conflict is usually triggered by stakeholders who receive clearly incongruent messages signaled by the self-narrative of the family and the collective narrative of the business (compared Fig. 22.2).

Building an FBG identity—a collective family-business identity—is a time-consuming and constant process of formulation, edition, and appreciation or rejection of some elements of the narrative that is being shaped, as Czarniawska-Joerges, (1994) suggest. Why is this process so tedious? The reason is that families may be unaware of the lack of congruence between family collective identity and organizational identity. This is also the result of the deeply ingrained identity that the founder has imprinted onto the family and the business. Often it represents the soul of the enterprising family, its traditions, and the heroic narrative of the founder. It is particularly the case in single business families, in which family members refer to themselves as *brewers* (if the legacy business is a brewery), *bakers* (if their legacy business is a bakery), or *publishers* (if their legacy business is a publishing house). These business families who are successful in walking through their identity development reject the omnipresent heroic narrative of the business founder and integrate the *owner-investor identity*. This leads to the construction of a new collective identity (Brown, 2006) of the enterprising family that encompasses both the entire portfolio of businesses and family investments. Not only would such an FBG send congruent signals about family self-narrative and the collective external narrative, but it would also build the meta-identity (see Fig. 22.3).

In summary, we illustrate how the process of identity development unfolds with the case study of the Rubin family and the evolution of their portfolio from Liverpool Shoe Company to Pentland Group, with JD Sports, a chain of retail shops forming bulk of their portfolio. We support our theorizing with the proposed model of three-stage identity development depicted in Fig. 22.4.

Our research contributes to the practice in several ways. First, we highlight that business families tend to be highly attached to their legacy identity and may not at times, realize the necessity to adapt their identity toward FBG meta-identity, which would reflect their entire portfolio of businesses. Second, we prove that the family collective identity needs to evolve toward FBG identity and this needs to be done intentionally! Third, by illustrating our theorizing with the case of the Rubin family and their Pentland Group, we build on bright spots in emotionally overlooked business units, allowing business families to navigate away from ill-advised strategies and unnecessary family conflicts.

We contribute to the literature on family business and identity in several different ways. First, in our theorizing, we go beyond the dynamic view of the development of an enterprising family (Controlling Owner Company, Sibling Partnership, and Cousin Consortium in Gersick et al., 1997) and the three-circle model (Tagiuri & Davis, 1992) and extend it by acknowledging that many business families are in fact owners of multiple businesses at the same time (Zellweger et al., 2012). Second, we propose that there are specific notions and processes—signaling, self-narrative, collective external narrative,

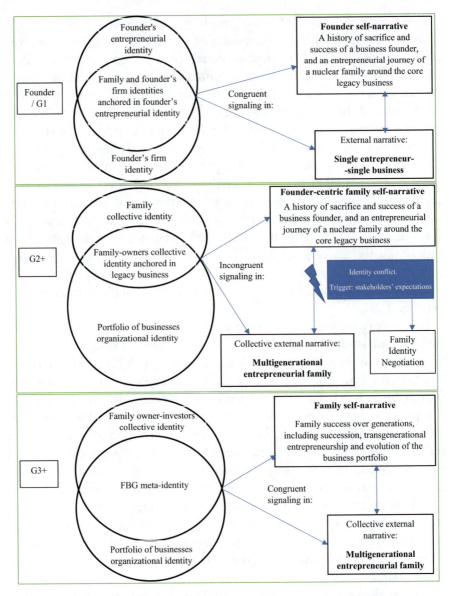

Fig. 22.4 Identity development. From founder's identity to FBG meta-identity

identity conflicts, multiple identities, development of collective family identity and organizational identity—that hinder or accelerate the evolution of FBG identity over time, as the nature of the family involvement and the scope of the enterprising portfolio evolves. Third, we integrate the *social identity theory* (Tajfel & Turner, 1979, 1986), which describes how persons define their identity based on their social context (Burke, 2003; Fiske & Taylor,

1991) with the organizational identity theory (Albert & Whetten, 1985) and mold it into a complex *collective identity* (Brown, 2006; Parada & Dawson, 2017) of FBGs that is an accumulation of collective family identity and the portfolio of businesses organizational identity. Further, by studying the *identity development* in the context of the dynamically evolving FBG, we contribute to the identity literature by showing how identity conflicts are resolved (Shepherd & Haynie, 2009) over time, and highlight the importance of identity evolution to match the different identities that emerge from various social systems.

Finally, our chapter aid practitioners by shedding light on the process of identity evolution that is needed in the conversation of business families as they expand their family base and business base. How they create their self-narrative and how they develop an external narrative can result in a positive or negative bias in the eyes of external stakeholders. Moreover, the ability to develop the FBG meta-identity is the foundation for building a long-lasting, dynamic, and durable governance system.

Recommendations for Further Research

This study, while profound and adding to different streams of literature, is not without its limitations. Our research reaches out to a single case study only. Thus, we attempted to illustrate the phenomenon of FBG meta-identity development by proposing a theoretical model, which is partly based on the literature available and partly on our own experiences, observations, and empirical evidence of business families. This research could be expanded further by developing an empirical work based on a qualitative methodology to explore in-depth how business families resolve their identity conflicts as they evolve from a founder firm to an FBG. Such an investigation may allow us to confirm the pathway presented in this chapter, as well as potentially expand the number and type of pathways observed in cases of other business families, who rebuild their identity toward FBG meta-identity.

Further, our study brings only one illustration of a UK-based company. However, the cultural aspects may affect the way families construct their identities. Therefore, building on a cross-cultural sample of multiple case studies could enrich our knowledge of how identity development is not only socially constructed but also culturally constructed.

Finally, our conceptual work opens the door for a diversity of practitioner projects and applied research. For example, it may serve as a basis for potential consultancy projects that aim to help business families by raising their awareness of their multiple identities, the need to identify their blind spots, or upcoming identity conflicts, as well as equipping them with adequate tools to navigate the conversations toward developing their FBG-meta identity.

References

Albert, S. & Whetten, D. A. (1985), *Organizational identity*, In L. L. Cummings and B. M. Staw, (Eds), Research in organizational behavior, 7, JAI Press, pp. 263–295.

Ashforth, B. E., Kreiner, G. E., & Fugate, M. (2000). All in a day's work: Boundaries and micro role transitions. *Academy of Management Review, 25*(3), 472–491.

Berger, A. R., & Janoff-Bulman, R. (2006). Costs and satisfaction in close relationships: The role of loss–gain framing. *Personal Relationships, 13*, 53–68.

Boivie, S., Lange, D., McDonald, M. L., & Westphal, J. D. (2011). Me or we: The effects of CEO organizational identification on agency costs. *Academy of Management Journal, 54*(3), 551–576.

Boje, D. M. (1998). The postmodern turn from stories-as-objects to stories-in-context methods. *Research Methods Forum, 3*, 1–8.

Brown, A. D. (2006). A narrative approach to collective identities. *Journal of Management Studies, 43*(4), 731–753.

Burke, P. J. (2001). *Relationships among multiple identities.* The Future of Identity Theory and Research, a Guide for a New Century Conference, Bloomington, Indiana.

Burke, P. J. (2003). Relationships among multiple identities. In P. J. Burke, T. J. Owens, R. T. Serpe, & P. A. Thoits (Eds.), *Advances in identity theory and research* (pp. 95–114). Kluwer Academic/Plenum Publishers.

Cannella, A. A., Jr., Jones, C. D., & Withers, M. C. (2015). Family-versus lone-founder-controlled public corporations: Social identity theory and boards of directors. *Academy of Management Journal, 58*(2), 436–459.

Cantor, N., & Mischel, W. (1979). Traits as prototypes: Effects on recognition memory. *Journal of Personality and Social Psychology, 35*, 38–44.

Cheng, C.Y.J., Au, K., Widz, M., & Jen, M. (2021). *The governance marathon: Dynamic durability in entrepreneurial families amid disruptions.* Boston, MA: 2086 Society & the Family Firm Institute.

Chreim, S., Williams, B. E., & Hinings, C. R. (2007). Interlevel influences on the reconstruction of professional role identity. *Academy of Management Journal, 50*(6), 1515–1539.

Chua, J. H., Chrisman, J. J., & Chang, E. P. (2004). Are family firms born or made? An exploratory investigation. *Family Business Review, 17*(1), 37–54.

Chua, J. H., Chrisman, J. J., & Sharma, P. (1999). *Defining the family business by behavior.*

Corley, K. G., & Gioia, D. A. (2004). Identity ambiguity and change in the wake of a corporate spin-off. *Administrative Science Quarterly, 49*(2), 173–208.

Czarniawska-Joerges, B. (1994). Narratives of individual and organizational identities. *Annals of the International Communication Association, 17*(1), 193–221.

Danes, S. M., & Olson, P. D. (2003). Women's role involvement in family businesses, business tensions, and business success. *Family Business Review, 16*(1), 53–68.

Dieleman, M. (2019). Reaping what you sow: The family firm innovation trajectory. *Journal of Family Business Strategy, 10*(4), 100–248.

Dobrev, S. D., & Barnett, W. P. (2005). Organizational roles and transition to entrepreneurship. *Academy of Management Journal, 48*(3), 433–449.

Dutton, J. E., Dukerich, J. M., & Harquail, C. V. (1994). Organizational images and member identification. *Administrative Science Quarterly*, 239–263.

Empson, L. (2004). Organizational identity change: Managerial regulation and member identification in an accounting firm acquisition. *Accounting, Organizations and Society, 29*(8), 759–781.

Fauchart, E., & Gruber, M. (2011). Darwinians, communitarians, and missionaries: The role of founder identity in entrepreneurship. *Academy of Management Journal, 54*(5), 935–957.

Fiske, S. & Taylor, S. (1991). *Social cognition* (2nd ed.). McGraw-Hill Book Company.

Ford, J. D., & Ford, L. W. (1995). The role of conversations in producing intentional change in organizations. *Academy of Management Review, 20*(3), 541–570.

Gersick, K., Davis, J. A., Hampton, M. M., & Lansberg, I. (1997). *Generation to generation: Life cycles of the family business*. Harvard Business Press.

Giordano, P. C. (2003). Relationships in adolescence. *Annual Review of Sociology, 29*, 257–281.

Goldbart, S., & DiFuria, J. (2009). Money and meaning: Implementation of effective family governance structures. *Journal of Practical Estate Planning, 11*(6), 79.

Goldberg, S., Grusec, J. E., & Jenkins, J. M. (1999). Confidence in protection: Arguments for a narrow definition of attachment. *Journal of Family Psychology, 13*, 475–483.

Hatch, M. J., & Schultz, M. (2002). The dynamics of organizational identity. *Human Relations, 55*(8), 989–1018.

Kenyon-Rouvinez, D. & Widz, M. (2019a). *Pentland brands: Succession dilemma (A)*, IMD- IMD-7–2052.

Kenyon-Rouvinez, D. & Widz, M. (2019b). *Pentland brands: Succession dilemma (B)*, *I*MD- IMD-7–2053.

Knoester, C., Petts, R. J., & Eggebeen, D. J. (2007). Commitments to fathering and the well-being and social participation of new, disadvantaged fathers. *Journal of Marriage and Family, 69*, 991–1004.

Lechner, V. (1993). Racial group responses to work and parent care. *Families in Society: Journal of Contemporary Human Services, 74*, 93–103.

Leleux, B., Widz, M. (2017). Pentland group: A family of brands. Lessons from the winner of the 2017 IMD Global Family Business Award. *Tomorrow's Challenges*. IMD.

Leleux, B. & Widz, M. (2018). *Pentland group: A family of brands*. IMD- IMD-7–1937.

Michael-Tsabari, N., Labaki, R., & Zachary, R. K. (2014). Toward the cluster model: The family firm's entrepreneurial behavior over generations. *Family Business Review, 27*(2), 161–185.

Miller, D., Le Breton-Miller, I., & Lester, R. H. (2011). Family and lone founder ownership and strategic behaviour: Social context, identity, and institutional logics. *Journal of Management Studies, 48*(1), 125.

Nag, R., Corley, K. G., & Gioia, D. A. (2007). The intersection of organizational identity, knowledge, and practice: Attempting strategic change via knowledge grafting. *Academy of Management Journal, 50*(4), 821–847.

Oertel, S., & Thommes, K. (2018). History as a source of organizational identity creation. *Organization Studies, 39*(12), 1709–1731.

Parada, M. J., & Dawson, A. (2017). Building family business identity through transgenerational narratives. *Journal of Organizational Change Management*, 30(2), 344–356.

Parada, M. J., & Viladás, H. (2010). Narratives: A powerful device for values transmission in family businesses. *Journal of Organizational Change Management, 23*(2), 166–172.

Parada, M. J., Akhter, N., Basco, R., Discua Cruz, A., & Fitz-Koch, S. (2019). Understanding the dynamics of business group development: A transgenerational perspective. *In The Family Business Group Phenomenon* (pp. 201–222). Palgrave Macmillan.

Rautiainen, M., Rosa, P., Pihkala, T., Parada, M. J., & Cruz, A. D. (2019). *The family business group phenomenon*. Palgrave.

Ravasi, D., & Schultz, M. (2006). Responding to organizational identity threats: Exploring the role of organizational culture. *Academy of Management Journal, 49*(3), 433–458.

Schneper, W. D., Celo, S., & Jain, N. K. (2008). Agents, altruism, and corporate governance: The impact of family ownership on non-executive compensation and training. *Proceedings of ASBBS, 15*(1).

Shepherd, D., & Haynie, J. M. (2009). Family business, identity conflict, and an expedited entrepreneurial process: A process of resolving identity conflict. *Entrepreneurship Theory and Practice, 33*(6), 1245–1264.

Sieger, P., Zellweger, T., Nason, R. S., & Clinton, E. (2011). Portfolio entrepreneurship in family firms: A resource-based perspective. *Strategic Entrepreneurship Journal, 5*(4), 327–351.

Stryker, S., & Burke, P. J. (2000). The past, present, and future of an identity theory. *Social Psychology Quarterly, 63*, 284–297.

Stryker, A., & Statham, A. (1985). Symbolic interaction and role theory. In G. Lindsey & L. Aronsen (Eds.), *Handbook of social psychology* (3rd ed., pp. 311–378). McGraw Hill.

Tagiuri, R., & Davis, J. A. (1992). On the goals of successful family companies. *Family Business Review, 5*(1), 43–62.

Tajfel, H. & Turner, J.C. (1979). *An integrative theory of intergroup conflict*. In W. Austin & S. Worchel (Eds.), *The social psychology of intergroup relations* (pp. 33–47). Brooks/Cole.

Tajfel, H., & Turner, J. C. (1986). The social identity theory of intergroup behavior. In S. Worchel & W. Austinn (Eds.), *Psychology of intergroup relations* (2nd ed., pp. 2–24). Nelson-Hall.

Thomsen, S., & Pedersen, T. (2000). Ownership structure and economic performance in the largest European companies. *Strategic Management Journal, 21*(6), 689–705.

Ward, J. (2016). *Perpetuating the family business: 50 lessons learned from long lasting, successful families in business*. Springer.

Wasserman, N. (2006). Stewards, agents, and the founder discount: Executive compensation in new ventures. *Academy of Management Journal, 49*(5), 960–976.

Whetten, D. A., & Godfrey, P. C. (Eds). (1998). *Identity in organizations: Building theory through conversations*. Sage Publications, Inc.

Widz, M. (2017). *Pentland group. building a family of brands for the world to love, generation after generation*. Family Business Network Polaris Report.

Zellweger, T. M., Nason, R. S., & Nordqvist, M. (2012). From longevity of firms to transgenerational entrepreneurship of families: Introducing family entrepreneurial orientation. *Family Business Review, 25*(2), 136–155.

Part V

Conclusions

23

Understanding the Dynamics of FBGs: Avenues for Further Research

Naveed Akhter, Allan Discua Cruz, Kajari Mukherjee, Maria José Parada⍟, Timo Pihkala, and Marita Rautiainen

The main interest of this book has dealt with the inherent strengths of FBGs, widening our understanding of their sustainability, competitiveness, and development. This book highlights that research conducted on the internal dynamics of FBGs is sparse. The phenomenon has remained severely understudied around the world.

This book compiles together a wide collection of viewpoints on the internal dynamics in FBGs and opens new research opportunities. In this chapter concluding the book, we highlight some of the new possible avenues for further research. We discuss research gaps related to FBGs vis-á-vis Innovation, Entrepreneurship, Strategy and resources, Identity, Sustainability, and Ownership and Governance, respectively.

N. Akhter
Jönköping International Business School (JIBS), Jönköping, Sweden
e-mail: naveed.akhter@ju.se

A. D. Cruz
Department of Entrepreneurship and Strategy, Lancaster University Management School, Lancaster, UK
e-mail: a.discuacruz@lancaster.ac.uk

© The Author(s), under exclusive license to Springer Nature Switzerland AG 2023
M. Rautiainen et al. (eds.), *The Palgrave Handbook of Managing Family Business Groups*, https://doi.org/10.1007/978-3-031-13206-3_23

Innovation

In family business research, the innovation paradox has been studied thoroughly. Empirical research has shown that family businesses use less inputs for innovation compared to non-family businesses at the same time as they produce higher outputs in innovation compared to non-family businesses (Duran et al., 2016). To a large extent, these empirical studies have been conducted in simple family businesses, or the possible group structures in the sample cases have been ignored. In this book, the studies on FBG innovation (e.g., *Giannini & Iacobucci*; *Pihkala, Rautiainen & Akhter*) suggest that business group structures provide benefits for innovation. Those benefits include, e.g., FBGs' ability to use internal resources and finance for innovation, the ability to centralize innovation in the group due to the task division within the business group, and large groups' possibilities to invest in R&D. It is evident that we must raise new questions about FBG innovation.

First, FBGs need their own innovation paradox analysis. FBGs have been shown to finance innovation within the group (see, e.g., *Giannini and Iacobucci*), and simultaneously exploit and benefit from internal spillovers of innovation activities, thus increasing synergy effects in the group structure. Should this be the case, it would mean that for FBGs, the innovation paradox would be even larger than for simple FBs. However, due to the complexity of FBGs as organizations, the FBGs' inputs for innovation would be more difficult to identify than in simple FBs, and analyzing the eventual paradox would need extra effort.

Second, since large FBGs have good access to finance and resources for innovation, and a high ability to control innovation spillover within the

---

K. Mukherjee
Department of Organisation Behavior and Human Resources Management, Indian Institue of Management Indore (IIM), Indore, India
e-mail: kajari@iimidr.ac.in

M. J. Parada
Department of Strategy and General Management, ESADE Business School, Sant Cugat del Vallès, Spain
e-mail: mariajose.parada@esade.edu

T. Pihkala (✉) · M. Rautiainen
School of Engineering Science, LUT University, Lahti, Finland
e-mail: timo.pihkala@lut.fi

M. Rautiainen
e-mail: marita.rautiainen@lut.fi

23 Understanding the Dynamics of FBGs: Avenues for Further Research 621

group, it is likely that for FBGs, innovation may appear less risky, more controlled, and manageable than for simple FBs. Furthermore, due to their size and ability for innovation management, they are capable of investing in high R&D expenditures with more ambitious goals. Due to these benefits arising from the character of FBGs, we suggest that FBGs can initiate more diversifying innovation projects without risking their sustainability. More research is needed to uncover the risk-bearing behavior of FBGs and especially those mechanisms or managerial patterns that the FBG owners and/or managers apply for innovation.

Third, we raise the question on the organization of innovation in FBGs. Earlier research (e.g., Rautiainen et al., 2021) and chapters in this book (*Sabyasachi* et al.; *Konsti-Laakso* et al.) have shown that FBGs may systematically employ innovation sourcing strategies. In FBGs, the acquisition of businesses may be a parallel method for innovation with the traditional internal innovation process. Simultaneously, the study by *Cheng and King* in this volume suggests that some FBGs may manage systematically their innovation investments in different risk categories. The decision-making on the allocation of innovation investments would provide important insights into the strategic development of FBGs.

Entrepreneurship

FBGs can be understood through diverse lenses that delve into the dynamics of entrepreneurship. Scholars have suggested that when new economic activities are added to old ones in existing organizations, entrepreneurship is often manifested as growth rather than as the creation of new organizations which may bring issues in our understanding of how a collection of firms comes into existence (Lockett et al., 2011). The chapters in this book suggest that a portfolio of family owned and controlled firms does not emerge in a vacuum; rather, it is often the result of a complex development including the entrepreneurial pursuits of one or more members of families in business throughout time. Until recently, very little attention has been paid to this phenomenon from an entrepreneurial perspective (Rautiainen et al., 2019; Rosa et al., 2014). This is surprising as studies highlight the long-standing presence, diversity, and entrepreneurial outcomes of family businesses around the world (Iacobucci & Rosa, 2010; Lubinski et al., 2013). Our understanding of family business groups should improve when we analyze the entrepreneurial dynamics undertaken by members of a family in business (Discua Cruz & Basco, 2018).

622   N. Akhter et al.

From an individual perspective, entrepreneurs who are involved in the development of multiple ventures differ from serial entrepreneurs, who establish several companies but own only one company at the time (Michael-Tsabari et al., 2014; Ucbasaran et al., 2001; Westhead & Wright, 1998). According to Huovinen and Tihula (2008), there is a unique development of entrepreneurial knowledge when organizing and managing start-up firms as individual or collective networks of firms. Family business groups benefit from entrepreneurs who have proposed many ideas, learned from their mistakes, and started again in the processes leading to the emergence of several firms. Moreover, the focus on portfolio entrepreneurship research has often concentrated on the relationship between entrepreneurship and the entrepreneur's context. Portfolio entrepreneurs have been found to be more motivated, innovative, and prone to take risks when compared with entrepreneurs who have only one business (Alsos & Carter, 2006; Alsos et al., 2014). The ability to leverage high-discretion slack resources, legitimacy, learning, and experimentation across loosely coupled ventures may provide family business groups a unique set of characteristics, through entrepreneurs, to develop new firms, penetrate new markets, and remain resilient through adversity (Discua Cruz et al., 2019; McGaughey, 2007).

The studies on FBGs, however, suggest that family owners may act as individual entrepreneurs at the same time as they are FBG owners. Such unique duality provides an interesting context for further studies. In this volume, *Ceron, Cruz and Parada* and *Sorvisto, Rautiainen, Pihkala, and Parada* suggest that aligning the individual entrepreneurial aspirations with the collective FBG aims may need special attention. From the perspective of ambidexterity, the creative tension between exploration and exploitation may grow from the balance between entrepreneurial owners and large corporate business volumes. This suggests that the co-existence of collective ownership and entrepreneurial persons participating in the FBG ownership match well with the ambidexterity argument. However, more research is needed on the ways in which FBGs reach the balance between exploration and exploitation—that is, how do FBG owners combine individual and organizational ambidexterity within the FBG?

While the individual perspective of portfolio entrepreneurship for family firms has received growing attention, the collective dimension is beginning to gain momentum. Ownership of small firms commonly involves relatives or partners who are directly involved in their management. In family businesses, some entrepreneurial families create teams of family members who found and develop several businesses over time (Discua Cruz et al., 2013; Iacobucci & Rosa, 2010). Scott and Rosa (1999) found that the natural growth process

23 Understanding the Dynamics of FBGs: Avenues for Further Research   623

of starting firms is not about increasing the size of a single firm, but about "growing the clusters of companies under the control of the entrepreneur or entrepreneurial team." In addition, Iacobucci and Rosa (2010), whose study focuses on the operations of entrepreneurial team dynamics in multiple business contexts, suggest that one of the main reasons for the formation and expansion of business groups is the need to create an entrepreneurial team, which is achieved by giving minority shares in the new ventures to others, mainly former employees.

Few studies have considered the family entrepreneurial team as a key unit of analysis in FBG studies, yet the findings so far show promise in understanding how this phenomenon unfolds in diverse contexts. For example, Alsos et al. (2014) suggest that portfolio management should be studied as a process, and that special attention should be paid to the composition of stakeholders in each component of the portfolio. Huovinen and Tihula (2008) note that portfolio entrepreneurship is more like a team sport than an individual sport and this offers good learning opportunities. Discua Cruz et al. (2013) studied portfolio businesses in Honduras and found that business groups' succession processes often entail keeping the family in the business through the development of a portfolio of businesses. This keeps the family in business, not the business in the family. In a recent study, Discua Cruz et al. (2021) relied on entrepreneurial opportunities, linguistic and stewardship perspectives to discover how family members developed portfolio businesses. They noticed that family members form groups committed to being in business together for the long term, and these family groups have a collectivist approach to opportunities and resources. Entrepreneurship within the context of a family entrepreneurial team can also relate to the context of family cycles or transitions. Such cycles, which may also include critical incidents and how they may affect the development of a family business group, have received scant attention. For example, recent studies suggest that when the untimely or anticipated death of family members occurs, there is immediate action required by family members to keep a group of family businesses operating while pondering about new business ideas (Discua Cruz & Hamilton, 2022).

Thus, from an entrepreneurial perspective, researchers highlight that further insight into a collective approach (Discua Cruz et al., 2013) may provide insight into the way family entrepreneurship unfolds (Randerson et al., 2015). Recent studies reveal that aspects related to identity, which revolves around the perception of a family as an entrepreneurial group needs further study as well as the way things are done may change or evolve over time suggesting attention to understudied aspects such as culture (Fitz-Koch et al., 2019). Relevant questions relate to: How do families in business rely on their identity as entrepreneurs in the process leading to create/acquire a new firm for their existing portfolio? What team level resources are produced and leveraged when pursuing new family businesses in the context of a family business group? What are the main influences on an entrepreneurial culture within the context of a family business group?

The basic theoretical framework around such approaches may relate more to strategic orientation for entrepreneurial value. Business group formation is a process that evolves over time, so such research requires a longitudinal research design where entrepreneurship is monitored over a period of years (Iacobucci & Rosa, 2010). Such strategic orientation may relate to unpicking a co-evolutionary perspective, where the development of a portfolio of business may have a long-term orientation including diverse opportunities, risk management, and diverse approaches to entrepreneurship (Litz, 2008; Lumpkin & Brigham, 2011). General questions may relate to: How do families in business make sense of their long-term approach to entrepreneurship when developing a new business venture? What factors are believed to create value in the approach of a family in business to the development of a new business venture?

Strategy and Resources

Earlier research and several chapters in this book have shown that FBGs are complex organizations with varying ownership arrangements, diverse structures, and multiple lines of business. In addition to business strategies, FBGs also have corporate strategies and ownership strategies affecting the direction, investments, development, and synergies within the business group. In this volume, *Sorvisto* et al. suggest that ownership strategies may take different forms depending on the needs in the FBG. That is, ownership strategies are created for a specific need, and they need to be updated accordingly. No research has been done on the development—or evolution—of ownership strategies. We suggest that uncovering the timely development of ownership strategies is vital for understanding the survival and success of FBGs. In line, it is likely that in the process of ownership strategy creation or update, the role of one or a few persons in the owning family is central. Earlier research on family businesses (Kelly et al., 2000) has suggested that the family leader's role may be critical for the success of an FB. Subsequently, we suggest that further studies are needed to uncover the individual owner's role in creating an

23 Understanding the Dynamics of FBGs: Avenues for Further Research

ownership strategy for FBGs. Parallel to ownership strategies, FBGs expand their businesses following corporate and business strategies.

In this book, *Mendoza* et al. analyze the growth strategies of Catalonian FBGs, and *Akhter and Lesage* explore the strategic redeployment of resources and exit in family business portfolios. Dealing with innovative initiatives, opportunities for business acquisitions or needs for internal development of business lines, FBGs need to allocate their resources. In other words, FBGs are bound to have internal competition of resources. In the competition, the winning criteria may be related to a number of things—ranging from profitability estimates or risk management to the family owners' personal preferences. In this perspective, the effect of family ownership on the FBG resource allocation is especially interesting. New research is needed on the question, how do owning families make decisions on resource allocation? How do families deal with the competition on internal resources?

Identity

Family business groups—and family businesses in general—are institutions with strong identities that guide their development, choices, transitions, and survival. The phenomenon is two sided: Family-related emotions are anchoring the business development into long-lasting continuum of legacy, values, identities, and cultures. At the same time, the development of the business affects the owning family in several ways. This relationship is suggested to contain paradoxes and conflict both inside the family and with the external stakeholders.

In this volume, *Cheng and King* raised the question, how does the change from family business to business family affect the family identity? While it is evident that the family identities are affecting the development of the FBG, relatively little is known about the relationship. Only some family businesses develop into business families owning large FBGs. Bearing this in mind, more research is needed to understand the relationship between family identity and FBG development. Can the family transition be managed, promoted, supported, or speeded up? In the process of transition, the owning family members may have different ideas about the future family identity, and conflicts are likely to arise and affect the family and the business. How do owning families transform and manage their conflicting multiple identities during the growth of the FBG?

As suggested by *Witz and Parada*, family business identities are socially created and they are affected by the external stakeholders, as well. Witz and

Parada build on the idea of self—and external narratives that participate in the construction of the business family identity. While the process is likely to resemble evolution rather than a managed project, the family is likely to affect the formation of the external narratives. In this context, the concepts such as socio-emotional wealth, corporate social responsibility, and sustainability embeddedness become important. Early evidence suggests that families seek to strengthen their external image and narratives of responsibility, sustainability, and ethical conduct. In terms of FBG development, little is known, how do these aspirations affect or resonate with the growth of the FBG? More research is warranted on the role and effect of family identities on the FBG development and growth.

Sustainability

There is a growing need and attention of family business scholars to address the issues of sustainability and responsibility. Family businesses are generally considered to be more responsible in terms of social and environmental sustainability (Arregle et al., 2007; James, 1999; Miller & Le Breton-Miller, 2005). In this book, *Ramirez-Pasillas, Saari, and Lundberg* addressed the topic of sustainability embeddedness and family business groups. The diversity in family business groups in terms of businesses, ownership, and management could pose challenges and advantages for sustainability. It has been recognized that family firms owning multiple businesses contribute to social and economic aspects due to their wide prevalence in developing economies. In the case of FBGs in developed economies, the economic and social effects are still largely uncovered. It is likely that their relative importance is not as high as in developing economies, but, at the same time, as large-scale businesses with concentrated ownership structures, they have potential to make important impacts.

In addition to the economic effects of the FBGs, also the effects related to ecological and ethical development need to be considered. The issue has remained largely unstudied and contains a wide range of interesting starting points for research. In this volume, *Liang and Carney* suggest that FBG owners identify and respond to the political pressures in the environment and develop personalized governance mechanisms to manage with the pressures.

In terms of FBG organization, how do FBGs implement owners' sustainability aspirations into the multiple businesses within the FBG? This question has close resemblance with studies on strategy implementation. How can same ideas, measures, and indicators of sustainability be applied into a

23 Understanding the Dynamics of FBGs: Avenues for Further Research

single business level of a diversified business group? Furthermore, as the FBG owners may differ in their motivations to pursuit sustainability goals, these differences may be reflected in the operation of the single businesses. Finally, as the FBGs often operate both internationally and locally, they meet competing interests in terms of sustainability in their different business contexts. Further research is needed to uncover how do family business groups manage diversity in their different contexts and contribute to the local environment?

Ownership and Governance

The development of ownership theory has followed two separate lines—the first has been dealing with the phenomenon of ownership, its various dimensions, and their effects on businesses (Nordqvist, 2005; Pierce et al., 2001). Here, ownership is considered as rights, responsibilities, legacy, feelings, or identity. In this volume, *Heino, Rautiainen, and Ikäheimonen* build on the concept of territoriality and suggest that individual owners' motivation to partake in FBG ownership and governance structures is based on their need to defend their ownership position, i.e., territory. This perspective is novel for the research on FBGs. Territoriality may have important consequences on the continuity of the FBG and the dynamics within the business family. We suggest that further studies are needed to understand the relationship between individual needs for territory and the joint ownership in FBGs.

The second line focusing on ownership theory has been more instrumental: focusing on ownership as an activity—that is those modes of operations, mechanisms, ways of affecting things, and guiding the strategies in family businesses. In this perspective, ownership can be seen as a resource, competence, and capability (Foss et al., 2021; Habbershon & Pistrui, 2002), that can make the difference in terms of FBG survival or success. However, along with the growth of the business group, the families are evolving and introducing new generations. As the complexity and entropy grow in both the business and the family, specific measures need to be taken to ensure the survivability of the complex structure. In this volume, *Ikäheimonen, Rautiainen, and Goel* discuss the concept of governing ownership. They point out that without specific measures, ownership cannot become a resource. The question arises, how do we create engaged ownership in large family business groups? Early evidence suggests that family councils, ownership strategies, family offices, and other informal governance structures may be critical to keep the family members attached to the business. *Liljeström* et al.

(in this volume) present a framework for analyzing informal governance mechanisms and suggest that they may be necessary ingredients for the effectiveness of FBG governance. However, more research is needed to uncover the prerequisites for ownership to take its place as a resource for FBGs.

Taken together, this book highlights the importance of FBGs in diverse contexts. Further work is needed to understand how such phenomenon unfolds around the world. This book opens the door for academics to consider diverse perspectives to unpack the factors that make FBGs unique as well as the approach and rationale of the families behind them over generations.

References

Alsos, G. A., & Carter, S. (2006). Multiple business ownership in the Norwegian farm sector: Resource transfer and performance consequences. *Journal of Rural Studies, 22*, 313–322.

Alsos, G. A., Carter, S., & Ljunggren, E. (2014). Kinship and business: How entrepreneurial households facilitate business growth. *Entrepreneurship & Regional Development, 26*(1–2), 97–122. https://doi.org/10.1080/08985626.2013.870235

Arregle, J. L., Hitt, M. A., Sirmon, D. G., & Very, P. (2007). The development of organizational social capital: Attributes of family firms. *Journal of Management Studies, 44*(1), 73–95.

Discua Cruz, A., & Basco, R. (2018). Family perspective on entrepreneurship. In R. V. Turcan & N. M. Fraser (Eds.), *The Palgrave handbook of multidisciplinary perspectives on entrepreneurship* (pp. 147–175). Springer International Publishing. https://doi.org/10.1007/978-3-319-91611-8_8

Discua Cruz, A., & Hamilton, E. (2022). Death and entrepreneuring in family businesses: A complexity and stewardship perspective. *Entrepreneurship & Regional Development*.

Discua Cruz, A., Hamilton, E., & Jack, S. L. (2019). Understanding the small family business: Past, present and future: International small business journal. *International Small Business Journal*, Special Virtual Issue. https://journals.sagepub.com/page/isb/collections/understanding-the-small-family-business

Discua, A., Hamilton, E., & Jack, S. L. (2021). Understanding entrepreneurial opportunities through metaphors: A narrative approach to theorizing family entrepreneurship. *Entrepreneurship & Regional Development, 33*(5–6), 405–426. https://doi.org/10.1080/08985626.2020.1727089

Discua, A., Howorth, C., & Hamilton, E. (2013). Intrafamily entrepreneurship: The formation and membership of family entrepreneurial teams. *Entrepreneurship*

Theory & Practice, 37(1), 17–46. https://doi.org/10.1111/j.1540-6520.2012.005 34.x

Duran, P., Kammerlander, N., Van Essen, M., & Zellweger, T. (2016). Doing more with less: Innovation input and output in family firms. *Academy of Management Journal, 59*(4), 1224–1264.

Fitz-Koch, S., Cooper, S., & Discua Cruz, A. (2019). Entrepreneurship and rural family identity: Understanding portfolio development in a family farm business. In M. Rautiainen, P. Rosa, T. Pihkala, M. J. Parada, & A. D. Cruz (Eds.), *The family business group phenomenon: Emergence and complexities* (pp. 353–383). Springer International Publishing. https://doi.org/10.1007/978-3-319-98542-8_14

Foss, N. J., Klein, P. G., Lien, L. B., Zellweger, T., & Zenger, T. (2021). *Ownership Competence. 1*(2), 302–328.

Habbershon, T. G., & Pistrui, J. (2002). Enterprising families domain: Family-influenced ownership groups in pursuit of transgenerational wealth. *Family Business Review, 15*(3), 223–237.

Huovinen, J., & Tihula, S. (2008). Entrepreneurial learning in the context of portfolio entrepreneurship. *International Journal of Entrepreneurial Behaviour & Research, 14*(3), 152–171.

Iacobucci, D., & Rosa, P. (2010). The growth of business groups by habitual entrepreneurs: The role of entrepreneurial teams. *Entrepreneurship Theory & Practice, 34*(2), 351–377. https://doi.org/10.1111/j.1540-6520.2010.00378.x

James, H. S. (1999). Owner as manager, extended horizons and the family firm. *International Journal of the Economics of Business, 6*(1), 41–55.

Kelly, L. M., Athanassiou, N., & Crittenden, W. F. (2000). Founder centrality and strategic behavior in the family-owned firm. *Entrepreneurship Theory & Practice, 25*(2), 27–42.

Litz, R. A. (2008). Two sides of a one-sided phenomenon: Conceptualizing the family business and business family as a möbius strip. *Family Business Review, 21*(3), 217–236. https://doi.org/10.1111/j.1741-6248.2008.00124.x

Lockett, A., Wiklund, J., Davidsson, P., & Girma, S. (2011). Organic and acquisitive growth: Re-examining, testing and extending penrose's growth theory. *Journal of Management Studies, 48*(1), 48–74. https://doi.org/10.1111/j.1467-6486.2009.00879.x

Lubinski, C., Fear, J., & Pérez, P. F. (2013). *Family multinationals: Entrepreneurship, governance, and pathways to internationalization.* Routledge.

Lumpkin, G. T., & Brigham, K. H. (2011). Long-term orientation and intertemporal choice in family firms. *Entrepreneurship Theory & Practice, 35*(6), 1149–1169. https://doi.org/10.1111/j.1540-6520.2011.00495.x

McGaughey, S. L. (2007). Hidden ties in international new venturing: The case of portfolio entrepreneurship. *Journal of World Business, 42*(3), 307–321.

Michael-, N., Labaki, R., & Zachary, R. K. (2014). Toward the cluster model the family firm's entrepreneurial behavior over generations. *Family Business Review, 27*(2), 161–185. https://doi.org/10.1177/0894486514525803

Miller, D., & Le Breton-Miller, I. (2005). *Managing for the long run: Lessons in competitive advantage from great family businesses.* Harvard Business Press.

Nordqvist, M. (2005). *Understanding the role of ownership in strategizing: A study of family firms.* Jönköping University.

Pierce, J. L., Kostova, T., & Dirks, K. T. (2001). Toward a theory of psychological ownership in organizations. *Academy of Management Review, 26*(2), 298–310.

Randerson, K., Bettinelli, C., Fayolle, A., & Anderson, A. (2015). Family entrepreneurship as a field of research: Exploring its contours and contents. *Journal of Family Business Strategy, 6*(3), 143–154. https://doi.org/10.1016/j.jfbs.2015.08.002

Rautiainen, M., Rosa, P., Pihkala, T., Parada, M. J., & Discua Cruz, A. (Eds.). (2019). *The family business group phenomenon: Emergence and complexities.* Palgrave Macmillan. https://doi.org/10.1007/978-3-319-98542-8

Rautiainen, M., Konsti-Laakso, S. & Pihkala, T. (2021). Innovation in family business group—beyond R&D-perspective. In A. Calabro, (Ed.). *A research agenda for family business.* E Elgar.

Rosa, P., & Scott, M. (1999). Entrepreneurial diversification, business-cluster formation, and growth. *Environment and Planning c: Government and Policy, 17*(5), 527–547.

Rosa, P., Howorth, C., & Discua, A. (2014). Habitual and portfolio entrepreneurship and the family in business. In L. Melin, M. Nordqvist, & P. Sharma (Eds.), *The SAGE handbook of family business* (pp. 364–382). Sage.

Ucbasaran, D., Westhead, P., & Wright, M. (2001). The focus of entrepreneurial research: Contextual and process issues. *Entrepreneurship Theory & Practice, 25*(4), 57–80.

Westhead, P., & Wright, M. (1998). Novice, portfolio, and serial founders in rural and urban areas. *Entrepreneurship Theory & Practice, 22*(4), 63–100.

Index

A

acquisition 26, 56, 137, 142, 195, 381, 383, 464, 477, 603, 621
Aditya Birla Group (ABG) 169, 171, 408, 413
affiliation
  affiliate company 49, 50, 52, 55–59, 61, 404
  family affiliation 400
  group affiliation 83, 390
agency
  agency cost 4, 22, 86, 88, 194
  agency costs of ownership 3
  agency theory 6, 86, 223, 226, 248
alliance 131, 139, 172, 173, 520
  interorganizational alliance 178
Amadeus database 83, 90
ambidexterity 7, 16, 20, 21, 23, 24, 29, 40, 42
  individual ambidexterity (IA) 23, 28, 42
  organizational ambidexterity (OA) 16, 20, 42, 125, 133, 134, 151, 152, 622

Argentina 131, 132, 141, 142, 145–147, 195
Asia 130, 241, 245, 250, 268, 509
  Asian Economy(ies) 8, 256, 258, 260

B

board of directors 8, 83, 89, 144, 146, 147, 202, 204, 211, 227, 228, 249, 284, 285, 320, 335
Bolivia 132, 147, 148
Brazil 131, 141–144, 146, 147, 195
business
  business family 10, 16, 191, 192, 204, 258, 275, 276, 281, 288, 290, 430, 502, 518, 524, 534, 537–539, 549–552, 556, 558–562, 564–566, 570, 571, 573–575, 577–582, 588, 589, 591, 596, 605, 606, 625–627
  business group 2, 20, 38, 39, 50–52, 54, 56, 58, 59, 160–163, 167, 169, 171, 173, 175, 177, 178, 180–182, 202,

© The Editor(s) (if applicable) and The Author(s), under exclusive
license to Springer Nature Switzerland AG 2023
M. Rautianen et al. (eds.), *The Palgrave Handbook of Managing Family Business Groups*,
https://doi.org/10.1007/978-3-031-13206-3

631

632 Index

217, 245, 267, 276, 280, 281, 284, 285, 287, 292, 305–307, 319, 322, 330, 332–336, 341, 343, 346, 347, 350, 351, 362–367, 378–385, 395–397, 399, 403, 404, 406, 411, 416, 419, 431, 432, 438, 439, 441–450, 472, 539, 550, 560, 620, 623, 624, 627

business growth 130, 175, 193, 211, 333, 343, 408

business model 151, 152, 181, 182, 411, 430, 433, 450, 537, 539

business group (BG) 2–4, 6, 10, 15, 16, 20, 25, 38, 42, 49–60, 82, 85, 86, 89, 94, 110, 111, 117, 118, 125, 126, 130, 131, 134, 135, 149, 151, 152, 307–309, 318, 319, 322, 329–336, 341, 343, 346–348, 350, 361–367, 379–384, 394, 396, 400, 403–409, 412, 415, 416, 418, 419, 429–432, 438, 439, 441–444, 446–450, 460, 468, 482, 487, 507, 525, 531, 549–551, 560, 562, 563, 577, 579, 581, 620–627

C

capability
  dynamic capability 7, 519
  enterprising capability 193
  innovation capability 410, 419

capital
  capital market 8, 49–53, 55–60, 172, 394, 405
  equity capital 51, 56
  financial capital 73, 191, 247, 413, 560
  human capital 181, 191, 208, 406, 416, 475

internal capital 3, 8, 49–53, 55–60, 365, 394, 405

internal capital market 8, 49–53, 55–60, 365, 394

non-financial capital 560

social capital 177, 213, 308, 390, 407, 408, 462, 524, 534

Carvajal Group 140

case study
  case study analysis 330, 463
  case study method 69, 280, 329, 366, 408, 525
  single case study 280, 366, 611

Catalonia 83, 84, 88–91, 117

Cencosud group 151

Chile 129, 131, 132, 145, 146, 151, 195

China 162, 242, 243, 245, 252, 253, 258, 478

Colombia 131–133, 138, 140, 146, 147

complex adaptive system 268, 269, 271

complexity 84, 86, 93, 208, 225, 231, 236, 268, 269, 273, 276, 290, 291, 333, 366, 510, 627
  complexity theory 281
  organizational complexity 20, 597

conglomerate 5, 84, 85, 130, 138, 190, 195, 418
  conglomerate structure 203

corporate
  corporate governance 15, 172, 202, 230, 247–250, 290, 299, 300, 304, 309, 310, 432, 444, 530, 531, 536
  corporate ownership 160, 245
  corporate social responsibility 146, 432, 433, 626
  corporate strategy 82, 118, 227, 411, 414
  corporate structure 85, 94, 106, 137, 241, 342

corporate sustainability 430–437, 439–442, 444, 448
corporate social responsibility (CSR) 146, 432, 433, 626
corporation 84, 87, 143, 147, 248, 302, 334, 348, 418, 436, 437, 537, 565
cousin consortium 189, 196, 208, 209, 272, 334, 608
COVID-19 433, 434, 561, 574
culture 129, 173, 179, 181, 191, 207, 274, 308, 348, 407, 418, 478, 523, 540, 562, 624
  organizational culture 151, 207

D

diversification
  diversification strategy 83, 87
  geographic diversification 87, 88, 106, 110, 117, 118
  product diversification 86, 88, 101, 117
  related diversification 171, 384
  unrelated diversification 87, 118, 382, 384

E

economy
  developed economy 4, 83, 85, 118
  developing economy 3, 4, 84, 626
  emerging economy 129, 167, 419
effectuation 550, 560
  effectuation theory 578
El Salvador 137, 138, 195
embeddedness 254, 436, 437, 448
  sustainability embeddedness 10, 431, 435–438, 441–450, 626
emerging countries 51, 125
emerging market 15, 50, 53, 130, 241, 246, 404, 409
enterprising family 210, 552, 580

entrepreneur
  habitual entrepreneur 552, 560
  portfolio entrepreneur 5, 67, 73, 75, 193, 549–551, 560, 571, 577, 578, 580, 581, 622, 623
  serial entrepreneur 138, 622
entrepreneurial
  behavior 86, 87, 126, 127, 498, 551, 579
  growth 7
  identity 229, 533, 541, 588, 593, 594, 596
  mindset 149, 151, 181, 192, 196, 203, 206, 207, 397
  orientation 128, 196, 570
  team 127, 623
  values 127, 128, 206, 211, 212, 624
  venturing 560
entrepreneurship
  corporate entrepreneurship 343
  entrepreneurship Committee 204
  habitual entrepreneurship 552, 560
  intergenerational entrepreneurship 196
  portfolio entrepreneurship 5, 16, 67, 75, 460, 550, 551, 558, 560, 563, 577, 580, 581, 622
  serial entrepreneurship 138
  sustainable entrepreneurship 432
  transgenerational entrepreneurship 5, 9, 127, 192, 205, 206, 212, 213, 218, 517, 522, 539, 552
exit
  business exit 8, 66–68, 71, 576
  entrepreneurial exit 65, 66, 69, 74
  exit strategy 71
  involuntary exit 68
exploratory study 7, 83, 550

634 Index

F

Falabella Group 146
families-in-business 550–552, 560,
 561, 570, 574, 575, 577–582
familiness 181, 191, 395, 407, 433,
 521, 537, 550
family
 business-owning family 20
 extended family 175, 177, 179,
  181, 235, 334
 family council 175, 232, 277,
  345, 531, 533–535, 537, 569,
  627
 family entrepreneurship 82,
  539–541, 623
 family firm 5, 20, 22, 43, 70, 75,
  82, 89, 167, 177, 204, 234,
  328, 365, 389, 390, 393, 394,
  397, 399, 404, 408, 433, 470,
  472, 476, 478, 481, 482, 487,
  488, 551, 580
 family identity 10, 27, 38, 42,
  335, 340, 344, 345, 349, 350,
  487, 550, 551, 560, 574,
  578–581, 588, 589, 592, 593,
  597, 603, 604, 608, 610, 611,
  625, 626
 family leader 16, 22, 26, 29, 41,
  42, 173, 293, 530, 537, 556
 family legacy 27, 182, 204, 205,
  480, 481, 485, 517, 518, 552
 family logic 161, 169, 171, 173,
  181, 182
 family meeting 175, 231, 285,
  288
 family members 2–6, 10, 21, 27,
  28, 72, 74, 84, 89, 127, 133,
  152, 164, 170, 171, 173, 175,
  176, 178, 193, 204, 208, 211,
  212, 224–228, 230, 232, 233,
  235, 248, 250, 254, 255, 268,
  269, 271, 273–277, 284–289,
  291, 292, 305, 306, 318, 322,
  328, 329, 333–336, 340–346,

  348–350, 393, 395, 399, 405,
  407, 433, 441, 460, 462, 469,
  470, 472–475, 479–482,
  497–499, 502, 503, 508–510,
  513, 523, 524, 527, 530,
  532–540, 542, 550, 561, 562,
  564, 568–571, 573, 576,
  587–589, 592, 595, 596, 598,
  602, 604, 608, 609, 622, 623,
  625, 627
 family office 202, 204, 209, 211,
  535
 family owners 2, 5, 6, 15, 16, 20,
  22, 25, 27, 28, 66, 67, 69–74,
  76, 87, 177, 178, 225, 227,
  232, 248, 249, 268–271,
  275–279, 284–286, 288–291,
  293, 317, 318, 322, 325, 330,
  340–346, 348, 350, 392, 393,
  396, 435, 460, 462, 497, 499,
  502, 596, 598, 605, 622, 625
 family ownership 21, 22, 81, 85,
  160, 177, 196, 203, 230, 232,
  254, 255, 267, 269, 272, 273,
  280, 284, 287, 293, 306, 319,
  322, 341, 345, 393, 405, 434,
  435, 440, 463, 468, 482, 502,
  587, 625
 family values 133, 178, 206, 210,
  213, 218, 230, 252, 341, 344,
  468, 469, 478, 487, 573, 587
 family wealth 170, 178, 231,
  232, 250, 271, 276, 293, 361,
  393, 435, 480, 538, 539
family business
 family business identity 562, 588,
  608
 family business legacy 209
 family business portfolio 66–69,
  71, 74–76, 625
 family business succession 228,
  230, 234, 328
 family business system 21, 22, 86,
  208

Index **635**

family business group (FBG)
emergence of 181
entrepreneurial FBG 193
evolution 10, 160–162, 202, 218,
242, 243, 459, 460, 498, 551
family business group strategy
173
FBG governance structure 29, 38
multigenerational FBG 191, 208,
242
Family Business Network (FBN) 430
family-controlled business group 177
Finland 280, 281, 508
Fortaleza Group 147

G

generation
founding generation 82, 481, 561
multigenerational 152, 191, 195,
210, 272, 560, 597, 604
Gerdau Group 142
goal
economic goals 6, 24, 29, 118,
273, 288, 439, 447, 498, 504
goal congruence 269, 270, 274,
288–290
non-economic goals 6, 24, 28,
29, 118, 273, 288, 439, 442,
447, 462, 498
governance
corporate governance 15, 172,
202, 230, 247–250, 290, 299,
300, 304, 305, 309, 444, 530,
531, 537
external governance mechanisms
248
FBG governance 9, 16, 29, 38,
43, 192, 242, 274, 275, 277,
288, 292, 628
formal governance 191, 218, 277,
300, 301, 305, 306, 309

governance mechanisms 38, 196,
210, 249, 274, 302, 405, 626,
628
governance practices 8, 9, 191,
192, 213, 231, 242, 247, 249,
259, 270, 299–311
governance structures 8, 27, 28,
196, 209, 210, 212, 217, 218,
242, 243, 247, 259, 268, 274,
276, 287, 308, 539, 627
governance system 8, 9, 22, 192,
224, 269, 270, 279, 287
informal governance 9, 277,
299–306, 308–311, 627, 628
internal governance mechanisms
249
organizational governance 242
growth
business growth 130, 175, 193,
211, 333, 343, 408
economic growth 58, 242, 252,
255, 434
organic growth 202, 589, 597
Grupo Carso 136, 137, 150
Grupo Poma 138

H

holding
holding board 203, 607
holding company 98, 137, 160,
169–171, 177, 203, 209, 290,
335, 465, 550, 556, 565
holding structure 333–335, 343,
344

I

identity
collective identity 26, 230, 321,
342, 345, 552, 588, 590, 591,
595–598, 602–605, 608, 609,
611

636 **Index**

family collective identity 590,
595, 596, 603, 604, 608, 609
family identity 10, 27, 38, 42,
335, 340, 344, 345, 349, 350,
487, 550, 560, 574, 578, 580,
581, 588, 589, 593, 603, 604,
608, 611, 625
FBG identity 589, 590, 592, 604,
605, 607–610
identity conflict 589, 591, 592,
597, 604–606, 610–612
investor identity 589, 605
organizational identity 549–551,
558–560, 563, 566, 570,
577–582, 587, 589–593, 596,
597, 603, 604, 608–611
owner identity 569, 578, 592,
598
ownership identity 549, 551
social identity theory 591, 610
immaterial property right (IPR) 382
India 159–165, 167, 168, 175, 176,
179–182, 404, 405, 408–414,
435, 507
Indonesia 130, 461, 463, 477, 487
innovation
external innovation 365, 383, 384
inbound innovation 392
innovation management 9,
361–364, 378, 380, 383–385,
392, 409, 410, 419, 621
innovation process 362–366, 381,
382
innovation sourcing 5, 362, 378,
398, 621
innovation strategy 381, 391
internal innovation 364, 365,
380–382, 384, 621
open innovation 5, 9, 389–392,
395–399, 418, 419, 520
outbound innovation 390, 392,
398, 399
parallel innovation strategy 363,
381

radical innovation 364, 447–449
institution
institutional environment 8, 10,
128, 129, 167, 169, 173, 177,
181, 182, 503, 505
institutional subsystem 251
institutional theory 6, 86
institutional trust 243–245,
249–251, 253, 256–260
institutional void 84, 85, 118,
159, 160, 162, 164, 165, 167,
169, 181, 241, 243, 252, 253,
405, 409, 560
intergenerational flourishing 10,
518, 519, 525, 527, 540, 542
interlocking directorship 274
international
internationalization 7, 86, 88,
107, 111, 118, 145, 193, 231,
253, 589, 597
international organization 254
Italy 59, 110, 128, 259

J

Jacto Group 143
Japan 84, 143, 162, 190, 246, 248,
253, 382, 405, 505, 506
John Nurminen family Business 508
joint venture 96, 301, 333, 379,
397, 398, 464, 484

K

knowledge sharing 10, 286, 291,
518–520, 524, 525, 527, 530,
538, 540–542
Korea 84, 190, 242, 243, 245, 246,
254, 255, 258

L

Latin America 15, 84, 111, 112,
114, 125, 126, 128, 131, 132,
134, 135, 138, 140, 144, 145,

149, 151, 152, 189, 190, 195, 196, 258, 405, 527
Lee Kum Kee Group 564, 568
legacy business 32, 69, 71, 74, 193, 203, 550, 551, 558, 559, 561, 562, 564, 565, 568, 569, 571, 572, 574, 576, 577, 588, 589, 593, 594, 596–598, 602–605, 609
legal entity 405, 406
life cycle 232, 271, 276, 397, 405
longitudinal study 581
Luen Thai Group 565, 569

M

Mahindra group 408, 415, 418
Malaysia 242, 243, 245, 255, 258
management 4, 531, 537, 587, 624, 626
  portfolio management 250, 565, 623
mergers and acquisitions 193, 604
Mexico 110, 130–133, 136–139, 147, 195, 526, 527, 529, 531
minority share holding 54, 55, 117, 274, 605
Motta Group 139
multidivision
  multidivisional company 54
  multidivisional firm 60
  multidivisional holding 190
  multidivisional organization 249
  multidivisional structure 248
multigenerational family 606
multinational company 137
multiple case 69, 329, 611
  multiple case analysis 319
  multiple case study 69, 329

N

narrative construction 498, 504, 626

O

organizational identity theory 550, 578, 591
owner
  entrepreneurial owner 248, 394, 398, 622
  family business owner 8, 173, 348–350, 361, 363, 365, 379, 598, 608
  multiple business owner 68
  owners' council 284, 290
ownership
  business ownership 68, 226, 232, 250, 267, 272, 292, 399, 551, 573
  collective ownership 228, 345, 349, 570, 622
  cross-ownership 334
  governing ownership system 8
  joint ownership 394, 627
  legal-economic ownership 320, 321, 325, 341
  legal ownership 318, 320, 325, 340–343, 347, 348, 350, 499, 513
  multiple business ownership 68
  ontology of ownership 500
  ownership competence 224, 276
  ownership governance 270, 275–281, 287, 288, 290–293
  ownership paradox 224
  ownership strategy 224–236, 284, 624, 625
  ownership values 224
  psychological ownership 224, 232, 318, 320–322, 324, 326, 328, 336, 340, 343, 347, 348, 350
  pyramidal ownership 85, 88, 231, 379, 405
  social ownership 320, 321, 342, 347, 350
  socio-symbolic ownership 321

638   Index

P

Pakistan 66, 69, 76, 190, 253
Panama 132, 138–140
paradox
  organizational paradox 27, 561
  paradoxical tension 10, 550, 551,
    558, 560, 562, 566, 576–582
  paradox theory 578, 579, 582
parent company 90–92, 94–96, 103,
  106, 438, 442, 445, 448
path dependency 366
Peikko group 379
Pentland Group 590, 594, 602, 603,
  609
Peru 110, 131, 132, 140, 141, 146,
  147, 195
pivot 502, 574, 576
political
  political control 252
  political elites 242
  political party 245
  political power 245, 253, 318,
    327, 342
  political ties 242, 253
  political uncertainty 8
portfolio
  multi-business portfolio 551, 556,
    562, 580
  portfolio business 623
  portfolio companies 416, 418,
    419, 556
  portfolio entrepreneurship (PE)
    16, 67, 73, 75, 460, 549–551,
    560, 563, 571, 577, 579–582,
    622
  portfolio strategy 551, 572, 579
  portfolio value creation 571, 577
pyramid
  pyramidal group 94, 195
  pyramid ownership 85, 379, 405
  pyramid structure 322

Q

qualitative research method 319

R

R&D
  R&D activity 50
  R&D expenditure 364, 621
  R&D intensity 364
  R&D investment 56–60
  R&D propensity 56
regional innovation system 394
Reliance Group 164, 165, 169, 172
research method 67, 319
resilience 55, 126, 160, 242, 443,
  450, 498, 503, 509
resource
  allocation of resource 49, 203,
    408
  physical resource 246, 324
  resource allocation 4, 51, 54,
    58–60, 193, 300, 364, 625
  resource management 5, 6, 8,
    66–72, 74–76, 365
  resource recycling 73
  resource redeployment 68
resource-based
  theory 6
restructuring 71, 72, 254, 259, 565,
  574, 576
Romero Group 140, 150

S

SABI database 83, 90
semi-pyramidal structure 94, 106
semi-structured interview 194, 319,
  330, 563
sensegiving 498–501, 504, 509
sensemaking 378, 498–505, 509,
  510, 513, 559, 561, 606
single case study 280, 366, 611
small and medium sized businesses
  (SME) 52, 55, 57, 252, 366

socio-emotional wealth (SEW) 10, 22, 224, 340, 626

Soni Family Business Group 29, 30

Spain 83, 84, 89–91, 106, 110, 140, 259, 430

spillover
  innovation spillover 620
  knowledge spillover 56, 365, 382
  spillover effect 382

stakeholder
  external stakeholder 8, 10, 278, 435, 440, 444, 445, 447, 449, 474, 510, 513, 559, 589, 597, 603, 604, 611, 625
  non-family stakeholder 435, 441

standalone firm 50, 53, 58, 59, 407

start-up 50, 172, 230, 364, 378, 380, 382, 383, 413, 416, 418, 419, 622

stewardship 259, 440, 467, 470, 474, 477, 481, 488, 559, 569, 623
  stewardship theory 224

strategic management 7, 23, 218, 227, 230, 274, 391, 434, 521

strategy
  long-term strategy 173
  succession strategy 30, 39, 175

subsidiary 50, 88, 138, 190, 202, 281

survival
  organizational survival 42
  survivability 11, 15, 26, 29, 32, 42, 472, 519, 627

sustainability
  corporate sustainability 430–436
  cross-generational sustainability 435
  family sustainability spectrum 449
  sustainability embeddedness 10, 431, 432, 436–438, 441–444, 446–449, 626

sustainable development goals (SDGs) 430, 432

Sweden 259, 446

system
  family system 127, 407
  social system 163, 227, 318, 325
  subsystem 228, 251, 267, 269, 271–273, 275, 579

systems theory 6, 228, 362

T

tacit knowledge 213, 521–523, 530

Tata Group 160, 169, 170, 172, 409, 418, 507

Techint Group 144, 145

temporal evolution 361, 363, 380

territory
  control-oriented territoriality 325–327, 342, 343, 350
  identity-oriented territoriality 325, 326, 343, 345, 350
  territorial behavior 8
  territoriality 6, 317–319, 322, 324–327, 329, 330, 332, 336, 340, 342, 345–351, 627

three circle model 194

Toyoda Family Business Group (TFBG) 505

transaction cost theory 6

transgenerational
  transgenerational entrepreneurship 5, 9, 127, 192, 205, 206, 212, 213, 218, 517, 522, 539, 552
  transgenerational FBG 39, 192
  transgenerational intention 25–27, 29, 39, 40, 42, 133
  transgenerational succession 20
  transgenerational succession strategy 30
  transgenerational value creation 191
  transgenerational wealth 271, 559

640 Index

triangulation 148

V

value creation 9, 131, 151, 166, 169, 170, 193, 208, 212, 213, 218, 445, 558, 572
Venezuela 195
vision
  entrepreneurial vision 210, 212

family vision 209, 285, 287, 289, 291, 488
long-term vision 39, 190, 203, 268, 437
owner's vision 212

W

wealth accumulation 21, 231, 271

Printed in the United States
by Baker & Taylor Publisher Services